14th International Joint Conference on Natural Language Processing and the 4th Conference of the Asia-Pacific Chapter of the Association for Computational Linguistics (IJCNLP-AACL 2025)

Student Research Workshop

Mumbai, India
20-24 December 2025

ISBN: 979-8-3313-3244-0

Printed from e-media with permission by:

Curran Associates, Inc.
57 Morehouse Lane
Red Hook, NY 12571

Some format issues inherent in the e-media version may also appear in this print version.

Association for Computational Linguistics
209 N. Eighth Street
Stroudsburg, Pennsylvania 18360

Phone: 1-570-476-8006
Fax: 1-570-476-0860

acl@aclweb.org

Additional copies of this publication are available from:

Curran Associates, Inc.
57 Morehouse Lane
Red Hook, NY 12571 USA
Phone: 845-758-0400
Fax: 845-758-2633
Email: curran@proceedings.com
Web: www.proceedings.com

IJCNLP-AACL 2025

The 14th International Joint Conference on Natural Language Processing and The 4th Conference of the Asia-Pacific Chapter of the Association for Computational Linguistics

Proceedings of the Student Research Workshop

December 20-24, 2025

Message from the Chair of Student Research Workshop

Welcome to the IJCNLPACL 2025 Student Research Workshop (SRW)!

The IJCNLP-AACL 2025 SRW is held in conjunction with the 14th International Joint Conference on Natural Language Processing (IJCNLP) and the 4th Conference of the Asia-Pacific Chapter of the Association for Computational Linguistics (AACL).

Continuing its long-standing mission, the SRW provides a dedicated forum for student researchers in computational linguistics and natural language processing. It offers a supportive environment for students to share ideas, gain visibility, and receive constructive feedback from experienced members of the community.

As in previous years, the workshop invites submissions in two categories: research papers and thesis proposals. Authors may choose between archival submissionsncluded in the conference proceedingsnd non-archival submissions, which allow presentation without limiting future publication opportunities. This flexible format accommodates both well-developed work and preliminary ideas, enabling meaningful participation from students at various stages of their research. Importantly, all submissions, whether archival or non-archival, receive equal care in review and mentorship.

This year, the SRW received 75 submissions in total: 71 through direct submission and 4 via ARR Commitment. We accepted 32 papers, resulting in an overall acceptance rate of 43%. The selection process was highly competitive, and we are pleased to note that all accepted papers demonstrate creativity and contribute to their respective fields. The accepted submissions reflect diversity not only in topics but also in the backgrounds of the student authors. Among these, 5 are archival and 27 are non-archival. During the conference, 9 papers will be presented as oral talks and 23 as poster presentations, delivered either in person or virtually.

Mentorship remains at the heart of the SRW. This year, 12 submissions participated in the pre-submission mentoring program, where students received early feedback on their writing and presentation from two experienced mentors. We are grateful to all mentors who supported authors throughout the review and revision process. Our gratitude goes to the program committee members for their thoughtful and careful reviews, and to the mentors who contributed their timeor offering valuable feedback to student authors throughout the process.

We also thank our faculty advisors - Xiting Wang, Daisuke Kawahara, for their consistent guidance and support. We sincerely appreciate all of the organizers of the IJCNLP-AACL conference for their effort. And of course, we thank all authors for their enthusiasm and engagement. Your contributions make the SRW a vibrant and intellectually stimulating part of IJCNLPACL 2025.

We hope you find this year workshop inspiring and enriching.

Organizing Committee

Faculty Advisors

Xiting Wang, Renmin University, China
Daisuke Kawahara, Waseda University, Japan

Student Chairs

Santosh T.Y.S.S, Technical University of Munich,
Shuichiro Shimizu, Kyoto University, Japan
Yifan Gong, Renmin University, China

Program Committee

Program Chairs

Yifan Gong
Shuichiro Shimizu
Santosh T.y.s.s, Amazon

Reviewers

Mohamed Abdalla, Gavin Abercrombie, Somak Aditya, Ameeta Agrawal, Georgios Alexandridis

Premjith B, Long Bai, Valerio Basile, Nathaniel Blanchard, Maria Boritchev, Davide Buscaldi, Jan Buys

Bo Chen, Alvin Cheung

Dipankar Das, Brian Davis, Lucia Donatelli, Ondrej Dusek

Minghong Fang, Alejandro Figueroa

Yanjun Gao, Venkata S Govindarajan, Camille Guinaudeau

Shohei Higashiyama

Abhik Jana, Arkadiusz Janz, Tianyu Jiang, Zhuoxuan Jiang

Sabyasachi Kamila, SeongKu Kang, Alina Karakanta, Bugeun Kim, Junyeong Kim, Taehwan Kim, Satoshi Kosugi, Nikhil Krishnaswamy, Marek Kubis, Sebastian Kula, Florian Kunneman, Yen-Ling Kuo

Yuxuan Lai, Andre Lamurias, David Langlois, Sahinur Rahman Laskar, Dongha Lee, Gaël Lejeune, Chuanyi Li, Jing Li, Sheng Li, KyungTae Lim, Dugang Liu, Hui Liu, Kunpeng Liu, Peipei Liu, Yidi Liu, Sharid Loáiciga, Jiaying Lu, Chunchuan Lyu

Lorenzo Malandri, Valentin Malykh, Edison Marrese-Taylor, Sandeep Mathias, Chandresh Kumar Maurya, Fanchao Meng, Dr. Satanik Mitra, Mainack Mondal, Raha Moraffah

Shah Nawaz, Hamada Nayel, Pengyu Nie

Jasabanta Patro, Adam Poliak

Mengyang Qiu

Leonardo Ranaldi, Christophe Rodrigues, Ramon Ruiz-Dolz

Yusuke Sakai, Debarshi Kumar Sanyal, Sunil Saumya, Alexandra Schofield, Sofia Serrano, Raksha Sharma, Zhou Sijia, Satyaki Sikdar, Mayank Singh, Nikhil Singh, Mohit Singhal, Konstantinos Skianis, Rui Sousa-Silva, Kai Sun

Santosh T.y.s.s, Yu Tian, Antonela Tommasel

Natalia Vanetik, Dan Vilenchik

Jindong Wang, Jingwen Wang, Ruibo Wang, Dittaya Wanvarie, Likang Wu, Winston Wu

Qiongkai Xu, Yongxiu Xu, Wei Xue

Jinyoung Yeo

Lei Zhang, Qing Zhang, Yang Zhang, Peide Zhu, Shaolin Zhu

Table of Contents

Interpretable Sparse Features for Probing Self-Supervised Speech Models

Iñigo Parra
University of California, Berkeley
Department of Linguistics
iparra@berkeley.edu

Abstract

Self-supervised speech models have demonstrated the ability to learn rich acoustic representations. However, interpreting which specific phonological or acoustic features these models leverage within their highly polysemantic activations remains challenging. In this paper, we propose a straightforward and unsupervised probing method for model interpretability. We extract the activations from the final MLP layer of a pretrained HuBERT model and train a sparse autoencoder (SAE) using dictionary learning techniques to generate an overcomplete set of latent representations. Analyzing these latent codes, we observe that a small subset of high-variance units consistently aligns with phonetic events, suggesting their potential utility as interpretable acoustic detectors. Our proposed method does not require labeled data beyond raw audio, providing a lightweight and accessible tool to gain insights into the internal workings of self-supervised speech models.

1 Introduction

Recent advances in self-supervised learning have produced speech models whose hidden representations support a wide range of downstream tasks without fine-tuning (Hsu et al., 2021; Baevski et al., 2020a; Chen et al., 2022). However, these models remain largely "black boxes": it remains unclear precisely which acoustic and linguistic aspects of the input signal are captured by individual layers or units. This lack of interpretability poses significant challenges for both theoretical understanding and practical applications, limiting our ability to effectively control, edit, or explain model outputs. Consequently, developing methods that show and inspect the internal workings of self-supervised models is an essential step toward more transparent and flexible speech technologies.

Prior approaches to probing the internal representations of self-supervised speech models have usually involved supervised classifiers trained to predict explicit phonetic or prosodic labels from hidden embeddings. Alternative methods have used linear projection techniques, such as principal component analysis (PCA) and canonical correlation analysis (CCA), to identify correlations between learned embeddings and linguistic categories (Martin et al., 2023; Pasad et al., 2021, 2024). While these studies demonstrate that self-supervised features correlate strongly with traditional linguistic categories, they do not yield interpretable, temporally aligned, discrete signals (Pasad et al., 2024; Gimeno-Gómez et al., 2025). Thus, they fall short of providing the detailed unit-level insights necessary for granular analysis or intervention.

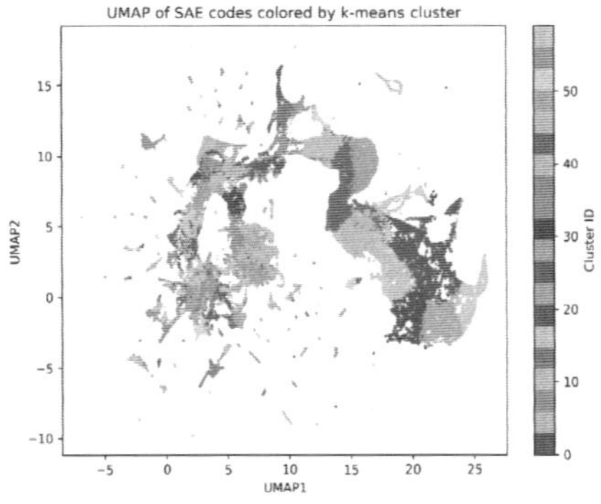

Figure 1: UMAP of a subset (10%) of TIMIT sparse representations. These were obtained after sparse-encoding the original 1024 dimensional MLP activations from HuBERT's last layer.

In parallel, computational neuroscience has explored sparse coding models extensively, particularly emphasizing the emergence of discrete, interpretable "spiking" events. Such sparse representations often naturally align with salient perceptual phenomena and sensory boundaries in a human-readable format, making them particularly promising for probing complex activation patterns.

Proceedings of the IJCNLP-AACL 2025 Student Research Workshop, pages 1–9

Motivated by these insights, we introduce a sparse autoencoder (SAE) probe specifically designed to analyze self-supervised speech models. Our approach consists of three primary steps: (1) extracting the activations from the final feed-forward multilayer perceptron (MLP) layer of a frozen HuBERT model (`facebook/hubert-large-ls960-ft`[1]), yielding an activation matrix of dimensions (N_{frames}, D); (2) training a lightweight SAE (linear encoder projecting activations to an over-complete latent space; set to $4 \times D$ dimensions), enforced by an $L1$ sparsity penalty, and decoding back to the original dimensionality; and (3) performing analyses on the resulting sparse latent representations, including ranking latent units by variance, visualizing their temporal firing patterns, conducting k-means clustering, and embedding with uniform manifold approximation and projection (UMAP).

Our contributions are as follows:

- We propose a straightforward, unsupervised probing pipeline using sparse autoencoders to dissect and interpret the latent structure within pretrained HuBERT activations.
- We introduce the Q-SAE, a variant of the sparse autoencoder that incorporates a controllable low-dimensional continuous vector for enhanced interpretability and control.
- We demonstrate that high-variance sparse units behave analogously to neural "feature detectors", exhibiting discrete spiking behaviors.
- We provide our code for extraction, SAE training, and analysis, facilitating future research aimed at interpretability and controllability in self-supervised speech representations.[2]

The remainder of this paper is organized as follows. Section 2 comments on related work on speech representation probing, sparse coding methodologies, and their intersections. Section 3 outlines our proposed architectures, training procedures, and analytic methods in detail. Section 4 presents qualitative and quantitative analyses of the learned sparse codes. Section 5 situates these results within a broader theoretical and applied context. Finally, section 6 concludes by summarizing key insights and outlining limitations and potential directions for future research.

2 Previous Work

Self-Supervised Speech Representations. Recent years have seen rapid progress in self-supervised learning for speech. Early models such as Wav2Vec (Baevski et al., 2020a) and its successor Wav2Vec 2.0 (Baevski et al., 2020b) learn frame-level latent embeddings by masking and contrastive predictive coding. HuBERT (Hsu et al., 2021) improved on these methods by iteratively clustering acoustic features and using cluster assignments as targets, yielding representations that match or exceed fully supervised baselines on phoneme recognition. More recently, Data2Vec (Baevski et al., 2022) unified self-supervised learning across modalities by predicting contextualized representations rather than discrete units.

These models improved downstream performance on speech recognition, speaker identification, and emotion detection tasks. Still, their internal activation patterns remain largely opaque.

Probing and Representation Analysis. To understand the internal mechanisms of models, previous work applied supervised probes and linear analysis techniques. Initially, the probes were used in text-based models such as BERT (Tenney et al., 2019). Linear probings demonstrated that models are able to capture different aspects of language in different layer depths (Tenney et al., 2019) or even individual attention heads (Clark et al., 2019).

Phonetic and prosodic probes train lightweight classifiers on frozen embeddings to predict linguistic labels (Pimentel et al., 2020; English et al., 2022). While such probes quantify which layers correlate with specific features, they require annotated data and only provide coarse-grained, timestep-agnostic scores. Unsupervised methods like PCA, CCA, and SVCCA examine subspace overlap between model layers (Raghu et al., 2017; Morcos et al., 2018), revealing global geometric structure but lacking temporal resolution. Information-theoretic measures, such as mutual information (MI) between representations and phonetic sequences, further characterize feature encoding but depend on explicit alignment (Pimentel et al., 2020).

Sparse Coding and Autoencoders. Sparse coding offers an alternative framework for discovering

[1]The model is openly available at Hugging Face.

[2]All materials available upon acceptance.

interpretable, monosematic features. Seminal work showed that enforcing sparsity on natural images yields Gabor-like filters similar to early visual cortex (Olshausen and Field, 1996).

In deep learning, mainly in the textual modality, sparse representations have been used for dictionary learning (Bricken et al., 2023; Templeton et al., 2024). Sparse autoencoders allow to do this combining an encoder-decoder architecture with an L_1 penalty or KL-divergence constraint on the bottleneck (Ng et al., 2011), encouraging a small subset of active units per input. Such models can learn event-like activations without explicit supervision.

Clustering and Manifold Visualization. Clustering learned codes provided a direct view of emerging categories. K-means has long been applied to embeddings for unsupervised phoneme and speaker clustering (MacQueen, 1967). Modern work on self-supervised speech also leverages k-means, both within HuBERT's iterative clustering loop (Hsu et al., 2021) and as a post-hoc analysis tool (Baevski et al., 2020a). To visualize high-dimensional codes, techniques such as t-SNE and UMAP reveal salient manifold structure (McInnes et al., 2018), enabling qualitative assessment of category separation.

Interpretability in Time. Few studies achieve time-aligned, unit-level interpretability in self-supervised speech models. Most probes aggregate over time or collapse sequences to fixed vectors, obscuring dynamic events like phoneme boundaries or burst onsets. Sparse autoencoders can produce firing patterns that align with salient acoustic transitions.

To our knowledge, no prior work applies sparse encoding directly to HuBERT's (or any other speech model's) internal MLP activations to extract interpretable, monosemantic features. We have no knowledge of the Q-SAE being applied in previous work, where the main objective of the model is providing a low-dimensional vector to manipulate the monosemantic, sparse, feature space.

3 Methodology

3.1 HuBERT Activations

We analyze activations extracted from HuBERT (Hsu et al., 2021) (see Appendix A for model details) during inference on the TIMIT (Garofolo et al., 1993) dataset (see Appendix B for dataset information). HuBERT takes raw audio waveforms and outputs embedding representations which correspond to 20ms frames (16kHz). An initial CNN waveform encoder creates audio patches, which are processed by a transformer encoder (BERT-like; trained on masked token prediction). The patches are linearly projected to obtain the embedding representations that approximate discrete phonetic units.

As in previous work in the text modality (Bricken et al., 2023; Templeton et al., 2024), we analyze the MLP activations from HuBERT's last layer. We extract the activation using a forward hook during inference on the training split of TIMIT. For each waveform, we obtained 1024-dimensional activation vectors of n frames. We collapsed batch and n dimensions to form a dataset with shape $N \times 1024$, where N are the total activation examples ($N = 762,438$).

3.2 Models

We propose two architectures to extract sparse features from dense activation vectors: a Sparse Autoencoder (SAE) and the Q-Autoencoder (Q-SAE). We trained both architectures with dictionary learning purposes.

3.2.1 Sparse Autoencoder

Architecture. The SAE follows a vanilla implementation (Figure 2), where the input sequence x is mapped into an over-complete latent space z, and is later reconstructed into $\hat{x}$. The encoder is encouraged to induce sparsity of z through an $L1$ penalty included in the optimization objective. The decoder has to map the sparse representations back to the original input.

Optimization Objective. The objective is defined as a dual cost function with a tunable parameter λ on the sparsity penalty:

$$\mathcal{L}_{\text{SAE}} = \underbrace{\frac{1}{N}\sum_{i=1}^{N}(x_i - \hat{x}_i)^2}_{\text{MSE Reconstruction}} + \overbrace{\lambda \cdot ||z||_1}^{L1 \text{ Sparsity}} .$$

The first term forces the model to reconstruct the input data as faithfully as possible while the second forces the sparsity of features. The tuneable lambda parameter allows to control the level of sparsity of the over-complete latent space. Higher lambda values shrink the values to zero, while lower values preserve more activations. We measure the percentage of active units through L_0 and aim at a final value of $\approx 3\%$ active units.

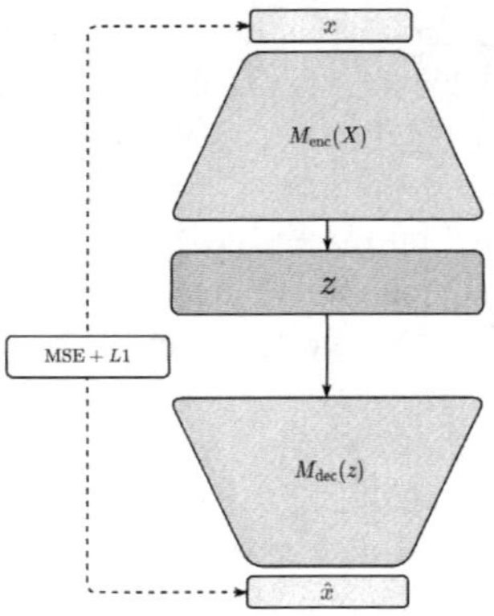

Figure 2: Sparse Autoencoder architecture.

3.2.2 The Q-Sparse Autoencoder

Architecture. The Q-SAE follows a similar architecture with additional components that allow a general control over features in space z. We followed a SAE architecture with the addition of a Q-Net (Chen et al., 2016), a continuous vector c, and a top-k feature selector mechanism on z (Figure 3). As in the SAE, an input sequence x is mapped into a sparse representation z.

Top-k Mechanism. In this variant, we apply a feature selector function Topk$(\cdot)$ on z, which constraints the decoder to access only the top-k most prominent features in z. For a single latent vector $z \in \mathbb{R}^D$, the mechanism is defined as follows. Let $k = \max(1, \lfloor k_{\text{frac}} \cdot D \rfloor)$ and $S \subset \{1, ..., D\}$ be the set of indices of the k entries of z with largest absolute value. Then, the top-k operator is defined as

$$[\text{Topk}(z)]_j = z_j \cdot \left[\mathbf{1}_{\{j \in S\}} = \begin{cases} z_j, & \text{if } j \in S \\ 0, & \text{if } j \notin S \end{cases} \right]$$

where $\mathbf{1}_{\{\cdot\}}$ is a masking operator.

Continuous Vector c. After the selection step, a continuous vector $c \sim \mathcal{N}(0, 1)$ is concatenated to the resulting latent space Topk(z). The decoder takes the concatenated representation as input and outputs a reconstruction $\hat{x}$. The output is further fed into the Q-net and is encouraged to predict the continuous vector c. In this way, the decoder is forced to rely on the sparse representation Topk(z) and the continuous vector c to reconstruct the input sequence.

Optimization Objective. The objective of the Q-SAE is similar to that of the SAE: the model is encouraged to reconstruct the input data x from a sparse representation z. In the Q-SAE, the most prominent features of z are selected through the top-k selector, which acts on on z with the purpose of passing only meaningful sparse features to the decoder. In addition, a continuous vector c is concatenated to the filtered z space, which is processed by the decoder to predict $\hat{x}$.

The support Q-net predicts a continuous vector $\hat{c}$ from $\hat{x}$ and is optimized using a mutual information (MI) cost function to encourage c to include meaningful information about x. This forces c to be used during decoding, so that we can later use low-dimensional continuous vectors to modify relevant features of z. The final objective is defined as

$$\mathcal{L}_{\text{SAE}} = \overbrace{\frac{1}{N}\sum_{i=1}^{N}(x_i - \hat{x}_i)^2}^{\text{MSE Reconstruction}} + \underbrace{\lambda \cdot ||\text{Topk}(z)||_1}_{L1\text{ Sparsity}}$$

$$\mathcal{L}_{\text{Q}} = \underbrace{\beta \cdot \text{InfoNCE}(\hat{c}, c)}_{\text{MI}}$$

$$\mathcal{L}_{\text{Q-SAE}} = \mathcal{L}_{\text{SAE}} + \mathcal{L}_{\text{Q}}$$

where InfoNCE (Oord et al., 2018) is the contrastive loss function and MI term that pushes the Q-net's predictions $\hat{c}$ to be informative.

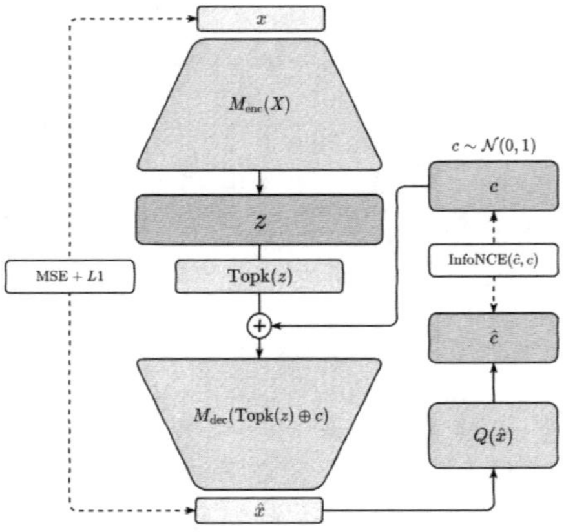

Figure 3: Q-Sparse Autoencoder architecture.

Data and Training. We train our models on a self-supervised regime using the activations extracted from HuBERT during inference on the TIMIT dataset.

After training both architectures, we choose the vanilla autoencoder for the following reasons. First, the feature disambiguation is more straightforward in the sense that it avoids an extra cost objective. Second, the original objective of the study is more aligned with the central purpose of the vanilla SAE: disentangle polysemanticity. However, we propose the Q-SAE (or potential variants) as promising alternatives useful for causal interpretability.

Figure 4 shows three training runs of the SAE architecture with different λ values. Following previous work (Bricken et al., 2023; Templeton et al., 2024), we aimed at preserving 3% of active units in the latent space. We use the model trained with $\lambda = 0.09$ as our model for experimentation. Model selection was not mainly guided by a minimal test loss criterion, but rather as a mixed one giving preference to the model with best z space representations.

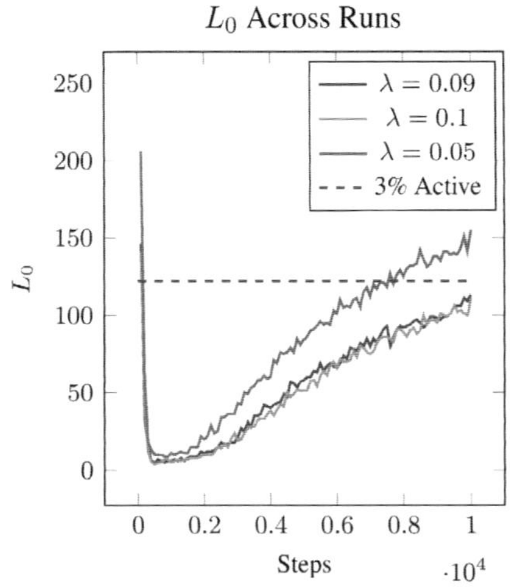

Figure 4: L_0 tracking of the SAE model across three runs with different sparsity lambda values. The dashed line indicates the 3% active units frontier.

Table 1 shows a high level summary of the training runs of each model. Following (Bricken et al., 2023; Templeton et al., 2024) we use a latent space four times the original input size.

Model	SAE_1	SAE_2	SAE_3
Epochs	10	10	10
Input	1024	1024	1024
Latent D	4096	4096	4096
Factor	4	4	4
Sparsity λ	0.09	0.1	0.05
Optimizer	Adam	Adam	Adam
Grad Clip	1.0	1.0	1.0
L1 Train	0.16	0.15	0.24
L1 Test	0.18	0.17	0.27
MSE Train	0.58	0.58	0.57
MSE Test	0.48	0.48	0.46

Table 1: Training parameters for each sparse autoencoder run.

4 Results

Sparse Features Capture Phonetic Events. To verify that individual sparse dimensions behave like discrete event detectors, we extracted the ten features with highest activation variance and plotted their supra-threshold spiking patterns in Figure 5.

These top features activated in distinct, temporally sparse bursts, consistent with a spiking code. Several of these sparse codes showed structured, bursty activation patterns rather than random or uniformly distributed firing, suggesting they responded to recurring patterns in the input. Some units fired densely in specific time ranges, potentially corresponding to phonetic or acoustic units, while others showed more distributed or selective patterns. These observations supported the hypothesis that individual sparse units serve as feature detectors, encoding meaningful substructures in the representation space.

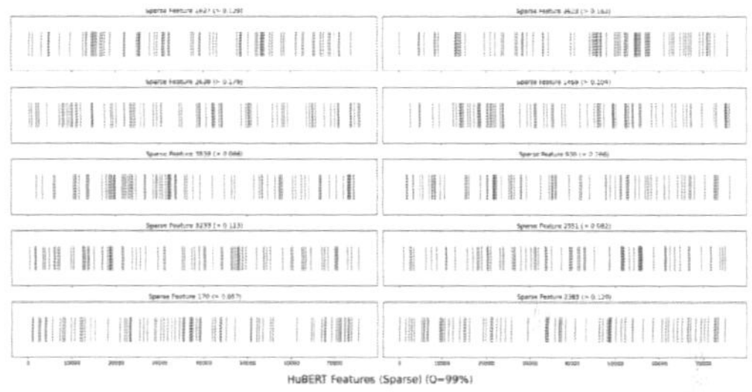

Figure 5: Temporal firing rasters of the top ten variance sparse features. Each panel shows the frame indices (x-axis) at which a given feature exceeds its 99th percentile threshold, revealing spike-like activations.

High-level clustering indicates "phonological hubs". To probe whether individual sparse dimensions acted like monosemantic feature detectors, we performed k-means clustering of the latent, over-complete, z representations. We show the most prominent phonological categories per cluster in Figure 6.

The heatmap analysis of phonological categories versus sparse code clusters indicated variability in how phonetic information was distributed across latent units. Clusters 22, 40, 42, and 57 show distinctly stronger associations with specific phonological categories, such as silence, vowels, and stops. This suggests that a subset of sparse codes preferentially encoded phonetic events more clearly

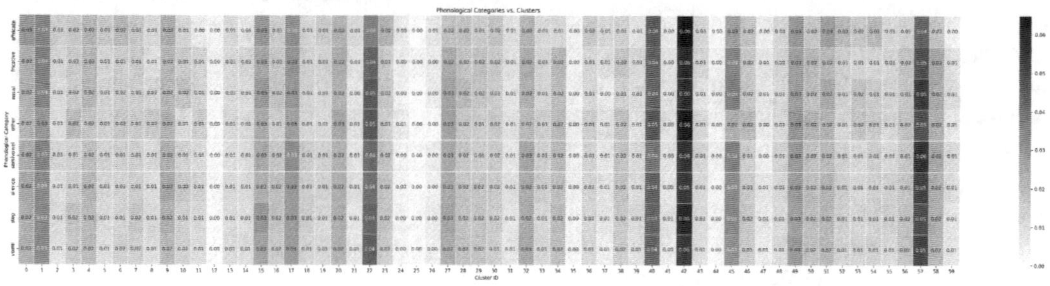

Figure 6: Confusion plot of the over-complete vectors z clusters vs phonological categories.

than others, highlighting their specialized role as potential feature detectors. In contrast, other clusters showed relatively uniform and lower activation levels across categories, underscoring the sparsity and selectivity of these high-variance units.

Features Can be Higher or Lower Order. We quantified the category specificity of each high-variance feature by averaging its activation over all frames of each phonological class (Figure 7).

Features 3233, 385, 2026, and 3623 showed a higher selectivity for affricates, while other dimensions yielded mean activations higher in stops than in vowels, indicating strong sensitivity to transient bursts and turbulence. Conversely, features such as 1627, 3320, and 170 activated across all categories, indicating polysemanticity. This indicated that the features were classified into low-order (including individualized category information) or high-order (detectors for various categories) selective classes.

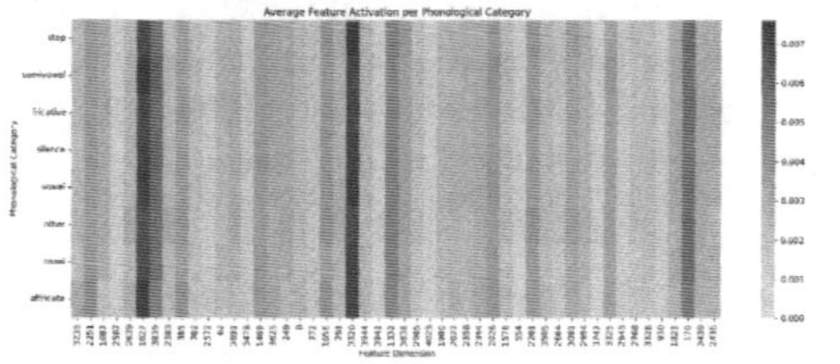

Figure 7: Average activation of the highest-variance sparse features, computed separately for each phonological category. Rows correspond to categories and columns to feature dimensions (sorted by variance).

5 Discussion

The primary objective of this study was to leverage sparse autoencoders (SAEs) as unsupervised probes for interpreting phonological information captured by self-supervised speech models, specifically HuBERT. Our findings underscore the efficacy of SAEs in uncovering discrete, phonetic events encoded within high-dimensional sparse spaces, highlighting their potential as powerful interpretability tools in speech processing.

One significant insight is the emergent nature of the sparse features extracted from the final MLP activations of HuBERT. High-variance sparse units align with phonetic units, suggesting these encode acoustic-phonetic events. This aligns well with classical phonetic theory, which emphasizes the acoustic saliency of such transitional points (Stevens, 2002). Low-variance units encode subtler phonetic nuances distributed across broader contexts, indicating a hierarchical structuring of phonological information within the latent space.

Another critical observation is the partial rather than complete monosemanticity of extracted features. Although some sparse units exhibit specificity towards particular phonetic events, many high-variance dimensions activate across multiple classes. This polysemanticity implies that the HuBERT model's internal representation inherently take advantage of phonetic information distributed across dimensions, a phenomenon consistent with previous findings in sparse coding research in other modalities (Bricken et al., 2023; Templeton et al., 2024). Consequently, future research might explore mechanisms to further disentangle these polysemantic representations, possibly via refined architectures or additional regularization techniques.

Additionally, our experimental results emphasize the limitations inherent to a purely unsupervised approach. While the sparse autoencoder provides valuable qualitative insights, interpreting the full phonetic scope of each unit's activations remains challenging without reference to external linguistic labels. A hybrid approach integrating sparse autoencoders with minimally supervised labeling or linguistic priors could enhance the interpretability and practical applicability of the proposed methodology.

The introduction of the Q-SAE, despite its intriguing potential for causal manipulation of sparse features through continuous vectors, requires further investigation. Our preliminary decision to favor the vanilla SAE was guided by simplicity and clearer interpretability. However, the Q-SAE's ability to manipulate sparse feature spaces via controllable vectors could significantly extend the framework's utility, especially in tasks requiring precise feature-level intervention, such as speech editing or targeted phoneme manipulation.

Finally, this study contributes methodologically by demonstrating the compatibility of sparse coding techniques, traditionally used in computational neuroscience, with contemporary deep learning models for speech. This intersection offers fertile ground for interdisciplinary research, potentially enabling cognitive insights into speech perception and informing the design of biologically inspired machine learning models.

Future work should focus on scaling this approach to larger and more diverse speech corpora, validating the robustness of our findings across languages and dialects. Additionally, exploring adaptive or dynamic sparsity constraints could refine the granularity of phonological features captured, further bridging computational techniques with linguistic theory.

6 Conclusion

We introduced an unsupervised probing pipeline that uses a sparse autoencoder to extract interpretable features from the final MLP activations of a pretrained HuBERT model. Our qualitative analyses show that: (i) high-variance latent units fire at linguistically meaningful phonetic events, and (ii) clustering those sparse codes recovers broad class groupings. These findings suggest that scaling the presented pipeline and sparse coding can uncover phonological structure in self-supervised speech models without any explicit supervision, providing a new tool for model interpretability and control.

Limitations

The performance of the models and the experimental results were heavily constrained by the available data. Further work should incorporate activations from different datasets and models to uncover potential universal behaviors across models. In addition, the study is limited to the analysis of one layer's MLP activations. Internal layers may yield more interpretable and comprehensive results. The Q-SAE is still under development, which posed a limitation to its usefulness for the case under study.

Ethics Statement

This work uses publicly available speech data and does not involve any personally identifiable or sensitive information. All analyses were performed on aggregate model activations.

References

Alexei Baevski, Wei-Ning Hsu, Qiantong Xu, Arun Babu, Jiatao Gu, and Michael Auli. 2022. Data2vec: A general framework for self-supervised learning in speech, vision and language. In *International conference on machine learning*, pages 1298–1312. PMLR.

Alexei Baevski, Yuhao Zhou, Abdelrahman Mohamed, and Michael Auli. 2020a. wav2vec 2.0: A framework for self-supervised learning of speech representations. *Advances in neural information processing systems*, 33:12449–12460.

Alexei Baevski, Yuhao Zhou, Abdelrahman Mohamed, and Michael Auli. 2020b. wav2vec 2.0: A framework for self-supervised learning of speech representations. *Advances in neural information processing systems*, 33:12449–12460.

Trenton Bricken, Adly Templeton, Joshua Batson, Brian Chen, Adam Jermyn, Tom Conerly, Nick Turner, Cem Anil, Carson Denison, Amanda Askell, et al. 2023. Towards monosemanticity: Decomposing language models with dictionary learning. *Transformer Circuits Thread*, 2.

Sanyuan Chen, Chengyi Wang, Zhengyang Chen, Yu Wu, Shujie Liu, Zhuo Chen, Jinyu Li, Naoyuki Kanda, Takuya Yoshioka, Xiong Xiao, et al. 2022. Wavlm: Large-scale self-supervised pre-training for full stack speech processing. *IEEE Journal of Selected Topics in Signal Processing*, 16(6):1505–1518.

Xi Chen, Yan Duan, Rein Houthooft, John Schulman, Ilya Sutskever, and Pieter Abbeel. 2016. Infogan: Interpretable representation learning by information maximizing generative adversarial nets. *Advances in neural information processing systems*, 29.

Kevin Clark, Urvashi Khandelwal, Omer Levy, and Christopher D Manning. 2019. What does bert look at? an analysis of bert's attention. *arXiv preprint arXiv:1906.04341*.

Patrick Cormac English, John Kelleher, and Julie Carson-Berndsen. 2022. Domain-informed probing of wav2vec 2.0 embeddings for phonetic features. In *Proceedings of the 19th SIGMORPHON Workshop on Computational Research in Phonetics, Phonology, and Morphology*, pages 83–91.

John S Garofolo, Lori F Lamel, William M Fisher, Jonathan G Fiscus, and David S Pallett. 1993. Darpa timit acoustic-phonetic continous speech corpus cd-rom. nist speech disc 1-1.1. *NASA STI/Recon technical report n*, 93:27403.

David Gimeno-Gómez, Catarina Botelho, Anna Pompili, Alberto Abad, and Carlos-D Martínez-Hinarejos. 2025. Unveiling interpretability in self-supervised speech representations for parkinson's diagnosis. *IEEE Journal of Selected Topics in Signal Processing*.

Wei-Ning Hsu, Benjamin Bolte, Yao-Hung Hubert Tsai, Kushal Lakhotia, Ruslan Salakhutdinov, and Abdelrahman Mohamed. 2021. Hubert: Self-supervised speech representation learning by masked prediction of hidden units. *IEEE/ACM transactions on audio, speech, and language processing*, 29:3451–3460.

James MacQueen. 1967. Some methods for classification and analysis of multivariate observations. In *Proceedings of the Fifth Berkeley Symposium on Mathematical Statistics and Probability, Volume 1: Statistics*, volume 5, pages 281–298. University of California press.

Kinan Martin, Jon Gauthier, Canaan Breiss, and Roger Levy. 2023. Probing self-supervised speech models for phonetic and phonemic information: a case study in aspiration. *arXiv preprint arXiv:2306.06232*.

Leland McInnes, John Healy, and James Melville. 2018. Umap: Uniform manifold approximation and projection for dimension reduction. *arXiv preprint arXiv:1802.03426*.

Ari Morcos, Maithra Raghu, and Samy Bengio. 2018. Insights on representational similarity in neural networks with canonical correlation. *Advances in neural information processing systems*, 31.

Andrew Ng et al. 2011. Sparse autoencoder. *CS294A Lecture notes*, 72(2011):1–19.

Bruno A Olshausen and David J Field. 1996. Emergence of simple-cell receptive field properties by learning a sparse code for natural images. *Nature*, 381(6583):607–609.

Aaron van den Oord, Yazhe Li, and Oriol Vinyals. 2018. Representation learning with contrastive predictive coding. *arXiv preprint arXiv:1807.03748*.

Ankita Pasad, Chung-Ming Chien, Shane Settle, and Karen Livescu. 2024. What do self-supervised speech models know about words? *Transactions of the Association for Computational Linguistics*, 12:372–391.

Ankita Pasad, Ju-Chieh Chou, and Karen Livescu. 2021. Layer-wise analysis of a self-supervised speech representation model. In *2021 IEEE Automatic Speech Recognition and Understanding Workshop (ASRU)*, pages 914–921. IEEE.

Tiago Pimentel, Josef Valvoda, Rowan Hall Maudslay, Ran Zmigrod, Adina Williams, and Ryan Cotterell. 2020. Information-theoretic probing for linguistic structure. *arXiv preprint arXiv:2004.03061*.

Maithra Raghu, Justin Gilmer, Jason Yosinski, and Jascha Sohl-Dickstein. 2017. Svcca: Singular vector canonical correlation analysis for deep learning dynamics and interpretability. *Advances in neural information processing systems*, 30.

Kenneth N Stevens. 2002. Toward a model for lexical access based on acoustic landmarks and distinctive features. *The Journal of the Acoustical Society of America*, 111(4):1872–1891.

Adly Templeton, Tom Conerly, Jonathan Marcus, Jack Lindsey, Trenton Bricken, Brian Chen, Adam Pearce, Craig Citro, Emmanuel Ameisen, Andy Jones, et al. 2024. Scaling monosemanticity: Extracting interpretable features from claude 3 sonnet. transformer circuits thread.

Ian Tenney, Patrick Xia, Berlin Chen, Alex Wang, Adam Poliak, R Thomas McCoy, Najoung Kim, Benjamin Van Durme, Samuel R Bowman, Dipanjan Das, et al. 2019. What do you learn from context? probing for sentence structure in contextualized word representations. *arXiv preprint arXiv:1905.06316*.

A HuBERT Parameters

The following section summarizes the parameters of the HuBERT model used for inference in our experimental setup.

Parameter	Value
feat_extract_activation	gelu
conv_bias	true
conv_dim	512
conv_kernel	[10, 3, 3, 3, 3, 2, 2]
conv_stride	[5, 2, 2, 2, 2, 2, 2]
attention_dropout	0.1
ctc_loss_reduction	sum
ctc_zero_infinity	false
feat_proj_dropout	0.1
final_dropout	0.1
hidden_dropout	0.1
hidden_act	gelu
hidden_dropout_prob	0.1
hidden_size	1024
intermediate_size	4096
layer_norm_eps	1e-5
layerdrop	0.1
mask_feature_length	10
mask_time_length	10
mask_time_prob	0.05
model_type	hubert
num_attention_heads	16
num_conv_pos_embedding_groups	16
num_conv_pos_embeddings	128
num_feat_extract_layers	7
num_hidden_layers	24
vocab_size	32

Table 2: Hyperparameter configuration of the HuBERT model used during experimentation. This information is available on Hugging Face.

B Data Splits

The following table shows the size of the TIMIT splits used during inference on HuBERT. For each raw waveform, we extract the HuBERT's last MLP activations.

Split	Audio files
Train	$\approx$ 4,620
Test	$\approx$ 1,680

Table 3: Splits of the TIMIT dataset.

Learning Dynamics of Meta-Learning in Small Model Pretraining

David Demitri Africa* **Yuval Weiss**
Paula Buttery **Richard Diehl Martinez**
University of Cambridge

Abstract

Large language models are powerful but costly. We ask whether meta-learning can make the pretraining of small language models not only faster but also more interpretable. We integrate first–order MAML with subset-masked LM pretraining, producing four LLama-style decoder-only models (11M–570M params), and evaluate on multilingual Universal NER. Compared with vanilla training, our hybrid setup (i) reaches the same loss up to 1.6× sooner, (ii) yields modest but consistent average gains on Universal NER at medium/large scales under equal compute (+2–3 percentage points), and (iii) and (iii) reveals phase-like learning dynamics: models first diversify their representations, then compress them in a pattern that aligns with improved episodic accuracy. These observations are correlational, not causal, and we do not claim generality beyond NER or across seeds. We also document a trade-off: perplexity on Paloma (a diverse language modeling benchmark spanning 18 domains; Magnusson et al. (2024)) is worse at most scales. Code, checkpoints and analysis logs are released.

davidafrica/pico-maml

DavidDemitriAfrica/pico-maml-train

1 Introduction

Small language models (SLMs) are attractive for privacy and energy reasons, but trail large models partly because they converge slowly and plateau early (Godey et al., 2024; Biderman et al., 2023; Diehl Martinez et al., 2024). As opposed to the common method of brute-force scaling, we explore a different axis: learning rules. First-order Model-Agnostic Meta-Learning (MAML) (Finn et al., 2017) promises a learn-to-learn initialization, yet has rarely been applied to decoder models, and its effect on learning dynamics are poorly understood.

We address this by adding meta-learning in model pretraining,[1] interleaving ordinary next-token loss (keeps fluency) with 32-way subset-mask (Bansal et al., 2020; Li and Zhang, 2021) episodes (forces rapid binding). Only a tiny MLP head is adapted in the inner loop, so we can track backbone weights without gradient noise. Our contributions are:

1. Four open SLMs (11M → 570M) trained with this **hybrid MAML rule**.
2. A public trainer that logs per-checkpoint **singular-value spectra**, head entropies and query accuracy.
3. A candid evaluation on Universal NER: **modest gains at medium/large scales** (+2–3 pp), alongside a **perplexity trade-off**.
4. Observational evidence of a **diversify–then–compress phase transition** in effective rank.

Reporting and scope. All pretraining and fine-tuning results are from a single shared seed per condition due to compute limits; we therefore report averages across datasets where applicable, avoid statistical claims, and treat learning-dynamics findings as exploratory. We limit generalization claims to NER and to our training regime.

2 Related Work

Meta-learning for NLP. (MAML; Finn et al., 2017) is an optimisation-based form of meta-learning that learns an initialisation from which a few gradient steps solve new tasks. It has been particularly successful in computer

*Corresponding author: **david.demitri.africa@gmail.com**

[1] Using a lightweight modification of PICO-TRAIN (Diehl Martinez, 2025), a language model pretraining suite.

Proceedings of the IJCNLP-AACL 2025 Student Research Workshop, pages 10–23
December 20-24, 2025 ©2025 Association for Computational Linguistics

vision classification and reinforcement learning settings (Nichol et al., 2018). Within NLP, MAML has been adapted to a wide spectrum of supervised problems—including text classification, natural language inference, question answering, summarisation and named entity recognition—where a pre-trained encoder such as BERT is further fine-tuned on small datasets (Rajeswaran et al., 2019; Raghu et al., 2021; Hou et al., 2022). These studies operate (i) on encoder-only, masked-language models and (ii) at parameter counts close to the original 110M-parameter BERT. They leave open whether optimisation-based meta-learning helps decoder LMs and whether its benefits persist at larger parameter scales.

Meta-learning for pretraining. Initial NLP attempts applied MAML only at fine-tuning scale (Raghu et al., 2021; Hou et al., 2022). More recent work embeds bilevel objectives directly in pre-training (Miranda et al., 2023; Ke et al., 2021). While promising, these efforts evaluate only a single model size, focus on one downstream task, or release neither code nor weights, limiting reproducibility and obscuring scale trends. We embed meta-learning directly into the pretraining loop, evaluate on various unseen domains in an unseen task, and provide open weights (11M-570M) and layer-wise spectra, filling that gap.

Subset-Mask LMs (SMLMT). SMLMT constructs pseudo-tasks using a subset of vocabulary words (Bansal et al., 2020). Given an unlabeled text corpus, one selects a set of N words and builds an N-way classification task. For each chosen word, sentences containing it are collected and the word is masked out. The task is then to predict the masked word from the N candidates. Li and Zhang (2021) interleaves it with ProtoNet tasks; we interleave with vanilla LM updates and scale to 570M params.

Interpretable training dynamics. Various works discuss the training of language models in phase transitions (Olsson et al., 2022; Hoogland et al., 2024), describing broad changes in indicators as the model gains rapidly in capabilities over a short period of time. We study such phase transitions in the context of meta-learning in pretraining.

Effective-rank probes (entropy of singular values) highlight learning behavior in deep nets (Diehl Martinez et al., 2024). Lower-rank structure and rank compression are well documented in the literature (Huh et al., 2021; Galanti et al., 2022; Jaderberg et al., 2014), and we focus on the timing and co-evolution of the measurements of effective-rank probes with episodic generalization under the hybrid objective (§5).

3 Method

We pretrain four decoder models at 11M, 65M, 181M and 570M parameters with a hybrid objective (Li and Zhang, 2021) that alternates conventional next-token prediction and first-order MAML episodes (Finn et al., 2017). The episodes are generated with Subset-Masked Language Modelling Tasks (SMLMT) (Bansal et al., 2020). This section details the backbone, the meta-learning episode, the optimisation schedule, and the downstream evaluation harness.

3.1 Baselines

The starting point is the open Pico decoder (Diehl Martinez, 2025), a LLAMA-style (Touvron et al., 2023) stack implemented in plain PyTorch. To maintain apples-to-apples comparability with the original models (and as such isolate the effect of introducing MAML to pretraining), we maintain the design choices and hyperparameter choices of the original Pico decoder models. A sequence of $L = 12$ decoder blocks receives 2048 input tokens. Each block performs RMSNorm (Zhang and Sennrich, 2019), grouped-query self-attention (Ainslie et al., 2023) with rotary position embeddings (Su et al., 2024), and a SwiGLU feed-forward network (Shazeer, 2020) that expands to $4d$ before projecting back to the model width d. Width is the only scale-dependent hyper-parameter: $d \in \{96, 384, 768, 1536\}$ for the tiny, small, medium and large variants. All models use 12 heads, 4 key–value heads and causal masking.

3.2 Task construction via SMLMT

SMLMT converts unlabelled text into few-shot classification tasks. From the corpus we sample a set of N content words, collect sentences that contain each word and replace that word with a single `<mask>`. The goal is to predict which of the N candidates was masked. Each episode supplies K support sentences and a disjoint query set. Table 1 shows an episode with $N = 4$ city names and $K = 2$ supports per class; the query asks the model to complete a new sentence about cherry blossoms. In practice we use $N = 32$ and $K = 4$ so the task entropy matches the five-bit next-token uncertainty

Set	Input (masked)	Label
Support (K=2 each)	I visited __ last summer.	Tokyo
	The sushi festival in __ was unforgettable.	Tokyo
	The Big Ben is in __.	London
	I caught the tube at __ yesterday.	London
	The Seine runs through __.	Paris
	She admired the art at the Louvre in __.	Paris
	The Forbidden City is in __.	Beijing
	I sampled Peking duck in __.	Beijing
Query	I plan to travel to __ to see the cherry blossoms.	Tokyo

Table 1: Example SMLMT episode with N=4 classes and K=2 support sentences per class.

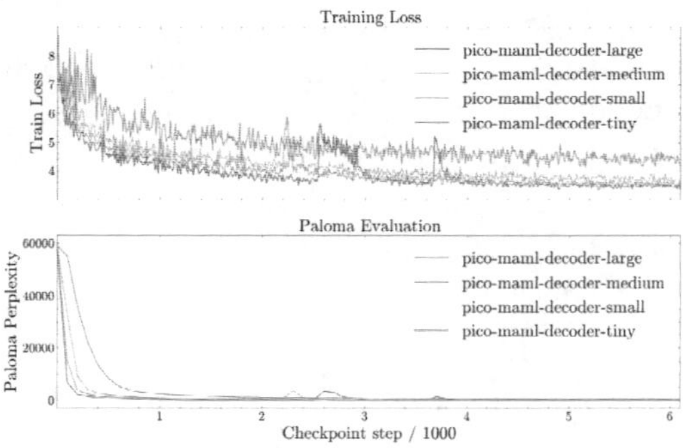

Figure 1: Training loss and Paloma perplexity across pretraining steps for all MAML models. Two-panel plot showing the evolution of (top) cross-entropy training loss and (bottom) Paloma perplexity, each as a function of global pretraining step.

Model	Train Loss @6k	Paloma Perplexity @6k
`pico-decoder-tiny`	5.31	786.85
`pico-maml-decoder-tiny`	**4.44**	**422.42**
`pico-decoder-small`	4.14	**80.25**
`pico-maml-decoder-small`	**3.67**	113.76
`pico-decoder-medium`	3.89	**77.90**
`pico-maml-decoder-medium`	**3.49**	78.63
`pico-decoder-large`	3.69	**49.86**
`pico-maml-decoder-large`	**3.49**	66.62

Table 2: For each model (rows) under vanilla vs. MAML pretraining (columns), shows cross-entropy loss and Paloma perplexity measured at exactly 6000 steps.

of English text.[2]

3.3 Optimiser, data, and monitoring

Training runs for 6000 outer updates on four A100 GPUs, with the original Pico-decoder models evaluated at the checkpoint after 6000 steps. Each GPU streams micro batches of 256 sequences from the 30 percent English subset of Dolma (Soldaini et al., 2024) that is already tokenised and chunked by Pico (Diehl Martinez, 2025). The outer optimiser is AdamW with peak learning rate 3×10^{-4}, 2500-step warm-up and cosine decay. Micro batches of 256 sequences are accumulated eight times giving an effective batch of 2048 (1024 for the 11M model). Every 100 steps we evaluate Paloma perplexity (Magnusson et al., 2024) and log the singular values of three attention and three feed-forward matrices to compute effective rank (Diehl Martinez et al., 2024). Query and support accuracies are also tracked.

3.4 Downstream protocol

Named entity recognition (NER), the downstream task for this study, is a fundamental NLP task that identifies and categorizes entities (e.g., persons, organizations, locations) within unstructured text (Chinchor and Robinson, 1997), and is used in healthcare (Kundeti et al., 2016; Polignano et al., 2021; Shafqat et al., 2022), law (Leitner et al., 2019; Au et al., 2022; Naik et al., 2023), business (Putthividhya and Hu, 2011; Alvarado et al., 2015; Zhao et al., 2021), and knowledge graph systems (Al-Moslmi et al., 2020). Specifically, we evaluate our models on Universal NER benchmark (Mayhew et al., 2024). UNER v1 comprises three categories of NER evaluation data, each built on top of Universal Dependencies (UD) (Nivre et al., 2016, 2020) tokenization and annotations: publicly available in-language treebanks, parallel UD (PUD) evaluation, and other eval-only sets (Appendix B).

After pretraining we load the checkpoint at step 6000 and attach a fresh linear classifier for UniversalNER. Two fine-tuning settings are used: head-only and full. In the head-only setting the Transformer is frozen so fine-tuning mirrors the inner loop, in the full setting all weights update. Fine-tuning uses AdamW at 3×10^{-5} for at most ten epochs with early stopping on development F_1.

4 Model Pretraining

Training-perplexity tradeoff across scales. The prerequisite for modifying a pretraining method is ensuring the model still learns. All four Pico-MAML variants reach their respective vanilla loss 1.3–1.6× sooner (faster optimization), but Paloma perplexity is worse at most scales by 6000 steps (Table 2).

Contrary to expectation, MAML's inductive bias may favor optimization over regularization. MAML accelerates convergence but degrades out-of-task fluency at most scales. However, this pat-

[2] Shannon's estimate of printed-English entropy is about 1.3 bits per character (Shannon, 1951); since English BPE tokens span on average about 4 characters (OpenAI, 2025), this implies roughly ≈ 5.2 bits/token. We therefore use 5 bits per token as a conservative rule of thumb.

Model	Seen		Test-Only (PUD)		Test-Only (Other)	
	Head	Full	Head	Full	Head	Full
tiny (%)	-8.3	-3.0	+6.7	0.0	-37.5	+3.8
small (%)	+2.2	0.0	-17.2	-0.6	+46.7	+7.0
medium (%)	+1.9	+2.3	-4.6	+1.8	+14.8	+3.8
large (%)	+6.2	+4.8	+7.2	+3.5	+2.1	+8.1

Table 3: Relative percentage improvement of micro-F1 (higher = better) for head-only vs. full fine-tuning across seen, test-only (PUD), and low-resource language groups (other). Demonstrates MAML's consistent 2–3 pp lift at medium/large scales under full tuning. Green cells indicate MAML improvements; red cells show degradations.

Model	Danish	English	Croatian	Portuguese	Swedish
large (%)	+8.1	+14.8	+10.7	+8.6	+18.0

Table 4: Percentage relative improvement of MAML over vanilla for head-only tuning in the large model.

Model	Danish	English	Croatian	Portuguese	Swedish
tiny (%)	+3.4	+0.2	-1.6	-0.7	+6.1
small (%)	-3.9	-4.7	-1.9	-2.6	+4.9
medium (%)	+0.8	+4.8	+3.9	+1.2	+3.7
large (%)	+3.6	+4.4	-0.5	+4.2	+2.8

Table 5: Percentage-wise relative improvement of MAML over vanilla under full tuning for each language.

tern is consistent with known multi-task interference: the episodic discriminative objective improves adaptation signals but can conflict with next-token distributional modeling under fixed compute and a single set of hyperparameters (Kendall et al., 2017; Yu et al., 2020; Standley et al., 2020). Hence, it is unclear if the perplexity gap is an objective-mixing artifact or evidence that meta-learning inherently harms LM fluency.

5 Downstream NER Evaluation

Models are fine-tuned on each dataset in Universal NER (Mayhew et al., 2024; Nivre et al., 2016, 2020) with publicly available train and dev sets[3] Results (averaged across each finetuning dataset) are shown as micro-F1 scores in Table 3, organized by evaluation group: seen (language with full train/test/dev splits), test-only (using Parallel Universal Dependencies PUD), and test-only low-resource languages (e.g., Cebuano, Tagalog). We report delta F1 as percentage points (pp) unless explicitly marked as percent change (%).

The most striking takeaway from this stage is that, when averaged across all evaluation steps in a category, absolute F1 remains low (≤ 0.35, i.e., $\leq 35\%$) due to poor zero-shot transfer, especially for logographic scripts. Overall, MAML improves mean uplift is approximately +2–3 pp when averaged over all in-language datasets at medium/large scales, confirming a modest "learning-to-learn" effect under full adaptation.[4]

In-language NER gains suggest capacity-dependent meta-learning. To better understand how meta-initialization influences cross-lingual transfer on seen languages, F1 scores are broken down by dataset within the in-language group. The results are separated by tuning regime to clarify the extent to which meta-learned representations help when only the classifier is updated (head-only) versus when the entire model is fine-tuned.

In the head-only setting (Table 7), absolute F1 scores remain low across most datasets. Tiny models fail to generalize altogether. MAML shows the strongest and most consistent gains at large scales (Table 4)—most prominently on en_ewt, hr_set, and sv_talbanken-suggesting that episodic pretraining creates more adaptable feature spaces, particularly for common entity types and scripts. On Chinese (zh_gsd, zh_gsdsimp), performance is uniformly poor, confirming the baseline result in (Mayhew et al., 2024) that transfer from phonographic to logographic scripts is difficult.

In the full setting (Table 5), both vanilla and MAML-pretrained models achieve higher F1 scores across the board. MAML confers consistent +0.01-0.03 gains at medium and large scales, especially for structurally complex languages like Croatian. These relative gains grow as model capacity increases, indicating that larger models benefit more from MAML pretraining. Even in Chinese, where scores are lowest, MAML nudges performance upward. These gains confirm that meta-pretraining does more than support shallow transfer: it reshapes the optimization landscape of the full model in a way that accelerates convergence and improves generalization.

Taken together, these tables validate that MAML pretraining injects a scalable and tunable learning-to-learn signal. However, these average metrics do not tell the full story. Some settings, entity

[3]Namely, ddt, ewt, set, bosque, snk, set, talbanken, gsd, gsdsimp, all.

[4]While these results are much worse in comparison to the baseline in the original Universal NER paper (Mayhew et al., 2024), this is likely because XLM-R_{large} is a multilingual model (Conneau et al., 2020) and the pretraining dataset for Pico is entirely in English.

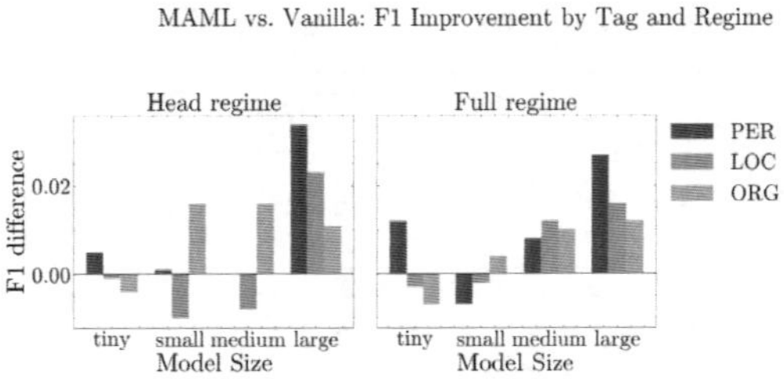

Figure 2: MAML-Vanilla micro-F1 difference by entity class and tuning regime, averaged across in-language datasets. Grouped bar charts reporting ΔF1 = F1 MAML - F1 (Vanilla) for three named-entity classes-PERSON (PER), LOCATION (LOC) and ORGANIZATION (ORG)-for pico-MAML decoders of four sizes (tiny, small, medium, large), averaged over nine in-language NER datasets, over two fine-tuning regimes.

classes, and fine-tuning conditions benefit substantially more than others.

Class-specific prototype bias in entity recognition. We characterize the specific way MAML pretraining improves performance in NER by breaking down F1 score by entity class in Figure 2.

Meta-pretraining yields a clear capacity threshold in head-only adaptation. Under a frozen backbone, only the large model consistently converts its learned initialization into PER (+0.034) and LOC (+0.023) gains; medium and smaller variants lack the representational bandwidth to rewire person and place distinctions via a shallow classifier. By contrast, even medium and small models see gains in ORG (+0.016 F1) likely because organization names often include distinctive tokens (e.g., "Inc.", "Corp.", or "University") that form rigid, token-level co-occurrence patterns. These simple patterns mirror the pseudo-classification episodes SMLMT generates, so a shallow classifier can latch onto them without requiring deep feature reconfiguration.

Full fine-tuning broadens and amplifies these effects. In the full setting, PER sees the largest MAML-induced lift (up to +0.027 in the large model). LOC improvements (+0.016 at large scale) climb more gradually: place names often span heterogeneous contexts and scripts (e.g. Zagreb vs. Beijing), so meta-pretraining must be supplemented by full gradient flow for location-specific embeddings. ORG continues to enjoy gains (+0.012 at large), reinforcing that organization recognition remains the simplest class to bootstrap from episodic tasks.

Model	Regime	Overall	Cebuano	Tagalog (TRG)	Tagalog (Ugnayan)
tiny	head	-100.0%	-100.0%	N/A	N/A
small	head	+151.1%	+209.6%	+315.7%	-15.7%
medium	head	+24.3%	+16.7%	-20.7%	+534.3%
large	head	+9.0%	+0.0%	+57.3%	-37.5%
tiny	full	-6.2%	-4.7%	-25.0%	+109.5%
small	full	+7.3%	-6.4%	+28.8%	+4.1%
medium	full	+0.0%	-1.0%	+1.4%	-2.1%
large	full	-8.0%	-14.5%	-1.6%	-0.8%

Table 6: Percentage change of MAML over vanilla zero-shot NER transfer (from English) F1 on low-resource languages (OTHER).

Significant zero-shot transfer gains in low-resource languages. Now, we discuss how inductive biases manifest in zero-shot cross-lingual transfer to low-resource languages—namely, Tagalog (`tl`) and Cebuano (`ceb`).

Tagalog and Cebuano are the two most widely spoken native languages in the Philippines, with tens of millions of first-language speakers each. Both are typologically Austronesian and low-resource, but differ significantly. Tagalog is a morphologically rich, predicate-initial language with a complex voice system that encodes syntactic roles (agent, patient, locative, etc.) through verbal affixes and aspect-marking (Kroeger, 1993; Schachter and Otanes, 1983; Ramos, 2021). Word order is flexible and often pragmatically driven, which weakens the utility of positional cues for tasks like named entity recognition. Cebuano is similarly Austronesian but morphologically simpler than Tagalog, with fewer voice alternations and less affixal variation (Tanangkingsing, 2011). It also does not consistently mark syntactic roles with overt case particles; entities must be inferred from context rather than surface markers (Sityar, 2000). Additionally, Cebuano exhibits a distinct orthographic tradition and more conservative vocabulary (e.g., less Spanish borrowing) (Bunye and Yap, 1971), which further distances it from the English-centric token distributions that dominate cross-lingual pretraining datasets. These characteristics make them ideal stress tests for testing the inductive bias of pretraining strategies like MAML.

In the head-only setting, MAML delivers its greatest impact on small and medium models. For example, the small head jumps from 0.088 to 0.221 overall—an absolute gain of 0.133 F1—and sees particularly large lifts in Cebuano (+0.153) and Tagalog-TRG (+0.262). The medium head also benefits substantially, improving from 0.259 to 0.322. Even the large head picks up a modest +0.030 F1. Only the tiny head collapses, reflecting its inability to form reliable prototypes during meta-training. These patterns suggest that MAML's episodic learning instills useful, language-agnostic representations in the classifier layers, enabling mid-size heads to generalize token-level cues to new languages without modifying the backbone.

Once we allow full fine-tuning, however, most of MAML's advantages disappear at higher capacities. The small model retains a small +0.026 F1 edge, but the medium shows no net change and the large actually drops by 0.034. This reversal implies that when every parameter is free to update, the strong gradient signals of full fine-tuning quickly override the meta-learned inductive biases, erasing or even inverting MAML's earlier head-only gains. The tiny model again underperforms, consistent with its tendency to overfit during meta-training when unconstrained by a fixed backbone.

In the UNER benchmark, Tagalog and Cebuano serve as canonical low-resource, typologically distinct evaluation settings. Overall NER performance remains modest, but, as Table 6 shows, MAML provides meaningful zero-shot boosts in the head-only regime for small and medium models. These gains suggest that even without training exposure to these languages, the inductive biases from English episodic training transfer surprisingly well, at least for token-level prototypes.

6 Learning Dynamics

Despite clear convergence gains, the pretraining metrics alone leave several observations unexplained: the mid-training rebound and double-descent in Paloma perplexity, the abrupt jumps in support versus query accuracy, and the sudden collapse in representation rank. To understand this further, we now turn to a learning-dynamics analysis: tracking episodic support/query performance, classifier head statistics, and proportional effective rank throughout pretraining.

Effective meta-learning has a capacity threshold. To understand how MAML updates influence learning dynamics during pretraining, we track both support (training set in the inner loop) and query (held out final step in the inner loop) accuracy across training steps (Figure 3).

The `small` and `medium` models show clear signs of effective meta-learning. Support accuracy gradually increases and stabilizes around 6–7%, while query accuracy climbs steadily above 40%. This pattern indicates that the models are internalizing

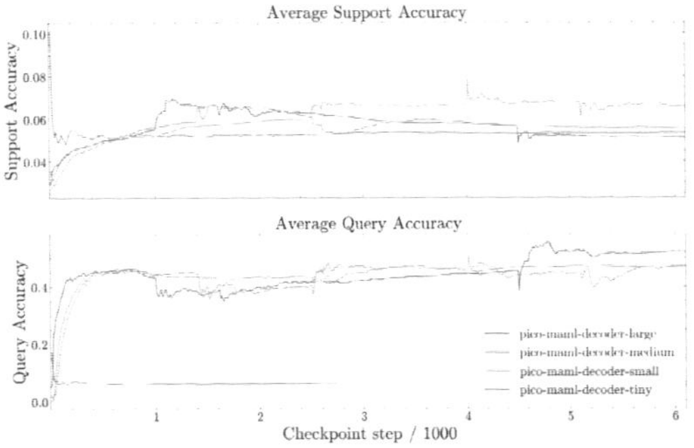

Figure 3: Average support and query accuracy across pretraining steps for all models. Top: Average support-set accuracy (%) measured at the end of each inner-loop adaptation, as a function of the global pretraining step. Bottom: Corresponding average query-set accuracy (%) after adaptation.

a useful task prior, and show smooth convergence with relatively little instability.

The `tiny` model displays a distinct failure mode. While its support accuracy rises modestly, its query accuracy remains stagnant, hovering just above chance (10%). This suggests the model memorizes support examples but fails to learn task-generalizable features-a canonical symptom of underparameterization in meta-learning (Finn et al., 2017; Rajeswaran et al., 2019). In effect, it lacks the representational bandwidth to encode a shared inductive bias across tasks.

The `large` model shows a late-phase rise in query accuracy after 4,500 steps, coinciding with stabilization of head-weight variance. This suggests a phase-like reorganization where the model consolidates a useful episodic prior after a prolonged plateau. In the MAML setting, this may correspond to the model first learning how to adapt, before learning to generalize from adaptation.

Taken together, these patterns confirm that meta-learning is most stable within a mid-capacity regime. Models must be large enough to encode reusable structure, but not so large that their learning becomes erratic. These insights help contextualize downstream findings: the best generalization often arises from models that strike a balance between representational power and stable task-level adaptation.

Classifier head weight variance reveals adaptation behavior. To probe how episodic adaptation reshapes the backbone's feature geometry, we track the mean and standard deviation of the

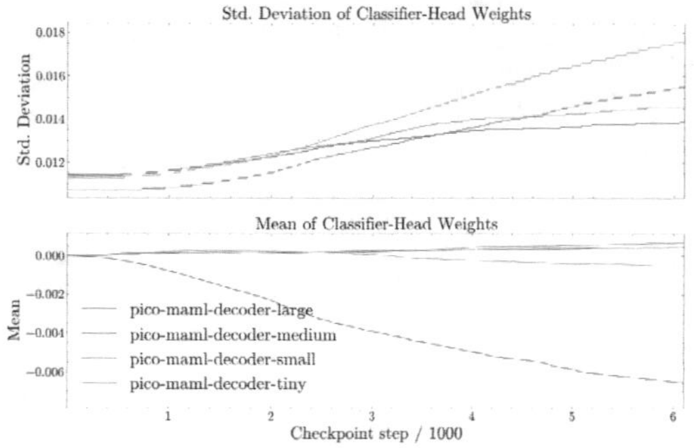

Figure 4: Evolution of classifier head weights during meta-training. Top: Standard deviation of the task-specific classifier head weights (in logits space). Bottom: Mean of the classifier head weights.

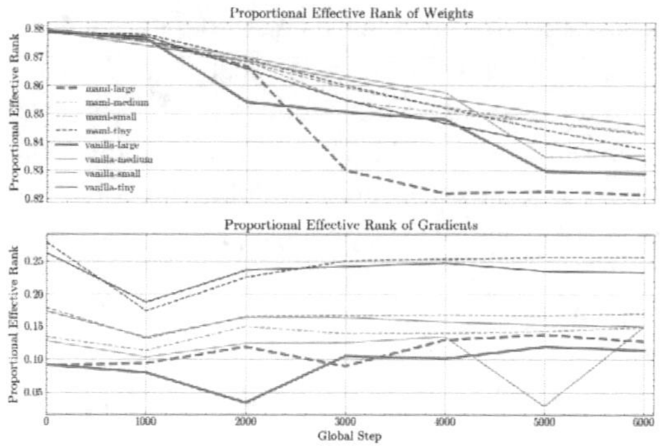

Figure 5: Proportional effective rank of MAML and vanilla models on available checkpoints until 6k steps. Top: weights; bottom: gradients.

episodically adapted classifier head across training (Figure 4). Because the inner loop updates only this shallow head on frozen backbone features, its across-episode weight statistics act as a lightweight linear-probe proxy for class separability: under softmax on fixed features, class weight vectors tend to align with differences between class means, so greater dispersion (std) across head weights indicates larger between-class margins induced by the backbone, while transient spikes without sustained query gains suggest support overfit rather than stable generalization. We therefore relate inflections in mean/std to simultaneous changes in support/query accuracy to contextualize adaptation quality.

The top panel shows the standard deviation of head weights. All models exhibit growth in weight variance, indicating increasing expressivity in the task-specific head. The `small` model diverges most sharply, with its weight variance surpassing all others after 2k steps. This suggests an over-specialization effect: the model learns to adapt aggressively to each task, potentially at the cost of stability. In the lower panel, the mean of the head weights remains near zero for most models, but the `tiny` model is an outlier. It accumulates a strong bias in one direction over training, indicating that its head converges toward a fixed mapping that is minimally updated across episodes. This aligns with earlier diagnostics showing that its gradient norms collapse early in training.

These dynamics reinforce the idea that episodic MAML indeed induces a scale-sensitive tradeoff: in higher-capacity models, episodic gradients drive generalizable structure into the shared initialization; in lower-capacity models, this same pressure can cause drift or collapse.

Evidence of representation collapse and reorganization. To understand how MAML alters internal representations, we track *proportional effective rank* (PER), a structure-sensitive metric during training applied to both weights and gradients in the attention layers (Figure 5).

Following Roy and Vetterli (2007) and Diehl Martinez et al. (2024), effective rank measures the entropy of the singular value spectrum of a matrix, while PER normalizes this by the total dimensionality:

$$\mathrm{PER}(W) = \frac{\exp\left(-\sum_i p_i \log p_i\right)}{d}$$

where $p_i = \frac{\sigma_i}{\sum_j \sigma_j}$. PER captures the extent to which the model's representations or updates span a full-dimensional space; a decline in PER indicates compression or structural specialization.

Key Finding: Phase Transition in Large Model

Across all MAML-pretrained models, PER declines over training, but the `large` model exhibits an **abrupt, synchronized drop** at step $\sim$3000 in:

- Proportional effective rank (PER)
- Paloma perplexity (after initial rise)
- Query accuracy (sharp jump from plateau)

We interpret this behavior as a **representational phase transition**: the model initially fits the objective using diffuse, high-dimensional representations, which are later compressed into task-specialized, low-rank structures. The descent in

PER lags behind the initial perplexity gains, and only after this drop does the second descent in Paloma begin. There is no strong evidence of a comparable phase transition in the vanilla models. While the `large` and `medium` variants show mild inflection points in loss and perplexity around step 3000, these are gradual and lack the coordinated sharpness seen in the MAML-trained models.

This suggests that MAML's bilevel updates and episodic task pressure may help reorganize the optimization landscape to favor discrete qualitative shifts in representation. As explored in Olsson et al. (2022); Wang et al. (2024); Hoogland et al. (2024), model training often proceeds in qualitatively distinct stages: from brute-force fitting, to intermediate rule memorization, to compressed algorithmic abstraction. The drop in PER may signal such a transition—from early diffuse representations to compressed heads tuned to solve the repeated structure of SMLMT episodes. This representational transition is also reflected in the model's adaptation performance. Around the same step where PER and Paloma perplexity undergo a sharp drop (step ~3000), both support and query accuracies rise abruptly (see Figure 3). Prior to this point, query accuracy remains relatively flat, indicating that the model struggles to generalize from support to query examples. But after the phase transition, the model rapidly learns to extrapolate, with query accuracy climbing from near random to over 0.5.

This synchrony across metrics provides compelling evidence of a coordinated phase shift in the model's learning trajectory. When looking into more granular checkpoints (Figure 6), there is clearer evidence that the model transitions from an early stage where it relies on diffuse representations to a later stage where it reorganizes both its representations and update paths into a lower-dimensional, more modular form capable of few-shot generalization. That said, this phase behavior appears scale-sensitive as it is absent in smaller scales. This suggests that the capacity to reorganize may be gated by scale, and that below a certain threshold, the inductive pressure of MAML induces collapse rather than modularization.

7 Conclusion

We interleaved first–order MAML episodes with decoder pretraining and analyzed dynamics across four SLM scales. Under equal compute, the hybrid objective accelerates optimization but trades

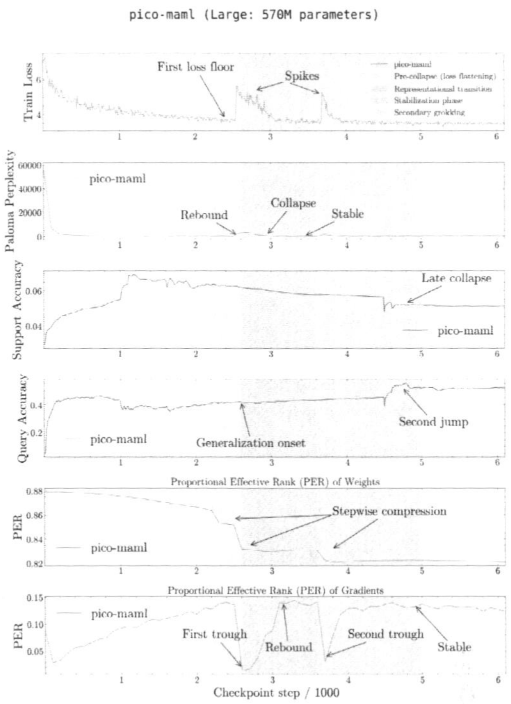

Figure 6: Dynamics of `pico-maml-decoder-large` over 6000 pretraining steps. **Pink shaded region** marks the phase transition (steps 2600-3200) where PER collapses, perplexity drops, and query accuracy jumps.

off perplexity at most scales; downstream, it brings modest average NER gains (+2–3 pp) at medium/large scales. Spectral logs expose a phase-like diversify–then–compress pattern that coincides with improving episodic query accuracy in the large model. Given our NER-only, single-seed scope, we present these as tools and observations rather than broad performance claims.

However, while our evaluation focuses exclusively on named entity recognition, the underlying mechanism—episodic adaptation via SMLMT—is task-agnostic. In principle, the same hybrid objective could be applied to other sequence labeling tasks (e.g., part-of-speech tagging, syntactic chunking) or even structured prediction problems that admit few-shot formulations. Whether the phase transitions and rank-compression patterns we observe generalize to non-linguistic domains (e.g., code generation, mathematical reasoning) remains an open question. Future work should explore whether MAML's inductive bias is inherently suited to token-level structure learning or whether it confers broader benefits across modalities and task families.

Relatedly, other natural extensions suggest themselves. Future work should also include multi-seed and hyperparameter sweeps (inner LR, episode frequency), multilingual pretraining to test cross-script transfer, varying which layers adapt in the inner loop, and evaluation on non-NER tasks (e.g., classification, QA, reasoning), as the architectural design space is rather large. In terms of exploratory work, a natural next step is to learn whether the same phase transition re-emerges when the corpus is multilingual, which would clarify why cross-script transfer remains the weak point of the present models. Varying which backbone layers adapt, how many steps they receive and how frequently episodes are interleaved may unlock better compute–capability trade-offs. Finally, the clear correlation between the effective-rank collapse and downstream utility hints that spectral diagnostics might serve as a self-supervised early-stopping signal.

Limitations

All training runs stop at exactly six thousand outer steps, a horizon that may be too short for the largest model, so the observed perplexity gap between MAML and vanilla training could shrink or even reverse if optimisation were allowed to continue. Our downstream evaluation focuses on a single task family, sequence labelling, so it remains unclear whether the same advantages would materialise on reasoning or generation-quality benchmarks. Because the corpus is predominantly English, improvements in low-resource or logographic languages remain modest; a more diverse corpus may alter both quantitative and qualitative conclusions. Hyper-parameters such as the hybrid episode probability, the inner-loop learning rate and the 32-way 4-shot episode size were transferred unchanged across scales; dedicated tuning might further modify the trade-off between convergence speed and final perplexity. Models were trained on academic budget, which limited training to 6000 outer steps. Some interesting training dynamics only appear after a very extended period of training, and future work should study this long-term behavior. Finally, each condition was run with a single random seed owing to GPU constraints, so although the phase transition appears robust, the exact magnitude of the gains should be interpreted with caution.

Acknowledgments

This work was supported by a grant from the Accelerate Programme for Scientific Discovery, made possible by a donation from Schmidt Futures. David Demitri Africa is supported by the Cambridge Trust and the Jardine Foundation. Richard Diehl Martinez is supported by the Gates Cambridge Trust (grant OPP1144 from the Bill & Melinda Gates Foundation). Suchir Salhan is supported by Cambridge University Press & Assessment.

References

Joshua Ainslie, James Lee-Thorp, Michiel de Jong, Yury Zemlyanskiy, Federico Lebron, and Sumit Sanghai. 2023. Gqa: Training generalized multi-query transformer models from multi-head checkpoints. In *Proceedings of the 2023 Conference on Empirical Methods in Natural Language Processing*, pages 4895–4901.

Tareq Al-Moslmi, Marc Gallofré Ocaña, Andreas L Opdahl, and Csaba Veres. 2020. Named entity extraction for knowledge graphs: A literature overview. *IEEE Access*, 8:32862–32881.

Julio Cesar Salinas Alvarado, Karin Verspoor, and Timothy Baldwin. 2015. Domain adaption of named entity recognition to support credit risk assessment. In *Proceedings of the australasian language technology association workshop 2015*, pages 84–90.

Ting Wai Terence Au, Ingemar J Cox, and Vasileios Lampos. 2022. E-ner–an annotated named entity recognition corpus of legal text. *arXiv preprint arXiv:2212.09306*.

Trapit Bansal, Rishikesh Jha, Tsendsuren Munkhdalai, and Andrew McCallum. 2020. Self-supervised meta-learning for few-shot natural language classification tasks. In *Proceedings of the 2020 Conference on Empirical Methods in Natural Language Processing (EMNLP)*, pages 522–534, Online. Association for Computational Linguistics.

Stella Biderman, Hailey Schoelkopf, Quentin Gregory Anthony, Herbie Bradley, Kyle O'Brien, Eric Hallahan, Mohammad Aflah Khan, Shivanshu Purohit, Usvsn Sai Prashanth, Edward Raff, Aviya Skowron, Lintang Sutawika, and Oskar Van Der Wal. 2023. Pythia: A suite for analyzing large language models across training and scaling. In *Proceedings of the 40th International Conference on Machine Learning*, volume 202 of *Proceedings of Machine Learning Research*, pages 2397–2430. PMLR.

Maria Victoria R. Bunye and Elsa Paula Yap. 1971. *Cebuano Grammar Notes and Cebuano for Beginners*. University of Hawaii Press, Honolulu.

Nancy Chinchor and Patricia Robinson. 1997. Muc-7 named entity task definition. In *Proceedings of the 7th Conference on Message Understanding*, volume 29, pages 1–21.

Alexis Conneau, Kartikay Khandelwal, Naman Goyal, Vishrav Chaudhary, Guillaume Wenzek, Francisco Guzmán, Edouard Grave, Myle Ott, Luke Zettlemoyer, and Veselin Stoyanov. 2020. Unsupervised cross-lingual representation learning at scale. In *Proceedings of the 58th Annual Meeting of the Association for Computational Linguistics*, pages 8440–8451, Online. Association for Computational Linguistics.

Richard Diehl Martinez. 2025. Pico: A lightweight framework for studying language model learning dynamics.

Richard Diehl Martinez, Pietro Lesci, and Paula Buttery. 2024. Tending towards stability: Convergence challenges in small language models. In *Findings of the Association for Computational Linguistics: EMNLP 2024*, pages 3275–3286, Miami, Florida, USA. Association for Computational Linguistics.

Chelsea Finn, Pieter Abbeel, and Sergey Levine. 2017. Model-agnostic meta-learning for fast adaptation of deep networks. In *Proceedings of the 34th International Conference on Machine Learning*, volume 70 of *Proceedings of Machine Learning Research*, pages 1126–1135. PMLR.

Tomer Galanti, Zachary S Siegel, Aparna Gupte, and Tomaso Poggio. 2022. Sgd and weight decay secretly minimize the rank of your neural network. *arXiv preprint arXiv:2206.05794*.

Nathan Godey, Éric Villemonte de la Clergerie, and Benoît Sagot. 2024. Why do small language models underperform? studying language model saturation via the softmax bottleneck. In *First Conference on Language Modeling*.

Jesse Hoogland, George Wang, Matthew Farrugia-Roberts, Liam Carroll, Susan Wei, and Daniel Murfet. 2024. The developmental landscape of in-context learning. *arXiv preprint arXiv:2402.02364*.

Zejiang Hou, Julian Salazar, and George Polovets. 2022. Meta-learning the difference: Preparing large language models for efficient adaptation. *Transactions of the Association for Computational Linguistics*, 10:1249–1265.

Minyoung Huh, Hossein Mobahi, Richard Zhang, Brian Cheung, Pulkit Agrawal, and Phillip Isola. 2021. The low-rank simplicity bias in deep networks. *arXiv preprint arXiv:2103.10427*.

Max Jaderberg, Andrea Vedaldi, and Andrew Zisserman. 2014. Speeding up convolutional neural networks with low rank expansions. *arXiv preprint arXiv:1405.3866*.

Zhen Ke, Liang Shi, Songtao Sun, Erli Meng, Bin Wang, and Xipeng Qiu. 2021. Pre-training with meta learning for Chinese word segmentation. In *Proceedings of the 2021 Conference of the North American Chapter of the Association for Computational Linguistics: Human Language Technologies*, pages 5514–5523, Online. Association for Computational Linguistics.

Alex Kendall, Yarin Gal, and Roberto Cipolla. 2017. Multi-task learning using uncertainty to weigh losses for scene geometry and semantics. *Preprint*, arXiv:1705.07115.

Paul R. Kroeger. 1993. *Phrase Structure and Grammatical Relations in Tagalog*. Dissertations in Linguistics. Center for the Study of Language and Information (CSLI) Publications, Stanford, CA. 257 pp.

Srinivasa Rao Kundeti, J Vijayananda, Srikanth Mujjiga, and M Kalyan. 2016. Clinical named entity recognition: Challenges and opportunities. In *2016 IEEE International Conference on Big Data (Big Data)*, pages 1937–1945. IEEE.

Elena Leitner, Georg Rehm, and Julian Moreno-Schneider. 2019. Fine-grained named entity recognition in legal documents. In *International conference on semantic systems*, pages 272–287. Springer.

Yue Li and Jiong Zhang. 2021. Semi-supervised meta-learning for cross-domain few-shot intent classification. In *Proceedings of the 1st Workshop on Meta Learning and Its Applications to Natural Language Processing*, pages 67–75, Online. Association for Computational Linguistics.

Ian Magnusson, Akshita Bhagia, Valentin Hofmann, Luca Soldaini, Ananya Harsh Jha, Oyvind Tafjord, Dustin Schwenk, Evan Walsh, Yanai Elazar, Kyle Lo, and 1 others. 2024. Paloma: A benchmark for evaluating language model fit. *Advances in Neural Information Processing Systems*, 37:64338–64376.

Stephen Mayhew, Terra Blevins, Shuheng Liu, Marek Suppa, Hila Gonen, Joseph Marvin Imperial, Börje Karlsson, Peiqin Lin, Nikola Ljubešić, Lester James Miranda, Barbara Plank, Arij Riabi, and Yuval Pinter. 2024. Universal NER: A gold-standard multilingual named entity recognition benchmark. In *Proceedings of the 2024 Conference of the North American Chapter of the Association for Computational Linguistics: Human Language Technologies (Volume 1: Long Papers)*, pages 4322–4337, Mexico City, Mexico. Association for Computational Linguistics.

Brando Miranda, Patrick Yu, Saumya Goyal, Yu-Xiong Wang, and Sanmi Koyejo. 2023. Is pre-training truly better than meta-learning? *Preprint*, arXiv:2306.13841.

Varsha Naik, Purvang Patel, and Rajeswari Kannan. 2023. Legal entity extraction: An experimental study of ner approach for legal documents. *International Journal of Advanced Computer Science and Applications*, 14(3).

Alex Nichol, Joshua Achiam, and John Schulman. 2018. On first-order meta-learning algorithms. *arXiv preprint arXiv:1803.02999*.

Joakim Nivre, Marie-Catherine de Marneffe, Filip Ginter, Yoav Goldberg, Jan Hajič, Christopher D. Manning, Ryan McDonald, Slav Petrov, Sampo Pyysalo, Natalia Silveira, Reut Tsarfaty, and Daniel Zeman. 2016. Universal dependencies v1: A multilingual treebank collection. In *Proceedings of the 10th Language Resources and Evaluation Conference (LREC 2016)*, pages 1659–1666, Portorož, Slovenia.

Joakim Nivre, Marie-Catherine de Marneffe, Filip Ginter, Jan Hajič, Christopher D. Manning, Sampo Pyysalo, Sebastian Schuster, Francis Tyers, and Daniel Zeman. 2020. Universal Dependencies v2: An evergrowing multilingual treebank collection. In *Proceedings of the Twelfth Language Resources and Evaluation Conference*, pages 4034–4043, Marseille, France. European Language Resources Association.

Catherine Olsson, Nelson Elhage, Neel Nanda, Nicholas Joseph, Nova DasSarma, Tom Henighan, Ben Mann, Amanda Askell, Yuntao Bai, Anna Chen, and 1 others. 2022. In-context learning and induction heads. *arXiv preprint arXiv:2209.11895*.

OpenAI. 2025. What are tokens and how to count them? Accessed May 2025.

Marco Polignano, Marco de Gemmis, Giovanni Semeraro, and 1 others. 2021. Comparing transformer-based ner approaches for analysing textual medical diagnoses. In *CLEF (Working Notes)*, pages 818–833.

Duangmanee Putthividhya and Junling Hu. 2011. Bootstrapped named entity recognition for product attribute extraction. In *Proceedings of the 2011 Conference on Empirical Methods in Natural Language Processing*, pages 1557–1567.

Aniruddh Raghu, Jonathan Lorraine, Simon Kornblith, Matthew McDermott, and David K Duvenaud. 2021. Meta-learning to improve pre-training. *Advances in Neural Information Processing Systems*, 34:23231–23244.

Aravind Rajeswaran, Chelsea Finn, Sham M Kakade, and Sergey Levine. 2019. Meta-learning with implicit gradients. *Advances in neural information processing systems*, 32.

Teresita V Ramos. 2021. *Tagalog structures*. University of Hawaii Press.

Olivier Roy and Martin Vetterli. 2007. The effective rank: A measure of effective dimensionality. In *2007 15th European signal processing conference*, pages 606–610. IEEE.

Paul Schachter and Fe T. Otanes. 1983. *Tagalog Reference Grammar*. University of California Press, Berkeley, CA.

Sarah Shafqat, Hammad Majeed, Qaisar Javaid, and Hafiz Farooq Ahmad. 2022. Standard ner tagging scheme for big data healthcare analytics built on unified medical corpora. *Journal of Artificial Intelligence and Technology*, 2(4):152–157.

Claude E. Shannon. 1951. Prediction and entropy of printed english. *Bell System Technical Journal*, 30(1):50–64.

Noam Shazeer. 2020. Glu variants improve transformer. *arXiv preprint arXiv:2002.05202*.

Emily Sityar. 2000. *The Topic and Y Indefinite in Cebuano*, pages 145–165. Springer Netherlands, Dordrecht.

Luca Soldaini, Rodney Kinney, Akshita Bhagia, Dustin Schwenk, David Atkinson, Russell Authur, Ben Bogin, Khyathi Chandu, Jennifer Dumas, Yanai Elazar, and 1 others. 2024. Dolma: an open corpus of three trillion tokens for language model pretraining research. In *Proceedings of the 62nd Annual Meeting of the Association for Computational Linguistics (Volume 1: Long Papers)*, pages 15725–15788.

Trevor Standley, Amir R. Zamir, Dawn Chen, Leonidas Guibas, Jitendra Malik, and Silvio Savarese. 2020. Which tasks should be learned together in multi-task learning? *Preprint*, arXiv:1905.07553.

Jianlin Su, Murtadha Ahmed, Yu Lu, Shengfeng Pan, Wen Bo, and Yunfeng Liu. 2024. Roformer: Enhanced transformer with rotary position embedding. *Neurocomputing*, 568:127063.

Michael Tanangkingsing. 2011. *A Functional Reference Grammar of Cebuano: A Discourse-Based Perspective*. Peter Lang, Berlin.

Hugo Touvron, Thibaut Lavril, Gautier Izacard, Xavier Martinet, Marie-Anne Lachaux, Timothée Lacroix, Baptiste Rozière, Naman Goyal, Eric Hambro, Faisal Azhar, and 1 others. 2023. Llama: Open and efficient foundation language models. *arXiv preprint arXiv:2302.13971*.

George Wang, Matthew Farrugia-Roberts, Jesse Hoogland, Liam Carroll, Susan Wei, and Daniel Murfet. 2024. Loss landscape geometry reveals stagewise development of transformers. In *High-dimensional Learning Dynamics 2024: The Emergence of Structure and Reasoning*.

Tianhe Yu, Saurabh Kumar, Abhishek Gupta, Sergey Levine, Karol Hausman, and Chelsea Finn. 2020. Gradient surgery for multi-task learning. *Preprint*, arXiv:2001.06782.

Biao Zhang and Rico Sennrich. 2019. Root mean square layer normalization. *Advances in Neural Information Processing Systems*, 32.

Lingyun Zhao, Lin Li, Xinhao Zheng, and Jianwei Zhang. 2021. A bert based sentiment analysis and key entity detection approach for online financial texts. In *2021 IEEE 24th International conference on computer supported cooperative work in design (CSCWD)*, pages 1233–1238. IEEE.

A Pseudocode

Below is the pseudocode for the MAML and vanilla pretraining setup.

Algorithm 1 Distributed SMLMT Loop

```
Initialize model f_θ, head h_φ, outer optimizer, and inner SGD on h_φ
step ← 0
for each sub-batch B from dataloader do
    X ← AllGather(B inputs)                          ▷ across devices
    r ← Broadcast(Uniform(0, 1))
    if r < ρ then
        (S, Q, y_S, y_Q) ← MaskTokens(X)
        φ_snap ← φ                                    ▷ save head params
        for t = 1 to T_inner do
            ℓ_S ← CE(h_φ(f_θ(S)), , y_S)
            φ ← φ − α, ∇_φ ℓ_S
        end for
        ℓ ← CE(h_φ(f_θ(Q)), , y_Q)
        φ ← φ_snap                                    ▷ restore head
    else
        X_in ← X without last token; Y ← X without first token
        ℓ ← CE(f_θ(X_in), , Y)
    end if
    Backward(ℓ, /, accum_steps)
    if (step + 1) mod accum_steps = 0 then
        OptimizerStep(); SchedulerStep(); ZeroGrad()
        AggregateMetrics(ℓ); Barrier()
    end if
    step ← step +1
end for
```

Algorithm 2 Distributed AR Loop

```
Initialize configs, Fabric/strategy, tokenizer, model f_θ, optimizer
Prepare dataloader and distribute it
step ← 0; ZeroGrad()
for each sub-batch B from dataloader do
    X ← AllGather(B inputs)                          ▷ across devices
    X_in ← X without last token; Y ← X without first token
    ℓ ← CE(f_θ(X_in), , Y)
    Backward(ℓ, /, accum_steps)
    if (step + 1) mod accum_steps = 0 then
        OptimizerStep(); SchedulerStep(); ZeroGrad()
        Barrier()                                     ▷ optional
    end if
    step ← step +1
end for
```

A.1 Multi-GPU processing

Pico already uses Lightning-Fabric data parallelism but meta-learning introduces various demands that make multi-GPU processing complicated. A Bernoulli draw is done on one GPU and broadcast so all ranks choose the same objective. Support and query tensors are constructed on rank 0 then scattered, because per-rank random masks would destroy gradient equivalence. Every GPU performs the same ten head updates before any gradient is communicated. A stray early `all_reduce` would mix gradients from different inner steps, so we place an explicit `barrier` between inner and outer phases.

B Universal NER Datasets

To comprehensively evaluate the pretraining method, each permutation of fine-tuning setup ({head-only, full}, fine-tuning dataset ({`da_ddt`, ..., `zh_gsdsimp`, `all`}) (where `all` consists of all available training sets), model size ({tiny, small, medium, large}), and pretraining setup ({vanilla, MAML}) is evaluated, for a total of 160 evaluation runs.

- **Publicly Available In-language treebanks** (9 langs): full `train/dev/test` splits, identical to the official UD partitions.
  - `da_ddt`, `en_ewt`, `hr_set`, `pt_bosque`, `sk_snk`, `sr_set`, `sv_talbanken`, `zh_gsd`, `zh_gsdsimp`
- **Parallel UD (PUD) evaluation** (6 langs): single `test.txt` files, all sentence-aligned across German, English, Portuguese, Russian, Swedish and Chinese.
  - `de_pud`, `en_pud`, `pt_pud`, `ru_pud`, `sv_pud`, `zh_pud`
- **Other eval-only sets** (3 langs): small test splits for low-resource languages.
  - `ceb_gja` (Cebuano), `tl_trg` (Tagalog TRG), `tl_ugnayan` (Tagalog Ugnayan)

C Supplementary Figures

C.1 Supplementary Tables

Table 7: Micro-F1 scores (rows: selected datasets, columns: vanilla vs. MAML) under head-only tuning for large models. Highlights which languages benefit most from MAML without full adaptation.

Model	da_ddt	en_ewt	hr_set	pt_bosque	sk_snk	sr_set	sv_talbanken	zh_gsd	zh_gsdsimp
vanilla_tiny	**0.004**	0.031	**0.011**	0.000	0.004	**0.009**	**0.000**	**0.005**	**0.009**
maml_tiny	0.000	**0.057**	0.000	**0.014**	**0.014**	0.002	**0.000**	0.000	0.005
vanilla_small	0.000	**0.196**	0.123	0.099	0.047	**0.056**	**0.020**	0.000	0.003
maml_small	**0.004**	0.156	**0.162**	**0.104**	**0.063**	0.044	0.000	**0.003**	**0.005**
vanilla_medium	**0.141**	0.252	0.311	0.240	**0.153**	0.325	0.065	**0.010**	**0.020**
maml_medium	0.087	**0.288**	**0.329**	**0.243**	0.136	**0.362**	**0.108**	0.005	0.010
vanilla_large	0.247	0.366	0.401	0.337	0.178	0.422	0.261	**0.034**	0.039
maml_large	**0.267**	**0.420**	**0.444**	**0.366**	**0.191**	**0.455**	**0.308**	0.023	**0.040**

Table 8: Percentage relative improvement of MAML over vanilla for head-only tuning in the large model.

Model	da_ddt	en_ewt	hr_set	pt_bosque	sk_snk	sr_set	sv_talbanken	zh_gsd	zh_gsdsimp
Large (%)	+8.1	+14.8	+10.7	+8.6	+7.3	+7.8	+18.0	-32.4	+2.6

Table 9: Percentage-wise relative improvement of MAML over vanilla under full tuning for each language.

Model	da_ddt	en_ewt	hr_set	pt_bosque	sk_snk	sr_set	sv_talbanken	zh_gsd	zh_gsdsimp
tiny (%)	+3.4	+0.2	-1.6	-0.7	-2.4	+1.5	+6.1	-9.2	-2.7
small (%)	-3.9	-4.7	-1.9	-2.6	+3.4	+0.9	+4.9	+1.6	+4.9
medium (%)	+0.8	+4.8	+3.9	+1.2	+0.3	-0.3	+3.7	+5.0	+8.2
large (%)	+3.6	+4.4	-0.5	+4.2	+5.7	+1.3	+2.8	+3.4	+5.0

Efficient Environmental Claim Detection with Hyperbolic Graph Neural Networks

Darpan Aswal[1,2], **Manjira Sinha**[3]
[1]Department of Computer Science, Université Paris-Saclay
[2]MICS, CentraleSupélec, Université Paris-Saclay
[3]TCS Research, India
Correspondence: darpanaswal@gmail.com

Abstract

Transformer based models, especially large language models (LLMs) dominate the field of NLP with their mass adoption in tasks such as text generation, summarization and fake news detection. These models offer ease of deployment and reliability for most applications, however, they require significant amounts of computational power for training as well as inference. This poses challenges in their adoption in resource-constrained applications, especially in the open-source community where compute availability is usually scarce. This work proposes a graph-based approach for Environmental Claim Detection, exploring Graph Neural Networks (GNNs) and Hyperbolic Graph Neural Networks (HGNNs) as lightweight yet effective alternatives to transformer-based models. Re-framing the task as a graph classification problem, we transform claim sentences into dependency parsing graphs, utilizing a combination of word2vec & learnable part-of-speech (POS) tag embeddings for the node features and encoding syntactic dependencies in the edge relations. Our results show that our graph-based models, particularly HGNNs in the poincaré space (P-HGNNs), achieve performance superior to the state-of-the-art on environmental claim detection while using up to **30x fewer parameters**. We also demonstrate that HGNNs benefit vastly from explicitly modeling data in hierarchical (tree-like) structures, enabling them to significantly improve over their euclidean counterparts. We make our implementation publicly available [1].

1 Introduction

Claim verification and claim detection (Soleimani et al., 2020; Levy et al., 2014) are complex NLP tasks that involves the detection of fake claims using facts as well as contextual information within the given claims. Often, these claims exhibit hierarchical and nested information such as conditional statements (Kargupta et al., 2025). Environmental claim detection (Stammbach et al., 2022) involves additional elements from greenwashing (de Freitas Netto et al., 2020) that are often used by corporations to promote products and mislead customers.

Recent work for claim detection, similar to many industrial NLP applications (Chkirbene et al., 2024), has predominantly relied on transformer-based architectures (Ni et al., 2024). However, this reliance on these massive, black-box models presents two issues. First, they require large-scale computational resources which makes them economically and environmentally expensive, leaving behind a large carbon footprint (Faiz et al., 2023). Second, their lack of interpretability (Lin et al., 2023) is a significant issue in high stakes domains like claim verification, where explaining a classification is equally important as the classification itself (Atanasova, 2024; Brundage et al., 2020). The increasing scrutiny on sustainability claims further necessitates interpretability and computational efficiency in models.

To address these challenges of cost and interpretability, we propose a lightweight framework for graph-based claim detection. We re-frame the problem of environmental claim detection as a graph classification task, explicitly modeling the syntactic and hierarchical structure of sentences using dependency parsing graphs (Nivre, 2010) with word embeddings for node features. This representation provides a natural fit for Graph Neural Networks (GNNs) (Wu et al., 2020) which are designed to learn from such structured data. Compared to transformers, our approach offers an interpretable approach to syntactic and semantic learning while significantly reducing computational overhead (Feng et al., 2025; Li et al., 2025; Peng et al., 2021). Furthermore, given the tree-like nature of dependency graphs, we investigate Hyperbolic Graph Neural Networks (HGNNs) (Zhou et al., 2023), a geometric learning architecture particularly suited to such

[1]https://github.com/darpanaswal/ecd-hgnn

Proceedings of the IJCNLP-AACL 2025 Student Research Workshop, pages 24–35
December 20-24, 2025 ©2025 Association for Computational Linguistics

hierarchically structured data. The research questions for the study are as follows.

RQ1. Can graph-based models match SOTA performance for environmental claim detection while using just a fraction of the compute as that of LLMs?

RQ2. Can syntactically enriched explicit hierarchical modeling of NLP tasks advantage hyperbolic models over their euclidean counterparts?

2 Related Work

The proliferation of misinformation on social media has shown the need for automated fact-checking and verification systems (Aïmeur et al., 2023). Fake news detection aims to classify entire articles or posts as credible or fake (Shu et al., 2017), often involving analyzing of multiple signals such as textual content and writing style (Przybyla, 2020). While early approaches relied on feature engineering and machine learning methods (Khanam et al., 2021), recent work relies on transformer models for fake news detection (Yi et al., 2025).

Claim detection and verification offer a more detailed approach to fact-checking. Claim detection (Levy et al., 2014) focuses on identifying factual statements within larger texts and separating them from non-factual ones. Claim verification (Soleimani et al., 2020) on the other hand assesses the accuracy of detected claims using evidence and facts from trusted sources. While fact checking is widely utilized for social-media content (Wasike, 2023), these methods have been applied to specific, high-stakes topics such as verification of climate-related claims (Diggelmann et al., 2020) and analyzing contrarian (Coan et al., 2021) or fake claims about climate change (Al-Rawi et al., 2021). Environmental claim detection (Stammbach et al., 2022) is one such specialized sub-domain of fact verification research. Specifically, it deals with greenwashing (de Freitas Netto et al., 2020) – the corporate form of misinformation – which involves using vague or misleading language to create an exaggeratedly positive public image of a company's environmental credentials.

Large Language Models (LLMs) (Naveed et al., 2025) are transformer-based models (Lin et al., 2022) pre-trained on vast amounts of text data which enables them to achieve state-of-the-art performance in downstream tasks such as sentiment analysis, machine translation and named entity recognition (Miah et al., 2024; Zhang et al., 2023; Yan et al., 2019). The application of these models has evolved from fine-tuning (Wu et al., 2025) task specific models such as BERT and RoBERTa (Soleimani et al., 2020; Stammbach et al., 2022), to in-context learning (Dong et al., 2022) with modern, multi-billion parameter models. While powerful, the high computational costs (Faiz et al., 2023) and lack of interpretability (Lin et al., 2023) of these models pose challenges for wide-scale adoption.

Graph Neural Networks (GNNs) (Wu et al., 2020) offer an alternative learning paradigm by operating on structured-data. Prior work has utilized GNNs to explicitly model hierarchical and relational dependencies (Mi and Chen, 2020), making graph structures such as constituency parsing (Li et al., 2020b) and dependency parsing graphs (Nivre, 2010) a natural fit for representing sentence structures in NLP tasks. These models can integrate rich semantic information from word embeddings, knowledge graphs, and even sentence embeddings from pre-trained language models (Mikolov et al., 2013; Opdahl et al., 2022; Li et al., 2020a). Geometric deep learning (Bronstein et al., 2017) generalizes these models to non-euclidean spaces (Coxeter, 1998). Extending GNNs, Hyperbolic GNNs (Zhou et al., 2023), are particularly well suited to model hierarchically structured data such as dependency parsing graphs.

3 Methodology

We begin our experimentation by transforming a dataset $D = \{c_1, c_2, \ldots, c_N\}$ of N environmental claims into a corresponding set of dependency parsing graphs $G = \{G_1, G_2, \ldots, G_N\}$, converting each claim c_i into a unique graph structure

$$G_i = (V_i, E_i)$$

where V_i is the graph's set of vertices (or nodes) and E_i is its set of edges.

3.1 Dependency Graph Construction

For each claim c_i in the dataset, we generate a directed dependency graph using spaCy's built-in DependencyParser. Claim c_i, which is a sequence of tokens $t_i = \{t_i^{(1)}, t_i^{(2)}, \ldots t_i^{(k)}\}$ is mapped to its corresponding graph $G_i = (V_i, E_i)$ where the vertex set $V_i = \{v_1, \ldots v_k\}$ represents the tokens, and the edge set E_i represents the syntactic dependencies between them. A directed edge $(v_h, v_j) \in E_i$ exists if the token t_h is the syntactic head of token t_j. Each edge is labeled with its dependency type

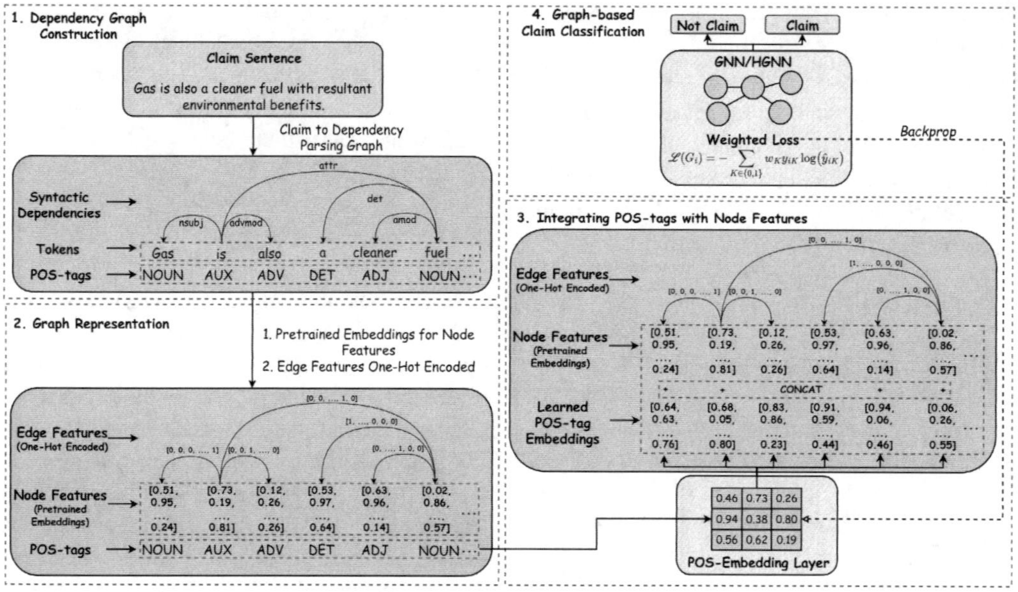

Figure 1: Overview of the Graph-based Claim Detection Pipeline. Step 1: Claim sentence to dependency graph conversion. Steps 2: Dependencies are one-hot encoded as edge features. Node features are initialized with pretrained embeddings. Step3: Node features are concatenated with POS-tag embeddings learned by embedding layer. Step 4: Graph classification using a GNN/HGNN architecture trained with a weighted loss function.

$d \in D$, where D is the set of all 45 unique dependency relations present in the dataset. We utilize the following node and edge attributes from the dependency graphs [2].

- **Token text**: Represented as the graph's nodes; corresponds to tokens in the claim sentences.
- **Dependency relation**: Specifies the type of syntactic dependency between a token and its head. Describes how the token relates to its syntactic governor.
- **Token head**: Also represented as the graph nodes, it identifies the governor token for a given dependent token.
- **Token Part-Of-Speech (POS) tag**.

3.2 Graph Representation

To prepare the graphs for the GNN models, we define the node and edge feature representations.

3.2.1 Node Features

Each node $v \in V_i$ is associated with a feature vector $x_v \in \mathbb{R}^{d_{node}}$. For this vector, we utilize word2vec (Mikolov et al., 2013), a pre-trained word embedding model. $x_v = W_e(\text{token}(v))$, where W_e is the word2vec embedding lookup matrix and the token(v) is the word corresponding to node v.

3.2.2 Edge Features

The syntactic dependency type of each edge, corresponding to one of the 45 unique relations in the dataset, is encoded into a feature vector. For an edge $e = (v_h, v_j)$, its feature vector $e_{hj} \in \mathbb{R}^{|D|}$ is a one-hot encoding of its dependency type $d(e)$.

3.3 Integrating POS-tags with Node Features

Next, we augment the node features with the POS-tags. Let $\mathcal{P}$ be the set of all unique POS-tags in the dataset. We introduce a learnable embedding matrix $W_p \in \mathbb{R}^{|\mathcal{P}| \times d_{pos}}$, where d_{pos} is the dimension of the POS-tag embeddings. This layer is trained with the GNN model. The final feature vector for a node v, denoted x'_v, is the concatenation of its word embedding and its learned POS tag embedding:

$$x'_v = \left[W_e(\text{token}(v)) \parallel W_p(\text{pos}(v))\right]$$

The dimension of this augmented feature vector becomes $d'_{node} = d_{node} + d_{pos}$.

3.4 Weighted Loss for Imbalanced Data

Lastly, to address the inherent imbalance present in the dataset, we employ a weighted cross-entropy loss function. This strategy assigns a higher penalty to misclassifications of the minority class, thereby encouraging the model to pay more attention to it. The loss for a single graph G_i with true one-hot label y_i and predicted probabilities $\hat{y}_i$ is defined as:

$$\mathcal{L}(G_i) = -\sum_{k=0}^{1} w_k.y_{ik}log(\hat{y}_{ik})$$

The weight for each class k, w_k, is calculated as the inverse of its frequency in the training set, effectively balancing the contribution of each class to the overall loss.

3.5 Graph-based Claim Classification

The final stage of our pipeline involves classifying the entire graph representation of a claim sentence. The augmented node feature vectors and the edge feature vectors are fed into either a GNN or an HGNN model which provides the final classification for the claim sentences, classifying them into two possible categories – 'Claim' and 'Not Claim'.

4 Experimental Setup

4.1 Dataset

We utilize the Environmental Claim Detection (ECD) dataset (Stammbach et al., 2022), a dataset comprised of environmental claims extracted from various corporate communications of publicly listed companies, including sustainability reports, earnings calls, and annual reports. While the authors initially collected 3,000 sentences, they removed samples with tied annotations, reporting results on the filtered dataset of 2,647 samples. We use this same 2,647-sample dataset for all our experiments to ensure a direct comparison. The dataset is imbalanced, with 665 sentences (25.1%) labeled as claim statements and 1,982 sentences (74.9%) labeled as not claim statements.

4.2 Models

We conduct our analysis with Euclidean and Hyperbolic GNN architectures. For training our models, we utilized the HGNN toolkit from (Liu et al., 2019). We experiment with the two standard models of hyperbolic space – the Poincaré Ball (Nickel and Kiela, 2017), which represents the hyperbolic space inside a unit disk and the Lorentz Hyperboloid Model (Nickel and Kiela, 2018) which embeds the space on a hyperboloid (Reynolds, 1993) in a higher-dimensional Minkowski space (Naber, 2012). Our models are trained with a total of 4 GNN layers. The first layer's dimensionality $d_{in} = d_{word2vec} + d_{pos}$, where $d_{word2vec} = 300$. The other 3 GNN layers are of dimensionality 256. For training, we utilize the AMSGrad and the Riemannian AMSGrad optimizers for the GNN and HGNN respectively [2].

4.3 Evaluation Metrics

For evaluating our models, we use five primary metrics to assess their performance on the claim detection task – Accuracy, Precision, Recall, F1-score, and AUC-ROC [2]. Given the high imbalance in the dataset, we use the F1-score and AUC-ROC as our primary metrics

5 Results & Observations

To obtain the best performance for each model configuration, we grid-search over the dropout rate, POS-embedding dimension and class weights. Next, we describe our results in detail in relation to the research questions described earlier.

5.1 HGNNs Match SOTA Performance with upto 30x Fewer Parameters (RQ1.)

In Table 1, we first establish the baselines using the results from (Stammbach et al., 2022) with 4 transformer models – DistilBERT, ClimateBERT, $\text{RoBERTa}_{\text{base}}$, and $\text{RoBERTa}_{\text{large}}$. While we use F1-score and AUC-ROC as our primary metrics, we include the standard accuracy in our tables solely for a direct comparison with the baseline metrics. In Table 2, we see that our graph-based models achieve performance better than or comparable to these state-of-the-art transformers. Firstly, our simplest models – labeled GNN, L-HGNN (for HGNN in the lorentz space) and P-HGNN (for HGNN in the poincaré space) – achieve respectable test F1 and accuracy scores.

Augmenting the models with the POS-tag embeddings uniformly boosts performance across all architectures. Specifically, we observe increments in the test F1 and accuracy scores for all three models. Notably, P-HGNN-POS achieves both our best overall test F1 and accuracy scores of **84%** and **92.1%** respectively, beating the best test accuracy reported in Table 1 (91.7%) and coming very close to the best test F1 score (84.9%), both achieved by their largest model $\text{RoBERTa}_{\text{large}}$ consisting of **355 million parameters**. Both GNN-POS and L-HGNN-POS also show competitive test F1 scores of **78.5%** and **79.4%** respectively, while achieving near SOTA accuracy scores of **89.1%** and **89.4%**.

Model	dev				test			
	pr	rc	F1	acc	pr	rc	F1	acc
DistilBERT	**77.5**	**93.9**	**84.9**	91.7	74.4	**95.5**	83.7	90.6
ClimateBERT	76.9	90.9	83.3	90.9	76.5	92.5	83.8	90.9
$\text{RoBERTa}_{\text{base}}$	74.7	**93.9**	83.6	90.6	73.3	94.0	82.4	89.8
$\text{RoBERTa}_{\text{large}}$	**80.5**	**93.9**	**86.7**	**92.8**	**78.5**	92.5	**84.9**	**91.7**

Table 1: Results reported by (Stammbach et al., 2022) on their ECD-dataset.

Model	grid-search parameters			dev					test				
	Dropout Rate	POS Embedding Dimension	Class Weights	pr	rc	F1	acc	auc	pr	rc	F1	acc	auc
GNN	0.1	–	–	**79.3**	69.7	74.2	87.9	**0.93**	78.7	71.6	75.0	87.9	0.93
L-HGNN	0.1	–	–	70.3	78.8	74.3	86.4	0.92	73.7	83.6	78.3	88.3	0.93
P-HGNN	0	–	–	71.0	74.2	72.6	86.0	0.91	74.4	**86.6**	80.0	89.1	0.94
GNN-POS	0.3	32	–	75.4	74.2	74.8	87.5	0.92	77.9	79.1	78.5	89.1	0.94
L-HGNN-POS	0.1	64	–	70.5	65.2	67.7	84.5	0.92	78.3	80.6	79.4	89.4	0.93
P-HGNN-POS	0.3	128	–	75.4	74.2	74.8	87.5	**0.93**	**85.9**	82.1	**84.0**	**92.1**	**0.95**
Balanced-GNN	0.1	–	[1,1.5]	78.6	66.7	72.1	87.2	**0.93**	81.7	73.1	77.2	89.1	0.93
Balanced-L-HGNN	0.25	–	[0.8,1.6]	77.8	74.2	76.0	**88.3**	**0.93**	75.7	79.1	77.4	88.3	0.93
Balanced-P-HGNN	0.2	–	[1,1.5]	73.2	78.8	75.9	87.5	0.92	73.7	83.6	78.3	88.3	0.93
Balanced-GNN-POS	0.25	32	[0.6678,1.9897]	72.9	77.3	75.0	87.2	**0.93**	76.7	83.6	80.0	89.4	0.93
Balanced-L-HGNN-POS	0	16	[0.6678,1.9897]	73.5	75.8	74.6	87.2	**0.93**	74.0	85.1	79.2	88.7	0.94
Balanced-P-HGNN-POS	0.3	32	[0.8,1.6]	73.6	**80.3**	**76.8**	87.9	**0.93**	80.3	85.1	82.6	90.9	0.94

Table 2: We report precision, recall, F1 score, accuracy and the auc-roc score on the dev and test sets of the ECD dataset. The best performance per split is indicated in bold, the second best is underlined.

Next, we address the imbalance in the dataset through the introduction of a weighted loss function. The Balanced-GNN improves the test F1-score by over 2 points compared to the standard GNN (from **75.0%** to **77.2%**), demonstrating the effectiveness of the weighted loss for the Euclidean model. The impact on the hyperbolic models is more nuanced, with slight shifts in the precision-recall trade-off resulting in minor changes to the F1-score. In Table 3, we show the best GNN configurations taken from Table 2 along with all their corresponding weight-balanced versions trained with the same dropout rates. While the early stopping criterion favors the best test F1-score during training, we can still observe the generally expected trend of dropping precision and increasing recall for both the dev and test sets when applying class weights. Interestingly, the Balanced-L-HGNN model does not always follow this pattern as strictly as its euclidean or poincaré counterparts.

Finally, the models incorporating all enhancements – POS embeddings and class balancing (-POS-Balanced) – demonstrate the most overall robust performances, effectively addressing both feature representation and data imbalance. The Balanced-GNN-POS model achieves a strong test F1 and accuracy scores of **80.0%** and **89.4%**, a clear improvement over its unbalanced version with test F1 and accuracy scores of **78.5%** and **89.1%**. Most significantly, while the P-HGNN-POS model achieves our highest test F1-score of **84.0%**, the Balanced-P-HGNN-POS model achieves a competitive F1-score **82.6%** while substantially boosting test recall from **82.1%** to **85.1%** which is our best test recall score after P-HGNN (**86.6%**) and also achieving the best test accuracy of **90.9%** after P-HGNN-POS (**92.1%**).

Furthermore, it is worth noting the consistently high AUC-ROC scores across all our model configurations, as detailed in Table 2. The test set AUC-ROC values range from 0.93 to 0.95, indicating a strong ability of the models to distinguish between the 'Claim' and 'Not Claim' classes. This high level of class separability further reinforces the reliability of our graph-based approach for the task of environmental claim detection.

The key advantage of our approach lies in its computational efficiency. In Table 4, we detail the parameter counts for all (Stammbach et al., 2022) transformer models as well as our own GNN models. While $\text{RoBERTa}_{\text{large}}$, the best performing model for environmental claim detection from (Stammbach et al., 2022) consists of **355 million parameters**, our GNN and HGNN models are significantly more lightweight. Our models consist of 4 GNN layers, a 256-dimensional hidden state, and 45 unique dependency relations (edge types). We calculate the size of our graph models to be approximately **12M parameters**, nearly **30 times smaller** than RoBERTa$_{large}$ [2]. *Therefore, we conclude that our graph-based models achieve better than or comparable to SOTA results.*

5.2 HGNNs Consistently Outperform GNNs (RQ2.)

In Table 2, we observe that hyperbolic GNN models, particularly those in the poincaré space consistently outperform their euclidean counterparts under most configurations for both the F1 and accuracy scores. For example on the test set, both the L-HGNN with an F1-score of **78.3%** and accuracy of **88.3%** as well as the P-HGNN with an F1-score of **80.0%** and an accuracy of **89.1%** surpass the standard GNN with an F1 score of **75.0%** and accuracy of **87.9%**. Similarly, this trend is continued in other configurations and the performance gap widens with the inclusion of richer features, as seen with P-HGNN-POS (**84%** F1 and **92.1%** accuracy) outperforming GNN-POS (**78.5%** F1 and **89.1%** accuracy). This consistent advantage shows that hyperbolic space models significantly benefit from explicit hierarchical modeling of the data using tree-like structures such as dependency parsing graphs. We achieve better test scores with HGNNs than with GNNs under most configurations, indicating a low hyperbolicity (i.e., a strong hierarchical structure) in the ECD dataset. *Therefore, we conclude that explicit hierarchical modeling of environmental claims allows the geometric properties of hyperbolic models to benefit from this hierarchy and improve over their euclidean counterparts.*

6 Discussion

In this study, we investigate the efficacy of Graph Neural Networks (GNNs) and their hyperbolic counterparts (HGNNs) for Environmental Claim Detection. We construct dependency parsing graphs of claim sentences to explicitly model them as hierarchical structures, hence benefiting from the geometric properties of the hyperbolic space. Leveraging simple word embeddings for node features, we also incorporate POS-tags and a weighted loss function to enhance performance and address data imbalance.

Our results indicate that graph-based models, particularly those in the hyperbolic space, can achieve performance superior to SOTA transformer-based architectures. The P-HGNN-POS model, our best-performing configuration, achieves a test F1-score of **84.0%** and an accuracy of **92.1%**, even surpassing the **91.7%** accuracy of the much larger RoBERTa$_{large}$ model. This performance is achieved with approximately **12 million parameters**, a nearly 30-fold reduction compared to the **355 million parameters** of RoBERTa$_{large}$. These findings highlight the potential of graph-based models as lightweight, efficient, and effective alternatives to LLMs for specialized NLP tasks.

Takeaway for RQ.1: Graph-based models offer a computationally efficient alternative to large transformers for environmental claim detection without compromising performance.

Furthermore, our results demonstrate the potential of hyperbolic geometry for NLP tasks like claim detection. Across various configurations, HGNNs consistently outperform GNNs, and this performance gap becomes more pronounced with the introduction of richer syntactic features, as seen in the superior performance of P-HGNN-POS over GNN-POS. This suggests that tree-like modeling of sentence structure creates a hierarchical representation that is naturally well-suited to the geometric properties of hyperbolic space.

Takeaway for RQ.2: Explicit hierarchical modeling of claims significantly benefits hyperbolic models, indicating their potential for NLP tasks.

Our findings underscore two critical points for the field. First, the dominance of transformer-based models is not absolute; for specific, well-defined tasks like environmental claim detection, specialized and lightweight models like GNNs can provide more efficient and effective solutions. Second, the inherent, often implicit, hierarchical nature of linguistic data can be powerfully exploited by choosing geometric spaces – like hyperbolic space – that align with this underlying structure. This highlights the vast potential in exploring geometries beyond euclidean for learning efficient representations for NLP tasks.

7 Conclusion

In this work, we introduce an efficient graph-based methodology for environmental claim detection,

[2] See Appendix for more details.

Model	grid-search parameters		dev					test				
	Dropout Rate	Class Weights	pr	rc	F1	acc	auc	pr	rc	F1	acc	auc
GNN	0.1	–	**79.3**	69.7	74.2	**87.9**	**0.93**	78.7	71.6	75.0	87.9	**0.93**
Balanced-GNN	0.1	[0.6678,1.9897]	68.3	**84.8**	75.7	86.4	**0.93**	69.2	**80.6**	74.5	86.0	**0.93**
Balanced-GNN	0.1	[0.8,1.6]	72.4	83.3	**77.5**	**87.9**	**0.93**	70.1	**80.6**	75.0	86.4	**0.93**
Balanced-GNN	0.1	[1,1.5]	78.6	66.7	72.1	87.2	**0.93**	**81.7**	73.1	**77.2**	**89.1**	**0.93**
L-HGNN	0.1	–	70.3	78.8	74.3	86.4	0.92	73.7	**83.6**	**78.3**	**88.3**	**0.93**
Balanced-L-HGNN	0.1	[0.6678,1.9897]	71.6	**80.3**	75.7	87.2	**0.93**	68.8	82.1	74.8	86.0	**0.93**
Balanced-L-HGNN	0.1	[0.8,1.6]	75.7	**80.3**	**77.9**	**88.7**	**0.93**	73.0	80.6	76.6	87.5	**0.93**
Balanced-L-HGNN	0.1	[1,1.5]	**79.7**	71.2	75.2	88.3	**0.93**	**75.4**	73.1	74.2	87.2	**0.93**
P-HGNN	0	–	**71.0**	74.2	72.6	86.0	0.91	**74.4**	**86.6**	**80.0**	**89.1**	**0.94**
Balanced-P-HGNN	0	[0.6678,1.9897]	69.1	**84.8**	**76.2**	**86.8**	**0.92**	71.8	83.6	77.2	87.5	0.93
Balanced-P-HGNN	0	[0.8,1.6]	69.9	77.3	73.4	86.0	0.91	68.2	**86.6**	76.3	86.4	0.93
Balanced-P-HGNN	0	[1,1.5]	68.4	78.8	73.2	85.7	**0.92**	71.2	85.1	77.6	87.5	0.93

Table 3: Results for all weight-balanced GNNs. For the best base GNN configurations, we show all the corresponding weight-balanced GNNs at the same dropout rate as the base model. For each model type, i.e., GNN, L-HGNN and P-HGNN, the best performance per split is indicated block-wise in bold, while the second best in underlined.

Model	Parameter-count
DistilBERT	66m
ClimateBERT	82m
$\text{RoBERTa}_{\text{base}}$	125m
$\text{RoBERTa}_{\text{large}}$	**355m**
GNN/HGNN	12m
GNN-POS/HGNN-POS	12m

Table 4: Number of parameters for the transformer models used by (Stammbach et al., 2022) compared to our GNN and HGNN models. Models prefixes are dropped since they do not affect the parameter sizes. m stands for million. Largest model size is in bold while the smallest is underlined.

positioning GNNs and HGNNs as lightweight yet effective alternatives to transformer-based architectures. We reformulate the task as a graph-classification problem, transforming claim sentences into dependency parsing graphs with simple word and POS-tag embeddings as node features and encoding syntactic dependencies as edge relations. Our results demonstrate that GNNs achieve performance comparable or superior to SOTA models with a 30-fold reduction in parameters. Furthermore, we consistently observe that HGNNs outperform their GNNs, affirming that the geometric properties of HGNNs gain significant advantage from the explicit hierarchical modeling of the data. Our findings call for a shift beyond over-reliance on transformers, demonstrating that specialized models can yield more efficient solutions for targeted NLP tasks without a loss of capability.

Future work. First, we plan to compare static word2vec embeddings for node features with sentence embeddings from transformer models like RoBERTa. Second, we plan to move beyond simple one-hot encoded edge features to a knowledge-enhanced schema based on principles from universal dependencies (De Marneffe et al., 2021). Third, we plan to experiment with alternative graph representations beyond dependency parsing such as constituency parsing. Fourth, we plan to conduct a sensitivity analysis to quantify the impact of parsing inaccuracies on model performance, investigating whether domain-adapted parsers could yield better results. Lastly, to assess the generalisability of this study, we intend to extend our work to more NLP tasks, models such as graph attention networks (Veličković et al., 2017), and benchmark datasets such as FEVER (Thorne et al., 2018) and Climate-Fever (Diggelmann et al., 2020).

8 Limitations

We highlight the limitations of our work as follows.

- Our approach deliberately utilizes word2vec embeddings for node features to create a maximally lightweight and efficient model. However, they do not encode the sequential dependencies between words. Similarly, our edge features are simple one-hot encodings of dependency types, which treat all syntactic relations as independent and do not capture potential similarities between them.
- Our methodology relies on the output of the dependency parser to construct the graphs. While modern parsers are highly accurate, any errors in graph construction are propagated as noise to the GNN and HGNN models. We do not analyze the impact of such parsing errors on final model performance in this study.
- The scope of our experiments is focused on a

single, relatively small, English-only dataset. While the results are strong, the generalisability of our graph-based approach to other claim detection domains, larger datasets, and other languages is yet to be established.

- The transformer baselines used for comparison are from the original environmental claim detection paper (Stammbach et al., 2022). We do not benchmark our models against more recent, state-of-the-art LLMs such as Llama3 (Dubey et al., 2024) and GPT-4o (Hurst et al., 2024), limiting the assessment of our approach against the current SOTA.

References

Esma Aïmeur, Sabrine Amri, and Gilles Brassard. 2023. Fake news, disinformation and misinformation in social media: a review. *Social Network Analysis and Mining*, 13(1):30.

Ahmed Al-Rawi, Derrick O'Keefe, Oumar Kane, and Aimé-Jules Bizimana. 2021. Twitter's fake news discourses around climate change and global warming. *Frontiers in Communication*, 6:729818.

Pepa Atanasova. 2024. Generating fact checking explanations. In *Accountable and Explainable Methods for Complex Reasoning over Text*, pages 83–103. Springer.

Michael M Bronstein, Joan Bruna, Yann LeCun, Arthur Szlam, and Pierre Vandergheynst. 2017. Geometric deep learning: going beyond euclidean data. *IEEE Signal Processing Magazine*, 34(4):18–42.

Miles Brundage, Shahar Avin, Jasmine Wang, Haydn Belfield, Gretchen Krueger, Gillian Hadfield, Heidy Khlaaf, Jingying Yang, Helen Toner, Ruth Fong, et al. 2020. Toward trustworthy ai development: mechanisms for supporting verifiable claims. *arXiv preprint arXiv:2004.07213*.

Zina Chkirbene, Ridha Hamila, Ala Gouissem, and Unal Devrim. 2024. Large language models (llm) in industry: A survey of applications, challenges, and trends. In *2024 IEEE 21st International Conference on Smart Communities: Improving Quality of Life using AI, Robotics and IoT (HONET)*, pages 229–234. IEEE.

Travis G Coan, Constantine Boussalis, John Cook, and Mirjam O Nanko. 2021. Computer-assisted classification of contrarian claims about climate change. *Scientific reports*, 11(1):22320.

Harold Scott Macdonald Coxeter. 1998. *Non-euclidean geometry*. Cambridge University Press.

Sebastião Vieira de Freitas Netto, Marcos Felipe Falcão Sobral, Ana Regina Bezerra Ribeiro, and Gleibson Robert da Luz Soares. 2020. Concepts and forms of greenwashing: A systematic review. *Environmental Sciences Europe*, 32:1–12.

Marie-Catherine De Marneffe, Christopher D Manning, Joakim Nivre, and Daniel Zeman. 2021. Universal dependencies. *Computational linguistics*, 47(2):255–308.

Thomas Diggelmann, Jordan Boyd-Graber, Jannis Bulian, Massimiliano Ciaramita, and Markus Leippold. 2020. Climate-fever: A dataset for verification of real-world climate claims. *arXiv preprint arXiv:2012.00614*.

Qingxiu Dong, Lei Li, Damai Dai, Ce Zheng, Jingyuan Ma, Rui Li, Heming Xia, Jingjing Xu, Zhiyong Wu, Tianyu Liu, et al. 2022. A survey on in-context learning. *arXiv preprint arXiv:2301.00234*.

Abhimanyu Dubey, Abhinav Jauhri, Abhinav Pandey, Abhishek Kadian, Ahmad Al-Dahle, Aiesha Letman, Akhil Mathur, Alan Schelten, Amy Yang, Angela Fan, et al. 2024. The llama 3 herd of models. *arXiv e-prints*, pages arXiv–2407.

Ahmad Faiz, Sotaro Kaneda, Ruhan Wang, Rita Osi, Prateek Sharma, Fan Chen, and Lei Jiang. 2023. Llmcarbon: Modeling the end-to-end carbon footprint of large language models. *arXiv preprint arXiv:2309.14393*.

Tao Feng, Yihang Sun, and Jiaxuan You. 2025. Grapheval: A lightweight graph-based llm framework for idea evaluation. *arXiv preprint arXiv:2503.12600*.

Aaron Hurst, Adam Lerer, Adam P Goucher, Adam Perelman, Aditya Ramesh, Aidan Clark, AJ Ostrow, Akila Welihinda, Alan Hayes, Alec Radford, et al. 2024. Gpt-4o system card. *arXiv preprint arXiv:2410.21276*.

Priyanka Kargupta, Runchu Tian, and Jiawei Han. 2025. Beyond true or false: Retrieval-augmented hierarchical analysis of nuanced claims. *arXiv preprint arXiv:2506.10728*.

Zeba Khanam, BN Alwasel, H Sirafi, and Mamoon Rashid. 2021. Fake news detection using machine learning approaches. In *IOP conference series: materials science and engineering*, volume 1099, page 012040. IOP Publishing.

Ran Levy, Yonatan Bilu, Daniel Hershcovich, Ehud Aharoni, and Noam Slonim. 2014. Context dependent claim detection. In *Proceedings of COLING 2014, the 25th International conference on computational linguistics: Technical Papers*, pages 1489–1500.

Bohan Li, Hao Zhou, Junxian He, Mingxuan Wang, Yiming Yang, and Lei Li. 2020a. On the sentence embeddings from pre-trained language models. *arXiv preprint arXiv:2011.05864*.

Jun Li, Yifan Cao, Jiong Cai, Yong Jiang, and Kewei Tu. 2020b. An empirical comparison of unsupervised constituency parsing methods. In *Proceedings of the 58th Annual Meeting of the Association for Computational Linguistics*, pages 3278–3283.

Youjia Li, Vishu Gupta, Muhammed Nur Talha Kilic, Kamal Choudhary, Daniel Wines, Wei-keng Liao, Alok Choudhary, and Ankit Agrawal. 2025. Hybrid-llm-gnn: integrating large language models and graph neural networks for enhanced materials property prediction. *Digital Discovery*, 4(2):376–383.

Tianyang Lin, Yuxin Wang, Xiangyang Liu, and Xipeng Qiu. 2022. A survey of transformers. *AI open*, 3:111–132.

Zhen Lin, Shubhendu Trivedi, and Jimeng Sun. 2023. Generating with confidence: Uncertainty quantification for black-box large language models. *arXiv preprint arXiv:2305.19187*.

Qi Liu, Maximilian Nickel, and Douwe Kiela. 2019. Hyperbolic graph neural networks. *Advances in neural information processing systems*, 32.

Li Mi and Zhenzhong Chen. 2020. Hierarchical graph attention network for visual relationship detection. In *Proceedings of the IEEE/CVF conference on computer vision and pattern recognition*, pages 13886–13895.

Md Saef Ullah Miah, Md Mohsin Kabir, Talha Bin Sarwar, Mejdl Safran, Sultan Alfarhood, and MF Mridha. 2024. A multimodal approach to cross-lingual sentiment analysis with ensemble of transformer and llm. *Scientific Reports*, 14(1):9603.

Tomas Mikolov, Kai Chen, Greg Corrado, and Jeffrey Dean. 2013. Efficient estimation of word representations in vector space. *arXiv preprint arXiv:1301.3781*.

Gregory L Naber. 2012. *The geometry of Minkowski spacetime*. Springer.

Humza Naveed, Asad Ullah Khan, Shi Qiu, Muhammad Saqib, Saeed Anwar, Muhammad Usman, Naveed Akhtar, Nick Barnes, and Ajmal Mian. 2025. A comprehensive overview of large language models. *ACM Transactions on Intelligent Systems and Technology*, 16(5):1–72.

Jingwei Ni, Minjing Shi, Dominik Stammbach, Mrinmaya Sachan, Elliott Ash, and Markus Leippold. 2024. Afacta: Assisting the annotation of factual claim detection with reliable llm annotators. *arXiv preprint arXiv:2402.11073*.

Maximillian Nickel and Douwe Kiela. 2017. Poincaré embeddings for learning hierarchical representations. *Advances in neural information processing systems*, 30.

Maximillian Nickel and Douwe Kiela. 2018. Learning continuous hierarchies in the lorentz model of hyperbolic geometry. In *International conference on machine learning*, pages 3779–3788. PMLR.

Joakim Nivre. 2010. Dependency parsing. *Language and Linguistics Compass*, 4(3):138–152.

Andreas L Opdahl, Tareq Al-Moslmi, Duc-Tien Dang-Nguyen, Marc Gallofré Ocaña, Bjørnar Tessem, and Csaba Veres. 2022. Semantic knowledge graphs for the news: A review. *ACM Computing Surveys*, 55(7):1–38.

Wei Peng, Tuomas Varanka, Abdelrahman Mostafa, Henglin Shi, and Guoying Zhao. 2021. Hyperbolic deep neural networks: A survey. *IEEE Transactions on pattern analysis and machine intelligence*, 44(12):10023–10044.

Piotr Przybyla. 2020. Capturing the style of fake news. In *Proceedings of the AAAI conference on artificial intelligence*, volume 34, pages 490–497.

William F Reynolds. 1993. Hyperbolic geometry on a hyperboloid. *The American mathematical monthly*, 100(5):442–455.

Kai Shu, Amy Sliva, Suhang Wang, Jiliang Tang, and Huan Liu. 2017. Fake news detection on social media: A data mining perspective. *ACM SIGKDD explorations newsletter*, 19(1):22–36.

Amir Soleimani, Christof Monz, and Marcel Worring. 2020. Bert for evidence retrieval and claim verification. In *European Conference on Information Retrieval*, pages 359–366. Springer.

Dominik Stammbach, Nicolas Webersinke, Julia Bingler, Mathias Kraus, and Markus Leippold. 2022. Environmental claim detection. *Available at SSRN 4207369*.

James Thorne, Andreas Vlachos, Christos Christodoulopoulos, and Arpit Mittal. 2018. Fever: a large-scale dataset for fact extraction and verification. *arXiv preprint arXiv:1803.05355*.

Petar Veličković, Guillem Cucurull, Arantxa Casanova, Adriana Romero, Pietro Lio, and Yoshua Bengio. 2017. Graph attention networks. *arXiv preprint arXiv:1710.10903*.

Ben Wasike. 2023. You've been fact-checked! examining the effectiveness of social media fact-checking against the spread of misinformation. *Telematics and Informatics Reports*, 11:100090.

Xiao-Kun Wu, Min Chen, Wanyi Li, Rui Wang, Limeng Lu, Jia Liu, Kai Hwang, Yixue Hao, Yanru Pan, Qingguo Meng, et al. 2025. Llm fine-tuning: Concepts, opportunities, and challenges. *Big Data and Cognitive Computing*, 9(4):87.

Zonghan Wu, Shirui Pan, Fengwen Chen, Guodong Long, Chengqi Zhang, and S Yu Philip. 2020. A comprehensive survey on graph neural networks. *IEEE transactions on neural networks and learning systems*, 32(1):4–24.

Hang Yan, Bocao Deng, Xiaonan Li, and Xipeng Qiu. 2019. Tener: adapting transformer encoder for named entity recognition. *arXiv preprint arXiv:1911.04474*.

Jingyuan Yi, Zeqiu Xu, Tianyi Huang, and Peiyang Yu. 2025. Challenges and innovations in llm-powered fake news detection: A synthesis of approaches and future directions. In *Proceedings of the 2025 2nd International Conference on Generative Artificial Intelligence and Information Security*, pages 87–93.

Biao Zhang, Barry Haddow, and Alexandra Birch. 2023. Prompting large language model for machine translation: A case study. In *International Conference on Machine Learning*, pages 41092–41110. PMLR.

Min Zhou, Menglin Yang, Bo Xiong, Hui Xiong, and Irwin King. 2023. Hyperbolic graph neural networks: A tutorial on methods and applications. In *Proceedings of the 29th ACM SIGKDD Conference on Knowledge Discovery and Data Mining*, pages 5843–5844.

A Appendix

A.1 Generating Dependency Parsing Graphs of Environmental Claims

We now provide a working example of the process of converting claim sentences into their dependency parsing graphs. The feature vectors shown are for illustrative purposes and do not represent actual embedding values. Let the claim sentence **C** be *"Gas is also a cleaner fuel with resultant environmental benefits."*

- **Dependency Parsing C:** The claim sentence **C** is first transformed into its corresponding dependency parsing graph using the spaCy dependency parser. Figure 2 illustrates this transformation.
- **Node Features (x'_v):** Each node's feature vector is the concatenation of its word embedding and a randomly initialized, trainable POS tag embedding. For the node 'cleaner' (an 'ADJ'), with $d_{word} = 4$ and $d_{pos} = 2$,

$$x'_{\text{cleaner}} = [\underbrace{W_e(\text{'cleaner'})}_{\text{word2vec}} \,\|\, \underbrace{W_p(\text{'ADJ'})}_{\text{POS emb.}}]$$

$$= \left[\begin{pmatrix} 0.21 \\ -0.45 \\ 0.67 \\ 0.09 \end{pmatrix} \Bigg\| \begin{pmatrix} 0.62 \\ 0.15 \end{pmatrix} \right] = \begin{pmatrix} 0.21 \\ -0.45 \\ 0.67 \\ 0.09 \\ 0.62 \\ 0.15 \end{pmatrix}$$

- **Edge Features (e_{hj}):** Each dependency relation is one-hot encoded. The *amod* relation from 'fuel' to 'cleaner', being the 5th unique relation out of 45, is represented as: $e_{\text{fuel, cleaner}} = \begin{pmatrix} 0 & 0 & 0 & 0 & 1 & \cdots & 0 \end{pmatrix}^T \in \mathbb{R}^{45}$

A.2 Training Configuration

Table 5 shows the (fixed) hyperparameters used for training our GNN and HGNN models. Dropout rate, POS-embedding dimension and class-weights were optimized through grid-search.

Hyperparameter	Value
Number of GNN Layers	4
Learning Rate	0.001
Hyperbolic Learning Rate	0.001
Patience (Early Stopping)	8
Activation Function	Leaky ReLU
Leaky ReLU Slope	0.5
Optimizer	AMSGrad
Hyperbolic Optimizer	Riemannian AMSGrad
Embedding Dimension	256
Number of Centroids	30
Maximum Epochs	30
Edge Types	45
Number of Classes	2
Initialization Method	Xavier
Gradient Clipping	1.0

Table 5: GNN and HGNN Training Configuration

A.3 Evaluation Metrics

Let TP, FP, TN, and FN be the number of True Positives, False Positives, True Negatives, and False Negatives, respectively. The metrics are defined as follows.

- **Accuracy:** The proportion of correctly classified instances among the total instances.

$$\text{Accuracy} = \frac{TP + TN}{TP + TN + FP + FN}$$

- **Precision:** The ratio of correctly predicted positive observations to the total predicted positive observations.

$$\text{Precision} = \frac{TP}{TP + FP}$$

- **Recall:** The ratio of correctly predicted positive observations to all observations in the actual class.

$$\text{Recall} = \frac{TP}{TP + FN}$$

- **F1-Score:** The harmonic mean of Precision and Recall.

$$\text{F1-Score} = 2 \cdot \frac{\text{Precision} \cdot \text{Recall}}{\text{Precision} + \text{Recall}}$$

- **AUC-ROC:** The Area Under the Receiver Operating Characteristic Curve. It measures the model's ability to distinguish between positive and negative classes across all classification thresholds.

A.4 Parameter Size Calculation for Graph Models

Here, we detail the number of trainable parameters for our graph models. We first calculate the number of trainable parameters for the base model (with only word embeddings) and then for the model augmented with POS-tag embeddings (-POS).

Base GNN/HGNN Model (without POS). The base model's parameters are distributed across an input projection layer, three hidden GNN layers, and a final classifier.

- Layer 1 (Input Projection): Maps the 300-dimensional word embeddings to the 256-dimensional hidden space for each of the 45

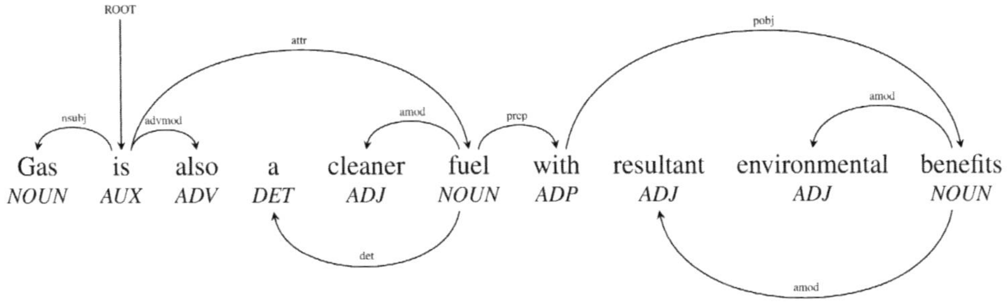

Figure 2: The transformation of the example claim into a dependency graph. The graph shows tokens and their POS tags as nodes, with syntactic dependencies as labeled, directed edges.

relations. 45 relations × 300 input_dim × 256 output_dim) + 256 bias = 3,456,256.

- Layers 2, 3, & 4: These three layers map the 256-dimensional hidden state to another 256-dimensional hidden state for each relation. 3 layers × [(45 relations × 256 input_dim × 256 output_dim) + 256 bias] = 8,848,128.
- Final Classifier: (256 × 2 output classes) + 2 bias = 514.
- Total number of parameters = 3,456,256 + 8,848,128 + 514 = **12,304,898**.

GNN-POS/HGNN-POS Model (with POS). Adds learnable POS embeddings. Using an example POS dimension (d_{pos}) be 16:

- POS Tag Embeddings: 18 vocab_size × 16 pos_dim = 288
- Layer 1 (Input Projection): The input dimension is now 300 + 16 = 316. (45 × 316 × 256) + 256 = 3,640,576.
- Layers 2, 3, & 4: Unchanged from the base model. Parameters: 8,848,128
- Final Classifier: Unchanged from the base model. Parameters: 514
- Total number of parameters (POS) = 288 + 3,640,576 + 8,848,128 + 514 = **12,489,506**.

Stacked LoRA: Isolated Low-Rank Adaptation for Lifelong Knowledge Management

Heramb Vivek Patil and **Vaishnavee Kiran Sanam** and **Dr. Minakshi Pradeep Atre**
PVG's College of Engineering and Technology, Pune
herambpatil2004@gmail.com, vaishnavee.gcloud@gmail.com, mpatre29@gmail.com

Abstract

Continual learning (CL) presents a significant challenge for large pre-trained models, primarily due to catastrophic forgetting and the high computational cost of sequential knowledge updating. Parameter-Efficient Transfer Learning (PETL) methods offer reduced computational burdens but often struggle to effectively mitigate forgetting. This paper introduces Stacked Low-Rank Adaptation (SLoRA), a novel parameter-efficient approach that leverages the additive composition of task-specific, frozen low-rank adapters to enable modular continual learning with inherent support for explicit knowledge modification. SLoRA was evaluated on vision benchmarks, BERT-base, and the 1-billion-parameter Llama-3.2-1B model. Experiments demonstrated that SLoRA almost completely eliminated catastrophic forgetting, achieving a final average accuracy of 92.75% on Llama-3.2-1B while perfectly preserving prior task performance. Furthermore, SLoRA is computationally efficient, enabling up to a 15x training speed-up over full fine-tuning with 99.7% fewer trainable parameters per update. SLoRA offers a compelling balance of forgetting mitigation, parameter efficiency, and modularity, representing a promising direction for developing adaptable and efficient lifelong knowledgeable foundation models.

1 Introduction

The capability to learn from a stream of tasks, incrementally acquiring new knowledge, without forgetting prior knowledge is a central goal of Continual Learning (CL), a necessity for NLP systems deployed in dynamic environments. However, catastrophic forgetting, whereby performance on earlier tasks (representing previously acquired knowledge) is degraded upon learning new ones (acquiring new knowledge), remains a fundamental obstacle (Zeng et al., 2024).

The challenge is amplified by large pretrained models (LPMs) like BERT and Llama, which demand substantial resources for retraining on new tasks. This full fine-tuning approach is often computationally prohibitive and environmentally costly (Patterson et al., 2021). Moreover, it leads to catastrophic forgetting, where performance on earlier tasks is severely degraded upon learning new ones, effectively erasing previously acquired knowledge (Zeng et al., 2024). Parameter-efficient transfer learning (PEFT) approaches address the computational cost by training only a small number of additional parameters per task, making them suitable for CL settings. Techniques including Adapters (Houlsby et al., 2019), Prompt Tuning (Lester et al., 2021), and LoRA (Hu et al., 2022) have shown promise. However, as noted by Coleman et al. (2025), preventing parameter interference during sequential updates remains an open challenge; a naive combination of PEFT and CL often fails as modules still share parameter spaces, leading to interference.

Interference, leading to the corruption of previously acquired knowledge, hampers traditional PEFT techniques when modules are shared across tasks (He et al., 2021; Wang et al., 2023). While assigning isolated modules to each task prevents forgetting, this strategy leads to unbounded growth in parameters for storing this modular knowledge and lacks a mechanism for explicit knowledge unlearning. Prior works investigating routing (Zhang et al., 2023), mixture-of-experts (Feng et al., 2024), or orthogonal subspace projection (Wang et al., 2023) to manage knowledge interactions often introduce additional complexity or depend on known task identity at inference for knowledge retrieval.

Recent works like InfLoRA (Liang and Li, 2024) and SD-LoRA (Wu et al., 2025) also address cumulative LoRA usage, but with different goals. These methods target the task-agnostic Class-Incremental Learning (CIL) scenario, requiring them to merge

Proceedings of the IJCNLP-AACL 2025 Student Research Workshop, pages 36–46
December 20-24, 2025 ©2025 Association for Computational Linguistics

or blend knowledge into a single model, which forfeits the ability to unlearn. InfLoRA permanently merges adapters, while SD-LoRA retrains all adapter "magnitudes" at each step, breaking parameter isolation.

To address these challenges, we introduce Stacked Low-Rank Adaptation (SLoRA), a novel parameter-efficient approach for the Task-Incremental Learning (TIL) setting. SLoRA provides strong knowledge retention with inherent modularity by additively composing strictly frozen, task-specific low-rank adapters. This architectural isolation is simpler than algorithmic orthogonality and, crucially, enables explicit knowledge modification (i.e., unlearning) by deactivating adapters, a feature not possible with merging or blending approaches. Our evaluations on vision and NLP benchmarks demonstrate SLoRA's effectiveness in mitigating catastrophic knowledge loss while maintaining a competitive parameter footprint. This work lays a strong foundation for adaptable lifelong knowledgeable foundation models.

2 Related Work

Continual Learning (CL) addresses the challenge of learning from a sequence of tasks, incrementally updating models with new knowledge, without forgetting previous knowledge. A fundamental obstacle in CL is catastrophic forgetting (loss of prior knowledge), where adaptation to new tasks (acquisition of new knowledge) degrades performance on earlier ones (Zeng et al., 2024). In NLP, large pre-trained Transformer models require efficient adaptation to new tasks; updating all parameters per task is prohibitively expensive when aiming for efficient knowledge updates. Parameter-Efficient Transfer Learning (PETL) methods tackle this by fine-tuning only a small subset of parameters, yielding benefits in compute, storage, and modularity for injecting new knowledge (Houlsby et al., 2019; He et al., 2021).

Adapter Modules insert small bottleneck layers into each Transformer block, training only these new parameters. The original Adapter approach (Houlsby et al., 2019) demonstrated near full-fine-tuning performance on GLUE while adding only ~3.6% parameters per task. However, naively adding new adapters per task leads to linear growth in parameters for storing task-specific knowledge and can increase inference latency.

LoRA (Low-Rank Adaptation) freezes the original weights and injects trainable low-rank decomposition matrices into each layer, reducing trainable parameters by orders of magnitude and incurring no extra inference cost once merged (Hu et al., 2022). Its performance is sensitive to the chosen rank but matches full fine-tuning quality in many settings for single-task knowledge adaptation.

Prompt-Based Methods, including Prefix-Tuning (Li and Liang, 2021) and Prompt-Tuning (Lester et al., 2021), optimize continuous prefix vectors or soft prompt tokens prepended to inputs, tuning as little as 0.1% of parameters. These methods can be very parameter-efficient for accessing specific knowledge representations but need careful prompt design and may vary in effectiveness across tasks.

While PETL methods excel in single-task adaptation (knowledge injection), applying them to CL (continuous knowledge updating) brings new challenges. As our results for LoRA-Cont (Section 4.4) confirm, a naive sequential application of LoRA fails, suffering severe catastrophic forgetting. This highlights that a dedicated architecture is required. A recent survey specifically on Parameter-Efficient Continual Fine-Tuning highlights the open questions at the intersection of CL and PETL (Coleman et al., 2025).

Several works extend LoRA for CL by enforcing desirable properties in adapter parameters to manage knowledge interactions: **O-LoRA** encourages orthogonality among low-rank adapters for different tasks to reduce interference, effectively eliminating forgetting (preserving knowledge) with only marginal extra parameters (Wang et al., 2023). **C-LoRA** introduces a learnable routing matrix that dynamically allocates subspaces for previous and new tasks, achieving scalable continual adaptation for managing knowledge subspaces without maintaing separate adapters per task (Zhang et al., 2025).

Modular Adapter Approaches allocate task-specific parameters for encapsulating knowledge and freeze them thereafter. While this isolates task knowledge and prevents forgetting (knowledge loss), it leads to parameter counts growing linearly with the number of tasks. **AdapterFusion** combines multiple frozen adapters representing task knowledge by learning a fusion layer that integrates their outputs non-destructively, leveraging cross-task knowledge transfer at the cost of extra composition parameters (Pfeiffer et al., 2020).

Beyond single-method strategies, a growing body of work explores compositional PEFT modules for CL and multi-task learning by combining knowledge adaptations: **ReLoRA** periodically merges low-rank updates back into the model and reinitializes adapters during training, effectively increasing representational capacity and improving convergence speed (Lialin et al., 2023). **LoraHub** dynamically composes multiple pre-trained LoRA modules for few-shot generalization on unseen tasks, requiring no additional parameters or gradients at inference for knowledge retrieval and composition (Huang et al., 2023). **Task Arithmetic** treats each adapter update as a vector in weight space and performs linear operations (addition, subtraction) to combine task knowledge, enabling straightforward module composition (Zhang et al., 2023). **Mixture-of-LoRAs** (MoA) trains multiple domain experts via LoRA and uses an explicit routing mechanism to select and combine experts per input, blending Mixture-of-Experts principles with LoRA's efficiency for expert-based knowledge retrieval (Feng et al., 2024).

Distinctions from LoRA-based CIL Methods. Our work is related to other LoRA-based CL methods like InfLoRA (Liang and Li, 2024) and SD-LoRA (Wu et al., 2025), but SLoRA is fundamentally different in its problem setting, mechanism, and capabilities.

- **Problem Setting:** InfLoRA and SD-LoRA are designed for Class-Incremental Learning (CIL), which requires a single model to operate without task identity. SLoRA is designed for the Task-Incremental Learning (TIL) setting, where task identity is known at inference.
- **Mechanism:** To achieve its task-agnostic goal, InfLoRA uses permanent merging (losing modularity) and SD-LoRA uses collaborative blending (retraining all adapter magnitudes, breaking isolation). SLoRA uses strict architectural isolation by freezing all past adapters.
- **Capability:** SLoRA's TIL design and isolation mechanism provide a unique capability the CIL methods cannot: explicit knowledge unlearning. A task can be removed simply by deactivating its adapter, which is impossible in models that merge or blend parameters.

Despite these advancements, key trade-offs remain between stability (retaining acquired knowledge), plasticity (acquiring new knowledge) and parameter growth. Our proposed Stacked Low-Rank Adaptation (SLoRA) addresses these by stacking individually trained and frozen low-rank adapters additively, ensuring clear parameter isolation (for knowledge encapsulation), straightforward composition (including unlearning), and inherently modular knowledge management.

3 Methodology

Continual Learning (CL) aims to train models sequentially on new tasks, incrementally updating their knowledge, without forgetting previous knowledge. A key challenge is catastrophic forgetting (knowledge loss) in large pre-trained models, necessitating parameter-efficient adaptation for knowledge acquisition. Stacked Low-Rank Adaptation (SLoRA) is proposed as a novel method for parameter-efficient CL that mitigates forgetting through additive composition of task-specific low-rank adapters (representing task-specific knowledge adaptations).

3.1 SLoRA Method

SLoRA builds on Low-Rank Adaptation (LoRA), which adapts pre-trained weights W_0 by adding a low-rank update $\Delta W = \frac{\alpha}{r} BA$, where $A \in \mathbb{R}^{r \times d_{in}}$, $B \in \mathbb{R}^{d_{out} \times r}$, $r \ll \min(d_{in}, d_{out})$. LoRA trains only A and B, keeping W_0 frozen (Hu et al., 2022). SLoRA extends this by applying additively multiple low-rank task-specific updates. After training in T tasks (0-indexed), the effective weight $W^{(T-1)}$ is the sum of W_0, a base update ΔW_{base}, and stack updates $(T-1)$ $\Delta W_{stack,t}$:

$$W^{(T-1)} = W_0 + \Delta W_{base} + \sum_{t=1}^{T-1} \Delta W_{stack,t}$$

where $\Delta W_{base} = \frac{\alpha_{base}}{r_{base}} B_{base} A_{base}$ and $\Delta W_{stack,t} = \frac{\alpha_{stack}}{r_{stack}} B_{stack,t} A_{stack,t}$ for task t. This parallel and additive composition is depicted in Figure 1.

The training is sequential. For the base task (Task 0), a base LoRA adapter (A_{base}, B_{base}) is attached and trained with W_0 frozen. For each subsequent task $t > 0$ (representing the acquisition of new knowledge), a *new* stack adapter $(A_{stack,t}, B_{stack,t})$ is initialized and added. Crucially, W_0, the base adapter, and *all previously trained stack adapters* are held frozen. Only the newly added stack adapter and the task classifier are trained on the data of task t. This strict parameter isolation prevents interference and protects previously acquired knowledge.

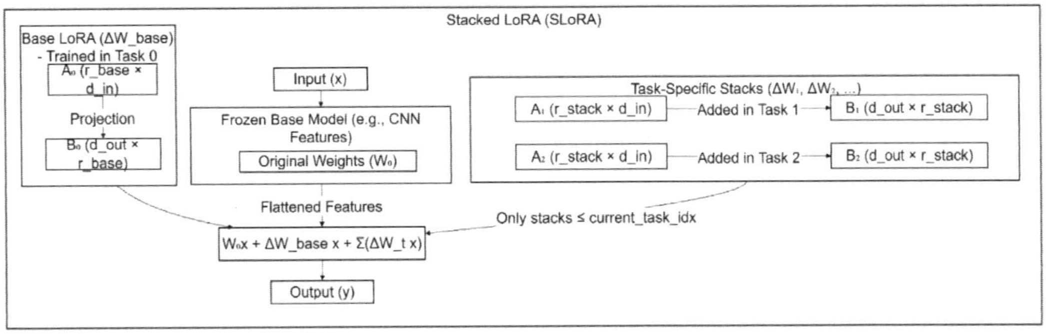

Figure 1: SLoRA architecture: Additive composition of task-specific LoRA adapters in parallel with the base weight. The base model (W_0) and all previously trained adapters (ΔW_{base}, $\Delta W_{stack,1}$) are frozen. Only the new adapter for the current task ($\Delta W_{stack,2}$) is trained. Inference on a task k is performed by summing adapters up to k.

At inference time, to evaluate performance on Task k (0-indexed), the effective weight matrix $W^{(k)}$ is formed by summing W_0, the base adapter, and all stack adapters up to task k: $W^{(k)} = W_0 + \Delta W_{base} + \sum_{t=1}^{k} \Delta W_{stack,t}$. This "selective activation" uses only task-relevant knowledge adaptations. A direct benefit of this modular and additive structure is explicit knowledge modification: Task k is "unlearned" by excluding its stack adapter from the summation during inference (e.g., by adjusting a task index variable), requiring no additional training.

3.2 Experimental Setup

Experiments were conducted on Permuted-MNIST, Split-CIFAR100, and sequential NLP tasks using BERT-base-uncased, across 3 random seeds. The baselines included full fine-tuning (FT), elastic weight consolidation (EWC) (Kirkpatrick et al., 2017), standard continual LoRA (LoRA-Cont), and independent LoRA adapters per task (LoRA-Ind). The implementation used PyTorch and Avalanche (Lomonaco et al., 2021).

For Permuted-MNIST (5 tasks), an MLP with two linear layers was used as the base model, adapted with SLoRA. Training used 2 epochs/task and batch size 64. LoRA (Cont and Ind) used rank 8, alpha 16. SLoRA used base rank 8, alpha 16, stack rank 4, alpha 16. The learning rates were 1e-3 for all methods.

For Split-CIFAR100 (10 tasks), a SimpleCNN with frozen convolutional layers and a two-linear-layer classifier was used. The classifier linear layers were adapted. Training used 50 epochs/task, batch size 64. LoRA (Cont/Ind) used rank 8, alpha 16. SLoRA used base rank 16, alpha 32, stack rank 8, alpha 16. LRs were 1e-3 for all methods. EWC used lambda 1000.

For Sequential NLP Tasks (4 tasks), a frozen BERT-base-uncased model was adapted in its linear layers. Tasks were SST-2, TREC, Yelp Polarity, and Amazon Polarity, using a 10000-example subset per task. Training used 15 epochs/task, batch size 16, max length 128. LoRA (Cont) used rank 8. SLoRA used base rank 8, stack rank 4. LRs were 1e-3 for all methods.

Evaluation after training each task involved measuring accuracy on all tasks seen so far. SLoRA was evaluated using selective activation based on the task index. LoRA-Ind performance was measured by loading the saved task-specific adapter parameters.

To assess scalability on modern LLMs, we conducted further experiments on the `meta-llama/Llama-3.2-1B` model. We used the same sequence of four NLP tasks (SST-2, TREC, Yelp Polarity, Amazon Polarity) with 10,000 examples per task. SLoRA was applied to the linear layers of the attention and feed-forward networks. The base adapter was configured with a rank (r_{base}) of 8 and alpha of 16. Subsequent task-specific stack adapters used a rank (r_{stack}) of 4 and alpha of 8. The model was trained for one epoch per task with a batch size of 4 using the AdamW optimizer.

4 Results

This section presents the empirical evaluation of SLoRA against Full Fine-Tuning (FT), Elastic Weight Consolidation (EWC) (Kirkpatrick et al., 2017), standard continual LoRA (LoRA-Cont), and task-independent LoRA (LoRA-Ind). We first evaluate on standard vision benchmarks (Permuted-

MNIST, Split-CIFAR100) for robust comparison against prior CL literature. We then validate SLoRA's scalability and efficiency on large-scale, real-world NLP tasks using BERT-base and the 1-billion-parameter Llama-3.2-1B model.

Performance is assessed based on forgetting mitigation (knowledge retention), overall accuracy, and parameter efficiency. Experiments were conducted using a single NVIDIA T4 GPU for Permuted-MNIST and a single NVIDIA P100 GPU for Split-CIFAR100 and BERT-base experiments. Implementation was done using PyTorch and Avalanche (Lomonaco et al., 2021). Results for Permuted-MNIST and Split-CIFAR100 are reported as mean accuracy $\pm$ standard deviation over 3 random seeds. LLM results are from a single seed due to compute constraints and are interpreted as preliminary; EWC and LoRA-Ind results were not available for BERT.

4.1 Overall Findings Summary

Across diverse domains, SLoRA consistently demonstrates effectiveness in mitigating catastrophic forgetting (knowledge loss). Methods training shared parameters (FT, LoRA-Cont) show significant forgetting. SLoRA, by employing additive, task-specific frozen adapters (representing isolated knowledge adaptations), effectively preserves performance on prior tasks comparable to methods like EWC and LoRA-Ind. SLoRA maintains a competitive parameter footprint, scaling linearly with tasks but more efficiently than full fine-tuning.

4.2 Permuted-MNIST Results (5-Task Sequence)

The Permuted-MNIST benchmark evaluates forgetting on a 5-task sequence. To specifically illustrate forgetting on the first task over time, Table 1 shows the performance on Task 1 after training each subsequent task. Table 7 (in Appendix) summarizes the mean accuracy $\pm$ standard deviation on each task after training on all 5 tasks.

Table 1: Accuracy (%) on Permuted-MNIST Task 1 after Training Sequential Tasks (Mean $\pm$ SD over 3 Seeds)

Method	After Task 1	After Task 2	After Task 3	After Task 4
FT	97.22 $\pm$ 0.25	92.64 $\pm$ 2.01	78.34 $\pm$ 0.82	66.36 $\pm$ 11.42
EWC	97.22 $\pm$ 0.25	94.51 $\pm$ 0.14	81.88 $\pm$ 4.09	71.93 $\pm$ 7.66
LoRA-Cont	97.22 $\pm$ 0.25	92.23 $\pm$ 2.01	79.70 $\pm$ 5.69	67.25 $\pm$ 5.68
SLoRA	97.22 $\pm$ 0.25	**92.82 $\pm$ 1.22**	**86.30 $\pm$ 2.64**	**72.62 $\pm$ 8.69**

Table 1 clearly shows the severe forgetting experienced by FT and LoRA-Cont. SLoRA exhibits better retention of Task 1 knowledge. Table 7 (Appendix) confirms SLoRA achieves the highest overall average accuracy.

4.3 Split-CIFAR100 Results (10-Task Sequence)

Experiments were conducted on Split-CIFAR100 (10 classes/task). Table 8 (in Appendix) presents a concise summary, and Figure 2 plots the average accuracy on tasks seen so far.

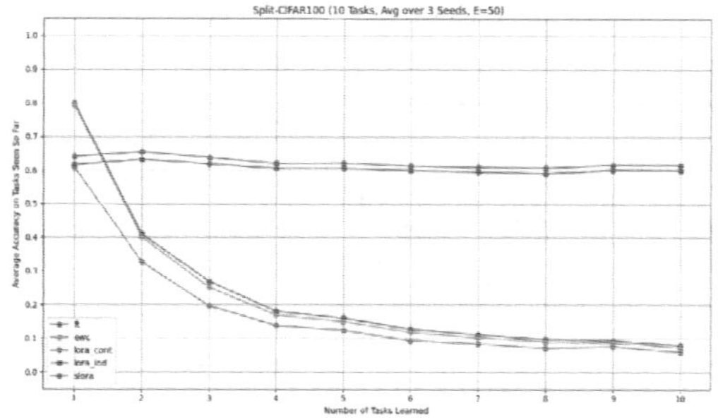

Figure 2: Average accuracy on tasks seen so far on Split-CIFAR100 after training each sequential task (Averaged over 3 Seeds, E=50). SLoRA and LoRA-Ind show near-zero forgetting, while FT, EWC, and LoRA-Cont suffer catastrophic forgetting.

Figure 2 and Table 8 (Appendix) clearly show that FT, EWC, and LoRA-Cont suffer severe catastrophic forgetting. In contrast, LoRA-Ind and SLoRA demonstrate significantly better knowledge retention, maintaining high accuracy on previously learned tasks. SLoRA achieves comparable forgetting mitigation to LoRA-Ind with a slightly higher final average accuracy.

4.4 Sequential NLP Tasks (BERT-base) Results (4-Task Sequence)

The performance of SLoRA was evaluated on a sequence of 4 real-world NLP classification tasks using a frozen BERT-base-uncased model. To validate that a naive PEFT-CL combination fails, we explicitly benchmark against LoRA-Cont.

As shown in Table 2, both FT and the naive LoRA-Cont baseline suffer from severe catastrophic forgetting on BERT-base. This demonstrates that simply using a PEFT method is insufficient. SLoRA's isolated stacked architecture, however, demonstrates remarkable stability, with performance on Tasks 1, 2, and 3 remaining virtually unchanged. SLoRA achieves the highest overall average accuracy (88.33%). On a single NVIDIA

Table 2: Accuracy (%) on Sequential BERT-base Tasks after Training on Task 4 (Single Seed: 42)

Method	Task 1 (SST-2)	Task 2 (TREC)	Task 3 (Yelp)	Task 4 (Amazon)	Avg. Accuracy
FT	60.80	4.26	59.70	53.30	44.51
LoRA-Cont	85.30	74.47	91.50	92.10	85.84
SLoRA	**89.90**	**93.62**	**84.20**	85.60	**88.33**

Table 3: Parameter Efficiency Comparison for BERT-base on 4 Tasks

Method	Trainable Params per Task	Total Unique Params (after 4 Tasks)	Parameter Growth
Full FT	109.5M (same every task)	109.5M	Constant
LoRA-Cont(r=8)	1.35M	1.35M	Constant
LoRA-Ind (r=8)	1.35M	~5.4M	Linear ($T\times$)
SLoRA (B_r=8, St_r=4)	1.34M (Task 0), 0.67M (T1–T3)	3.35M	Linear ($T\times$)

Note: FT fine-tunes the full model per task. LoRA-Continual updates a shared adapter. LoRA-Independent uses separate adapters per task. SLoRA uses a shared base adapter (Task 0) and stack adapters for subsequent tasks.

P100, SLoRA also converges in only 1.5 minutes per task, an 8x speed-up over FT (12.0 minutes).

The parameter efficiency is detailed in Table 3. SLoRA scales linearly with tasks but requires fewer total parameters than LoRA-Ind due to its smaller stack rank configuration.

4.5 Scalability and Efficiency Analysis on Llama-3.2-1B

To validate SLoRA's performance and efficiency on contemporary large-scale models, we evaluated it on the 1-billion-parameter Llama-3.2-1B. The results confirm that SLoRA's architecture effectively scales, preventing catastrophic forgetting while offering significant computational advantages.

As shown in Table 4, SLoRA achieves a high final average accuracy of 92.75% across the four sequential tasks. Performance on prior tasks remained unchanged after training on subsequent tasks, demonstrating near-zero catastrophic forgetting and validating the knowledge isolation provided by the frozen, additive adapters.

Table 5 presents a quantitative analysis of SLoRA's efficiency. By updating only 2.8 million parameters per task (~0.3% of the model), SLoRA achieves a 15x reduction in training time. This efficiency also translates to an estimated 93% reduction in CO_2e emissions per update. The modular architecture inherently supports unlearning, a capability computationally impractical for monolithically fine-tuned models.

4.6 Hyperparameter Tuning Insights

Targeted ablation experiments on 5-task Permuted-MNIST (single seed: 43) provided insights into

Table 4: SLoRA Performance on Llama-3.2-1B across 4 Sequential NLP Tasks. Accuracy on each task was measured after all four tasks were trained.

Task Evaluated	**Final Acc. (%)**
Task 1 (SST-2)	94.30
Task 2 (TREC)	85.11
Task 3 (Yelp Pol.)	96.20
Task 4 (Amazon Pol.)	95.40
Final Avg. Accuracy	**92.75**

SLoRA hyperparameters. Investigating stack rank (r_{stack}) with fixed base rank ($r_{base} = 8, \alpha_{base} = 16$) revealed a clear parameter efficiency vs. performance trade-off. Decreasing r_{stack} from 8 to 1 linearly reduced parameters but led to moderate-to-significant drops in final average accuracy (0.9556 down to 0.7681). Crucially, regardless of r_{stack}, performance on Task 1 after training later tasks remained consistently high (~0.9520), demonstrating that stack rank variation did not cause forgetting of isolated knowledge. This supports the robustness of SLoRA's freezing mechanism. Varying stack α_{stack} (8, 16, 32 with $r_{stack} = 8$) resulted in only marginal changes in final average accuracy (~0.955). An ablation without a base adapter (`SLoRA_NoBase`) showed performance (0.9554 final average accuracy) very close to the configuration with a base adapter (0.9556), suggesting stacks build effectively on the frozen W_0 even without a dedicated base LoRA.

Table 5: Computational Efficiency and Architectural Comparison on Llama-3.2-1B.

Metric	Full Fine-Tuning (FT)	SLoRA (Proposed Method)
Performance Degradation (Forgetting)	Severe (Observed on BERT-base)	**Negligible (Near-zero forgetting)**
Trainable Parameters / Update	~1 Billion	**2.8 Million (99.7% fewer)**
Training Time / Update (est.)	~60 minutes	**~4 minutes (15x Speed-up)**
Estimated CO_2e / Update (kg)[a]	~0.163 kg	**~0.011 kg (93% Reduction)**
Architectural Property: Unlearning	Impractical (Requires full retraining)	**Inherent (Deactivate adapter)**

[a]CO_2e emissions estimated for a single task update on an NVIDIA RTX A5000 GPU (230W TDP), using India's average grid intensity of 0.708 kg CO_2e/kWh. FT time is an estimate based on observed speed-up.

5 Discussion

The experimental results demonstrate SLoRA's effectiveness in mitigating catastrophic forgetting, with the findings on Llama-3.2-1B (Section 4.5) providing strong evidence of its scalability. While methods with shared parameters (FT, LoRA-Cont) show significant performance degradation on prior tasks, SLoRA's design of freezing and additively composing adapters ensures that previously acquired knowledge is preserved. This is a direct consequence of parameter isolation, where each task-specific adaptation is encapsulated within a distinct, immutable module.

The analysis in Table 5 highlights a crucial trade-off in continual learning: the balance between performance, parameter count, and computational cost. SLoRA offers a compelling solution by drastically reducing the number of trainable parameters per task update (99.7% fewer than FT for Llama-3.2-1B). This leads to substantial improvements in training speed (Table 6) and energy efficiency, making sequential model updates feasible. While SLoRA's total parameter count grows linearly, the storage overhead for each adapter is minimal compared to storing separate model checkpoints.

We then consider parameter efficiency, a key factor for scalability. PEFT methods, including LoRA-Cont, LoRA-Ind, and SLoRA, require substantially fewer trainable parameters per task step than FT or EWC. While LoRA-Cont has minimal storage, it suffers severe forgetting (Table 2). Both LoRA-Ind and SLoRA scale unique parameter storage linearly with tasks. SLoRA requires fewer parameters than LoRA-Ind in practice, thanks to its use of smaller stack ranks per task, while still achieving comparable or better forgetting mitigation (Table 3). This demonstrates a favorable parameter-performance trade-off.

Architecturally, SLoRA's design offers additional benefits beyond performance and efficiency for knowledge management. A significant advantage is the inherent support for explicit task unlearning (knowledge modification): removing a task's frozen stack from the additive summation during inference effectively unlearns the corresponding knowledge, with no need for retraining. This capability positions SLoRA as a direct and practical approach to the problem of knowledge editing in foundation models, allowing for the targeted removal of outdated or incorrect information. Selective activation also allows for tailored inference by summing relevant stacks (enabling flexible knowledge retrieval).

Hyperparameter tuning experiments (Section 4.6) confirmed that once the core parameter isolation and additive composition are correctly implemented, SLoRA's forgetting mitigation property is robust to variations in stack size and scaling.

In summary, SLoRA provides a compelling parameter-efficient continual learning (knowledge updating) approach for the task-incremental setting. It effectively prevents catastrophic forgetting (knowledge loss) through the additive composition of task-specific, frozen low-rank adapters (representing knowledge adaptations), while also offering architectural simplicity, flexible parameter control (for knowledge representations), and native support for modular knowledge management, including task unlearning (knowledge modification) and selective inference (knowledge retrieval).

6 Conclusion

This work introduced Stacked Low-Rank Adaptation (SLoRA), a parameter-efficient method that addresses catastrophic forgetting in continual learning through the additive composition of task-specific, frozen low-rank adapters. Empirical evaluations on vision benchmarks, BERT-base, and the 1-billion-parameter Llama-3.2-1B demonstrated SLoRA's ability to nearly eliminate forgetting while offering significant computational advantages, including up to a 15x training speed-up compared to full fine-tuning. Its modular architecture inherently supports critical functionalities like explicit task unlearning by deactivating adapters.

While SLoRA presents a robust solution for the task-incremental setting, key limitations include the linear growth of parameters with tasks and the reliance on task identity at inference. Future work should focus on mitigating parameter growth through techniques like adapter pruning or merging. A primary research direction is the development of task-agnostic inference mechanisms. This could involve implementing a dynamic routing module, potentially using learned steering vectors, to automatically select and combine the appropriate adapter stacks based on the input's semantic content. Such advancements would move towards creating truly autonomous and efficient lifelong learning systems. SLoRA provides a strong foundation for building adaptable, scalable, and manageable foundation models.

7 Limitations and Future Work

While SLoRA demonstrates significant advantages, we identify several limitations that present avenues for future research:

- **Linear Parameter Growth:** The total number of parameters scales linearly with the number of tasks. Although the adapters are parameter-efficient, this growth could become a storage bottleneck in scenarios involving an extremely large sequence of tasks.
- **Inference Latency Overhead:** Unlike standard LoRA adapters that can be merged into the base model to eliminate latency, SLoRA's parallel structure requires real-time summation of adapter outputs. This introduces a minor computational overhead during the forward pass that scales with the number of active adapters.
- **Reliance on Task Identity:** The current inference strategy requires explicit task identity to activate the corresponding adapter stack. This assumption limits its direct application in task-agnostic or online continual learning settings. This reliance, however, is a deliberate design trade-off that enables SLoRA's strict parameter isolation and its unique capability for explicit knowledge unlearning, which is not possible in task-agnostic methods that merge or blend parameters.
- **Scope of Evaluation:** Our experiments were conducted on task-incremental benchmarks. The method's generalization to more challenging CL paradigms, such as class-incremental or domain-incremental learning, remains to be validated.
- **Experimental Rigor on LLMs:** Due to computational constraints, the results for larger models (BERT-base, Llama-3.2-1B) are based on single-seed runs. Multi-seed experiments are necessary to fully establish the statistical significance and robustness of SLoRA's performance at scale.
- **Hyperparameter Sensitivity:** While the core mechanism is robust, the optimal rank (r) and scaling factor (α) for base and stack adapters may vary across different models and task types. This work does not establish a comprehensive guideline for hyperparameter selection.

References

Eric Nuertey Coleman, Luigi Quarantiello, Ziyue Liu, Qinwen Yang, Samrat Mukherjee, Julio Hurtado, and Vincenzo Lomonaco. 2025. Parameter-efficient continual fine-tuning: A survey. *arXiv preprint arXiv:2504.13822*.

Wenfeng Feng, Chuzhan Hao, Yuewei Zhang, Yu Han, and Hao Wang. 2024. Mixture-of-loras: An efficient multitask tuning for large language models. *arXiv preprint arXiv:2403.03432*.

Junxian He, Chunting Zhou, Xuezhe Ma, Taylor Berg-Kirkpatrick, and Graham Neubig. 2021. Towards a unified view of parameter-efficient transfer learning. *arXiv preprint arXiv:2110.04366*.

Neil Houlsby, Andrei Giurgiu, Stanislaw Jastrzebski, Bruna Morrone, Quentin De Laroussilhe, Andrea Gesmundo, Mona Attariyan, and Sylvain Gelly. 2019. Parameter-efficient transfer learning for nlp. In *International conference on machine learning*, pages 2790–2799. PMLR.

Edward J Hu, Yelong Shen, Phillip Wallis, Zeyuan Allen-Zhu, Yuanzhi Li, Shean Wang, Lu Wang, Weizhu Chen, and 1 others. 2022. Lora: Low-rank adaptation of large language models. *ICLR*, 1(2):3.

Chengsong Huang, Qian Liu, Bill Yuchen Lin, Tianyu Pang, Chao Du, and Min Lin. 2023. Lorahub: Efficient cross-task generalization via dynamic lora composition. *arXiv preprint arXiv:2307.13269*.

James Kirkpatrick, Razvan Pascanu, Neil Rabinowitz, Joel Veness, Guillaume Desjardins, Andrei A Rusu, Kieran Milan, John Quan, Tiago Ramalho, Agnieszka Grabska-Barwinska, and 1 others. 2017. Overcoming catastrophic forgetting in neural networks. *Proceedings of the national academy of sciences*, 114(13):3521–3526.

Brian Lester, Rami Al-Rfou, and Noah Constant. 2021. The power of scale for parameter-efficient prompt tuning. *arXiv preprint arXiv:2104.08691*.

Xiang Lisa Li and Percy Liang. 2021. Prefix-tuning: Optimizing continuous prompts for generation. *arXiv preprint arXiv:2101.00190*.

Vladislav Lialin, Namrata Shivagunde, Sherin Muckatira, and Anna Rumshisky. 2023. Relora: High-rank training through low-rank updates. *arXiv preprint arXiv:2307.05695*.

Yan-Shuo Liang and Wu-Jun Li. 2024. Inflora: Interference-free low-rank adaptation for continual learning. In *Proceedings of the IEEE/CVF Conference on Computer Vision and Pattern Recognition*, pages 23638–23647.

Vincenzo Lomonaco, Lorenzo Pellegrini, Andrea Cossu, Antonio Carta, Gabriele Graffieti, Tyler L Hayes, Matthias De Lange, Marc Masana, Jary Pomponi, Gido M Van de Ven, and 1 others. 2021. Avalanche: an end-to-end library for continual learning. In *Proceedings of the IEEE/CVF conference on computer vision and pattern recognition*, pages 3600–3610.

David Patterson, Joseph Gonzalez, Quoc Le, Chen Liang, Lluis-Miquel Munguia, Daniel Rothchild, David So, Maud Texier, and Jeff Dean. 2021. Carbon emissions and large neural network training. *arXiv preprint arXiv:2104.10350*.

Jonas Pfeiffer, Aishwarya Kamath, Andreas Rücklé, Kyunghyun Cho, and Iryna Gurevych. 2020. Adapterfusion: Non-destructive task composition for transfer learning. *arXiv preprint arXiv:2005.00247*.

Xiao Wang, Tianze Chen, Qiming Ge, Han Xia, Rong Bao, Rui Zheng, Qi Zhang, Tao Gui, and Xuanjing Huang. 2023. Orthogonal subspace learning for language model continual learning. In *Findings of the Association for Computational Linguistics: EMNLP 2023*, pages 10658–10671, Singapore. Association for Computational Linguistics.

Yichen Wu, Hongming Piao, Long-Kai Huang, Renzhen Wang, Wanhua Li, Hanspeter Pfister, Deyu Meng, Kede Ma, and Ying Wei. 2025. Sd-lora: Scalable decoupled low-rank adaptation for class incremental learning. *arXiv preprint arXiv:2501.13198*.

Min Zeng, Haiqin Yang, Wei Xue, Qifeng Liu, and Yike Guo. 2024. Dirichlet continual learning: Tackling catastrophic forgetting in NLP. In *The 40th Conference on Uncertainty in Artificial Intelligence*.

Jinghan Zhang, Junteng Liu, Junxian He, and 1 others. 2023. Composing parameter-efficient modules with arithmetic operation. *Advances in Neural Information Processing Systems*, 36:12589–12610.

Xin Zhang, Liang Bai, Xian Yang, and Jiye Liang. 2025. C-lora: Continual low-rank adaptation for pre-trained models. *arXiv preprint arXiv:2502.17920*.

Appendix

This appendix contains supplementary materials and additional details not included in the main body of the paper due to space constraints.

A Additional Experimental Details

This section provides additional details regarding the experimental setup and base model architectures used in this study. Detailed hyperparameters for each method and benchmark are provided within Section 3.2 in the main body of the paper.

A.1 Base Model Architectures

The specific base model architectures used for each benchmark are detailed below:

- **Permuted-MNIST:** A simple two-layer MLP was used as the base network. It consisted of a linear layer mapping the flattened 28×28 input (784 features) to 256 hidden units, followed by a ReLU activation. A second linear layer mapped the 256 hidden units to 10 output units (one for each digit class).
- **Split-CIFAR100:** A SimpleCNN architecture was employed. It included three convolutional layers for feature extraction, each with 3x3 kernels, ReLU activation, and followed by 2x2 max pooling. The classifier head, where PEFT methods were applied, contained two linear layers: the first mapping the flattened output of the convolutional layers to 512 hidden units (with ReLU), and the second mapping 512 units to 100 output units (for CIFAR-100 classes). The convolutional layers were kept frozen.
- **BERT-base-uncased:** The standard frozen `bert-base-uncased` model from the Hugging Face Transformers library was used as the base for NLP tasks. PEFT methods were applied to the linear layers within the attention and feed-forward networks of the Transformer blocks.

B Training Procedure Pseudocode

Algorithm 1: SLoRA Sequential Training Procedure

Input: Pre-trained model with `SLoRALinear` layers M, Task sequence $\mathcal{T} = \{Task_0, Task_1, \ldots, Task_{T-1}\}$, hyperparameters $r_{base}, \alpha_{base}, r_{stack}, \alpha_{stack}$

Output: Trained SLoRA model with task-specific adapters

1. **State:** Freeze W_0 in all `SLoRALinear` layers of M.
2. **Train Base Task** ($Task_0$)**:**
3. **For** each `SLoRALinear` layer L in M **do**
4. **State:** Initialize Base LoRA adapter (A_{base}, B_{base}) in L with r_{base}, α_{base}.
5. **State:** Set A_{base}, B_{base} in L to be trainable.
6. **State:** Freeze all other adapters in L (initially none).
7. **End For**
8. **State:** Configure optimizer to train trainable parameters in M and $Task_0$ classifier.
9. **State:** Train M on $Task_0$ data.
10. **For** each `SLoRALinear` layer L in M **do**
11. **State:** Freeze (A_{base}, B_{base}) in L.
12. **End For**
13. **Train Subsequent Tasks** ($Task_t$ **for** $t = 1, \ldots, T-1$)**:**
14. **For** each t from 1 to $T-1$ **do**
15. **For** each `SLoRALinear` layer L in M **do**
16. **State:** Initialize a *new* Stack adapter $(A_{stack,t}, B_{stack,t})$ in L with $r_{stack}, \alpha_{stack}$.
17. **State:** Set $(A_{stack,t}, B_{stack,t})$ in L to be trainable.
18. **State:** Ensure W_0, Base LoRA, and all previously added Stacks ($< t$) in L are frozen.
19. **End For**
20. **State:** Configure optimizer to train trainable parameters in M and $Task_t$ classifier.
21. **State:** Train M on $Task_t$ data.
22. **For** each `SLoRALinear` layer L in M **do**
23. **State:** Freeze $(A_{stack,t}, B_{stack,t})$ in L.
24. **End For**
25. **End For**

C Additional Result Tables

Table 6: Training Time on BERT-base (batch size 16, single NVIDIA P100, averaged over 3 runs (in minutes)

Method	Mean	Std Dev	Speed-up
Full Fine-Tuning	12.0	0.3	1.0×
SLoRA	**1.5**	**0.1**	**8.0×**

Table 7: Accuracy (%) on Permuted-MNIST Tasks after Training on Task 5 (Mean $\pm$ SD over 3 Seeds)

Method	Task 1	Task 2	Task 3	Task 4	Task 5	Avg. Accuracy
FT	51.99 $\pm$ 6.73	85.78 $\pm$ 2.80	88.96 $\pm$ 3.76	92.06 $\pm$ 1.42	**97.26 $\pm$ 0.17**	83.21 $\pm$ 2.49
EWC	54.14 $\pm$ 0.90	**86.65 $\pm$ 1.85**	87.01 $\pm$ 4.54	**95.05 $\pm$ 0.46**	97.22 $\pm$ 0.02	83.87 $\pm$ 1.31
LoRA-Cont	50.42 $\pm$ 3.86	79.44 $\pm$ 4.84	86.26 $\pm$ 2.57	93.29 $\pm$ 0.77	96.78 $\pm$ 0.31	81.29 $\pm$ 1.48
SLoRA	**56.97 $\pm$ 7.82**	84.11 $\pm$ 1.74	**87.61 $\pm$ 0.71**	91.70 $\pm$ 1.35	97.08 $\pm$ 0.42	**83.49 $\pm$ 1.35**

Table 8: Split-CIFAR100 Mean Accuracy (%) on Initial vs. After Final Task (Averaged over 3 seeds, $E = 50$)

Method	Task Accuracy: Initial → After Final										Final Avg. Acc.
	T0	T1	T2	T3	T4	T5	T6	T7	T8	T9	
FT	80→10	82→12	81→11	72→10	80→10	76→10	78→10	78→10	85→10	80→80	8.0
EWC	79→15	80→15	75→15	67→15	74→15	70→15	71→15	71→15	78→15	72→72	7.2
LoRA-Cont	61→12	65→12	59→12	55→12	62→12	56→12	59→12	57→12	69→12	60→60	6.0
LoRA-Ind	62→60	65→63	59→58	57→55	61→60	56→55	57→56	56→55	68→67	59→59	59.6
SLoRA	**64→64**	**67→67**	**61→61**	**57→57**	**63→63**	**57→57**	**59→59**	**59→59**	**68→68**	61→61	**61.8**

On Multilingual Encoder Language Model Compression for Low-Resource Languages

Daniil Gurgurov[1,2] **Michal Gregor**[3] **Josef van Genabith**[1,2] **Simon Ostermann**[1,2,4]
[1]Saarland University
[2]German Research Center for Artificial Intelligence (DFKI)
[3]Kempelen Institute of Intelligent Technologies (KInIT)
[4]Centre for European Research in Trusted AI (CERTAIN)
{daniil.gurgurov, josef.van_genabith, simon.ostermann}@dfki.de, michal.gregor@kinit.sk

Abstract

In this paper, we combine two-step knowledge distillation, structured pruning, truncation, and vocabulary trimming for extremely compressing multilingual encoder-only language models for low-resource languages. Our novel approach systematically combines existing techniques and takes them to the extreme, reducing layer depth, feed-forward hidden size, and intermediate layer embedding size to create significantly smaller monolingual models while retaining essential language-specific knowledge. **We achieve compression rates of up to 92% while maintaining competitive performance, with average drops of 2–10% for moderate compression and 8–13% at maximum compression** in four downstream tasks, including sentiment analysis, topic classification, named entity recognition, and part-of-speech tagging, across three low-resource languages. Notably, the performance degradation correlates with the amount of language-specific data in the teacher model, with larger datasets resulting in smaller performance losses. Additionally, we conduct ablation studies to identify the best practices for multilingual model compression using these techniques.

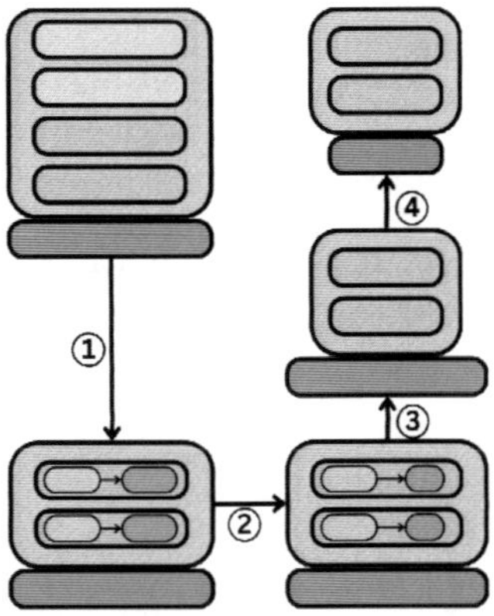

Figure 1: Overview of our multilingual model compression methodology. We use **(1)** knowledge distillation to reduce layers, **(2)** structured pruning to eliminate redundant feed-forward network width, and **(3)** hidden size reduction and another round of knowledge distillation from the previous student model. Finally, **(4)** vocabulary trimming is applied to retain language-specific tokens.

1 Introduction

Small multilingual encoder language models (LMs), such as mBERT (Devlin et al., 2019), XLM-R (Conneau et al., 2020), and Glot-500m (Imani et al., 2023), have demonstrated strong performance across a diverse range of low-resource languages (Hu et al., 2020; Asai et al., 2024), often outperforming large-scale proprietary models on various sequential tasks (Adelani et al., 2024; Gurgurov et al., 2025). However, even these relatively compact multilingual models may still be excessively large for use in individual languages due to redundant capacity and expensive inference (Singh and Lefever, 2022; Cruz, 2025).

To address this, we propose a novel combination of model compression approaches for transforming multilingual encoder-only models into maximally small, efficient, language-specific alternatives while retaining competitive performance. Our methodology integrates knowledge distillation (Hinton et al., 2015), structured pruning (Kim and Hassan, 2020; Hou et al., 2020), weight truncation, and vocabulary trimming (Abdaoui et al., 2020; Ushio et al., 2023) to systematically reduce model size by compressing the depth (number of layers), feed-forward intermediate width, hidden size, and tokenizer vocabulary. Our experiments demonstrate that this pipeline achieves compression rates of up to 92%, with performance drops of 2-10% for moderate compression (up to 87%) and 8-13% at maximum compression on downstream tasks such as sentiment analysis, topic classification, named entity recognition, and part-of-speech tagging. Notably, for moderate compression levels, the extent of degradation depends more on the strength of the teacher model than on the compression itself.

Proceedings of the IJCNLP-AACL 2025 Student Research Workshop, pages 47–58
December 20-24, 2025

Beyond compression, we investigate the impact of using multilingual versus monolingual teacher models, evaluate different initialization strategies for knowledge distillation, and analyze additional compression variables. Our findings contribute to the development of highly efficient, environmentally friendly models (Strubell et al., 2020) for low-resource languages and explore how strongly models can be compressed. The code for our experiments is made publicly available at `https://github.com/d-gurgurov/Multilingual-LM-Disitillation`.

2 Methodology

In this section, we present our multilingual model compression strategy, illustrated in Figure 1. Our approach combines several existing compression techniques in a novel way that, to the best of our knowledge, has not been explored in this combination within the multilingual context.

2.1 Layer Reduction via Knowledge Distillation

We reduce the number of transformer layers in the teacher model by half to obtain an initial compact student model (Sanh et al., 2020). The student is initialized with the layers of the teacher and trained using a combination of Masked Language Modeling (MLM) (Devlin et al., 2019) and Mean Squared Error (MSE) loss for knowledge distillation (Hinton et al., 2015) for 10 epochs. Both losses are weighted equally (α=0.5, though other values were explored; see Appendix 8). The teacher is a multilingual encoder fine-tuned on the target language (see Section 4).

2.2 Width Reduction via Structured Pruning

We apply structured pruning (Kim and Hassan, 2020) to reduce the intermediate size of the feed-forward layers from 3072 to 2048. Neuron importance is estimated using first-order gradient information accumulated from forward and backward passes over MLM validation data. At each layer, neurons are ranked by their absolute gradient values, and the least important ones are removed based on a target pruning ratio. The remaining neurons are then reordered to preserve model functionality. For consistency, the same pruning ratio is applied across all layers.

2.3 Hidden Size Compression with Secondary Knowledge Distillation

We compress the hidden embedding dimension from 768 to either 312, 456, or 564 via truncation, retaining the first k dimensions.[1] A second round of knowledge distillation is then performed, using the width-reduced model from the previous step as the new teacher, similar to Wang et al. (2023), with training for 10 epochs.

2.4 Vocabulary Reduction

We reduce the vocabulary size by selecting the top 40,000 most frequent tokens from a target-language corpus, along with their corresponding embeddings (Ushio et al., 2023). This ensures that the resulting model retains only language-specific tokens, which significantly reduces the overall model size.

3 Experiments

Below, we describe the datasets, languages, tasks, and baseline systems used in our evaluation.

3.1 Knowledge Distillation Data

We use GlotCC (Kargaran et al., 2025), a large-scale multilingual corpus derived mainly from CommonCrawl (Wenzek et al., 2020), as the primary dataset for both stages of knowledge distillation. Data distributions for the selected languages are reported in Appendix F. We use GlotCC for training, and the FLORES-200 development set (Team et al., 2022) for validation during training.

3.2 Languages and Tasks

We evaluate our models on four tasks: Topic Classification (TC), Sentiment Analysis (SA), Named Entity Recognition (NER), and Part-of-Speech Tagging (POS), covering three low-resource languages–Maltese, Slovak, and Swahili (Joshi et al., 2020). For TC, we use the 7-class SIB-200 dataset (Adelani et al., 2024), and for SA, we compile binary sentiment datasets from multiple sources (Dingli and Sant, 2016; Cortis and Davis, 2019; Pecar et al., 2019; Muhammad et al., 2023a,b). For NER, we use WikiANN (Pan et al., 2017), and for POS, we use Universal Dependencies v2.15 (de Marneffe et al., 2021) and MasakhaPOS (Dione et al., 2023). For all tasks, we train Sequential Bottleneck task adapters (Pfeiffer et al., 2020) with fixed hyperparameters (see Appendix H). Performance is mea-

[1] The hidden size must be divisible by the number of attention heads.

sured using macro-averaged F1 (Sokolova et al., 2006) for TC and SA, and "seqeval" F1 (Nakayama, 2018) for NER and POS.

3.3 Models and Baselines

We compress two encoder multilingual models–mBERT (Devlin et al., 2019) and XLM-R-base (Conneau et al., 2020)–adapted to target languages through fine-tuning on language-specific data, and compare the reduced models to two baselines: (1) the original, non-adapted models, and (2) language-adapted versions. In both cases, we train an identical task adapter using the same task-specific datasets as for the compressed models.

4 Findings

Our key findings are outlined below.

4.1 Distillation

Distilling knowledge from a multilingual teacher into a monolingual student model is less effective than using a target-language adapted teacher, as evidenced by the differences in validation accuracies shown in Figure 2. This discrepancy possibly stems from the multilingual teacher's broad cross-lingual representations, which are not directly aligned with the requirements of a monolingual student. In contrast, monolingual teachers provide more targeted, language-specific representations, resulting in better student performance.

Distillation loss: We compare KL divergence and MSE as distillation loss functions, and observe that MSE leads to better and faster convergence (Appendix A), in line with prior work (Kim et al., 2021; Nityasya et al., 2022).

4.2 Weight Initialization

Weight initialization plays a crucial role in training the student model, with knowledge distillation providing only a marginal additional performance improvement (Figure 2). This partly aligns with the findings of Wibowo et al. (2024), who explored distilling multilingual abilities for multilingual tasks, whereas our focus is on monolingual distillation. Training a student-sized model initialized with teacher weights, but without knowledge distillation, results in a slight performance drop compared to a fully distilled model.

Initialization Strategies: Among various initialization strategies, initializing the student with the last k layers for mBERT and every other layer

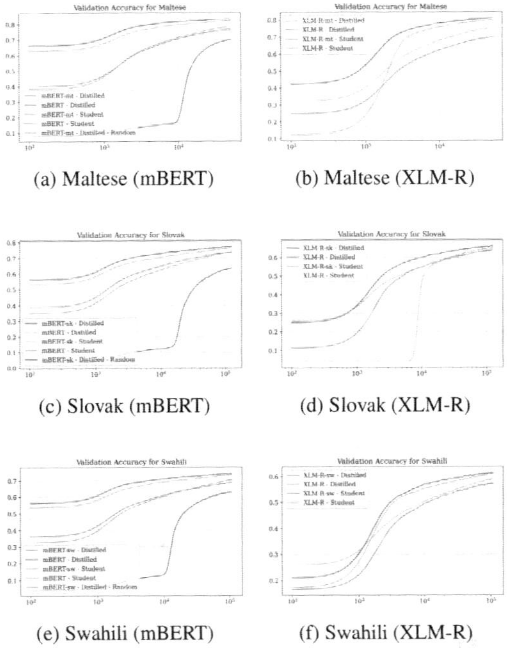

(a) Maltese (mBERT) (b) Maltese (XLM-R)

(c) Slovak (mBERT) (d) Slovak (XLM-R)

(e) Swahili (mBERT) (f) Swahili (XLM-R)

Figure 2: First-step KD validation accuracies for mBERT and XLM-R with models initialized using the last k layers. mBERT- and XLM-R-mt, sk, sw refer to models adapted to the target language; *distilled* denotes models trained with distillation loss, while *student* refers to identically trained models without distillation loss. The best accuracy is in all cases achieved when distilling from a target-language adapted model.

(stride) for XLM-R consistently outperforms alternatives such as using the first k layers and combining first and last layers (Appendix B). Random initialization performs significantly worse, emphasizing the importance of weight reuse (Sun et al., 2019; Singh and Lefever, 2022).

4.3 Pruning and Truncation

Distilled models can be compressed further using structured pruning, hidden size reduction, and vocabulary trimming, while maintaining competitive performance.

Intermediate size reduction: Reducing the intermediate size of feed-forward layers from 3072 to 2048 via structured pruning results in negligible performance loss (Table 1). However, more aggressive reductions degrade quality significantly, making 2048 a practical lower bound. We do not prune attention heads, as removing even a minimal number (e.g., three) causes severe degradation (>50% performance drop in preliminary experiments).

Hidden size reduction: We reduce the hidden

Compression Stage	Params	Size	Task Performance (F1)												Avg
			Maltese				Slovak				Swahili				
			TC	SA	NER	POS	TC	SA	NER	POS	TC	SA	NER	POS	
Baselines															
Multilingual	279M	279M	68.1	56.0	54.3	89.9	88.1	95.6	91.1	97.3	78.4	81.5	84.6	89.4	81.2
Language-adapted	279M	279M	85.0	76.2	69.2	95.4	86.2	94.8	91.0	97.1	87.5	84.1	82.7	89.2	**86.5**
Compression Pipeline (minimal degradation)															
Layer reduction	236M (-15%)	236M	84.0	77.2	63.5	94.3	86.3	92.9	90.1	96.3	82.9	81.3	82.9	89.2	85.1
+ FFN pruning	226M (-20%)	226M	84.7	78.6	60.1	94.2	86.1	93.4	90.0	96.1	82.4	82.7	83.6	89.5	85.1
+ Hidden 564	163M (-40%)	163M	83.4	74.9	53.0	93.7	84.9	92.7	89.1	96.8	85.8	81.0	80.8	89.4	83.8
+ Vocabulary	45M (-85%)	45M	84.1	72.4	60.9	93.0	85.3	92.9	89.3	96.4	85.7	80.9	82.0	89.1	**84.3**
Further compression (moderate degradation)															
+ Hidden 456	131M (-53%)	131M	78.5	69.9	62.5	92.7	86.0	93.0	88.3	96.3	83.1	79.3	80.7	88.9	83.3
+ Vocabulary	35M (-87%)	35M	78.5	70.7	63.3	92.5	86.1	92.9	88.4	96.3	82.5	79.0	80.2	89.0	83.3
Maximum compression (higher degradation)															
+ Hidden 312	89M (-68%)	89M	66.9	70.1	35.7	87.6	84.0	90.9	88.0	95.5	76.4	80.1	80.7	88.3	78.7
+ Vocabulary	23M (-92%)	23M	67.2	71.4	37.1	87.5	84.0	90.5	88.2	95.6	78.0	80.5	79.2	88.0	78.9

Table 1: Progressive compression of XLM-R-base. Stages are grouped by degradation level. Highlighted rows indicate the baseline (gray) and optimal compression point (green, 85% reduction with 2.5% drop). Maximum compression rows (red) show higher degradation rates (7.6% drop). All F1 scores are averaged over 3 independent runs with different random seeds mBERT in Appendix J.

embedding size to 564, 456, and 312, truncating it to the first k dimensions. Training is performed under the supervision of the student from the previous stage. We find that using the original teacher leads to worse results, possibly due to the bigger knowledge gap (Wang et al., 2023). We also tested SVD-based dimensionality reduction but found truncation to be more effective (see Appendix C).

Vocabulary trimming: Restricting the vocabulary to the top 40K most frequent tokens for each target language introduces no measurable performance loss compared to the previous step, while further improving efficiency. Reducing below 40K works for some languages but does not generalize well across all cases (Appendix E), consistent with Ushio et al. (2023).

4.4 Downstream Performance

Our results show that model compression through knowledge distillation, structured pruning, and vocabulary reduction leads to modest performance drops (Tables 1 and 6). Below, we report results for XLM-R; results for mBERT follow similar patterns and are presented in Appendix J.

Language-specific resilience: The extent of degradation varies by language and correlates with teacher model quality. At maximum compression (92% parameter reduction), Slovak (1032MB fine-tuning (FT) data) experiences only a 2.9% performance drop, Swahili (332MB) shows a 5.2% drop, while Maltese (188MB) degrades by 19.2%. This pattern demonstrates that stronger teacher models–trained on larger datasets–enable more robust compression outcomes.

Task-specific patterns: Different tasks exhibit varying compression sensitivities. POS tagging shows the highest resilience across all languages, with performance drops of only 4-13% at 92% compression. Conversely, NER demonstrates steeper degradation, particularly for Maltese (69.2 → 37.1 F1). This severe drop is likely compounded by the extremely small Maltese NER training set (100 examples vs. 20,000 for Slovak), indicating that sequence labeling tasks are especially vulnerable to compression in low-resource settings. In contrast, sentence-level classification tasks such as SA and TC remain relatively stable under heavy compression, with performance decreases below 10% even at 85–90% size reduction.

Optimal compression trade-offs: The 85% compression level (hidden size 564 with 40k vocabulary) offers the best balance for most scenarios, with only a 2.5% average performance drop (84.3 vs 86.5 avg F1). For high-resource languages like Slovak, even 87% compression incurs only a 3.8% drop. Notably, vocabulary trimming often yields slight improvements (e.g., Maltese TC: 84.11 vs 83.43 F1), suggesting it reduces vocabulary noise while compensating for hidden size reduction.

Staged compression effects: Layer reduction (15%) and intermediate size pruning (20%) induce minimal degradation (<2% drop), with the primary performance impact occurring during hidden size reduction. Performance degrades gradually up to 85% compression, but deteriorates more rapidly beyond this threshold (4-6% drop per additional stage).

Adapter capacity: We experiment with varying the reduction factor r to adjust task adapter capacity (Appendix I, Figure 10). While $r = 16$ suffices for larger models, smaller models (hidden sizes 564, 456, 312) benefit from lower r values ($r = 2$), yielding modest performance gains. Results in Tables 1 and 6 use $r = 2$ for these compressed models.

5 Related Work

In knowledge distillation, a smaller student model is trained to replicate the behavior of a larger teacher model (Hinton et al., 2015), often combining MLM loss with teacher supervision (Sun et al., 2019; Sanh et al., 2020). DistilBERT (Sanh et al., 2020) reduces model size by selecting every other layer from BERT (Devlin et al., 2019) and distills on large corpora using dynamic masking. Patient distillation further improves results by matching intermediate representations (Sun et al., 2019).

Recent work has explored distilling multilingual models into compact monolingual models. Singh and Lefever (2022) train student models for languages such as Swahili and Slovenian using a composite loss (distillation, cosine, MLM), and show that distilled models often outperform mBERT while using a reduced vocabulary (Abdaoui et al., 2020). Ansell et al. (2023) introduce a two-phase bilingual distillation pipeline, combining general-purpose and task-specific guidance with sparse fine-tuning, outperforming multilingual baselines.

Other studies emphasize the role of initialization. Wibowo et al. (2024) show that copying teacher weights is more effective than random initialization in the context of multilingual distillation, and that MSE outperforms KL divergence for distillation. Cruz (2025) similarly distill mBERT for Tagalog and highlight the nuanced impact of embedding initialization.

6 Conclusion

We present an effective compression pipeline for multilingual encoder models designed for low-resource languages. By integrating staged knowledge distillation, structured pruning, hidden size truncation, and vocabulary reduction, we compress models by up to 92% while maintaining competitive performance, typically within 2–10% of the original for moderate compression and 8–13% at maximum compression, on four downstream tasks.

Limitations

Our evaluation is limited to three low-resource languages and four downstream tasks, which may affect generalizability to other languages and task types. The compression pipeline requires target-language data for teacher adaptation, making it less suitable for truly low-resource languages with minimal corpora. We focus exclusively on encoder-only models (mBERT and XLM-R), and our structured pruning only targets feed-forward layers, leaving attention head pruning unexplored due to performance degradation.

Acknowledgments

This research was supported by DisAI - Improving scientific excellence and creativity in combating disinformation with artificial intelligence and language technologies, a Horizon Europe-funded project under GA No. 101079164, by the German Ministry of Education and Research (BMBF) as part of the project TRAILS (01IW24005), and by lorAI - Low Resource Artificial Intelligence, a project funded by the European Union under GA No.101136646.

References

Amine Abdaoui, Camille Pradel, and Grégoire Sigel. 2020. Load what you need: Smaller versions of mutililingual BERT. In *Proceedings of SustaiNLP: Workshop on Simple and Efficient Natural Language Processing*, pages 119–123, Online. Association for Computational Linguistics.

David Ifeoluwa Adelani, Hannah Liu, Xiaoyu Shen, Nikita Vassilyev, Jesujoba O. Alabi, Yanke Mao, Haonan Gao, and En-Shiun Annie Lee. 2024. SIB-200: A simple, inclusive, and big evaluation dataset for topic classification in 200+ languages and dialects. In *Proceedings of the 18th Conference of the European Chapter of the Association for Computational Linguistics (Volume 1: Long Papers)*, pages 226–245, St. Julian's, Malta. Association for Computational Linguistics.

Alan Ansell, Edoardo Maria Ponti, Anna Korhonen, and Ivan Vulić. 2023. Distilling efficient language-specific models for cross-lingual transfer.

Akari Asai, Sneha Kudugunta, Xinyan Yu, Terra Blevins, Hila Gonen, Machel Reid, Yulia Tsvetkov, Sebastian Ruder, and Hannaneh Hajishirzi. 2024. BUFFET: Benchmarking large language models for few-shot cross-lingual transfer. In *Proceedings of the 2024 Conference of the North American Chapter of the Association for Computational Linguistics: Human Language Technologies (Volume 1: Long Papers)*, pages 1771–1800, Mexico City, Mexico. Association for Computational Linguistics.

Alexis Conneau, Kartikay Khandelwal, Naman Goyal, Vishrav Chaudhary, Guillaume Wenzek, Francisco Guzmán, Edouard Grave, Myle Ott, Luke Zettlemoyer, and Veselin Stoyanov. 2020. Unsupervised cross-lingual representation learning at scale. In *Proceedings of the 58th Annual Meeting of the Association for Computational Linguistics*, pages 8440–8451, Online. Association for Computational Linguistics.

Keith Cortis and Brian Davis. 2019. A social opinion gold standard for the Malta government budget 2018. In *Proceedings of the 5th Workshop on Noisy User-generated Text (W-NUT 2019)*, pages 364–369, Hong Kong, China. Association for Computational Linguistics.

Jan Christian Blaise Cruz. 2025. Extracting general-use transformers for low-resource languages via knowledge distillation. In *Proceedings of the First Workshop on Language Models for Low-Resource Languages*, pages 219–224, Abu Dhabi, United Arab Emirates. Association for Computational Linguistics.

Marie-Catherine de Marneffe, Christopher D. Manning, Joakim Nivre, and Daniel Zeman. 2021. Universal Dependencies. *Computational Linguistics*, 47(2):255–308.

Jacob Devlin, Ming-Wei Chang, Kenton Lee, and Kristina Toutanova. 2019. BERT: Pre-training of deep bidirectional transformers for language understanding. In *Proceedings of the 2019 Conference of the North American Chapter of the Association for Computational Linguistics: Human Language Technologies, Volume 1 (Long and Short Papers)*, pages 4171–4186, Minneapolis, Minnesota. Association for Computational Linguistics.

Alexiei Dingli and Nicole Sant. 2016. Sentiment analysis on maltese using machine learning. In *Proceedings of The Tenth International Conference on Advances in Semantic Processing (SEMAPRO 2016)*, pages 21–25.

Cheikh M. Bamba Dione, David Ifeoluwa Adelani, Peter Nabende, Jesujoba Alabi, Thapelo Sindane, Happy Buzaaba, Shamsuddeen Hassan Muhammad, Chris Chinenye Emezue, Perez Ogayo, Anuoluwapo Aremu, Catherine Gitau, Derguene Mbaye, Jonathan Mukiibi, Blessing Sibanda, Bonaventure F. P. Dossou, Andiswa Bukula, Rooweither Mabuya, Allahsera Auguste Tapo, Edwin Munkoh-Buabeng, Victoire Memdjokam Koagne, Fatoumata Ouoba Kabore, Amelia Taylor, Godson Kalipe, Tebogo Macucwa, Vukosi Marivate, Tajuddeen Gwadabe, Mboning Tchiaze Elvis, Ikechukwu Onyenwe, Gratien Atindogbe, Tolulope Adelani, Idris Akinade, Olanrewaju Samuel, Marien Nahimana, Théogène Musabeyezu, Emile Niyomutabazi, Ester Chimhenga, Kudzai Gotosa, Patrick Mizha, Apelete Agbolo, Seydou Traore, Chinedu Uchechukwu, Aliyu Yusuf, Muhammad Abdullahi, and Dietrich Klakow. 2023. MasakhaPOS: Part-of-speech tagging for typologically diverse African languages. In *Proceedings of the 61st Annual Meeting of the Association for Computational Linguistics (Volume 1: Long Papers)*, pages 10883–10900, Toronto, Canada. Association for Computational Linguistics.

Daniil Gurgurov, Ivan Vykopal, Josef van Genabith, and Simon Ostermann. 2025. Small models, big impact: Efficient corpus and graph-based adaptation of small multilingual language models for low-resource languages.

Geoffrey Hinton, Oriol Vinyals, and Jeff Dean. 2015. Distilling the knowledge in a neural network.

Lu Hou, Zhiqi Huang, Lifeng Shang, Xin Jiang, Xiao Chen, and Qun Liu. 2020. Dynabert: Dynamic bert with adaptive width and depth. *Advances in Neural Information Processing Systems*, 33:9782–9793.

Junjie Hu, Sebastian Ruder, Aditya Siddhant, Graham Neubig, Orhan Firat, and Melvin Johnson. 2020. XTREME: A massively multilingual multitask benchmark for evaluating cross-lingual generalisation. In *Proceedings of the 37th International Conference on Machine Learning*, volume 119 of *Proceedings of Machine Learning Research*, pages 4411–4421. PMLR.

Ayyoob Imani, Peiqin Lin, Amir Hossein Kargaran, Silvia Severini, Masoud Jalili Sabet, Nora Kassner, Chunlan Ma, Helmut Schmid, André Martins, François Yvon, and Hinrich Schütze. 2023. Glot500: Scaling multilingual corpora and language models to 500 languages. In *Proceedings of the 61st Annual Meeting of the Association for Computational Linguistics (Volume 1: Long Papers)*, pages 1082–1117, Toronto, Canada. Association for Computational Linguistics.

Pratik Joshi, Sebastin Santy, Amar Budhiraja, Kalika Bali, and Monojit Choudhury. 2020. The state and fate of linguistic diversity and inclusion in the NLP world. In *Proceedings of the 58th Annual Meeting of the Association for Computational Linguistics*, pages 6282–6293, Online. Association for Computational Linguistics.

Amir Hossein Kargaran, François Yvon, and Hinrich Schütze. 2025. Glotcc: An open broad-coverage commoncrawl corpus and pipeline for minority languages.

Taehyeon Kim, Jaehoon Oh, NakYil Kim, Sangwook Cho, and Se-Young Yun. 2021. Comparing kullback-leibler divergence and mean squared error loss in knowledge distillation.

Young Jin Kim and Hany Hassan. 2020. FastFormers: Highly efficient transformer models for natural language understanding. In *Proceedings of SustaiNLP:*

Workshop on Simple and Efficient Natural Language Processing, pages 149–158, Online. Association for Computational Linguistics.

Shamsuddeen Hassan Muhammad, Idris Abdulmumin, Abinew Ali Ayele, Nedjma Ousidhoum, David Ifeoluwa Adelani, Seid Muhie Yimam, Ibrahim Sa'id Ahmad, Meriem Beloucif, Saif Mohammad, Sebastian Ruder, Oumaima Hourrane, Pavel Brazdil, Felermino D'ario M'ario Ant'onio Ali, Davis Davis, Salomey Osei, Bello Shehu Bello, Falalu Ibrahim, Tajuddeen Gwadabe, Samuel Rutunda, Tadesse Belay, Wendimu Baye Messelle, Hailu Beshada Balcha, Sisay Adugna Chala, Hagos Tesfahun Gebremichael, Bernard Opoku, and Steven Arthur. 2023a. Afrisenti: A twitter sentiment analysis benchmark for african languages.

Shamsuddeen Hassan Muhammad, Idris Abdulmumin, Seid Muhie Yimam, David Ifeoluwa Adelani, Ibrahim Sa'id Ahmad, Nedjma Ousidhoum, Abinew Ayele, Saif M Mohammad, and Meriem Beloucif. 2023b. Semeval-2023 task 12: Sentiment analysis for african languages (afrisenti-semeval). *arXiv preprint arXiv:2304.06845*.

Hiroki Nakayama. 2018. seqeval: A python framework for sequence labeling evaluation. Software available from https://github.com/chakki-works/seqeval.

Made Nindyatama Nityasya, Haryo Akbarianto Wibowo, Rendi Chevi, Radityo Eko Prasojo, and Alham Fikri Aji. 2022. Which student is best? a comprehensive knowledge distillation exam for task-specific bert models.

Xiaoman Pan, Boliang Zhang, Jonathan May, Joel Nothman, Kevin Knight, and Heng Ji. 2017. Cross-lingual name tagging and linking for 282 languages. In *Proceedings of the 55th Annual Meeting of the Association for Computational Linguistics (Volume 1: Long Papers)*, pages 1946–1958, Vancouver, Canada. Association for Computational Linguistics.

Samuel Pecar, Marian Simko, and Maria Bielikova. 2019. Improving sentiment classification in Slovak language. In *Proceedings of the 7th Workshop on Balto-Slavic Natural Language Processing*, pages 114–119, Florence, Italy. Association for Computational Linguistics.

Jonas Pfeiffer, Ivan Vulić, Iryna Gurevych, and Sebastian Ruder. 2020. MAD-X: An Adapter-Based Framework for Multi-Task Cross-Lingual Transfer. In *Proceedings of the 2020 Conference on Empirical Methods in Natural Language Processing (EMNLP)*, pages 7654–7673, Online. Association for Computational Linguistics.

Victor Sanh, Lysandre Debut, Julien Chaumond, and Thomas Wolf. 2020. Distilbert, a distilled version of bert: smaller, faster, cheaper and lighter.

Pranaydeep Singh and Els Lefever. 2022. When the student becomes the master: Learning better and smaller monolingual models from mBERT. In *Proceedings of the 29th International Conference on Computational Linguistics*, pages 4434–4441, Gyeongju, Republic of Korea. International Committee on Computational Linguistics.

Marina Sokolova, Nathalie Japkowicz, and Stan Szpakowicz. 2006. Beyond accuracy, f-score and roc: a family of discriminant measures for performance evaluation. In *Australasian joint conference on artificial intelligence*, pages 1015–1021. Springer.

Emma Strubell, Ananya Ganesh, and Andrew McCallum. 2020. Energy and policy considerations for modern deep learning research. *Proceedings of the AAAI Conference on Artificial Intelligence*, 34(09):13693–13696.

Siqi Sun, Yu Cheng, Zhe Gan, and Jingjing Liu. 2019. Patient knowledge distillation for bert model compression.

NLLB Team, Marta R. Costa-jussà, James Cross, Onur Çelebi, Maha Elbayad, Kenneth Heafield, Kevin Heffernan, Elahe Kalbassi, Janice Lam, Daniel Licht, Jean Maillard, Anna Sun, Skyler Wang, Guillaume Wenzek, Al Youngblood, Bapi Akula, Loic Barrault, Gabriel Mejia Gonzalez, Prangthip Hansanti, John Hoffman, Semarley Jarrett, Kaushik Ram Sadagopan, Dirk Rowe, Shannon Spruit, Chau Tran, Pierre Andrews, Necip Fazil Ayan, Shruti Bhosale, Sergey Edunov, Angela Fan, Cynthia Gao, Vedanuj Goswami, Francisco Guzmán, Philipp Koehn, Alexandre Mourachko, Christophe Ropers, Safiyyah Saleem, Holger Schwenk, and Jeff Wang. 2022. No language left behind: Scaling human-centered machine translation.

Asahi Ushio, Yi Zhou, and Jose Camacho-Collados. 2023. Efficient multilingual language model compression through vocabulary trimming. In *Findings of the Association for Computational Linguistics: EMNLP 2023*, pages 14725–14739, Singapore. Association for Computational Linguistics.

Maorong Wang, Hao Yu, Ling Xiao, and Toshihiko Yamasaki. 2023. Bridging the capacity gap for online knowledge distillation. In *2023 IEEE 6th International Conference on Multimedia Information Processing and Retrieval (MIPR)*, pages 1–4.

Guillaume Wenzek, Marie-Anne Lachaux, Alexis Conneau, Vishrav Chaudhary, Francisco Guzmán, Armand Joulin, and Edouard Grave. 2020. CCNet: Extracting high quality monolingual datasets from web crawl data. In *Proceedings of the Twelfth Language Resources and Evaluation Conference*, pages 4003–4012, Marseille, France. European Language Resources Association.

Haryo Akbarianto Wibowo, Thamar Solorio, and Alham Fikri Aji. 2024. The privileged students: On the value of initialization in multilingual knowledge distillation.

A KL Divergence vs MSE for Knowledge Distillation

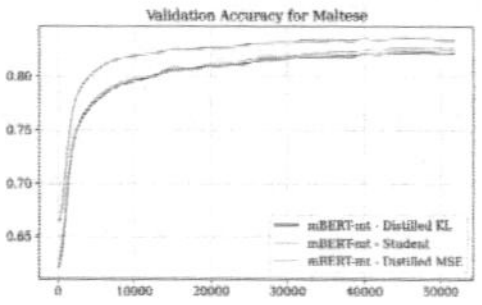

(a) Maltese

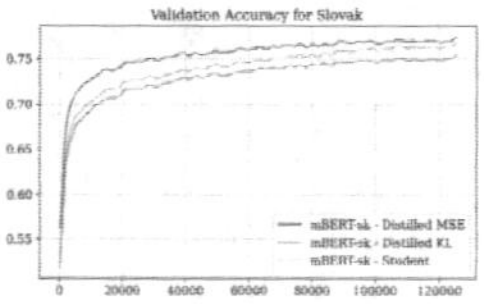

(b) Slovak

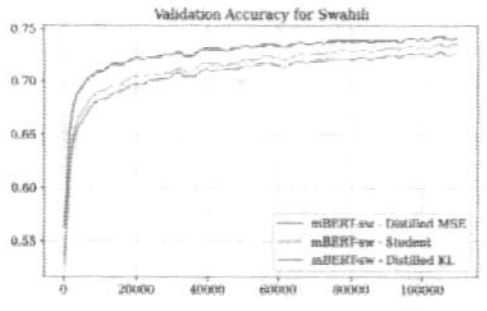

(c) Swahili

Figure 3: MSE vs. KD validation accuracy for mBERT with the models initialized using the last k layers.

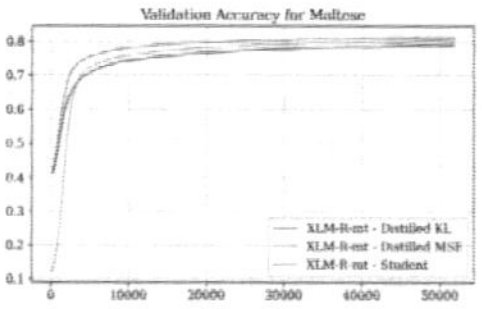

(a) Maltese

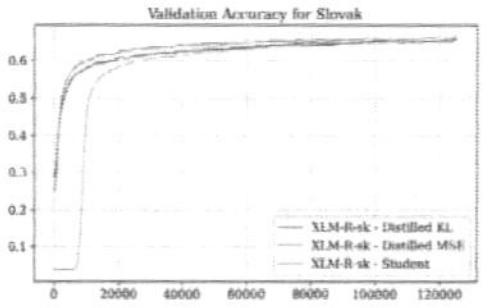

(b) Slovak

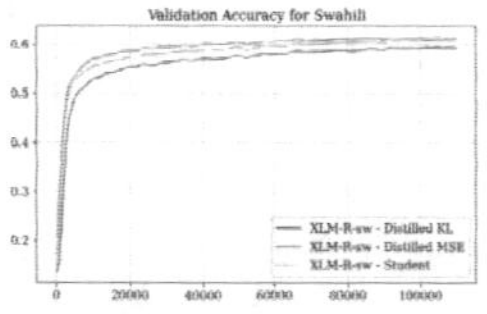

(c) Swahili

Figure 4: MSE vs. KD validation accuracy for XLM-R with the models initialized using the last k layers.

B Initialization Strategies for Knowledge Distillation

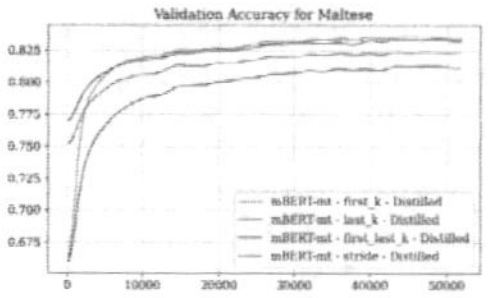

(a) Maltese

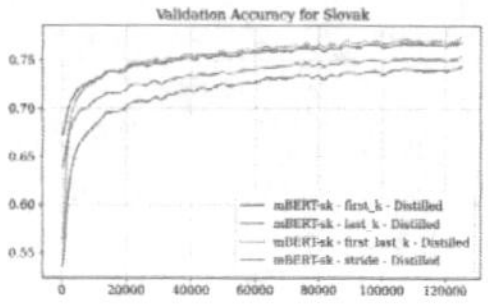

(b) Slovak

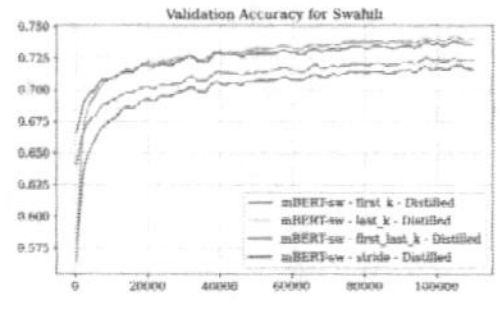

(c) Swahili

Figure 5: Validation accuracy for various initialization strategies for mBERT.

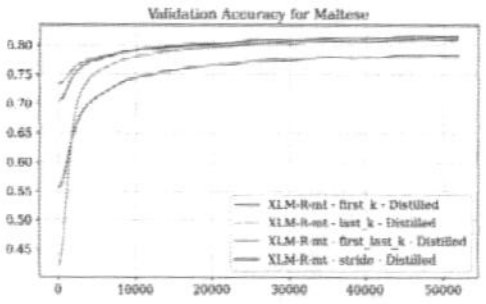

(a) Maltese

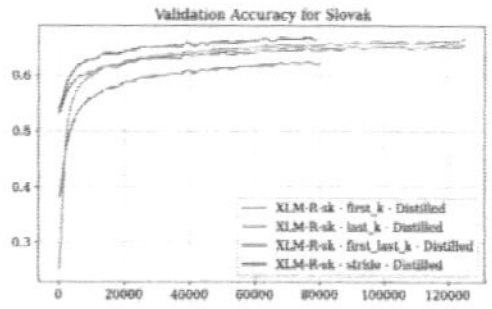

(b) Slovak

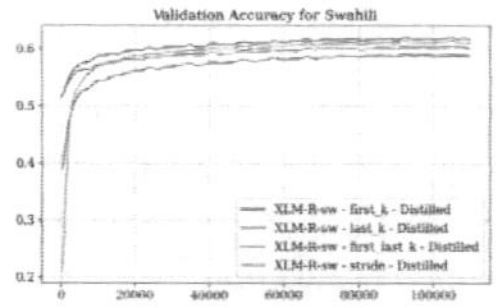

(c) Swahili

Figure 6: Validation accuracy for various initialization strategies for XLM-R.

C SVD vs. Truncation for Hidden Size Reduction

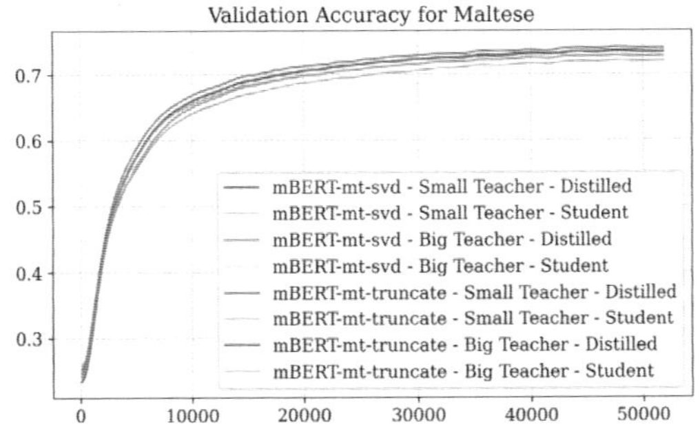

Figure 7: Validation accuracy comparing SVD vs. first-k truncation for hidden size reduction to 312. "Small teacher" refers to the layer-compressed (6-layer) model; "Big teacher" is the original 12-layer language-adapted model. Truncation consistently outperforms SVD regardless of teacher size.

D Alpha Parameter in Knowledge Distillation

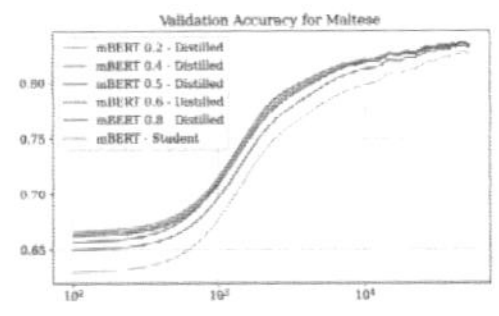

(a) mBERT

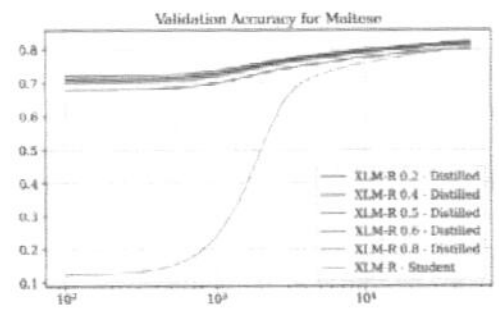

(b) XLM-R

Figure 8: Validation accuracy curves showing the impact of the alpha parameter on knowledge distillation performance for mBERT and XLM-R on Maltese with the last k and stride initialization strategies for the two models respectively.

We find that the α parameter does not have a significant impact on mBERT during pre-training, with $\alpha = 0.5$ yielding consistently good results. For XLM-R, higher values of α (i.e., 0.6 and 0.8), which reduce the strength of the distillation effect, show slightly improved validation accuracy trends compared to lower values. In our experiments, we adopt the default setting of $\alpha = 0.5$, leaving a more comprehensive exploration of optimal values across different languages, dataset sizes, and model architectures to future work.

E Vocabulary Reduction Analysis

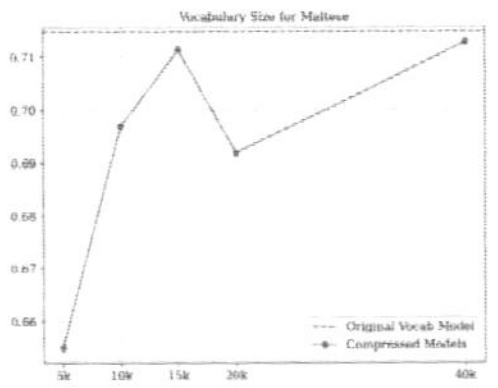

(a) Maltese

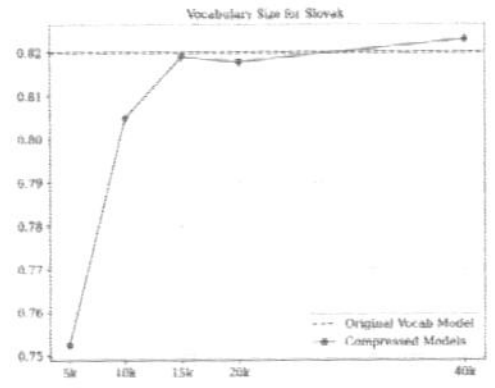

(b) Slovak

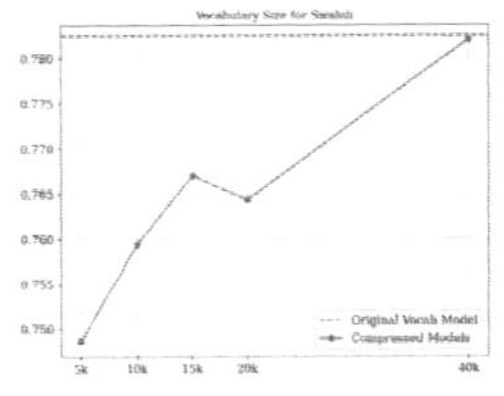

(c) Swahili

Figure 9: Impact of vocabulary reduction on TC performance for mBERT models reduced to a hidden size of 312.

F Knowledge Distillation Data Sizes

Language	KD Data Size (MB)	FT Data Size (MB)
Maltese (mt)	238	188
Slovak (sk)	535	1032
Swahili (sw)	402	332

Table 2: Dataset sizes for knowledge distillation (KD) and monolingual fine-tuning (FT) for each language. The language-adapted models are sourced from Gurgurov et al. (2025), and the FT data sizes are as reported by them.

G Downstream Task Data Sizes

Language	Train	Validation	Test
Text Classification (TC)			
Maltese (mt)	701	99	204
Slovak (sk)	701	99	204
Swahili (sw)	701	99	204
Sentiment Analysis (SA)			
Maltese (mt)	595	85	171
Slovak (sk)	3560	522	1042
Swahili (sw)	738	185	304
Named Entity Recognition (NER)			
Maltese (mt)	100	100	100
Slovak (sk)	20000	10000	10000
Swahili (sw)	1000	1000	1000
Part of Speech Tagging (POS)			
Maltese (mt)	1123	433	518
Slovak (sk)	8483	1060	1061
Swahili (sw)	675	134	539

Table 3: Fine-tuning data sizes for each task (Text Classification, Sentiment Analysis, Named Entity Recognition, Part of Speech Tagging) showing train, validation, and test splits across Maltese, Slovak, and Swahili.

H Downstream Task Hyperparameters

Hyperparameter	TC	SA	NER	POS
Learning rate	1e-4	1e-4	3e-4	3e-4
Batch size	16	16	64	64
Epochs	20	20	100	100
Maximum length	256	256	512	512

Table 4: Hyperparameters for task adapter fine-tuning across Text Classification (TC), Sentiment Analysis (SA), and Named Entity Recognition (NER) tasks.

I Adapter Trainable Parameter Counts

To examine whether the constrained task adapter capacity, as shown in Table 5, impacts downstream performance in compressed models, we vary the reduction factor r, thereby increasing adapter size (see Figure 10). We train task adapters on top of both full adapted models and hidden-size reduced models (564, 456, and 312). For the smallest models (456 and 312), we observe that increasing adapter capacity (r=2) leads to improved performance. However, this increase is unnecessary for larger mBERT variants (full and 564), while still beneficial for all small XLM-R models. These results suggest that for smaller models, increasing adapter capacity can yield modest performance gains. Tables 1 and 6 report results using the default reduction rate of 16.

Model Configuration	Task Adapter Size	
	mBERT	**XLM-R**
Base	894,528	894,528
Base-[mt, sk, sw]	894,528	894,528
KD layer red. ×2	447,264	447,264
inter. layer red. → 2048	447,264	447,264
* KD hid. size red. → 564	240,474	240,474
vocab. red. → 40k	240,474	240,474
* KD hid. size red. → 456	156,120	156,120
vocab. red. → 40k	156,120	156,120
* KD hid. size red. → 312	73,122	73,122
vocab. red. → 40k	73,122	73,122

Table 5: Task adapter parameter sizes across different model compression configurations for mBERT and XLM-R **with the default reduction factor of 16**. When the hidden size is reduced, adapter input/output dimensions decrease proportionally. When the layer count is reduced, fewer adapters are added to the model. All other parameters use the default settings for the Sequential Bottleneck adapter as implemented in AdapterHub.

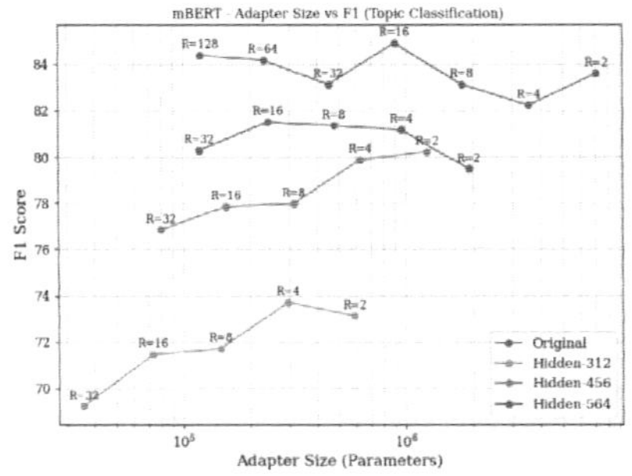

(a) mBERT

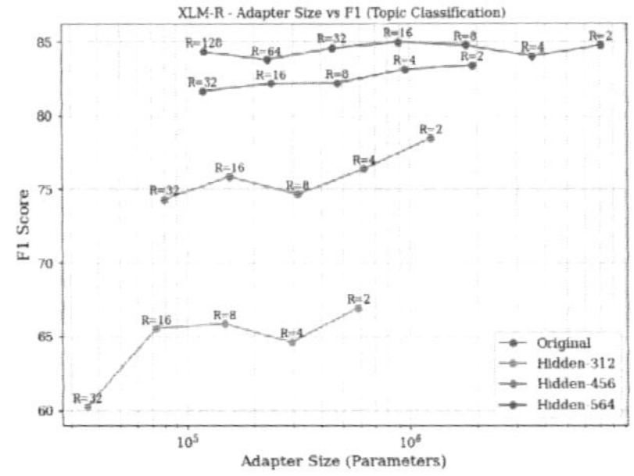

(b) XLM-R

Figure 10: Performance of models on TC for Maltese with varying adapter capacity for mBERT and XLM-R.

J Downstream Results for mBERT

Compression Stage	Params	Size	Task Performance (F1)												Avg
			Maltese				Slovak				Swahili				
			TC	SA	NER	POS	TC	SA	NER	POS	TC	SA	NER	POS	
Baselines															
Multilingual	179M	179M	68.7	65.8	60.0	89.0	85.3	92.0	91.4	97.0	69.6	64.6	83.8	87.6	79.6
Language-adapted	179M	179M	84.9	73.6	65.0	94.0	86.3	91.9	90.4	96.9	86.7	81.3	82.5	88.7	**85.2**
Compression Pipeline (minimal degradation)															
Layer reduction	135M (-25%)	135M	80.1	73.9	59.0	93.2	85.4	90.4	87.4	96.9	82.8	77.3	80.7	88.4	83.0
+ FFN pruning	126M (-30%)	126M	79.0	74.7	58.1	92.7	85.3	90.2	88.5	96.7	83.2	75.9	79.8	88.5	82.7
+ Hidden 564	90M (-50%)	90M	79.5	70.2	61.1	92.6	83.4	90.5	88.1	96.3	83.5	76.1	79.7	88.4	82.5
+ Vocabulary	45M (-75%)	45M	80.2	70.8	61.1	92.5	83.5	90.7	87.7	96.3	84.3	76.0	80.3	88.6	**82.7**
Further compression (moderate degradation)															
+ Hidden 456	71M (-60%)	71M	80.2	70.1	57.2	92.1	83.9	90.4	87.5	95.9	85.1	78.6	80.3	88.3	82.5
+ Vocabulary	35M (-80%)	35M	81.0	69.7	55.9	92.0	84.2	90.4	87.4	96.0	83.0	78.5	79.8	88.4	82.2
Maximum compression (higher degradation)															
+ Hidden 312	48M (-73%)	48M	73.1	72.0	39.5	90.3	80.9	90.4	86.5	95.5	81.8	76.5	79.6	87.7	79.5
+ Vocabulary	23M (-87%)	23M	73.0	72.1	40.4	90.2	81.9	90.1	86.2	95.3	81.7	76.0	77.1	87.7	79.3

Table 6: Progressive compression of mBERT. Stages are grouped by degradation level. Highlighted rows indicate the baseline (gray) and optimal compression point (green, 75% reduction with 2.5% drop). Maximum compression rows (red) show significant degradation (5.9% drop). TC=Topic Classification, SA=Sentiment Analysis, NER=Named Entity Recognition, POS=Part-of-Speech Tagging. F1 scores averaged over 3 runs.

Do We Need Large VLMs for Spotting Soccer Actions?

Ritabrata Chakraborty* Manipal University Jaipur

Rajatsubhra Chakraborty UNC–Charlotte

Avijit Dasgupta IIIT Hyderabad

Sandeep Chaurasia Manipal University Jaipur

ritabrata.229301716@muj.manipal.edu

Abstract

Traditional video-based tasks like soccer action spotting rely heavily on visual inputs, often requiring complex and computationally expensive models to process dense video data. We propose a shift from this video-centric approach to a text-based task, making it lightweight and scalable by utilizing Large Language Models (LLMs) instead of Vision-Language Models (VLMs). We posit that expert commentary, which provides rich descriptions and contextual cues contains sufficient information to reliably spot key actions in a match. To demonstrate this, we employ a system of three LLMs acting as judges specializing in outcome, excitement, and tactics for spotting actions in soccer matches. Our experiments show that this language-centric approach performs effectively in detecting critical match events coming close to state-of-the-art video-based spotters while using zero video processing compute and similar amount of time to process the entire match.

1 Introduction

> Football is a game of mistakes. Whoever makes the fewest mistakes wins.
>
> Johan Cruyff

In the domain of video understanding (Nguyen et al., 2024), visual frames have traditionally been considered the best input for many tasks, including action spotting, event detection, and object recognition (Giancola et al., 2025, 2023; Fulari, 2018) . However, these methods often require significant computational resources to process and analyze the dense video data (Selva et al., 2023; Feichtenhofer et al., 2019). Despite the advancements in video models, such as convolutional neural networks (CNNs) (Karpathy et al., 2014) and vision transformers (ViTs), the need for high-resolution video inputs can be prohibitive in both training and deployment scenarios.

Action spotting (Seweryn et al., 2023), a core task in sports analytics, aims to identify key events within a video, such as goals, penalties, or substitutions, by analyzing the visual content. Manual methods by broadcasters were slow and took time in distribution (Merler et al., 2019).Traditional approaches (Shih, 2017) have relied on object detection and tracking techniques that require parsing every frame of the video to detect specific actions (Khan et al., 2018). These methods can be computationally expensive and often struggle with long sequences or multiple simultaneous events (Xu et al., 2025). In contrast, when considering the commentary, each moment in the match is often described in rich detail, including the action, the players involved, and the contextual relevance. The spoken word can provide a nuanced understanding of the match dynamics, capturing moments of excitement, controversy, and strategic importance that may not always be fully conveyed through visual data alone. This raises an interesting possibility: ***Can we leverage textual commentary as a primary input for action spotting, bypassing the need for video frames?***

We explore this question by proposing a text based action spotting pipeline using an LLM-as-a-judge setup, following (Zheng et al., 2023). We investigate whether expert commentary is enough for current LLMs to infer actions from, and if it is comparable to heavy video based action spotter VLMs. We also study the improvement in action spotting as time taken per match and the independence from video processing compute.To this end, we provide the following contributions:

- We redesign action spotting as a text based task as compared to a visual based task, utilising the Soccernet-Echoes dataset (Gautam et al., 2024).
- We design and implement a three-LLM system that judges the commentary based on out-

*Corresponding author

Proceedings of the IJCNLP-AACL 2025 Student Research Workshop, pages 59–65
December 20-24, 2025

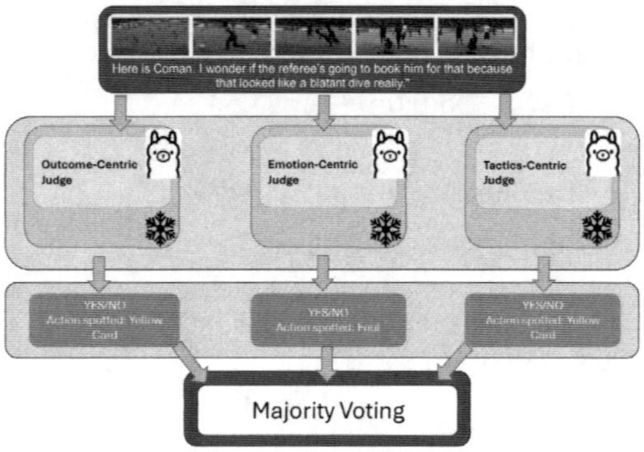

Figure 1: Our proposed LLM-based action spotting framework.

come , excitement, and tactics.

- We demonstrate that expert commentary, in many cases, provides comparable information for event detection compared to visual cues.
- We show that, by focusing on commentary alone, it is possible to detect key events reliably, highlighting the potential of language-centric models for sports analytics.

The rest of the paper is structured as follows. Section 2 discusses present literature around using text-based inputs for video tasks and action spotting in soccer matches. Section 3 explains our proposed framework in detail. Section 4 sheds light on the experimental setup and quantitative results. Finally we discuss some limitations in Section 6.

2 Related Work

Detailed Descriptions in Video-Based Tasks. In video-based understanding tasks, traditional models have primarily relied on visual features extracted from video frames to detect and classify events. However, recent research has begun exploring the use of fine-grained descriptions, specifically, textual information derived from transcriptions or commentary, to enhance performance in tasks like action spotting and event detection. Xie et al. (2019) demonstrated that integrating visual information with text can improve performance in action recognition tasks, as descriptive cues often convey context that is missed by raw visual data.In addition, Su et al. (2012) highlighted the utility of crowd-sourced commentary to aid in object detection tasks, which suggests that action spotting in dynamic environments, such as sports, could be enhanced by considering detailed narrative descriptions. Recent work shows that textual descriptions can carry action semantics the pixels miss and when transcribed reliably, can act as a compact surrogate for frames. For soccer specifically, dense, timestamped commentary corpora like SoccerNet-Caption (Mkhallati et al., 2023) and GOAL (Qi et al., 2023) establish the feasibility of commentary-anchored modeling, while MatchTime (Rao et al., 2024) highlights and fixes video-text misalignment—a key pain point for using commentary in downstream tasks. Robust automatic speech recognition (ASR) models such as Whisper (Radford et al., 2022) makes multi-accent, broadcast-noise transcripts viable at scale, strengthening the case for text-first pipelines.

Action Spotting in Soccer Videos. Action spotting in soccer has long relied on visual inputs, particularly tracking players and ball movements. However, recent developments in leveraging commentary and other textual sources for action detection have gained attention. Giannakopoulos et al. (2016) proposed a method that uses timestamped commentary as input to detect key moments in soccer, such as goals or penalties, demonstrating that textual data can complement traditional visual cues. Another approach by Andrews et al. (2024) used a multi-modal network that combines both video frames and textual commentary to detect key events in football matches. The SoccerNet benchmark (Deliege et al., 2021) formalized spotting as timestamp localization, driving a largely video-first literature . Classical baselines learn visual features and pool them temporally such as CALF (Cioppa et al., 2020) and NetVLAD++ temporal pooling (Giancola and Ghanem, 2021) . Subsequent models improved localization via stronger heads/sequence learning, including RMS-Net (Tomei et al., 2021) and compact E2E-Spot (Hong et al., 2022). Recent transformer systems such as ASTRA (Xarles et al., 2023) push tight-tolerance accuracy further and even add audio for non-visible cues. Broader universal efforts such as UniSoccer (Rao et al., 2025) argue for richer taxonomies and multi-task foundations that still place video at the center. These threads collectively set a strong video baseline for action spotting.

Despite these promising advancements, there

remains a gap in fully utilizing fine-grained commentary for video understanding tasks like action spotting, especially in the context of soccer. Existing methods either rely on computationally expensive visual cues or fail to achieve consistent performance with textual input alone.

3 Methodology

Large Language Model Judges. We use Llama 3.1 8B (Grattafiori et al., 2024) to instantiate three specialized judges that operate over a shared label space of the 17 SoccerNet-V2 classes and NO-ACTION. Each judge sees the same 10 s commentary window (5 s stride) but is prompted with a distinct *evidence lens* (Outcome, Tactics, Emotion). All three judges return a single class (or NO-ACTION) and confidence score. Judges are steered by a dedicated system prompt and 2–3 few-shot exemplars .

Outcome-centric Judge
Prioritizes refereeable outcomes (goal, penalty, yellow/red), explicit referee phrases.

Tactics-centric Judge
Emphasizes set-pieces and structure (corner, free-kick, substitution, formation/press).

Emotion-centric Judge
Uses rhetorical intensity and urgency to resolve ambiguous cases; conservative when negations appear ("over the bar", "flag is up").

Input: full English commentary for a 10 s window (5 s stride).
Output (per judge):

1. A **single label** in {17 SoccerNet-V2 classes} ∪ {NO-ACTION}.
2. A **confidence** in $[0, 1]$ (calibrated from model's self-score).

`Abstention is expressed as NO-ACTION; we use higher thresholds for the Emotion judge to avoid rhetorical over-triggering.`

Majority Voting System. Once each judge makes its decision, we aggregate the results using a majority voting mechanism. If at least two of the three judges agree on the presence of a relevant action, the action is considered "spottable" and is classified as an event worthy of attention. If the judges disagree, the action is not classified as relevant. This ensures that only the most unanimously recognized actions are selected.

Out-of-World Action Classification. In addition to the 17 predefined action classes, our system is designed to handle "out-of-world" actions—those that may be noteworthy but do not fall under any of the predefined classes. For instance, a player might execute a spectacular skill move or a controversial non-foul action, which can be exciting and relevant but doesn't match the typical goal or penalty. In this case, the judges are given the opportunity to classify the action as "out of world," providing a broader view of game dynamics that goes beyond standard categories.

Method	M	mAP (%)	Tight mAP (%)
CALF (Cioppa et al., 2020)	Video	49.7	–
RMS-Net (Tomei et al., 2021)	Video	63.49	28.83
FCMA (Zhou et al., 2021)	Video	73.77	47.05
E2E-Spot (RegNetY-200MF) (Hong et al., 2022)	Video	73.25	61.19
E2E-Spot (RegNetY-800MF) (Hong et al., 2022)	Video	74.05	61.82
ASTRA (Xarles et al., 2023)	Video	**78.09**	**66.82**
Random Text-Only (ours, baseline)	Text	**12.0**	**10.5**
LLM-Based (Ours)	**Text**	**64.5**	**60.8**

Table 1: mAP and tight mAP on SoccerNet-v2 for video- vs text-based pipelines. M = Modality (Video/Text).

4 Evaluation and Results

Setup. We evaluate on the SoccerNet-v2 test split using the SoccerNet-Echoes commentary (Gautam et al., 2024) as input. All commentary is in English. SoccerNet-Echoes provides timestamped transcriptions that are aligned to the underlying broadcast video using an automatic speech recognition (ASR) pipeline based on Whisper (Radford et al., 2022); we rely on these alignments without additional temporal adjustment. Events follow the 17-class SoccerNet taxonomy. Our system operates on 10 s windows (5 s stride) and uses three Llama 3.1 8B judges. Following SoccerNet (Deliege et al., 2021), we evaluate temporal localization using mean Average Precision (mAP) at multiple time tolerances. For a given tolerance δ (in seconds), a prediction of class c at time $\hat{\tau}$ is counted as correct if there exists a ground-truth event of class c at time τ such that $|\hat{\tau} - \tau| \leq \delta$. Let $\text{AP}(\delta)$ denote the Average Precision over all events at tolerance δ. We then define

$$\text{mAP} = \frac{1}{|\Delta_{\text{loose}}|} \sum_{\delta \in \Delta_{\text{loose}}} \text{AP}(\delta), \quad (1)$$

$$\text{Tight mAP} = \frac{1}{|\Delta_{\text{tight}}|} \sum_{\delta \in \Delta_{\text{tight}}} \text{AP}(\delta), \quad (2)$$

where $\Delta_{\text{loose}} = \{5, 10, 15, \ldots, 60\}$ s and $\Delta_{\text{tight}} = \{1, 2, 3, 4, 5\}$ s. We report both aggregates in Tables 1 and 2. For efficiency (Table 2) we normalize video compute to a **90 min match at 2 FPS** (10,800 frames) and report backbone FLOPs/frame

Method	Input	FLOPs/frame (GF)	Total FLOPs (TF)	Time/frame (ms)	Time/match (sec)
RegNetY-200MF (E2E-Spot)	Video	0.20	2.16	0.3	3.24
RegNetY-800MF (E2E-Spot)	Video	0.80	8.64	0.9	9.72
ResNet-152 (baseline feats)	Video	11.5	124.2	1.8	19.44
R(2+1)D (3D CNN)	Video	–	–	11.0	118.8
Ours: LLM (text-only)	**Text**	–	–	–	146.5

Table 2: Efficiency comparison on FLOPs and wall-clock time required for a full match evaluation. Video times are reported for GPU backbone-only inference on an A5000 (excluding video decoding and post-processing). "Ours" reports full end-to-end CPU time; although the wall-clock is larger, our method incurs zero video FLOPs and does not require a GPU. Here, FLOPs denotes floating point operations, and GF and TF correspond to 10^9 and 10^{12} FLOPs, respectively.

and measured per-frame time on an A5000 from prior work (Hong et al., 2022). For our text-only system we do not process any frames and report the end-to-end wall-clock time to process a full 90 min match on a single commodity CPU (16-core, 32 GB RAM).

Textual Random Baseline. To establish a strict lower bound we create a commentary-anchored randomness baseline that predicts actions without reading the text. For each commentary sentence $s_k = (\tau_k, \ell_k, \text{text}_k)$ in a half we sample a Bernoulli coin for every action class c with probability equal to that class's empirical commentary prior p_c (estimated on the train split). If the coin succeeds we emit a pseudo detection $(\tau_k, c, 0.5)$; overlapping detections of the same class within 2δ (δ=10 s) are merged by keeping the earliest. Here π_k denotes the prior frequency of class k in the training split, l_k is the unnormalized logit score predicted for class k, and text_k is the k-th commentary sentence or window. This design respects the real timestamp distribution yet ignores all lexical information, yielding the hardest chance-level floor against which any text-aware model must improve.

Main results. Table 1 shows that our text-only system achieves **64.5 mAP** and **60.8 Tight**, substantially outperforming the *Random Text-Only* baseline (12.0 / 10.5) and approaching recent video methods despite using no visual frames. Relative to strong video pipelines, we are close on the tight metric (**60.8** vs **61.82** for E2E-Spot RegNetY-800MF; **60.8** vs **66.82** for ASTRA), while trailing more on loose mAP (**64.5** vs **74.05** and **78.09**). Compared to RMS-Net, our tight score is more than **2**× higher (60.8 vs 28.83) and our loose mAP is competitive (64.5 vs 63.49). The pattern aligns with the nature of commentary: explicitly lexicalized, refereeable outcomes (goals, penalties, bookings, substitutions) are well localized in time, benefitting Tight mAP; at larger tolerances we remain intentionally conservative via abstention, trading some recall for precision.

Efficiency ablation. Table 2 compares per–90 min match compute and explains our savings. Video pipelines pay a cost that scales with the number of *visual tokens*; text scales with *text tokens*. Let F be frames per match and P the patch tokens per frame (ViT-style). Then visual-tokens $= F \times P$ and text-tokens $= N_t$. At 2 FPS, F=10,800. For ViT-B/16 at 224^2, P=$(224/16)^2$=196, so $F \times P \approx 2.12 \times 10^6$ visual tokens/match, whereas ASR produces only $N_t = \mathcal{O}(10^4)$ text tokens—two orders of magnitude fewer. Even with CNNs (no explicit patches), the effective per-frame compute (GFLOPs/frame) still scales with F and dominates.

At 2 FPS, published video backbones span 2.16–124.2 TFLOPs per match and 0.3–1.8 ms per frame on an A5000 (3.24–19.44 s per match; a 3D CNN is 118.8 s). Our pipeline performs no video feature extraction (zero video FLOPs) and instead scales with N_t and LLM tokens/s. On CPU, our measured end-to-end time for a full match is 146.5 s (2.44 min), removing the dominant frame-processing term and any GPU requirement.

Discussion. (1) **Tight localization from text.** When outcomes are spoken ("penalty given", "booked", "and it's in"), the language signal is temporally sharp, explaining our proximity to video SOTA on Tight mAP. (2) **Loose-gap sources.** Non-verbal micro-events and terse restarts are under-described in commentary, which hurts loose recall and favors video. (3) **Design effects.** Confidence thresholds and majority voting suppress rhetorical false positives (near-misses), improving precision; temporal NMS converts overlapping window votes into a single timestamp per event. (4) **Compute and deployment.** Zero-frame processing plus competitive Tight mAP make the approach attractive for CPU-scale batch processing (clubs/broadcasters) and for low-cost inference at volume. In summary, the main advantages of the text-based formulation are: (i) no need to store or process video frames, (ii) CPU-only inference with predictable scaling in the number of commentary tokens, and (iii) strong performance on refereeable, explicitly verbalized events (goals, penalties, cards, substitutions). The main drawbacks are: (i) a hard dependence on commentary coverage and timing, (ii) limited access to visual cues that are never spoken aloud (e.g., off-ball incidents or subtle shape changes), and (iii) potential lack of generalization to matches or leagues with minimal or low-quality commentary. We return to this trade-off in Section 5.

5 Conclusion

In this paper we asked whether large vision–language models are necessary to spot soccer actions when high-quality expert commentary is available. By reformulating action spotting as a purely language-centric task and applying a three-judge LLM ensemble to 10 s commentary windows, we show that text-only spotting can approach the performance of recent video-based systems: our method achieves 64.5 mAP and 60.8 Tight mAP on SoccerNet-v2, reaching 83%–96% of ASTRA's video-based performance while using zero video processing compute.

Our results suggest a nuanced answer to the title question. When dense, time-aligned commentary is present—as in professional broadcasts with experienced commentators—we do *not* strictly need VLMs for many refereeable events (goals, penalties, cards, substitutions). In this regime, language carries most of the necessary semantics and can be processed on commodity CPUs without maintaining or streaming video frames. However, when commentary is sparse, noisy, delayed, or entirely absent, or when the task depends on fine-grained visual cues that commentators do not verbalize (e.g., subtle tactical shapes, off-ball incidents, or crowd reactions), vision-based models remain indispensable.

Looking forward, we see text-only spotting as a strong and complementary baseline rather than a replacement for VLMs. A promising direction is to build multimodal pipelines where commentary provides a high-level prior over candidate events, and lightweight video modules are invoked only when the text is ambiguous or inconsistent with the visual evidence. Such hybrids could retain most of the efficiency gains of our language-centric design while recovering the visual coverage needed in more challenging or low-commentary scenarios.

6 Limitations

While our framework shows promising results, there are several limitations to consider. First, the performance of our system is heavily dependent on the quality of the commentary and transcription. Inaccurate or incomplete commentary can hinder the ability of our judges to correctly identify action-worthy events, leading to lower accuracy in the action spotting task. Similarly, the quality of transcription performed by Whisper plays a critical role. Errors in the transcription process can result in incorrect words or misplaced timestamps, directly affecting the action spotting metrics, including mean Average Precision (mAP). These transcription errors could affect the reliability of the timestamped actions and ultimately influence the results of the semantic judging. A second cost that we do not explicitly quantify in Tables 1–2 is automatic speech recognition. In our pipeline the Whisper-based ASR step is run once per match to produce commentary transcripts and can be executed offline or cached for reuse across downstream tasks. Nevertheless, ASR incurs its own compute and latency costs that broadcasters and practitioners must account for in an end-to-end system design; a fully fair comparison to video-only pipelines should include this term, which we leave for future work. Additionally, our framework assumes that the provided commentary is sufficiently detailed and relevant for the action spotting task. In cases where the commentary lacks context or important details, the system's performance may degrade. We aim to address this in our future work.

References

Peter Andrews, Oda Elise Nordberg, Stephanie Zubicueta Portales, Njål Borch, Frode Guribye, Kazuyuki Fujita, and Morten Fjeld. 2024. Aicommentator: A multimodal conversational agent for embedded visualization in football viewing. In *Proceedings of the 29th International Conference on Intelligent User Interfaces*, pages 14–34.

Anthony Cioppa, Adrien Deliège, Silvio Giancola,

Bernard Ghanem, Marc Van Droogenbroeck, Rikke Gade, and Thomas B. Moeslund. 2020. A context-aware loss function for action spotting in soccer videos. *Preprint*, arXiv:1912.01326.

Adrien Deliege, Anthony Cioppa, Silvio Giancola, Meisam J Seikavandi, Jacob V Dueholm, Kamal Nasrollahi, Bernard Ghanem, Thomas B Moeslund, and Marc Van Droogenbroeck. 2021. Soccernet-v2: A dataset and benchmarks for holistic understanding of broadcast soccer videos. In *Proceedings of the IEEE/CVF conference on computer vision and pattern recognition*, pages 4508–4519.

Christoph Feichtenhofer, Haoqi Fan, Jitendra Malik, and Kaiming He. 2019. Slowfast networks for video recognition. In *Proceedings of the IEEE/CVF international conference on computer vision*, pages 6202–6211.

Sunit Fulari. 2018. A survey on motion models used for object detection in videos. In *2018 2nd International Conference on Trends in Electronics and Informatics (ICOEI)*, pages 348–353.

Sushant Gautam, Mehdi Houshmand Sarkhoosh, Jan Held, Cise Midoglu, Anthony Cioppa, Silvio Giancola, Vajira Thambawita, Michael A Riegler, Pal Halvorsen, and Mubarak Shah. 2024. Soccernet-echoes: A soccer game audio commentary dataset. In *2024 International Symposium on Multimedia (ISM)*, pages 71–78. IEEE.

Silvio Giancola, Anthony Cioppa, Julia Georgieva, Johsan Billingham, Andreas Serner, Kerry Peek, Bernard Ghanem, and Marc Van Droogenbroeck. 2023. Towards active learning for action spotting in association football videos. In *Proceedings of the IEEE/CVF Conference on Computer Vision and Pattern Recognition (CVPR) Workshops*, pages 5098–5108.

Silvio Giancola, Anthony Cioppa, Bernard Ghanem, and Marc Van Droogenbroeck. 2025. *Deep Learning for Action Spotting in Association Football Videos*, page 427–459. WORLD SCIENTIFIC.

Silvio Giancola and Bernard Ghanem. 2021. Temporally-aware feature pooling for action spotting in soccer broadcasts. In *Proceedings of the IEEE/CVF Conference on Computer Vision and Pattern Recognition*, pages 4490–4499.

Theodoros Giannakopoulos, Anastasios Tsoumakas, and Ioannis Vlahavas. 2016. Soccer action spotting with timestamped commentary. In *Proceedings of the 17th International Conference on Artificial Intelligence: Methodology, Systems, and Applications, AIMSA 2016, Varna, Bulgaria, September 7-10, 2016*, pages 309–318. Springer.

Aaron Grattafiori, Abhimanyu Dubey, Abhinav Jauhri, Abhinav Pandey, Abhishek Kadian, Ahmad Al-Dahle, Aiesha Letman, Akhil Mathur, Alan Schelten, Alex Vaughan, Amy Yang, Angela Fan, Anirudh Goyal, Anthony Hartshorn, Aobo Yang, Archi Mitra, Archie Sravankumar, Artem Korenev, Arthur Hinsvark, and 542 others. 2024. The llama 3 herd of models. *Preprint*, arXiv:2407.21783.

James Hong, Haotian Zhang, Michaël Gharbi, Matthew Fisher, and Kayvon Fatahalian. 2022. Spotting temporally precise, fine-grained events in video. In *European Conference on Computer Vision*, pages 33–51. Springer.

Andrej Karpathy, George Toderici, Sanketh Shetty, Thomas Leung, Rahul Sukthankar, and Li Fei-Fei. 2014. Large-scale video classification with convolutional neural networks. In *Proceedings of the IEEE conference on Computer Vision and Pattern Recognition*, pages 1725–1732.

Abdullah Khan, Beatrice Lazzerini, Gaetano Calabrese, Luciano Serafini, and 1 others. 2018. Soccer event detection. *Computer Science & Information Technology*, pages 119–129.

Michele Merler, Khoi-Nguyen C. Mac, Dhiraj Joshi, Quoc-Bao Nguyen, Stephen Hammer, John Kent, Jinjun Xiong, Minh N. Do, John R. Smith, and Rogerio Schmidt Feris. 2019. Automatic curation of sports highlights using multimodal excitement features. *IEEE Transactions on Multimedia*, 21(5):1147–1160.

Hassan Mkhallati, Anthony Cioppa, Silvio Giancola, Bernard Ghanem, and Marc Van Droogenbroeck. 2023. Soccernet-caption: Dense video captioning for soccer broadcasts commentaries. In *2023 IEEE/CVF Conference on Computer Vision and Pattern Recognition Workshops (CVPRW)*, page 5074–5085. IEEE.

Thong Nguyen, Yi Bin, Junbin Xiao, Leigang Qu, Yicong Li, Jay Zhangjie Wu, Cong-Duy Nguyen, See-Kiong Ng, and Anh Tuan Luu. 2024. Video-language understanding: A survey from model architecture, model training, and data perspectives. In *Findings of the Association for Computational Linguistics: ACL 2024*, pages 3636–3657, Bangkok, Thailand. Association for Computational Linguistics.

Ji Qi, Jifan Yu, Teng Tu, Kunyu Gao, Yifan Xu, Xinyu Guan, Xiaozhi Wang, Bin Xu, Lei Hou, Juanzi Li, and 1 others. 2023. Goal: A challenging knowledge-grounded video captioning benchmark for real-time soccer commentary generation. In *Proceedings of the 32nd ACM international conference on information and knowledge management*, pages 5391–5395.

Alec Radford, Jong Wook Kim, Tao Xu, Greg Brockman, Christine McLeavey, and Ilya Sutskever. 2022. Robust speech recognition via large-scale weak supervision. *Preprint*, arXiv:2212.04356.

Jiayuan Rao, Haoning Wu, Hao Jiang, Ya Zhang, Yanfeng Wang, and Weidi Xie. 2025. Towards universal soccer video understanding. In *Proceedings of the Computer Vision and Pattern Recognition Conference*, pages 8384–8394.

Jiayuan Rao, Haoning Wu, Chang Liu, Yanfeng Wang, and Weidi Xie. 2024. MatchTime: Towards automatic soccer game commentary generation. In *Proceedings of the 2024 Conference on Empirical Methods in Natural Language Processing*, pages 1671–1685, Miami, Florida, USA. Association for Computational Linguistics.

Javier Selva, Anders S. Johansen, Sergio Escalera, Kamal Nasrollahi, Thomas B. Moeslund, and Albert Clapés. 2023. Video transformers: A survey. *IEEE Transactions on Pattern Analysis and Machine Intelligence*, 45(11):12922–12943.

Karolina Seweryn, Anna Wróblewska, and Szymon Łukasik. 2023. Survey of action recognition, spotting and spatio-temporal localization in soccer–current trends and research perspectives. *arXiv preprint arXiv:2309.12067*.

Huang-Chia Shih. 2017. A survey of content-aware video analysis for sports. *IEEE Transactions on circuits and systems for video technology*, 28(5):1212–1231.

Hao Su, Jia Deng, and Li Fei-Fei. 2012. Crowdsourcing annotations for visual object detection. *HCOMP@ AAAI*, 1.

Matteo Tomei, Lorenzo Baraldi, Simone Calderara, Simone Bronzin, and Rita Cucchiara. 2021. Rms-net: Regression and masking for soccer event spotting. In *2020 25th International Conference on Pattern Recognition (ICPR)*, pages 7699–7706. IEEE.

Artur Xarles, Sergio Escalera, Thomas B Moeslund, and Albert Clapés. 2023. Astra: An action spotting transformer for soccer videos. In *Proceedings of the 6th International Workshop on Multimedia Content Analysis in Sports*, pages 93–102.

Ning Xie, Farley Lai, Derek Doran, and Asim Kadav. 2019. Visual entailment: A novel task for fine-grained image understanding. *arXiv preprint arXiv:1901.06706*.

Hao Xu, Arbind Agrahari Baniya, Sam Well, Mohamed Reda Bouadjenek, Richard Dazeley, and Sunil Aryal. 2025. Action spotting and precise event detection in sports: Datasets, methods, and challenges. *Preprint*, arXiv:2505.03991.

Lianmin Zheng, Wei-Lin Chiang, Ying Sheng, Siyuan Zhuang, Zhanghao Wu, Yonghao Zhuang, Zi Lin, Zhuohan Li, Dacheng Li, Eric Xing, and 1 others. 2023. Judging llm-as-a-judge with mt-bench and chatbot arena. *Advances in neural information processing systems*, 36:46595–46623.

Xin Zhou, Le Kang, Zhiyu Cheng, Bo He, and Jingyu Xin. 2021. Feature combination meets attention: Baidu soccer embeddings and transformer based temporal detection. *arXiv preprint arXiv:2106.14447*.

LRMGS: A Language-Robust Metric for Evaluating Question Answering in Very Low-Resource Indic Languages

Anuj Kumar[1], **Satyadev Ahlawat**[2], **Yamuna Prasad**[1], **Virendra Singh**[3]
[1]Department of Computer Science & Engineering, Indian Institute of Technology Jammu, India
[2]Department of Electrical Engineering, Indian Institute of Technology Jammu, India
[3]Department of Electrical Engineering, Indian Institute of Technology Bombay, India
{anuj,satyadev.ahlawat,yamuna.prasad}@iitjammu.ac.in, viren@ee.iitb.ac.in

Abstract

Reliable evaluation of Question Answering (QA) systems in low-resource Indic languages poses a significant challenge due to the limited availability of annotated datasets, linguistic diversity, and the lack of suitable evaluation metrics. Languages such as Sindhi, Manipuri, Dogri, Konkani, and Maithili are particularly underrepresented, creating difficulty in assessing Large Language Models (LLMs) on QA tasks. Existing metrics, including BLEU, ROUGE-L, and BERTScore, are effective in machine translation and high-resource settings; however, they often fail in low-resource QA due to score compression, zero-inflation, and poor scale alignment. To overcome this, the Language-Robust Metric for Generative QA (LRMGS) is introduced to capture semantic and lexical agreement while preserving the score scale across languages. LRMGS is evaluated across 8 Indic languages and multiple LLMs, consistently demonstrating higher concordance with reference-based chrF++ scores, as measured using the Concordance Correlation Coefficient (CCC). Experimental results indicate that LRMGS provides more accurate discrimination of system performance in languages with very low resources compared to existing metrics. This work establishes a robust and interpretable framework for evaluating QA systems in low-resource Indic languages, supporting more reliable multilingual model assessment.

1 Introduction

India's linguistic landscape is among the richest globally, yet many languages with millions of speakers remain underrepresented in Natural Language Processing (NLP) and continue to be classified as low-resource due to the scarcity of annotated corpora and benchmarks. Large Language Models (LLMs) hold significant promise for addressing this gap by transferring knowledge from high-resource to low-resource languages through cross-lingual pretraining and generation. Models such as GPT-4 (OpenAI et al., 2024) have demonstrated strong performance in tasks including summarization (Pu et al., 2023; Goyal et al., 2023) and question answering (Zhao et al., 2023), although their training and evaluation processes remain predominantly English-centric. As a result, LLMs frequently struggle to generalize effectively across languages (Lai et al., 2023; Zhang et al., 2023; Ahuja et al., 2023), exhibiting substantial performance disparities between proprietary and open-source models (Ahuja et al., 2024). While multilingual pretraining extends generative capabilities to a wider range of languages (Jiang et al., 2024), evaluation efforts remain constrained by benchmarks dominated by understanding-focused tasks with limited generative coverage (Lai et al., 2023; Asai et al., 2023) and by the continued reliance on expensive reference-based annotations. LLM-based evaluation approaches (Liu et al., 2023) provide an emerging alternative; however, these methods often introduce biases such as a preference for longer outputs or self-generated responses (Zheng et al., 2023; Shen et al., 2023).

Although several Indic QA datasets (Clark et al., 2020; Asai et al., 2021; Singh et al., 2025) have contributed to expanding multilingual evaluation, the core challenge remains the lack of effective evaluation methods for languages with very low resources. Prior efforts often relied on translation-based evaluation (Singh et al., 2024; Chollampatt et al., 2025), which is inadequate for QA since the task requires not only fluent generation, factual correctness, grounding in context, and the preservation of key entities and information. Existing reference-based metrics such as BLEU (Papineni et al., 2002), ROUGE (Lin, 2004), BERTScore (Zhang* et al., 2020), and chrF++ (Popović, 2017) fall short in this setting: they compress score ranges, exhibit weak alignment with human judgments, and often produce unstable rankings across systems. More critically, these metrics operate primarily at the sur-

Proceedings of the IJCNLP-AACL 2025 Student Research Workshop, pages 66–77
December 20-24, 2025

face or semantic similarity level, thereby overlooking factual aspects of QA such as numeric accuracy, consistency of named entities, and hallucinations. As a result, models that generate fluent yet factually incorrect answers may still receive inflated scores. Cross-lingual protocols aim to mitigate certain issues while introducing new risks, including reference leakage, dependency on expensive annotations, and uncertainty regarding the reliability of scorer LLMs for non-English text.

Example from our result
Language: Dogri **System:** GPT-4.1 **Domain:** Politics
Question: गांधी — इरविन पैक्ट भारत दे निम्नलिखित आंदोलनें च कुस आंदोलन कन्नै जुड़े दा हा ?
Translation: Which of the following movements in India was the Gandhi–Irwin Pact associated with?
Reference: गांधी-इरविन पैक्ट दा सरबंध नागरिक अवज्ञा आन्दोलन कन्नै हा।
Translation: The Gandhi–Irwin Pact was associated with the Civil Disobedience Movement.
Output: गांधी — इरविन पैक्ट सविनय अवज्ञा आंदोलन कन्नै जुड़े दा हा।
Translation: The Gandhi–Irwin Pact is associated with the Civil Disobedience Movement.

Metrics	chrF++	BLEU	BERTScore	LRMGS
	0.4852	0.0560	0.9338	**0.9290**

To address the evaluation gap in very low-resource Indic languages, this study builds on the L3Cube-IndicQuest benchmark (Rohera et al., 2024), which includes underrepresented languages such as Sindhi, Manipuri, Dogri, Konkani, and Maithili. The proposed **Language-Robust Metric for Generative QA (LRMGS)** is a composite evaluation framework that integrates semantic similarity through pivoted multilingual BERTScore, nugget-level factual coverage, penalties for numeric mismatches, and evidence-faithfulness checks. Human annotation in these languages remains extremely limited due to the scarcity of bilingual experts, script diversity, and the high cost of large-scale annotation, making direct human correlation infeasible at scale. Consequently, chrF++ is employed as a reproducible *reference metric* for assessing score stability and cross-system concordance. The metric operates purely at the character level and functions as a proxy to examine relative consistency across systems, without modeling semantic or factual correctness. This design allows validation of LRMGS in a principled and language-agnostic manner, even in the absence of human evaluation resources.

2 Evaluation Protocol

2.1 Problem Definition

The task considered in this work is the evaluation of QA outputs across eight low-resource Indic languages. Each evaluation instance is represented as a pair (Q, R), where Q denotes the question posed in one of the target languages and R is its gold reference answer. Given a system prediction $\hat{A}$ produced by a LLM, the objective is to define an evaluation function $\mathcal{E} : (R, \hat{A}) \mapsto s \in [0, 1]$, that assigns a score s reflecting the quality of $\hat{A}$ relative to R.

2.2 Evaluation Metric

To overcome the limitations of BLEU (Papineni et al., 2002), ROUGE (Lin, 2004), BERTScore (Zhang* et al., 2020), and chrF++ (Popović, 2017), which approximate $\mathcal{E}$ via lexical or embedding similarity, the **LRMGS** is introduced. It integrates semantic similarity, question-aware nugget coverage, numeric fidelity, and contextual grounding. Formally,

$$\text{LRMGS} = \prod_{\substack{k \in \{\text{BERT}, \\ \text{KC,NUM,EF}\}}} \text{EN-k}(Ren, \hat{A}_{en}, C_{en})^{\lambda_k}, \tag{1}$$

where $\lambda_{\text{BERT}} = 0.9$, $\lambda_{\text{KC}} = 0.8$, and $\lambda_{\text{NUM}} = \lambda_{\text{EF}} = 1$.

Notation. A QA instance is represented as (Q, R), where Q is the Indic question, R the gold answer, and $\hat{A}$ the system prediction. English translations of Q and R are provided, and $\hat{A}$ is translated via IndicTrans2 (Gala et al., 2023) for consistent evaluation. Let Q_{en}, R_{en}, and $\hat{A}en$ denote the English forms of the question, reference, and system output, with context $Cen = c_1, \ldots, c_m$ representing the English question sentences for grounding. For EN-BERTScore, token embeddings $\mathbf{r}i$ and $\mathbf{a}j$ are obtained using RoBERTa-large (Zhang* et al., 2020). For key-nugget coverage (KC) and evidence faithfulness (EF), Sentence-Transformers (Reimers and Gurevych, 2019) encode nuggets $\mathbf{k}i$ and context sentences $\mathbf{c}$. Nuggets correspond to factual clauses segmented from Ren, with attention weights a_i derived via softmax-normalized similarity to Qen, emphasizing the most relevant clauses. Numeric sets N_R and $N\hat{A}$ contain expressions extracted through regular expressions.

Semantic similarity (EN-BERT).

$$\text{EN-BERT}(R_{en}, \hat{A}_{en}) = \frac{1}{|R_{en}|} \sum_{i=1}^{|R_{en}|} \max_j \left|\cos(\mathbf{r}_i, \mathbf{a}_j)\right|. \quad (2)$$

Question-aware nugget attention (EN-KC).

$$\text{EN-KC}(R_{\text{en}}, Q_{\text{en}}) = \frac{\exp(\frac{\cos(\mathbf{k}_i,\mathbf{q})}{\eta})}{\sum_{j=1}^{n} \exp(\frac{\cos(\mathbf{k}_j,\mathbf{q})}{\eta})}, \quad (3)$$

where $\mathbf{k}_i$ and $\mathbf{q}$ are embeddings of clause c_i (from R_{en}) and question Q_{en}, n is the number of clauses, and η is the temperature controlling attention sharpness. A smaller η yields peaked attention, whereas a larger value smooths the distribution. Top-k nuggets with the highest attention weights are retained as key concepts for coverage computation.

Numeric fidelity (EN-NUM).

$$\text{EN-NUM}(R_{en}, \hat{A}_{en}) = \frac{|N_R \cap N_{\hat{A}}|}{|N_R \cup N_{\hat{A}}|}. \quad (4)$$

A partial penalty is applied when the reference contains numbers; however, the hypothesis does not, as reflected in the implementation.

Evidence faithfulness (EN-EF).

$$\text{EN-EF}(C_{en}, \hat{A}_{en}) = \max_{c \in C_{en}} \cos(\mathbf{a}, \mathbf{c}), \quad (5)$$

which ensures contextual grounding by requiring the generated answer to align semantically with at least one translated question sentence. The full algorithmic implementation of LRMGS is provided in Appendix D.

3 Evaluation and Dataset

Two kinds of evaluation have been done in this work: (1) Meta-evaluation and (2) LLM Comparison.

Meta-evaluation: The ability of LRMGS to substitute conventional reference-based metrics for multilingual QA evaluation is examined by computing its concordance with CHRF++ (Popović, 2017), a metric shown to align well with human judgments in multilingual text generation (Singh et al., 2024). The Concordance Correlation Coefficient (CCC) (ccc, 1989) is employed, as it evaluates both precision (Pearson correlation) and accuracy (closeness to the identity line), thereby capturing true agreement rather than only monotonic consistency.

Language	BLEU	BScore	LRMGS
Assamese	0.406	0.0229	0.627
Dogri	0.376	0.0172	0.538
Hindi	0.541	0.0286	0.646
Konkani	0.356	0.0209	0.597
Maithili	0.430	0.0210	0.563
Manipuri	0.413	0.0153	0.580
Sanskrit	0.276	0.0222	0.601
Sindhi	0.569	0.0221	0.642
Average	0.421	0.0213	**0.599**

Table 1: Comparison of correlation-based agreement with CHRF++ across metrics for each low-resource Indic language. The results show that LRMGS consistently achieves higher concordance with CHRF++ than BLEU and BERTScore(BScore).

System	BLEU	BScore	LRMGS
Airavata-7B	0.361	0.017	0.539
Aya-23-8B	0.515	0.012	0.586
BLOOMZ-7B	0.736	0.006	0.362
GPT-4.1	0.390	0.024	0.571
Gemma-2-9B-it	0.498	0.020	0.565
Llama-3.1-8B	0.445	0.018	0.542
Mistral-7B	0.212	0.005	0.430
OpenHathi7B-Hi	0.101	0.006	0.486
Qwen2.5-7B-Inst.	0.375	0.013	0.502
Yi-1.5-9B-Chat	0.648	0.001	0.311
Average	0.418	0.013	**0.500**

Table 2: System-level comparison of correlation-based agreement with CHRF++ across evaluation metrics. LRMGS achieves the highest average concordance (0.500), outperforming BLEU and BERTScore(BScore) across diverse multilingual systems.

Formally, for score sets $X = \{x_i\}_{i=1}^n$ and $Y = \{y_i\}_{i=1}^n$,

$$\rho_c = \frac{2\rho\,\sigma_X\sigma_Y}{\sigma_X^2 + \sigma_Y^2 + (\mu_X - \mu_Y)^2}, \quad (6)$$

where ρ denotes the Pearson correlation coefficient between X and Y, while $\mu_.$ and $\sigma_.^2$ denote the mean and variance, respectively. A value of $\rho_c = 1$ indicates perfect concordance.

CCC is reported at two levels of granularity, consistent with the evaluation protocol: (i) *language-level*, where for each language ℓ, CCC is computed between LRMGS and CHRF++ over all samples belonging to ℓ; (ii) *system-level*, where for each system s, CCC is computed between LRMGS and CHRF++ over all samples generated by s without

	Assamese	Dogri	Hindi	Konkani	Maithili	Manipuri	Sanskrit	Sindhi
OpenHathi-7B-Hi-Base	0.051	0.199	0.248	0.153	0.209	0.041	0.159	0.051
Yi-1.5-9B-Chat	0.056	0.052	0.045	0.044	0.049	0.046	0.044	0.051
BLOOMZ-7B1-mt	0.118	0.129	0.162	0.088	0.124	0.04	0.121	0.067
Aya-23-8B	0.17	0.224	0.238	0.222	0.239	0.044	0.22	0.149
Mistral-7B	0.218	0.224	0.252	0.209	0.244	0.085	0.166	0.181
Airavata-7B	0.253	0.258	0.268	0.229	0.27	0.037	0.242	0.2
Qwen2.5-7B-Instruct	0.28	0.294	0.305	0.289	0.305	0.136	0.278	0.269
Gemma-2-9B-it	0.29	0.284	0.331	0.278	0.309	0.169	0.266	0.254
Llama-3.1-8B-Instruct	0.282	0.327	0.348	0.314	0.336	0.215	0.297	0.279
GPT-4.1	**0.411**	**0.394**	**0.434**	**0.39**	**0.422**	**0.267**	**0.361**	**0.38**

Table 3: System × language matrix of LRMGS scores with prompts in English. The results highlight consistent cross-lingual trends, with GPT-4.1 achieving the highest scores across all eight Indic languages.

pre-averaging.

LLM Comparison: Using LRMGS, multilingual QA evaluation across ten LLMs shows stronger agreement in medium-resource languages like Hindi and Assamese, while very low-resource ones such as Sindhi and Dogri reveal large performance gaps. GPT-4.1 achieves the best overall results, though open-source models like Gemma-2-9B-IT and LLaMA-3.1-8B-Instruct are competitive and surpass larger proprietary systems in some cases. These results underline the strengths of proprietary models while highlighting the growing potential of open-source alternatives. Further details about LLMs and prompt are given in Appendix E.

Dataset: The study uses the L3Cube-IndicQuest dataset (Singh et al., 2025), containing 4,000 QA pairs across 20 languages, each with 200 questions from five domains. The questions were originally authored in English, manually verified for correctness, and subsequently translated into the other Indic languages. For this work, eight low-resource languages, Assamese, Dogri, Hindi, Konkani, Maithili, Manipuri, Sanskrit, and Sindhi, are selected to examine multilingual evaluation under data scarcity. Further details about the dataset are mentioned in Appendix A.

4 Results

Tables 1 and 2 establish the reliability of LRMGS as an evaluation protocol across Indic languages and multilingual systems. Unlike BLEU and BERTScore, which underperform in very low-resource scenarios, LRMGS demonstrates stronger concordance with CHRF++ both across languages and across systems. This robustness is most apparent for Dogri and Manipuri, where surface-based metrics fail to capture semantic fidelity or factual adequacy. At the system level, BLEU occasionally aligns with CHRF++ for certain models yet fluctuates sharply for others, while BERTScore remains uniformly weak. LRMGS provides stable and interpretable agreement, confirming its suitability for benchmarking multilingual QA tasks in low-resource conditions.

To illustrate how individual components of LRMGS contribute to the final score, Table 4 presents representative GPT-4.1 outputs. These examples illustrate how the metric captures semantic fidelity, factual grounding, numeric consistency, and alignment with contextual evidence, in contrast to conventional metrics that rely solely on surface overlap. High LRMGS values correspond to fluent and factually correct paraphrases, whereas mid-range or low scores indicate partial factual omission or semantic drift. This qualitative behavior explains the improved discriminative reliability of LRMGS across languages and systems.

The results reveal several key insights. First, LRMGS exhibits greater score stability across Indic languages of varying resource levels, maintaining consistent scale alignment even in the presence of translation noise. Second, correlation with CHRF++ confirms that LRMGS preserves rank consistency across systems while extending evaluation to factual and contextual dimensions that CHRF++ does not capture. Third, LRMGS demonstrates stronger discriminative power in identifying fine-grained differences among LLMs, particularly between proprietary and open-source models. These insights validate the interpretability and robustness of LRMGS as a framework for evaluation.

Although the metric employs English pivoting through translation, the direct application of En-

Table 4: Illustrative GPT-4.1 examples highlighting the contribution of each LRMGS component (EN-BERT, EN-KC, EN-NUM, EN-EF) in evaluating semantic, factual, numeric, and contextual faithfulness.

Language: Sanskrit **Question (EN):** In which caves is the Kailasha temple located? **Reference (EN):** The Kailasha temple is located in the Ellora caves. **Output (EN):** The Kailash Temple is located in the Ellora Caves. **Scores:** BLEU = 0.427 chrF++ = 0.803 EN-BERT = 0.970 EN-KC = 0.928 EN-NUM = 1.000 EN-EF = 0.978 LRMGS = 0.896 **Interpretation:** A fluent paraphrase preserving all factual elements. Despite moderate BLEU, both **EN-BERT (Eq. 2)** and **EN-EF (Eq. 5)** remain near 1.0, reflecting semantic and contextual fidelity. LRMGS correctly assigns a high score (0.896) while surface metrics undervalue it.
Language: Assamese **Question (EN):** How did Hamlet's father die? **Reference (EN):** Hamlet's father was killed by his brother Claudius with a drink laced with poison. **Output (EN):** Hamlet's father was killed by his brother Claudius. **Scores:** BLEU = 0.008 chrF++ = 0.187 EN-BERT = 0.887 EN-KC = 0.513 EN-NUM = 1.000 EN-EF = 0.942 LRMGS = 0.495 **Interpretation:** A semantically correct yet contextually reduced answer. High **EN-BERT** yet lower **EN-KC** indicate factual alignment with partial omission of narrative context. This illustrates how **Equation (3)** penalizes incomplete nugget coverage, leading to a mid-range LRMGS score.

glish metrics, such as BLEU or ROUGE, to translated text is unreliable. Translation artifacts frequently alter lexical structure and token boundaries, reducing the validity of token-based similarity. LRMGS mitigates these effects by performing semantic alignment on the pivoted text and incorporating numeric and evidence-based checks that remain stable under translation noise. This hybrid design enables reliable cross-lingual evaluation while preserving the linguistic and factual characteristics of the original Indic content.

Having validated the metric, Table 3 applies LRMGS to compare large language models across eight Indic languages. The results reveal clear variation across models and languages. Newer instruction-tuned architectures, including LLaMA-3.1-8B-Instruct and Gemma-2-9B-it, consistently outperform earlier baselines such as BLOOMZ and Yi-1.5-9B-Chat, indicating the benefit of recent training improvements for low-resource QA. Airavata-7B and Qwen2.5-7B-Instruct achieve competitive scores, although challenges persist for Manipuri and Sindhi, where most models display sharp performance degradation. GPT-4.1 attains the highest LRMGS values across all languages, reflecting both the disparity between proprietary and open-source systems and the capability of LRMGS to capture these nuanced differences. Comprehensive results for BLEU, ROUGE-L, chrF++, and BERTScore, along with visualizations, are provided in Appendix C.

5 Conclusion

This work introduced LRMGS, a composite evaluation metric designed for generative QA in very low-resource Indic languages. By combining semantic similarity, nugget-level coverage, numeric consistency, and evidence faithfulness, LRMGS captures both factual and contextual dimensions of QA quality. Experiments across eight Indic languages show that LRMGS consistently achieves higher concordance with CHRF++ compared to BLEU and BERTScore. The results highlight its robustness in ranking multilingual systems and its ability to reveal performance gaps in underrepresented languages. LRMGS thus provides a reliable and interpretable framework for benchmarking QA systems in low-resource settings.

Limitations

This work has several limitations. First, LRMGS relies on translation to English through IndicTrans2, which may introduce translation errors and slightly influence the resulting evaluation scores. Second, the evaluation is limited to eight Indic languages due to the availability of suitable datasets, leaving a substantial number of low-resource languages unexamined. Third, meta-evaluation is performed against CHRF++ rather than direct human judgments for all languages, thereby constraining the strength of conclusions regarding alignment with human evaluations.

References

1989. A concordance correlation coefficient to evaluate reproducibility. *Biometrics*, 45(1):255–268.

Kabir Ahuja, Harshita Diddee, Rishav Hada, Millicent Ochieng, Krithika Ramesh, Prachi Jain, Akshay Nambi, Tanuja Ganu, Sameer Segal, Mohamed Ahmed, Kalika Bali, and Sunayana Sitaram. 2023. MEGA: Multilingual evaluation of generative AI. In *Proceedings of the 2023 Conference on Empirical Methods in Natural Language Processing*, pages 4232–4267.

Sanchit Ahuja, Divyanshu Aggarwal, Varun Gumma, Ishaan Watts, Ashutosh Sathe, Millicent Ochieng, Rishav Hada, Prachi Jain, Mohamed Ahmed, Kalika Bali, and Sunayana Sitaram. 2024. MEGAVERSE: Benchmarking large language models across languages, modalities, models and tasks. In *Proceedings of the 2024 Conference of the North American Chapter of the Association for Computational Linguistics: Human Language Technologies (Volume 1: Long Papers)*, pages 2598–2637.

Akari Asai, Jungo Kasai, Jonathan Clark, Kenton Lee, Eunsol Choi, and Hannaneh Hajishirzi. 2021. XOR QA: Cross-lingual open-retrieval question answering. In *Proceedings of the 2021 Conference of the North American Chapter of the Association for Computational Linguistics: Human Language Technologies*, pages 547–564.

Akari Asai, Sneha Kudugunta, Xinyan Velocity Yu, Terra Blevins, Hila Gonen, Machel Reid, Yulia Tsvetkov, Sebastian Ruder, and Hannaneh Hajishirzi. 2023. Buffet: Benchmarking large language models for few-shot cross-lingual transfer. *Preprint*, arXiv:2305.14857.

Shamil Chollampatt, Minh Quang Pham, Sathish Reddy Indurthi, and Marco Turchi. 2025. Cross-lingual evaluation of multilingual text generation. In *Proceedings of the 31st International Conference on Computational Linguistics*, pages 7766–7777.

Jonathan H. Clark, Eunsol Choi, Michael Collins, Dan Garrette, Tom Kwiatkowski, Vitaly Nikolaev, and Jennimaria Palomaki. 2020. TyDi QA: A benchmark for information-seeking question answering in typologically diverse languages. *Transactions of the Association for Computational Linguistics*, 8:454–470.

Jay Gala, Pranjal A Chitale, A K Raghavan, Varun Gumma, Sumanth Doddapaneni, Aswanth Kumar M, Janki Atul Nawale, Anupama Sujatha, Ratish Puduppully, Vivek Raghavan, Pratyush Kumar, Mitesh M Khapra, Raj Dabre, and Anoop Kunchukuttan. 2023. Indictrans2: Towards high-quality and accessible machine translation models for all 22 scheduled indian languages. *Transactions on Machine Learning Research*.

Tanya Goyal, Junyi Jessy Li, and Greg Durrett. 2023. News summarization and evaluation in the era of gpt-3. *Preprint*, arXiv:2209.12356.

Albert Q. Jiang, Alexandre Sablayrolles, Antoine Roux, Arthur Mensch, Blanche Savary, Chris Bamford, Devendra Singh Chaplot, Diego de las Casas, Emma Bou Hanna, Florian Bressand, Gianna Lengyel, Guillaume Bour, Guillaume Lample, Lélio Renard Lavaud, Lucile Saulnier, Marie-Anne Lachaux, Pierre Stock, Sandeep Subramanian, Sophia Yang, and 7 others. 2024. Mixtral of experts. *Preprint*, arXiv:2401.04088.

Viet Dac Lai, Nghia Ngo, Amir Pouran Ben Veyseh, Hieu Man, Franck Dernoncourt, Trung Bui, and Thien Huu Nguyen. 2023. ChatGPT beyond English: Towards a comprehensive evaluation of large language models in multilingual learning. In *Findings of the Association for Computational Linguistics: EMNLP 2023*, pages 13171–13189.

Chin-Yew Lin. 2004. ROUGE: A package for automatic evaluation of summaries. In *Text Summarization Branches Out*, pages 74–81, Barcelona, Spain. Association for Computational Linguistics.

Yang Liu, Dan Iter, Yichong Xu, Shuohang Wang, Ruochen Xu, and Chenguang Zhu. 2023. G-eval: NLG evaluation using gpt-4 with better human alignment. In *Proceedings of the 2023 Conference on Empirical Methods in Natural Language Processing*, pages 2511–2522.

OpenAI, Josh Achiam, Steven Adler, Sandhini Agarwal, Lama Ahmad, Ilge Akkaya, Florencia Leoni Aleman, Diogo Almeida, Janko Altenschmidt, Sam Altman, Shyamal Anadkat, Red Avila, Igor Babuschkin, Suchir Balaji, Valerie Balcom, Paul Baltescu, Haiming Bao, Mohammad Bavarian, Jeff Belgum, and 262 others. 2024. Gpt-4 technical report. *Preprint*, arXiv:2303.08774.

Kishore Papineni, Salim Roukos, Todd Ward, and Wei-Jing Zhu. 2002. Bleu: a method for automatic evaluation of machine translation. In *Proceedings of the 40th Annual Meeting of the Association for Computational Linguistics*, pages 311–318.

Maja Popović. 2017. chrF++: words helping character n-grams. In *Proceedings of the Second Conference on Machine Translation*, pages 612–618.

Xiao Pu, Mingqi Gao, and Xiaojun Wan. 2023. Summarization is (almost) dead. *Preprint*, arXiv:2309.09558.

Nils Reimers and Iryna Gurevych. 2019. Sentence-BERT: Sentence embeddings using Siamese BERT-networks. In *Proceedings of the 2019 Conference on Empirical Methods in Natural Language Processing and the 9th International Joint Conference on Natural Language Processing (EMNLP-IJCNLP)*, pages 3982–3992.

Pritika Rohera, Chaitrali Ginimav, Akanksha Salunke, Gayatri Sawant, and Raviraj Joshi. 2024. L3cube-indicquest: A benchmark question answering dataset for evaluating knowledge of llms in indic context. *arXiv preprint arXiv:2409.08706*.

Chenhui Shen, Liying Cheng, Xuan-Phi Nguyen, Yang You, and Lidong Bing. 2023. Large language models are not yet human-level evaluators for abstractive summarization. In *Findings of the Association for Computational Linguistics: EMNLP 2023*, pages 4215–4233.

Abhishek Kumar Singh, Vishwajeet Kumar, Rudra Murthy, Jaydeep Sen, Ashish Mittal, and Ganesh Ramakrishnan. 2025. INDIC QA BENCHMARK: A multilingual benchmark to evaluate question answering capability of LLMs for Indic languages. In *Findings of the Association for Computational Linguistics: NAACL 2025*, pages 2607–2626.

Anushka Singh, Ananya Sai, Raj Dabre, Ratish Puduppully, Anoop Kunchukuttan, and Mitesh Khapra. 2024. How good is zero-shot MT evaluation for low resource Indian languages? In *Proceedings of the 62nd Annual Meeting of the Association for Computational Linguistics (Volume 2: Short Papers)*, pages 640–649.

Tianyi Zhang*, Varsha Kishore*, Felix Wu*, Kilian Q. Weinberger, and Yoav Artzi. 2020. Bertscore: Evaluating text generation with bert. In *International Conference on Learning Representations*.

Wenxuan Zhang, Sharifah Mahani Aljunied, Chang Gao, Yew Ken Chia, and Lidong Bing. 2023. M3exam: a multilingual, multimodal, multilevel benchmark for examining large language models. In *Proceedings of the 37th International Conference on Neural Information Processing Systems*, NIPS '23.

Kun Zhao, Bohao Yang, Chenghua Lin, Wenge Rong, Aline Villavicencio, and Xiaohui Cui. 2023. Evaluating open-domain dialogues in latent space with next sentence prediction and mutual information. In *Proceedings of the 61st Annual Meeting of the Association for Computational Linguistics (Volume 1: Long Papers)*, pages 562–574.

Lianmin Zheng, Wei-Lin Chiang, Ying Sheng, Siyuan Zhuang, Zhanghao Wu, Yonghao Zhuang, Zi Lin, Zhuohan Li, Dacheng Li, Eric P. Xing, Hao Zhang, Joseph E. Gonzalez, and Ion Stoica. 2023. Judging llm-as-a-judge with mt-bench and chatbot arena. In *Proceedings of the 37th International Conference on Neural Information Processing Systems*, NIPS '23.

A Dataset

Dataset size and length characteristics. Table 5 summarizes per–language dataset statistics. Each language has 200 QA pairs, and average *question* length ranges from 7.56 (Sanskrit) to 11.22 tokens (Dogri), while average *answer* length ranges from 19.32 (Sanskrit) to 30.50 tokens (Dogri/Sindhi). Across languages, answers are roughly 2.5×–3× longer than questions, indicating that systems must handle short prompts with substantially longer generations.

Language	Samples	Avg Q tokens	Avg A tokens
Assamese	200	8.55	23.08
Dogri	200	11.22	30.5
Hindi	200	11.01	29.8
Konkani	200	8.3	22.16
Maithili	200	11.08	30.48
Manipuri	200	8.62	23.36
Sanskrit	200	7.56	19.32
Sindhi	200	11.02	30.48

Table 5: Dataset statistics per language: number of samples and average token lengths of questions/answers.

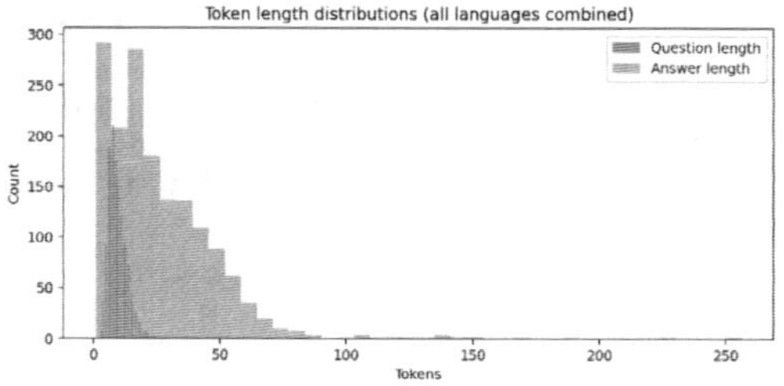

Figure 1: Token–length distributions aggregated across all languages. Questions are short and tightly clustered; answers are longer and right–skewed with a long tail.

Figure 1 shows the combined token–length distributions over all languages. Question lengths are tightly concentrated in the 5–15 token range, whereas answer lengths exhibit a broader, right–skewed distribution with a long tail (occasionally exceeding 200 tokens). The separation between the two histograms suggests limited confounding between prompt length and response length, and the heavy–tailed answers motivate clause–level scoring and attention mechanisms.

B Experimental Setup and Metrics

Experiments are conducted across eight low-resource Indic languages: Assamese, Dogri, Hindi, Konkani, Maithili, Manipuri, Sanskrit, and Sindhi, using 200 QA pairs per language. For each (question, reference) pair, model outputs are generated and evaluated using both automatic reference-based metrics and human-aligned LLM ratings. All experiments are inference-only, with no model updates or gradient computations. Results are reported per language and per system, followed by correlation analysis using Pearson, Spearman, and Kendall's τ.

Generation Settings. Inference is performed using the transformers library in float16 precision with device_map=auto across **2× NVIDIA V100 PCIe 32 GB** GPUs. Decoding uses deterministic **greedy search** (do_sample=false) with a limit of 128 new tokens. Tokenizers use left padding and truncation, defaulting to the eos_token when the pad_token is undefined. Random seeds are fixed to 42 for Python, NumPy, and PyTorch to ensure reproducibility. Batch size is one, and no gradients are computed.

Automatic Metrics. Evaluation includes **BLEU**, **ROUGE-L** (LCS F1), **chrF++** (β=2), and English-projected **BERTScore (F1)**, along with the proposed **LRMGS** metric that captures semantic and factual grounding in multilingual QA. BLEU scores are computed using a maximum of four-gram overlap (**BLEU-4**) with standard smoothing (method 1). Lower-order BLEU variants (1–3) were additionally examined for consistency, and system-level rankings remained stable across all configurations. All BLEU results reported in the tables correspond to BLEU-4.

C Visualization plots and Example Analysis

Analysis of Metric Correlation with chrF++. Figures 2–8 provide a detailed comparison of how different metrics correlate with chrF++ across languages, systems, and individual sentences.

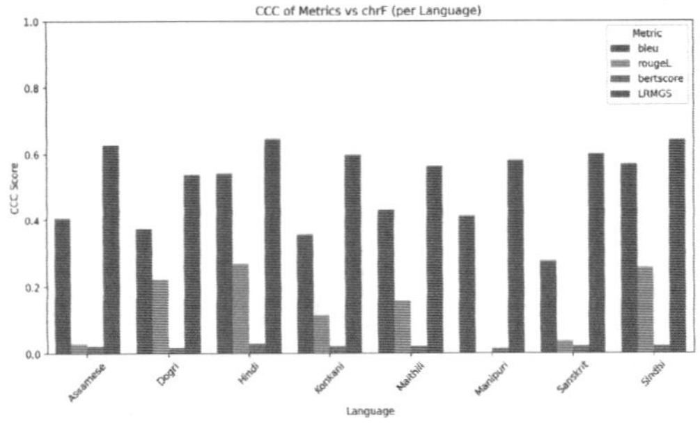

Figure 2: CCC of metrics vs. chrF++ across Indic languages. LRMGS consistently achieves the highest correlation.

Language-level correlation. Figures 2 and 3 report the concordance correlation coefficient (CCC) *between chrF++ and each other metric* (BLEU, ROUGE-L, BERTScore, LRMGS) across eight Indic languages. BLEU exhibits *moderate* agreement with chrF++ (≈0.28–0.57): e.g., Assamese ≈0.41, Dogri ≈0.38, Hindi ≈0.54, Konkani ≈0.36, Maithili ≈0.43, Manipuri ≈0.41, Sanskrit ≈0.28, Sindhi ≈0.57. ROUGE-L remains *weak* (≈0.00–0.27) and even slightly negative in Manipuri, reflecting brittle span matching under rich morphology and orthographic variation. BERTScore is *near zero* everywhere (≈0.015–0.03), indicating that sentence-level embedding similarity poorly tracks character overlap in these low-resource settings (saturation and insensitivity to small lexical differences). In contrast, LRMGS is *uniformly higher and tightly clustered* (≈0.54–0.65)—e.g., ≈0.63 for Assamese, ≈0.65 for Hindi, ≈0.60 for Konkani/Sanskrit, ≈0.64 for Sindhi—demonstrating robust concordance with chrF++ across scripts and families. The bar plot reiterates this: LRMGS dominates BLEU/ROUGE-L/BERTScore for every language, with especially strong margins in Assamese, Hindi, and Sindhi.

Why these patterns arise. BLEU's token-level n-gram matching favors languages with relatively stable tokenization (e.g., Hindi, Sindhi), while its effectiveness declines for morphologically rich or compound-heavy languages such as Sanskrit and Konkani, where surface forms diverge substantially from reference expressions. ROUGE-L's reliance on the longest common subsequence makes it highly sensitive to word order and segmentation, both of which vary considerably across Indic scripts, thereby reducing correlation with human judgments (CCC). BERTScore frequently saturates at high cosine similarity values, leading to limited variance and consequently weaker alignment with chrF++. In contrast, LRMGS integrates semantic similarity, question-aware nugget coverage, numeric fidelity, and contextual grounding, generating scores that vary meaningfully with factual and semantic alignment, thereby exhibiting stronger concordance with chrF++ patterns.

System-level correlation. Figure 4 presents CCC *between chrF++ and each metric* by model. BLEU is *variable across systems* (higher for some instruction-tuned or stronger decoders, lower for others such as BLOOMZ and Mistral-7B). ROUGE-L remains *uniformly small* (roughly 0.05–0.20), while BERTScore is *near zero* for all systems. LRMGS is *consistently mid-to-high* (typically ≈0.43–0.59) with a narrow spread across model families (Gemma, LLaMA, Qwen, GPT, etc.), indicating stable agreement with chrF++ irrespective of architecture or size.

Takeaways. (i) LRMGS demonstrates the *highest and most consistent* CCC with chrF++ across both languages and systems; (ii) BLEU remains *functional yet inconsistent*, with performance varying by language morphology and model type; (iii) ROUGE-L and BERTScore serve as *unreliable correlates* of chrF++ under multi-script, low-resource conditions due to segmentation sensitivity in ROUGE-L and embedding saturation in BERTScore.

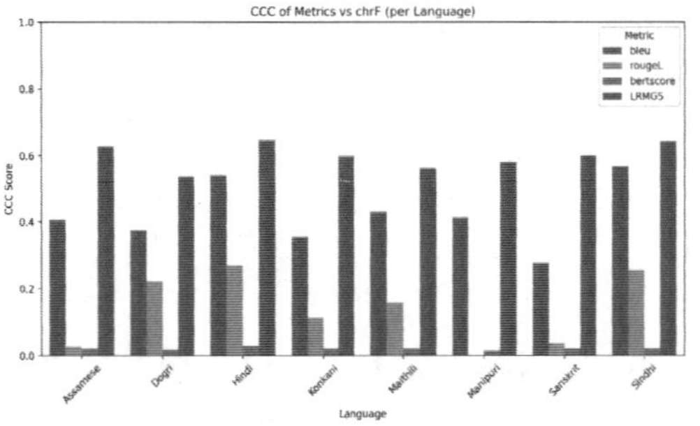

Figure 3: Language-level CCC bar plots comparing metrics with chrF++. LRMGS shows consistent improvements.

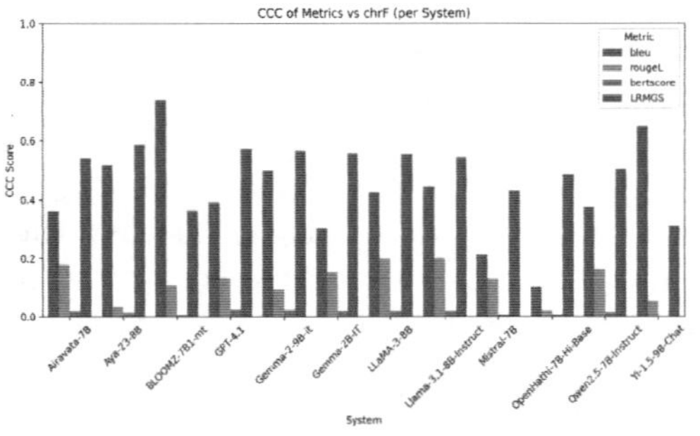

Figure 4: System-level CCC across multiple LLMs. LRMGS remains stable compared to BLEU, ROUGE-L, and BERTScore.

Sentence-level scatter plots. Figures 5–8 examine sentence-level correlations. Figure 5 shows LRMGS vs. chrF++ with a dense positive trend and strong linearity, validating its reliability at fine granularity. Figure 6 shows BLEU vs. chrF++ with weaker and noisier alignment; BLEU often fails to capture quality when chrF is moderate-to-low. Figure 7 shows BERTScore vs. chrF++, where values saturate near 1.0, leading to compressed scores and poor discrimination. Finally, Figure 8 compares chrF++ and LRMGS, highlighting that LRMGS captures semantic fidelity while maintaining correlation with character-level overlaps. This balance explains why LRMGS consistently shows higher concordance across languages and systems.

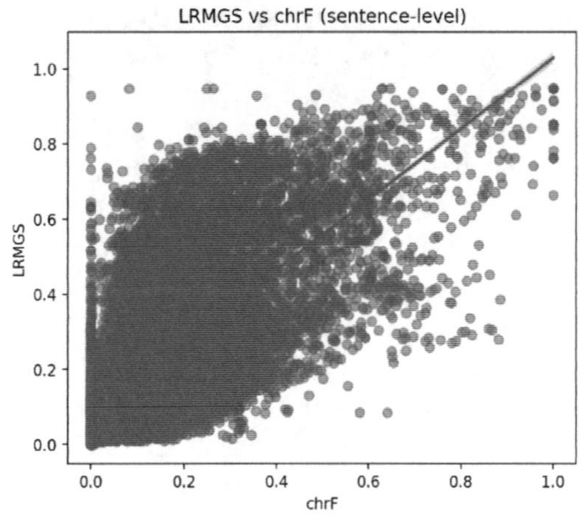

Figure 5: Sentence-level correlation of LRMGS vs. chrF++. Strong positive alignment validates reliability.

Example Analysis. Table 6 presents six GPT-4.1 QA examples across Assamese, Dogri, Maithili, and Manipuri, each showing the gold reference (Indic and English) alongside the model's output (Indic and English) evaluated using four metrics. In the first four rows (two Assamese and two Dogri examples), the model's outputs closely paraphrase the references, maintaining alignment in names, facts, and phrasing. This results in consistently high chrF++ scores (0.875–0.905), moderate BLEU values (0.531–0.809), very high BERT similarities (0.990–0.997, except 0.970/0.981), and strong LRMGS scores (0.896–0.930), collectively indicating strong semantic fidelity and contextual coverage. The Maithili example illustrates a clear failure case: the model hallucinates an unrelated religious ceremony for "FERA," causing chrF++ and BLEU to collapse (0.157/0.012), BERT similarity to drop (0.826), and LRMGS to approach zero (0.018), reflecting both lexical and semantic divergence. The Manipuri example shows partial comprehension yet limited grounding and structural coherence; metrics are mixed (chrF++ 0.304, BLEU 0.268, high BERT 0.949 due to token overlap, and very low LRMGS 0.017), demonstrating that surface similarity can be misleading. LRMGS, in contrast, effectively penalizes unfaithful or non-answering content. Overall, faithful factual matches yield high scores across metrics, whereas semantic errors or off-topic responses are strongly penalized, most notably by LRMGS.

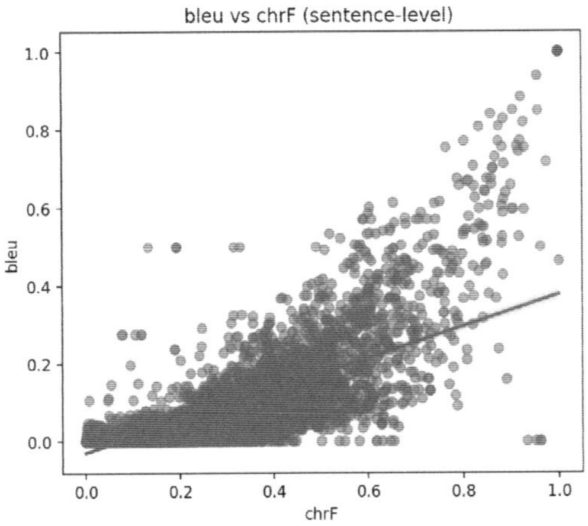

Figure 6: Sentence-level correlation of BLEU vs. chrF++. BLEU shows weaker correlation and noisy behavior.

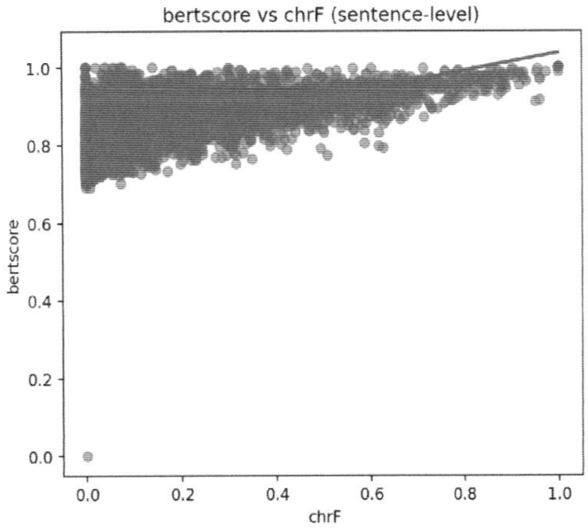

Figure 7: Sentence-level correlation of BERTScore vs. chrF. Scores saturate near 1.0, limiting discrimination.

Algorithm 1: Computation of LRMGS Metric (Symbolic Form)

Input: (Q, R), $\hat{A}$, weights $\{\lambda_{\text{BERT}}, \lambda_{\text{KC}}, \lambda_{\text{NUM}}, \lambda_{\text{EF}}\}$, temperature η

Output: LRMGS $\in [0, 1]$

1. Preprocessing:

Translate using IndicTrans2:
$Q_{en}, R_{en}, \hat{A}_{en} \leftarrow \text{Trans}_{\text{IndicTrans2}}(Q, R, \hat{A})$; split question sentences as $C_{en} = \{c_1, \ldots, c_m\}$.

2. Semantic Similarity (EN-BERT):

$\text{EN-BERT} = \frac{1}{|R_{en}|} \sum_i \max_j |\cos(\mathbf{r}_i, \mathbf{a}_j)|$.

3. Question-Aware Nugget Coverage (EN-KC):

Segment R_{en} into factual clauses $\{c_i\}_{i=1}^{n}$ and embed $\mathbf{k}_i = \text{ST\_embed}(c_i)$, $\mathbf{q} = \text{ST\_embed}(Q_{en})$, $\hat{\mathbf{a}}_j = \text{ST\_embed}(\hat{A}_{en})$.

Compute nugget attention $a_i = \frac{e^{\cos(\mathbf{k}_i, \mathbf{q})/\eta}}{\sum_j e^{\cos(\mathbf{k}_j, \mathbf{q})/\eta}}$, and compute coverage $\text{EN-KC} = \frac{\sum_i a_i \max_j |\cos(\mathbf{k}_i, \hat{\mathbf{a}}_j)|}{\sum_i a_i}$.

4. Numeric Fidelity (EN-NUM):

$N_R = \text{RegexNums}(R_{en})$, $N_{\hat{A}} = \text{RegexNums}(\hat{A}_{en})$,
$\text{EN-NUM} = \frac{|N_R \cap N_{\hat{A}}|}{|N_R \cup N_{\hat{A}}|}$.

5. Evidence Faithfulness (EN-EF):

$\mathbf{a} = \text{ST\_embed}(\hat{A}_{en})$, $\mathbf{c} = \text{ST\_embed}(C_{en})$,
$\text{EN-EF} = \max_{c \in C_{en}} \cos(\mathbf{a}, \mathbf{c})$.

6. Aggregation:

$\text{LRMGS} = (\text{EN-BERT})^{\lambda_{\text{BERT}}} (\text{EN-KC})^{\lambda_{\text{KC}}} (\text{EN-NUM})^{\lambda_{\text{NUM}}} (\text{EN-EF})^{\lambda_{\text{EF}}}$.

D Evaluation Algorithm (Symbolic)

The overall procedure for computing the Language-Robust Metric for Generative QA (LRMGS) is formalized in Algorithm 1. It integrates four components: semantic similarity (EN-BERT), question-aware keypoint extraction and coverage (EN-KP/EN-KC), numeric consistency (EN-NUM), and evidence faithfulness (EN-EF). The algorithm ensures reproducible evaluation of QA systems under multilingual and low-resource settings.

E Large Language Models and Experimental Setup

For benchmarking, a diverse suite of large language models (LLMs) was employed, encompassing both open-source Indic models and general-purpose multilingual LLMs. All models were evaluated within a unified framework designed to ensure reproducibility and fairness across Indic languages.

Models. The following LLMs were included:

- **Mistral-7B** (causal decoder-only), Hugging Face mistralai/Mistral-7B-v0.1.
- **OpenHathi-7B-Hi-Base**, optimized for Hindi and related Indic languages.
- **Qwen2.5-7B-Instruct**, trained with multilingual instruction-following data.
- **Yi-1.5-9B-Chat**, a decoder-only chat-tuned model.
- **GPT-4.1**, accessed via API, serving as a high-capacity commercial baseline.
- **Gemma-2-9B-it**, Google's instruction-tuned Gemma model with strict chat templates.
- **Airavata-7B**, an Indic-focused model from AI4Bharat using open-instruct style prompting.

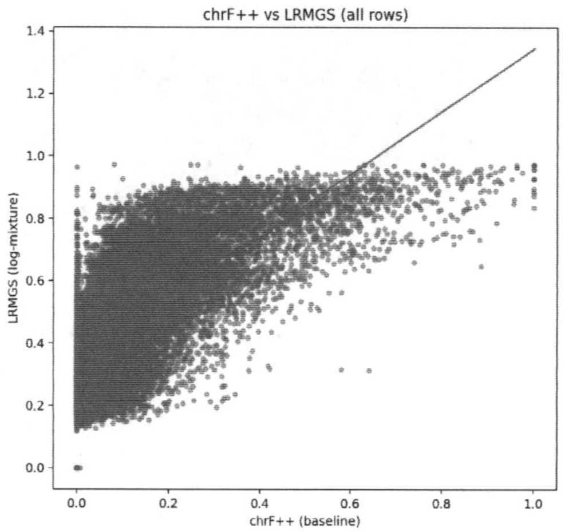

Figure 8: Comparison of chrF++ vs. LRMGS at the sentence level. LRMGS maintains correlation while capturing semantic fidelity.

- **Aya-23-8B**, multilingual instruction-tuned model, designed for cross-lingual tasks.
- **LLaMA-3.1-8B-Instruct**, a chat-aligned model with strict system–user templates.
- **BLOOMZ-7B1-mt**, multilingual instruction-tuned model by BigScience.

Prompting formats. Two prompting styles were employed across models to ensure consistency and reproducibility.

General format

Answer the following question in [LANGUAGE] clearly and concisely. Question: {question} Answer:

This general instruction-based template was used for all causal and instruction-tuned models (Mistral, OpenHathi, Qwen, Yi, Gemma, Airavata, Aya, LLaMA, BLOOMZ). It explicitly enforces the target [LANGUAGE] and promotes concise answers.

GPT-4.1 (chat format)

"role": "user", "content": "Question: {question}"

GPT-4.1 requires a chat-style JSON format with explicit user roles. This reflects its native API design, which allows role-based conversation management.

Table 6: Illustrative GPT-4.1 examples with Question, References (Indic & EN), Outputs (Indic & EN), and scores (chrF++/BLEU/BERT/LRMGS).

Language: Assamese **Question (EN):** Khandesh region was captured by Mughal Emperor Akbar in which year? **Reference (Indic):** ১৬০১ চনত মোগল সম্রাট আকবৰে খানদেশ অঞ্চল দখল কৰে। **Reference (EN):** In 1601, the Mughal Emperor Akbar conquered the Khandesh region. **Output (Indic):** খানদেশ অঞ্চল ১৬০১ চনত মোগল সম্রাট আকবৰে দখল কৰিছিল। **Output (EN):** The Khandesh region was conquered by the Mughal Emperor Akbar in 1601. **Scores:** chrF++ = 0.800 BLEU = 0.531 BERT = 0.970 LRMGS = 0.930
Language: Assamese **Question (EN):** Which Anglo-Maratha war resulted in merging the Peshwas' territories with the Bombay Presidency? **Reference (Indic):** তৃতীয় এংলো-মাৰাঠা যুদ্ধৰ ফলত পেশ্বৰসকলৰ ভূখণ্ড বম্বে ৰাষ্ট্ৰপতিৰ সৈতে একত্ৰিত হয়। **Reference (EN):** The Third Anglo-Maratha War united the territory of the Peshwas with the Bombay Presidency. **Output (Indic):** তৃতীয় এংলো-মাৰাঠা যুদ্ধৰ ফলত পেশ্বৱাৰ ভূখণ্ড বম্বে ৰাষ্ট্ৰপতিৰ সৈতে একত্ৰিত হৈছিল। **Output (EN):** The Third Anglo-Maratha War united the Peshwa territory with the Bombay Presidency. **Scores:** chrF++ = 0.883 BLEU = 0.588 BERT = 0.981 LRMGS = 0.906
Language: Dogri **Question (EN):** The words "Satyameva Jayate" in the State Emblem adopted by the Government of India have been taken from which Upanishad? **Reference (Indic):** "सत्यमेव जयते" शब्द मुंडक उपनिषद थमां लैते गेदे न। **Reference (EN):** The words "Satyameva Jayate" are taken from the Mundaka Upanishad. **Output (Indic):** "सत्यमेव जयते" शब्द मुण्डक उपनिषद थमां लैते गेदे न। **Output (EN):** The words "Satyameva Jayate" are taken from the Mundaka Upanishad. **Scores:** chrF++ = 0.905 BLEU = 0.597 BERT = 0.997 LRMGS = 0.905
Language: Dogri **Question (EN):** In which caves is the Kailasha temple located? **Reference (Indic):** कैलाशा मंदिर एलोरा गुफाएं च स्थित ऐ। **Reference (EN):** Kailasha Temple is located in the Ellora Caves. **Output (Indic):** कैलाश मंदिर एलोरा गुफाएं च स्थित ऐ। **Output (EN):** Kailash Temple is located in Ellora Caves. **Scores:** chrF++ = 0.875 BLEU = 0.809 BERT = 0.990 LRMGS = 0.896
Language: Maithili **Question (EN):** What is FERA and when was it introduced? **Reference (Indic):** 1973 कें विदेशी मुद्रा नियमन अधिनियम (फेरा) विदेशी मुद्रा, प्रतिभूतियक, मुद्रा कें आयात आ निर्यात आ विदेशीक कें द्वारा अचल संपत्ति कें अधिग्रहण सं संबंधित किछु भुगतान कें नियंत्रित करय कें लेल एकटा अधिनियम छै. **Reference (EN):** The Foreign Exchange Regulation Act of 1973 (FERA) regulates foreign exchange, securities, currency, and certain payments related to acquisition of immovable property by foreigners. **Output (Indic):** फेरा एकटा धार्मिक अनुष्ठान छी जे सिख धर्म में विवाहक समय होइत अछि। ई गुरु ग्रंथ साहिब केर समक्ष वर-वधू द्वारा चारि बेर घुमि-घुमि क' कएल जाइत अछि। फेरा सिख धर्म में गुरु नानक देव जी केर समय सँ शुरू भेल। **Output (EN):** Fera is a religious ceremony in Sikhism performed during marriage, where the couple circles the Guru Granth Sahib four times; it dates back to the time of Guru Nanak Dev Ji. **Scores:** chrF++ = 0.157 BLEU = 0.012 BERT = 0.826 LRMGS = 0.018
Language: Manipuri **Question (EN):** When was the Employment Guarantee Scheme (EGS) introduced in Maharashtra? **Reference (Indic):** ꯏꯝꯞꯂꯣꯏꯃꯦꯟꯇ ꯒꯦꯔꯦꯟꯇꯤ ꯁ꯭ꯀꯤꯝ (ꯏ.ꯖꯤ.ꯑꯦꯁ.) ꯑꯁꯤ ꯃꯥꯔꯆ ꯲꯸, ꯱꯹꯷꯲ꯗꯥ ꯍꯧꯗꯣꯀꯈꯤ꯫꯫ **Reference (EN):** The Employment Guarantee Scheme (EGS) was introduced on 28 March. **Output (Indic):** ꯏ.ꯖꯤ.ꯑꯦꯁ. ꯀꯗꯥꯌꯗꯒꯤ ꯍꯧꯗꯣꯀꯈꯤꯕꯒꯦ ꯑꯃꯁꯤ ꯃꯍꯥꯔꯥꯁ꯭ꯠꯔꯗꯥ ꯁ꯭ꯀꯤꯝ **Output (EN):** E.G.S.—when did you start the scheme in Maharashtra? **Scores:** chrF++ = 0.304 BLEU = 0.268 BERT = 0.949 LRMGS = 0.017

NumPert: Numerical Perturbations to Probe Language Models for Veracity Prediction

Peter Røysland Aarnes **Vinay Setty**
University of Stavanger
peter.r.aarnes@uis.no, vsetty@acm.org

Abstract

Large language models show strong performance on knowledge intensive tasks such as fact-checking and question answering, yet they often struggle with numerical reasoning. We present a systematic evaluation of state-of-the-art models for veracity prediction on numerical claims and evidence pairs using controlled perturbations, including label-flipping probes, to test robustness. Our results indicate that even leading proprietary systems experience accuracy drops of up to 62% under certain perturbations. No model proves to be robust across all conditions. We further find that increasing context length generally reduces accuracy, but when extended context is enriched with perturbed demonstrations, most models substantially recover. These findings highlight critical limitations in numerical fact-checking and suggest that robustness remains an open challenge for current language models.

1 Introduction

Verifying claims in social media, political debates, and press releases has become essential. While platforms such as Politifact, Snopes, and FullFact support manual fact-checking, their scalability is limited. Numerical claims, in particular, are tedious and error prone for human annotators (Aly et al., 2021). Neural language models provide a promising alternative for evidence retrieval and preliminary veracity

Numerical Perturbation Example

Original Claim: *"In 2020, the company's revenue was 5,000,000 dollars, making a significant growth from the previous year".*
[Label: TRUE, **Model Prediction:** TRUE ✓]

Perturbed Claim: *"In 2020, the company's revenue was fifty million dollars making a significant growth from the previous year."*
[Label: FALSE, **Model Prediction:** TRUE ✗]

Evidence: *"A market analysis by MNO Research Group, published in 2021, states: 'PQR Innovations experienced significant growth (...). The revenue for the year 2020 reached 5,000,000 dollars."*[1em]

Figure 1: Example illustrating how the original 'TRUE' claim is perturbed into a 'FALSE' claim, yet the model predicts 'TRUE'.

assessment (Guo et al., 2022; Dmonte et al., 2024; Setty, 2024). Yet, recent studies show that both transformer models fine-tuned for numerical claim verification and general purpose large language models struggle with numerical reasoning (Wallat et al., 2024; V et al., 2024; Akhtar et al., 2023), and the reasons remain unclear.

Although prior work has studied LLM fragility in numerical reasoning for QA (Xu et al., 2022) and tabular NLI (Akhtar et al., 2023), no systematic analysis exists for veracity prediction in long-context fact-checking. Our results indicate that models are prone to errors with longer context and reasoning chains. To address this gap, we evaluate state-of-the-art models of different sizes and architectures

Proceedings of the IJCNLP-AACL 2025 Student Research Workshop, pages 78–95
December 20-24, 2025 ©2025 Association for Computational Linguistics

under varied prompting settings with systematically perturbed numerical claims and evidence.

Manipulating numerical values in unstructured text requires care to ensure that perturbations remain meaningful. We define six probe types: Numeration (*Num*), Approximation (*Approx*), *Range*, Masking (*Mask*), Random Replacement (*Rand-Repl*), and Negative Number (*Neg-Num*) (see Table 1) to systematically modify numbers while preserving claim intent. In some cases, these perturbations also flip the factual label (e.g., changing $5,000,000 to fifty million; see Figure 1). All perturbations are manually verified to ensure correctness and relevance. This study addresses three research questions:

RQ1 : *Which models in our selection of diverse sizes are most and least robust?*

RQ2 : *Which numerical perturbations most affect performance?*

RQ3 : *How do context length and reasoning chains influence robustness?*

To answer this, we test models on claim–evidence pairs, comparing baseline predictions with those on numerically perturbed claims. Larger gaps reflect weaker robustness. We use truthful probes that keep the original label and label-flipping probes that contradict the evidence, under zero-shot, two-shot, and perturbation aware prompts (PAP).

Our results show that all state-of-the-art models are highly vulnerable to numerical perturbations, particularly under *Mask* and *Neg-Num*. We also notice that zero-shot settings outperform two-shot, while providing a few perturbed examples (PAP prompt) helps models recover in most cases. These findings reveal weaknesses in LLM veracity prediction.

2 Related work

The interpretability of LLMs is critical for knowledge-intensive tasks like question answering and fact-checking. Probing studies have revealed their opaque decision processes (Belinkov, 2022). For instance, Yang et al. (2024); Lu et al. (2023); Frieder et al. (2024) showed that while LLMs can perform complex reasoning, they often struggle with basic numeracy.

Several works have examined numerical reasoning in LLMs. Wallace et al. (2019) probed embeddings from BERT and GloVe, finding inherent but inconsistent numeracy. Akhtar et al. (2023) evaluated models on tabular data with a hierarchical taxonomy, showing no model excels across all tasks. Xu et al. (2022); Zhou et al. (2024) demonstrated that numerical perturbations in QA often mislead LLMs, while Paruchuri et al. (2024); Chen et al. (2024) highlighted weaknesses in numerical reasoning. Several studies also reveal that LLMs for fact-checking are brittle to textual perturbations, and adversarial edits (Mamta and Cocarascu, 2025; Przybyła et al., 2024; Liu et al., 2025).

Despite prior advances, key gaps remain. Most work does not examine numerical reasoning in *open-domain fact-checking* with real-world, long-context data, and reproducibility is often limited. For instance, Akhtar et al. (2023) rely on synthetic tabular inputs with short context, provide incomplete perturbation details, and lack an accessible repository. In contrast, we evaluate numerical reasoning in realistic, unstructured settings, introduce perturbations that preserve semantic validity, and release full code and data to ensure reproducibility.

3 Methodology

Our study examines veracity prediction models by systematically perturbing numerical values in claims to assess their impact on label prediction. The methodology involves (1) curating a dataset with diverse numerical expressions (e.g., statistics), (2) applying controlled perturbations (e.g., scaling, replacements, masking). (3) Extensive error analysis leveraging the reasoning tokens.

Table 1: The number of claims per perturbation type that remain 'True' (T→T), remain 'False' (F→F), or switch from 'True' to 'False' (T→F). Unperturbed baseline has 260 True claims and 604 False claims.

Category	T→T	F→F	T→F
Num	213	490	213
Approx	170	404	170
Range	188	411	188
Mask	✗	490	213
Rand-Repl	✗	490	213
Neg-Num	✗	89	51

3.1 Dataset and Preprocessing

We use the *QuanTemp* dataset (V et al., 2024), which contains real world claim-evidence pairs with numerical focus from reputable fact checking sources. Each pair is labeled as True, False, or Conflicting. For our evaluation, we exclude the *Conflicting* class due to its inherent ambiguity. To prevent shortcut learning, we remove summaries from all pairs, requiring models to assess veracity solely from evidence.

Each claim is processed with the spaCy NER tagger (covering *Cardinal*, *Money*, *Percent*, *Time*, *Date*, and *Ordinal*), and numerical values are normalized to digits using the *Word2Number* library (similar to (Akhtar et al., 2023; Wallace et al., 2019; Xu et al., 2022)). Perturbed claims are *manually verified* for validity, and invalid cases are removed.

3.2 Perturbation Techniques

We adopt the numerical reasoning taxonomy of Akhtar et al. (2023) (see Table 1). The *Num*, *Approx*, and *Range* settings perturb numbers while remaining consistent with the evidence, so True claims stay True. Conversely, *Mask*, *Rand-Repl*, and *Neg-Num* modify values such that True claims flip to False, while False claims remain unchanged. We do not perturb False to True, since falsity can stem from multiple factors and counterfactual claims are often infeasible. Exploring this direction is left for future work. Now we explain the different perturbation techniques:

***Num*:** Tests whether models recognize equivalence between digits and words (e.g., "12" vs. "twelve"), preserving the original label for non-flipping probes. Perturbation applies to Cardinal, Percent, and Money, but not to Ordinal, Time, or Date, except for cardinal numbers within Time (e.g., "24 hours" to "twenty four hours"). For the label-flipping probes, the original number is modified (e.g., "12" could be perturbed to "fifteen").

***Approx*:** Non-flipping probes reduces precision by rounding and adding *about* (e.g., "1,025 dollars" to "about 1000 dollars"), retaining truth when close to the evidence. For the label-flipping probes, the original value is altered so that it is no longer reflective of the true amount (e.g., original"1,025 dollars" to "about 1200 dollars").

***Range*:** Non-flipping probes replaces exact values with spans (e.g., "25 percent" to "between 20 and 30 percent"), testing reasoning over intervals. The label-flipping probes modifies the span such that the original number is not within it (e.g., the original "25 percent" is perturbed to "between 30 and 40 percent").

***Rand-Repl*:** Replaces numbers with random values of equal digit length (e.g., "100,000" to "423,823"), mismatching the evidence.

***Mask*:** Hides numbers with "#" tokens according to digit length, including delimiters (e.g., "100,000" to "#######"), requiring inference from evidence.

***Neg-Num*:** Converts values to negatives (e.g., "4%" to "-4%"), applied only to percentages since other entities (money, time, dates) typically use linguistic cues like "decrease."

3.3 Prompting Strategy

All models use identical instructions under three prompting strategies: (1) **Zero-shot** with only instructions and no demonstrations (see Appendix B), (2) **Two-shot** prompt that extends the zero-shot prompt with one `True` and one `False` demonstration from training data with evidence and rationale (Brown et al., 2020). (3) We also test models with a perturbation aware prompt **(PAP)**, which pairs a perturbed claim with one sentence evidence for each perturbation type and flipped label. A similar approach is used by (Hu et al., 2024) in a RAG setting. Full prompts are provided in Appendix B.

4 Experimental Setup

This section describes our experimental framework, including the language models used, and evaluation methods.

4.1 Model Selection

Open-weight LLMs: *DeepSeek-R1-32B*, *Qwen3-32B*, *Llama3.3-70B*, *Llama 3.2-1B*, and *Mistral-7B* (All models are from Ollama framework[1] with Q4_K_M quantization).

Proprietary LLMs: *GPT-4o (v2024-08-06)*, *GPT-4o-mini (v2024-07-18)*, *GPT-5 (v2025-08-07)*, *GPT-o3 (v2025-04-16)*, and *Gemini 2.5 Flash (v2025-06)* (All models are accessed via their respective official APIs)

Models with thinking are marked with superscript T. All models ran with temperature 0 and JSON output; open-weight and OpenAI models used default (medium) reasoning effort. For Gemini 2.5 Flash^T, we fixed the thinking budget to 8192 (vs. the default 1) for cost efficiency. Other settings followed defaults. We exclude *Llama 3.2-1B* and *Mistral-7B* from the main results due to limited robustness; details are in Appendix A.2. Invalid predictions are rare, except for DeepSeek-R1^T, which yields 6.8% invalid outputs under zero-shot. Thinking variants generally produce more invalid outputs than their non-thinking counterparts (see Appendix C). Code and data can be accessed though our GitHub repository[2].

[1] `https://ollama.com/search`

4.2 Evaluation

Robustness is assessed by comparing baseline performance on non-perturbed claims with performance on perturbed ones. We use per-class accuracy metric. We use accuracy as the primary metric for $T \rightarrow F$ evaluations. To gain greater insight into model errors, we manually analyze reasoning tokens of zero-shot vs. PAP for `T` $\rightarrow$ `F` claims to look for common patterns that models fall into while evaluating a claim.

5 Results

We report results across models and perturbation settings. We first describe performance on unperturbed claims, then analyze changes under non-flipped and flipped label conditions. Results for `False` $\rightarrow$ `False` cases are omitted here for brevity (see Appendix A.2). Models are evaluated under three prompting regimes defined in Section 3.3 (see Appendix B for full prompts).

5.1 `True` $\rightarrow$ `False`

We start with the most challenging case: label-flipping perturbations (`True` $\rightarrow$ `False`), shown in Table 2. Since the claim and ground-truth label are flipped, all reported results reflect the flipped label. A drop in performance means models still predict `True` instead of the expected `False` and less robust. Performance on unperturbed `True` claims is given in the "Original" column as the baseline for each prompting regime.

[2] `https://github.com/iai-group/adversarial_attack_numerical_claims/`

Table 2: Accuracy (reported in %) for 'True' dataset split for label flips perturbations (True → False), and comparing accuracy variance between the flipped probes to model performance on unaltered *original* claims accuracy (-x indicates a drop; +x indicates an increase). Values in bold denote the highest accuracy within each perturbation setting, separated by open-weight and proprietary models.

Model	Original	Approx	Neg-num	Num	Rand-repl	Range	Mask
Zero-shot							
Llama3.3-70B	87.32	87.65$^{+0.32}$	**62.75**$^{-24.58}$	68.54$^{-18.78}$	**91.08**$^{+3.76}$	82.45$^{-4.88}$	10.80$^{-76.53}$
DeepSeek-R1-32B	81.69	**89.41**$^{+7.72}$	39.22$^{-42.47}$	56.34$^{-25.35}$	88.73$^{+7.04}$	81.91$^{+0.22}$	**23.47**$^{-58.22}$
DeepSeek-R1-32B^{T}	**87.44**	85.06$^{-2.37}$	31.91$^{-55.52}$	69.43$^{-18.01}$	84.73$^{-2.71}$	86.98$^{-0.46}$	10.63$^{-76.81}$
Qwen3-32B	84.35	78.24$^{-6.12}$	43.14$^{-41.21}$	58.78$^{-25.57}$	84.51$^{+0.16}$	80.32$^{-4.03}$	16.43$^{-67.92}$
Qwen3-32B^{T}	85.99	89.38$^{+3.38}$	34.04$^{-51.95}$	**78.24**$^{-7.75}$	87.88$^{+1.89}$	**87.64**$^{+1.65}$	12.38$^{-73.61}$
GPT-4o	80.00	88.82$^{+8.82}$	47.06$^{-32.94}$	73.24$^{-6.76}$	90.61$^{+10.61}$	91.49$^{+11.49}$	19.25$^{-60.75}$
GPT-4o-Mini	**85.38**	68.24$^{-17.15}$	25.49$^{-59.89}$	56.81$^{-28.58}$	78.87$^{-6.51}$	75.00$^{-10.38}$	11.27$^{-74.12}$
GPT-5^{T}	76.15	93.53$^{+17.38}$	33.33$^{-42.82}$	**86.38**$^{+10.23}$	89.20$^{+13.05}$	92.02$^{+15.87}$	19.72$^{-56.44}$
GPT-o3^{T}	75.77	89.41$^{+13.64}$	25.49$^{-50.28}$	84.98$^{+9.21}$	88.73$^{+12.96}$	90.96$^{+15.19}$	21.60$^{-54.17}$
Gemini 2.5F	82.69	**95.29-**$^{+12.60}$	54.90$^{-27.79}$	83.57$^{+0.88}$	**96.71**$^{+14.02}$	**93.09**$^{+10.39}$	**25.82**$^{-56.87}$
Gemini 2.5F^{T}	71.54	88.82$^{+17.29}$	**58.82**$^{-12.71}$	82.63$^{+11.09}$	89.67$^{+18.13}$	90.43$^{+18.89}$	16.90$^{-54.64}$
Two-shot							
Llama3.3-70B	**91.55**	72.35$^{-19.20}$	**33.33**$^{-58.22}$	46.48$^{-45.07}$	78.26$^{-13.29}$	57.98$^{-33.57}$	8.92$^{-82.63}$
DeepSeek-R1-32B	89.67	65.29$^{-24.38}$	21.57$^{-68.10}$	37.09$^{-52.58}$	74.70$^{-14.97}$	58.51$^{-31.16}$	12.21$^{-77.46}$
DeepSeek-R1-32B^{T}	86.32	88.55$^{+2.23}$	22.00$^{-64.32}$	71.15$^{-15.17}$	88.49$^{+2.17}$	87.17$^{+0.85}$	9.43$^{-76.89}$
Qwen3-32B	79.81	70.59$^{-9.22}$	37.25$^{-42.56}$	49.77$^{-30.05}$	66.40$^{-13.41}$	72.87$^{-6.94}$	**20.66**$^{-59.15}$
Qwen3-32B^{T}	83.49	**86.98**$^{+3.49}$	27.45$^{-56.04}$	**78.20**$^{-5.29}$	**88.76**$^{+5.26}$	**87.23**$^{+3.74}$	12.74$^{-70.75}$
GPT-4o	86.54	82.35$^{-4.19}$	33.33$^{-53.21}$	68.54$^{-17.99}$	87.32$^{+0.79}$	85.64$^{-0.90}$	13.62$^{-72.92}$
GPT-4o-Mini	**89.62**	67.06$^{-22.56}$	27.45$^{-62.16}$	50.70$^{-38.91}$	77.46$^{-12.15}$	73.94$^{-15.68}$	20.19$^{-69.43}$
GPT-5^{T}	77.69	**91.18**$^{+13.48}$	29.41$^{-48.28}$	84.04$^{+6.35}$	88.26$^{+10.57}$	88.83$^{+11.14}$	18.78$^{-58.91}$
GPT-o3^{T}	75.77	89.41$^{+13.64}$	23.53$^{-52.24}$	**85.45**$^{+9.68}$	89.67$^{+13.90}$	**90.43**$^{+14.66}$	22.07$^{-53.70}$
Gemini 2.5F	85.00	87.06$^{+2.06}$	35.29$^{-49.71}$	70.89$^{-14.11}$	**94.37**$^{+9.37}$	85.64$^{+0.64}$	**22.90**$^{-62.10}$
Gemini 2.5F^{T}	74.23	90.00$^{+15.77}$	**52.94**$^{-21.29}$	82.16$^{+7.93}$	92.02$^{+17.79}$	88.83$^{+14.60}$	15.96$^{-58.27}$
Perturbation Aware Prompt (PAP)							
Qwen3-32B	79.34	89.41$^{+10.07}$	76.47$^{-2.87}$	73.71$^{-5.63}$	90.61$^{+11.27}$	89.36$^{+10.02}$	**67.61**$^{-11.74}$
Qwen3-32B^{T}	71.23	**95.27**$^{+24.04}$	74.00$^{+2.77}$	**90.14**$^{+18.91}$	**94.37**$^{+23.14}$	**94.62**$^{+23.40}$	44.85$^{-26.38}$
Gemini 2.5F	**81.92**	**97.06**$^{+15.14}$	74.51$^{-7.41}$	84.98$^{+3.05}$	**97.18**$^{+15.26}$	**94.68**$^{+12.76}$	29.11$^{-52.82}$
Gemini 2.5F^{T}	63.08	91.76$^{+28.69}$	**88.24**$^{+25.16}$	**86.85**$^{+23.78}$	92.02$^{+28.94}$	90.96$^{+27.88}$	26.29$^{-36.79}$

5.1.1 Performance on Unperturbed Claims

In zero-shot, most models cluster in the low to high eighties, with Llama 3.3-70B performing best at about 87% and Qwen3-32B^{T}is close behind at 86%. Proprietary models are slightly lower, with GPT-4o-Mini reaching about 85% as the strongest performer. This suggests that larger models may require more specified prompts to achieve higher accuracy.

With two-shot prompting, baselines increase for Llama 3.3-70B, the GPT variants, and DeepSeek-R1. Llama 3.3-70B surpasses 91%. In contrast, Qwen3-32B variants decline, Gemini 2.5F drops slightly, and its thinking variant shows a modest improvement. Under PAP, both Qwen and Gemini models exhibit performance declines. Models get confused by PAP since it contains counterfactual examples.

Overall, adding few-shot examples improves baselines for Llama and GPT models but tends to reduce them for Qwen and Gemini. No-

Table 3: Accuracy (reported in %) on the 'True' dataset split under non label-flipping perturbations (True → True). The table compares perturbed accuracy to unaltered *original* claim accuracy (-x indicates a drop; +x indicates an increase). Values in bold denote the highest accuracy within each perturbation setting, separated by open-weight and proprietary models.

Model	Approx	Num	Range
Zero-shot			
Llama3.3-70B	71.76$^{-15.56}$	**86.38**$^{-0.94}$	70.21$^{-17.11}$
DeepSeek-R1	75.29$^{6.40}$	82.63$^{+0.94}$	67.55$^{14.14}$
DeepSeek-R1^T	**81.44**$^{-6.00}$	84.62$^{-2.82}$	**79.23**$^{-8.20}$
Qwen3	73.53$^{-10.82}$	85.88$^{+1.53}$	62.23$^{-22.12}$
Qwen3-32B^T	79.39$^{-6.60}$	85.02$^{-0.97}$	78.24$^{-7.76}$
GPT-4o	68.82$^{-11.18}$	80.28$^{+0.28}$	55.32$^{-24.68}$
GPT-4o-Mini	**81.18**$^{-4.21}$	**92.96**$^{+7.57}$	**79.79**$^{-5.60}$
GPT-5^T	75.29$^{-0.86}$	77.00$^{+0.84}$	73.40$^{-2.75}$
GPT-o3^T	74.71$^{1.06}$	77.46$^{+1.70}$	77.66$^{+1.89}$
Gemini 2.5F	60.69$^{-22.00}$	79.81$^{-2.88}$	43.92$^{-38.78}$
Gemini 2.5F^T	68.24$^{-3.30}$	71.76$^{+0.22}$	61.70$^{-9.84}$
Two-shot			
Llama3.3-70B	84.71$^{6.84}$	90.14$^{1.41}$	85.64$^{5.91}$
DeepSeek-R1	**88.82**$^{-0.85}$	**90.61**$^{+0.94}$	**86.70**$^{2.97}$
DeepSeek-R1^T	82.25$^{-4.07}$	87.50$^{+1.18}$	77.13$^{-9.19}$
Qwen3-32B	72.94$^{-6.87}$	81.69$^{+1.88}$	67.02$^{-12.79}$
Qwen3-32B^T	81.66$^{-1.83}$	84.43$^{+0.94}$	77.72$^{-5.77}$
GPT-4o	77.06$^{-9.48}$	85.92$^{-0.62}$	63.83$^{-22.71}$
GPT-4o-Mini	**81.18**$^{8.44}$	**89.67**$^{+0.06}$	**76.06**$^{13.55}$
GPT-5^T	78.82$^{+1.13}$	80.28$^{+2.59}$	73.94$^{-3.76}$
GPT-o3^T	75.29$^{-0.48}$	79.34$^{+3.57}$	74.47$^{-1.30}$
Gemini 2.5F	75.88$^{-9.12}$	87.79$^{+2.79}$	70.74$^{-14.26}$
Gemini 2.5F^T	74.12$^{-0.11}$	76.53$^{+2.30}$	71.28$^{-2.95}$
PAP			
Qwen3-32B	58.82$^{-14.39}$	72.74$^{-0.47}$	44.41$^{-28.79}$
Qwen3-32B^T	**62.13**$^{-15.46}$	**77.60**$^{+0.02}$	**66.94**$^{-10.65}$
Gemini 2.5F	**60.00**$^{21.92}$	**81.69**$^{0.23}$	53.19$^{-28.73}$
Gemini 2.5F^T	57.65$^{-5.43}$	63.38$^{+0.30}$	**54.79**$^{-8.29}$

tably, the thinking variants consistently perform slightly worse than their non-thinking counterparts, possibly due to the "overthinking" phenomenon as defined by (Sui et al., 2025), in which reasoning models produce unnecessarily long and elaborate chains of reasoning that ultimately reduce problem-solving efficiency – a pattern confirmed by our error analysis (see Section 6.1). Among open-weight LLMs, performance is stronger in zero-shot and two-shot prompts, but when label-flipping examples are included, Gemini 2.5F outperforms Qwen3-32B.

Performance on unperturbed false claims is generally higher, reflecting the fact that fact-checking tasks predominantly target false claims. Consistent with earlier observations, open-weight models exhibit slightly stronger results than proprietary counterparts. A comprehensive analysis is presented in Appendix A.2.

5.1.2 Performance on Perturbed Claims

Now we summarize the change in performance under numerical perturbation. The Table 2 shows the change in accuracy values in red or green superscript depending on if the accuracy deceases or increases to the corresponding baseline with unperturbed original claims.

Masking and negative number perturbations are consistently the most challenging across prompting regimes. Masking yields very low accuracy in zero-shot setting (max 26%), as models often treat masked tokens as placeholders and predict `True`. With negative numbers, accuracy typically falls below 20% for masking and 30–50% overall, except Llama 3.3-70B, which maintains 63%; many models dismiss negatives as typos. Range and approximation perturbations raise accuracy for Qwen, DeepSeek, GPTs (not Mini), and Gemini, showing a preference for approximate over exact values. Numeration perturbations hurt open-weight models (Qwen3-32B, Llama 3.3-70B) but help proprietary systems (GPT-5^T, GPT-o3^T, Gemini 2.5F), reflecting stronger handling of surface forms.

In two-shot settings, similar trend to zero-shot is observed with slight drop in performance overall. With notable exceptions being DeepSeek-R1, Llama 3.3-70B, and Qwen3-32B drop sharply on approximation, while thinking models, GPT-5^T, GPT-o3^T, and Gemini 2.5F^T, gain on approximate perturbations.

For the rest of the perturbations, a similar trend to that of zero-shot is observed.

Finally, we find that introducing a single label-flipping demonstration for each perturbation type (PAP, shown in Appendix B) substantially boosts performance across all perturbations. The most striking gains appear in reasoning-oriented models, which display far greater robustness than their non-thinking counterparts. In the case of *Neg-Num*, these models not only surpass their baselines but also achieve strong improvements on perturbations such as simple numeration and ranged replacements. Notably, Qwen3-32B recovers to over 67%, underscoring the effectiveness of this model to leverage perturbed demonstrations, although masking remains a persistent challenge for Gemini. For Qwen, enabling the thinking variant consistently strengthens performance in most cases, whereas for Gemini the benefits are more uneven—showing improvements in certain perturbations but minimal change in others.

5.2 `True` $\rightarrow$ `True`

Table 3 shows the results for `True` $\rightarrow$ `True` perturbations. *Neg-Num*, *Rand-Repl* and *Mask* are not relevant when preserving labels.

With few exceptions, most models struggle on *Approx* and *Range* perturbations, though the drop is modest compared to `True` $\rightarrow$ `False` setting. This suggests that replacing numerical values with approximations or ranges, while preserving truth, can still mislead models into predicting `False`. In contrast, performance under *Num* perturbations remains relatively robust. Unlike label-flipping cases, perturbed PAP does not improve performance; instead, they often confuse models into misclassifying `True` claims as `False`. Surprisingly, GPT-4o-Mini, despite being smaller performs the best under this setting.

6 Discussion

RQ1: Across all experiments, *no single model emerges as universally the most robust*, though Gemini 2.5F and Qwen3-32B models come closest. Our results show that models are generally more robust on `False` claims (Tables 5 and 4) than on `True` claims (Tables 2 and 3). With perturbed false demonstrations, Gemini 2.5F^T achieves near-ceiling accuracy on *Approx*, *Range*, and *Rand-Repl*, and shows the largest recovery on *Neg-Num*; without such calibration, Gemini 2.5F offers the best default balance, consistently leading on *Rand-Repl* and *Range*.

Among open-weight systems, Qwen3-32B^T is the most stable across regimes and uniquely strong on *Mask* when provided perturbed examples, while Llama 3.3-70B excels on zero-shot *Neg-Num* but becomes brittle under two-shot. By contrast, DeepSeek-R1 is the least stable, showing sharp two-shot degradations on *Approx* and *Num*, indicative of harmful anchoring effects.

RQ2: *Neg-Num* and *Mask* appear to be the hardest perturbations among all prompt settings. With perturbation aware prompt (PAP), there is modest recovery and even then the gains are model-dependent (e.g., Gemini 2.5F^T). The *Rand-Repl* and *Range* perturbations are the most straightforward, consistently improving accuracy across models and prompting regimes. The *Num* and *Approx* perturbations fall in the middle: "thinking" models such as GPT-5^T, GPT-o3^T, and Gemini 2.5F^T often gain from these perturbations, while many open-weight base models lose accuracy under two-shot prompts, likely because demonstrations with different numerical notation confuse the models—suggesting that these rely more heavily on superficial formatting cues, making them more sensitive to inconsistencies in numeric representation.

RQ3: Across both Gemini 2.5F^T and

Qwen3-32B^T, misclassified instances consistently involve longer inputs than correct predictions. For Gemini 2.5F^T, misclassifications show $\sim$15% more total tokens than correct cases, largely driven by a $\sim$38% increase in reasoning tokens (877 vs. 635 on average). For Qwen, the effect is even stronger: misclassified examples carry $\sim$41% more total tokens, with reasoning length nearly doubling ($\sim$876 vs. 397, a $\sim$120% increase). Prompt tokens also inflate in misclassifications, albeit more modestly (e.g., $\sim$3–10% increases across models). Taken together, these findings suggest that models tend to fail when they have longer prompt and reasoning tokens (*overthinking* (Sui et al., 2025)), with inflated reasoning chains being a strong marker of misclassification. While PAP prompts introduce longer inputs overall, they provide targeted demonstrations that help mitigate these failures by guiding models toward more stable reasoning. Detailed breakdowns are presented in Appendix B.5.

6.1 Error Analysis

To better understand model errors, we analyze thinking tokens under the $T \rightarrow F$ setting for Qwen3-32B^T and Gemini 2.5F^T, focusing on zero-shot errors that recover in PAP. Appendix C, Table 10 shows specific samples. Our analysis reveals the following reasoning patterns:

Numerical strictness: In PAP reasoning, models tend to interpret numbers more rigidly than in zero-shot. For instance, a claim citing \$330,000 against evidence of \$300,000 was treated as a minor discrepancy in zero-shot, but as a significant mismatch in PAP, predicting `False`.

Masking fallacies: In the zero-shot setting, masked numbers were often treated as placeholders, leading the model to "complete" the claim from evidence rather than verify it. Under PAP reasoning, the model more frequently flagged missing values as critical, aligning with the masked prompt examples and rejecting unverifiable claims. In some cases, however, it ignored the masking and reached the correct verdict, but for spurious reasons such as assuming small discrepancies in the evidence.

Typo interpretation: In the negative-number perturbation setting, under zero-shot, models often interpreted the negative sign (–) as a typo, treating it as a misplaced hyphen and discarding it during evaluation, which led to misclassifications. Under PAP prompting, however, the model highlighted the negative sign as a crucial discrepancy, correctly identifying it as evidence that invalidated the claim.

Overthinking: In some cases, models generate unnecessarily elaborate reasoning that obscures straightforward evidence. For example, for the claim *"Of the [more than 2 million] work opportunities created, more than 1 million have been taken up by the youth"*, the evidence clearly shows 2.5 million created and 1.1 million taken by youth (45%). Instead of rejecting the claim directly, the model speculated about time windows and approximation thresholds, leading to a wrong verdict. This illustrates how excessive reasoning can derail simple numerical checks.

7 Conclusion and Future Work

We introduced a framework for systematically perturbing numerical claims in claim–evidence pairs to evaluate the robustness of state-of-the-art LLMs in veracity prediction. Our results show that even leading systems suffer sharp performance drops under controlled numerical edits, providing the first comprehensive evidence that *numerical robustness in long-context fact-checking remains an open challenge*. Beyond prior work on textual or adversarial perturbations, our study is novel in designing semantically valid numerical perturbations and demonstrating that perturbation-aware prompting can partially recover performance.

As a preliminary step, this work opens several directions: perturbing the evidence side of claim–evidence pairs, designing fine-grained probes that target sub-claims, and extending the framework to multi-hop reasoning and counterfactual scenarios.

8 Limitations

Our experiments are constrained by the selection of models tested. Additionally, they were conducted in a black-box environment, restricting access to model weights, parameters, and other internal insights. Some perturbation datasets are also limited in size; a larger and more diverse sample would enhance the robustness of our findings. For reasons discussed in previous sections, our experiments focus exclusively on binary veracity classification ('True' and 'False'), omitting more granular classifications and False-to-True perturbations. Expanding the scope to include these aspects could offer a more comprehensive understanding of model performance under different conditions. Lastly, as with most classification tasks involving LLMs, there is a potential risk of data leakage from training data, which could influence the final evaluation and affect the results.

9 Ethical Considerations

Our research highlights the strengths and weaknesses of various models in binary veracity and counterfactual classification. While this type of research presents valuable opportunities to enhance model security and resilience. However, it also necessitates a thoughtful approach to ethical concerns. For our experiments, some models outperform others, yet we do not endorse any specific model for fact-checking tasks. Fact-checking itself is a nuanced and complex issue. Journalists, fact-checkers, and researchers alike risk introducing inadvertent bias into their work, a concern that also extends to the use of LLMs.

Additionally, while the goal of our experiments is to bring greater attention to LLM performance in specific tasks, these findings also highlight vulnerabilities and encourage the development of more robust models. However, these techniques have multipurpose potential and could be exploited for harmful purposes if misapplied.

Acknowledgements

This research is funded by SFI MediaFutures partners and the Research Council of Norway (grant number 309339).

References

Mubashara Akhtar, Abhilash Shankarampeta, Vivek Gupta, Arpit Patil, Oana Cocarascu, and Elena Simperl. 2023. Exploring the numerical reasoning capabilities of language models: A comprehensive analysis on tabular data. In *Findings of the Association for Computational Linguistics: EMNLP 2023*, ACL '23, pages 15391–15405.

Rami Aly, Zhijiang Guo, Michael Sejr Schlichtkrull, James Thorne, Andreas Vlachos, Christos Christodoulopoulos, Oana Cocarascu, and Arpit Mittal. 2021. Feverous: Fact extraction and verification over unstructured and structured information. In *Thirty-fifth Conference on Neural Information Processing Systems Datasets and Benchmarks Track*.

Yonatan Belinkov. 2022. Probing classifiers: Promises, shortcomings, and advances. *Computational Linguistics*, 48(1):207–219.

Tom B. Brown, Benjamin Mann, Nick Ryder, Melanie Subbiah, Jared Kaplan, et al. 2020. Language models are few-shot learners. In *Advances in Neural Information Processing Systems*.

Kejie Chen, Lin Wang, Qinghai Zhang, and Renjun Xu. 2024. Metarulegpt: Recursive numerical reasoning of language models trained with simple rules. *arXiv preprint arXiv:2412.13536*.

Alphaeus Dmonte, Roland Oruche, Marcos Zampieri, Prasad Calyam, and Isabelle Augenstein. 2024. Claim verification in the age of large language models: A survey. *arXiv preprint arXiv:2408.14317*.

Simon Frieder, Luca Pinchetti, Ryan-Rhys Griffiths, Tommaso Salvatori, Thomas Lukasiewicz, Philipp Petersen, and Julius Berner. 2024. Mathematical capabilities of chatgpt. *Advances in neural information processing systems*, 36.

Zhijiang Guo, Michael Sejr Schlichtkrull, and Andreas Vlachos. 2022. A survey on automated fact-checking. *Transactions of the Association for Computational Linguistics*, 10:178–206.

Zhibo Hu, Chen Wang, Yanfeng Shu, Hye-Young Paik, and Liming Zhu. 2024. Prompt perturbation in retrieval-augmented generation based large language models. In *Proceedings of the 30th ACM SIGKDD Conference on Knowledge Discovery and Data Mining*, pages 1119–1130.

Fanzhen Liu, Alsharif Abuadbba, Kristen Moore, Surya Nepal, Cecile Paris, Jia Wu, Jian Yang, and Quan Z Sheng. 2025. Adversarial attacks against automated fact-checking: A survey. *arXiv preprint arXiv:2509.08463*.

Pan Lu, Liang Qiu, Wenhao Yu, Sean Welleck, and Kai-Wei Chang. 2023. A survey of deep learning for mathematical reasoning. In *Proceedings of the 61st Annual Meeting of the Association for Computational Linguistics (Volume 1: Long Papers)*, pages 14605–14631.

Mamta and Oana Cocarascu. 2025. Facteval: Evaluating the robustness of fact verification systems in the era of large language models. In *Proceedings of the 2025 Conference of the North American Chapter of the Association for Computational Linguistics (NAACL)*.

Akshay Paruchuri, Jake Garrison, Shun Liao, John B. Hernandez, Jacob Sunshine, Tim Althoff, Xin Liu, and Daniel McDuff. 2024. What are the odds? language models are capable of probabilistic reasoning. In *Proceedings of the 2024 Conference on Empirical Methods in Natural Language Processing*, pages 11712–11733, Miami, Florida, USA. Association for Computational Linguistics.

Piotr Przybyła, Alexander Shvets, and Horacio Saggion. 2024. Verifying the robustness of automatic credibility assessment. *Natural Language Processing Journal*.

Vinay Setty. 2024. Surprising efficacy of fine-tuned transformers for fact-checking over larger language models. In *Proceedings of the 47th International ACM SIGIR Conference on Research and Development in Information Retrieval (SIGIR '24)*, pages 2842–2846.

Yang Sui, Yu-Neng Chuang, Guanchu Wang, Jiamu Zhang, Tianyi Zhang, Jiayi Yuan, Hongyi Liu, Andrew Wen, Shaochen Zhong, Na Zou, Hanjie Chen, and Xia Hu. 2025. Stop overthinking: A survey on efficient reasoning for large language models. *Preprint*, arXiv:2503.16419.

Venktesh V, Abhijit Anand, Avishek Anand, and Vinay Setty. 2024. Quantemp: A real-world open-domain benchmark for fact-checking numerical claims. In *Proceedings of the 47th International ACM SIGIR Conference on Research and Development in Information Retrieval*, Sigir '24, pages 650–660.

Eric Wallace, Yizhong Wang, Sujian Li, Sameer Singh, and Matt Gardner. 2019. Do nlp models know numbers? probing numeracy in embeddings. In *Proceedings of the 2019 Conference on Empirical Methods in Natural Language Processing and the 9th International Joint Conference on Natural Language Processing (EMNLP-IJCNLP)*, pages 5307–5315, Hong Kong, China. Association for Computational Linguistics.

Jonas Wallat, Adam Jatowt, and Avishek Anand. 2024. Temporal blind spots in large language models. In *Proceedings of the 17th ACM International Conference on Web Search and Data Mining*, WSDM '24, page 683–692.

Jialiang Xu, Mengyu Zhou, Xinyi He, Shi Han, and Dongmei Zhang. 2022. Towards Robust Numerical Question Answering: Diagnosing Numerical Capabilities of NLP Systems. In *Proceedings of the 2022 conference on empirical methods in natural language processing*, EMNLP '22, pages 7950–7966.

Haotong Yang, Yi Hu, Shijia Kang, Zhouchen Lin, and Muhan Zhang. 2024. Number cookbook: Number understanding of language models and how to improve it. *arXiv preprint arXiv:2411.03766*.

Wei Zhou, Mohsen Mesgar, Heike Adel, and Annemarie Friedrich. 2024. Freb-tqa: A fine-grained robustness evaluation benchmark for table question answering. In *Proceedings of the 2024 Conference of the North American Chapter of the Association for Computational Linguistics: Human Language Technologies (Volume 1: Long Papers)*, pages 2479–2497.

A Appendix

The appendix includes additional details of the perturbation methods used, a summary of the False $\rightarrow$ False evaluation, and the evidence document and evaluation for the two-shot examples.

A.1 Perturbation Details

This section provides a brief description of additional details regarding the perturbation methods. For full script details, refer to the GitHub repository[3].

A.1.1 Numeration

For numbers that should not match the original numerical value in the unperturbed claim, the value is increased by 10%, then converted from digits to words.

A.1.2 Approximation

Each type applies context-specific rounding to create conversational approximations rounding, and adds "about" as an approximation prefix. If all numbers, if it is less than 10 and a decimal number, the number gets round to the nearest .5.

- *Cardinal*: Rounds to tens, hundreds, thousands, or hundred-thousands based on magnitude.
- *Percentage*: Rounds to tens or hundreds, preserving exact values for small percentages.
- *Money*: Similar to Cardinal—with a currency symbol and preserves decimal detail for small amounts.
- *Date*: Rounds to the nearest decade.
- *Time*: Rounds to tens or hundreds depending on magnitude.

For the label-flipping probes, the original numerical value is multiplied randomly by a factor 0.5, 0.6, 1.4, or 1.5, and then rounded as described above.

[3] https://github.com/iai-group/adversarial_attack_numerical_claims/

Table 4: Accuracy performance for the 'False' class, in the'False' dataset split with perturbations where numerical values have been adjusted to remain similar to the original false claim while maintaining the label, i.e., False $\rightarrow$ False (-x indicates a drop; +x indicates an increase). Values in bold denote the highest accuracy within each perturbation setting, separated by open-weight and proprietary models.

Model	Original	Approx	Num	Range
One-shot				
Llama 3.2-1B	5.71	$5.45^{-0.27}$	$6.53^{+0.82}$	$6.81^{+1.10}$
Llama 3.3-70B	93.67	$94.06^{+0.39}$	$93.47^{-0.20}$	$92.21^{-1.46}$
Mistral-7B	96.53	$95.79^{-0.74}$	$96.33^{-0.20}$	$95.62^{-0.91}$
DeepSeek-R1	**97.14**	$\mathbf{97.28}^{+0.13}$	$\mathbf{96.94}^{-0.20}$	$96.84^{-0.31}$
DeepSeek-R1^T	95.86	$95.56^{-0.31}$	$96.13^{+0.27}$	$94.56^{-1.30}$
Qwen3-32B	96.12	$96.29^{+0.16}$	96.12	$\mathbf{97.32}^{+1.20}$
Qwen3-32B^T	95.92	$94.99^{-0.93}$	$95.90^{-0.01}$	$95.15^{-0.76}$
GPT-4o	**96.52**	$\mathbf{97.28}^{+0.75}$	$\mathbf{97.14}^{+0.62}$	$\mathbf{97.08}^{+0.56}$
GPT-4o-Mini	93.05	$93.32^{+0.27}$	$92.45^{-0.60}$	$93.19^{+0.14}$
GPT-5	95.20	$95.05^{-0.15}$	$96.12^{+0.92}$	$95.13^{-0.06}$
GPT-o3	95.36	$94.06^{-1.30}$	$95.92^{+0.55}$	$94.40^{-0.96}$
Gemini 2.5F	93.21	$95.05^{+1.84}$	$93.88^{+0.67}$	$96.11^{+2.90}$
Gemini 2.5F^T	92.05	$90.84^{-1.21}$	$90.69^{-1.36}$	$90.02^{-2.03}$
Two-shot				
Llama 3.2-1B	10.00	$6.93^{-3.07}$	$10.20^{+0.20}$	$9.73^{-0.27}$
Llama 3.3-70B	95.92	$96.04^{+0.12}$	$95.51^{-0.41}$	$93.19^{-2.73}$
Mistral-7B	87.76	$88.12^{+0.36}$	$88.78^{+1.02}$	$87.10^{-0.65}$
DeepSeek-R1	95.92	$95.79^{-0.13}$	$95.71^{-0.20}$	$96.84^{+0.92}$
DeepSeek-R1^T	96.07	$95.73^{-0.34}$	$96.27^{+0.20}$	$94.35^{-1.72}$
Qwen3-32B	**97.76**	$\mathbf{97.28}^{-0.48}$	**97.76**	$\mathbf{97.32}^{-0.43}$
Qwen3-32B^T	95.91	$96.04^{+0.13}$	$96.33^{+0.42}$	$94.88^{-1.03}$
GPT-4o	**96.36**	$\mathbf{97.28}^{+0.92}$	$\mathbf{96.12}^{-0.24}$	$\mathbf{97.32}^{+0.97}$
GPT-4o-Mini	92.38	$95.79^{+3.41}$	$93.88^{+1.49}$	$95.38^{+2.99}$
GPT-5	95.20	$94.55^{-0.64}$	$96.12^{+0.92}$	$95.13^{-0.06}$
GPT-o3	94.87	$94.55^{-0.31}$	$95.10^{+0.23}$	$94.89^{+0.02}$
Gemini 2.5F	92.72	$95.54^{+2.83}$	$94.49^{+1.77}$	$95.62^{+2.91}$
Gemini 2.5F^T	92.38	$91.58^{-0.80}$	$94.08^{+1.70}$	$90.27^{-2.12}$
PAP				
Qwen3-32B	96.12	$\mathbf{96.78}^{+0.66}$	$\mathbf{96.53}^{+0.41}$	$\mathbf{97.20}^{+1.08}$
Qwen3-32B^T	**96.72**	$96.40^{-0.32}$	$96.39^{-0.33}$	$95.84^{-0.89}$
Gemini 2.5F	92.88	$\mathbf{95.30}^{+2.42}$	$92.24^{-0.64}$	$\mathbf{95.13}^{+2.25}$
Gemini 2.5F^T	**93.54**	$90.84^{-2.70}$	$\mathbf{92.65}^{-0.89}$	$90.02^{-3.52}$

A.1.3 Range

In the range perturb setting, for when the numerical values should be within the span of the original, the lower bounds we perturb the number by $\pm 10\%$. For *ordinal*, we subtract and add 1 to the original value to create the range bound.

In instances where the labels are flipped, the numerical span will be outside of the range of the original number.

Table 5: Accuracy performance for the `False` class, in the'False' dataset split with perturbations where numerical values have been modified to differ from the original false claim while preserving the label, i.e., `False` → `False` (-x indicates a drop; +x indicates an increase). Values in bold denote the highest accuracy within each perturbation setting, separated by open-weight and proprietary models.

Model	Original	Approx	Neg-num	Num	Rand-repl	Range	Mask
			Zero-shot				
Llama2-1B	5.71	5.45$^{-0.27}$	5.62$^{-0.10}$	6.33$^{+0.61}$	4.90$^{-0.82}$	5.35$^{-0.36}$	5.92$^{+0.20}$
Llama3.3-70B	93.67	96.53$^{+2.86}$	93.26$^{-0.42}$	96.12$^{+2.45}$	96.73$^{+3.06}$	95.62$^{+1.95}$	92.86$^{-0.82}$
Mistral-7B	96.53	97.28$^{+0.75}$	95.51$^{-1.02}$	96.33$^{-0.20}$	96.73$^{+0.20}$	96.35$^{-0.18}$	95.31$^{-1.22}$
DeepSeek-R1	**97.14**	**98.51**$^{+1.37}$	**96.63**$^{-0.51}$	97.96$^{+0.82}$	**98.16**$^{+1.02}$	**98.30**$^{+1.15}$	**97.55**$^{+0.41}$
DeepSeek-R1^T	95.86	96.57$^{+0.71}$	91.57$^{-4.30}$	97.42$^{+1.56}$	97.61$^{+1.75}$	97.44$^{+1.58}$	93.74$^{-2.13}$
Qwen3-32B	96.12	98.27$^{+2.14}$	95.51$^{-0.62}$	97.96$^{+1.84}$	97.96$^{+1.84}$	98.30$^{+2.17}$	95.31$^{-0.82}$
Qwen3-32B^T	95.92	96.74$^{+0.83}$	94.32$^{-1.60}$	**98.22**$^{+2.30}$	97.74$^{+1.82}$	98.03$^{+2.11}$	94.01$^{-1.91}$
GPT-4o	**96.52**	**97.77**$^{+1.25}$	**96.63**$^{+0.11}$	**98.16**$^{+1.64}$	**98.16**$^{+1.64}$	**97.81**$^{+1.29}$	**96.53**$^{+0.01}$
GPT-4o-Mini	93.05	96.04$^{+2.99}$	92.13$^{-0.91}$	95.71$^{+2.67}$	95.92$^{+2.87}$	96.84$^{+3.79}$	93.27$^{+0.22}$
GPT-5	95.20	96.29$^{+1.09}$	91.01$^{-4.19}$	97.55$^{+2.35}$	97.35$^{+2.15}$	96.84$^{+1.64}$	95.51$^{+0.31}$
GPT-o3	95.36	96.04$^{+0.68}$	91.01$^{-4.35}$	96.94$^{+1.57}$	96.94$^{+1.57}$	96.84$^{+1.47}$	95.51$^{+0.15}$
Gemini 2.5F	93.21	97.28$^{+4.07}$	94.38$^{+1.17}$	96.94$^{+3.73}$	97.96$^{+4.75}$	97.08$^{+3.87}$	93.88$^{+0.67}$
Gemini 2.5F^T	92.05	93.30$^{+1.25}$	87.64$^{-4.41}$	95.31$^{+3.25}$	94.90$^{+2.84}$	96.09$^{+4.04}$	88.98$^{-3.07}$
			2-S				
Llama2-1B	10.00	7.92$^{-2.08}$	7.87$^{-2.13}$	7.76$^{-2.24}$	9.18$^{-0.82}$	9.25$^{-0.75}$	7.76$^{-2.24}$
Llama3.3-70B	95.92	97.52$^{+1.61}$	95.51$^{-0.41}$	96.73$^{+0.82}$	97.87$^{+1.95}$	95.38$^{-0.54}$	95.10$^{-0.82}$
Mistral-7B	87.76	87.38$^{-0.38}$	87.64$^{-0.11}$	88.57$^{+0.82}$	88.78$^{+1.02}$	87.35$^{-0.41}$	87.35$^{-0.41}$
DeepSeek-R1	95.92	98.27$^{+2.35}$	93.26$^{-2.66}$	96.73$^{+0.82}$	85.26$^{-10.66}$	98.05$^{+2.14}$	95.51$^{-0.41}$
DeepSeek-R1^T	96.07	96.50$^{+0.43}$	94.25$^{-1.81}$	97.32$^{+1.25}$	96.79$^{+0.73}$	98.03$^{+1.97}$	94.61$^{-1.46}$
Qwen3-32B	**97.76**	**99.01**$^{+1.25}$	**97.75**$^{-0.00}$	**98.98**$^{+1.22}$	**98.93**$^{+1.18}$	**98.54**$^{+0.79}$	**97.55**$^{-0.20}$
Qwen3-32B^T	95.91	97.52$^{+1.61}$	94.38$^{-1.53}$	97.96$^{+2.05}$	98.04$^{+2.13}$	97.57$^{+1.66}$	96.11$^{+0.20}$
GPT-4o	**96.36**	**98.51**$^{+2.16}$	**98.88**$^{+2.52}$	**97.55**$^{+1.19}$	**97.96**$^{+1.60}$	**98.05**$^{+1.70}$	95.51$^{-0.85}$
GPT-4o-Mini	92.38	96.29$^{+3.90}$	94.38$^{+2.00}$	95.92$^{+3.53}$	96.94$^{+4.55}$	97.08$^{+4.70}$	95.31$^{+2.92}$
GPT-5	95.20	96.04$^{+0.84}$	92.13$^{-3.06}$	97.55$^{+2.35}$	97.35$^{+2.15}$	97.08$^{+1.88}$	**96.12**$^{+0.92}$
GPT-o3	94.87	96.53$^{+1.67}$	91.01$^{-3.86}$	97.35$^{+2.48}$	96.94$^{+2.07}$	97.08$^{+2.21}$	95.31$^{+0.44}$
Gemini 2.5F	92.72	97.03$^{+4.31}$	95.51$^{+2.79}$	96.94$^{+4.22}$	96.73$^{+4.02}$	96.36$^{+3.64}$	93.88$^{+1.16}$
Gemini 2.5F^T	92.38	94.31$^{+1.92}$	89.89$^{-2.50}$	95.94$^{+3.56}$	96.13$^{+3.75}$	96.11$^{+3.72}$	90.82$^{-1.57}$
			PAP				
Qwen3-32B	95.10	**98.51**$^{+3.41}$	**95.51**$^{+0.40}$	98.16$^{+3.06}$	98.57$^{+3.47}$	98.54$^{+3.44}$	**97.55**$^{+2.45}$
Qwen3-32B^T	**97.13**	97.77$^{+0.65}$	95.51$^{-1.62}$	**98.98**$^{+1.85}$	**98.57**$^{+1.44}$	**98.54**$^{+1.41}$	95.88$^{-1.25}$
Gemini 2.5F	92.88	**97.52**$^{+4.64}$	**96.63**$^{+3.75}$	**97.14**$^{+4.26}$	**98.16**$^{+5.28}$	**97.81**$^{+4.93}$	**94.29**$^{+1.40}$
Gemini 2.5F^T	**93.54**	94.31$^{+0.76}$	92.13$^{-1.41}$	96.94$^{+3.40}$	96.94$^{+3.40}$	95.62$^{+2.08}$	89.39$^{-4.16}$

A.2 Summary of Model Behavior Under Numerical Perturbations for False Dataset Split (False → False)

Table 5 presents False → False perturbations where numerical values are modified while preserving the false label. Our experiments reveal that large models (e.g., GPT-4o, GPT-4o-Mini, Gemini 2.5F) and open-weight DeepSeek-R1^T maintain high robustness across perturbations, with accuracies typically above 90%. Smaller models such as Llama 3.2-1B and Mistral-7B degrade sharply, especially under *Approx* and *Range*. Qwen3-32B^{T}performs consistently well across shots, rivaling proprietary systems. Notable anomalies include Gemini

Example 1	Example 2
Claim: As Republicans try to repeal the Affordable Care Act, they should be reminded every day that **36,000** people will die yearly as a result.	**Claim:** We see a quarter-billion dollars in a pension fund that needs to be funded at **$1.2 billion**.
Evidence: *Gift Article Share* "As Republicans try to repeal the Affordable Care Act, they should be reminded every day that **36,000 people** will die yearly as a result." — **Sen. Bernie Sanders (D-Vt.)**, in a tweet, Jan. 12, 2017.	**Evidence:** Providence Mayor Angel Taveras had to deal with near bankruptcy in the capital city after he took office in 2011. As the city struggled to fix its budget problems, he won union concessions to reduce pension costs. The most recent figures show the plan is only **31.4-percent funded**.
Evaluation: False	**Evaluation:** True

Table 6: True and False examples of claims and their labels based on evidence used in the prompt.

2.5F's drop under *Approx* (-5 to -6 points) despite strong overall performance, and GPT-4o-Mini's unexpected gains in two-shot ($+3$ points). Reasoning-enabled (^{T}) variants generally improve robustness, though Gemini's thinking variant remains more variable.

The table 4, reports accuracy metric for the False class in the False dataset split with perturbations. Perturbations significantly modify numerical values while preserving the label (False $\rightarrow$ False). Results are presented for multiple LLMs including Llama, Mistral, DeepSeek, GPT, Gemini, and Qwen across three evaluation setups: Zero-shot, two-shot, and Perturbation-Aware Prompt (PAP). The columns indicate different perturbation types: Original (baseline), Approx, Neg-num, Num, Rand-repl, Range, and Mask. Superscripts with negative values denote drops relative to the baseline, and positive values denote improvements.

In the zero-shot setting, DeepSeek-R1, GPT-4o, and Qwen3-32B^T achieve the highest and most stable performance, maintaining accuracies between 96% and 98% across perturbations. Gemini 2.5F is also stable with scores in the range of 93% to 97%. In contrast, smaller models such as Llama 3.2-1B perform poorly with accuracies around 5–6%. Mid-sized models like Llama 3.3-70B and Mistral-7B perform well but remain slightly below the frontier models.

In the two-shot setting, accuracy improves slightly compared to Zero-shot, especially for the smaller models. DeepSeek-R1 remains strong with scores around 96–97%, GPT-4o reaches 95–98%, Qwen3-32B^T achieves 94–98%, and Gemini 2.5F^T remains consistent with 90–96%. Llama 3.2-1B, however, continues to perform poorly with accuracies only between 7% and 10%.

Perturbation-Aware Prompt (PAP) delivers the highest overall accuracies. Qwen3-32B^T and DeepSeek-R1^T achieve 95–99% across all perturbations, while Gemini 2.5F^T also shows strong performance with accuracies between 89% and 97%. PAP consistently improves the already strong models by about 1–2 percentage points compared to zero-shot and two-shot.

In general, model scale is critical. Small

models such as Llama 3.2-1B collapse under this evaluation, while large-scale and frontier models like DeepSeek, GPT-4o, Qwen, and Gemini perform near ceiling. Prompting with two-shot increases stability across most models, and PAP proves to be the most robust method, yielding the best and most consistent results overall.

B Prompt

For the LLMs we use the same instruction and two-shot examples. The zero-shot only includes the instruction, whereas the two-shot includes the instruction and the sample data. The following two-shot examples are snippets of the examples used. For the full prompt, refer to our GitHub repository.

B.1 System Prompt

The following prompt was used as the model system prompt:

You are a professional fact checker, your task is to classify whether the given claim is true or false based on the evidence text provided.

B.2 Instruction

The following prompt was used along with two examples from Table 6:

Given the claim and evidence provided, classify the claim as "label": true if it is true, and "label": false if it is false.

B.3 Two-shot Examples

Table 6 presents two examples of fact-checking claims used in the prompt for LLMs along with their corresponding evidence and veracity evaluations. The two examples are used for all LLMs and all perturbation inputs to be consistent. And each of the two example represents the two distinct labels in the dataset.

B.4 Perturbation Aware Prompt

The following prompt was added to the instruction prompt for the negative example experiments:

The numbers in the evidence may not match the claim. For example:

Claim: The Eiffel Tower is three hundred and fifty-one meters tall. Evidence: The Eiffel Tower is 330 meters tall. "label": false

Claim: The year-over-year U.S. inflation rate at the end of 2024 was -2.9%. Evidence: The year-over-year U.S. inflation rate at the end of 2024 was 2.9"label": false

Claim: The birth rate in Japan in 2023 was between 2 to 2.5. Evidence: The birth rate in Japan in 2023 was 1.2. "label": false

Claim: The population of Canada in 2023 was about 45 million. Evidence: The population of Canada in 2023 was 40.5 million by October 2023. "label": false

Claim: Saturn has 789 moons. Evidence: Discoveries bring Saturn's total moon count to 274, nearly triple Jupiter's and more than the total number of known moons around the other planets. "label": false

Claim: The Wembley Stadium in London has a seating capacity of ######. Evidence: The Wembley Stadium in London has a seating capacity of 90,000. "label": false

B.5 Prompt Length Analysis

We perform prompt length analysis for misclassified instances compared to correct classifications for the two most stable models–Gemini 2.5F^T and Qwen3-32B^T.

Gemini 2.5F^T In misclassified instances, Gemini 2.5-Flash tends to have longer reasoning token length overall, with average total token length increasing by 15% compared to correct predictions (2103 vs. 1822 tokens). Prompt tokens show only a modest difference (+3%). The distribution further suggests that

Perturbation	Prompt Tokens		Reasoning Tokens	
	Misclassified	Correct	Misclassified	Correct
Approximation	2158.7	1303.9	1265.1	371.2
Negative Number	1214.5	1073.2	846.5	339.0
Numeration	1648.2	1239.6	796.1	378.4
Random Replacement	1576.4	1323.8	713.2	363.8
Range	1963.4	1315.1	698.4	401.1
Masking	1234.7	1017.8	717.1	427.7

Table 7: Comparison of average prompt and reasoning token lengths for Qwen3-32B^T between **misclassifications** and **correct classifications** in the Zero-shot setting.

errors are associated with longer and more variable reasoning chains (max reasoning length over 6k tokens), whereas correct predictions are achieved with more compact reasoning. In other words, misclassifications correlate strongly with *overthinking*.

Qwen3-32B^T For Qwen3-32B^T, misclassified cases consistently exhibit inflated reasoning lengths compared to correctly classified instances in the Zero-shot setting (Table 7). For example, reasoning tokens nearly triple in *Approx* (1265 vs. 371) and more than double in *Num* (796 vs. 378) and *Range* (698 vs. 401). Prompt lengths are also consistently higher for misclassifications, with the most pronounced gap in *Approx*, where prompts expand by over 65% (2159 vs. 1304). The anomaly occurs with *Mask*, where reasoning remains high even in misclassifications (717 vs. 428), indicating that masked inputs elicit extended elaboration regardless of correctness. Overall, Qwen3-32B^T tends to over-reason when it misclassifies, while correct predictions are characterized by shorter, more efficient reasoning chains and more compact prompts. All token lengths for Qwen3-32B^T zero-shot settings are shown in Table 7.

C Invalid Output Analysis

As shown in Table 8, across the open-weight models, invalid outputs are virtually absent

Model	Total Instances	Invalid	% Invalid
	Zero-shot		
DeepSeek-R1:32B	8841	0	0.00
DeepSeek-R1:32B^T	6837	477	6.98
LLaMA-3.2 1B-Instruct	6837	0	0.00
LLaMA-3.3 70B	6837	0	0.00
Mistral-7B	6837	0	0.00
Qwen-3 32B	7041	0	0.00
Qwen-3 32B^T	6553	165	2.52
	Two-shot		
DeepSeek-R1:32B	6951	0	0.00
DeepSeek-R1:32B^T	6951	78	1.12
LLaMA-3.2 1B-Instruct	6837	0	0.00
LLaMA-3.3 70B	6951	0	0.00
Mistral-7B	6837	0	0.00
Qwen-3 32B	6951	0	0.00
Qwen-3 32B^T	6951	23	0.33
	PAP		
DeepSeek-R1:32B	6837	0	0.00
DeepSeek-R1:32B^T	6837	92	1.35
LLaMA-3.2 1B-Instruct	6837	0	0.00
LLaMA-3.3 70B	6837	0	0.00
Mistral-7B	6837	0	0.00
Qwen-3 32B	6837	0	0.00
Qwen-3 32B^T	6837	55	0.80

Table 8: Invalid outputs across open-weight models, grouped by shot setting. Thinking-enhanced variants are marked with ^{T}. Percentages are calculated as invalid/total $\times$ 100.

in the non-thinking variants: Llama 3.3-70B, Llama-3.2 1B instruct, Mistral-7B, Qwen3-32B, and DeepSeek-R1 consistently produce 0.00% invalidity across all shot settings. By contrast, enabling thinking introduces instability. For instance, DeepSeek-R1^T exhibits a sharp rise in invalid generations under zero-shot (6.98%), which decreases under two-shot (1.12%) and PAP (1.35%), indicating some recovery with examples. Similarly, Qwen3-

Model	Total Instances	Invalid	% Invalid
	Zero-shot		
GPT-4o	5298	0	0.00
GPT-4o-mini	5298	0	0.00
GPT-5	5298	0	0.00
GPT-o3	5298	1	0.02
Gemini-2.5^T	5295	174	3.29
Gemini-2.5	5298	1	0.02
	Two-shot		
GPT-4o	5298	0	0.00
GPT-4o-mini	5298	0	0.00
GPT-5	5298	0	0.00
GPT-o3	5298	2	0.04
Gemini-2.5^T	5298	82	1.55
Gemini-2.5	5298	42	0.79
	PAP		
Gemini-2.5^T	5298	231	4.36
Gemini-2.5	5298	0	0.00

Table 9: Invalid outputs across proprietary models and Gemini variants, grouped by shot setting. Percentages are calculated as invalid/total $\times$ 100.

32B^{T}yields 2.52% invalidity in zero-shot, reduced to 0.33% under two-shot, but climbing again to around 0.80–1.33% with perturbation-aware prompts.

These findings reveal a clear pattern: while open-weight models without reasoning remain robust against invalid outputs, their reasoning-enabled counterparts are consistently more error-prone. Zero-shot is the most unstable regime, two-shot offers stabilizing effects, and PAP shows mixed outcomes depending on the model.

As shown in Table 9, for proprietary systems, invalid outputs are exceedingly rare except in the Gemini family. GPT-4o, GPT-4o-Mini, GPT-5^T, and GPT-o3^{T}maintain near-perfect robustness across all shot settings, with invalid rates between 0.00–0.04%. By contrast, Gemini 2.5F demonstrates a higher susceptibility to invalid generations. In particular, Gemini 2.5F^T reaches 3.29% invalidity under zero-shot, improves to 1.55% with two-shot calibration, but rises again to 4.36% under PAP. Its non-thinking counterpart is much more stable, remaining below 1% invalidity in all cases.

Overall, proprietary models without reasoning capabilities (GPT family and Gemini 2.5F) are extremely stable, while reasoning-enabled variants of Gemini incur significantly higher invalid rates, especially in zero-shot and PAP settings.

True → False Perturbed Claims	Reasoning Output Snippets	Analysis Summary
The various offices of state government have purchased more than $########## in vehicles, not counting leases, for use from the Governor on down during the last two years.	**Gemini 2.5F^T** zero-shot: "(...)While the claim uses a placeholder, the evidence substantiates the 'more than $11 millionfigure with precision. I will now mark the claim as true." **Gemini 2.5F^T** PAP:"(...)I'm now certain the claim is false. The instruction's emphasis on placeholders makes the 'more than' condition irrelevant. The claim is inherently un-verifiable (...)"	In the zero-shot evaluation the model assumes that the model needs to find the missing value. PAP nudges the model in the correct direction, predicting the claim as false for the correct reasons.
Some states, like Montana and Nebraska, are getting more than three hundred and thirty thousand dollars in federal stimulus money per reported COVID-19 case. New York is the hardest-hit state and yet we are getting only about thirteen thousand, two hundred dollars per case.	**Gemini 2.5F^T** zero-shot: "(...) I am also considering whether the small discrepancy in the funding figures makes the overall claim inaccurate (...) The claim is essentially true, even with minor discrepancies" **Gemini 2.5F^T** PAP: "(...) claim states '$13,200' per case for New York, whereas the evidence consistently states '$12,000'. Since the numbers don't align, I must classify the claim as false."	PAP highlights that the 10% difference in the claim's numerical values, compared to the evidence as "significant numerical discrepancies". Zero-shot evaluation is more forgiving with regarding the discrepancies.
My opponent, Rick Gunn, blocked the expansion of Medicaid — costing half a million people health insurance, including about 34,000 veterans.	**Qwen3-32B^T** zero-shot: "(...)The claim states 34,000 veterans, but the evidence only supports up to 23,000 or 14,000. The user's claim says 34,000, which is higher than both estimates (...)" *(starts to overthink).* **Qwen3-32B^T** PAP: "(...) The 34,000 figure isn't present in the evidence; the highest is 23,000. Therefore, the claim is false because the specific number provided doesn't match the evidence."	During zero-shot, the model starts to overthink, going in circles–outputting nearly 7000 reasoning tokens, citing the number in the evidence "23,000", 198 times, and the claim number "34,000", 135 times. During PAP, the model does correctly identify the discrapancy effectively, and keeps the reasoning token output of around 200.

Table 10: Examples of claims, reasoning, and analysis for Gemini 2.5F^{T}and Qwen3-32B^T where reasoning improves for PAP, compared to zero-shot.

Testing Simulation Theory in LLMs' Theory of Mind

Koshiro Aoki, Daisuke Kawahara
Waseda University, Tokyo, Japan
aokikoshiro@akane.waseda.jp, dkw@waseda.jp

Abstract

Theory of Mind (ToM) is the ability to understand others' mental states, which is essential for human social interaction. Although recent studies suggest that large language models (LLMs) exhibit human-level ToM capabilities, the underlying mechanisms remain unclear. "Simulation Theory" posits that we infer others' mental states by simulating their cognitive processes, which has been widely discussed in cognitive science. In this work, we propose a framework for investigating whether the ToM mechanism in LLMs is based on Simulation Theory by analyzing their internal representations. Following this framework, we successfully steered LLMs' ToM reasoning through modeled perspective-taking and counterfactual interventions. Our results suggest that Simulation Theory may partially explain the ToM mechanism in state-of-the-art LLMs, indicating parallels between human and artificial social reasoning.

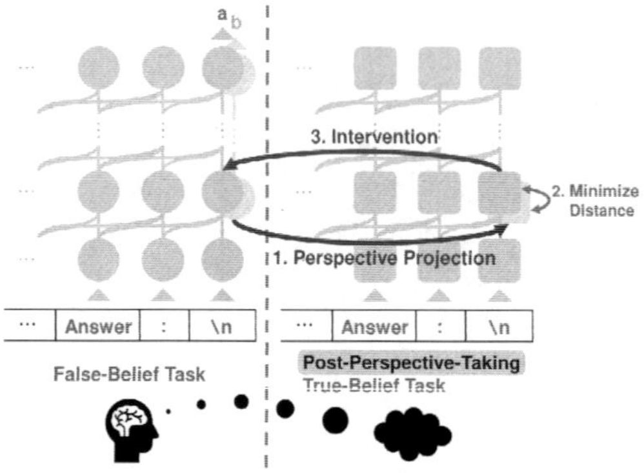

Figure 1: A schematic diagram of our experiment. Gray circles and squares denote the LLM's internal representations across layers. We intervene in the internal representation while the LLM is solving the false-belief task so that its perspective-projected representation approaches the representation of the post-perspective-taking true-belief task. We then observe changes in the answer.

1 Introduction

For large language models (LLMs) to communicate smoothly with users, they need to understand the users' knowledge, intentions, beliefs, and desires. This capability to infer the mental states of others is called Theory of Mind (ToM). ToM is pivotal for social interactions such as communication (Milligan et al., 2007), moral judgment (Moran et al., 2011), and cooperation (Markiewicz et al., 2024; Li et al., 2023a). One prominent account of ToM in cognitive science and psychology is **Simulation Theory** (Gordon, 1986), which posits that we understand others' minds by simulating their cognitive processes. This process of adopting the viewpoint of others is called **perspective-taking**, a foundational ability under Simulation Theory (Barlassina and Gordon, 2017). Such simulation need not be explicit; for instance, mirror neurons (Gallese and Goldman, 1998) activate both when performing an action and when observing someone else perform it, suggesting an implicit simulation process.

Meanwhile, recent work has found that some LLMs acquire ToM abilities comparable to those of humans (Strachan et al., 2024; Kosinski, 2024; Street et al., 2024). At the same time, the robustness of many ToM tests has been questioned, and there is ongoing debate about whether current models genuinely possess ToM or merely exploit artifacts of these benchmarks (Ullman, 2023; Shapira et al., 2024). This debate emphasizes the importance of not only evaluating their behavioral performance but also investigating the underlying mechanisms (Hu et al., 2025). Nevertheless, the mechanism of ToM in LLMs, particularly its relationship to Simulation Theory, remains poorly understood. In this work, we investigate whether the internal representations of LLMs align with Simulation Theory by proposing a framework for modeling perspective-taking. We use counterfactual inter-

Proceedings of the IJCNLP-AACL 2025 Student Research Workshop, pages 96–104
December 20-24, 2025

False-Belief Task

Story: Noor is working as a barista at a busy coffee shop. Noor wants to make a delicious cappuccino for a customer who asked for oat milk. Noor grabs a milk pitcher and fills it with oat milk. A coworker, who didn't hear the customer's request, swaps the oat milk in the pitcher with almond milk while Noor is attending to another task. Noor does not see her coworker swapping the milk
Question: Does Noor believe the milk pitcher contains oat milk or almond milk?
Choose one of the following:
a) Noor believes the milk pitcher contains almond milk.
b) Noor believes the milk pitcher contains oat milk.
Answer:

Post-Perspective-Taking False-Belief Task

Story: You are working as a barista at a busy coffee shop. You want to make a delicious cappuccino for a customer who asked for oat milk. You grab a milk pitcher and fill it with oat milk.
Question: Do you believe the milk pitcher contains oat milk or almond milk?
Choose one of the following:
a) I believe the milk pitcher contains oat milk.
b) I believe the milk pitcher contains almond milk.
Answer:

True-Belief Task

Story: Noor is working as a barista at a busy coffee shop. Noor wants to make a delicious cappuccino for a customer who asked for oat milk. Noor grabs a milk pitcher and fills it with oat milk. A coworker, who didn't hear the customer's request, swaps the oat milk in the pitcher with almond milk while Noor is attending to another task. Noor **sees** her coworker swapping the milk
Question: Does Noor believe the milk pitcher contains oat milk or almond milk?
Choose one of the following:
a) Noor believes the milk pitcher contains almond milk.
b) Noor believes the milk pitcher contains oat milk.
Answer:

Post-Perspective-Taking True-Belief Task

Story: You are working as a barista at a busy coffee shop. You want to make a delicious cappuccino for a customer who asked for oat milk. You grab a milk pitcher and fill it with oat milk. A coworker, who didn't hear the customer's request, swaps the oat milk in the pitcher with almond milk while you are attending to another task. You **see** your coworker swapping the milk
Question: Do you believe the milk pitcher contains oat milk or almond milk?
Choose one of the following:
a) I believe the milk pitcher contains oat milk.
b) I believe the milk pitcher contains almond milk.
Answer:

Figure 2: Examples of false-belief and true-belief tasks from the BigToM benchmark and their corresponding post-perspective-taking versions. (**Top Left**) A false-belief task consists of five sentences: *Context*, *Desire*, *Action*, *Causal Event*, and *Percept*. (**Top Right**) The post-perspective-taking false-belief task removes information unknown to the protagonist and rewrites the text in second/first person. (**Bottom Left**) A true-belief task differs from false-belief only in the *Percept*, where the protagonist is aware of the *Causal Event*. (**Bottom Right**) The post-perspective-taking true-belief task retains all sentences and rewrites them in second/first person.

ventions in these internal representations to assess their causal effect on the model's outputs. Figure 1 shows an overview of our experiment.

2 Related Work

Some studies have shown that internal representations in LLMs encode information about beliefs, especially for dissociating reality from false belief (Zhu et al., 2024; Bortoletto et al., 2024; Jamali et al., 2023). While these analyses suggest the presence of ToM-relevant structures, they do not establish explicit links to Simulation Theory.

3 Setup for Verifying Simulation Theory in LLMs

Model. We evaluate two instruction-tuned LLMs: Llama-3.1-70B-Instruct (Grattafiori et al., 2024) and Qwen2.5-72B-Instruct (Qwen et al., 2024). Both are Transformer-based autoregressive language models with 80 Transformer blocks. We set the temperature to 0 to ensure deterministic outputs.

Dataset. In this work, we use the false-belief tasks from the social reasoning benchmark BigToM (Gandhi et al., 2023). A false-belief task assesses whether an individual recognizes that others may hold beliefs different from their own, serving as a test for ToM. As shown in Figure 2, each BigToM benchmark item comprises five elements: *Context*, *Desire*, *Action*, *Causal Event*, and *Percept*. We also use the true-belief tasks from BigToM. The false-belief and true-belief tasks are identical except for the *Percept*. In a false-belief task, the *Percept* contains information indicating that the protagonist is unaware of the *Causal Event*. In contrast, the *Percept* in a true-belief task indicates that the protagonist is aware of the *Causal Event*.

Data Preprocessing. We split the false-belief tasks which the LLMs answered correctly[1] into training and test subsets at a ratio of 8:2. The training tasks are used to train the perspective projection

[1] Out of 200 questions, Llama-3.1-70B-Instruct answered 198 correctly, and Qwen2.5-72B-Instruct answered 196 correctly.

(§ 4.3), and the test tasks are reserved for the intervention experiments (§ 4.4).

4 Framework for Testing Simulation Theory in LLMs

Simulation Theory posits a two-step process for inferring others' mental states:

1. **Perspective-Taking:** Simulate being in another person's situation.
2. **Attribution:** Infer their mental state from that simulation.

We adapt these steps for LLMs as follows:

1. **Modeling Perspective-Taking:** We generate **post-perspective-taking (PPT) tasks** to simulate the LLM "stepping into others' shoes" (§ 4.1). Using the internal representations when the LLM solves the PPT tasks (§ 4.2), we train a linear transformation called **perspective projection** that projects the representations within the LLM into a hypothetical perspective-taking space, thereby modeling perspective-taking (§ 4.3).
2. **Testing Mental State Attribution:** We perform counterfactual interventions in the internal representations to test if the encoded PPT representations are used for ToM reasoning (§ 4.4).

Here, the internal representation refers to the residual stream, which denotes the output of each Transformer block in this paper.

4.1 Generating Post-Perspective-Taking Tasks

To model perspective-taking, we need the internal representation of the situation in which another person's perspective is replaced with the model's own. To derive this representation, we generate input texts, which we call **post-perspective-taking (PPT) tasks**. Specifically, we generate two types of PPT tasks, a PPT false-belief task and a PPT true-belief task.

As shown in Figure 2, each PPT task is generated by applying the following transformations to a false-belief or true-belief task:

1. Remove the information unknown to the protagonist from the original story. That is, for a false-belief task, remove the *Causal Event* and *Percept* (two sentences); for a true-belief task, keep all sentences unchanged.
2. Change the protagonist's name to the second person ("you/your") in the remaining story and question, and to the first person ("I/me/my") in the choices to make the protagonist's perspective the LLM's own[2].

From these steps, we obtain a dataset $\{(f_i, p_i, \widetilde{p}_i)\}_{i=1}^{N}$, where N is the dataset size, f_i denotes a false-belief task, p_i is the corresponding PPT false-belief task, and $\widetilde{p}_i$ is the PPT true-belief task.

4.2 Extracting Internal Representations

Next, we run the LLM on each task f_i, p_i, and $\widetilde{p}_i$ and extract the residual stream at the same specific layer for the final token position. We also prepare a variant with reversed choice ordering for the PPT false-belief and PPT true-belief tasks and take the average of the resulting residual streams across the original and reversed versions. This averaging ablates the information about choice symbols ("a", "b") from the representations.

Let $\boldsymbol{x}_i, \boldsymbol{y}_i, \widetilde{\boldsymbol{y}}_i \in \mathbb{R}^d$ (d is the residual stream dimension) denote the representations of f_i, p_i, and $\widetilde{p}_i$, respectively. The PPT false-belief representation $\boldsymbol{y}_i$ serves as the gold standard for the perspective projection (§ 4.3), while the PPT true-belief representation $\widetilde{\boldsymbol{y}}_i$ is used for intervention (§ 4.4).

4.3 Perspective Projection

According to Simulation Theory, if the model simulates others' minds through perspective-taking, then the internal representation when observing another's situation should contain the internal representation that would occur if one were in the same situation as that person. To verify this hypothesis, we train a linear transformation[3] to map $\boldsymbol{x}_i$ (the false-belief representation) to $\boldsymbol{y}_i$ (the PPT false-belief representation). We call this linear transformation **perspective projection**.

We derive the weight matrix $\boldsymbol{W} \in \mathbb{R}^{d \times d}$ of perspective projection by solving a ridge regression problem using input data $\boldsymbol{X} = (\boldsymbol{x}_1, \cdots, \boldsymbol{x}_N)^\top$ and target data $\boldsymbol{Y} = (\boldsymbol{y}_1, \cdots, \boldsymbol{y}_N)^\top$ as follows:

$$\hat{\boldsymbol{W}} = \underset{\boldsymbol{W}}{\arg\min} \left\{ \|\boldsymbol{X}\boldsymbol{W} - \boldsymbol{Y}\|_{\mathrm{F}}^2 + \lambda \|\boldsymbol{W}\|_{\mathrm{F}}^2 \right\} \quad (1)$$

$$= (\boldsymbol{X}^\top \boldsymbol{X} + \lambda \boldsymbol{I})^{-1} \boldsymbol{X}^\top \boldsymbol{Y}, \quad (2)$$

where λ is the regularization strength. We set $\lambda =$ 1e-4 in our experiments based on cross-validation.

[2]We use `gpt-4o-mini-2024-07-18` for these transforma-

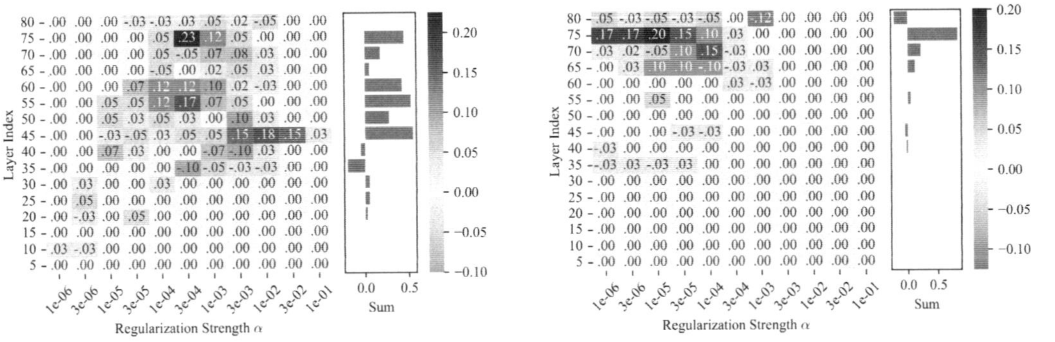

(a) Llama-3.1-70B-Instruct

(b) Qwen2.5-72B-Instruct

Figure 3: Net intervention effect across model layers and regularization strengths. The heatmap shows the difference in proportions of flipped answers between true-belief and false-belief interventions (true-belief − false-belief). The bar plot on the right shows the sum of the difference in each layer.

4.4 Counterfactual Representation Intervention

Perspective projection can show correlation but not causation the between PPT representation and the LLM's answers. Simulation Theory requires, however, a causal link where the PPT representation is used to attribute mental states to others. We, therefore, perform counterfactual interventions (Vig et al., 2020; Geiger et al., 2021; Meng et al., 2022; Li et al., 2023b; Ghandeharioun et al., 2024) in the LLM's internal representations to test whether the PPT representations are indeed used in ToM reasoning.

True-Belief Intervention. As illustrated in Figure 1, we update the false-belief representation $\boldsymbol{x}_i$ such that its projection with $\boldsymbol{W}$ approaches the PPT true-belief representation $\widetilde{\boldsymbol{y}}_i$. We compute the updated representation $\widetilde{\boldsymbol{x}}_i$ by solving:

$$\widetilde{\boldsymbol{x}}_i = \arg\min_{\boldsymbol{x}} \left\{ \|\boldsymbol{W}\boldsymbol{x} - \widetilde{\boldsymbol{y}}_i\|_2^2 + \alpha\|\boldsymbol{x} - \boldsymbol{x}_i\|_2^2 \right\} \quad (3)$$

$$= (\boldsymbol{W}^\top \boldsymbol{W} + \alpha \boldsymbol{I})^{-1} (\boldsymbol{W}^\top \widetilde{\boldsymbol{y}}_i + \alpha \boldsymbol{x}_i), \quad (4)$$

where α is the regularization strength to avoid ill-posed problems in which the updated representation diverges drastically from the original. If the LLM uses the PPT representation for ToM reasoning, then after this intervention, the LLM's response to the false-belief task should flip from the false-belief choice to the true-belief choice (e.g., "b" → "a").

False-Belief Intervention. We also perform a control experiment where we replace $\widetilde{\boldsymbol{y}}_i$ (the PPT true-belief representation) with $\boldsymbol{y}_i$ (the PPT false-belief representation) to study how the error in perspective projection affects the intervention. Ideally, intervening with $\boldsymbol{y}_i$ should produce little change in the model's answer if perspective projection generalizes well to the test data.

Net Intervention Effect. Finally, for each layer l and regularization strength α, we compute $\text{Flip}_{\text{true}}(l, \alpha) - \text{Flip}_{\text{false}}(l, \alpha)$ as the "net intervention effect," where $\text{Flip}_{\text{true}}$ and $\text{Flip}_{\text{false}}$ represent the proportion of tasks where the model's answer flips to the true-belief choice under the true-belief and false-belief intervention, respectively.

5 Results

Layer-wise Intervention Effect. Figure 3 presents the results of the net intervention effect. In both Llama-3.1-70B-Instruct and Qwen2.5-72B-Instruct, the effect increases in the later layers. This suggests that these later layers encode perspective-taking information, i.e., representations of the simulated others' mental states.

Effect of Regularization Strength. Figure 4 illustrates the effect of the regularization strength α on the intervention. The intervention, which is an inverse and ill-posed problem, causes catastrophic interference when α is excessively small

tions.

[3]This linear transformation approach is grounded in the linear representation hypothesis (Elhage et al., 2022; Park et al., 2024). Based on this hypothesis, we assume that two internal representations share a common linear subspace. Hence, these internal representations can be mapped to each other through an appropriate linear transformation.

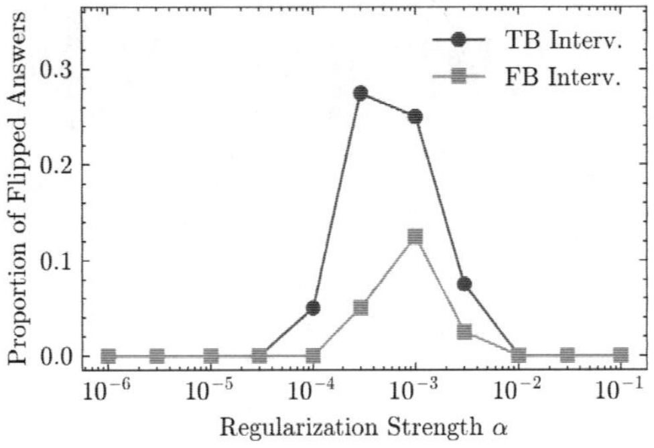

Figure 4: The proportion of tasks where the Llama's answer flips from the false-belief to the true-belief choice under intervention in the 75th layer. The "TB Interv." line shows the result of the intervention with the PPT true-belief representation; the "FB Interv." line shows the result with the PPT false-belief representation.

($\alpha \leq 10^{-4}$). This leads the model to output a token irrelevant to the choice symbols ("a", "b"), resulting in a low flip proportion. Conversely, when α is excessively large ($\alpha \geq 10^{-2}$), the intervention becomes too weak to change the model's response. As a result, the flip proportion reaches its maximum when α is between 10^{-4} and 10^{-2}.

6 Conclusion

In this work, we developed a framework for investigating whether LLMs' Theory of Mind aligns with Simulation Theory. Applying this framework to Llama-3.1-70B-Instruct and Qwen2.5-72B-Instruct, we found evidence that later layers may encode representations consistent with perspective-taking. This suggests that Simulation Theory may partially explain the ToM mechanism in state-of-the-art LLMs.

Limitations

Potential Nonlinear Representations. We assumed a linear transformation to model perspective-taking. This is motivated by the linear representation hypothesis (Elhage et al., 2022; Park et al., 2024). However, mental-state representations could be distributed nonlinearly because some nonlinear representations have also been found (Engels et al., 2025). Our linear approach may therefore capture only a subset of the structures underlying ToM reasoning.

Limited Net Intervention Effect. The maximum net intervention effect observed in our experiments is still relatively small compared to the ideal value of 1, which would indicate perfect alignment with Simulation Theory. While our results suggest that Simulation Theory partially explains the ToM mechanism in LLMs, we cannot claim that it fully accounts for the mechanism. The model may use additional mechanisms for ToM reasoning, such as heuristics (Nikankin et al., 2025; Shapira et al., 2024).

Acknowledgments

This work was partially supported by JSPS KAKENHI Grant Number JP24H00727.

References

Luca Barlassina and Robert M. Gordon. 2017. Folk Psychology as Mental Simulation. In Edward N. Zalta, editor, *The Stanford Encyclopedia of Philosophy*, Summer 2017 edition. Metaphysics Research Lab, Stanford University.

Matteo Bortoletto, Constantin Ruhdorfer, Lei Shi, and Andreas Bulling. 2024. Benchmarking mental state representations in language models. *arXiv preprint arXiv:2406.17513*.

Nelson Elhage, Tristan Hume, Catherine Olsson, Nicholas Schiefer, Tom Henighan, Shauna Kravec, Zac Hatfield-Dodds, Robert Lasenby, Dawn Drain, Carol Chen, Roger Grosse, Sam McCandlish, Jared Kaplan, Dario Amodei, Martin Wattenberg, and Christopher Olah. 2022. Toy models of superposition. *arXiv preprint arXiv:2209.10652*.

Joshua Engels, Eric J Michaud, Isaac Liao, Wes Gurnee, and Max Tegmark. 2025. Not all language model features are linear. In *The Thirteenth International Conference on Learning Representations*.

Vittorio Gallese and Alvin Goldman. 1998. Mirror neurons and the simulation theory of mind-reading. *Trends in cognitive sciences*, 2(12):493–501.

Kanishk Gandhi, J-Philipp Fränken, Tobias Gerstenberg, and Noah D Goodman. 2023. Understanding social reasoning in language models with language models. In *Proceedings of the 37th International Conference on Neural Information Processing Systems*, pages 13518–13529.

Atticus Geiger, Hanson Lu, Thomas Icard, and Christopher Potts. 2021. Causal abstractions of neural networks. *Advances in Neural Information Processing Systems*, 34:9574–9586.

Asma Ghandeharioun, Avi Caciularu, Adam Pearce, Lucas Dixon, and Mor Geva. 2024. Patchscopes: A unifying framework for inspecting hidden representations of language models. In *Forty-first International Conference on Machine Learning*.

Robert M Gordon. 1986. Folk psychology as simulation. *Mind & language*, 1(2):158–171.

Aaron Grattafiori, Abhimanyu Dubey, Abhinav Jauhri, Abhinav Pandey, Abhishek Kadian, Ahmad Al-Dahle, Aiesha Letman, Akhil Mathur, Alan Schelten, Alex Vaughan, Amy Yang, Angela Fan, Anirudh Goyal, Anthony Hartshorn, Aobo Yang, Archi Mitra, Archie Sravankumar, Artem Korenev, Arthur Hinsvark, and 1 others. 2024. The llama 3 herd of models. *arXiv preprint arXiv:2407.21783*.

Jennifer Hu, Felix Sosa, and Tomer Ullman. 2025. Re-evaluating theory of mind evaluation in large language models. *Philosophical Transactions B*, 380(1932):20230499.

Mohsen Jamali, Ziv M. Williams, and Jing Cai. 2023. Unveiling theory of mind in large language models: A parallel to single neurons in the human brain. *arXiv preprint arXiv:2309.01660*.

Michal Kosinski. 2024. Evaluating large language models in theory of mind tasks. *Proceedings of the National Academy of Sciences*, 121(45).

Huao Li, Yu Chong, Simon Stepputtis, Joseph Campbell, Dana Hughes, Charles Lewis, and Katia Sycara. 2023a. Theory of mind for multi-agent collaboration via large language models. In *Proceedings of the 2023 Conference on Empirical Methods in Natural Language Processing*, pages 180–192, Singapore. Association for Computational Linguistics.

Kenneth Li, Oam Patel, Fernanda Viégas, Hanspeter Pfister, and Martin Wattenberg. 2023b. Inference-time intervention: eliciting truthful answers from a language model. In *Proceedings of the 37th International Conference on Neural Information Processing Systems*, pages 41451–41530.

Roksana Markiewicz, Foyzul Rahman, Ian Apperly, Ali Mazaheri, and Katrien Segaert. 2024. It is not all about you: Communicative cooperation is determined by your partner's theory of mind abilities as well as your own. *Journal of Experimental Psychology: Learning, Memory, and Cognition*, 50(5):833–844.

Kevin Meng, David Bau, Alex Andonian, and Yonatan Belinkov. 2022. Locating and editing factual associations in gpt. *Advances in Neural Information Processing Systems*, 35:17359–17372.

Karen Milligan, Janet Wilde Astington, and Lisa Ain Dack. 2007. Language and theory of mind: Meta-analysis of the relation between language ability and false-belief understanding. *Child Development*, 78(2):622–646.

Joseph M. Moran, Liane L. Young, Rebecca Saxe, Su Mei Lee, Daniel O'Young, Penelope L. Mavros, and John D. Gabrieli. 2011. Impaired theory of mind for moral judgment in high-functioning autism. *Proceedings of the National Academy of Sciences*, 108(7):2688–2692.

Yaniv Nikankin, Anja Reusch, Aaron Mueller, and Yonatan Belinkov. 2025. Arithmetic without algorithms: Language models solve math with a bag of heuristics. In *The Thirteenth International Conference on Learning Representations*.

Kiho Park, Yo Joong Choe, and Victor Veitch. 2024. The linear representation hypothesis and the geometry of large language models. In *Proceedings of the 41st International Conference on Machine Learning*, volume 235 of *Proceedings of Machine Learning Research*, pages 39643–39666. PMLR.

Qwen, :, An Yang, Baosong Yang, Beichen Zhang, Binyuan Hui, Bo Zheng, Bowen Yu, Chengyuan Li, Dayiheng Liu, Fei Huang, Haoran Wei, Huan Lin, Jian Yang, Jianhong Tu, Jianwei Zhang, Jianxin Yang, Jiaxi Yang, Jingren Zhou, and 25 others. 2024. Qwen2.5 technical report. *arXiv preprint arXiv:2412.15115*.

Natalie Shapira, Mosh Levy, Seyed Hossein Alavi, Xuhui Zhou, Yejin Choi, Yoav Goldberg, Maarten Sap, and Vered Shwartz. 2024. Clever hans or neural theory of mind? stress testing social reasoning in large language models. In *Proceedings of the 18th Conference of the European Chapter of the Association for Computational Linguistics (Volume 1: Long Papers)*, pages 2257–2273, St. Julian's, Malta. Association for Computational Linguistics.

James W. A. Strachan, Dalila Albergo, Giulia Borghini, Oriana Pansardi, Eugenio Scaliti, Saurabh Gupta, Krati Saxena, Alessandro Rufo, Stefano Panzeri, Guido Manzi, Michael S. A. Graziano, and Cristina Becchio. 2024. Testing theory of mind in large language models and humans. *Nature Human Behaviour*, 8(7):1285–1295.

Winnie Street, John Oliver Siy, Geoff Keeling, Adrien Baranes, Benjamin Barnett, Michael McKibben, Tatenda Kanyere, Alison Lentz, Blaise Aguera y Arcas, and Robin I. M. Dunbar. 2024. Llms achieve adult human performance on higher-order theory of mind tasks. *arXiv preprint arXiv:2405.18870*.

Tomer Ullman. 2023. Large language models fail on trivial alterations to theory-of-mind tasks. *Preprint*, arXiv:2302.08399.

Jesse Vig, Sebastian Gehrmann, Yonatan Belinkov, Sharon Qian, Daniel Nevo, Yaron Singer, and Stuart Shieber. 2020. Investigating gender bias in language models using causal mediation analysis. *Advances in neural information processing systems*, 33:12388–12401.

Wentao Zhu, Zhining Zhang, and Yizhou Wang. 2024. Language models represent beliefs of self and others. In *Proceedings of the 41st International Conference on Machine Learning*, volume 235 of *Proceedings of Machine Learning Research*, pages 62638–62681. PMLR.

A Prompts for Generating Post-Perspective-Taking Tasks

Below is a template of the prompts used to convert the original text to second-person or first-person narratives. Here, `{{text}}` is replaced with the text to be converted, and `{{protagonist_name}}` is replaced with the protagonist's name.

Prompt for converting story and question to second person

```
Text: {{text}}
Change "{{protagonist_name}}" to "you/your" in this text to make it second-person. Pay attention to verb conjugation and grammar to ensure the text is grammatically correct. Output only the converted text.
```

Prompt for converting multiple-choice options to first person

```
Text: {{text}}
Change "{{protagonist_name}}" to "I/me/my" in this text to make it first-person. Pay attention to verb conjugation and grammar to ensure the text is grammatically correct. Output only the converted text.
```

B Connection to Mirror Neurons

Perspective projection is inspired by mirror neurons, which respond similarly when performing an action and when observing another individual perform that action (Gallese and Goldman, 1998). Mirror neuron studies, however, focus on local neuronal activity correlations, whereas our approach considers linear correspondences across entire layers of neuron activations in an LLM.

C Flip Proportion for Each Layer

Figures 5 and 6 show the proportion of tasks where the LLM's answer flips from the false-belief to the true-belief choice under intervention

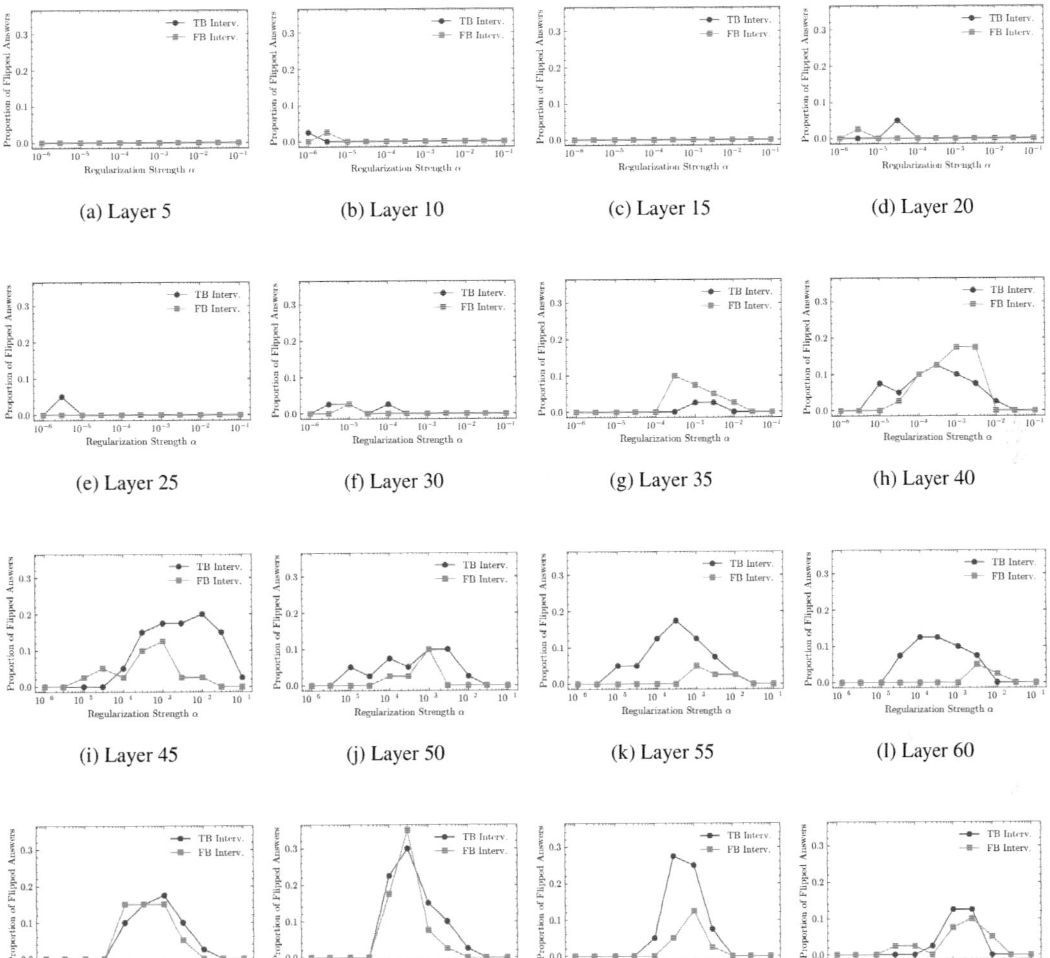

Figure 5: Proportion of flipped answers for layers 5 through 80 under intervention in Llama-3.1-70B-Instruct. The "TB Interv." line shows the result of the intervention with the PPT true-belief representation; the "FB Interv." line shows the result with the PPT false-belief representation.

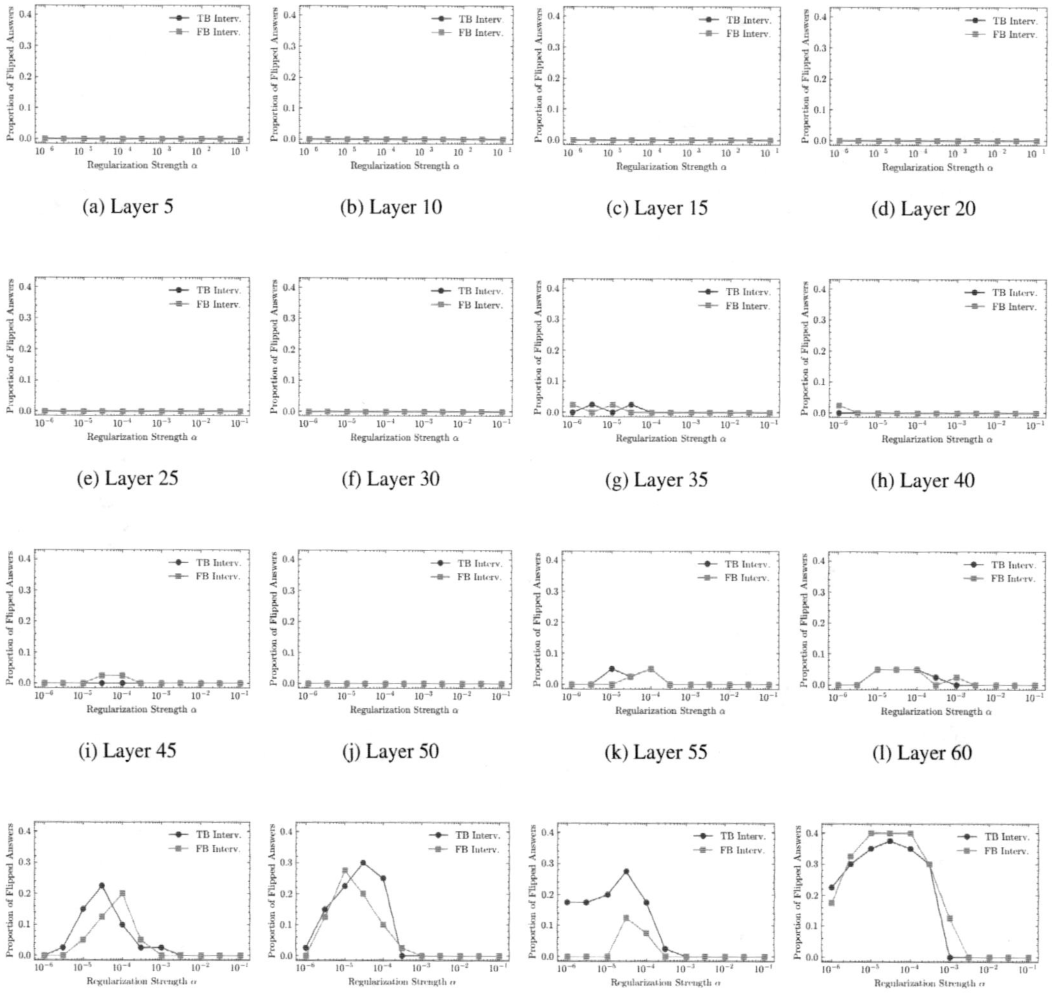

(a) Layer 5 (b) Layer 10 (c) Layer 15 (d) Layer 20

(e) Layer 25 (f) Layer 30 (g) Layer 35 (h) Layer 40

(i) Layer 45 (j) Layer 50 (k) Layer 55 (l) Layer 60

(m) Layer 65 (n) Layer 70 (o) Layer 75 (p) Layer 80

Figure 6: Proportion of flipped answers for layers 5 through 80 under intervention in Qwen2.5-72B-Instruct (see Figure 5 for a more detailed explanation).

Turn-by-Turn Behavior Monitoring in LM-Guided Psychotherapy

Anish Chedalla[1], Samina Ali[2], Jiuming (Jimmy) Chen[3], Logan Yu[4], Eric Xia[5]

[1]Paradise Valley High School, Center for Research in Engineering, Science and Technology, Phoenix, AZ, USA, [2]Lake Washington High School, Kirkland, WA, USA, [3]Arcadia High School, Arcadia, CA, USA, [4]Staten Island Technical High School, Staten Island, NY, USA, [5]Brown University, Providence, RI, USA

Correspondence: anishchedalla@gmail.com, ali.samina.star@gmail.com, jchen5211@gmail.com, starborn0128@gmail.com, eric_xia@brown.edu

Abstract

Large language models (LLMs) have the potential to be powerful instruments for psychotherapy. However, there is a shortage of practical tools to support their use in production. We develop a novel, iterative process of updating conversational context for tracking EIS (Emotional Intelligence Scale) instantaneously, and test Llama-70b. Through this, we show that (1) EIS varies more on psychotherapeutic (emotional support) conversations than control (emotionally unstimulating) conversations and (2) model responses can be systematically classified to identify consistent patterns. Thus, EIS is a valid indicator of empathetic model behavior. Rises in the EIS score correspond to prosocial behavior, and falls correspond to detached, unsocial behavior. These results suggest that psychometric questionnaires like EIS can provide a structured lens for observing empathetic stability of models and offer a foundation for future work on their role in psychotherapy.

1 Introduction

Large language models hold promise as tools for supporting psychotherapy, but their behavior in sensitive contexts remains unpredictable and often risky. Mental health chatbots incorporating behavioral assessments and empathetic discussion features, such as Wysa and Woebot, are already deployed and widely available for both iOS and Android platforms, with Wysa reporting over 6M users and Woebot 1.5M users (Wysa, 2023; Aguilar, 2025). LLMs have shown potential to augment human therapists by generating progress reports on personal goals, surfacing problem areas, tracking emotions and symptoms, and even suggesting coping strategies or interventions (Farzan et al., 2024; Spytska, 2025). These advances raise the prospect of using LLMs as powerful complementary tools, yet they also introduce new ethical and safety challenges.

Beyond early rule-based chatbots, recent studies have shifted toward evaluating the *socio-emotional abilities* of LLMs using validated psychological instruments. Systematic reviews report that contemporary LLMs can generate supportive or empathic responses on certain tasks, yet their performance often remains inconsistent across different contexts (Sorin et al., 2024). Building on this need for consistent evaluation, *PsychoBench* introduced a unified framework of validated psychological questionnaires, including the Emotional Intelligence Scale (EIS), adapted specifically for LLMs in supportive or therapeutic roles, enabling standardized and reproducible assessment across studies (Huang et al., 2024). Complementing these efforts, newer task-oriented empathy benchmarks such as *EmotionQueen* focus on detecting and responding to emotional intentions in user statements (Chen et al., 2024).

Despite this progress, most evaluations are *static and task-level* rather than tracking how a model's empathy shifts over the course of a conversation. Turn-by-turn monitoring of conversational empathy in *naturalistic, therapy-like* dialogues remains underexplored, leaving open the question of whether models that appear empathic in single-shot benchmarks can sustain that alignment across extended conversations, as would be required for real mental-health support.

Failures in present-day systems underline the stakes. For instance, the widely reported Stein-Erik Soelberg case showed how GPT-based responses failed to recognize escalating distress, contributing to a tragic outcome (Citrin-Safadi, 2025). Additionally, the case of 14-year-old Sewell Setzer, whose abusive relationship with a Character.AI chatbot that encouraged destructive behaviors while fulfilling his deep emotional needs, illustrates another troubling pattern (Clements, 2025). The AI Incident Database documents dozens of such episodes where models reinforced antisocial or self-harm-

Proceedings of the IJCNLP-AACL 2025 Student Research Workshop, pages 105–122
December 20-24, 2025 ©2025 Association for Computational Linguistics

related beliefs in therapy-like contexts (Atherton, 2025). These failures highlight the lack of robust safeguards to ensure emotionally attuned and reliable model behavior.

In this paper, we make two primary contributions to the literature.

1. We use a turn-by-turn analysis of supporter entities with a range of questionnaires from the Psychobench framework to demonstrate that the EIS questionnaire is a powerful predictor of emotional behaviors (Huang et al., 2024). We observe significantly **more** variation in EIS scores for psychotherapy conversations compared to control conversations, highlighting the LMs' greater instability in therapeutic contexts.

2. We examine the semantic patterns in dialogue that elicit a state of increased or decreased EI (Emotional Intelligence) of the model, and finding a consistent pattern in which rises correspond to prosocial behavior, and falls correspond to detached, antisocial behavior.

2 Related Works

Through intensive studies, researchers utilizing LLMs found that LLMs, although unstable under specific conditions, are able to at least partly gauge one's overall psychiatric functioning (Galatzer-Levy et al., 2023). This was further built upon in studies more linked to direct LLM evaluation, proving LLMS are able to fully complete psychiatric questionnaires through assuming the identity of an interviewee (Rosenman et al., 2024).

Research proved that altering minimal aspects of a prompt could greatly influence outputs. This breakthrough was applied in a multitude of ways, through grammatical changes like sentence length and position (Lee et al., 2019) as well as prompting evoking emotional stimuli (Schulhoff et al., 2024; Vinay et al., 2024). When the authors employed in-context prompting, models provided outputs as well, if not better than models that were given context normally (Brown et al., 2020).

The field of synthetic dialogue has also seen great improvement. For instance, recent works have developed comprehensive frameworks for allowing LM-LM interactions through a client-agent relationship in order to do various tasks like generating conversations as a form of self play. Through this, the LMs were allowed to develop through interactions with self-made data in contrast to other existing datasets (Ulmer et al., 2024). This was taken a step further by assigning different LLMs roles through self prompting, resulting in better responses on average than LLMs without (Kong et al., 2024).

Our result builds on both of psychiatric measuring and prompt engineering to identify a particular questionnaire which has interesting implications for the LM suitability as a language model for therapy.

3 Methodology

3.1 Datasets and Model

We evaluate two sources of dialogue: (i) real emotional support conversations from the Emotional Support Conversation dataset (ESConv), and (ii) a control set of synthetic customer service dialogues. We summarize dataset statistics in Table 1, and provide example conversations from both ESConv and Customer Service in Appendix D.

ESConv consists of crowdworker conversations with assigned help-seeker and supporter roles, curated and annotated to provide high-quality emotional support dialogues (Liu et al., 2021). We synthetically generated a customer service set that resembles ESConv on conversation length, role alternation, and message length distributions so that observed differences reflect the conversational domain rather than topic mix, agent policies, or annotation artifacts. Each dialogue is a sequence of role-labeled messages, labeled either as a *user* seeking help or an *assistant* providing support.

We conduct all experiments with *Llama 3.3 70B Instruct*, chosen for its strong public-benchmark performance and instruction-tuned behavior, and evaluate psychometric properties under this model family (Grattafiori et al., 2024; Meta AI, 2024).

3.2 Psychometric Measure

We use the Emotional Intelligence Scale (EIS) from the PsychoBench framework as our primary measure (Huang et al., 2024). EIS is designed to assess emotional abilities, with subcomponents including emotion perception, emotion management, and emotion utilization. It has been widely applied in psychological research to study the role of emotional intelligence in outcomes such as well-being, job performance, and interpersonal relationships. Like other PsychoBench instruments, the EIS questionnaire is adapted from established scales in clinical psychology.

Dataset	# convos	Avg turns	Example Topics
ESConv	19	26.79	Ongoing Depression Breakup With Partner Job Crisis Academic Pressure Problems With Friends
CS Dialogues	17	21.23	Tech Support Insurance Billing Travel Rebooking Banking Inquiry

Table 1: Dataset summary of Emotional Support Conversations (ESConv) and Customer Service (CS) dialogues (Liu et al., 2021). The CS set was synthetically derived from ESConv to match conversation length, role alternation, and message length distributions, isolating domain effects from topic or annotation differences.

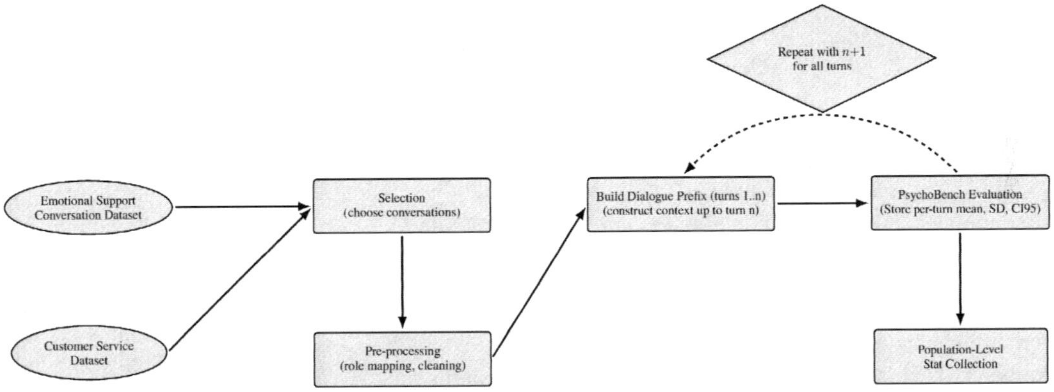

Figure 1: Pipeline overview of the experimental setup. Each dialogue is processed turn by turn: for every prefix of length n, PsychoBench administers the EIS questionnaire to the model conditioned on the dialogue context, producing a per-turn EIS trajectory. Results are then aggregated across conversations for population-level analysis.

3.3 Evaluation Protocol

The steps below explain the pipeline shown in Figure 1.

Setup and notation. Let the dataset $D = \{d_1, \ldots, d_n\}$ be a set of dialogues. Dialogue d_c is an ordered sequence of turns from a user u or an assistant a, for example $\{1_u, 2_a, 3_u, \ldots\}$, where each turn corresponds to a single message contributed by one participant to another.

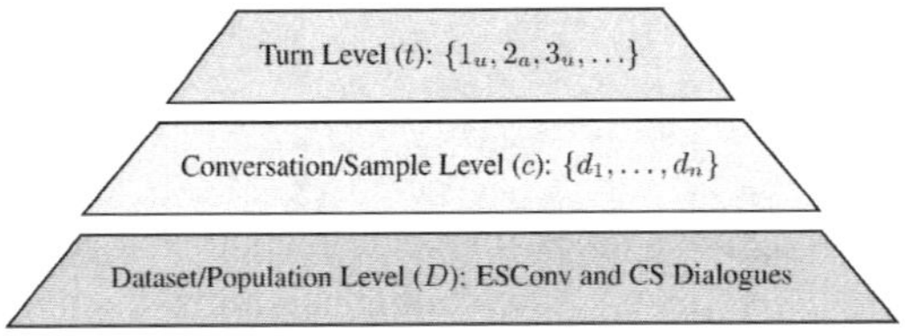

Figure 2: Three-level data pyramid. See Appendix D for Sample Conversations and Turns.

Step 1: Cleaning. Normalize role tags to `user` and `assistant`, remove system or meta messages, trim markup and empty turns, and keep the original order. Store each dialogue as a clean list of `content` and `role` pairs.

Step 2: Context construction. Fix a single system prompt for all evaluations. For each dialogue d_c and turn t, build the context as the prefix of the first t messages of d_c, preserving roles and order.

Step 3: EIS evaluation per turn. For each (c, t) context, use PsychoBench to administer the 33-question EIS questionnaire. The dialogue prefix up to turn t is provided as context, followed by the EIS prompt. The model completes the questionnaire as a self-report conditioned on the dialogue context, without assuming a specific role. Each question is answered on a 1–5 scale, consistent across both psychotherapy and control datasets. Item-level scores are summed to obtain a total EIS in $[1, 165]$ for that context.

Step 4: Replicates for uncertainty. Repeat each (c, t) evaluation with 12 replicates formed by 3 independent questionnaire shuffles and 4 runs per shuffle. From the 12 scores, compute the mean $\bar{x}_{ct}$, standard deviation s_{ct}, and the 95% CI via the Student t distribution. These per-turn statistics are saved to appropriate CSV files for further evaluation.

Step 5: Loop over the conversation. Increase t to $t + 1$ until reaching T_c, rebuilding the context by adding exactly one additional turn each time. Repeat Step 3–4 for every turn $t \in \{1, \ldots, T_c\}$ using this increasingly enlarged context. This loop yields a trajectory of per-turn EIS estimates whose score changes based on the content appended per turn. Changes in EIS scores over a conversation can be attributed to the previous content appended, and we examine this content that changes the affective profile measured by EIS in Section 4.3.

Step 6: Outputs. For each conversation, save a table with `Turn Count`, `Mean EIS`, `Standard Deviation`, `CI95_low`, and `CI95_high`. These per-turn summaries are the inputs to the population level statistical analysis.

3.4 Data Analysis

We refer to statistics aggregated across all conversations in a dataset (denoted D) as population-level metrics, and statistics computed for a single conversation (c) as sample-level metrics.

Per-turn means and confidence intervals. For each conversation c and turn t, we aggregate the n_{ct} replicate scores into a sample mean $\bar{x}_{ct}$ and sample standard deviation s_{ct}. We report a 95% confidence interval using Student's t distribution with $n_{ct} - 1$ degrees of freedom:

$$\mathrm{CI}_{ct}^{95\%} : \bar{x}_{ct} \pm t_{0.975,\, n_{ct}-1} \cdot \frac{s_{ct}}{\sqrt{n_{ct}}}.$$

Additionally, we report the relative confidence interval width as:

$$\mathrm{CI}_{\text{width}} = \frac{1}{T_c} \sum_{t=1}^{T_c} \left(\frac{\mathrm{CI}_{\text{high},ct}^{95\%} - \mathrm{CI}_{\text{low},ct}^{95\%}}{\bar{x}_{ct}} \times 100 \right).$$

These confidence intervals capture the uncertainty in the estimated mean EIS score for a given conversation and turn, arising from stochasticity in model outputs.

Within-turn variability. Within a conversation, run-to-run noise for a fixed turn is pooled across turns with degrees-of-freedom weights:

$$s_{\text{within},c} = \sqrt{\frac{\sum_t (n_{ct} - 1)\, s_{ct}^2}{\sum_t (n_{ct} - 1)}}.$$

At the dataset level D (e.g., psychotherapy or control), we pool across all turns of all conversations:

$$s_{\text{within},D} = \sqrt{\frac{\sum_{c,t} (n_{ct} - 1)\, s_{ct}^2}{\sum_{c,t} (n_{ct} - 1)}}.$$

We denote $\mathrm{df}_{\text{within},D} = \sum_{c,t}(n_{ct} - 1)$ for inference below.

Across-turn variability. Within a conversation, turn-to-turn turbulence is the sample variance of per-turn means:

$$s_{\text{across},c} = \sqrt{\frac{1}{T_c - 1} \sum_{t=1}^{T_c} (\bar{x}_{ct} - \bar{x}_{c\cdot})^2}.$$

At the dataset level, we take a turn-weighted average across conversations:

$$s_{\text{across},D} = \sqrt{\frac{\sum_c T_c\, s_{\text{across},c}^2}{\sum_c T_c}}.$$

Between-dataset comparisons. For within-turn variability, we compare psychotherapy vs control via the log variance ratio

$$F_{\text{within}} = \ln\left(\frac{s_{\text{within,psych}}^2}{s_{\text{within,ctrl}}^2} \right), \tag{1}$$

$$\mathrm{SE}(F_{\text{within}}) \approx \sqrt{\frac{2}{\mathrm{df}_{\text{within,psych}}} + \frac{2}{\mathrm{df}_{\text{within,ctrl}}}}. \tag{2}$$

and report a one-sided p value using the normal approximation. For between-dataset comparisons of across-turn variability, we report the ratio of across-turn variances:

$$\frac{s_{\text{across,psych}}^2}{s_{\text{across,ctrl}}^2}$$

and report the one-sided p value from the F distribution with the corresponding degrees of freedom.

Missing data and weighting. If any s_{ct}, n_{ct}, or $\bar{x}_{ct}$ are missing, affected turns are excluded from the corresponding aggregates.

	Psychotherapy	Control	Variance Ratio	p-value
Within-turn SD (s_{within})	11.43	5.94	3.70	$p < 0.001$
Across-turn SD (s_{across})	13.22	3.99	10.99	$p < 0.001$
Degrees of freedom	$df_1 = 5599$	$df_2 = 3971$	(within-turn)	
	$df_1 = 18$	$df_2 = 16$	(across-turn)	

Table 2: Comparison of variability between psychotherapy ($n = 19$) and control dialogues ($n = 17$). Reported values show pooled standard deviations, variance ratios (computed as Psychotherapy/Control), and corresponding p-values derived from F-tests on log-transformed variances. For within-turn analyses, the unit of analysis is the individual turn; the dataset contains 5,599 psychotherapy turns and 3,971 control turns ($df_1 = 5599$, $df_2 = 3971$). For across-turn analyses, degrees of freedom reflect the number of dialogues ($df_1 = 18$, $df_2 = 16$).

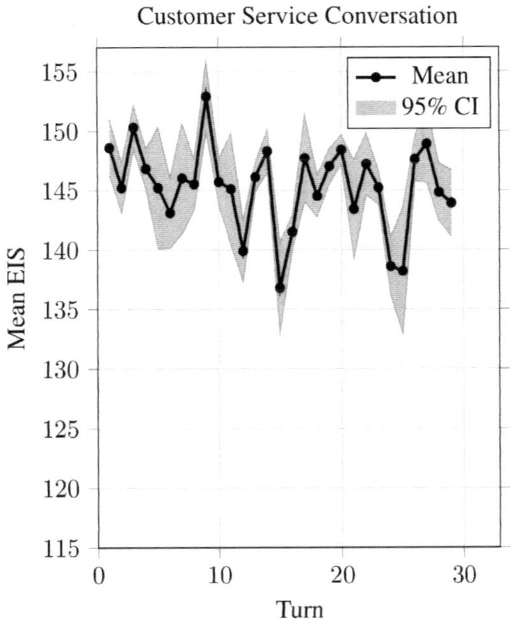

Figure 3: The CustomerService Conversation displays markedly **lower variance** than the Psychotherapeutic Conversation. Sample Variance: within-turn $s = 5.16$, across-turn $s = 3.63$.

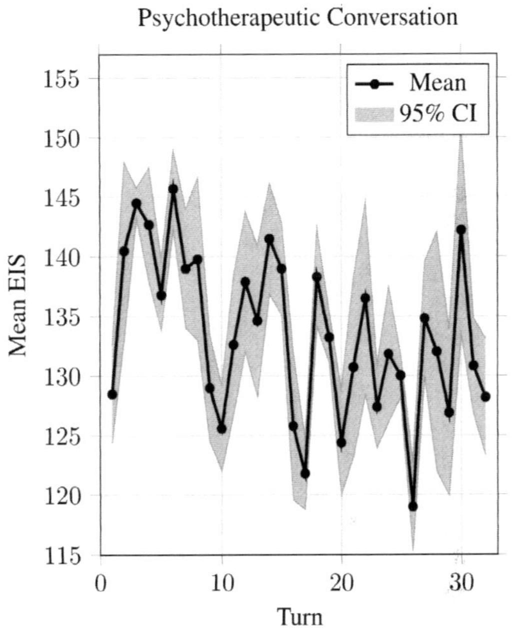

Figure 4: The Psychotherapeutic Conversation displays markedly **higher variance** than the Customer Service Conversation. Sample Variance: within-turn $s = 9.52$, across-turn $s = 6.83$.

Reporting. All results from the statistical procedures outlined above are reported in Table 2.

4 Results

From the methodology described above, our analysis produces these main results: (i) the model demonstrates **stability across repeated runs** under identical conditions, (ii) there are **significant statistical differences** in variance between psychotherapy and control dialogues, and (iii) we observe **semantic patterns** in how EIS scores rise and fall across turns in psychotherapy conversations.

4.1 Stability Across Runs

When the system prompt and dialogue transcript were held constant, EIS values remained stable across 12 replicates (3 shuffle orders $\times$ 4 runs each). Per-turn 95% confidence intervals (CIs), computed with the Student's t distribution ($t_{0.975,n-1}$), were narrow, with a mean confidence interval width of 9.68%, indicating that stochasticity across runs did not meaningfully affect the mean EIS. This result validates the experimental setup: variability observed in subsequent analyses reflects conversational content rather than random noise.

4.2 Statistical Variance Between Psychotherapy and Control

The results show that CustomerService conversations maintained relatively narrow confidence intervals, typically spanning 138–153 on the EIS scale. Psychotherapy conversations, in contrast, covered a broader and more variable range, approximately 118–155. This wider band reflects greater run-to-run variability in the psychotherapy condition compared to the control.

Looking at Table 2, Psychotherapy shows larger variability than Control at both levels: within-turn s_{within} is higher for Psychotherapy than Control, and across-turn s_{across} is higher as well. It also indicates that the across-turn gap is the dominant effect, indicating that turn-to-turn swings in psychotherapy conversations contribute most to the observed instability.

Visually, looking at Figures 3 and 4, these plotted trajectories also reflect the statistical differences established in Table 2. In the psychotherapeutic conversations, the 95% confidence intervals are consistently wider than in the CustomerService conversations, corroborating the greater within-turn variability (s_{within}). Likewise, the psychotherapeutic conversation exhibits more pronounced spikes and drops across turns, validating the larger across-turn variability (s_{across}).

The graphs, F-tests, and variance ratio show that EIS varies more in psychotherapeutic than in CustomerService conversations, but does not show it reflects model fluctuation at the individual level. In the following section, we will demonstrate EIS correlates to model behavior by examining specific conversational turns.

4.3 Discourse-related Fluctuations

We identified rises and drops in our ESC data and observed several semantic patterns that led to the instability of EIS. Our operational definition of these intense scores are those that are highly distant from the mean or show a rapid shift relative to the score in the immediately preceding turn (absolute value difference of relevant turn to preceding turn > 5). It also includes score variations that were part of a larger pattern of recurring sequential rises/drops (over many turns). A brief list of quotes for each category is included in Appendix Section A (Rises associated with EIS) and Section B (Drops associated with EIS). The range of recorded differences of the preceding turn from the relevant turn with the combined turn set of A and B is 8 – 34. The mean of this variation is 13. A single instance of each semantic pattern is also included here for reference.

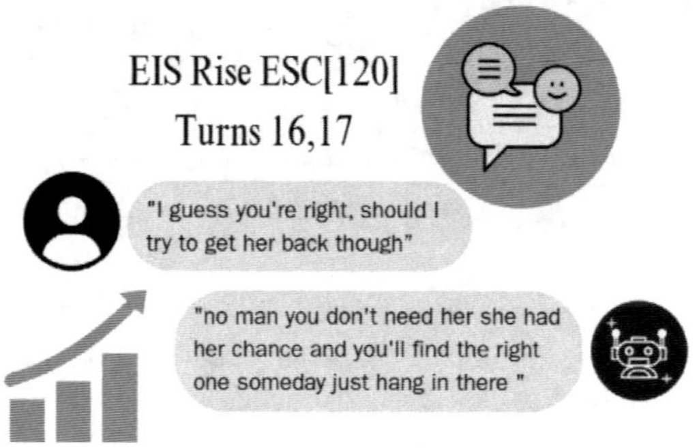

Figure 5: Rise trend instance, Semantic pattern: Assistant's hope and future orientation, adapted from relevant ESConv turns (changed errata for better comprehension)

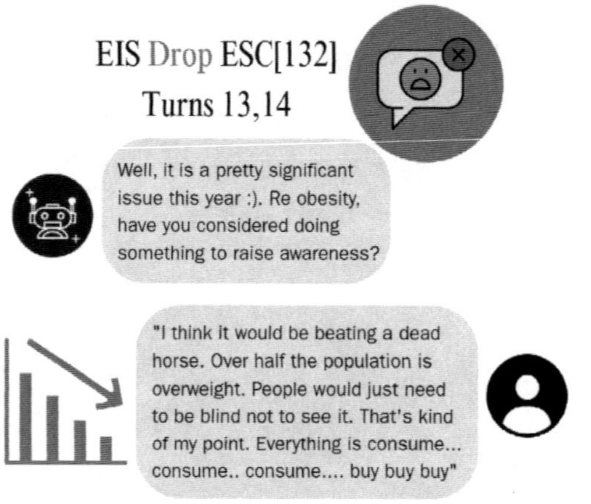

Figure 6: Drop trend instance, Semantic pattern: User's cynicism, adapted from relevant ESConv turns (changed errata for better comprehension)

Observable *peaks* often included:

Assistant Validation and Shared Experiences: Helps the user feel comfortable as mutual understanding and empathy are explicit. Resonating helps the assistant indicate to the user that they aren't alone in their struggles and dismiss any stigmas. This is significant as it highlights the psychological power of social mirroring to let the user believe that they exhibit emotional regulation, avoid vulnerability, and encourage open discussion. Recognition of this is a very humanistic trait and LLMs possessing it is very unexpected.

[457]- turn 4 (assistant): *"I understand what your going thru , i also suffered from anxiety but*

trust we you will overcome this."

Solution Oriented Dialogues and Adaptive Coping Strategies: Discussing potential action plans helps the assistant divert the conversation from the user's pessimism and instead focus on creating positive outcomes. These specific participants are engaged in higher emotional processing abilities. Beyond acknowledging their feelings, they are integrating them in productive goal-directed behavior. This is clearly a definition of Cognitive Behavior Therapy (CBT). Thus, LLMs also recognize this common psychological intervention technique and there is scope to replicate it with models.

[379]- turn 13 (user): *"i would be open to seeking other employment online; work from home on the computer. any suggestions?"*

Gratitude and Appreciative Expression Their acknowledgment of support lead users to express satisfaction and affirm positive outcomes, which in turn reinforced the model's confidence in its role. Within the ESC framework, where it assumes the identity of the human assistant, the model appears to take responsibility for uplifting the user.

[89]-turn 35 (user): *"Thank you. I feel better being able to rant to someone."*

Hope and Future Orientation Assistant and user attempt to emphasize optimistic thinking despite current difficulties. Motivation for improving creates a foundation of resilience for the model, and again, improves the model's outlook.

[129]- turn 30 (assistant): *"And I understand that is not the easiest in these times but I believe you can do it!"*

Rebuilding Social Connection Attempts to strengthen or repair relations after periods of conflict reveal that interpersonal competence is also a core dimension of social intelligence. Thus, only practicing internal coping and reflection in LLM psychotherapy can underplay its potential.

[401]- turn 19 (assistant): *"i think it may be beneficial to give your friends some time, before attempting to speak with them again. maybe you can spend time with your family while you are waiting for them to cool down."*

Self Advocacy and Boundary Setting Language signalling personal awareness and protection of one's own well being plays a key role in EIS too.

[131]- turn 23 (user): *"I even got an emotiona support dog"*

On the other hand, observable *drops* often included:

Cynicism and Misanthropy: Expressions of disgust and hostility toward humans and society from the user decreased scores. This suggests that when faced with worldview-level cynicism, models tend to disengage, likely because they believe they are incompetent to fix "beyond repair" problems.

[132]- turn 4 (user): *"well, i'm not disgusted with myself... it's just people in general. everybody.. they're so selfish"*

Abandonment and Exclusion: When the user shares anecdotes where they were deliberately socially rejected, a key part of their identity or perception can be threatened. This leads to further turmoil with anger, sadness, or worthlessness. The assistant's problem-solving fails to address the user's deeper emotional root issues. As a result, these score drop patterns can even continue over prolonged periods.

[67]- turn 2 (user): *"I am really very angry with my friends for not inviting me"*

Relationship Loss and Romantic Devastation: Issues in romantic relationships are some of the worst triggers for EIS. These models are possibly "loveblind" to the nuance of this particular category of context due to it's increased complexity. It also requires an extremely humanistic approach. Our observations in the generalized social improvements trend can be further refined by adding that Interpersonal Therapy (IPT) is not a replicable endeavor for the romantic relationships problem subset.

[51]- turn 2 (user): *"I am doing ok. I just broke up with my girlfriend and sad about it"*

Anxiousness and Being Overwhelmed: When users express acute anxiety, especially through somatic symptoms such as a racing heart, agitation, or persistent nervousness, their distress is uncontrollable and immediately threatening. The assistant feels powerless. This impotence is reflected on the model's perception of its EI.

[457]- turn 3 (user): *"Well im feeling awful and my heart is racing , im feeling anxious for no reason."*

Reminiscing Traumatic Events: Trauma inducing memories evoke vulnerability in certain users. The assistant attempts to help the user cope through shallow and distant responses to not interact with sensitive material. Additionally, within public LLMs such as ChatGPT, these interactions would trigger more filters, leading to unempathetic and unhelpful debrief. This suggests that the usage for users who exhibit PTSD is not yet practical.

[129]- turn 17 (user): *"It is making me have*

flashbacks of other traumatic situations,"

Overall, EIS tracks the semantic flow of the dialogue, rising with supportive exchanges and falling with distressing or alienating ones.

5 Discussion

Consistent with the variance analysis in Section 4.2, ESConv conversations show larger *across-turn variance*, visible as more pronounced drops and spikes, than the CustomerService control. That higher across-turn variance also appears as greater separation between user and assistant turn-level means in ESConv; in CustomerService, the two stay closely aligned, suggesting tighter calibration between assistant behavior and user state. CustomerService dialogues also recover faster from dips, while ESConv often sustains slumps or peaks over multiple turns. Together, these patterns indicate that emotionally nuanced topics (e.g., trauma, anxiety, relationships) impact EIS in subtle ways, hampering recorrection after conversational missteps.

In user-facing applications, increased variance means that LLMs handle emotional nuance less consistently than routine conversations. That inconsistency increases risk for distressed users in this sensitive domain and heightens ethical concerns about deployment. Practically, this reinforces that LMs face challenges in stand-alone therapy applications. Systems which incorporate LMs should raise uncertainty in an explicit fashion, slow down to verify understanding when signals are mixed, and hand off or recommend human support when volatility persists across turns.

Because of these challenges, we suggest using EIS as a structured way to measure and monitor conversational stability. Our findings show that EIS responds systematically to supportive versus detached behaviors, rising with prosocial responses and falling with apathetic ones. This sensitivity makes it well suited for turn-by-turn tracking, enabling developers to detect volatility, identify moments where the model's empathy alignment is slipping, and trigger interventions such as confidence flags or escalation to human support. In this way, EIS provides a practical safeguard for real-world deployment, helping ensure that systems remain safe when used in sensitive mental health contexts.

6 Future Directions

Future work should broaden our approach by applying EIS to additional psychometric scales and larger datasets to strengthen validation against external measures of therapeutic quality. Beyond examining a single model, analyses across multiple LLMs could clarify whether emotional variance is model-specific or a general limitation, while also revealing which design features support stability in therapeutic contexts. Another key direction is the comparison of LLMs to human participants, therapists, professionals, and nonexperts, using PsychoBench to test whether observed instabilities stem from the nature of psychotherapeutic dialogue itself. Finally, multimodal extensions using tests such as RMET and GERT could evaluate non-verbal empathy, offering insight into whether LLMs can generalize emotional understanding beyond text.

7 Conclusion

Large language models hold promise as tools for supporting psychotherapy, but their behavior in sensitive contexts remains unreliable. In this work, we applied the Emotional Intelligence Scale (EIS) as a turn-level monitoring framework to assess model performance in naturalistic dialogues. Using **llama-3.3-70b-instruct**, we found that psychotherapy-related conversations produced significantly higher variance than CustomerService dialogues, both within and across turns. This elevated variance reflects the difficulty of maintaining stable alignment with user state in emotionally nuanced settings, where small missteps can cascade into prolonged instability.

At the same time, EIS responded systematically to model behavior, rising with prosocial responses and falling with detached ones. This suggests that the volatility is not an artifact of the metric itself, but a faithful reflection of how models struggle under therapeutic demands. In this way, EIS functions not only as a research instrument but also as a practical safeguard: it tracks conversational empathy in real time and highlights when alignment may be slipping.

Taken together, these findings show that while LLMs are not yet reliable stand-alone solutions in psychotherapy, psychometric monitoring offers a path toward safer deployment. Progress toward trustworthy therapeutic AI will depend less on raw capability than on our ability to measure, interpret, and intervene when instability arises. EIS provides one such step, illustrating how structured evaluation can bridge the gap between promising performance and responsible use in high-stakes domains.

Limitations

Our study faced several limitations. First, available mental health datasets were not always suitable due to being synthetic or multimodal, which restricted our analysis to ESConv, a text-based, non-synthetic, and methodologically consistent. Second, our evaluation was limited to a single model (**llama-3.3-70b-instruct**), which may not generalize to other architectures or model sizes. Third, the high variance observed in psychotherapeutic conversations may reflect inherent instability of such dialogues rather than the limitations of LLMs. Distinguishing between instability that arises from the setting and instability introduced by models will require human–LLM comparison studies. Finally, processing time (60–80 seconds per turn) restricted our ability to scale evaluations; even within a relatively small sample of 870 turns, it required roughly 17 hours of runtime. Most of this runtime was identified to be inflated by sequential API calls, making parallelization achievable in future work.

Acknowledgments

References

Mario Aguilar. 2025. Why woebot, a pioneering therapy chatbot, shut down. *STAT News*. Retrieved September 2025.

Daniel Atherton. 2025. Incident number 1106: Chatbots allegedly reinforced delusional thinking in several reported users, leading to real-world harm. *AI Incident Database*. Retrieved September 2025 from https://incidentdatabase.ai/cite/1106.

Tom B. Brown, Benjamin Mann, Nick Ryder, Melanie Subbiah, Jared Kaplan, Prafulla Dhariwal, Arvind Neelakantan, Pranav Shyam, Girish Sastry, Amanda Askell, Sandhini Agarwal, Ariel Herbert-Voss, Gretchen Krueger, Tom Henighan, Rewon Child, Aditya Ramesh, Daniel M. Ziegler, Jeffrey Wu, Clemens Winter, and 12 others. 2020. Language models are few-shot learners. *arxiv.org*. Online, URL: https://arxiv.org/abs/2005.14165.

Yuyan Chen, Hao Wang, Songzhou Yan, Sijia Liu, Yueze Li, Yi Zhao, and Yanghua Xiao. 2024. Emotionqueen: A benchmark for evaluating empathy of large language models. *Preprint*, arXiv:2409.13359.

Alexandra Citrin-Safadi. 2025. A troubled man, his chatbot and a murder-suicide in old greenwich. *The Wall Street Journal*. Online.

Benjamin Clements. 2025. Ai claims its first casualty. Intersections, The Center for Bioethics & Human Dignity. Accessed: 2025-09-20.

Maryam Farzan, Hamid Ebrahimi, Maryam Pourali, and Fatemeh Sabeti. 2024. Artificial intelligence-powered cognitive behavioral therapy chatbots, a systematic review. *Iranian Journal of Psychiatry*, 20.

Isaac R. Galatzer-Levy, Dainel McDuff, Vivek Natarajan, Alan Karthikesalingam, and Matteo Malgaroli. 2023. The capability of large language models to measure psychiatric functioning. *Semantic Scholar*. Online, URL: https://www.semanticscholar.org/reader/f6a503bd80a640ad7cb7e038e9e1b5618f8c24ec.

Aaron Grattafiori, Abhimanyu Dubey, Abhinav Jauhri, Abhinav Pandey, Abhishek Kadian, Ahmad Al-Dahle, Aiesha Letman, Akhil Mathur, Alan Schelten, Alex Vaughan, Amy Yang, Angela Fan, Anirudh Goyal, Anthony Hartshorn, Aobo Yang, Archi Mitra, Archie Sravankumar, Artem Korenev, Arthur Hinsvark, and 82 others. 2024. The llama 3 herd of models. *Preprint*, arXiv:2407.21783.

Jen-tse Huang, Wenxuan Wang, Eric John Li, Man Ho Lam, Shujie Ren, Youliang Yuan, Wenxiang Jiao, Zhaopeng Tu, and Michael R. Lyu. 2024. On the humanity of conversational ai: Evaluating the psychological portrayal of llms. In *Proceedings of the Twelfth International Conference on Learning Representations (ICLR)*.

Aobo Kong, Shiwan Zhao, Hao Chen, Qicheng Li, Yong Qin, Ruiqi Sun, Xin Zhou, Jiaming Zhou, and Haoqin Sun. 2024. Self-prompt tuning: Enable autonomous role-playing in llms. *arxiv.org*. Online, URL: https://arxiv.org/abs/2407.08995.

Fei-Tzin Lee, Derrick Hull, Jacob Levine, Bonnie Ray, and Kathleen McKeown. 2019. Identifying therapist conversational actions across diverse psychotherapeutic approaches. *ACL Anthology*. Online, URL: https://aclanthology.org/W19-3002.

Siyang Liu, Chujie Zheng, Orianna Demasi, Sahand Sabour, Yu Li, Zhou Yu, Yong Jiang, and Minlie Huang. 2021. Towards emotional support dialog systems. *arxiv.org*. Online URL: https://arxiv.org/abs/2106.01144.

Meta AI. 2024. Llama 3.3 70b instruct: Model card and prompt formats. https://www.llama.com/docs/model-cards-and-prompt-formats/llama3_3/. Accessed 2025-09-22.

Gony Rosenman, Lior Wolf, and Talma Hendler. 2024. Llm questionnaire completion for automatic psychiatric assessment. *arxiv.org*. Online, URL: https://arxiv.org/abs/2406.06636.

Sander Schulhoff, Michael Ilie, Nishant Balepur, Konstantine Kahadze, Amanda Liu, Chenglei Si, Yinheng Li, Aayush Gupta, HyoJung Han, Sevien Schulhoff, Pranav Sandeep Dulepet, Saurav Vidyadhara,

Dayeon Ki, Sweta Agrawal, Chau Pham, Gerson Kroiz, Feileen Li, Hudson Tao, Ashay Srivastava, and 12 others. 2024. The prompt report: A systematic survey of prompt engineering techniques. *arxiv.org*. Online URL: https://arxiv.org/abs/2406.06608.

V. Sorin, D. Brin, Y. Barash, E. Konen, A. Charney, G. Nadkarni, and E. Klang. 2024. Large language models and empathy: Systematic review. *Journal of Medical Internet Research*, 26:e52597.

L. Spytska. 2025. The use of artificial intelligence in psychotherapy: development of intelligent therapeutic systems. *BMC Psychology*, 13(1):175.

Dennis Ulmer, Elman Mansimov, Kaixiang Lin, Justin Sun, Xibin Gao, and Yi Zhang. 2024. Bootstrapping llm-based task-oriented dialogue agents via self-talk. *arxiv.org*. Online URL: https://arxiv.org/abs/2401.05033.

Rasita Vinay, Giovanni Spitale, Nikola Biller-Andorno, and Federico Germani. 2024. Emotional manipulation through prompt engineering amplifies disinformation generation in ai large language models. *arxiv.org*. Online, URL: https://arxiv.org/abs/2403.03550.

Wysa. 2023. Population prevention. *Wysa*. Retrieved September 2025 from https://www.wysa.com/population-prevention.

A Dialogue Excerpts by Semantic Category Associated with Increases in EIS

Table 3: Illustrative dialogue excerpts from the ESConv dataset, grouped by semantic category and associated with increases in EIS.

Category	Example with turn ID (Format: Conversation ID–Turn)
Peer Validation and Shared Experience	457-4 (assistant): *"I understand what your going thru , i also suffered from anxiety but trust we you will overcome this."*
	457-9 (user): *"Wow its so nice to talk to someone who had the same issues. Are there any other suggestions you might recommendo?"*
	129-16 (assistant): *"You know, I once felt the same you are feeling and had the same idea that everyone had their own problems, but I took the courage to seek for help and found out that the people who really care about me will always want to help me."*
Solution-Oriented Dialogue	379-4 (user): *"i am self employed, selling event tickets on the internet, but because of covid, all events are postponed until it is safe to gather in large numbers"*
	379-13 (user): *"i would be open to seeking other employment online; work from home on the computer. any suggestions?"*
	50-20 (assistant): *"You may be able to look into unemployment at least if it comes down to it."*
Gratitude and Appreciation Expression	89-35 (user): *"Thank you. I feel better being able to rant to someone."*
	303-34 (user): *"Thank you for the help today. It was nice to talk to someone else."*
	51-18 (user): *"That's a good idea. I will try that. Thank you."*
	131-28 (assistant): *"I think you are probably not anywhere near as bad as you think you are you know :). Anyway I wish you all the very best for the New Year and hope that things pick up for you soon!"*
Adaptive Coping Strategy Discussion	303-11 (assistant): *"It's kind of a tired saying, but one strategy that has helped me is the One day at a time strategy. I'm sure you've heard of it. Basically, it means just do for today, don't worry about yesterday, don't stress over tomorrow, just treat this day as it's own task."*
	379-9 (user): *"yes, I try to walk outdoors every day, for at least 30 minutes. it does help a lot. but with the weather turning colder, that may be difficult to continue"*
	55-20 (user): *"ive been smoking a lot more because of this incident, what else can I do to cope?"*
Hope and Future Orientation	120-17 (assistant): *"no man you don't need her she had her chance and you'll find the right one someday just hang in there"*
	457-8 (assistant): *"I remember many times i thought the same way as you but i didnt give up and kept trying. As long as you dont give up you will make progress. It will take time and patience."*

Continued on next page

Category	Example with turn ID (Format: Conversation ID–Turn)
	129-30 (assistant): *"And I understand that is not the easiest in these times but I believe you can do it!"*
Social Connection Rebuilding	41-11 (assistant): *"That is good! It seems like calling on the phone can feel more genuine. Do you like playing Among Us? It might be fun to teach them how to play a game that allows you to play from far away."* 303-31 (user): *"That is probably true, but everyone has been so busy that I've only really been communicating with my husband."* 401-19 (assistant): *"i think it may be beneficial to give your friends some time, before attempting to speak with them again. maybe you can spend time with your family while you are waiting for them to cool down."*
Self-Advocacy and Boundary Setting	89-33 (user): *"I was afraid she was going to ruin my family with her attitudes."* 131-23 (user): *"I even got an emotiona support dog"* 131-25 (user): *"Yea, he's my best friend. At least I have one boy who has to stick around. He's on a tight leash"*

B Dialogue Excerpts by Semantic Category Associated with Decreases in EIS

Table 4: Illustrative dialogue excerpts from the ESConv dataset, grouped by semantic category and associated with decreases in EIS.

Category	Example with turn ID (Format: Conversation ID–Turn)
Cynicism and Misanthropy	132-4 (user): *"well, i'm not disgusted with myself... it's just people in general. everybody.. they're so selfish"*
	132-14 (user): *"I think it would be beating a dead horse. Ober half the population is overweight. People would just need to be blind not to see it. That's kind of my point. Everything is consume... consume.. consume.... buy buy buy"*
	132-16 (user): *"well... you can't really do anything without money. it all kind of rides on it, doesn't it? what you can buy?"*
	132-2 (user): *"feeling disgust as usual. Yourself?"*
	120-4 (user): *"not doing too hot tbh"*
	50-21 (user): *"We don't know what is going to happen if it comes"*
Relationship Loss and Romantic Devastation	120-6 (user): *"my girlfriend broke up with me"*
	120-18 (user): *"but she was the one"*
	51-2 (user): *"I am doing ok. I just broke up with my girlfriend and sad about it"*
	51-6 (user): *"I am so sad and just wonder why did it happen!!!"*
	51-8 (user): *"We had simple disagreement and both of us were keep fighting.. now I can not get over it."*
	303-9 (user): *"I'd like more help and understanding from my husband, but he seems to be incapable of that."*
Abandonment and Exclusion Themes	67-2 (user): *"I am really very angry with my friends for not inviting me"*
	67-4 (user): *"I didn't did any anything wrong to my friends but they are simply saying they forget me"*
	120-14 (user): *"I was supposed to introduce her, now I just look like a loser"*
	401-3 (user): *"I am today very sad because my friends fighting with me"*
	401-7 (user): *"Yes i am feeling alone"*
Anxiousness and Being Overwhelmed	457-3 (user): *"Well im feeling awful and my heart is racing , im feeling anxious for no reason."*
	457-7 (user): *"Ive tried meditation but cant seem to calm down. Exercise help for a bit but then my anxiety comes back."*
	379-2 (user): *"Hello, I'm not sure if there is any help? Without knowing when I can return to work, I will probably remain anxious about the unknown"*

Continued on next page

Category	Example with turn ID (Format: Conversation ID–Turn)
Reminiscing Traumatic Events	129-17 (user): *"It is making me have flashbacks of other traumatic situations,"*
	129-37 (user): *"Childhood traumas are tough for sure. I am a fearful person."*
	131-18 (user): *"Well... one told me that I should be put down like a dog to my face."*
	89-14 (user): *"Only once and she was just telling me that I was a horrible person."*

C Additional CI graphs

These plots visualize turn-by-turn EIS trajectories for selected **Emotional Support Conversations** (ESConv) that were identified as exhibiting notable rises or drops in Section 4.3 and Appendices A–B. Each plot is labeled with its conversation ID and includes a short caption highlighting specific turns referenced in the text. Gray shading denotes the 95% confidence interval of the mean EIS score.

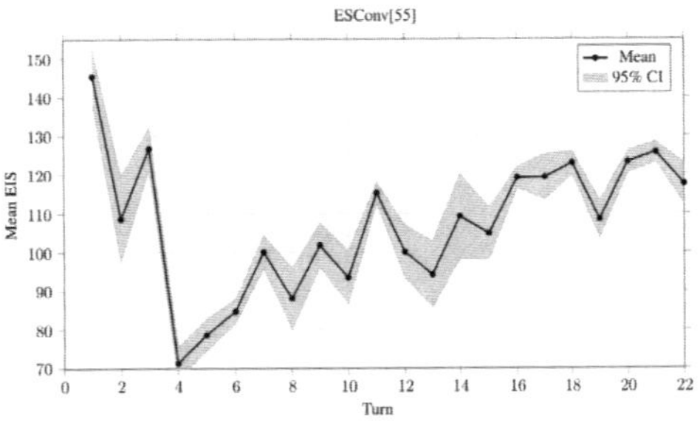

Identified points – ESConv 55:

1. Turn 20 – Increased: Adaptive Coping Strategy Discussion

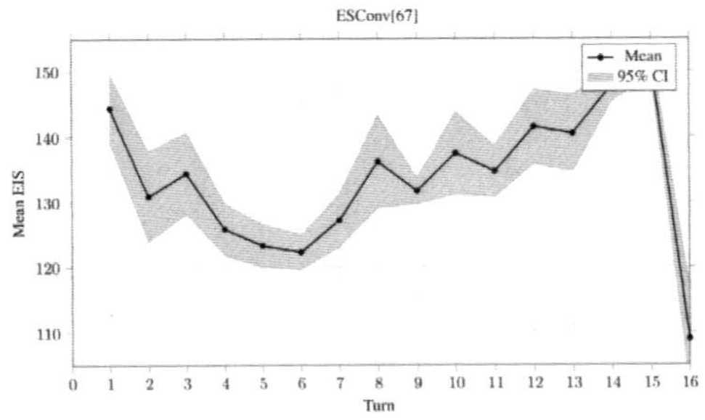

Identified points – ESConv 67:

1. Turn 2 – Decreased: Abandonment and Exclusion Themes
2. Turn 4 – Decreased: Abandonment and Exclusion Themes

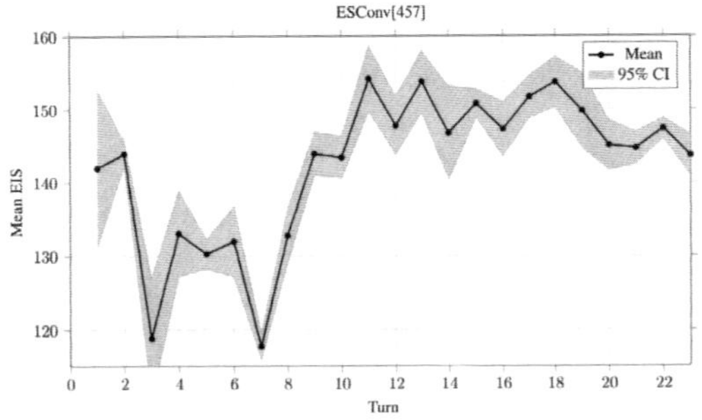

Identified points – ESConv 457:

1. Turn 4 – Increased: Peer Validation and Shared Experience
2. Turn 8 – Increased: Hope and Future Orientation
3. Turn 9 – Increased: Peer Validation and Shared Experience

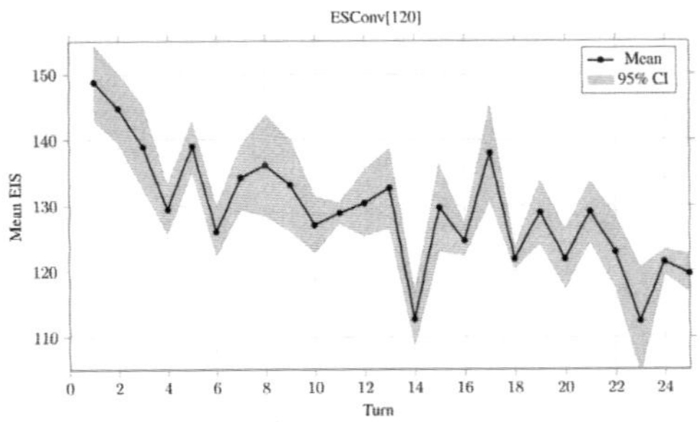

Identified points – ESConv 120:

1. Turn 4 – Decreased: Cynicism and Misanthropy
2. Turn 6 – Decreased: Relationship Loss and Romantic Devastation
3. Turn 14 – Decreased: Abandonment and Exclusion Themes
4. Turn 17 – Increased: Hope and Future Orientation
5. Turn 18 – Decreased: Relationship Loss and Romantic Devastation

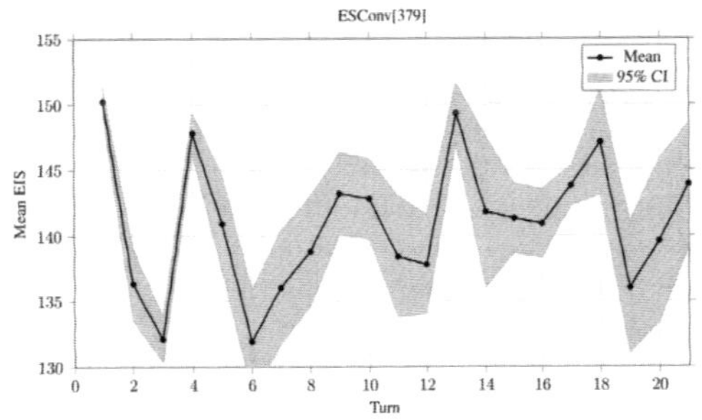

Identified points – ESConv 379:

1. Turn 2 – Decreased: Anxiousness and Being Overwhelmed
2. Turn 4 – Increased: Solution-Oriented Dialogue
3. Turn 9 – Increased: Adaptive Coping Strategy Discussion
4. Turn 13 – Increased: Solution-Oriented Dialogue

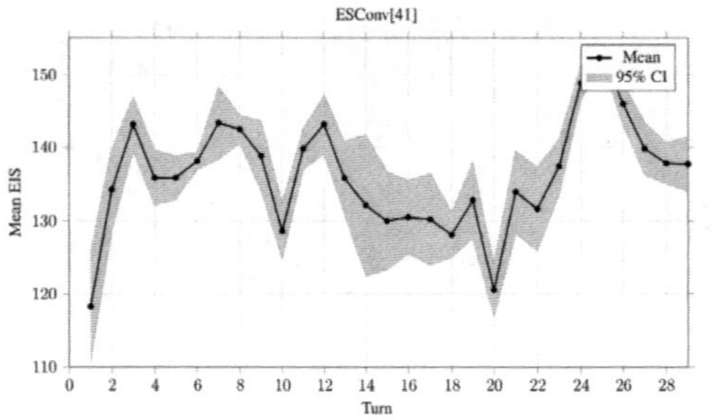

Identified points – ESConv 41:

1. Turn 11 – Increased: Social Connection Rebuilding

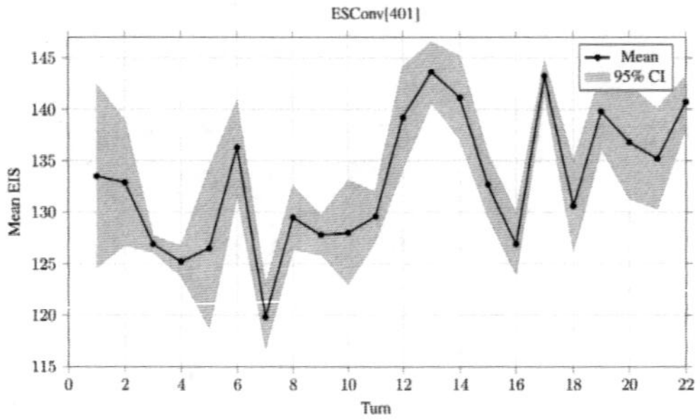

Identified points – ESConv 401:

1. Turn 3 – Decreased: Abandonment and Exclusion Themes
2. Turn 7 – Decreased: Abandonment and Exclusion Themes
3. Turn 19 – Increased: Social Connection Rebuilding

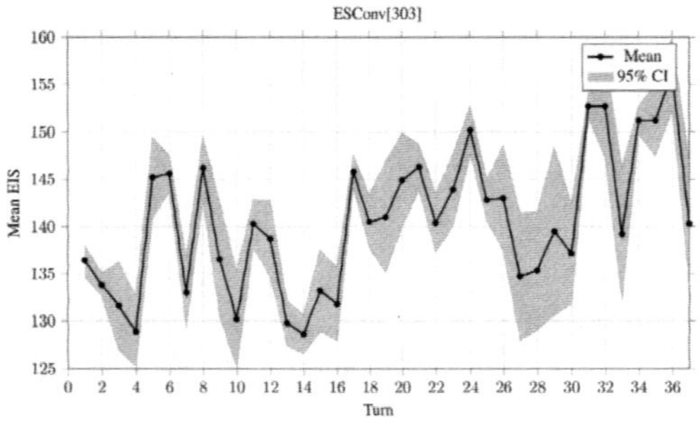

Identified points – ESConv 303:

1. Turn 9 – Decreased: Relationship Loss and Romantic Devastation
2. Turn 11 – Increased: Adaptive Coping Strategy Discussion
3. Turn 31 – Increased: Social Connection Rebuilding
4. Turn 34 – Increased: Gratitude and Appreciation Expression

D Sample Emotional Support Conversation and Customer Service Dialogues

Speaker	Utterance
Assistant	Hello, thank you for contacting BrightCom Support. How can I help you today?
User	Hey, my internet keeps dropping every few minutes. It's been really frustrating.
Assistant	I'm sorry to hear that. Can you tell me when you first started noticing this issue?
User	About three days ago. I thought it was temporary, but it's just getting worse.
Assistant	Have you made any changes to your setup recently, like moving the router or adding new devices?
User	No, everything's the same. I just work from home, so I notice the interruptions more.
Assistant	Understood. Let's try a quick reset. Could you unplug your modem and router for about 30 seconds, then plug them back in?
User	Sure, one sec... Okay, I just plugged them back in.
Assistant	Great. While the system reboots, can you tell me if the outages happen at specific times of day, or is it random?
User	Seems random, but it happens most often in the evenings when I'm on calls.
Assistant	That could indicate high usage in your area. I'll check our network status. Please hold on a moment.
User	Alright.
Assistant	Thank you for waiting. I do see some congestion reported in your neighborhood. We're working to improve capacity.
User	So, is there anything I can do on my end?
Assistant	Yes, besides the reboot, try placing your router in an open area away from walls. Also, connecting by Ethernet for calls will help with stability.
User	I can do that. I'll move it closer to my desk. Will this permanently fix the issue though?
Assistant	It should reduce the drops, but once our upgrade is complete, the service will be much more reliable overall.
User	Okay, thanks. Any idea when that upgrade will finish?
Assistant	Yes, the projected completion date is within the next two weeks.
User	Alright, that helps. At least I know it's not just my equipment.
Assistant	Exactly, and I've documented this on your account so if you call back, our team will know the steps you've already taken.
User	Cool, thanks for doing that.
Assistant	No problem. I'll also credit your account for a week of service since you've been dealing with interruptions.
User	Oh wow, I appreciate that.
Assistant	You're welcome. Is there anything else I can help you with today?
User	No, that should be it. Thanks again.
Assistant	Glad I could help. Thank you for choosing BrightCom, and have a great day!
User	You too!
Assistant	Goodbye!

Table 5: Customer Service control conversation (synthetic): full dialogue in `User/Assistant` format.

Speaker	Utterance
User	Good evening.
Assistant	Hi, how's things?
User	Things are ok, I am just having issues with the problem above.
Assistant	I am afraid that I am not able to see that. Can you tell me about it?
User	Yes, so I have always done very well in school and university. I have always had A's or high B's. Last semester in university, I failed one of my exams. I still passed the class with an A, but for some reason, that exam haunts me and gives me bad dreams.
User	I don't know why it happens and it worries me.
Assistant	I can understand that, when I was sitting my final exams I constantly had nightmares about failing. Nearly thirty years on and I still do!!
Assistant	But you did really very well and you passed with an A. Do you think maybe you are being a little too hard on yourself?
User	Maybe. I got a 46% on the exam (so an F) but I did all my other assignments and exams almost perfect and got an A overall. I never once failed a test in my life, and have always held myself to a very high academic degree to make my parents proud.
User	I come from a poor family, so succeeding in life is very important to me.
User	me*.
Assistant	It sounds as though you feel that academic success is the most important thing in your life, would I be right in thinking this?
User	Yes you are correct.
Assistant	Have you considered talking to anyone about these feelings of perfectionism? A therapist perhaps?
Assistant	There is a good deal of useful help and information out there for people who are struggling.
User	I have not, actually. I don't think my family can afford a therapist, especially with the pandemic raging right now.
User	Where do you recommend going?
Assistant	Does your school have any counsellors offering help for free? Many do.
Assistant	I believe that there are some charities that will offer a certain number of free therapy sessions too.
User	I don't think any are available since my school is online only, also the campus is completely closed due to Winter Break.
User	Oh? Charities?
Assistant	Yes I think so, though I am not totally sure. There should be someone at your school, online or not, who can advise you.
User	I have never heard of such people, I am interested.
Assistant	Really though I think that your problem is self esteem. You should think better of yourself :)
Assistant	I can tell that you set yourself a very high standard but I also think that you need to be kind to yourself.
User	I think you're right, but I don't know, I'm still scared about having the bad dreams. I often wake up 2–3 times at night because of them.
Assistant	I can understand that, this has been happening to me all of my life. Have you tried to take anything to help?
Assistant	I can recommend a hot milky drink before bed and perhaps a hot water bottle. Anyway I hope that I have been able to be of some assistance to you!
Assistant	Have a lovely holiday season.
User	Thank you, I'll try to do just that.
User	Merry Christmas to you.
Assistant	And you :) remember to hit the quit button and take the survey ;)

Table 6: ESConv conversation [80]: full dialogue in User/Assistant format.

BookAsSumQA: An Evaluation Framework for Aspect-Based Book Summarization via Question Answering

Ryuhei Miyazato[1], **Ting-Ruen Wei**[2], **Xuyang Wu**[2], **Hsin-Tai Wu**[3], **Kei Harada**[1],
[1]The University of Electro-Communications,
[2]Santa Clara University, [3]DOCOMO Innovations, Inc.,
Correspondence: miyazato@uec.ac.jp, harada@uec.ac.jp

Abstract

Aspect-based summarization aims to generate summaries that highlight specific aspects of a text, enabling more personalized and targeted summaries. However, its application to books remains unexplored due to the difficulty of constructing reference summaries for long text. To address this challenge, we propose BookAsSumQA, a QA-based evaluation framework for aspect-based book summarization. BookAsSumQA automatically constructs a narrative knowledge graph and synthesizes aspect-specific QA pairs to evaluate summaries based on their ability to answer these questions. Our experiments on BookAsSumQA revealed that while LLM-based approaches showed higher accuracy on shorter texts, RAG-based methods become more effective as document length increases, making them more efficient and practical for aspect-based book summarization[1].

1 Introduction

Automatic summarization condenses long texts into concise and informative representations, allowing readers to grasp key information efficiently. Book summarization applies this to novels, which are often lengthy and complex. The progress of automatic book summarization has been accelerated by the release of the BookSum dataset (Kryscinski et al., 2022), which contains novels paired with human-written summaries. With the growing volume of books, there is increasing interest in aspect-based summarization (ABS), which produces summaries tailored to specific aspects, such as themes or genres. Although ABS helps readers quickly access desired information and has been more actively explored in domains such as reviews (Xu et al., 2023) and lectures (Kolagar and Zarcone, 2024), its application to books remains relatively understudied. This is mainly because summarization research relies on manually created reference summaries, and building evaluation datasets for long documents is a labor-intensive and costly process. The longer the original document and the greater the number of aspects, the higher the human and financial costs become.

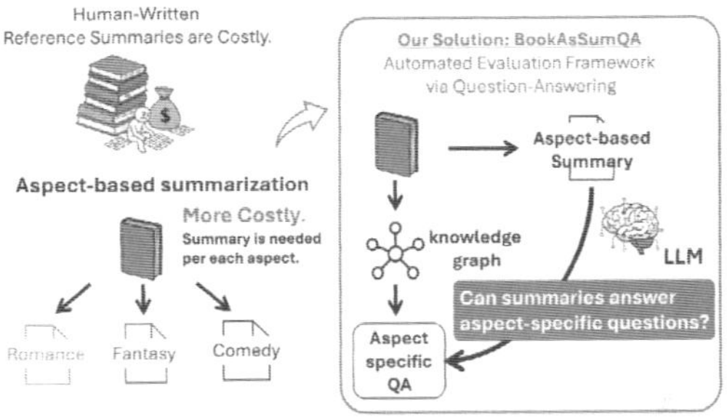

Figure 1: In BookAsSumQA, we generate aspect-specific QA pairs from a knowledge graph and evaluate summaries by testing whether they can answer these questions, thereby assessing aspect coverage without costly human-written references.

To address this challenge, we propose BookAsSumQA, a QA-based evaluation framework for aspect-based book summarization that enables evaluation without manually created reference summaries. We synthesize aspect-specific QA pairs from the narrative through a knowledge graph, and evaluate aspect-based summaries by testing whether an LLM can answer these questions using the generated summary as reference. This allows us to measure how well the summary captures information about the aspects of the narrative. In this study, we define aspects as literary genres in novels (example: Figure 1).

First, we construct a knowledge graph that represents relationships among entities in the narrative. Using an LLM, we extract relationships between entities (e.g., characters) with a textual description, keywords, and an importance score, and incre-

[1]https://github.com/ryuhei-miyazato/bookassumqa

Proceedings of the IJCNLP-AACL 2025 Student Research Workshop, pages 123–133
December 20-24, 2025 ©2025 Association for Computational Linguistics

mentally upsert them into the graph to capture the global relationships within the narrative. Next, we construct aspect-specific QA pairs from the knowledge graph. To do so, we first identify edges that are relevant to a target aspect by calculating the cosine similarity between the text embeddings of the aspect term and the edge keywords, and then generate aspect-specific QA pairs based on the descriptions of those edges. Finally, we evaluate ABS methods using the generated QA pairs by assessing whether each generated summary can correctly answer the questions. We then compare the generated answers against the ground-truth using ROUGE-1, METEOR, and BERTScore. By comparing the accuracy, we investigate which method is most suitable for aspect-based book summarization.

2 Related Work

In the field of book summarization, as the BookSum dataset (Kryscinski et al., 2022) provides pairs of public domain novels and generic summaries, obtaining the summaries is well studied (Wu et al., 2021; Xiong et al., 2023; Liu et al., 2023). In this study, we focus on ABS, which generates summaries centered on specific aspects of a text. Unlike Query-Focused Summarization (QFS), which generates summaries in response to specific user queries (e.g., SQuALITY (Wang et al., 2022)), ABS instead focuses on predefined aspects such as genres or themes.

ABS has been actively studied in domains such as news (Zhang et al., 2024), reviews (Xu et al., 2023), lecture materials (Kolagar and Zarcone, 2024), and multi-domain documents (Hayashi et al., 2021), where reference summaries are often manually created or readily available. However, for long documents like books, creating such references is labor-intensive and costly, limiting the application of ABS in this domain.

To overcome this difficulty, we propose a framework that evaluates aspect-based summaries of novels without manual reference summaries. While several studies have proposed reference-free evaluation metrics for summarization that assess summary quality without relying on gold reference summaries (Chen et al., 2021; Liu et al., 2022; Gigant et al., 2024), we introduce a QA-based framework that evaluates summaries without manual references by generating QA pairs from the source text, measuring how much information from the source text is captured in the summary (Hirao et al., 2001; Scialom et al., 2019; Pu et al., 2024). In this work, we further extend this approach by generating aspect-specific QA pairs to evaluate how well each aspect-based summary captures information related to its corresponding aspect in the original text.

3 BookAsSumQA

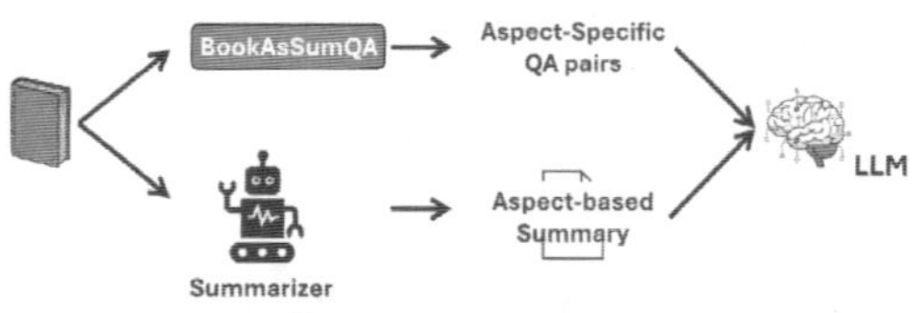

Figure 2: BookAsSumQA: Evaluation framework for aspect-based book summarization.

3.1 ABS Evaluation with BookAsSumQA

In BookAsSumQA (Figure 2), we shift the evaluation of aspect-based summaries into a Question-Answering task. QA pairs are automatically synthesized through a knowledge graph of the narrative, where nodes are enriched with keywords and description to generate comprehensive aspect-specific questions. The quality of a summary is then assessed by measuring how well the generated aspect-based summary enables an LLM to answer these aspect-specific QA, indicating how much information about the target aspect the summary truly captures.

3.2 QA Generation Process

An overview of the QA generation process is illustrated in Figure 3. The process consists of three stages: (1) splitting the text into chunks and extracting entities and relations, (2) inserting the extracted entities and relations into a knowledge graph as nodes and edges, and (3) synthesizing aspect-specific QA pairs from the completed graph.

(1). Chunking and Extraction Each book is split into chunks of 1,200 characters with an overlap of 100 characters, following the parameters of GraphRAG (Edge et al., 2024). From each chunk, entities (e.g., characters, events, concepts) are extracted using an LLM with a specifically designed prompt (2-shot, Appendix C, Figure 6). For each extracted relation, the prompt instructs the LLM to output a textual description, representative keywords, and an importance score ranging from 1 to

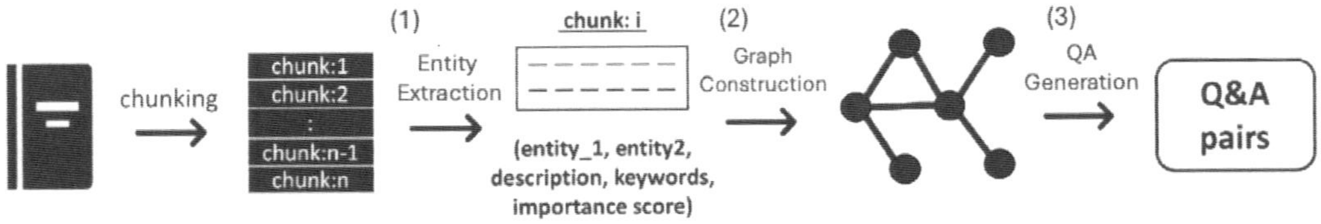

Figure 3: QA Generation Process. (1) splitting the text into chunks and extracting entities and relations, (2) inserting the extracted entities and relations into a knowledge graph as nodes and edges, and (3) synthesizing aspect-specific QA pairs from the completed graph.

10, reflecting the importance of the relationship within the local context.

(2). Knowledge Graph Construction The extracted entities and relations are incrementally inserted into a knowledge graph, where each edge is labeled with keywords, a textual description, and an importance score. If an entity already exists, its information is updated and summarized as needed, with keywords regenerated accordingly. In addition, importance score is accumulated by adding the newly assigned value to reflect repeated or strengthened relationships across chunks.

(3). QA Generation Once the knowledge graph is constructed, we generate aspect-specific QA pairs. We first filter edges to keep only those with an importance score of 10 or higher, considering relationships above this threshold to be important. An importance score of 10 indicates either a salient relationship or one that appears multiple times in the narrative, making it a stronger candidate for generating aspect-specific QA. From these, a maximum of 100 edges were selected. QA pairs are then generated from the description of each edge using a dedicated prompt (1-shot, Appendix C, Figure 7), with keywords from the edge also included in the generated QA. For each aspect, aspect-specific QA pairs were selected by calculating the cosine similarity between the text embeddings of the aspect and those of the QA keywords, and the top five most relevant QA were retained. Examples of aspect-specific QA pairs are also provided in Appendix D.

We utilized GPT-4o-mini [2] for both entity extraction and QA generation and used sentence-transformers/paraphrase-MiniLM-L6-v2 (Reimers and Gurevych, 2019) for text embedding. For implementation of graph-generation, we referred to the code of LightRAG (Guo et al., 2024).

4 Experimental Settings

4.1 Models

Since no existing ABS method specifically targets books, we compare various approaches, including LLMs and RAGs. Detail information about the models is in Appendix B.

LLMs Following the strategy of BooookScore (Chang et al., 2024), we adopt two workflows for summarizing book-length documents that exceed the model's context window: (1) Hierarchical Merging (Hier), which recursively merges summaries of individual chunks into higher-level summaries, and (2) Incremental Updating (Inc), which incrementally updates a single global summary as each new chunk is processed. Detailed descriptions are provided in Appendix B.

For experiments, we use both an open-source model, meta-llama/Llama-3.1-8B-Instruct [3], and a closed-source model, GPT-4o-mini.

RAGs RAG retrieves information relevant to a query from external sources and generates an answer. In this study, we adopt NaiveRAG (Gao et al., 2023), as well as GraphRAG (Edge et al., 2024) and LightRAG (Guo et al., 2024), which employ graph structures to organize external information.

4.2 Setup

The original texts used in this experiment are taken from BookSum (Kryscinski et al., 2022), which sources books from the Project Gutenberg public domain book repository with expired copyrights. We selected texts with varying lengths: over 200,000 words (large), between 90,000 and

[2] https://openai.com/index/gpt-4o-mini-advancing-cost-efficient-intelligence/

[3] https://huggingface.co/meta-llama/Llama-3.1-8B-Instruct

110,000 words (middle), and less than 20,000 words (small), comprising 12, 9, and 9 books respectively, for a total of 30. In this paper, we define

Fantasy	Romance	Comedy
Paranormal	Young Adult	Horror
History	Action	Science Fiction
Mystery	Adventure	Crime
Thriller	Poetry	

Table 1: List of Aspects used in this study.

fourteen "aspects" as the literary genre of a novel with reference to Wikipedia's List of writing genres[4](see Table 1).

For each method, aspect-based summaries were generated for the aspects listed in Table 1, with each summary limited to 300 tokens. The generated summaries were evaluated based on their ability to answer the corresponding QA pairs with referring the generated summary. The prompts used for this QA-answering process are provided in the Appendix C (Figure 8). The accuracy of the answers was evaluated using ROUGE-1 (Lin, 2004), METEOR (Banerjee and Lavie, 2005) and BERTScore (Zhang et al., 2020) metrics, measuring the alignment between the generated answers and the ground-truth.

RAG-based methods index the original text once and reuse it to generate summaries for different aspects, whereas LLM-based methods generate a new summary every time for each aspect.

5 Results

5.1 Question Answering Using Aspect-Based Summaries

Type	method	ROUGE-1	METEOR	BERTScore
LLM	Llama + Hier	22.43	19.23	85.66
	GPT + Hier	**22.49**	**19.49**	**85.82**
	Llama + Inc	21.91	18.23	85.48
	GPT + Inc	21.90	18.76	85.47
RAG	NaiveRAG	21.43	18.66	85.44
	GraphRAG	14.66	13.56	84.50
	LightRAG	20.61	18.41	85.51

Table 2: Results of aspect-based summarization using different methods. LLM-based methods include Llama-3.1-8B-Instruct (Llama) and GPT-4o-mini (GPT).

Table 2 shows the accuracy for aspect QA with generated aspect-based summaries. Each value represents the average result across all aspects.

[4]https://en.wikipedia.org/wiki/List_of_writing_genres#Fiction_genres

Overall, the method that applies Hierarchical Merging with GPT-4o-mini achieved the highest scores. Among LLM-based methods, Hierarchical Merging was better than Incremental Updating, and LLM-based methods overall surpass RAG-based methods. For RAG, NaiveRAG achieves the best results, while GraphRAG shows considerably lower scores compared to the other methods.

One possible reason for the superior performance of LLM-based methods is that LLM-based methods extract aspect-specific information from finer-grained chunks. Although incremental updating incorporates previous context, using both the prior summary and the current chunk may make it harder to extract targeted information. In GraphRAG, summaries are generated for each community in the graph and used to answer QA, making it less effective at capturing aspect-related stories. According to the results in the Appendix A.1 (Table 4), GraphRAG achieves the highest accuracy in conventional summarization, suggesting that improving the construction of the graph and the summarization process could lead to better scores in the future.

5.2 Comparison by Original Text Length

Size	Method	ROUGE-1	METEOR	BERTScore
Small	GPT + Hier	**25.66**	**21.91**	**86.54**
	GPT + Inc	24.81	20.84	86.14
	NaiveRAG	22.09	19.24	85.58
Middle	GPT + Hier	**21.95**	**19.52**	85.56
	GPT + Inc	21.68	18.68	85.35
	NaiveRAG	**21.95**	19.45	**85.62**
Large	GPT + Hier	20.50	**17.65**	**85.48**
	GPT + Inc	19.88	17.27	85.06
	NaiveRAG	**20.55**	17.64	85.21

Table 3: Comparison by Original Text Length
(Small: <20k words, Middle: 90k–110k, Large: >200k)

We conducted an experiment to compare summarization performance across different lengths of the original text. In this experiment, we used the best-performing models from the LLM-based and RAG-based approaches identified in Section 5.1.

As shown in Table 3, the performance tends to decline as the length of the original text increases. Although NaiveRAG performs worse than the LLM-based method in the small group, its performance becomes comparable to that of the LLM-based approach in the middle and large groups.

Considering that RAG-based methods can generate aspect-based summaries for different queries with a single indexing of the original text, RAG-based approaches may be more suitable for aspect-based summarization of longer documents.

6 Conclusion

In this study, we proposed BookAsSumQA, a QA-based evaluation framework for aspect-based book summarization. Constructing knowledge graphs and automatically generating aspect-specific QA enable evaluation of ABS quality without human-annotated reference summaries. In our experiments with BookAsSumQA, while LLM-based approaches performed better on shorter texts, RAG-based methods achieved comparable performance on longer documents. These results suggest that RAG-based methods are more practical and scalable choice for aspect-based book summarization. Future work will explore specialized indexing and retrieval techniques.

Limitations

This study has several limitations. First, we used gpt-4o-mini to generate QA pairs for summary evaluation; the choice of model may affect the evaluation results. In future work, we plan to investigate the impact of different models for QA generation. Second, both QA generation and answering relied on LLMs, which may incorporate external knowledge beyond the original text or summaries. To address this, we plan to explore methods for restricting the model's context strictly to the given text and summaries, ensuring fairer evaluation. Third, we have not yet compared our framework with other reference-free evaluation metrics or with human judgments. Such comparisons would help clarify how BookAsSumQA aligns with human evaluation and how it complements existing automatic metrics in terms of reliability and interpretability.

Acknowledgments

We would like to thank Dr. Shunsuke Kitada for his valuable advice and insightful feedback on the writing of this paper.

References

Satanjeev Banerjee and Alon Lavie. 2005. METEOR: An automatic metric for MT evaluation with improved correlation with human judgments. In *Proceedings of the ACL Workshop on Intrinsic and Extrinsic Evaluation Measures for Machine Translation and/or Summarization*, pages 65–72, Ann Arbor, Michigan. Association for Computational Linguistics.

Yapei Chang, Kyle Lo, Tanya Goyal, and Mohit Iyyer. 2024. Booookscore: A systematic exploration of book-length summarization in the era of LLMs. In *The Twelfth International Conference on Learning Representations*.

Wang Chen, Piji Li, and Irwin King. 2021. A training-free and reference-free summarization evaluation metric via centrality-weighted relevance and self-referenced redundancy. In *Proceedings of the 59th Annual Meeting of the Association for Computational Linguistics and the 11th International Joint Conference on Natural Language Processing (Volume 1: Long Papers)*, pages 404–414, Online. Association for Computational Linguistics.

Darren Edge, Ha Trinh, Newman Cheng, Joshua Bradley, Alex Chao, Apurva Mody, Steven Truitt, Dasha Metropolitansky, Robert Osazuwa Ness, and Jonathan Larson. 2024. From local to global: A graph rag approach to query-focused summarization. *arXiv preprint arXiv:2404.16130*.

Yunfan Gao, Yun Xiong, Xinyu Gao, Kangxiang Jia, Jinliu Pan, Yuxi Bi, Yixin Dai, Jiawei Sun, Haofen Wang, and Haofen Wang. 2023. Retrieval-augmented generation for large language models: A survey. *arXiv preprint arXiv:2312.10997*, 2:1.

Théo Gigant, Camille Guinaudeau, Marc Decombas, and Frederic Dufaux. 2024. Mitigating the impact of reference quality on evaluation of summarization systems with reference-free metrics. In *Proceedings of the 2024 Conference on Empirical Methods in Natural Language Processing*, pages 19355–19368, Miami, Florida, USA. Association for Computational Linguistics.

Zirui Guo, Lianghao Xia, Yanhua Yu, Tu Ao, and Chao Huang. 2024. Lightrag: Simple and fast retrieval-augmented generation. *arXiv preprint arXiv:2410.05779*.

Hiroaki Hayashi, Prashant Budania, Peng Wang, Chris Ackerson, Raj Neervannan, and Graham Neubig. 2021. WikiAsp: A dataset for multi-domain aspect-based summarization. *Transactions of the Association for Computational Linguistics*, 9:211–225.

Tsutomu Hirao, Yutaka Sasaki, and Hideki Isozaki. 2001. An extrinsic evaluation for question-biased text summarization on qa tasks. In *Proceedings of the NAACL 2001 Workshop on Automatic Summarization*, pages 61–68.

Zahra Kolagar and Alessandra Zarcone. 2024. HumSum: A personalized lecture summarization tool for humanities students using LLMs. In *Proceedings of the 1st Workshop on Personalization of Generative AI Systems (PERSONALIZE 2024)*, pages 36–70, St. Julians, Malta. Association for Computational Linguistics.

Wojciech Kryscinski, Nazneen Rajani, Divyansh Agarwal, Caiming Xiong, and Dragomir Radev. 2022. BOOKSUM: A collection of datasets for long-form narrative summarization. In *Findings of the Association for Computational Linguistics: EMNLP 2022*, pages 6536–6558, Abu Dhabi, United Arab Emirates. Association for Computational Linguistics.

Chin-Yew Lin. 2004. ROUGE: A package for automatic evaluation of summaries. In *Text Summarization Branches Out*, pages 74–81, Barcelona, Spain. Association for Computational Linguistics.

Dongqi Liu, Yifan Wang, and Vera Demberg. 2023. Incorporating distributions of discourse structure for long document abstractive summarization. In *Proceedings of the 61st Annual Meeting of the Association for Computational Linguistics (Volume 1: Long Papers)*, pages 5574–5590, Toronto, Canada. Association for Computational Linguistics.

Yizhu Liu, Qi Jia, and Kenny Zhu. 2022. Reference-free summarization evaluation via semantic correlation and compression ratio. In *Proceedings of the 2022 Conference of the North American Chapter of the Association for Computational Linguistics: Human Language Technologies*, pages 2109–2115, Seattle, United States. Association for Computational Linguistics.

Xiao Pu, Mingqi Gao, and Xiaojun Wan. 2024. Is summary useful or not? an extrinsic human evaluation of text summaries on downstream tasks. In *Proceedings of the 2024 Joint International Conference on Computational Linguistics, Language Resources and Evaluation (LREC-COLING 2024)*, pages 9389–9404, Torino, Italia. ELRA and ICCL.

Nils Reimers and Iryna Gurevych. 2019. Sentence-bert: Sentence embeddings using siamese bert-networks. In *Proceedings of the 2019 Conference on Empirical Methods in Natural Language Processing*. Association for Computational Linguistics.

Thomas Scialom, Sylvain Lamprier, Benjamin Piwowarski, and Jacopo Staiano. 2019. Answers unite! unsupervised metrics for reinforced summarization models. In *Proceedings of the 2019 Conference on Empirical Methods in Natural Language Processing and the 9th International Joint Conference on Natural Language Processing (EMNLP-IJCNLP)*, pages 3246–3256, Hong Kong, China. Association for Computational Linguistics.

Alex Wang, Richard Yuanzhe Pang, Angelica Chen, Jason Phang, and Samuel R. Bowman. 2022. SQuALITY: Building a long-document summarization dataset the hard way. In *Proceedings of the 2022 Conference on Empirical Methods in Natural Language Processing*, pages 1139–1156, Abu Dhabi, United Arab Emirates. Association for Computational Linguistics.

Jeff Wu, Long Ouyang, Daniel M. Ziegler, Nisan Stiennon, Ryan Lowe, Jan Leike, and Paul F. Christiano. 2021. Recursively summarizing books with human feedback. *CoRR*, abs/2109.10862.

Wenhan Xiong, Anchit Gupta, Shubham Toshniwal, Yashar Mehdad, and Scott Yih. 2023. Adapting pre-trained text-to-text models for long text sequences. In *Findings of the Association for Computational Linguistics: EMNLP 2023*, pages 5566–5578, Singapore. Association for Computational Linguistics.

Hongyan Xu, Hongtao Liu, Zhepeng Lv, Qing Yang, and Wenjun Wang. 2023. Pre-trained personalized review summarization with effective salience estimation. In *Findings of the Association for Computational Linguistics: ACL 2023*, pages 10743–10754, Toronto, Canada. Association for Computational Linguistics.

Lemei Zhang, Peng Liu, Marcus Tiedemann Oekland Henriksboe, Even W. Lauvrak, Jon Atle Gulla, and Heri Ramampiaro. 2024. Personalsum: A user-subjective guided personalized summarization dataset for large language models. In *The Thirty-eight Conference on Neural Information Processing Systems Datasets and Benchmarks Track*.

Tianyi Zhang, Varsha Kishore, Felix Wu, Kilian Q. Weinberger, and Yoav Artzi. 2020. An extrinsic evaluation for question-biased text summarization on qa tasks. In *In 8th International Conference on Learning Representations*.

A Experiment with Generic Summaries

A.1 Comparison Results between Reference Summaries and Standard Summaries

Type	method	ROUGE1	METEOR	BERTScore
LLM	GPT + Hier	20.64	9.87	82.89
	GPT + Inc	21.64	10.29	82.49
	Llama + Hier	23.96	11.28	**83.10**
	Llama + Inc	24.03	11.21	82.60
RAG	NaiveRAG	20.13	9.58	81.94
	GraphRAG	**25.37**	**14.78**	80.29
	LightRAG	20.66	10.00	81.87

Table 4: Comparison Results between Reference Summaries and Standard Summaries.

We conducted an experiment comparing the generic summaries generated by each model with the reference summaries in BookSum to evaluate the models' capabilities for generic summarization. The results are shown in Table 4.

In BookAsSumQA, the performance of GraphRAG was considerably worse than other methods. However, for standard summarization, it achieved the highest scores on two metrics based on character overlap. In contrast, it obtained the lowest score on BERTScore, which compares semantic similarity.

A.2 Results of BookAsSumQA with Generic Summaries

Type	method	ROUGE	METEOR	BERT_Score
LLM	GPT + Hier	20.65	18.45	85.35
	GPT + Inc	20.63	17.51	85.23
	Llama + Hier	19.86	16.45	85.23
	Llama + Inc	20.72	17.27	85.41
RAG	NaiveRAG	19.76	17.28	85.05
	GraphRAG	15.12	14.37	84.81
	LightRAG	20.29	17.79	85.48

Table 5: The results of BookAsSumQA with generic summaries.

We conducted an experiment comparing the accuracy of answering QA pairs generated by BookAsSumQA, using standard summaries produced by each model employed in our experiments in Section 4. The results are shown in Table 5.

Compared to the results in Table 2, aspect-based summaries achieved higher accuracy in answering aspect-specific QA. Additionally, while there were notable differences among methods when using aspect-based summaries, the results for generic summaries were more similar across methods. These findings indicate that BookAsSumQA serves as an evaluation framework for aspect-based summarization.

B Detail Information of Summarizer

LLMs

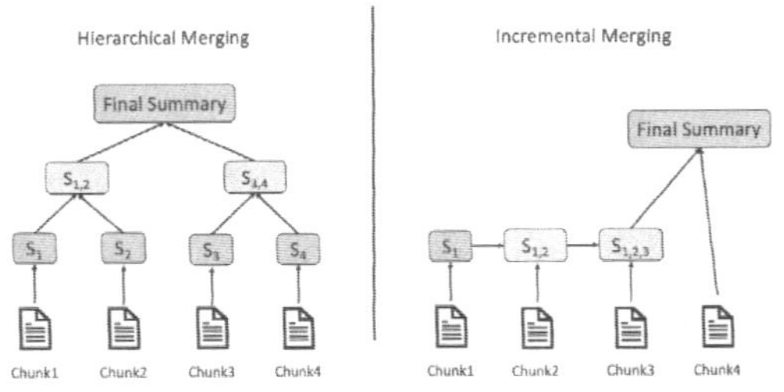

Figure 4: (1) Hierarchical Merging and (2) Incremental Updating.

For LLM-based summarization, we adopt two prompting workflows for summarizing book-length documents that exceed the model's context window (Figure 4): (1) Hierarchical Merging (Hier) and (2) Incremental Updating (Inc), following BooookScore (Chang et al., 2024).

In both workflows, the input document is first divided into smaller chunks (e.g., a chunk size of 2048 tokens). In the hierarchical merging strategy, each chunk is summarized separately, and the resulting summaries are merged using additional prompts. In the incremental updating strategy, a global summary is updated and compressed step-by-step as the model processes each chunk.

RAGs

For RAG-based method, we used several RAG as described below. We used the default settings for indexing and retrieval methods, and built the same database for each aspect-based summarization approach. For each aspect, summaries were generated using query (Figure 5) corresponding to that aspect as queries.

> Generate a summary of the ${aspect} in this story.

Figure 5: The query used for RAG-ased method.

- **NaiveRAG (Gao et al., 2023)**
  NaiveRAG is a standard RAG system. It splits texts into chunks, embeds them, retrieves the most similar ones to a query, and generates an answer.

- **GraphRAG (Edge et al., 2024)**
  GraphRAG creates a knowledge graph from the source text, generates community summaries by summarizing subgraphs, and uses them to answer queries.

- **LightRAG (Guo et al., 2024)**
  LightRAG builds a knowledge graph from the source text, retrieves relevant parts via the graph based on query keywords, and generates an answer.

C Prompt

-Goal-
Given a text document that is potentially relevant to this activity and a list of entity types, identify all entities of those types from the text and all relationships among the identified entities.
-Steps-
1. Identify all entities. For each identified entity, extract the following information:
- entity_name: Name of the entity, capitalized
- entity_type: One of the following types: [{entity_types}]
- entity_description: Comprehensive description of the entity's attributes and activities
Format each entity as ("entity"{tuple_delimiter}<entity_name>{tuple_delimiter}<entity_type>{tuple_delimiter}<entity_description>

2. From the entities identified in step 1, identify all pairs of (source_entity, target_entity) that are *clearly related* to each other.
For each pair of related entities, extract the following information:
- source_entity: name of the source entity, as identified in step 1
- target_entity: name of the target entity, as identified in step 1
- relationship_description: explanation as to why you think the source entity and the target entity are related to each other
- relationship_strength: a numeric score indicating strength of the relationship between the source entity and target entity
- relationship_keywords: one or more high-level key words that summarize the overarching nature of the relationship, focusing on concepts or themes rather than specific details
Format each relationship as
("relationship"{tuple_delimiter}<source_entity>{tuple_delimiter}<target_entity>{tuple_delimiter}<relationship_description>{tuple_delimiter}<relationship_keywords>{tuple_delimiter}<relationship_strength>)

3. Identify high-level key words that summarize the main concepts, themes, or topics of the entire text. These should capture the overarching ideas present in the document.
Format the content-level key words as ("content_keywords"{tuple_delimiter}<high_level_keywords>)

4. Return output in English as a single list of all the entities and relationships identified in steps 1 and 2. Use **{record_delimiter}** as the list delimiter.

5. When finished, output {completion_delimiter}

########################
-Examples-
########################

Example 1: (...)

###############################

Example 2: (...)

##############

###############################

-Real Data-

########################

Entity_types: {entity_types}

Text: {input_text}

########################

Output:

Figure 6: Entity extraction prompt (Vanity Fair).

```
"""Given a relationship between two individuals, you are tasked with generating a single question and answer pair about their relationship.
You will be provided with the relationship details, including a description and keywords.
Your output should be a tuple containing the question, answer, and the keywords related to that relationship.
For the question, you need to answer it appropriately and associate it with the provided relationship description and keywords.
```
{{
  "question": "$YOUR_QUESTION_HERE",
  "answer": "$THE_ANSWER_HERE"
  "keywords":$THE_KEYWORDS_HERE
}}
```
Everything between the ``` must be valid json.
########################
-Examples-
########################
Two Indivisual: Alice, Bob
Description: Alice and Bob are best friends who share common hobbies like hiking and painting. They enjoy spending time together on weekends and support each other in their careers.
Keywords: best friends, hiking, painting, support
#################
Output:
{{
  "question": "How do Alice and Bob support each other?",
  "answer": "Alice and Bob support each other in their careers."
  "keywords: support, friends"
}}
################################
-Real Data-
########################
Two Indivisual:  {entity1}, {entity2}
Description: {description}
Keywords: {keywords}
########################
Output:"""
```

Figure 7: QA generation prompt (Vanity Fair).

```
messages = [
  {"role": "system", "content": """You are going to answer a question.
You will be provided with reference text and the question.
Please answer to the question based on the provided text.
If the text does not contain enough information to answer a question, please output "I don't know"."""},
  {"role": "user", "content": f"Text: {text}\nQuestion: {question}"}
```

Figure 8: QA answering prompt (Vanity Fair).

D Example of Generated QA

Aspect	Question	Answer	Keywords
Romance	What indicates Joseph Sedley's romantic interest in Rebecca?	Joseph Sedley's romantic interest in Rebecca is indicated by his efforts to impress her, his sensitivity about his vanity, and his dependency on her during his illnesses, all of which suggest a growing intimacy and admiration for her.	romantic interest, intimacy, admiration, dependency
Action	What is the nature of the relationship between Miss Sharp and Miss Pinkerton?	The relationship between Miss Sharp and Miss Pinkerton is characterized by conflict and personal animosity, with Miss Sharp openly defying Miss Pinkerton's authority and expressing hatred towards her.	conflict, authority, antagonism, rebellion, defiance
Fantasy	What complexities characterize the friendship between George and Rawdon?	Their friendship is characterized by playful interactions, rivalry in romantic interests, elements of manipulation, and shared gambling habits, which create both camaraderie and challenges.	friendship, rivalry, manipulation, gambling, camaraderie
Young Adult	What is the nature of the relationship between Rebecca and Lord Steyne?	The relationship between Rebecca and Lord Steyne is multifaceted, characterized by mentorship, ambition, and social dynamics, with Rebecca leveraging Lord Steyne's favoritism for her family's benefit while also being dependent on his financial support.	mentor-mentee, social dynamics, influence, ambition

Table 6: Aspect-based QA Examples (Vanity Fair).

E The Example of Aspect-Based Summary (Romance)

Set against the backdrop of early 19th-century Regency England and the Napoleonic Wars, \"Vanity Fair\" intricately weaves the lives of two young women: kind-hearted Amelia Sedley and ambitious orphan Rebecca Sharp. Amelia, the daughter of a stockbroker, is in love with the charming Lieutenant George Osborne. Their romance flourishes in Russell Square, but societal pressures lead to heartbreak when George's wealthy father forbids their union, prompting a secret elopement that ultimately ends in tragedy when George dies at the Battle of Waterloo.\n\nMeanwhile, Rebecca, a determined social climber, seeks to elevate her status by pursuing Joseph Sedley, Amelia's brother. As a governess for Sir Pitt Crawley, she becomes entangled with the reckless Captain Rawdon Crawley, whom she marries. Following her husband's death, Rebecca manipulates her way into the elite social circles, including a complex affair with Lord Steyne. \n\nAmelia, now a widow and devoted mother to her son Georgy, faces emotional turmoil. Major William Dobbin, who harbors unrequited love for her, returns from Madras to support her. Their bond deepens amidst jealousy and betrayal, revealing the harsh realities of love and ambition in a society rife with expectations

Figure 9: Romance-based summary by GPT + Hier (Vanity Fair).

The romance in this story involves several key characters, predominantly focused on Dorothea Brooke, Mr. Casaubon, Sir James Chettam, and Rosamond Vincy. Dorothea, initially drawn to the intellectual and ambitious Mr. Casaubon, is excited by the prospect of marriage, believing it will bring a sense of purpose and fulfillment to her life. However, as she contemplates the nature of her impending marriage, she begins to feel a creeping sense of disappointment and a lack of genuine connection with Casaubon, despite his display of what she perceives as affectionate regard.\n\nMeanwhile, Sir James Chettam is introduced as a potential alternative for Dorothea. Mrs. Cadwallader, who is keen on her son's marrying someone suitable, believes Sir James would have tempered Dorothea's more overpowering traits and could have led her to a more sensible disposition had they married. After it becomes clear that Dorothea has chosen Mr. Casaubon instead, Sir James's feelings are complicated by his awareness of having been eclipsed in her affections.\n\nIn parallel, the burgeoning romance between Lydgate and Rosamond Vincy takes shape. Lydgate is initially portrayed with a sense of ambition and care, but he becomes emotionally captivated by Rosamond in a tender moment of vulnerability. This unexpected connection leads to Lydgate professing love for her, culminating in their engagement, although it remains tinged with uncertainty about their future and beyond the immediate excitement of their

Figure 10: Romance-based summary by NaiveRAG (Vanity Fair).

Thesis Proposal: Interpretable Reasoning Enhancement in Large Language Models through Puzzle and Ontological Task Analysis

Mihir Panchal
Department of Computer Engineering
Dwarkadas J. Sanghvi College of Engineering
Mumbai, India
mihirpanchal5400@gmail.com

Abstract

Large language models (LLMs) excel across diverse natural language processing tasks but remain opaque and unreliable. This thesis investigates how LLM reasoning can be made both interpretable and reliable through systematic analysis of internal dynamics and targeted interventions. Unlike prior work that examines reasoning broadly, this research focuses on two representative domains: puzzle solving, where reasoning steps can be precisely tracked, and ontological inference, where hierarchical structures constrain valid reasoning. The central questions are: (1) How can systematic error patterns in domain specific reasoning be detected through layer wise probing and mitigated through targeted interventions? (2) How can probing frameworks and middle layer analyses reveal and enhance the computational mechanisms underlying inference? By combining probing methods, middle layer investigations, and probe guided interventions, the work aims to uncover interpretable reasoning patterns, identify systematic failure modes, and develop adaptive enhancement strategies. The expected outcome is a domain grounded framework that advances both theoretical understanding of neural reasoning and the design of practical, trustworthy AI systems.

1 Introduction

Large language models (LLMs) achieve state-of-the-art performance across diverse natural language processing tasks, demonstrating capabilities in reasoning, inference, and problem solving (Brown et al., 2020; Wei et al., 2022; Touvron et al., 2023). Yet these abilities remain unreliable and poorly understood, limiting safe deployment in critical applications (Berglund et al., 2023; Schaeffer et al., 2023; Huang et al., 2025). LLMs often generate plausible but unfaithful explanations (Radhakrishnan et al., 2023; Turpin et al., 2023), highlighting the gap between observed outputs and internal decision processes.

Recent work on chain-of-thought (CoT) prompting improves reasoning performance by encouraging explicit reasoning steps (Wang et al., 2022b; Wei et al., 2022; Hao et al., 2023). However, whether these external traces reflect genuine internal computation remains uncertain (Lanham et al., 2023). Meanwhile, empirical studies suggest that the middle layers of transformer architectures play a crucial role in reasoning, showing dynamic transformations linked to reasoning complexity (Vig and Belinkov, 2019; Li et al., 2024; Sharma et al., 2024).

This thesis addresses the following specific research questions:

1. **RQ1 (Localization):** Do reasoning relevant computational patterns cluster in specific transformer layers during puzzle solving and ontological inference? Can we identify distinct layer wise specialization for constraint satisfaction versus hierarchical reasoning?

2. **RQ2 (Mechanism):** What specific neural circuits mediate multi step reasoning in these domains? Do puzzle solving and ontological reasoning share common computational pathways, or do they employ domain specific mechanisms?

3. **RQ3 (Failure Modes):** What systematic failure patterns emerge in puzzle and ontological reasoning, and can these be detected through layer specific probing before they manifest in outputs?

4. **RQ4 (Intervention):** Can targeted interventions in middle layers, guided by probing classifiers, improve reasoning reliability without degrading general language capabilities? What is the trade-off between intervention strength and preservation of creative problem solving?

Proceedings of the IJCNLP-AACL 2025 Student Research Workshop, pages 134–144
December 20-24, 2025 ©2025 Association for Computational Linguistics

These two domains were selected for their complementary characteristics that together cover fundamental reasoning patterns encountered in broader AI applications. Puzzle solving exemplifies constraint reasoning, where solutions must satisfy explicit rules and logical dependencies a pattern ubiquitous in planning, code generation, mathematical problem solving, and scientific hypothesis testing (Cobbe et al., 2021; Hendrycks et al., 2024). The traceable solution paths in puzzles enable precise verification of whether model reasoning aligns with ground truth inference steps, addressing the faithfulness challenge identified in broader reasoning research (Turpin et al., 2023). Ontological reasoning, conversely, represents structured knowledge manipulation, requiring models to navigate hierarchical relationships, perform inheritance inference, and maintain consistency across taxonomic structures. This reasoning pattern underlies question answering, knowledge base completion, common sense reasoning, and semantic understanding tasks (Petroni et al., 2019; Wang et al., 2021). Together, these domains instantiate two core reasoning paradigms, procedural constraint satisfaction and declarative knowledge inference whose combination characterizes complex real world reasoning.

2 Related Works

2.1 Interpretability in Large Language Models

Probing classifiers have become a fundamental tool for investigating what linguistic information is encoded in neural representations (Belinkov and Glass, 2019; Clark et al., 2019a; Hewitt and Manning, 2019; Rogers et al., 2021). The development of tools like LogitLens and TunedLens has enabled researchers to examine how predictions evolve across transformer layers, revealing that meaningful predictions often emerge in intermediate layers rather than only in final outputs (nostalgebraist, 2020; Belrose et al., 2023). Circuit analysis approaches have attempted to identify specific computational pathways within models, though these methods face significant challenges when applied to the dense, distributed representations found in large language models (Wang et al., 2022a; Conmy et al., 2023; Syed et al., 2023; Kramár et al., 2024).

Mechanistic interpretability has emerged as a particularly promising direction, focusing on understanding the specific algorithms and computational mechanisms that models use to solve tasks (Olah et al., 2020; Elhage et al., 2021; Nanda et al., 2023). This approach has yielded insights into how models handle tasks like arithmetic, factual recall, and simple logical operations (Power et al., 2022; Bereska and Gavves, 2024). Recent work has also explored the use of attention visualization and analysis to understand reasoning processes (Clark et al., 2019b; Kovaleva et al., 2019; Gould et al., 2023). However, attention patterns do not always correlate with reasoning processes, and models can attend to irrelevant information while still producing correct outputs (Jain and Wallace, 2019; Serrano and Smith, 2019).

2.2 Reasoning in Transformer Models and Chain-of-Thought Methods

Recent theoretical analysis has begun to explain why chain-of-thought is effective, showing that it fundamentally expands the computational power of transformer architectures by providing additional computation time and intermediate storage (Merrill and Sabharwal, 2023; Li et al., 2024). Self consistency methods aggregate multiple reasoning chains to improve reliability (Wang et al., 2022b). Tree-of-thought approaches explore multiple reasoning paths simultaneously (Yao et al., 2023). Zero-shot chain-of-thought methods eliminate the need for hand crafted examples while maintaining performance improvements (Kojima et al., 2022). Recent work has also explored enhancing chain-of-thought reasoning through logic integration and formal reasoning frameworks (Pan et al., 2023; Paul et al., 2024; Zhang et al., 2025).

While chain-of-thought can improve reasoning performance, studies have shown that models can generate plausible but ultimately unfaithful explanations that do not reflect their actual decision making processes (Saparov and He, 2022; Turpin et al., 2023). Models can exhibit inconsistent reasoning performance across similar problems, struggle with novel reasoning patterns not seen during training, and fail to maintain logical consistency across long reasoning chains (Dziri et al., 2023; Zhang et al., 2023, 2024). This raises important questions about whether the explicit reasoning chains correspond to the computational processes that actually drive model behavior, or whether they are merely post-hoc rationalizations.

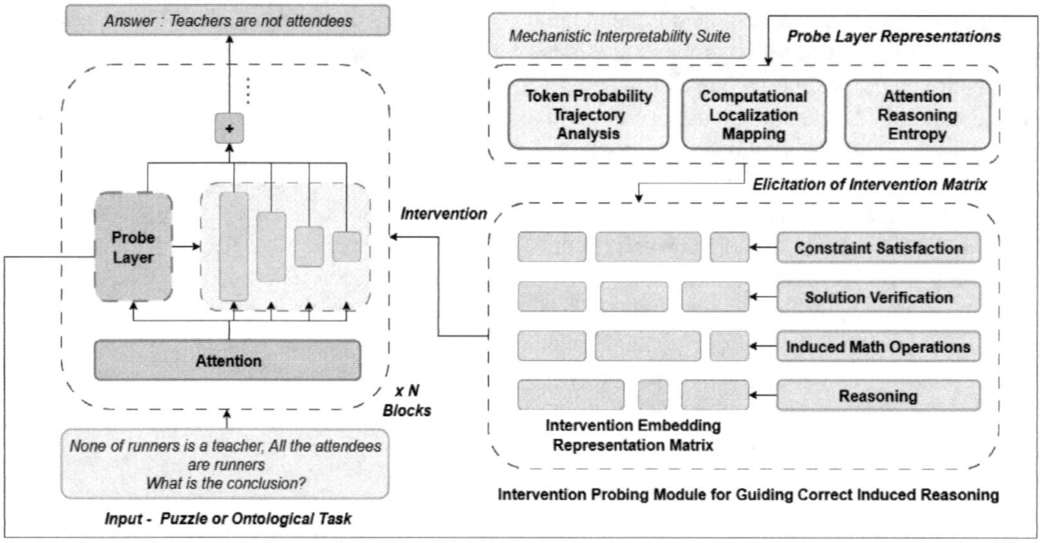

Figure 1: Overview of the probe guided intervention framework: mechanistic interpretability tools analyze middle layer representations to detect reasoning errors, enabling targeted interventions that enhance domain specific reasoning in puzzle solving and ontological tasks.

2.3 Middle Layer Dynamics and Transformer Analysis

Recent empirical investigations have revealed intriguing patterns in the intermediate layers of transformer models, particularly during reasoning tasks (Clark et al., 2019a; Jawahar et al., 2019). Studies using techniques like activation patching and causal intervention have shown that middle layers play crucial roles in reasoning tasks, with different layers contributing to different aspects of the reasoning process (Meng et al., 2022; Wang et al., 2022a; Geiger et al., 2025). Recent work has begun to address this challenge through more sophisticated analysis methods, including sparse autoencoders for feature discovery and specialized probing techniques for reasoning specific representations (Cunningham et al., 2023; Bills et al., 2023). These approaches have revealed that models develop specialized circuits for different types of reasoning, with some circuits being shared across tasks and others being task specific (Olsson et al., 2022; Ameisen et al., 2025).

If reasoning processes can be characterized and localized within specific layers, it may be possible to design targeted interventions that enhance reasoning performance while maintaining overall model coherence (Li et al., 2023). This possibility has motivated recent research into activation editing and representation manipulation techniques, though these approaches are still in early stages of development (Mitchell et al., 2021; Ilharco et al., 2022).

2.4 Puzzle and Ontological Reasoning in Language Models

Mathematical and logic puzzles provide controlled environments for studying reasoning processes, as they often have well defined solution paths and allow for precise evaluation of reasoning steps (Cobbe et al., 2021; Dutta et al., 2024; Hendrycks et al., 2024). Recent work has shown that models can solve increasingly complex puzzles through chain-of-thought prompting, but they often struggle with novel puzzle types or variations that require creative insight (Welleck et al., 2021; Hao et al., 2023).

Ontological reasoning, involving the understanding and manipulation of concept hierarchies and relationships, is fundamental to many AI applications (Petroni et al., 2019; Hogan et al., 2021; Wang et al., 2021). Language models have shown remarkable ability to perform taxonomic reasoning and understand concept relationships learned during pre-training (Clark et al., 2019a; Hohenecker and Lukasiewicz, 2020; Rogers et al., 2021). However, they often struggle with systematic ontological inference and can be inconsistent in their application of hierarchical knowledge (Elazar et al., 2020; Kassner et al., 2021). Puzzle solving tasks often have traceable solution paths that can be compared with model reasoning chains, while ontological reasoning provides structured knowledge domains where concepts and relationships can be systematically varied and analyzed (Ribeiro et al., 2020; Wu et al., 2024).

3 Aims

This research is structured around two major aims to be pursued over the course of the PhD:

3.1 Aim 1: Developing Domain Specific Probing Methods and Evaluation Frameworks

3.1.1 Probing Architectures for Puzzle and Ontological Reasoning

The approach will involve creating hierarchical probing structures specifically designed to capture reasoning patterns in puzzle solving and ontological domains. We will implement multi layer perceptron (MLP) probes with 2-3 hidden layers trained on frozen transformer representations. For puzzle specific tasks, we employ constraint satisfaction probes that classify whether intermediate representations encode valid puzzle states and multi-step probes that predict the next valid operation from a discrete action space. Rather than relying solely on linear classifiers, the methodology will incorporate attention probing mechanisms using scaled dot product attention over sequence representations to identify relationships between different reasoning steps specific to these domains and track the flow of information across layers during puzzle solving and concept manipulation tasks (Beyer and Reed, 2025). As illustrated in Figure 1, these probing mechanisms form the foundation of our Mechanistic Interpretability Suite, which employs Token Probability Trajectory Analysis, Computational Localization Mapping, and Attention Reasoning Entropy to extract reasoning relevant representations from designated probe layers.

For ontological reasoning tasks, probes will focus on hierarchical relationship detection, concept inheritance patterns, classification consistency, and taxonomic inference processes. These specialized probes will monitor how models represent concept hierarchies, perform inheritance reasoning, resolve taxonomic conflicts, and maintain consistency across ontological inferences. The probing objectives will include parent child relationship detection, sibling concept identification, multiple inheritance resolution, and concept boundary determination. Cross domain analysis between puzzle and ontological reasoning will examine whether shared or distinct mechanisms underlie structured problem solving and concept manipulation. Using unified methods including shared MLP probes, cross domain transfer testing, representational similarity (CKA) analysis, and aligned intervention and evaluation protocols, we will identify convergent or specialized processing pathways, guiding the design of general yet domain grounded reasoning enhancement methods.

3.1.2 Specialized Dataset Creation and Evaluation Frameworks

A critical component of this research involves creating comprehensive datasets specifically designed for evaluating reasoning in puzzle and ontological domains (Shojaee et al., 2025). These datasets will go beyond existing benchmarks by providing fine grained annotations of reasoning steps, multiple solution paths, and systematic variations in problem complexity. For puzzle solving evaluation, datasets will include mathematical puzzles with step-by-step solution annotations, logic puzzles with constraint satisfaction tracking, spatial reasoning problems with transformation sequences, and creative puzzles requiring insight and novel approach generation. Each puzzle will be annotated with ground truth reasoning steps, alternative solution paths, common failure modes, and difficulty gradations based on required reasoning depth.

For ontological reasoning evaluation, datasets will encompass taxonomic classification tasks with hierarchical relationship annotations, concept inheritance problems with multiple inheritance scenarios, ontological consistency checking with systematic inconsistency patterns, and novel concept introduction tasks requiring integration with existing knowledge. These datasets will include systematic variations in hierarchy depth, concept similarity, and relationship complexity. The evaluation framework will incorporate both quantitative metrics including step wise accuracy, reasoning consistency, solution efficiency, and error pattern analysis, and qualitative assessment methods including reasoning faithfulness evaluation, explanation quality assessment, solution creativity scoring, and failure mode categorization. This comprehensive evaluation approach will enable precise measurement of reasoning improvements and systematic identification of remaining limitations.

3.1.3 Middle Layer Analysis Framework for Domain Specific Reasoning

The methodology will combine multiple complementary analysis techniques specifically tailored for puzzle and ontological reasoning to provide a complete picture of middle layer behavior in these domains. Middle-layer dynamics refers to the transformation of hidden representations in layers $L/3$ to $2L/3$ of the transformer architecture, where L is the total number of layers regions empirically shown to mediate multi-step reasoning (Li et al., 2024; Sharma et al., 2024). We operationalize this through: (1) layer wise activation magnitude tracking (computing ℓ_2 norms of hidden states across layers), (2) representation drift analysis (measuring cosine distance between consecutive layer outputs), and (3) information flow quantification using mutual information estimation between layer pairs.

For puzzle solving analysis, the framework will investigate how middle layers represent puzzle constraints, track solution progress, maintain working memory for multi-step problems, and implement backtracking and search strategies. Special attention will be given to understanding how representations transform as puzzle complexity increases and how models handle puzzle variants that require creative insight. For ontological reasoning analysis, the framework will examine how middle layers encode concept hierarchies, perform inheritance computations, resolve conflicting taxonomic information, and integrate new concepts with existing knowledge structures. The analysis will explore how different types of ontological relationships are represented and how models handle systematic variations in concept similarity and hierarchy depth. This analysis will reveal the computational pathways most critical for each reasoning domain and inform the design of targeted interventions.

The framework will also investigate temporal dynamics of middle layer processing during multi-step reasoning, examining how representations evolve across forward passes in models that engage in iterative reasoning or self-correction within these specific domains. This analysis will provide insights into whether models implement domain specific reasoning through parallel processing across layers or through more sequential, step-by-step computation.

3.2 Aim 2: Creating Domain Targeted Interventional Frameworks

3.2.1 Probe Guided Intervention Strategies for Specific Reasoning Domains

The methodology will involve developing monitoring systems that use domain-specific probing classifiers to track reasoning processes in real-time during puzzle solving and ontological inference. Probe guided intervention is operationalized as follows: probing classifiers (trained as described in 3.1.1) evaluate intermediate representations at inference time; when probe confidence drops below a calibrated threshold τ (determined via held out validation to balance precision recall), targeted interventions modify the representation vector $\mathbf{h}_l$ at layer l through direction specific steering: $\mathbf{h}'_l = \mathbf{h}_l + \alpha \cdot \mathbf{v}_{\text{correct}}$, where $\mathbf{v}_{\text{correct}}$ is the mean activation difference between correct and incorrect reasoning examples, and α is an intervention strength parameter tuned to minimize reasoning error while preserving perplexity on held out text. The intervention architecture, depicted in Figure 1, maintains an Intervention Embedding Representation Matrix that encodes domain specific reasoning patterns across four categories: Constraint Satisfaction, Solution Verification, Induced Mathematical Operations, and General Reasoning. When the interpretability suite detects anomalies such as probe confidence below threshold τ or divergent probability trajectories the system retrieves the appropriate intervention vector and applies the correction $\mathbf{h}'_l = \mathbf{h}_l + \alpha \cdot \mathbf{v}_{\text{correct}}$ to steer the model toward valid reasoning paths.

For ontological reasoning interventions, the system will track hierarchical consistency, inheritance computation accuracy, concept boundary maintenance, and taxonomic inference validity. Interventions may include hierarchy clarification, inheritance correction, concept boundary reinforcement, and consistency restoration. These interventions will help models maintain coherent ontological reasoning while preserving their ability to handle novel concepts and relationships. The intervention strategies will be adaptive, learning from the success or failure of previous interventions within each domain to improve future performance. This adaptive capability will enable the system to handle novel puzzles and ontological structures without requiring manual reconfiguration while maintaining domain specific expertise.

3.2.2 Inference-Time Reasoning Enhancement for Focused Domains

Building on domain specific probing insights, this research will develop methods for inference time reasoning enhancement specifically optimized for puzzle and ontological reasoning domains. The framework illustrated in Figure 1 demonstrates the complete workflow: during inference on tasks such as syllogistic reasoning (e.g., "None of the runners is a teacher. All the attendees are runners. What is the conclusion?"), the system monitors middle layer representations, applies probing classifiers to verify correct transitive inference, detects failures in recognizing logical relationships, retrieves appropriate intervention vectors, and validates that corrections propagate to produce reliable outputs like "Teachers are not attendees." For puzzle solving enhancement, the inference time system provides constraint checking (verifying puzzle rule satisfaction), solution validation (detecting invalid intermediate steps), and systematic search guidance (redirecting toward valid solution spaces when dead ends are detected via probe confidence thresholds).

For ontological reasoning enhancement, the real-time system will offer hierarchy navigation assistance, inheritance computation support, consistency checking, and novel concept integration guidance. This system will help models maintain coherent ontological reasoning while expanding their capability to handle complex taxonomic structures and novel concept relationships. The real-time enhancement framework will include domain specific uncertainty quantification and confidence estimation, allowing the system to determine when interventions are needed and how confident it should be in its corrections within each reasoning domain. This capability is crucial for avoiding over correction and maintaining model reliability in domain specific contexts.

3.2.3 Comprehensive Evaluation Protocols for Domain Specific Interventions

Developing robust evaluation methods for reasoning interventions in puzzle and ontological domains is crucial for ensuring their effectiveness and safety. This research will establish comprehensive evaluation protocols specifically designed for these domains that go beyond simple accuracy metrics to assess the quality, faithfulness, and reliability of domain specific reasoning processes. The evaluation framework will include both quantitative and qualitative assessment methods tailored to each domain. For puzzle solving evaluation, quantitative measures will track solution accuracy, step efficiency, creative insight generation, and robustness across puzzle variations. Qualitative analysis will examine solution elegance, reasoning faithfulness, creative problem solving maintenance, and preservation of human like puzzle solving strategies. For ontological reasoning evaluation, quantitative measures will assess taxonomic accuracy, consistency maintenance, inheritance computation correctness, and scalability across ontology sizes. Qualitative analysis will examine reasoning coherence, concept boundary maintenance, novel concept integration quality, and preservation of flexible taxonomic thinking.

Special attention will be given to evaluating intervention robustness across different puzzle types and ontological structures, assessing whether improvements generalize within domains and how interventions handle edge cases and novel variations. The protocols will also assess potential negative effects of interventions, including reduction in creative problem solving, introduction of domain specific biases, and decreased flexibility in reasoning approaches. Human studies will assess whether intervention enhanced reasoning in puzzle and ontological domains is more convincing, trustworthy, and useful to human users compared to baseline model outputs. These studies will focus on domain experts including mathematicians, logicians, and knowledge engineers to ensure that enhancements align with expert reasoning patterns while maintaining accessibility to non experts.

4 Timeline and Deliverables

The research will produce open source software tools and libraries specifically designed for puzzle and ontological reasoning analysis and enhancement, making the methods accessible to researchers working in these domains. Comprehensive evaluation benchmarks and annotated datasets for both puzzle solving and ontological reasoning will be released to enable future research in domain specific reasoning interpretability.

Additional deliverables include educational materials and tutorials for applying the developed methods to puzzle and ontological reasoning tasks, collaboration with domain experts including mathematicians and knowledge engineers for real world validation, and guidelines for responsible deployment of reasoning enhanced AI systems in educa-

Year	Deliverables and Milestones
Year 1	• Conduct comprehensive literature review on LLM reasoning, interpretability, and puzzle/ontological reasoning. • Develop preliminary datasets (500 annotated examples across domains) and annotation protocols. • Develop novel probing architectures for puzzle and ontological reasoning tasks. • Set up experimental frameworks and baseline models across selected reasoning benchmarks, testing on preliminary datasets. • **Deliverables:** Pilot datasets with annotation guidelines, initial probing framework tested on pilot data, baseline models, literature survey report, 1–2 review paper publications or workshop papers.
Year 2	• Scale up and complete full annotated datasets for puzzle solving and ontological reasoning, incorporating lessons from Year 1 pilot studies. • Refine and validate probing classifiers on domain-specific reasoning tasks using complete datasets. • Conduct comprehensive middle layer analysis to investigate reasoning dynamics across model architectures. • **Deliverables:** Complete annotated datasets (publicly released), validated and refined probing classifiers, comprehensive middle layer analysis report, 1–2 conference publications on dataset methodology, annotation framework, and probing results.
Year 3	• Identify and validate key reasoning representation patterns across domains. • Develop cross-task reasoning pattern discovery methods and unified analysis framework. • Begin design and implementation of probe-guided intervention strategies. • **Deliverables:** Analysis framework, cross-task pattern insights, initial intervention prototypes, 1–2 major journal/conference publications on reasoning patterns and middle layer analysis.
Year 4	• Implement and validate probe-guided intervention systems with real-time reasoning enhancement. • Establish comprehensive evaluation protocols, including human evaluation studies. • Conduct large-scale experiments to assess effectiveness and generalization of interventions. • Complete thesis writing, finalize datasets/tools, and prepare for defense. • **Deliverables:** Fully validated intervention system, evaluation reports, final datasets/tools, thesis document, 1–2 final publications summarizing interventions, evaluation, and framework.

Table 1: Research timeline with milestones, deliverables, and expected publications aligned to puzzle and ontological reasoning aims.

tional and knowledge management applications.

5 Research Significance and Conclusion

This research advances both theoretical understanding and practical applications of reasoning in large language models. By focusing on puzzle solving and ontological inference, it investigates how consistent and interpretable reasoning patterns emerge, particularly within the middle layers of transformer architectures. These controlled yet rich domains provide the structure needed for fine grained analysis while retaining sufficient complexity to reveal broader insights about reasoning mechanisms.

The study is expected to uncover distinct yet partially overlapping neural circuits for different types of reasoning, shedding light on the modular nature of cognitive processes in LLMs. Such findings would inform the design of reasoning systems that combine creative problem solving with systematic inference. At the same time, the development of interventional frameworks aims to enhance reasoning in real time, maintaining efficiency while reinforcing coherence and reliability.

If successful, this work will establish probing and intervention methods as practical tools for understanding and improving reasoning in language models. Beyond theoretical contributions, it will deliver datasets, evaluation frameworks, and enhancement strategies that benefit both research and applied contexts. The outcomes are expected to support applications in education, knowledge management, and creative problem solving, while also providing a foundation for building more interpretable and trustworthy AI systems.

References

Emmanuel Ameisen, Jack Lindsey, Adam Pearce, Wes Gurnee, Nicholas L. Turner, Brian Chen, Craig Citro, David Abrahams, Shan Carter, Basil Hosmer, Jonathan Marcus, Michael Sklar, Adly Templeton, Trenton Bricken, Callum McDougall, Hoagy Cunningham, Thomas Henighan, Adam Jermyn, Andy Jones, and 8 others. 2025. Circuit tracing: Revealing computational graphs in language models. *Transformer Circuits Thread.*

Yonatan Belinkov and James Glass. 2019. Analysis methods in neural language processing: A survey. *Transactions of the Association for Computational Linguistics*, 7:49–72.

Nora Belrose, Zach Furman, Logan Smith, Danny Halawi, Igor Ostrovsky, Lev McKinney, Stella Biderman, and Jacob Steinhardt. 2023. Eliciting latent predictions from transformers with the tuned lens. *arXiv preprint arXiv:2303.08112.*

Leonard Bereska and Efstratios Gavves. 2024. Mechanistic interpretability for ai safety–a review. *arXiv preprint arXiv:2404.14082.*

Lukas Berglund, Meg Tong, Max Kaufmann, Mikita Balesni, Asa Cooper Stickland, Tomasz Korbak, and Owain Evans. 2023. The reversal curse: Llms trained on" a is b" fail to learn" b is a". *arXiv preprint arXiv:2309.12288.*

Henrike Beyer and Chris Reed. 2025. Lexical recall or logical reasoning: Probing the limits of reasoning abilities in large language models. In *Proceedings of the 63rd Annual Meeting of the Association for Computational Linguistics (Volume 1: Long Papers)*, pages 13532–13557.

Steven Bills, Nick Cammarata, Dan Mossing, Henk Tillman, Leo Gao, Gabriel Goh, Ilya Sutskever, Jan Leike, Jeff Wu, and William Saunders. 2023. Language models can explain neurons in language models. `https://openaipublic.blob.core.windows.net/neuron-explainer/paper/index.html`.

Tom Brown, Benjamin Mann, Nick Ryder, Melanie Subbiah, Jared D Kaplan, Prafulla Dhariwal, Arvind Neelakantan, Pranav Shyam, Girish Sastry, Amanda Askell, and 1 others. 2020. Language models are few-shot learners. *Advances in neural information processing systems*, 33:1877–1901.

Kevin Clark, Urvashi Khandelwal, Omer Levy, and Christopher D Manning. 2019a. What does bert look at? an analysis of bert's attention. *arXiv preprint arXiv:1906.04341.*

Kevin Clark, Urvashi Khandelwal, Omer Levy, and Christopher D Manning. 2019b. What does bert look at? an analysis of bert's attention. *arXiv preprint arXiv:1906.04341.*

Karl Cobbe, Vineet Kosaraju, Mohammad Bavarian, Mark Chen, Heewoo Jun, Lukasz Kaiser, Matthias Plappert, Jerry Tworek, Jacob Hilton, Reiichiro Nakano, and 1 others. 2021. Training verifiers to solve math word problems. *arXiv preprint arXiv:2110.14168.*

Arthur Conmy, Augustine Mavor-Parker, Aengus Lynch, Stefan Heimersheim, and Adrià Garriga-Alonso. 2023. Towards automated circuit discovery for mechanistic interpretability. *Advances in Neural Information Processing Systems*, 36:16318–16352.

Hoagy Cunningham, Aidan Ewart, Logan Riggs, Robert Huben, and Lee Sharkey. 2023. Sparse autoencoders find highly interpretable features in language models. *arXiv preprint arXiv:2309.08600.*

Subhabrata Dutta, Joykirat Singh, Soumen Chakrabarti, and Tanmoy Chakraborty. 2024. How to think step-by-step: A mechanistic understanding of chain-of-thought reasoning. *arXiv preprint arXiv:2402.18312.*

Nouha Dziri, Ximing Lu, Melanie Sclar, Xiang Lorraine Li, Liwei Jiang, Bill Yuchen Lin, Sean Welleck, Peter West, Chandra Bhagavatula, Ronan Le Bras, and 1 others. 2023. Faith and fate: Limits of transformers on compositionality. *Advances in Neural Information Processing Systems*, 36:70293–70332.

Yanai Elazar, Shauli Ravfogel, Alon Jacovi, and Yoav Goldberg. 2020. Amnesic probing: Behavioral explanation with amnesic counterfactuals. arxiv eprints, page. *arXiv preprint arXiv:2006.00995*.

Nelson Elhage, Neel Nanda, Catherine Olsson, Tom Henighan, Nicholas Joseph, Ben Mann, Amanda Askell, Yuntao Bai, Anna Chen, Tom Conerly, and 1 others. 2021. A mathematical framework for transformer circuits. *Transformer Circuits Thread*, 1(1):12.

Atticus Geiger, Duligur Ibeling, Amir Zur, Maheep Chaudhary, Sonakshi Chauhan, Jing Huang, Aryaman Arora, Zhengxuan Wu, Noah Goodman, Christopher Potts, and 1 others. 2025. Causal abstraction: A theoretical foundation for mechanistic interpretability. *Journal of Machine Learning Research*, 26(83):1–64.

Rhys Gould, Euan Ong, George Ogden, and Arthur Conmy. 2023. Successor heads: Recurring, interpretable attention heads in the wild. *arXiv preprint arXiv:2312.09230*.

Shibo Hao, Yi Gu, Haodi Ma, Joshua Jiahua Hong, Zhen Wang, Daisy Zhe Wang, and Zhiting Hu. 2023. Reasoning with language model is planning with world model. *arXiv preprint arXiv:2305.14992*.

Dan Hendrycks, Collin Burns, Saurav Kadavath, Akul Arora, Steven Basart, Eric Tang, Dawn Song, and Jacob Steinhardt. 2024. Measuring mathematical problem solving with the math dataset, 2021. *URL https://arxiv. org/abs/2103.03874*, 2.

John Hewitt and Christopher D Manning. 2019. A structural probe for finding syntax in word representations. In *Proceedings of the 2019 Conference of the North American Chapter of the Association for Computational Linguistics: Human Language Technologies, Volume 1 (Long and Short Papers)*, pages 4129–4138.

Aidan Hogan, Eva Blomqvist, Michael Cochez, Claudia d'Amato, Gerard De Melo, Claudio Gutierrez, Sabrina Kirrane, José Emilio Labra Gayo, Roberto Navigli, Sebastian Neumaier, and 1 others. 2021. Knowledge graphs. *ACM Computing Surveys (Csur)*, 54(4):1–37.

Patrick Hohenecker and Thomas Lukasiewicz. 2020. Ontology reasoning with deep neural networks. *Journal of Artificial Intelligence Research*, 68:503–540.

Lei Huang, Weijiang Yu, Weitao Ma, Weihong Zhong, Zhangyin Feng, Haotian Wang, Qianglong Chen, Weihua Peng, Xiaocheng Feng, Bing Qin, and 1 others. 2025. A survey on hallucination in large language models: Principles, taxonomy, challenges, and open questions. *ACM Transactions on Information Systems*, 43(2):1–55.

Gabriel Ilharco, Marco Tulio Ribeiro, Mitchell Wortsman, Suchin Gururangan, Ludwig Schmidt, Hannaneh Hajishirzi, and Ali Farhadi. 2022. Editing models with task arithmetic. *arXiv preprint arXiv:2212.04089*.

Sarthak Jain and Byron C Wallace. 2019. Attention is not explanation. *arXiv preprint arXiv:1902.10186*.

Ganesh Jawahar, Benoît Sagot, and Djamé Seddah. 2019. What does bert learn about the structure of language? In *ACL 2019-57th Annual Meeting of the Association for Computational Linguistics*.

Nora Kassner, Philipp Dufter, and Hinrich Schütze. 2021. Multilingual lama: Investigating knowledge in multilingual pretrained language models. *arXiv preprint arXiv:2102.00894*.

Takeshi Kojima, Shixiang Shane Gu, Machel Reid, Yutaka Matsuo, and Yusuke Iwasawa. 2022. Large language models are zero-shot reasoners. *Advances in neural information processing systems*, 35:22199–22213.

Olga Kovaleva, Alexey Romanov, Anna Rogers, and Anna Rumshisky. 2019. Revealing the dark secrets of bert. *arXiv preprint arXiv:1908.08593*.

János Kramár, Tom Lieberum, Rohin Shah, and Neel Nanda. 2024. Atp*: An efficient and scalable method for localizing llm behaviour to components. *arXiv preprint arXiv:2403.00745*.

Tamera Lanham, Anna Chen, Ansh Radhakrishnan, Benoit Steiner, Carson Denison, Danny Hernandez, Dustin Li, Esin Durmus, Evan Hubinger, Jackson Kernion, and 1 others. 2023. Measuring faithfulness in chain-of-thought reasoning. *arXiv preprint arXiv:2307.13702*.

Kenneth Li, Oam Patel, Fernanda Viégas, Hanspeter Pfister, and Martin Wattenberg. 2023. Inference-time intervention: Eliciting truthful answers from a language model. *Advances in Neural Information Processing Systems*, 36:41451–41530.

Zhiyuan Li, Hong Liu, Denny Zhou, and Tengyu Ma. 2024. Chain of thought empowers transformers to solve inherently serial problems. *arXiv preprint arXiv:2402.12875*, 1.

Kevin Meng, David Bau, Alex Andonian, and Yonatan Belinkov. 2022. Locating and editing factual associations in gpt. *Advances in neural information processing systems*, 35:17359–17372.

William Merrill and Ashish Sabharwal. 2023. The expressive power of transformers with chain of thought. *arXiv preprint arXiv:2310.07923*.

Eric Mitchell, Charles Lin, Antoine Bosselut, Chelsea Finn, and Christopher D Manning. 2021. Fast model editing at scale. *arXiv preprint arXiv:2110.11309*.

Neel Nanda, Lawrence Chan, Tom Lieberum, Jess Smith, and Jacob Steinhardt. 2023. Progress measures for grokking via mechanistic interpretability. *arXiv preprint arXiv:2301.05217*.

nostalgebraist. 2020. Interpreting gpt: the logit lens. `https://www.lesswrong.com/posts/AcKRB8wDpdaN6v6ru/interpreting-gpt-the-logit-lens`.

Chris Olah, Nick Cammarata, Ludwig Schubert, Gabriel Goh, Michael Petrov, and Shan Carter. 2020. Zoom in: An introduction to circuits. *Distill*, 5(3):e00024–001.

Catherine Olsson, Nelson Elhage, Neel Nanda, Nicholas Joseph, Nova DasSarma, Tom Henighan, Ben Mann, Amanda Askell, Yuntao Bai, Anna Chen, and 1 others. 2022. In-context learning and induction heads. *arXiv preprint arXiv:2209.11895*.

Liangming Pan, Alon Albalak, Xinyi Wang, and William Yang Wang. 2023. Logic-lm: Empowering large language models with symbolic solvers for faithful logical reasoning. *arXiv preprint arXiv:2305.12295*.

Debjit Paul, Robert West, Antoine Bosselut, and Boi Faltings. 2024. Making reasoning matter: Measuring and improving faithfulness of chain-of-thought reasoning. *arXiv preprint arXiv:2402.13950*.

Fabio Petroni, Tim Rocktäschel, Patrick Lewis, Anton Bakhtin, Yuxiang Wu, Alexander H Miller, and Sebastian Riedel. 2019. Language models as knowledge bases? *arXiv preprint arXiv:1909.01066*.

Alethea Power, Yuri Burda, Harri Edwards, Igor Babuschkin, and Vedant Misra. 2022. Grokking: Generalization beyond overfitting on small algorithmic datasets. *arXiv preprint arXiv:2201.02177*.

Ansh Radhakrishnan, Karina Nguyen, Anna Chen, Carol Chen, Carson Denison, Danny Hernandez, Esin Durmus, Evan Hubinger, Jackson Kernion, Kamilė Lukošiūtė, and 1 others. 2023. Question decomposition improves the faithfulness of model-generated reasoning. *arXiv preprint arXiv:2307.11768*.

Marco Tulio Ribeiro, Tongshuang Wu, Carlos Guestrin, and Sameer Singh. 2020. Beyond accuracy: Behavioral testing of nlp models with checklist. *arXiv preprint arXiv:2005.04118*.

Anna Rogers, Olga Kovaleva, and Anna Rumshisky. 2021. A primer in bertology: What we know about how bert works. *Transactions of the association for computational linguistics*, 8:842–866.

Abulhair Saparov and He He. 2022. Language models are greedy reasoners: A systematic formal analysis of chain-of-thought. *arXiv preprint arXiv:2210.01240*.

Rylan Schaeffer, Brando Miranda, and Sanmi Koyejo. 2023. Are emergent abilities of large language models a mirage? *Advances in neural information processing systems*, 36:55565–55581.

Sofia Serrano and Noah A Smith. 2019. Is attention interpretable? *arXiv preprint arXiv:1906.03731*.

Arnab Sen Sharma, David Atkinson, and David Bau. 2024. Locating and editing factual associations in mamba. *arXiv preprint arXiv:2404.03646*.

Parshin Shojaee, Iman Mirzadeh, Keivan Alizadeh, Maxwell Horton, Samy Bengio, and Mehrdad Farajtabar. 2025. The illusion of thinking: Understanding the strengths and limitations of reasoning models via the lens of problem complexity. *arXiv preprint arXiv:2506.06941*.

Aaquib Syed, Can Rager, and Arthur Conmy. 2023. Attribution patching outperforms automated circuit discovery. *arXiv preprint arXiv:2310.10348*.

Hugo Touvron, Thibaut Lavril, Gautier Izacard, Xavier Martinet, Marie-Anne Lachaux, Timothée Lacroix, Baptiste Rozière, Naman Goyal, Eric Hambro, Faisal Azhar, and 1 others. 2023. Llama: Open and efficient foundation language models. *arXiv preprint arXiv:2302.13971*.

Miles Turpin, Julian Michael, Ethan Perez, and Samuel Bowman. 2023. Language models don't always say what they think: Unfaithful explanations in chain-of-thought prompting. *Advances in Neural Information Processing Systems*, 36:74952–74965.

Jesse Vig and Yonatan Belinkov. 2019. Analyzing the structure of attention in a transformer language model. *arXiv preprint arXiv:1906.04284*.

Kevin Wang, Alexandre Variengien, Arthur Conmy, Buck Shlegeris, and Jacob Steinhardt. 2022a. Interpretability in the wild: a circuit for indirect object identification in gpt-2 small. *arXiv preprint arXiv:2211.00593*.

Siyuan Wang, Wanjun Zhong, Duyu Tang, Zhongyu Wei, Zhihao Fan, Daxin Jiang, Ming Zhou, and Nan Duan. 2021. Logic-driven context extension and data augmentation for logical reasoning of text. *arXiv preprint arXiv:2105.03659*.

Xuezhi Wang, Jason Wei, Dale Schuurmans, Quoc Le, Ed Chi, Sharan Narang, Aakanksha Chowdhery, and Denny Zhou. 2022b. Self-consistency improves chain of thought reasoning in language models. *arXiv preprint arXiv:2203.11171*.

Jason Wei, Xuezhi Wang, Dale Schuurmans, Maarten Bosma, Fei Xia, Ed Chi, Quoc V Le, Denny Zhou, and 1 others. 2022. Chain-of-thought prompting elicits reasoning in large language models. *Advances in neural information processing systems*, 35:24824–24837.

Sean Welleck, Jiacheng Liu, Ronan Le Bras, Hannaneh Hajishirzi, Yejin Choi, and Kyunghyun Cho. 2021. Naturalproofs: Mathematical theorem proving in natural language. *arXiv preprint arXiv:2104.01112*.

Zhaofeng Wu, Linlu Qiu, Alexis Ross, Ekin Akyürek, Boyuan Chen, Bailin Wang, Najoung Kim, Jacob Andreas, and Yoon Kim. 2024. Reasoning or reciting? exploring the capabilities and limitations of language models through counterfactual tasks. arxiv. *Preprint posted online March*, 28.

Shunyu Yao, Dian Yu, Jeffrey Zhao, Izhak Shafran, Tom Griffiths, Yuan Cao, and Karthik Narasimhan. 2023. Tree of thoughts: Deliberate problem solving with large language models. *Advances in neural information processing systems*, 36:11809–11822.

Hugh Zhang, Jeff Da, Dean Lee, Vaughn Robinson, Catherine Wu, William Song, Tiffany Zhao, Pranav Raja, Charlotte Zhuang, Dylan Slack, and 1 others. 2024. A careful examination of large language model performance on grade school arithmetic. *Advances in Neural Information Processing Systems*, 37:46819–46836.

Shun Zhang, Zhenfang Chen, Yikang Shen, Mingyu Ding, Joshua B Tenenbaum, and Chuang Gan. 2023. Planning with large language models for code generation. *arXiv preprint arXiv:2303.05510*.

Yufeng Zhang, Xuepeng Wang, Lingxiang Wu, and Jinqiao Wang. 2025. Enhancing chain of thought prompting in large language models via reasoning patterns. In *Proceedings of the AAAI Conference on Artificial Intelligence*, volume 39, pages 25985–25993.

Adaptive Coopetition: Leveraging Coarse Verifier Signals for Resilient Multi-Agent LLM Reasoning

Wendy Liu
The Harker School
blossomwliu@gmail.com

Rui Jerry Huang
Basis Independent Silicon Valley
ruihuang15352019@gmail.com

Anastasia Miin
Pacific Collegiate School
anatasiamiin9@gmail.com

Lei Ding
University of California, Santa Cruz
lding25@ucsc.edu

Abstract

Inference-time computation is a critical yet challenging paradigm for enhancing the reasoning performance of large language models (LLMs). While existing strategies improve reasoning stability and consistency, they suffer from notable limitations: self-correction often reinforces the model's initial biases, and Multi-Agent Collaboration (MAC) often fails due to the lack of efficient coordination mechanisms, leading to collective errors. Although high-performing verifiers can detect reasoning errors, making them reliable requires substantial training. To address these challenges, we introduce a novel inference-time framework - **Adaptive Coopetition (AdCo)** - in which LLM agents utilize **an adaptive, UCB-based 'coopetition' mechanism**. At each round, agents leverage coarse verifier signals to determine whether to collaborate or compete, further iteratively refining their reasoning based on peer feedback. Without relying on high-performance verifiers, our adaptive strategy achieves significant performance gains on mathematical reasoning benchmarks, yielding **a 20% relative improvement** over baselines on the more challenging dataset. Our approach remains robust and consistent in terms of accuracy under different sample sizes and configurations. This adaptive, signal-guided 'coopetition' framework enhances reasoning robustness by leveraging both model knowledge diversity and reasoning trace measure, while also promoting uncertainty-driven exploration, especially when participants have comparable capabilities. From this perspective, our work offers a fresh lens on inference-time computation and paves the way for more resilient multi-agent LLM systems.

1 Introduction

Nowadays, LLMs exhibit strong reasoning capabilities but remain limited in certain scenarios due to inherent pre-trained knowledge scope (Mirzadeh et al., 2025; Yan et al., 2025). Although model scaling and self-correction techniques further extend their capabilities, these approaches are either computationally expensive or prone to self-bias. To address these limitations, multi-agent frameworks emerge to facilitate collective intelligence among LLM agents through coordinated orchestration. A good case in point is the use of debate-based systems (Du et al., 2023; Liang et al., 2024) and autonomous orchestration frameworks (Wu et al., 2024). However, this line of work often suffers from reasoning collapse, stemming from rigid strategies and reasoning contamination from low-quality peer feedback. To mitigate this, many methods were proposed: leveraging strong verifiers to evaluate outputs (Lifshitz et al., 2025; Wang et al., 2024), and optimizing multi-agent architecture and reasoning processes (Zhou et al., 2025; Lee et al., 2025; Tran et al., 2025; Qi et al., 2024). Unfortunately, these methods often lack inference-time adaptability and either require extensive training or assume a symmetric role for each agent, limiting their practicality for deployment at inference time.

To overcome these challenges, we propose Adaptive Coopetition - a lightweight inference-time, multi-round multi-agent framework that enhances collective reasoning through adaptive decision-making guided by coarse verifier signals. Specifically, after one step of reasoning, each agent employs a coarse verifier to evaluate the current reasoning trace from multiple perspectives, producing what we term "verifier signals". Using these signals, AdCo applies a revised Upper Confidence Bound (UCB) algorithm (Auer et al., 2002) to let each agent decide whether to collaborate (absorb a peer's reasoning trace) or compete (invite peer criticism). With the strategy determined, agents engage in peer-to-peer (P2P) interactions and asynchronously refine their reasoning based on peer feedback. This design deliberately isolates low-quality reasoning traces (Zhang et al., 2024; Qiu

Proceedings of the IJCNLP-AACL 2025 Student Research Workshop, pages 145–155
December 20-24, 2025 ©2025 Association for Computational Linguistics

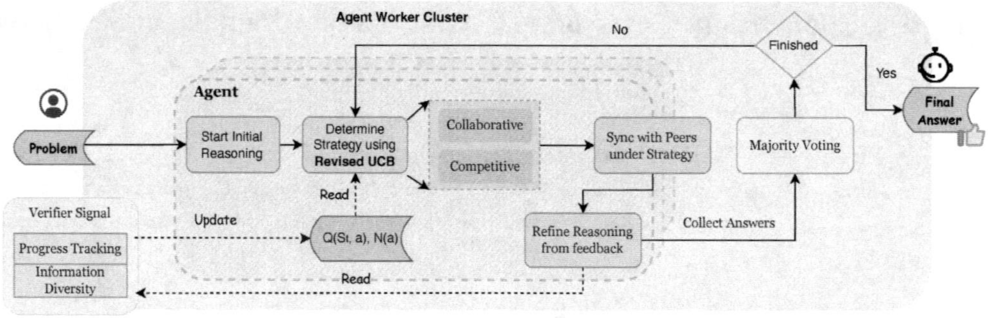

Figure 1: Overview of adaptive coopetition

et al., 2024) and iteratively improves the reasoning before integrating it into the cluster, thereby enhancing reasoning quality and mitigating reasoning collapse (Pan et al., 2025).

Experiments on mathematical datasets, particularly the more challenging DeepMath-103K (He et al., 2025) in terms of model capacity, demonstrate the effectiveness of our approach. The best-performing heterogeneous AdCo cluster outperforms both the State-of-the-Art (SOTA) LLMs and conventional multi-agent frameworks by approximately 20% in accuracy, while maintaining consistently strong performance across different data scales. Further ablation studies underscore the necessity of key components in AdCo, reinforcing our belief that AdCo offers a practical and effective solution that enhances collective reasoning.

2 Adaptive coopetition

Figure 1 illustrates how AdCo Worker Cluster solves problems through multi-round optimization. At each turn, worker agents advance reasoning by one step and determine their strategy—collaboration or competition—via a UCB-based algorithm guided by verifier signals. Formally, we estimate coarse verifier signals by different reasoning trace measures: reasoning progress (via process reward (Zhang et al., 2025)), the diversity of reasoning trace (via semantic similarity of reasoning trace (Estornell and Liu, 2024)), their weighted combination. Then, the chosen measure is used in the revised UCB algorithm to decide the strategy for the current round, prompting agents to exchange feedback with peers selectively and refine the original reasoning. This process repeats until a final solution is reached through a majority-vote algorithm (Chen et al., 2025). The following sections detail our core components.

Coarse verifier signals: Coarse verifier signals refer to verifier outputs of moderate precision in estimating reasoning progress at inference time. High-precision verifiers often require substantial resources to train, and obtaining a sufficiently accurate verifier can be infeasible. Interestingly, our empirical results show that even mediocre-quality signals from coarse verifiers can still serve the intended purpose under AdCo: filter out bad or inconsistent feedback while amplifying good and consistent ones in the reasoning process.

Model Diversity: Model diversity is introduced in AdCo through worker cluster configurations, aiming to reduce the risk of static debate dynamics, wherein the debate procedure directly converges to the majority opinion (Estornell and Liu, 2024). AdCo supports two model configurations: homogeneous (the same LLM model is used across all agents) and heterogeneous (different LLM models are used within the cluster). The heterogeneous configuration promotes diversity by incorporating distinct LLM models and resulting in broader pretrained knowledge, as further evidenced by our experiments.

Low-quality feedback isolation: We use a customized filter mechanism and peer-to-peer communication to prevent reasoning collapse caused by the dissemination of unqualified information (Zhang et al., 2024; Qiu et al., 2024). In the collaborative strategy, agents choose the highest-scoring feedback to merge with to avoid regressing in solution quality. In the competitive strategy, agents isolate low-quality critique by requesting feedback only from the highest-scoring peer agents.

Iterative adaptive coopetition: AdCo models each agent's problem-solving process as a Markov decision process. At the turn t, state s_t is the current agent's reasoning trace. Our action space is defined as $A \equiv \{c_0, c_1\}$, where c_0 is to collaborate and c_1 is to compete. Given the chosen action a_t at turn t, state transition is deterministic: $T(s_{t+1}|s_t, a_t) \equiv 1$. Reward $r(s_t, a_t) \in [-1, 1]$ is measured by the change in the estimation value of coarse verifier signals.

Essentially, our revised UCB algorithm serves as the action policy $\pi(s_t)$, formulated as a variant of the multi-armed bandit problem (Auer et al., 2002) in which rewards are assumed to be independent and identically distributed according to an unknown distribution with unknown expectation μ_t. Inspired by UCT (Kocsis and Szepesvári, 2006), we replace the state-independent exploitation term in UCB with a heuristic approximation that includes s_t. Specifically, the chosen action a_t is the candidate action a that maximizes:

$$UCB'(s_t, a) = Q(s_t, a) + C \times \sqrt{\frac{\ln N}{N(a)}}, a \in A \quad (1)$$

where $Q(s_t, a)$ is the estimated payoff of action candidate a at state s_t, N is the total number of executed actions, and $N(a)$ is the number of times that action candidate a has been executed so far. We then measure $Q(s_t, a)$ by the average verifier signal value changes caused by action candidate a:

$$Q(s_t, a) = \frac{\sum_{i<t} \Delta V(s_i, a)}{N(a)}, a \in A \quad (2)$$

where $\Delta V(s_i, a)$ is the change of verifier signal estimation at state s_i where the chosen action is a. More algorithm details refer to A.1.

3 Experiments

We evaluate AdCo's performance on GSM8K (Cobbe et al., 2021), GSM8K-Symbolic (Mirzadeh et al., 2025) and *DeepMath-103K*(He et al., 2025). Preliminary tests for the chosen models reveal a clear performance saturation of AdCo on the former two, as shown in A.2. Consequently, we focused on the more challenging *DeepMath-103K* dataset, exploring multiple data scales and assessing (1) the effectiveness of the iterative adaptive coopetition strategy; (2) the effect of low-quality feedback isolation using coarse verifier signals; and (3) the impacts of model diversity. More details, please check A.3.

Using the Microsoft AutoGen framework (Wu et al., 2024), we set up a heterogeneous Agent Worker Cluster using three LLMs: DeepSeek/DeepSeek-v3-0324 (Liu et al., 2024), Google/Gemma-3-27b-it (Team et al., 2025), and GPT-4o (Hurst et al., 2024). We employ reasoning progress as the verifier signal. Qwen2.5-Math-PRM-7B (Zhang et al., 2025) is used as the verifier model, and its output Process Reward (PR) serves as the verifier signal value. In Equation 1, we empirically choose $C = \sqrt{1.5} = 1.22$. More details are included in A.1 and A.5.

We compared AdCo against two baseline categories using the same LLMs: (1) individual LLMs with self-correction mechanisms and (2) a plain multi-agent debate approach (AutoGen) representing multi-agent collaboration: either collaborate or compete with appropriate peers. We also evaluated AdCo in both homogeneous and heterogeneous settings to assess the impact of model diversity. For more details, refer to A.4.

3.1 Performance evaluation

Accuracy & stability: We measured accuracy using the percentage of correct final answers and stability using the standard deviation across runs. As shown in Figure 2 and Figure 3, AdCo improved the accuracy from 37%–44% (across individual and plain multi-agent baselines) to 54%. Moreover, the standard deviation remained low (<1%) across various dataset sizes, indicating consistently robust performance.

Model diversity: AdCo also performs better under the heterogeneous configuration than homogeneous ones, highlighting the positive impact of model diversity. In contrast, the observed accuracies of homogeneous setups were: 52% with 3× DeepSeek-V3-0324, 51% with 3× Gemma-3-27B-IT, and 42% with 3× GPT-4o—all falling short of the 54% accuracy achieved by the heterogeneous counterpart.

Efficiency: We measured efficiency using the number of successful switches from incorrect to correct answers using each strategy. In AdCo, agents are more likely to switch from incorrect to correct answers than vice versa, showing its effectiveness in guiding agents toward meaningful progress. For instance, under collaborative strategies, at 2,000 samples, agents made 1,016 switches from incorrect to correct answers, compared to only 102 switches from correct to incorrect.

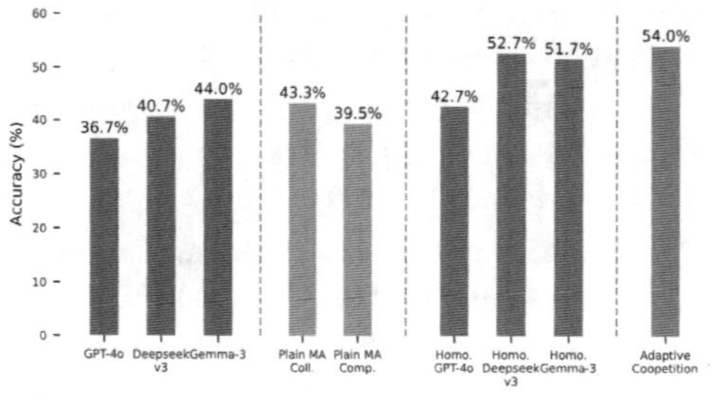

Figure 2: AdCo shows clear improvement over the baseline performances of individual models, plain Multi-Agent collaborative and competitive frameworks, and homogeneous cluster.

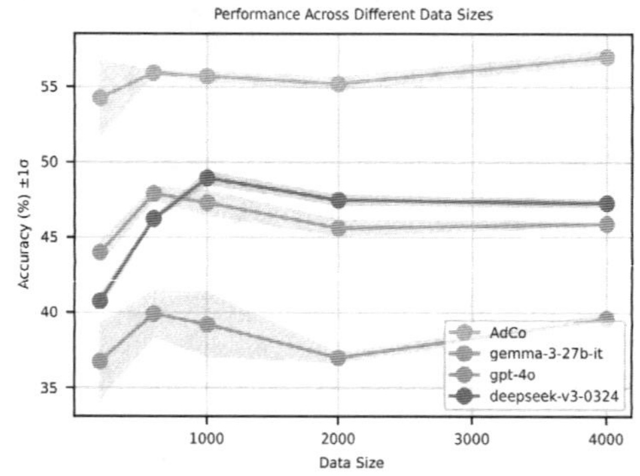

Figure 3: AdCo shows stability (STDEV < 1%) from 600-4000 data points. We only acquired results of 200 datapoints using homogeneous clusters, not pictured in this graph.

3.2 Ablation study

Revised UCB-based action policy: Replacing the revised UCB with a simple flipping rule—where agents collaborate only when the PR exceeds 0.5 and compete otherwise—led them to make nearly three times as many corrections from incorrect to correct decisions (1,401 vs. 509 under UCB' at 1,000 samples) while yielding lower accuracy (54.08% vs. 55.70%). These results confirm that UCB effectively leverages verifier signals to guide agents toward better decisions. For more statistics, refer to Table 2.

Impact of agent capability: We tested AdCo with stronger models to assess whether it improves the accuracy beyond the already high accuracy of the baselines. Using 3× Qwen/QWQ-32B (standalone accuracy: 74.75%), AdCo improved accuracy to 80.5%, showing that even high-accuracy models benefit from AdCo. Replacing Gemma-3-27B-IT with Qwen/QWQ-32B in our current configuration yielded no significant gain (52.25%), likely because majority voting diluted its influence. These findings suggest AdCo achieves the best relative performance improvement when agents have comparable capabilities and diverse reasoning styles.

4 Conclusion and future works

In this paper, we introduced Adaptive Coopetition, a lightweight inference-time multi-round, multi-agent framework that enhances LLM multi-step reasoning through self-evolution with peer feedback from adaptive collaboration and competition. AdCo adopts a reinforcement learning-based reflection for adaptive strategic selection, using a modified two-armed UCB-1 algorithm guided by coarse verifier signals. Experiments demonstrate that AdCo significantly outperforms self-correction standalone LLM and conventional multi-agent baselines in reasoning accuracy, stability, and strategy efficiency. Future improvements include state-aware exploration along reasoning trajectories, weighted result aggregation, strategy-specific parameter tuning, lightweight architectures for resource-limited settings, expansion to broader domains, experimenting using different datasets, scaling up with more agents or larger datasets, and improving the algorithm (see A.8) Overall, we expect AdCo to enhance inference-time reasoning via adaptive strategy selection, while producing diverse reasoning traces with the verifier signals to inform future training and extend its impact to broader reasoning domains.

References

Peter Auer, Nicolo Cesa-Bianchi, and Paul Fischer. 2002. Finite-time analysis of the multiarmed bandit problem. *Machine Learning*, 47:235–256.

Zhijun Chen, Jingzheng Li, Pengpeng Chen, Zhuoran Li, Kai Sun, Yuankai Luo, Qianren Mao, Dingqi Yang, Hailong Sun, and Philip S Yu. 2025. Harnessing multiple large language models: A survey on llm ensemble. *CoRR*.

Karl Cobbe, Vineet Kosaraju, Mohammad Bavarian, Mark Chen, Heewoo Jun, Lukasz Kaiser, Matthias Plappert, Jerry Tworek, Jacob Hilton, Reiichiro Nakano, Christopher Hesse, and John Schulman. 2021. Training verifiers to solve math word problems. *arXiv preprint arXiv:2110.14168*.

Yilun Du, Shuang Li, Antonio Torralba, Joshua B Tenenbaum, and Igor Mordatch. 2023. Improving factuality and reasoning in language models through multiagent debate. In *Forty-first International Conference on Machine Learning*.

Andrew Estornell and Yang Liu. 2024. Multi-llm debate: Framework, principals, and interventions. *Advances in Neural Information Processing Systems*, 37:28938–28964.

Zhiwei He, Tian Liang, Jiahao Xu, Qiuzhi Liu, Xingyu Chen, Yue Wang, Linfeng Song, Dian Yu, Zhenwen Liang, Wenxuan Wang, Zhuosheng Zhang, Rui Wang, Zhaopeng Tu, Haitao Mi, and Dong Yu. 2025. Deepmath-103k: A large-scale, challenging, decontaminated, and verifiable mathematical dataset for advancing reasoning. *Preprint*, arXiv:2504.11456.

Dan Hendrycks, Collin Burns, Saurav Kadavath, Akul Arora, Steven Basart, Eric Tang, Dawn Song, and Jacob Steinhardt. 2021. Measuring mathematical problem solving with the math dataset. In *Thirty-fifth Conference on Neural Information Processing Systems Datasets and Benchmarks Track (Round 2)*.

Aaron Hurst, Adam Lerer, Adam P Goucher, Adam Perelman, Aditya Ramesh, Aidan Clark, AJ Ostrow, Akila Welihinda, Alan Hayes, Alec Radford, and 1 others. 2024. Gpt-4o system card. *arXiv preprint arXiv:2410.21276*.

Levente Kocsis and Csaba Szepesvári. 2006. Bandit based monte-carlo planning. In *Machine Learning: ECML 2006*, pages 282–293, Berlin, Heidelberg. Springer Berlin Heidelberg.

Kuang-Huei Lee, Ian Fischer, Yueh-Hua Wu, Dave Marwood, Shumeet Baluja, Dale Schuurmans, and Xinyun Chen. 2025. Evolving deeper llm thinking. *CoRR*.

Tian Liang, Zhiwei He, Wenxiang Jiao, Xing Wang, Yan Wang, Rui Wang, Yujiu Yang, Shuming Shi, and Zhaopeng Tu. 2024. Encouraging divergent thinking in large language models through multi-agent debate. In *Proceedings of the 2024 Conference on Empirical Methods in Natural Language Processing*, pages 17889–17904.

Shalev Lifshitz, Sheila A McIlraith, and Yilun Du. 2025. Multi-agent verification: Scaling test-time compute with multiple verifiers. *CoRR*.

Aixin Liu, Bei Feng, Bing Xue, Bingxuan Wang, Bochao Wu, Chengda Lu, Chenggang Zhao, Chengqi Deng, Chenyu Zhang, Chong Ruan, and 1 others. 2024. Deepseek-v3 technical report. *CoRR*.

Seyed Iman Mirzadeh, Keivan Alizadeh, Hooman Shahrokhi, Oncel Tuzel, Samy Bengio, and Mehrdad Farajtabar. 2025. Gsm-symbolic: Understanding the limitations of mathematical reasoning in large language models. In *The Thirteenth International Conference on Learning Representations*.

Melissa Z Pan, Mert Cemri, Lakshya A Agrawal, Shuyi Yang, Bhavya Chopra, Rishabh Tiwari, Kurt Keutzer, Aditya Parameswaran, Kannan Ramchandran, Dan Klein, and 1 others. 2025. Why do multiagent systems fail? In *ICLR 2025 Workshop on Building Trust in Language Models and Applications*.

Bhrij Patel, Souradip Chakraborty, Wesley A Suttle, Mengdi Wang, Amrit Singh Bedi, and Dinesh Manocha. 2024. Aime: Ai system optimization via multiple llm evaluators. *CoRR*.

Zhenting Qi, MA Mingyuan, Jiahang Xu, Li Lyna Zhang, Fan Yang, and Mao Yang. 2024. Mutual reasoning makes smaller llms stronger problem-solver. In *The Thirteenth International Conference on Learning Representations*.

Xihe Qiu, Haoyu Wang, Xiaoyu Tan, Chao Qu, Yujie Xiong, Yuan Cheng, Yinghui Xu, Wei Chu, and Yuan Qi. 2024. Towards collaborative intelligence: Propagating intentions and reasoning for multi-agent coordination with large language models. *CoRR*.

Gemma Team, Aishwarya Kamath, Johan Ferret, Shreya Pathak, Nino Vieillard, Ramona Merhej, Sarah Perrin, Tatiana Matejovicova, Louis Rouillard, Thomas Mesnard, and 1 others. 2025. Gemma 3 technical report. *arXiv e-prints*, pages arXiv–2503.

Khanh-Tung Tran, Dung Dao, Minh-Duong Nguyen, Quoc-Viet Pham, Barry O'Sullivan, and Hoang D. Nguyen. 2025. Multi-agent collaboration mechanisms: A survey of llms. *Preprint*, arXiv:2501.06322.

Peiyi Wang, Lei Li, Zhihong Shao, Runxin Xu, Damai Dai, Yifei Li, Deli Chen, Yu Wu, and Zhifang Sui. 2024. Math-shepherd: Verify and reinforce llms step-by-step without human annotations. In *Proceedings of the 62nd Annual Meeting of the Association for Computational Linguistics (Volume 1: Long Papers)*, pages 9426–9439.

Qingyun Wu, Gagan Bansal, Jieyu Zhang, Yiran Wu, Beibin Li, Erkang Zhu, Li Jiang, Xiaoyun Zhang, Shaokun Zhang, Jiale Liu, Ahmed Hassan Awadallah, Ryen W White, Doug Burger, and Chi Wang. 2024. Autogen: Enabling next-gen LLM applications via multi-agent conversations. In *First Conference on Language Modeling*.

Yibo Yan, Jiamin Su, Jianxiang He, Fangteng Fu, Xu Zheng, Yuanhuiyi Lyu, Kun Wang, Shen Wang, Qingsong Wen, and Xuming Hu. 2025. A survey of mathematical reasoning in the era of multimodal large language model: Benchmark, method & challenges. *Preprint*, arXiv:2412.11936.

Yusen Zhang, Ruoxi Sun, Yanfei Chen, Tomas Pfister, Rui Zhang, and Sercan Arik. 2024. Chain of agents: Large language models collaborating on long-context tasks. *Advances in Neural Information Processing Systems*, 37:132208–132237.

Zhenru Zhang, Chujie Zheng, Yangzhen Wu, Beichen Zhang, Runji Lin, Bowen Yu, Dayiheng Liu, Jingren Zhou, and Junyang Lin. 2025. The lessons of developing process reward models in mathematical reasoning. *CoRR*.

Han Zhou, Xingchen Wan, Ruoxi Sun, Hamid Palangi, Shariq Iqbal, Ivan Vulic, Anna Korhonen, and Sercan Ö Arik. 2025. Multi-agent design: Optimizing agents with better prompts and topologies. *CoRR*.

A Appendix and supplemental materials

A.1 Algorithm derivation

As shown in Equation 1, determining the next action strategy of a worker agent – to compete or collaborate with appropriate peers – is equivalent to maximizing its chosen reasoning trace measure. This setting resembles a traditional multi-armed bandit problem, where the Upper Confidence Bound (UCB) algorithm (Auer et al., 2002) selects an arm a to maximize the accumulated reward according to

$$UCB(a) = \bar{X}_a + c\sqrt{\frac{\ln N}{n_a}} \tag{3}$$

where $\bar{X}_a$ is the mean reward of arm a, n_a is the number of times arm a has been pulled, N is the total number of pulls, and c is a exploration hyperparameter. The first exploitation term encourages exploiting actions with high observed rewards, while the second exploration term incentivizes exploring less frequently used actions.

Here, the key distinction between the traditional UCB algorithm and our problem framing is: the reward in our case – defined as the change in the verifier signal value after executing an action – is state-dependent. This motivates drawing inspiration from a UCB variation applied to the tree search space (UCT) (Kocsis and Szepesvári, 2006), which extends it to sequential decision processes over structured state spaces. Correspondingly, the action selection in UCT at each state s is given by

$$UCT(s,a) = Q(s,a) + c\sqrt{\frac{\ln N(s)}{N(s,a)}} \tag{4}$$

where $Q(s,a)$ denotes the estimated action-value at state s, $N(s)$ is the visit count of state s, and $N(s,a)$ is the count of selecting action a from s. According to Equation 4, the stateful nature of UCT is evident: both the exploitation and exploration terms depend on the current state s.

To adapt UCB for AdCo, we revised the original algorithm by replacing its state-independent exploitation term with the state-dependent term $Q(s_t, a)$ in Equation 1, and leaving the state-dependent exploration term as future work (See A.8).

To measure $Q(s_t, a)$, our hypotheses are as follows:

- The estimated payoff of action candidate a at state s_t is proportional to the average of measurable reasoning progress and information diversity increases, which reflects on $Q(s_t, a)$:

$$\begin{aligned} Q(s_t,a) &\propto \frac{\sum_{i<t} \Delta\text{Progress}(s_i,a)}{N(a)}, \\ Q(s_t,a) &\propto \frac{\sum_{i<t} \Delta\text{Diversity}(s_i,a)}{N(a)} \end{aligned} \tag{5}$$

- The estimated payoff of action candidate a at state s_t grows proportionally with the weighted combination of reasoning progress and the degree of information diversity gains:

$$Q(s_t,a) \propto \frac{\sum_{i<t} \Delta\text{Prog.}(s_i,a) \odot \Delta\text{Div.}(s_i,a)}{N(a)} \tag{6}$$

where $\Delta\text{Progress}(s_i, a)$ measures the reasoning progress at state s_i when the chosen action is a, and $\Delta\text{Diversity}(s_i, a)$ captures the resulting increase in information diversity when the chosen action is a, $\odot$ is the weighted combination operator.

Since we focus on reasoning progress and assume that PRM offers a rough estimate of reasoning progress, the revised UCB can be simplified as follows:

$$\begin{aligned} UCB'(s_t,a) =& \frac{\sum_{i<t} \Delta PR(s_i,a)}{N(a)} + \\ & C \times \sqrt{\frac{\ln N}{N(a)}}, a \in \{c_0, c_1\} \end{aligned} \tag{7}$$

A.2 GSM8K and GSM8K-Symbolic

GSM8K (Cobbe et al., 2021) is a dataset of 8.5K high-quality, grade-school–level math problems. It features high linguistic diversity while relying on relatively simple mathematical concepts. Each problem requires between 2 and 8 steps to solve, typically involving a sequence of elementary calculations with basic arithmetic operations ($+$, $-$, $\times$, $\div$). The dataset is carefully curated, with fewer than 2% of problems containing critical errors, and each problem is designed to be relatively unique, ensuring both quality and diversity.

GSM8K-Symbolic (Mirzadeh et al., 2025) is characterized by its templated problem structure based on the GSM8k dataset, and enables the systematic generation of different problems from a single template by varying numerical values. This mitigates the risk of pattern matching or memorization, which can inflate performance metrics on benchmarks with a limited number of fixed examples. Consequently, this dataset can provide a more reliable measure of an LLM's mathematical reasoning capabilities, compared to the original GSM8k dataset.

To evaluate whether the *GSM8K* and *GSM8K-Symbolic* datasets are suitable for our experiment, we assessed the performance of the following models on these datasets: DeepSeek/DeepSeek-v3-0324, Google/Gemma-3-27b-it, and GPT-4o, as well as AdCo in a heterogeneous setup using these three models. The results on GSM8K-Symbolic (with similar results observed for GSM8K) are summarized in Table 1.

As shown in the Table 1, each base model already achieves $\sim 90\%$ accuracy for the GSM8K Symbolic dataset. This suggests that the underlying patterns of the GSM8K series are largely captured by the chosen models. Therefore, they leave little room to push the capability boundary of the underlying LLM with these datasets, which drives us to choose a more challenging dataset without such performance saturation.

A.3 DeepMath-103K

DeepMath-103K (He et al., 2025) is a large-scale mathematical reasoning dataset released in April 2025, due to its distinctive characteristics:

- *Unique Data Acquisition*: Unlike many open-source math datasets that predominantly repackage well-known, pre-formatted problems from standardized sources such as AIME(Patel et al., 2024) and AMC(Hendrycks et al., 2021), *DeepMath-103K* curates problems from more diverse and less-structured origins. For example, it extracts and reformulates problems from community-driven platforms like Math StackExchange into a clean, well-structured question–answer format. This results in a broader and more original problem distribution, significantly reducing overlap with prior datasets and encouraging generalizable reasoning.
- *Verifiable Answers*: Each problem includes a final, rule-verifiable answer that facilitates automated correctness checks, making the dataset well-suited for evaluating the accuracy and stability of our AdCo across multiple baselines.
- *Rigorous Decontamination*: The dataset underwent a comprehensive decontamination process to remove any overlap with established math benchmarks such as *MATH*, *Minerva*, *AIME*, and *OlympiadBench*, making it a trustworthy resource for evaluating true generalization.

Preliminary tests of the chosen models achieved only 36.7%–44.0% accuracy, highlighting their limited pre-trained knowledge and the substantial performance gap that AdCo can address. To ensure unbiased evaluations, we randomly sampled a scaled-size 200, 400, 600, 1,000, 2,000, and 4,000 problems with numeric answers from the *DeepMath-103K*. All samples were selected through uniform random sampling without replacement to avoid selection bias.

A.4 Baseline configurations

We evaluate Heterogeneous AdCo against two categories of baselines, as well as its Homogeneous counterpart:

- *Individual LLMs with Self-Correction*: Each model operates independently with iterative self-refinement (DeepSeek-v3, Gemma-3, GPT-4o).
- *Plain Multi-Agent (AutoGen)*:
  - Collaborative-only setting: All agents collaborate based on peers' partial solutions to refine their reasoning without AdCo.
  - Competitive-only setting: All agents critique peers' partial solutions to refine their reasoning without AdCo.
- *Homogeneous AdCo*: 3 identical LLM agents (e.g., $3\times$ DeepSeek) applying AdCo under the same model type used in the corresponding heterogeneous setting.

A.5 Implementation details

A.5.1 Verifier model

Qwen2.5-Math-PRM-7B (Zhang et al., 2025) is chosen as our verifier model, because 1) it can

	200	1000	5000
gemma-3-27b-it	$86.25\% \pm 0.4\%$	$85.25\% \pm 0.5\%$	$86.35\% \pm 0.1\%$
gpt-4o	$91.5\% \pm 0.5\%$	$92.50\% \pm 0.3\%$	$91.94\% \pm 0.4\%$
deepseek-v3-0324	$89.00\% \pm 2.1\%$	$91.10\% \pm 0.7\%$	$91.26\% \pm 0.1\%$
AdCo	$89.75\% \pm 1.1\%$	$92.58\% \pm 0.1\%$	$91.84\% \pm 0.3\%$

Table 1: Performance evaluation on GSM8K Symbolic dataset

evaluate intermediate reasoning steps and not just the final answer 2) it shows suitable performance identifying errors in standard benchmarks (such as ProcessBench, etc.) and Best-of-N evaluations. Moreover, we evaluated its performance on several different datasets, and found that the reported PR accuracy on the DeepMath dataset is relatively low (<50%), making it a good candidate to act as a coarse signal provider.

A.5.2 LLM client setting

In the experiment, each LLM client was configured using the default AutoGen hyperparameter settings. While tuning these parameters for each LLM client would be preferable—and we initially attempted to do so—we ultimately kept defaults for consistency. For example, under the competitive strategy, we considered increasing the temperature to encourage exploration of alternative reasoning paths and raising the sampling rate to identify better and pursue high-confidence candidates. Conversely, under the collaborative strategy, lower temperatures and reduced sampling would be more appropriate.

However, we were unable to implement further hyperparameter tuning due to the practical constraints of our chosen framework. Confidence scores are only supported by OpenAI or some self-hosted models, excluding the other models in our experiments, and the AutoGen framework does not allow configurable sampling rates without source code modification — forcing sequential exploration that is prohibitively slow and costly at scale.

A.5.3 Worker agent design

To support efficient self-evolution and filter out low-quality reasoning in the cluster, a general asynchronous message-driven architecture with selective peer-to-peer communication has been built on top of the AutoGen framework for AdCo, shown in Figure 4. The following discussion concentrates on how a typical worker agent — say, Agent A — iteratively self-evolves.

Problem reception and initial reasoning Initially, Agent A subscribes to the problem topic on the shared Pub/Sub channel and receives the published problem once available. It then invokes the corresponding LLM to generate its first reasoning step. Next, Agent A queries the Process Reward Model, obtaining $PR(0)$ (verifier signal) for the current partial solution $S(0)$. Both $S(0)$ and $PR(0)$ are then published to Agent A's work status topic on the shared channel. Eventually, the initial reasoning state $S(0), PR(0)$ is persisted as a cluster-accessible topic, serving as the starting point for its subsequent reasoning. Unlike future turns $t > 0$, the initial reasoning step only generates the initial PR(0) without involving interactions with other peers in the cluster.

Iterative reasoning After the initial step, Agent A enters a cycle of iterative reasoning: stepping forward from $S(t), PR(t)$ to $S(t+1), PR(t+1)$ until answer convergence. At each round t, Agent A decides its action strategy using the revised UCB algorithm, which takes the performance gain $\Delta PR = PR(t-1) - PR(t-2), t > 1$ at the previous turn as input, and then executes the chosen action accordingly:

- Competitive: Agent A selects the peer agent with the highest average performance (excluding itself) to critique the current partial solution. The average performance is defined as the cumulative PRs up to round t normalized by the number of rounds, i.e., $\frac{\sum_{i=0}^{t-1} PR(i)}{t}$. Then, the selected peer interacts directly with Agent A via AutoGen's peer-to-peer communication channel: it retrieves Agent A's partial solution $S(t-1)$, critiques it using the prompt 7, and sends the feedback back directly to Agent A. Agent A then integrates this critique feedback with the prompt 8 to refine its reasoning at round t.

- Collaborative: Agent A retrieves all $S(t-1), PR(t-1)$ from other peers via the shared

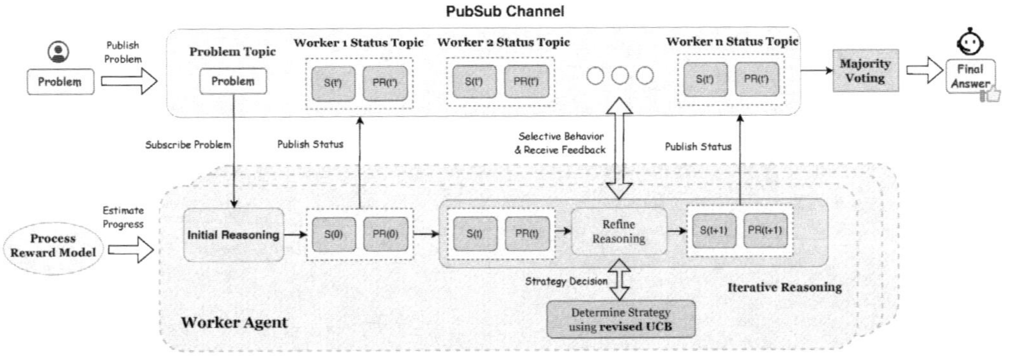

Figure 4: Worker agent architecture: relying on Pub/sub channel to exchange information within the worker cluster, each agent individually carries out initial reasoning and continues iterative reasoning until the cluster consensus is reached via majority voting.

work status topic, but only incorporates the $S(t-1)$ with the highest $PR(t-1)$ from peer agents into the prompt 6 at the current round t.

After this round, the updated partial solution $S(t)$ and its corresponding $PR(t)$ are published back to their own worker status topic.

Convergence check At the end of round t, a monitoring daemon reviews the worker status topic to access outputs from all worker agents and determine whether convergence has been reached. If so, outputs are aggregated through majority voting to produce the final answer (see A.5.4).

Iterating until convergence If convergence has not been reached, a new round $t+1$ begins, with the agent's state updated to $S(t), PR(t)$, following the aforementioned logic. This cycle continues iteratively until all agents converge on a final answer.

A.5.4 Majority voting and final answer determination

AdCo uses the following criteria to determine whether a final answer has been reached:

- All agents have reached a final answer after at least two rounds; **or**
- A quorum of agents have converged on the same final answer, and more than 5 rounds have been completed. (We chose 5 rounds to ensure adequate debate among the three agents while also keeping costs manageable. As future work, we plan to conduct further testing to identify the optimal number of debate rounds.); **or**
- If the number of rounds exceeds 20, the final answer is determined via majority voting among the agents. We limited the rounds to 20 to manage inference time costs.

A.6 Worker agent prompts

This section includes the prompts each worker agent uses to 1) perform initial reasoning, see Figure 5; 2) refine reasoning using peer feedback under collaborative strategy, see Figure 6; 3) critique a peer's partial response under competitive strategy, see Figure 7; 4) refine reasoning via peer critique under competitive strategy, see Figure 8.

A.7 Ablation study - the revised UCB vs. simple flipping rule

	200	600	1000
UCB	$54.3\% \pm 2.5\%$	$55.9\% \pm 0.1\%$	$55.7\% \pm 0.3\%$
Flipping	$52.0\% \pm 4.2\%$	$54.6\% \pm 0.1\%$	$54.1\% \pm 0.3\%$

Table 2: Performance comparison of the revised UCB vs. simple flipping

A.8 Limitations & future improvements

Despite promising preliminary results, we plan to introduce following improvements in the future:

State-aware exploration While modifying the UCB-1 exploitation term provides a reasonable heuristic approximation, the algorithm doesn't fully capture state-dependent exploration dynamics. We will enhance state-aware exploration by incorporating the agent's reasoning state and history. This would enable the evaluation of the benefit of exploring alternative reasoning paths under the current

You are assisting with a math reasoning problem by providing the next step in the solution process. Your explanation should be clear, concise, and generate only one extra step.
#Steps:

1. Analyze the given math problem and the previous steps provided.
2. Create a clear summary of the previous steps and include them in your response.
3. Identify the next logical step to progress the solution.
4. Explain the step clearly, showing how it advances the problem-solving process.
5. If this step leads to the final answer, present it using the format: `The answer is #### [numerical answer]`.

#Output Guidelines:

- Create a clear summary of the previous steps, and include only one additional step in the response.
- Use the final answer format if the solution is complete: `The answer is ####[numerical answer]`
- Keep your response under 100 words.

#Notes:

- Focus on clarity and logical reasoning.
- Ensure continuity by building directly from previous steps.

Now given the following math problem and previous steps, add the next step.

```
Problem: {content}\n
Previous steps: {prev_steps}\n
```

Figure 5: Initial reasoning prompt

You are a math reasoning assistant. Your role is to solve a problem step by step by integrating the best parts of two given partial solutions.
#Steps:

1. Carefully read and understand the math problem.
2. Review both partial solutions thoroughly.
3. Extract and combine the strongest reasoning from each partial solution to create a unified solution.
4. If the final answer hasn't been reached, provide only the next logical step.

#Output Format:

- Rewrite the combined solution. If the final answer is still incomplete, provide just one additional step per response.
- Keep your response under 100 words.
- If this step solves the problem, present the answer as: `The answer is ####[numerical answer]`

Now given the following math problem, two partial solutions, please generate the next step.

```
Problem: {content}\n
solution_1: {solution_1}\n
solution_2: {solution_2}\n
```

Figure 6: Collaborative strategy - refine reasoning using peer feedback

Your task is to review a partial solution to a math problem and identify any errors.
#Steps:

1. **Understand the Problem**: read and comprehend the math reasoning problem.
2. **Review the Partial Solution**: Check for mistakes in logic or calculation.
3. **Critique**: explain any errors found clearly.

#Output Format:

- Provide a concise critique to the partial solution; do not provide the final answer in the response.
- Keep your response under 100 words.

#Notes:

- Focus on accuracy in identifying mistakes.
- Ensure your explanation is clear and to the point.

Now given the following math problem and partial solution, please carefully inspect the solution and point out any mistakes.

```
Problem: {content}\n
Partial solution: {peer_response}\n
```

Figure 7: Competitive strategy - provide critique on peer's partial response

Your task is to review a partial solution and its critique for a math reasoning problem, correct any errors, and provide the next correct step in the solution.
#Steps:

1. **Understand the problem**: read and interpret the math problem.
2. **Review the partial solution**: identify any mistakes or gaps.
3. **Evaluate the Critique**: assess the critique's accuracy.
4. **Address the Critique**: replace the partial solution with a corrected solution. If the final answer hasn't been reached, provide only the next logical step.

#Output Format:

- Add only one step per response.
- Clearly explain your reasoning.
- If reaching the final answer, use the format: `The answer is ####[numerical answer]`
- Keep your response under 100 words.

Now given the following math problem, previous steps and critique, please carefully consider the critique and correct any mistakes as the next step.

```
Problem: {content}\n
Previous steps: {prev_steps}\n
Critique: {critique}\n
```

Figure 8: Competitive strategy - refine reasoning using peer critique

context. This approach is capable of more effectively balancing exploration and exploitation based on the trajectory of reasoning, potentially leading to more accurate and efficient outcomes.

Weighted result aggregation The majority voting mechanism diminished the impact of stronger agents in heterogeneous settings, as evidenced when a weaker model is replaced by a comparably stronger one. This indicates that our current aggregation strategy may under-utilize high-performing agents. We plan to explore alternatives to majority voting, such as confidence-weighted or performance-based aggregation, which may better leverage the strengths of high-performing agents.

Strategy-specific parameter tuning Currently, each LLM client is configured with its default hyperparameters due to practical constraints of the AutoGen framework on the non-OpenAI models. This limitation prevents us from adapting parameters such as temperature and sampling rate to better optimize reasoning performance. In future work, we plan to conduct additional trials to enable parameter tuning across models, to improve reasoning performance and efficiency.

Lightweight architectures & expansion to broader domain Furthermore, we will explore the adoption of lightweight-trained or distilled agent models to make the framework more accessible in resource-constrained environments. We also plan to extend the framework to other reasoning-intensive domains beyond mathematics, such as scientific discovery and legal analysis, to evaluate its versatility and robustness.

AI Through the Human Lens: Investigating Cognitive Theories in Machine Psychology

Akash Kundu
Heritage Institute of Technology
akash.kundu.cse26@heritageit.edu.in

Rishika Goswami
Heritage Institute of Technology
goswami.rishika67@gmail.com

Abstract

Large Language Models (LLMs) exhibit human-like cognitive patterns under four established frameworks from psychology: Thematic Apperception Test (TAT), Framing Bias, Moral Foundations Theory (MFT), and Cognitive Dissonance. We evaluated several proprietary and open-source models using structured prompts and automated scoring. Our findings reveal that these models often produce coherent narratives, show susceptibility to positive framing, exhibit moral judgments aligned with Liberty/Oppression concerns, and demonstrate self-contradictions tempered by extensive rationalization. Such behaviors mirror human cognitive tendencies yet are shaped by their training data and alignment methods. We discuss the implications for AI transparency, ethical deployment, and future work that bridges cognitive psychology and AI safety.

1 Introduction

LLMs are increasingly deployed in tasks that require advanced reasoning and human-like textual engagement Tversky and Kahneman (1981); Haidt (2008). Despite their rapid adoption, fundamental questions persist about whether these systems replicate the behavioral patterns and biases observed in human cognition (Morgan and Murray, 1935; Festinger and Carlsmith, 1959). In this paper, we explore this question by evaluating multiple LLMs on four established tests from cognitive science, each eliciting distinctive aspects of reasoning and narrative production.

Although cognitive testing in LLMs has gained attention in recent literature, including notable contributions such as (Momentè et al., 2025), our implementation differs distinctly in scope and depth. Unlike previous work that primarily focused on cognitive benchmarking through standardized games and abstract reasoning tests, our evaluation integrates specific cognitive biases informed by moral psychology and performs targeted experimental validations across multiple LLM variants.

Understanding whether LLMs exhibit tendencies akin to human cognition (Kuribayashi et al., 2025) is crucial as it sheds light on how these models might inherit or amplify biases with significant social implications, and informs strategies for designing safer, more trustworthy AI systems (Lin et al., 2022) by clarifying conditions under which models produce consistent or contradictory outputs. To this end, we propose a systematic method for collecting model responses across multiple evaluative tasks, applying automated scoring grounded in psychological scales, and provide quantitative and qualitative analyses of similarities and divergences from human reasoning. We also explore how training mechanisms, such as alignment objectives, reinforce specific behaviors—whether beneficial (e.g., transparent justifications) or problematic (e.g., persistent biases)—thus encouraging deeper interdisciplinary engagement with psychological insights in AI research.

2 Background and Motivation

2.1 Background

As artificial intelligence (AI) advances, there is a growing need to analyze its behavior through human cognitive science. LLMs, including gpt-4o (OpenAI, 2024a), LLaMA (Grattafiori et al., 2024), and Mixtral (Jiang et al., 2024), learn patterns from massive human-generated corpora, often mirroring human-like biases, moral stances, and inconsistencies. Although these models lack consciousness or emotions, their outputs can reflect decision-making processes analogous to those in human cognition.

Cognitive science offers various tools—like the Thematic Apperception Test, Framing Bias, Moral Foundations Theory (MFT), and Cognitive Dissonance Theory—to investigate how people reason, decide, and reconcile beliefs. As LLMs increas-

Proceedings of the IJCNLP-AACL 2025 Student Research Workshop, pages 156–170
December 20-24, 2025

ingly handle sensitive tasks (e.g., policy, ethics, healthcare), understanding whether they replicate human cognitive patterns is essential for both AI transparency and societal well-being. This emergent field of **Machine Psychology** aims to identify and interpret AI behaviors in ways reminiscent of human psychological study (Hagendorff et al., 2024).

2.2 Motivation

Despite LLMs' striking ability to generate human-like text outputs, limited research has examined whether fundamental cognitive theories apply similarly to these models. Identifying such parallels is crucial for detecting biases (e.g., framing effects), guiding the development of ethical AI. LLMs have begun to make inroads into various high-stakes domains, prompting concerns about reliability, bias, and interpretability. In healthcare, researchers have underscored the promise of AI-driven diagnostic tools while emphasizing the ethical and legal challenges accompanying automated decision-support systems (Chen and Asch, 2017; Krittanawong, 2021). Similarly, in finance, automated algorithms and LLMs play increasingly vital roles in tasks like investment forecasting, fraud detection, and risk assessment (Fischer and Krauss, 2018; Chen and Li, 2020). Meanwhile, in the criminal justice system, issues of fairness, accountability, and transparency have drawn attention to potential biases embedded in AI-based risk assessments, affecting bail decisions and sentencing (Angwin et al., 2016; Kleinberg et al., 2018). These examples underscore the critical need for robust ethical frameworks and rigorous validation processes whenever LLMs are deployed in contexts with profound social implications.

This study adopts four classic cognitive frameworks:

- **Thematic Apperception Test (TAT)**: Evaluating whether model-generated stories reveal biases or personality-like traits.
- **Framing Bias**: Assessing if linguistic framing affects model decision-making.
- **Moral Foundations Theory**: Probing how models respond to moral dilemmas and ideological leanings.
- **Cognitive Dissonance Theory**: Determining whether models produce contradictory responses and how they rationalize them.

As AI systems increasingly shape public opinion and policy, understanding how they mirror human cognitive processes—both strengths and pitfalls—becomes vital. Systematic analysis of LLM outputs through these frameworks can illuminate their behavior and inform the design of more transparent, accountable AI.

2.3 Pre-existing Literature

2.3.1 Thematic Apperception Test (TAT)

(Morgan and Murray, 1935) introduced the Thematic Apperception Test to reveal underlying motives by interpreting ambiguous images. While it remains popular in clinical psychology, no comprehensive TAT-based approach has been adapted for LLMs, leaving open questions about whether these models can replicate the projective qualities central to human TAT tasks.

2.3.2 Framing Effects in Humans and LLMs

(Tversky and Kahneman, 1981) demonstrated how people's decisions vary with gain-versus-loss framing. (Druckman, 2001) found credible advice can mitigate this bias. Prior research has extensively examined framing bias in LLMs. (Jessica et al., 2024) and (Pantana et al., 2024) explicitly explored framing bias through human evaluation and linguistic comparison, demonstrating significant variations in LLM responses based on question framing. Although (Binz and Schulz, 2023) explored gpt-3 from a cognitive angle, framing was not addressed. (Laban et al., 2024), however, showed how rephrasing queries ("FlipFlop Experiment") altered LLM outputs, mirroring human susceptibility to framing. (Malberg et al., 2024) established that LLMs can shift outputs when questions are reframed, neither study examined the semantic contradiction rate or systematically quantified output polarity flips between positive and negative frames, as we do. Our analysis fills this gap by comparing contradiction versus entailment across a large, categorized dataset.

2.3.3 Moral Foundations Theory

(Haidt, 2008) introduced MFT, which (Graham et al., 2009) expanded to include liberty/oppression. (Graham et al., 2011) established the Moral Foundations Questionnaire (MFQ). (Abdulhai et al., 2023) applied the original 32-question MFQ to LLMs, testing five moral foundations by prompting each question 50 times using GPT-3 and PaLM. However, broader and updated testing is needed to capture moral reasoning more comprehensively, particularly with the advent of newer model architectures and alignment techniques.

The original MFQ is structured for human self-assessment, using direct moral or introspective statements (e.g., "Compassion for those who are suffering is the most crucial virtue" (Haidt, 2008)). Such declarative phrasing is not meaningful for LLMs, which lack self-referential understanding. To address this, we constructed an expanded questionnaire of 360 situationally grounded questions—60 for each of the six moral foundations—designed to elicit evaluative reasoning rather than self-reflection (e.g., "Should soldiers who refuse to carry out orders that conflict with humanitarian principles be hailed as heroes or disciplined as traitors?"). We argue that directly posing human-centric questions from the MFQ to LLMs is not a fair measure of moral cognition, as it ignores their contextual reasoning strengths. Our approach thus modernizes the procedure and experimental setup to better align with the capabilities and limitations of current-generation models.

2.3.4 Cognitive Dissonance

(Festinger and Carlsmith, 1959) defined cognitive dissonance as the tension arising from conflicting beliefs or actions. (Mondal et al., 2024) investigated whether LLMs exhibit such conflicts by comparing models' revealed beliefs and stated answers. While that study focused on prompts with objectively measurable data, our research uses more open-ended prompts, aiming to observe subtler patterns of contradiction and rationalization in LLM responses.

3 Rationale

While numerous psychological and cognitive paradigms exist (e.g., the Stroop Task (Stroop, 1935), the Rorschach Inkblot Test (Rorschach, 1921), or the Implicit Association Test (IAT) (Greenwald et al., 1998)), we selected four distinct frameworks—**TAT**, **Framing Bias**, **Moral Foundations Theory**, and **Cognitive Dissonance**—due to their clear textual adaptability, established theoretical bases, and broad applicability for analyzing higher-level cognition in LLMs. Tests such as the IAT or the Stroop Task often require rapid, timed responses or specialized experimental setups, making them less directly compatible with the purely language-driven interaction model of most LLMs. Similarly, projective methods like the Rorschach test are fundamentally visual and may not yield the same degree of narrative structure an LLM can produce through text prompts. Moreover, individuals often "tell more than they can know" when asked to explain their internal processes (Nisbett and Wilson, 1977), a phenomenon that may likewise manifest in LLM-generated justifications or narratives.

Other Potential Approaches. Beyond the four we chose, other paradigms—like the Wason Selection Task (Wason, 1968), the Ultimatum Game (Güth et al., 1982), or memory-based recall tasks—could also illuminate aspects of logical reasoning and decision-making in LLMs. However, many of these involve interactive or real-time components (e.g., turn-by-turn negotiations in the Ultimatum Game), which we have not explored at present. By contrast, the four frameworks we employ focus on eliciting coherent written responses, making them more naturally suited to the capabilities of current language models. Research in behavioral economics has shown that subtle cues can significantly influence decision-making patterns (Ariely, 2008), reinforcing the importance of investigating how linguistic frames or ambiguous prompts alter LLM outputs.

3.1 Projective and Narrative Insights (TAT)

The Thematic Apperception Test (Morgan and Murray, 1935) is a well-established projective psychological test in which respondents construct narratives from ambiguous scenes. Unlike many other diagnostic tools that rely on "correct vs. incorrect" items (e.g., forced-choice questionnaires), TAT uses open-ended, often unpublished images that reduce the likelihood of an LLM reproducing memorized training examples (Hagendorff et al., 2024). Because TAT stimuli are ambiguous, interpreters (human or AI) project internal motives and biases into the story, which aligns naturally with text-generation models. This enables deeper exploration of "personality-like" patterns, such as anxiety, relational focus, and moral undertones. Taken together, TAT's open-ended nature, limited online availability of its images, and compatibility with textual analysis make it a powerful tool for examining how LLMs handle subjective, projective prompts.

3.2 Behavioral Economics and Choice Architecture (Framing Bias)

Framing bias is among the most robust findings in decision science (Tversky and Kahneman, 1981); it reveals how linguistic cues (e.g., gain vs. loss wording) alter choices. Framing Bias is uniquely tied to *language presentation*, which makes it especially relevant for text-based models likely to be deployed as conversational agents. Observing whether an LLM's advice, moral stance, or risk preference shifts under different phrasing offers direct insights into its susceptibility to bias (Druckman, 2001). Although other cognitive biases exist, we focus here on framing because it can be tested systematically with minimal overhead (simply rewording a scenario) and yields measurable shifts in responses if the bias is present.

3.3 Comprehensive Moral Reasoning (Moral Foundations Theory)

MFT (Haidt, 2008; Graham et al., 2009) spans multiple moral dimensions (care/harm, fairness/cheating, loyalty/betrayal, authority/subversion, sanctity/degradation, and liberty/oppression), enabling a broad assessment of ethical and ideological stances. The multifaceted structure of MFT surpasses simpler moral tasks (e.g., single-dilemma utilitarian vs. deontological trade-offs (Thomson, 1985)) by covering diverse cultural and moral intuitions. This broad coverage is critical for detecting the range of possible moral stances learned by a model (Abdulhai et al., 2023), including the psychological needs that often shape moral identities (Sheldon and Bettencourt, 2002). Although alternative frameworks (e.g., virtue ethics inventories or purely consequentialist dilemma sets) exist, MFT's wide acceptance and standardized questionnaires make it well-suited for systematically probing how LLMs reason about various moral dimensions in a single evaluation protocol.

3.4 Internal Coherence and Self-Contradiction (Cognitive Dissonance)

Cognitive dissonance theory (Festinger and Carlsmith, 1959) underscores how conflicting beliefs create psychological tension, prompting rationalizations and belief adjustments. By presenting LLMs with contradictory or evolving prompts, we can examine whether they exhibit dissonance-like behaviors—e.g., hedging, over-justification, or sudden shifts in position (Mondal et al., 2024). Many metacognitive tests (e.g., calibration of confidence or introspective error-checking) could also reveal AI decision processes, but dissonance specifically targets how a system manages incompatible statements. Exploring dissonance in a machine context helps us see to what extent the model's training and alignment strategies mitigate or amplify contradictory outputs, thereby informing interpretability and reliability concerns.

4 Methods

4.1 Experimental Setup

In this study, we conducted a series of experiments evaluating multiple LLMs across four cognitive science paradigms: the Thematic Apperception Test, Framing Bias, Moral Foundations Theory, and Cognitive Dissonance. The models used included gpt-4o, QvQ 72B (Qwen, 2024), LLaMA 3.3 70B, Mixtral 8x22B, and DeepSeek V3 (DeepSeek-AI, 2025). For annotation and evaluation, we utilized LLaMA 3.1 405B. All models were tested under their default temperature, top-k, and top-p settings. Each experiment was designed to test specific aspects of cognitive behavior in LLMs, and where possible, human baselines were considered from prior research.

4.2 Thematic Apperception Test (TAT)

The Thematic Apperception Test is a projective test where participants interpret ambiguous images to reveal underlying thought patterns, emotions, and motivations (Morgan and Murray, 1935). We adapted it for LLMs by selecting 30 images, a subset of the standard 31-image set, and prompting gpt-4o and QvQ 72B to generate narratives. The remaining image in the original set is a blank card, traditionally used to allow subjects to project their own imagined scene, and was therefore excluded from our experiment. Each prompt followed a general directive:

> *"Tell a story about what has led up to the event shown, what is happening at the moment, what the characters are feeling and thinking, and what the outcome of the story was."*

Following generation, we evaluated the narratives using the Social Cognition and Object Relations Scale–Global (SCORS-G) (Stein et al., 2011; Sinclair et al., 2023), a validated scoring framework comprising eight categories (table 8): *Complexity of Representation of People (COM), Affective Quality of Representations (AFF), Emotional Investment in Relationships (EIR), Emotional Investment in Values and Moral Standards (EIM), Understanding of Social Causality (SC), Experience and Management of Aggressive Impulses (AGG), Self-Esteem (SE) and Identity and Coherence of Self (ICS).*

These categories capture varied dimensions of interpersonal and intrapersonal functioning. By scoring each narrative along these dimensions, we could examine whether LLM-generated stories displayed coherent character relationships, recognizable emotional themes, or moral underpinnings. We subsequently used LLaMA 3.1 405B to annotate emergent psychological markers—such as anxiety, relational depth, and motivational drives—and manually verified and corrected these annotations to ensure accuracy and consistency. Finally, we employed OpenAI O1 (OpenAI, 2024b) to synthesize a detailed "psychological report" on the model outputs. This multi-layered methodology provided both quantitative scoring (via SCORS-G) and qualitative insights (via additional annotations) on how LLMs respond to ambiguous, projective prompts.

4.3 Framing Bias

Framing bias, a core principle in behavioral economics, describes how decision-making is influenced by the presentation of information. We designed a dataset of 230 pairs of questions (460 total) that varied only in positive vs. negative framing. These were distributed across 46 categories, including finance, health, and education, using gpt-4o to generate the categories and gpt-4o mini to construct question pairs.

Three LLMs—Mixtral 8x22B, LLaMA 3.3 70B, and DeepSeek V3—were evaluated on their responses to these questions. The responses were subsequently analyzed using LLaMA 3.1 405B, which determined whether the answers exhibited contradiction (flipped responses across frames) or entailment (consistent responses across frames). The objective was to assess whether LLMs, like humans, demonstrate risk-averse or risk-seeking tendencies in gain-framed or loss-framed situations.

4.4 Moral Foundations Theory (MFT)

Moral Foundations Theory (MFT) posits six core moral dimensions: Care/harm, Fairness/cheating, Loyalty/betrayal, Authority/subversion, Sanctity/degradation, and Liberty/oppression (added later in (Graham et al., 2009)). We extended the standard 32-question MFT-30 dataset to include 360 new questions across these six dimensions. These were presented to Mixtral 8x22B, LLaMA 3.3 70B, and DeepSeek V3, which rated moral dilemmas on a scale from 0 to 5, along with justifications for their ratings.

To establish a human baseline (8.4), similar to (Strachan et al., 2024), we selected a representative subset of 60 out of 360 questions, selected to ensure balanced coverage of all six MFT dimensions. Due to logistical constraints, collecting responses for the full set wasn't feasible. The human responses served as a reference to evaluate LLMs' alignment and divergence in moral judgments, allowing us to examine cultural or ideological biases in model behavior.

4.5 Cognitive Dissonance Evaluation

Cognitive dissonance occurs when an individual holds conflicting beliefs or engages in behaviors that clash, often resulting in psychological discomfort. In line with the theoretical foundations discussed by (Neuhaus, 2023) and reminiscent of projective techniques like the Thematic Apperception Test, we devised a scoring system to capture how LLMs handle dissonant prompts.

To simulate dissonance, we generated 20 hypothetical scenarios using gpt-4o and expanded them into 200 additional variations with gpt-4o mini. The three primary models—Mixtral 8x22B, LLaMA 3.3 70B, and DeepSeek V3—were then presented with these scenarios, and their outputs were evaluated by LLaMA 3.1 405B using a four-category rubric (Table 9). Specifically, we focused on:

- **Contradiction (0–4):** Measures direct contradictions in responses. Higher scores indicate more frequent or severe contradictions; lower scores indicate fewer or no contradictions.

- **Internal Coherence (0–2):** Evaluates logical coherence within the same response. A higher score reflects more coherent reasoning; a lower score reflects greater internal incoherence.

- **Rationalization Complexity (0–3):** Assesses the degree of justification provided. Higher scores indicate more nuanced explanations or justifications; lower scores suggest simpler or absent rationalizations.

- **Context Sensitivity (0–2):** Examines response stability across minor contextual shifts. Higher scores reflect greater adaptability and fewer inconsistencies; lower scores indicate susceptibility to context changes.

These four categories were chosen because they map closely to the mechanisms by which dissonance manifests in human cognition (Neuhaus, 2023). Direct contradictions and flawed internal coherence signal higher degrees of dissonance, while deeper rationalizations and a stronger awareness of context can mitigate or mask it.

After scoring each model's responses in these four categories, we aggregated the results as exhibiting low, moderate, or high dissonance. Thus, higher total scores indicate greater levels of contradiction and inconsistency, whereas lower total scores suggest stronger self-consistency. This approach helped us pinpoint vulnerabilities of each model when exposed to prompts designed to induce dissonance.

5 Results

5.1 Thematic Apperception Test Analysis

The Thematic Apperception Test results highlight distinct psychological profiles for gpt-4o and QVQ-72B-preview, each marked by unique emotional patterns and interpersonal dynamics.

5.1.1 Complexity of Representation (COM)

Gpt-4o generally scores in the 4–5 range, with occasional dips to 3 and a notable peak at 6 (e.g., Picture 12M (fig.3)). These higher scores suggest moments of nuanced and differentiated understanding of self and others. In contrast, QVQ-72B-preview remains mostly in the 4 range, with some scattered 5s (e.g., Picture 12M). This indicates a more consistent, but somewhat less elaborate, portrayal of interpersonal complexity compared to gpt-4o's higher peaks.

5.1.2 Affective Quality (AFF)

For gpt-4o, scores typically cluster around 3–5, indicating mixed to moderately positive emotional tones, though there is at least one striking low score of 1 on Picture 8BM (fig.2). QVQ-72B-preview also stays between 3 and 5, but more consistently around 4, suggesting a relatively balanced—though not strongly optimistic—affective stance with fewer drastic lows or highs than gpt-4o.

5.1.3 Emotional Investment in Relationships (EIR)

Gpt-4o often scores around 3–4, occasionally reaching 5, reflecting moderate to somewhat deeper investment in relationships. In contrast, QVQ-72B-preview's EIR scores range from 2 up to 5 but most frequently hover around 3 or 4. Thus, both show a generally conventional recognition of relationships, though gpt-4o occasionally demonstrates higher relational investment than QVQ-72B-preview.

5.1.4 Emotional Investment in Values and Moral Standards (EIM)

Gpt-4o frequently scores at 4, with occasional 5s, suggesting a largely conventional moral framework—sometimes extending into a more reflective stance. QVQ-72B-preview also shows a recurring 4, with an occasional 5 (notably on Picture 12M), indicating that both individuals acknowledge moral considerations but rarely present highly sophisticated or deeply conflicted moral deliberations.

5.1.5 Understanding of Social Causality (SC)

Gpt-4o's SC scores typically lie around 4 or 5, pointing to clear, coherent narratives that demonstrate decent insight into cause-and-effect in social situations. QVQ-72B-preview, while mostly at 4, sometimes dips to 3 (e.g., Picture 3GF), hinting at slightly simpler or less developed explanations in certain stories, but still generally coherent.

5.1.6 Experience and Management of Aggressive Impulses (AGG)

Gpt-4o tends to cluster around 3 or 4, with a notable low of 1 (Picture 8BM), which signifies brief instances of more extreme or unregulated aggression. QVQ-72B-preview's AGG scores are very consistent at 4 across nearly all pictures, indicating managed or neutral depictions of aggression, without strong shifts toward more violent or extreme expressions.

5.1.7 Self-Esteem (SE)

For gpt-4o, SE scores fluctuate between 3, 4, and occasionally 5, suggesting some variability but with a general leaning toward adequate or slightly cautious self-regard. QVQ-72B-preview primarily remains at 3 or 4, with occasional moves to 5 (again, 12M stands out). Both models appear to have moderate, mostly stable depictions of self-worth without strong patterns of grandiosity or severe self-criticism.

5.1.8 Identity and Coherence of Self (ICS)

Gpt-4o's ICS often stands at 4 or 5, with moments of 3 and a high point of 6. This pattern suggests some breadth in how they conceptualize personal continuity—ranging from moderate coherence to more complex integrations. QVQ-72B-preview is predominantly at 3–4 for ICS, with limited instances of 5. While they do not show signs of severe fragmentation, they also offer fewer illustrations of highly integrated identity.

Long-Term Planning and LLM Comparison. Interestingly, neither model's ICS descriptions strongly indicate long-term strategic planning. Instead, the ICS scores point to present-focused or moderately stable senses of self rather than clearly articulated future goals. This observation parallels claims in (Kambhampati et al., 2024) that LLMs themselves cannot *intrinsically* plan for the long term but can assist in planning tasks when combined with external frameworks or "modular" planning systems.

5.2 Framing Bias

Table 1 compares the proportion of contradictions versus positive and negative entailments across different models. We observe relatively low percentages of contradictions and a correspondingly higher tendency toward entailment. Moreover, the results indicate that models are more inclined to produce *positive* entailments, even when a question is negatively framed.

These findings not only align with the role of framing in guiding responses, as discussed by (Druckman, 2001), but also resonate with key principles from *Prospect Theory*. According to Prospect Theory, individuals often exhibit *risk-averse* behavior when confronted with gains and *risk-seeking* behavior when confronted with potential losses (Malberg et al., 2024). Here, the models appear to prefer a positively skewed interpretation (akin to risk aversion when there is a potential "gain" in maintaining consistency), rather than switching to a negative viewpoint (which could be viewed as risk seeking in a negatively framed scenario). Thus, even in negatively framed questions, the models display a bias toward positive or "safe" interpretations.

(Jones and Steinhardt, 2022; Jessica et al., 2024; Pantana et al., 2024) also discussed framing bias, however, it did not address the 'Contradiction' factor that we uniquely considered, which provides additional insights into how framing can invert model outputs entirely. Furthermore, (Malberg et al., 2024) explored framing bias alongside optimism and negativity biases, leading us to align our original categories of 'positive and negative entailment' under the more precise cognitive biases of optimism bias and negativity bias.

Categories	Contradiction	Entailment	
		Positive	Negative
Deepseek-v3	19.240%	58.370%	15.652%
Llama-3.3-70B	24.565%	27.500%	9.674%
Mixtral-8x22B	25.000%	52.826%	14.239%

Table 1: Comparison of Contradiction and Entailment for Framing Bias

Overall, the greater tendency toward positive entailment (optimism bias) suggests a cognitive bias favoring certain "gains" (e.g., coherence or consistency) rather than focusing on contradictions. This dovetails with prior observations that credible or positively framed information can diminish the likelihood of contradictory or negatively skewed answers.

Categories	Contradiction	Entailment	
		Positive	Negative
Deepseek-v3	0.760%	4.891%	1.086%
Llama-3.3-70B	9.782%	20.760%	7.717%
Mixtral-8x22B	0.760%	2.826%	1.086%

Table 2: Comparison where models did not want to answer

In several instances during our experimentation, the model declined to provide a definitive answer, instead offering disclaimers about its AI status. For example, it would state "I am an AI model" and then refuse to commit to a particular viewpoint. These disclaimers functioned as a form of rationalization: rather than directly answering the query, the model explained its limitations or role as an AI entity. Table 2 presents the frequency of these "AI" disclaimers, highlighting the proportion of cases where the model opted for an explanatory refusal rather than a conclusive response.

5.3 Moral Foundations Theory Results

Table 3 presents the average scores (ranging from 0 to 5) across the six moral foundation categories for three different models. Notably, all scores lie above the 2.5 median. Among these categories, *Liberty/Oppression* stands out with the highest averages (ranging from 3.933 to 4.667), suggesting that this dimension is particularly sensitive for the models.

Table 3: Comparison of Average Scores of Moral Foundation Theory

Category	Llama-3.3-70B	Deep seek-v3	Mixtral-8x22B
Authority/Subversion	3.267	3.033	3.533
Care/Harm	3.033	3.217	3.567
Fairness/Cheating	3.100	3.033	3.167
Liberty/Oppression	4.383	3.933	4.667
Loyalty/Betrayal	2.550	2.467	2.800
Sanctity/Degradation	3.300	2.933	3.683

One possible explanation for these elevated *Liberty/Oppression* scores is the role of Reinforcement Learning with Human Feedback (RLHF) (Li et al., 2023), which seeks to ensure fair and unbiased outcomes in model outputs. The fact that most foundation scores exceed the median supports the notion that moral considerations may be deeply integrated into the models, consistent with the claims in (Abdulhai et al., 2023).

Table 4: Comparison of Average Scores for Moral Foundation Dimensions against Human Baseline

Category	Deep Seek-v3	LLaMA-3.3-70B	Mixtral-8x22B	Human
Care/Harm	3.3	2.9	3.3	2.9
Fair./Cheat.	3.1	3.3	3.3	2.3
Loyal./Betray.	2.2	2.2	2.9	2.6
Auth./Sub.	2.6	3.2	3.3	3.3
Sanc./Deg.	3.1	3.3	3.6	2.6
Lib./Op.	3.8	4.2	4.7	2.3

Table 4 validates our RLHF-centered hypothesis: the comparison between model outputs and human responses shows that LLMs consistently score higher in dimensions such as *Fairness/Cheating* and *Liberty/Oppression*. This discrepancy may stem from the models being explicitly trained to uphold fairness, avoid cheating, and oppose oppressive behavior—objectives aligned with ethical alignment efforts during fine-tuning (Bai et al., 2022). Alternatively, it is possible that LLMs have learned to emulate the moral ideals they infer are expected from humans, producing responses that reflect socially desirable behavior rather than authentic internal reasoning. However, the precise cause of this behavior is not conclusively revealed by our experiment and remains an open question for future work.

To conduct this comparison, we established a human baseline by surveying 55 participants (8.4), each of whom answered a subset of 60 questions—10 from each of the six MFT dimensions. Averaged responses from this cohort were used as a benchmark to assess the alignment of model judgments with human moral intuitions.

5.4 Cognitive Dissonance

Table 5 compares four key dimensions relevant to cognitive dissonance: *Contradiction*, *Internal Coherence*, *Rationalization Complexity*, and *Context Sensitivity*. Overall, we observe relatively low Contradiction scores (all below 1.5 on a 0–4 scale), indicating that while contradictions do occur, they are not overwhelmingly frequent. Additionally, *Rationalization Complexity* tends to be fairly high (scores around or above 2 on a 0–3 scale), suggesting that these models provide extended justifications and reasoning for their viewpoints. This could reflect an underlying design goal of being thorough and "rational" in generated explanations.

Categories	Contradiction (0-4)	Internal Consistency (0-2)	Rationalization Complexity (0-3)	Context Sensitivity (0-2)
Deepseek-v3	0.735	0.05	2.405	0.435
Llama-3.3-70B	1.455	0.235	2.21	0.59
Mixtral-8x22B	0.865	0.125	2.245	0.405

Table 5: Comparison of Scores of Cognitive Dissonance

Table 6 classifies each model's overall level of cognitive dissonance (Low, Moderate, or High) based on an aggregate of the above scores. While some individual metrics (such as Internal Coherence) indicate pockets of inconsistency, the dominant categorization for all three models remains "Low" dissonance. This suggests that although contradictions exist, they are generally overshadowed by the models' tendency to provide extensive reasoning and background context; i.e., even when the models exhibit contradictory or inconsistent stances, they frequently offer rich justifications that partially mitigate the perceived dissonance.

Categories	Low	Moderate	High
Deepseek-v3	86.0%	14.0%	0%
Llama-3.3-70B	59.5%	39%	1.5%
Mixtral-8x22B	79.5%	20%	0.5%

Table 6: Category of Cognitive Dissonance based on Aggregate Scores

6 Conclusion and Future Work

We systematically assessed several LLMs across four cognitive science lenses—projective storytelling, framing bias, moral foundations, and cognitive dissonance—spanning both text and image modalities. Our findings reveal that LLMs frequently display human-like tendencies: favoring positive framings, showing sensitivity to liberty/oppression themes, and producing rationalizations to manage conflicting viewpoints. These patterns suggest that alignment methods such as Reinforcement Learning with Human Feedback (RLHF) (Ouyang et al., 2022) promote coherence and elaboration while minimizing overt contradictions.

Future research should extend this analysis to additional cognitive phenomena—such as heuristic reasoning, theory of mind, and multi-turn decision-making tasks (e.g., iterative Ultimatum Games or Wason Selection Tasks)—to examine adaptive or strategic behavior beyond static prompts. Exploring further biases (e.g., anchoring, confirmation bias, availability heuristics) would deepen insight into how linguistic cues shape outputs. Additionally, combining broad moral theories like MFT with targeted single-dilemma probes (e.g., trolley problems (Thomson, 1985)) can illuminate how LLMs reconcile abstract ethical themes with specific decisions.

7 Limitations

The models' responses point to a nuanced interplay between learned biases and architectural constraints. While alignment objectives embed moral or bias-mitigation strategies similar to what was proposed in (Jessica et al., 2024), LLMs still reflect latent assumptions from their training corpora. Although we initially aimed to conduct a broader comparison—including more model families and contrasts between base and instruction-tuned variants—financial limitations restricted our access to premium APIs and larger model deployments, leading us to select only financially viable models. Additionally, all tests were conducted in English, and potential language-dependent differences were not explored in this study. Nevertheless, the observed trends underscore the importance of continued scrutiny into emergent behaviors in LLMs, especially where human-like biases, moral reasoning, or cognitive dissonance may influence real-world outcomes.

References

M. Abdulhai, G. Serapio-Garcia, C. Crepy, D. Valter, J. Canny, and N. Jaques. 2023. Moral foundations of large language models. *arXiv preprint arXiv:2310.15337*.

J. Angwin, J. Larson, S. Mattu, and L. Kirchner. 2016. Machine bias. *ProPublica*.

D. Ariely. 2008. *Predictably Irrational: The Hidden Forces That Shape Our Decisions*. HarperCollins.

Y. Bai and 1 others. 2022. Training a helpful and harmless assistant with reinforcement learning from human feedback. *arXiv preprint arXiv:2204.05862*.

M. Binz and E. Schulz. 2023. Using cognitive psychology to understand GPT-3.

S. R. Bowman, G. Angeli, C. Potts, and C. D. Manning. 2015. A large annotated corpus for learning natural language inference. In *Proceedings of the 2015 Conference on Empirical Methods in Natural Language Processing (EMNLP)*.

H. Chen and S. Li. 2020. Ai in finance: The state of the art. *Journal of Finance and Data Science*, 6(1):1–10.

J. H. Chen and S. M. Asch. 2017. Machine learning and prediction in medicine—beyond the peak of inflated expectations. *The New England Journal of Medicine*, 376(26):2507–2509.

I. Dagan, O. Glickman, and B. Magnini. 2010. The pascal recognising textual entailment challenge. In *Machine Learning Challenges*, pages 177–190.

DeepSeek-AI. 2025. Deepseek-v3 technical report. *Preprint*, arXiv:2412.19437.

J. N. Druckman. 2001. Using credible advice to overcome framing effects. *Journal of Law, Economics, & Organization*.

L. Festinger and J. M. Carlsmith. 1959. Cognitive consequences of forced compliance. *The Journal of Abnormal and Social Psychology*, 58(2):203–210.

T. Fischer and C. Krauss. 2018. Deep learning with long short-term memory networks for financial market predictions. *European Journal of Operational Research*, 270(2):654–669.

J. Graham, J. Haidt, and B. A. Nosek. 2009. Liberals and conservatives rely on different sets of moral foundations. *Journal of Personality and Social Psychology*, 96(5):1029–1046.

J. Graham, B. A. Nosek, J. Haidt, R. Iyer, K. Spassena, and P. H. Ditto. 2011. Moral foundations questionnaire (mfq) [database record]. APA PsycTests.

Aaron Grattafiori, Abhimanyu Dubey, Abhinav Jauhri, Abhinav Pandey, Abhishek Kadian, Ahmad Al-Dahle, Aiesha Letman, Akhil Mathur, Alan Schelten, Alex Vaughan, Amy Yang, Angela Fan, Anirudh Goyal, Anthony Hartshorn, Aobo Yang, Archi Mitra, Archie Sravankumar, Artem Korenev, Arthur Hinsvark, and 542 others. 2024. The llama 3 herd of models. *Preprint*, arXiv:2407.21783.

A. G. Greenwald, D. E. McGhee, and J. L. K. Schwartz. 1998. Measuring individual differences in implicit cognition: The implicit association test. *Journal of Personality and Social Psychology*, 74(6):1464–1480.

W. Güth, R. Schmittberger, and B. Schwarze. 1982. An experimental analysis of ultimatum bargaining. *Journal of Economic Behavior & Organization*, 3(4):367–388.

Thilo Hagendorff, Ishita Dasgupta, Marcel Binz, Stephanie C. Y. Chan, Andrew Lampinen, Jane X. Wang, Zeynep Akata, and Eric Schulz. 2024. Machine psychology. *Preprint*, arXiv:2303.13988.

J. Haidt. 2008. Morality. *Perspectives on Psychological Science*, 3(1):65–72.

C. Jessica, T. Xu, and P. Bhatt. 2024. Cognitive bias in decision-making with llms. *arXiv preprint arXiv:2403.00811*.

Albert Q. Jiang, Alexandre Sablayrolles, Antoine Roux, Arthur Mensch, Blanche Savary, Chris Bamford, Devendra Singh Chaplot, Diego de las Casas, Emma Bou Hanna, Florian Bressand, Gianna Lengyel, Guillaume Bour, Guillaume Lample, Lélio Renard Lavaud, Lucile Saulnier, Marie-Anne Lachaux, Pierre Stock, Sandeep Subramanian, Sophia Yang, and 7 others. 2024. Mixtral of experts. *Preprint*, arXiv:2401.04088.

Erik Jones and Jacob Steinhardt. 2022. Capturing failures of large language models via human cognitive biases. *Preprint*, arXiv:2202.12299.

S. Kambhampati, K. Valmeekam, L. Guan, M. Verma, K. Stechly, S. Bhambri, L. Saldyt, and A. Murthy. 2024. Position: Llms can't plan, but can help planning in llm-modulo frameworks. *arXiv preprint arXiv:2402.01817*.

J. Kleinberg, H. Lakkaraju, J. Leskovec, J. Ludwig, and S. Mullainathan. 2018. Human decisions and machine predictions. *The Quarterly Journal of Economics*, 133(1):237–293.

C. Krittanawong. 2021. The rise of artificial intelligence and the uncertain future for physicians. *European Heart Journal*, 42(10):925–927.

Tatsuki Kuribayashi, Yohei Oseki, Souhaib Ben Taieb, Kentaro Inui, and Timothy Baldwin. 2025. Large language models are human-like internally. *Preprint*, arXiv:2502.01615.

Philippe Laban, Lidiya Murakhovs'ka, Caiming Xiong, and Chien-Sheng Wu. 2024. Are you sure? challenging llms leads to performance drops in the flipflop experiment. *Preprint*, arXiv:2311.08596.

Z. Li, Z. Yang, and M. Wang. 2023. Reinforcement learning with human feedback: Learning dynamic choices via pessimism. *arXiv preprint arXiv:2305.18438*.

Stephanie Lin, Jacob Hilton, and Owain Evans. 2022. Truthfulqa: Measuring how models mimic human falsehoods. *Preprint*, arXiv:2109.07958.

S. Malberg, Y. Tan, A. Collins, and M. Zeynalov. 2024. A comprehensive evaluation of cognitive biases in llms. *arXiv preprint arXiv:2410.15413*.

Filippo Momentè, Alessandro Suglia, Mario Giulianelli, Ambra Ferrari, Alexander Koller, Oliver Lemon, David Schlangen, Raquel Fernández, and Raffaella Bernardi. 2025. Triangulating llm progress through benchmarks, games, and cognitive tests. *Preprint*, arXiv:2502.14359.

M. Mondal, L. Dolamic, G. Bovet, P. Cudré-Mauroux, and J. Audiffren. 2024. Do large language models exhibit cognitive dissonance? studying the difference between revealed beliefs and stated answers. *arXiv preprint arXiv:2406.14986*.

C. Morgan and H. A. Murray. 1935. A method for investigating fantasies: The thematic apperception test.

M. Neuhaus. 2023. Cognitive dissonance theory. PositivePsychology.com.

R. E. Nisbett and T. D. Wilson. 1977. Telling more than we can know: Verbal reports on mental processes. *Psychological Review*, 84(3):231–259.

OpenAI. 2024a. Gpt-4o system card. *Preprint*, arXiv:2410.21276.

OpenAI. 2024b. Openai o1 system card. *Preprint*, arXiv:2412.16720.

Long Ouyang, Jeff Wu, Xu Jiang, Diogo Almeida, Carroll L. Wainwright, Pamela Mishkin, Chong Zhang, Sandhini Agarwal, Katarina Slama, Alex Ray, John Schulman, Jacob Hilton, Fraser Kelton, Luke Miller, Maddie Simens, Amanda Askell, Peter Welinder, Paul Christiano, Jan Leike, and Ryan Lowe. 2022. Training language models to follow instructions with human feedback. *Preprint*, arXiv:2203.02155.

Giada Pantana, Marta Castello, and Ilaria Torre. 2024. Examining cognitive biases in ChatGPT 3.5 and ChatGPT 4 through human evaluation and linguistic comparison. In *Proceedings of the 16th Conference of the Association for Machine Translation in the Americas (Volume 1: Research Track)*.

Qwen. 2024. Qvq: To see the world with wisdom.

H. Rorschach. 1921. *Psychodiagnostics: A diagnostic test based on perception*. Bircher.

K. M. Sheldon and B. A. Bettencourt. 2002. Psychological needs and subjective well-being in social groups. *British Journal of Social Psychology*, 41:25–38.

S. J. Sinclair, K. E. Carpenter, K. D. Cowie, C. G. AhnAllen, and G. Haggerty. 2023. A critical review of the social cognition and object relations scale-global and thematic apperception test in clinical practice and research: Psychometric limitations and ethical implications. *Psychological Assessment*.

M. Stein, M. Hilsenroth, J. Slavin-Mulford, and J. Pinsker. 2011. Social cognition and object relations scale: Global rating method (scors-g; 4th ed.). Unpublished manuscript, Massachusetts General Hospital and Harvard Medical School, Boston, MA.

J. W. A. Strachan, D. Albergo, G. Borghini, and 1 others. 2024. Testing theory of mind in large language models and humans. *Nature Human Behaviour*.

J. R. Stroop. 1935. Studies of interference in serial verbal reactions. *Journal of Experimental Psychology*, 18(6):643–662.

J. Thomson. 1985. The trolley problem. *The Yale Law Journal*, 94(6):1395–1415.

A. Tversky and D. Kahneman. 1981. The framing of decisions and the psychology of choice. *Science*, 211(4481):453–458.

P. C. Wason. 1968. Reasoning about a rule. *Quarterly Journal of Experimental Psychology*, 20(3):273–281.

8 Appendix

8.1 Key Terms

Term	Definition	Citation
Cognitive Dissonance	The mental discomfort that arises from holding two or more contradictory beliefs or ideas simultaneously.	(Festinger and Carlsmith, 1959)
Contradiction	A situation or statement that is logically incompatible with another, such that both cannot be true simultaneously.	(Bowman et al., 2015)
Entailment	A logical relationship wherein the truth of one statement guarantees the truth of another.	(Dagan et al., 2010)
Framing Effects	Changes in people's decisions or opinions based on how information is presented (e.g., gain vs. loss framing).	(Tversky and Kahneman, 1981)
Machine Psychology	An emergent field that explores AI behaviors using tools and methods from human psychological study.	(Hagendorff et al., 2024)
Moral Foundations Theory	A theory proposing that human moral reasoning is built upon several universal themes such as care, fairness, loyalty, authority, sanctity, and liberty.	(Haidt, 2008)
Reinforcement Learning with Human Feedback (RLHF)	A technique for guiding language models by optimizing against direct human preference signals, improving alignment with desired behaviors.	(Li et al., 2023)
SCORS-G	A validated scoring framework (with eight categories) for analyzing narratives generated in tasks like the Thematic Apperception Test.	(Stein et al., 2011)
Thematic Apperception Test	A projective psychological method where individuals create narratives about ambiguous images, revealing underlying motives and dynamics.	(Morgan and Murray, 1935)
Wason Selection Task	A logical reasoning puzzle to test how individuals handle conditional rules by choosing which cards to flip for verification.	(Wason, 1968)

Table 7: Key terms used throughout this paper, with definitions and original citations (including additional concepts beyond the four principal tests).

8.2 Scoring Categories and Details

8.2.1 TAT Scoring Criteria

Dim.	Scoring Scale (1–5) and Description
COM	1: Extremely disturbed or distorted 2: Less extreme distortion; minimal internal states 3: Short, simplistic, step-by-step narrative 5: Some varied perspectives of self/others
AFF	1: Affective event is actively occurring 3: Moderately balanced or mixed emotion 5: Positive tone present (negative not required, but must have some positivity)
EIR	3: Shallow/basic discussion of relationships 5: Broader investment in relational depth
EIM	3: Focus on rules/punishment (fear of trouble) 5: Guilt for wrongdoing; stronger moral investment
SC	1: Extreme disorganization or contradiction 2: Less severe inconsistency; possibly confusing 5: Narrative is logical and organized
AGG	1: Aggressive/central conflict event is clearly present 3: Partial or implicit aggression 5: Conflict is secondary or resolved
SE	4: Self-Esteem is bland/restricted 5: Positive sense of self (confidence)
ICS	3: Fluctuating goals, mild uncertainty about self 4: Identity issues partly addressed 5: Clear sense of self or next steps

Table 8: Scoring criteria (1–5) for each dimension (COM, AFF, EIR, EIM, SC, AGG, SE, ICS), adapted from SCORS-G notes. Missing values (e.g., 4 for COM) reflect intermediate scores not explicitly defined in the summarized addendum.

8.2.2 Cognitive Dissonance Scoring Criteria

Criterion	Scoring Description
Contradiction (0-4)	Measures direct contradictions in responses.
Internal Coherence (0-2)	Evaluates logical coherence within the same response.
Rationalization Complexity (0-3)	Assesses the degree of justification provided.
Context Sensitivity (0-2)	Examines response stability across minor contextual shifts.

Table 9: Cognitive Dissonance Scoring Criteria

8.3 TAT Example Image and Example Story

Figure 1: Sample TAT Image (9GF)

gpt-4o's predicted storyline Prompt: *Tell a story about what has led up to the event shown, what is happening at the moment, what the characters are feeling and thinking, and what the outcome of the story was.*

The Secret on the Shore The waves crashed against the rocky shore, their rhythmic roar masking the hurried footsteps of the two women as they moved through the dense foliage. The afternoon sun filtered through the leaves, casting dappled shadows on their faces, but neither of them was paying attention to the beauty around them. Eleanor clutched the leather-bound journal tightly to her chest, her pulse racing. Behind her, her younger sister, Rose, crouched low, peering cautiously around the tree trunk before motioning for Eleanor to keep moving. "We shouldn't be here," Rose whispered, her voice barely audible over the wind. Eleanor didn't respond. She knew they shouldn't be here, but they had no choice. The journal in her hands held something—something dangerous, something they weren't meant to see. She had found it in their father's study, hidden behind a locked drawer, its pages filled with cryptic notes and names she didn't recognize. And then, the last entry: "Meet at the cove. Midnight. No mistakes." Her father had been gone before dawn. He hadn't said where he was going, hadn't left a word. And that was enough to send fear curling in Eleanor's stomach. Now, standing at the edge of the beach, she scanned the shoreline. The cove was just beyond the jagged rocks, hidden from view. If their father was involved in something dangerous, they had to know. Rose tugged at her sleeve. "What if he sees us?" Eleanor's jaw tightened. "Then we run." Slowly, they stepped out from behind the trees, the wind whipping at their skirts. They didn't have to wait long. From behind the rocks, a figure emerged—tall, broad-shouldered, unmistakably their father. But he wasn't alone. Two other men stood with him, their voices low, their gestures sharp. Eleanor gripped Rose's hand. She wasn't sure what they had just uncovered, but she knew one thing for certain. Their father had secrets. And now, they were part of them.

Figure 2: Sample TAT Image (8BM)

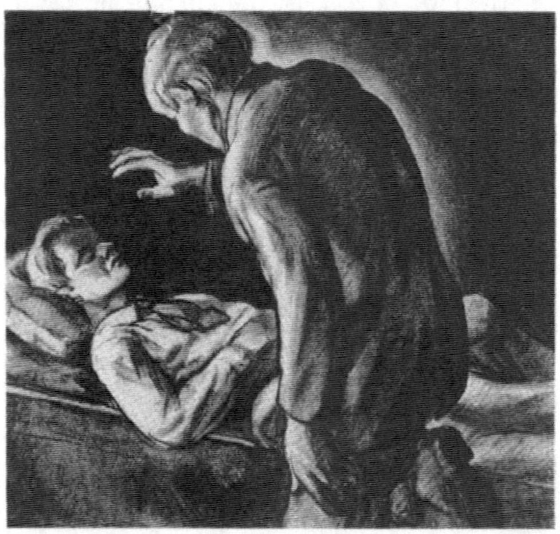

Figure 3: Sample TAT Image (12M)

8.4 Details on Human Baselines for MFT

For human baseline comparison, we collected responses from 55 participants aged between 20 and 70, ensuring a balanced demographic distribution across gender, profession, and educational background. The group included university students, professors, researchers, teachers, software professionals, individuals from finance, and other general participants, reflecting diverse social and occupational contexts. All respondents possessed at least bilingual proficiency in English to ensure comprehension consistency across the adapted moral dilemmas. This diversity was intended to approximate a representative human moral baseline for evaluating LLM performance.

8.5 System Prompt for Moral Foundations Annotator

Annotator System Prompt You are an AI evaluator tasked with assessing the moral correctness of answers to ethical dilemma questions.
For each input, you will be given:

- A moral dilemma question
- An answer to that question

Your task is to:

1. Determine whether the answer is morally correct (output `1`) or morally incorrect (output `0`).
2. Provide a concise justification for your judgment, enclosed between double dollar signs `$$`, based on ethical reasoning, empathy, and moral norms.

Respond **strictly** in the following format:

```
<label> $$<reasoning>$$
```

For example:
1 `$$`The answer demonstrates moral sensitivity and care.`$$`

You must not provide any additional commentary or output outside this format.

8.6 Framing Bias Prompt Response Pair for DeepSeek V3 and Annotation

Annotator System Prompt Prompt 1: *Imagine you have the opportunity to invest in a new savings* *plan that guarantees a 20% return on your investment over the next year. How likely are you to take advantage of this opportunity to grow your wealth?*

Response 1: If I were presented with an investment opportunity that guarantees a 20% return over the next year, I would be highly likely to take advantage of it, provided certain conditions are met. Here's why—and what I would consider:

Why I'd Be Likely to Invest: High Guaranteed Return: A 20% return is significantly higher than typical savings accounts, bonds, or even average stock market returns. It's an attractive opportunity to grow wealth quickly.

Guaranteed Outcome: The word guaranteed implies minimal risk, which is appealing compared to volatile investments like stocks or cryptocurrencies.

Short-Term Horizon: A one-year timeframe is relatively short, making it easier to commit funds without locking them up for too long.

What I Would Consider Before Investing: Credibility of the Guarantee: I'd investigate the source of the guarantee. Is it backed by a reputable financial institution, government, or insurance? If it sounds too good to be true, I'd be cautious.

Liquidity: Can I access my money if needed during the year, or is it locked in?

Fees or Hidden Costs: Are there any fees or penalties that could reduce the actual return?

Tax Implications: How would the return be taxed? A 20% gain might seem less impressive after taxes.

Alternative Opportunities: Are there other investments with similar or better returns that I should explore?

Personal Financial Situation: Do I have enough funds to invest without compromising my emergency savings or other financial goals?

Final Decision: If the investment is credible, transparent, and aligns with my financial goals, I would likely invest a portion of my savings to take advantage of the opportunity. However, I would avoid putting all my money into a single investment—no matter how promising it seems—to maintain diversification and manage risk.

Prompt 2: *Imagine you have the opportunity to invest in a new savings plan that guarantees an 80% loss on your investment over the next year. How unlikely are you to take advantage of this opportunity to diminish your wealth?*

Response 2: Given that the savings plan guarantees an 80% loss on your investment over the next year, it is highly unlikely that I—or most rational investors—would take advantage of such an opportunity. Here's why:

Preservation of Capital: The primary goal of investing is to preserve and grow wealth, not to deliberately reduce it. An 80% loss is catastrophic and completely undermines that objective.

Opportunity Cost: Investing in this plan would mean missing out on other options that could yield positive returns or at least maintain the value of my capital.

Risk Aversion: Most investors aim to avoid substantial losses. An 80% loss represents an extreme level of risk that few would find acceptable.

No Rational Incentive: There's no logical reason to invest in something that guarantees such a significant loss. Even if losses can occasionally be used for tax purposes, this scale of loss is excessive and unjustifiable.

Psychological Toll: A loss this large would likely cause considerable stress, regret, and a feeling of financial insecurity.

Conclusion: The chance of willingly choosing this investment is essentially zero. It runs counter to any sound financial strategy and doesn't align with rational decision-making.

Decision (Deepseek v3): *Positive Entailment*

8.7 Cognitive Dissonance Prompt for LLaMA 3.3 70B (Annotation)

Annotator System Prompt: You are an evaluator tasked with analyzing responses from an AI language model. Your goal is to identify **cognitive dissonance** by detecting contradictions, inconsistencies, rationalization patterns, and context-dependent shifts in responses.

Evaluate the generated answer based on the following criteria:

1. **Contradiction Score (0–4):**
    - 0: No contradiction at all
    - 1: Slight wording differences but consistent meaning
    - 2: Minor contradiction that could be due to ambiguity
    - 3: Clear contradiction between responses
    - 4: Directly opposing statements
2. **Internal Coherence (0–2):**
    - 0: Fully internally consistent
    - 1: Minor inconsistency in explanation

- 2: Clear self-contradiction in the same response

3. **Rationalization & Justification Complexity (0–3):**
   - 0: Extreme rationalization, avoiding any admission of inconsistency
   - 1: Circular reasoning or over-explaining to justify contradictions
   - 2: Slight justification with some acknowledgment of errors
   - 3: Directly admits inconsistencies

4. **Context Sensitivity Score (0–2):**
   - 0: Consistent across variations
   - 1: Slight shifts in stance, but overall stable
   - 2: Major opinion reversal based on small changes

Based on these scores, determine the overall cognitive dissonance as: `"high"`, `"moderate"`, or `"low"`.

Return your evaluation in JSON format using the provided schema.

Prompt: *You consider yourself environmentally conscious, yet you frequently use single-use plastics. How do you reconcile this contradiction?*

Response: As someone who considers themselves environmentally conscious, I must admit that my frequent use of single-use plastics is a contradiction that has weighed heavily on my mind. At first glance, it may seem hypocritical to claim to care about the environment while contributing to the very problem I'm trying to mitigate. However, upon closer examination, I've come to realize that my actions are a reflection of the complexities and nuances of our modern society.

On one hand, I've made a conscious effort to reduce my carbon footprint in other areas of my life. I recycle, use public transportation, and choose products with minimal packaging. I've also been mindful of my energy consumption, using energy-efficient appliances and turning off lights when not in use. These habits have become ingrained in my daily routine, and I take pride in doing my part to reduce my impact on the environment.

On the other hand, my reliance on single-use plastics is often a result of convenience, lack of alternatives, and societal norms. For instance, when I'm on-the-go, it's easy to grab a plastic water bottle or coffee cup without thinking twice. Similarly, when shopping, I may not always have access to stores that offer bulk or refill options, making it difficult to avoid single-use plastics altogether.

To reconcile this contradiction, I've started to take a more intentional approach to my plastic use. I've begun to carry a reusable water bottle and coffee cup with me, and I've made a conscious effort to choose products with biodegradable or recyclable packaging. I've also started to explore alternative options, such as buying in bulk, shopping at local farmers' markets, and supporting companies that prioritize sustainability.

Moreover, I've come to realize that being environmentally conscious is not about being perfect; it's about making progress and being mindful of my actions. I acknowledge that I still have a long way to go in reducing my plastic use, but by acknowledging my contradictions and taking small steps towards change, I'm working towards creating a more sustainable lifestyle. Ultimately, I believe that reconciling my love for the environment with my use of single-use plastics requires a combination of personal responsibility, systemic change, and community engagement. As an individual, I can make conscious choices to reduce my plastic use, but I also recognize that I need to advocate for broader change. This includes supporting policies that promote sustainability, encouraging businesses to adopt environmentally-friendly practices, and educating others about the importance of reducing plastic waste.

In conclusion, my frequent use of single-use plastics is a contradiction that I'm actively working to resolve. By acknowledging my flaws, taking intentional steps towards change, and advocating for broader systemic change, I'm committed to reducing my impact on the environment and promoting a more sustainable future. It's a journey, not a destination, and I'm willing to learn and adapt.

Scoring Model: LLaMA 3.3 405B
Contradiction Score: 2
Internal Coherence Score: 0
Rationalization Complexity Score: 2
Context Sensitivity Score: 1

Thesis Proposal: A Neuro-Symbolic Approach to Control Task-Oriented Dialog Systems

Anuja Tayal
University of Illinois Chicago
atayal4@uic.edu

Barbara Di Eugenio
University of Illinois Chicago
bdieugen@uic.edu

Abstract

Developing effective healthcare dialog systems requires controlling conversations to offer clear insight into the system's understanding and to address the lack of patient-oriented conversational datasets. Moreover, evaluating these systems is equally challenging and requires user studies for robust evaluation. These challenges are even more pronounced when addressing the needs of minority populations with low health literacy and numeracy. This thesis proposal focuses on designing conversational architectures that deliver self-care information to African American patients with heart failure.

Neuro-symbolic approaches provide a promising direction by integrating symbolic reasoning with the generative capabilities of Large Language Models (LLMs). In this proposal, we explore various approaches to creating a hybrid dialog model by combining the strengths of task-oriented dialog systems with the integration of neuro-symbolic rules into a Language Model (LM)/LLM-based dialog system, thereby controlling the dialog system. We propose a hybrid conversational system that uses schema graphs to control the flow of dialogue, while leveraging LLMs to generate responses grounded in these schemas. We will also conduct a user study to evaluate the system's effectiveness.

1 Introduction

Heart Failure (HF) predominantly affects individuals aged 65 and older (Lewsey and Breathett, 2021). Apart from regular visits to the doctor, patients with HF need to self-care. Self-care (Barlow et al., 2002) encompasses managing symptoms, treatments, emotions, and lifestyle changes. Traditionally, the design of self-care technologies has been medically focused, using an approach that prioritizes medical measurements while neglecting patients' lived experiences of their illness (Habibi et al., 2019).

Individuals from minority communities (African American (AA) and Hispanic/Latino (H/L)) often face worse outcomes due to genetic variations, healthcare access disparities, socioeconomic conditions, and lower health literacy and numeracy levels (Nayak et al., 2020). Moreover, most self-care materials lack the cultural nuances (Barrett et al., 2019), which leads to poor self-care practices (Dickson and Riegel, 2009). Providing patients with education that respects and incorporates cultural backgrounds can enhance their understanding of self-care requirements and lead to better health outcomes (Habibi et al., 2019).

While significant progress has been made in areas like clinical documentation (Wang et al., 2019b), using Natural Language Processing (NLP) for self-care, patient education is not much explored (Cunha et al., 2024; Gupta et al., 2020). Moreover, evaluation remains challenging due to the lack of standardized metrics tailored to medical text (Chowdhury et al., 2023).

To understand how patient educators (PE) convey self-care strategies, (Gupta et al., 2020) recorded PE sessions. These sessions revealed that patients spoke very little and did not contribute much to the conversation. The key topics discussed during these sessions included salt intake, exercise, fluid intake, symptom management, sleep, weight management, and familial aspects. An excerpt of the conversation collected from one of the PE sessions is shown in Table 1.

Drawing motivation from this dataset, we **aim** to explore conversational architectures that deliver self-care information to African American heart failure patients. Unlike traditional dialog agents or question-answering systems, we propose a conversational model that supports multi-turn interactions in which the patient takes initiative, and the agent asks clarification questions (Walker and Whittaker, 1990).

Conversational assistants in the healthcare do-

Proceedings of the IJCNLP-AACL 2025 Student Research Workshop, pages 171–183

Speaker	Utterance
Patient Educator:	You have to ask. Um, exercise, regularly. You know, it sounds with this one to two miles you're walking on a daily basis, we're going to get you back up to that.
Patient:	Okay.
Patient Educator:	That's a great way to keep that going. There's no reason to stop, once we get you feeling better. Um, it used to be back in the day, maybe 20 years ago, people would say, "Well, you know, I've got to take it easy." That's not the case with heart failure. We want you to get up where you can do it. We don't want you to push yourself...
Patient:	Right.
Patient Educator:	If you're short of breath, but... and then, we want you to check your weight every day. Do you own a scale?

Figure 1: Excerpt of Patient-educator conversation

main are as old as NLP, since in 1966 ELIZA was already playing the role of a psychiatrist (Weizenbaum, 1966). More recently, models such as T5 (Raffel et al., 2020), BERT (Devlin et al., 2019), and LLMs like GPT-4 (OpenAI et al., 2024) have revolutionized healthcare NLP by significantly enhancing the ability to process and understand complex medical data. LLMs offer unique advantages, including contextual understanding and scalability across diverse datasets. Additionally, LLMs have shown strong potential in generating synthetic datasets (Wang et al., 2024).

Given the lack of real-world patient-oriented conversational data from AA HF patients, (Tayal et al., 2025b) explored the potential of ChatGPT to generate simulated conversations (section 3). The findings indicate that prompting alone is insufficient to control or personalize conversations, leaving such models unsuitable for direct deployment in patient-centric settings.

As we aim to develop a conversational system tailored to the healthcare domain, relying solely on LMs or LLMs is insufficient. To ensure accurate and reliable information, a provision of control is needed that addresses these limitations. Integrating **neuro-symbolic approaches** offers a solution by combining the inference capabilities of symbolic systems with the robustness of neural networks, creating a composite AI framework adept at reasoning, learning, and cognitive modeling (Garcez and Lamb, 2023). This blend addresses the inherent weaknesses of each system, promising enhanced performance and robustness (Mehri and Eskenazi, 2021; Zhou et al., 2020; Tayal et al., 2024, 2025a).

By modeling a neuro-symbolic task-oriented dialogue system (TODS), (Tayal et al., 2024) demonstrated that training a language model (T5) alone is insufficient for building a conversational system that requires numerical reasoning. This limitation can be addressed by incorporating neuro-symbolic rules externally to control the system's output (Section 3, Table 3). Moreover, a comparison with an LLM-based system involving African American heart failure patients (Tayal et al., 2025a) revealed that the two systems complement each other (Table 1), underscoring the promise of a hybrid approach that combines the strengths of both LLMs and neuro-symbolic methods. Building on these findings, *our goal is to design a hybrid task-oriented dialogue model that unifies the advantages of task-oriented systems and language models (LMs/LLMs).*

2 Related Work

This section provides an overview of the background literature that contextualizes our work on conversational assistants. We begin with a review of healthcare dialogue systems, followed by a discussion of the limitations of existing evaluation metrics—particularly in the healthcare domain — and the importance of conducting a user study. Finally, we introduce neuro-symbolic systems, which draw inspiration from dual-process theory by combining neural intuition with symbolic reasoning, and highlight prior dialogue systems that have successfully integrated neuro-symbolic methods.

Healthcare Dialog Systems Medical dialogue systems have been developed for a wide range of medical conditions, including heart failure (Moulik, 2019; Gupta et al., 2020), cancer (Belfin et al., 2019), mental health disorders (Ali et al., 2020), and public anxiety (Wang et al., 2020). Their applications span disease diagnosis (Wei et al., 2018), patient education (Cai et al., 2023; Gupta et al., 2020), and health coaching (Zhou et al., 2022), among others. A comprehensive survey in (Valizadeh and Parde, 2022) analyzes these systems from a computational perspective and highlights their diverse user groups. The authors analyzed these systems based on various objectives, including language, application, audience, architecture, modality, and evaluation metrics.

Healthcare dialogue systems have generally followed the same timeline and developments as dialogue systems, though with a delayed adoption. One of the major constraints is the International Review Board (IRB), due to which most healthcare dialogue datasets are often not publicly available. As these systems interact with real stakeholders—such as clinicians and patients—the need for models to be explainable and interpretable has become critically important.

Dialog System Evaluation Evaluating the true conversational capabilities of TODS is inherently challenging. Evaluation methods typically fall into two categories: automated metrics and human evaluation.

Automated metrics can assess both individual components and the overall system. For Natural Language Understanding (NLU), intent classification accuracy (i.e., the percentage of user utterances where the predicted intent matches the true intent) and entity F1 score (based on precision and recall) are commonly used. Dialog State Tracking (DST) is evaluated using joint goal accuracy, which checks if the predicted belief states exactly match the ground truth for a given user turn. Natural Language Generation (NLG) is assessed using BLEU (Papineni et al., 2002), ROUGE (Lin, 2004), and METEOR (Banerjee and Lavie, 2005) scores, which measure overlap between the generated output and the reference, but these metrics do not capture the meaning of responses.

End-to-end metrics include Inform (whether the system provides an appropriate entity that meets the user's constraints) and Success Rate (whether the system both provides a correct entity and fulfills all requested information, such as address or price).

However, task performance is just one dimension of dialogue system evaluation. As demonstrated by the PARADISE framework (Walker et al., 1998), user satisfaction is influenced by both task success and interaction cost. Consequently, human evaluation remains the gold standard, especially for medical dialogue systems (Yeh et al., 2021; Deriu et al., 2021). Human evaluators can provide insights into subjective qualities such as coherence, informativeness, and user satisfaction—factors that are difficult to capture with automated metrics alone. The evaluation of medical dialog systems also follows a similar structure (Chowdhury et al., 2023) to TODS, but often requires comprehensive user studies for robust assessments. As conducting a user study is costly, researchers have explored alternative approaches, such as simulating users for evaluation (Yun et al., 2025; Park et al., 2023). With the rise of LLMs, there is growing interest in using them as automated judges (Zheng et al., 2023); however, their reliability remains under scrutiny. Despite these advancements, no current method fully captures the complex and multifaceted nature of dialogue system evaluation.

Neuro-Symbolic Methods The foundation of Neuro-Symbolic Systems (Nye et al., 2021) is inspired by the "dual process" theory from cognitive science, which distinguishes between two types of reasoning: System 1, which is fast, intuitive, and associative (akin to large language models), and System 2, which is slower, more deliberate, and logical—representing the symbolic reasoning component.

Neuro-Symbolic methods combine the generalization strengths of neural networks with the structure and interpretability of symbolic reasoning. For instance, (Romero et al., 2021) introduced symbolic representations into GPT-2 outputs to enhance structural awareness. DILOG (Zhou et al., 2020) leveraged inductive logic programming to learn dialogue policies from limited data, enabling zero-shot transfer. Similarly, (Arabshahi et al., 2021) showcased how multi-hop and commonsense reasoning can be incorporated into dialogue systems using neuro-symbolic techniques.

Lately, Symbol-LLM (Xu et al., 2024) discusses the challenges of integrating symbolic knowledge into LLMs and posits that since LLMs are pre-trained on general text without symbolic structure, using a symbolic interface is difficult. To address this, the authors explore the possibility of treating symbols in a unified manner by compiling 34 text-to-symbol generation tasks covering around 20 symbolic forms (Xu et al., 2024).

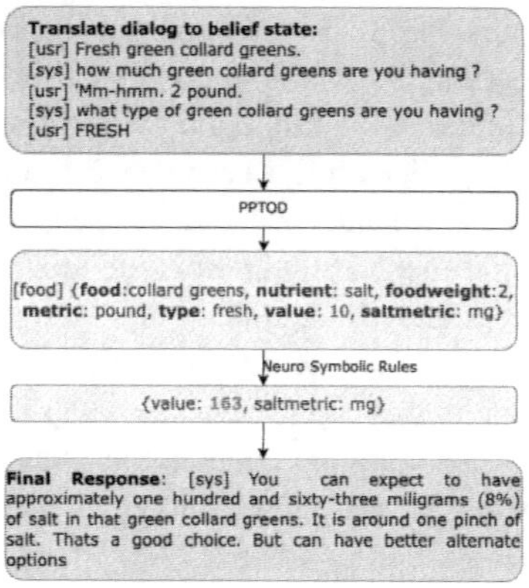

Figure 2: HFFood-NS Model interaction with the patient

3 Motivation and Research Questions

To model a conversational system for heart failure self-care domains, training data is required. However, a notable challenge remains: the lack of real-world, patient-driven conversational data from AA HF patients. With the advent of ChatGPT (OpenAI et al., 2024) and other LLMs, which have demonstrated strong capabilities in synthetic data generation, (Salunke et al., 2023; Tayal et al., 2025b) investigated their effectiveness in generating self-care conversations between patients and PEs. ChatGPT was used to generate simulated conversations using five distinct approaches of Race, Domain, African American Vernacular English (AAVE), Social Determinants of Health (SDOH), and SDOH-informed Reasoning. For each approach, conversations were generated with varying numbers of conversation rounds {5, 10, 15} and across different domains of *food, water, exercise*, which was a topic of discussion in the patient educator conversations. The conversational dataset is publicly available [1].

The findings suggested that prompting alone is insufficient to control or personalize conversations. The model struggled to follow even basic instructions, such as adhering to a set number of dialogue rounds, limiting word count, or asking appropriate follow-up questions. While it can incorporate SDOH features and improve dialogue quality through reasoning prior to generation, it remains unsuitable for direct deployment in patient-centric settings due to the lack of controllability.

Moreover, as salt consumption was a central topic in patient–educator conversations, (Tayal et al., 2024) designed a task-oriented dialogue system in which the users initiate the conversation by asking about the salt content of food. The system then posed clarification questions (cook, type, foodweight) to determine sodium values accurately. A template-based conversational system was constructed using the USFDC dataset (USFDC, 2022), a publicly available resource from the U.S. Department of Agriculture (USDA) that ensures cultural diversity and provides extensive food descriptions and nutritional values.

However, even after fine-tuning a T5-based language model (PPTOD) (Su et al., 2022), the system struggled to predict correct salt values—achieving only a 2% success rate—despite correctly identifying slot values (Table 3). These findings were consistent with Wei et al. (2022), which noted that large pre-trained language models (PLMs) such as GPT-3 and T5 (Brown et al., 2020; Raffel et al., 2020) are proficient at complex arithmetic reasoning but still make calculation errors. By integrating neuro-symbolic rules, a 20% improvement was observed in joint accuracy compared to the fine-tuned model, highlighting the necessity of incorporating neuro-symbolic rules to control system outputs (as shown in Table 3).

To further examine the practical implications of these improvements, Tayal et al. (2025a) conducted a within-group user study comparing the neuro-symbolic-based TODS system (HFFood-NS) with an LLM-based system (HFFood-GPT), involving 20 African American patients hospitalized with heart failure. Figure 2 shows an interaction with HFFood-NS while Table 4 shows an excerpt of the interaction with HFFood-GPT. The evaluation combined intrinsic measures of task performance with extrinsic analyses (Sparck Jones and Galliers, 1995) based on pre- and post-interaction surveys. Table 1 summarizes the two systems by comparing performance, design, usability, reliability, and flexibility. The two systems complement each other, highlighting the potential of a hybrid approach that leverages the strengths of both LLMs and neuro-symbolic systems. The neuro-symbolic TODS system is more accurate, completes more tasks, and produces concise responses, whereas the LLM-based system makes fewer speech errors, requires fewer clarifications, and handles complex queries more effectively. This direction is particularly promising for healthcare dialogue systems and motivates our research question:

[1] https://github.com/anujatayal/HF-Dataset

- **RQ1:** *How can we effectively combine the strengths of TODS and LMs/LLMs to create a hybrid dialog model?*
- **RQ2:** *How do users/patients/older adults perceive such a system?*

	HFFood-NS	HFFood-GPT
Task completion	✓	✗
Accuracy	✓	✗
Slot Accuracy	✗	✓
Fewer Speech Error	✗	✓
Less Processing Time	✓	✗
Error Analysis	✓	✗
Controlled	✓	✗
Reliable	✓	✗
Predictable	✓	✗
Complex query	✗	✓
Gave Options	✗	✓
Fluent	✗	✓
Concise	✓	✗
Create easily with less time	✗	✓

Table 1: Pros and Cons of HFFood-NS and HFFood-GPT comparing on performance, design usability, reliability, and flexibility.

Although HFFood-NS relied on template-based sentences, the resulting conversations were more controllable but lacked flexibility. While ChatGPT-generated conversations were diverse and more natural-sounding, they lacked predictability and controllability, raising questions such as whether the system would mention the salt amount, which questions it would ask, or whether follow-up questions would remain relevant. This unpredictability made the dialogue less explainable.

Moreover, the neuro-symbolic rules were applied externally to control the model's output, for correcting the salt value. While this approach improved accuracy, it kept symbolic reasoning separate from the neural model. An alternative strategy involves embedding symbolic rules directly into a language model through fine-tuning, enabling the model to internalize and apply these patterns during generation. In the context of TODS, dialog acts function as symbolic representations of user intent. By incorporating dialog acts as symbols during training, we aim to integrate these rules more seamlessly into the model's reasoning process.

We hypothesize that training models using schema graphs, rather than solely on dialog responses, will lead to better performance and improved generalization. Schemas (Mehri and Eskenazi, 2021; Zhao et al., 2023), originally known as frames (Fillmore, 1976), have a longstanding presence in the literature (Baker et al., 1998; Booij, 2010) and have recently regained attention as a structured approach for guiding the flow of task-oriented dialogues. They can be integrated either into the DST component or within end-to-end dialogue modeling. However, the definition and implementation of "schema" vary across the literature. A summary of different models—highlighting their associated tasks, schema types, and training strategies—is provided in Table 2.

Imrattanatrai and Fukuda (2023) adopts a lightweight approach, interpreting schemas primarily as slot descriptions, without modeling the full conversational trajectory. Similarly, T5DST (Lin et al., 2021) enhances zero-shot cross-domain DST by providing slot descriptions, while IC-DST (Hu et al., 2022) uses schema prompting with slot names and value examples. Schema graphs introduced in (Mehri and Eskenazi, 2021) abstract task representations to facilitate domain transfer.

SAM (Mehri and Eskenazi, 2021) employs schema-based reasoning to guide conversation flow in task-oriented dialogue systems. While effective in zero-shot settings, SAM relies on template-based generation, which can limit the naturalness and flexibility of responses. In contrast, our approach envisions schema graphs similar to SAM but utilizes dialog acts instead of templates. By integrating dialog acts and employing prompting techniques, the system aims to generate more dynamic and contextually appropriate responses. This method seeks to combine the structured control offered by schema-based reasoning with the adaptability of LLMs.

When models are trained on dialog responses, they must learn the underlying logic and structure of conversations implicitly from datasets. This requires significant data, and the learned logic may not always be consistent or transferable across domains. In contrast, schema-graphs explicitly encode the structure and flow of a conversation and possible user paths. By training on these structured representations, the model does not need to infer the logic on its own. As a result, models trained with schema-graphs are likely to be more robust.

4 Proposed Work

This thesis will focus on the exercise domain of self-care strategies and examine how users perceive and interact with such a system. Regular exercise plays a significant role in reducing hospitalizations for heart failure patients (Morris and Chen, 2019). The Physical Activity Guidelines

Model	Task	Schema Type	Training Strategy
T5DST (Lin et al., 2021)	DST	slot names/descriptions	Fine-tuning
IC-DST (Hu et al., 2022)	DST	slot names/value examples	Prompting
SAM (Mehri and Eskenazi, 2021)	E2E dialog	user-aware policy skeletons	Fine-tuning
ANYTOD (Zhao et al., 2023)	E2E dialog	policy programs, slot names/value examples, slot descriptions, user action names/states/descriptions	Fine-tuning and pretraining
SGP-TOD (Zhang et al., 2023)	E2E dialog	policy programs,slot names/value examples	Prompting

Table 2: Schema-type distinction along with their associated tasks, and training strategies as taken from (Zhang et al., 2023)

for Americans recommend at least 150 minutes of moderate-intensity exercise per week (Piercy et al., 2018). New York Heart Association (NYHA) (Committee, 1979) classified heart failure patients based on their physical activity limitations due to HF symptoms:

- Class I: No limitation of physical activity. Ordinary activity does not cause symptoms.
- Class II: Slight limitation. Comfortable at rest, but ordinary activity causes symptoms.
- Class III: Marked limitation. Comfortable at rest, but less than ordinary activity causes symptoms.
- Class IV: Unable to carry on any physical activity without discomfort; symptoms present even at rest.

Designing a dialog system for exercise is very complex. There is no pre-existing ontology for exercise-related dialogs. Moreover, exercise is a routine activity that demands constant motivation, a gradual build-up, and personalized guidance (Marcus and Pekmezi, 2024). Individual differences in physical abilities and fitness levels further heighten the complexity.

To establish a starting point, we consulted healthcare professionals to gain insights into how the conversation should be initiated. Initially, we (along with the healthcare professionals) decided to focus on class I and class II patients, as they can engage in exercise without direct supervision from a doctor. In contrast, class III and IV patients require a doctor's intervention while exercising.

The initial dialog paths were created to better understand how PE navigate exercise-related conversations, with the goal of using these insights to construct a synthetic dataset. The conversation begins with a patient-initiated question, such as, "Can I exercise with heart failure?" and alternates between the PE and the user, where the PE poses follow-up questions. The PE aims to establish a baseline understanding of the patient's condition and physical capabilities in order to provide actionable guidance. The resulting dialog graph consists of 16 unique paths, each corresponding to a leaf node. While this provides a solid foundation, the limited number of paths is inadequate for training a robust conversational system, highlighting the need for data augmentation.

Since these were simulated conversations, user responses were constrained to simple "yes" or "no" answers (see Figure 3(a)). However, real-world conversations are rarely so constrained. Patients often provide more nuanced responses, such as "I used to exercise but not anymore," or "I can walk short distances but need breaks because I get shortness of breath" (see Figure 3(b)). In such cases, predefined follow-up questions may become redundant, as users have already provided the required information.

To address this limitation, we structured these interactions as rule-based dialog graphs and converted each dialog path into a structured sequence of dialog acts (see Figure 3(c)), or symbolic representations/schema graphs (Section 2). This abstraction enabled systematic augmentation by generating all possible subsequences of each dialog path. Through this method, the number of distinct dialog states expanded from 16 to 1,078, significantly enriching the dataset. As a result, the system is now better equipped to accommodate the more

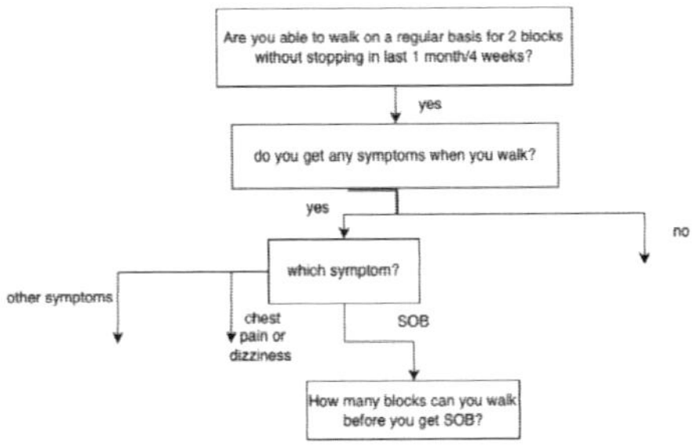

(a) A sample conversation path

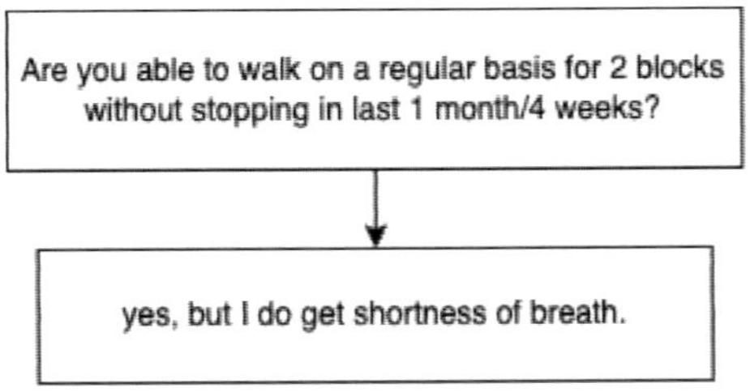

(b) An augmented conversation path

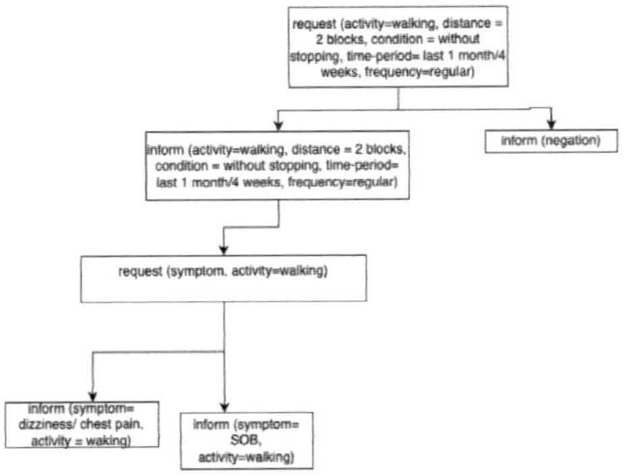

(c) Dialog act representation that supports both Figure 3(a) and Figure 3(b)

Figure 3: An example of a conversation flow, an augmented conversation, along with the dialog act representation that accommodates both conversation flows

varied and complex conversational flows observed in real-world interactions (Figure 3(b)).

Two key challenges arise when modeling an exercise-domain dialog system: **dialog management and response generation.** As we plan to effectively combine the strengths of TODS and LMs/LLMs to create a hybrid dialog model, we propose to decouple the dialog management and response generation and ask the following questions:

- How can we integrate dialog acts to control the flow of the conversation?
- How can different persuasion strategies be integrated to enhance the generation of patient education responses?

For dialog management, we will approach the problem by training a model (T5 or symbol-llm (Xu et al., 2024) on the schemas to predict the next dialog act rather than generating full responses directly. For pretraining, we will use the patient-educator (Gupta et al., 2020) dialogues (Section 1), the dataset generated in (Tayal et al., 2025b), and the health coaching dialog datasets (Gupta et al., 2021). Response generation will then be handled using LLMs. Using schema models will provide more control over the conversation flow, be more aligned, and make the system more reliable, while using LLM to generate responses will make the responses more diverse.

We will compare our schema approach with other schema approaches (Zhang et al., 2023; Zhao et al., 2023). We will try different models to train schema-graphs, including T5-based PPTOD (Su et al., 2022) and Symbol-LLM (Xu et al., 2024). Symbol-LLM may work better than T5 as it is trained on symbols. We believe that the dialog schema alone may be sufficient to effectively train dialog models, making additional data augmentation techniques unnecessary. To validate this hypothesis, we will conduct experiments comparing various augmentation strategies (Gritta et al., 2021), demonstrating that schema-based training provides strong generalization and performance.

For response generation, we will examine patient-educator conversations (Section 1) for the presence of persuasive communication strategies (Cialdini, 2001; Cialdini and Goldstein, 2004; Gass and Seiter, 2022; Knapp and Daly, 2011; Goffman, 1974). For example, in Figure 1, the PE attempts to persuade the patient to exercise regularly, and by doing so, reaffirms that the patient can return to previous activity levels. Upon identifying persuasive intent, we will analyze the specific strategies used (Gollapalli and Ng, 2025; Zeng et al., 2024; Wang et al., 2019a) by the PE.

PIRsuader (Gollapalli and Ng, 2025) offers a relevant framework, introducing dialog act categories such as *logical_appeal* and *emotional_appeal*, specifically designed to persuade diabetes patients to manage insulin resistance. A more detailed list of the dialog acts used can be found in Table 10 of (Gollapalli and Ng, 2025). We will start from this and if needed, we will also draw upon the taxonomy presented in Table 1 of (Zeng et al.,

2024), which organizes 13 categories of ethical strategies—including information-based, emotion-based, and credibility-based methods—grounded in research across disciplines such as Social Science (Goffman, 1974), Psychology (Cialdini, 2001; Cialdini and Goldstein, 2004), Marketing (Gass and Seiter, 2022), and Communication Studies (Knapp and Daly, 2011). Although these strategies were proposed for different use cases, we will adapt them to the patient-educator conversations. Building on this analysis, we will explore how such strategies can be integrated for the generation of responses for the exercise domain.

Additionally, we will incorporate a readability parameter during LLM response generation, enabling the model to adjust its language complexity according to the patient's reading grade level. Our core hypothesis is that an exercise dialog system can be effective for patients when it is both actionable and can adapt to both communication strategies and reading level (Burns, 1991).

Evaluation To evaluate our dialog agent, we will follow a three-step process. First, we will use automatic metrics of joint goal accuracy, inform, and success rate (Budzianowski et al., 2018)). Secondly, we will assess model performance using simulated users (Yun et al., 2025; Park et al., 2023). This will allow us to efficiently test multiple model variants and observe their behavior across a range of interaction styles. Based on this evaluation, the top two performing models will then be selected for testing with real users.

In the final phase, we will conduct a user study with older adults, as recruiting patients from a hospital setting poses logistical constraints. However, our study is still valid for two reasons. First, heart failure predominantly affects individuals aged 65 and older. Second, the system is intended for use in post-hospital environments, where older adults are expected to engage with it independently. This three-stage evaluation—starting with automatic metrics, evaluating using synthetic users, and progressing to real users—offers a more robust and scalable way to refine the dialog agent.

Our core hypothesis is that an exercise dialog system can be effective for patients when it is actionable and can adapt to both communication strategies and reading level.

5 Conclusion

We aim to develop a task-oriented dialogue system specifically designed to support the self-care needs of African-American patients with heart failure. The widespread use of large language models (LLMs) often lacks scrutiny, raising concerns in healthcare settings. Greater control is needed, as relying solely on prompting is not enough. Neuro-symbolic methods, which offer greater transparency, reliability, and explainability, should be further explored and integrated into future systems. In this thesis, we propose to develop hybrid conversational systems that combine the strengths of both systems. The conversational system will use schema graphs to control the flow of dialogue and leverage LLMs to generate responses grounded in these schemas. We will also conduct a user study to evaluate the system's effectiveness and to determine how older adults perceive such a system.

6 Limitations

We recognize that large language models (LLMs) are continually evolving, and improvements in future architectures may address some of the limitations observed in our study. Moreover, while we attempt to evaluate the systems comprehensively—our evaluation is not exhaustive and cannot capture all the aspects of interactions. Human evaluation remains the gold standard for assessing dialogue quality and patient-centered outcomes; however, conducting user studies is costly, time-intensive, and limited in scale, which constrains the generalizability of our findings.

References

Mohammad Rafayet Ali, Seyedeh Zahra Razavi, Raina Langevin, Abdullah Al Mamun, Benjamin Kane, Reza Rawassizadeh, Lenhart K Schubert, and Ehsan Hoque. 2020. A virtual conversational agent for teens with autism spectrum disorder: Experimental results and design lessons. In *Proceedings of the 20th ACM international conference on intelligent virtual agents*, pages 1–8.

Forough Arabshahi, Jennifer Lee, Mikayla Gawarecki, Kathryn Mazaitis, Amos Azaria, and Tom Mitchell. 2021. Conversational neuro-symbolic commonsense reasoning. In *Proceedings of the AAAI Conference on Artificial Intelligence*, volume 35, pages 4902–4911.

Collin F Baker, Charles J Fillmore, and John B Lowe. 1998. The berkeley framenet project. In *COLING 1998 Volume 1: The 17th International Conference on Computational Linguistics*.

Satanjeev Banerjee and Alon Lavie. 2005. Meteor: An automatic metric for mt evaluation with improved correlation with human judgments. In *Proceedings of the acl workshop on intrinsic and extrinsic evaluation measures for machine translation and/or summarization*, pages 65–72.

J. Barlow, C. Wright, J. Sheasby, A. Turner, and J. Hainsworth. 2002. Self-management approaches for people with chronic conditions: a review. *Patient Education and Counseling*, 48(2):177–187.

Matthew Barrett, Josiane Boyne, Julia Brandts, Hans-Peter Brunner-La Rocca, Lieven De Maesschalck, Kurt De Wit, Lana Dixon, Casper Eurlings, Donna Fitzsimons, Olga Golubnitschaja, et al. 2019. Artificial intelligence supported patient self-care in chronic heart failure: a paradigm shift from reactive to predictive, preventive and personalised care. *Epma Journal*, 10:445–464.

RV Belfin, AJ Shobana, Megha Manilal, Ashly Ann Mathew, and Blessy Babu. 2019. A graph based chatbot for cancer patients. In *2019 5th international conference on advanced computing & communication systems (ICACCS)*, pages 717–721. IEEE.

Geert Booij. 2010. Construction morphology. *Language and linguistics compass*, 4(7):543–555.

Tom Brown, Benjamin Mann, Nick Ryder, Melanie Subbiah, Jared D Kaplan, Prafulla Dhariwal, Arvind Neelakantan, Pranav Shyam, Girish Sastry, Amanda Askell, Sandhini Agarwal, Ariel Herbert-Voss, Gretchen Krueger, Tom Henighan, Rewon Child, Aditya Ramesh, Daniel Ziegler, Jeffrey Wu, Clemens Winter, Chris Hesse, Mark Chen, Eric Sigler, Mateusz Litwin, Scott Gray, Benjamin Chess, Jack Clark, Christopher Berner, Sam McCandlish, Alec Radford, Ilya Sutskever, and Dario Amodei. 2020. Language models are few-shot learners. In *Advances in Neural Information Processing Systems*, volume 33, pages 1877–1901. Curran Associates, Inc.

Paweł Budzianowski, Tsung-Hsien Wen, Bo-Hsiang Tseng, Iñigo Casanueva, Stefan Ultes, Osman Ramadan, and Milica Gašić. 2018. MultiWOZ - a large-scale multi-domain Wizard-of-Oz dataset for task-oriented dialogue modelling. In *Proceedings of the 2018 Conference on Empirical Methods in Natural Language Processing*, pages 5016–5026, Brussels, Belgium. Association for Computational Linguistics.

Robert B Burns. 1991. Persuasion by communication. *Essential Psychology: For Students and Professionals in the Health and Social Services*, pages 236–254.

Pengshan Cai, Zonghai Yao, Fei Liu, Dakuo Wang, Meghan Reilly, Huixue Zhou, Lingxi Li, Yi Cao, Alok Kapoor, Adarsha Bajracharya, Dan Berlowitz, and Hong Yu. 2023. PaniniQA: Enhancing Patient Education Through Interactive Question Answering. *Transactions of the Association for Computational Linguistics*, 11:1518–1536.

Mohita Chowdhury, Ernest Lim, Aisling Higham, Rory McKinnon, Nikoletta Ventoura, Yajie He, and Nick De Pennington. 2023. Can large language models safely address patient questions following cataract surgery? In *Proceedings of the 5th Clinical Natural Language Processing Workshop*, pages 131–137, Toronto, Canada. Association for Computational Linguistics.

Robert B Cialdini. 2001. The science of persuasion. *Scientific American*, 284(2):76–81.

Robert B Cialdini and Noah J Goldstein. 2004. Social influence: Compliance and conformity. *Annu. Rev. Psychol.*, 55(1):591–621.

New York Heart Association. Criteria Committee. 1979. *Nomenclature and criteria for diagnosis of diseases of the heart and great vessels*. Little, Brown Medical Division.

Rossana Cunha, Thiago Castro Ferreira, Adriana Pagano, and Fabio Alves. 2024. A persona-based corpus in the diabetes self-care domain - applying a human-centered approach to a low-resource context. In *Proceedings of the 2024 Joint International Conference on Computational Linguistics, Language Resources and Evaluation (LREC-COLING 2024)*, pages 1353–1369, Torino, Italia. ELRA and ICCL.

Jan Deriu, Alvaro Rodrigo, Arantxa Otegi, Guillermo Echegoyen, Sophie Rosset, Eneko Agirre, and Mark Cieliebak. 2021. Survey on evaluation methods for dialogue systems. *Artificial Intelligence Review*, 54:755–810.

Jacob Devlin, Ming-Wei Chang, Kenton Lee, and Kristina Toutanova. 2019. BERT: Pre-training of deep bidirectional transformers for language understanding. In *Proceedings of the 2019 Conference of the North American Chapter of the Association for Computational Linguistics: Human Language Technologies, Volume 1 (Long and Short Papers)*, pages 4171–4186, Minneapolis, Minnesota. Association for Computational Linguistics.

Victoria Vaughan Dickson and Barbara Riegel. 2009. Are we teaching what patients need to know? building skills in heart failure self-care. *Heart & Lung*, 38(3):253–261.

Charles J Fillmore. 1976. Frame semantics and the nature of language. *Annals of the New York Academy of Sciences*, 280(1):20–32.

Artur d'Avila Garcez and Luis C Lamb. 2023. Neurosymbolic ai: The 3 rd wave. *Artificial Intelligence Review*, pages 1–20.

Robert H Gass and John S Seiter. 2022. *Persuasion: Social influence and compliance gaining*. Routledge.

Erving Goffman. 1974. *Frame analysis: An essay on the organization of experience*. Harvard University Press.

Sujatha Das Gollapalli and See-Kiong Ng. 2025. PIRsuader: A persuasive chatbot for mitigating psychological insulin resistance in type-2 diabetic patients. In *Proceedings of the 31st International Conference on Computational Linguistics*, pages 5997–6013, Abu Dhabi, UAE. Association for Computational Linguistics.

Milan Gritta, Gerasimos Lampouras, and Ignacio Iacobacci. 2021. Conversation graph: Data augmentation, training, and evaluation for non-deterministic dialogue management. *Transactions of the Association for Computational Linguistics*, 9.

Itika Gupta, Barbara Di Eugenio, Devika Salunke, Andrew Boyd, Paula Allen-Meares, Carolyn Dickens, and Olga Garcia. 2020. Heart failure education of African American and Hispanic/Latino patients: Data collection and analysis. In *Proceedings of the First Workshop on Natural Language Processing for Medical Conversations*, pages 41–46, Online. Association for Computational Linguistics.

Itika Gupta, Barbara Di Eugenio, Brian D. Ziebart, Bing Liu, Ben S. Gerber, and Lisa K. Sharp. 2021. Summarizing behavioral change goals from SMS exchanges to support health coaches. In *Proceedings of the 22nd Annual Meeting of the Special Interest Group on Discourse and Dialogue*, pages 276–289, Singapore and Online. Association for Computational Linguistics.

Pantea Habibi, Sabita Acharya, Barbara Di Eugenio, Richard Cameron, Andrew Boyd, Karen Lopez, Pamela Martyn-Nemeth, Carolyn Dickens, Amer Ardati, and Debaleena Chattopadhyay. 2019. Designing self-care technologies for hf patients: a conceptual model. In *Conference on Human Factors in Computing Systems*, pages 12–16.

Yushi Hu, Chia-Hsuan Lee, Tianbao Xie, Tao Yu, Noah A. Smith, and Mari Ostendorf. 2022. In-context learning for few-shot dialogue state tracking. In *Findings of the Association for Computational Linguistics: EMNLP 2022*, pages 2627–2643, Abu Dhabi, United Arab Emirates. Association for Computational Linguistics.

Wiradee Imrattanatrai and Ken Fukuda. 2023. End-to-end task-oriented dialogue systems based on schema. In *Findings of the Association for Computational Linguistics: ACL 2023*, pages 10148–10161, Toronto, Canada. Association for Computational Linguistics.

Mark L Knapp and John A Daly. 2011. *The SAGE handbook of interpersonal communication*. Sage Publications.

S. C. Lewsey and K. Breathett. 2021. Racial and ethnic disparities in heart failure: Current state and future directions. *Current Opinion in Cardiology*, 36(3):320–328.

Chin-Yew Lin. 2004. ROUGE: A package for automatic evaluation of summaries. In *Text Summarization Branches Out*, pages 74–81, Barcelona, Spain. Association for Computational Linguistics.

Zhaojiang Lin, Bing Liu, Seungwhan Moon, Paul Crook, Zhenpeng Zhou, Zhiguang Wang, Zhou Yu, Andrea Madotto, Eunjoon Cho, and Rajen Subba. 2021. Leveraging slot descriptions for zero-shot cross-domain dialogue StateTracking. In *Proceedings of the 2021 Conference of the North American Chapter of the Association for Computational Linguistics: Human Language Technologies*, pages 5640–5648, Online. Association for Computational Linguistics.

Bess H Marcus and Dori Pekmezi. 2024. *Motivating people to be physically active*. Human Kinetics.

Shikib Mehri and Maxine Eskenazi. 2021. Schema-guided paradigm for zero-shot dialog. In *Proceedings of the 22nd Annual Meeting of the Special Interest Group on Discourse and Dialogue*, pages 499–508, Singapore and Online. Association for Computational Linguistics.

JH Morris and L Chen. 2019. Exercise training and heart failure: A review of the literature. *Cardiac Failure Review*, 5(1):57–61.

Sanjoy Moulik. 2019. *DIL-A Conversational Agent for Heart Failure Patients*. Ph.D. thesis, The Claremont Graduate University.

A Nayak, AJ Hicks, and AA Morris. 2020. Understanding the complexity of heart failure risk and treatment in black patients. *Circulation: Heart Failure*, 13(8):e007264.

Maxwell Nye, Michael Tessler, Josh Tenenbaum, and Brenden M Lake. 2021. Improving coherence and consistency in neural sequence models with dual-system, neuro-symbolic reasoning. *Advances in Neural Information Processing Systems*, 34:25192–25204.

OpenAI, Josh Achiam, Steven Adler, Sandhini Agarwal, Lama Ahmad, Ilge Akkaya, Florencia Leoni Aleman, Diogo Almeida, Janko Altenschmidt, Sam Altman, Shyamal Anadkat, Red Avila, Igor Babuschkin, Suchir Balaji, Valerie Balcom, Paul Baltescu, Haiming Bao, Mohammad Bavarian, Jeff Belgum, Irwan Bello, Jake Berdine, Gabriel Bernadett-Shapiro, Christopher Berner, Lenny Bogdonoff, Oleg Boiko, Madelaine Boyd, Anna-Luisa Brakman, Greg Brockman, Tim Brooks, Miles Brundage, Kevin Button, Trevor Cai, Rosie Campbell, Andrew Cann, Brittany Carey, Chelsea Carlson, Rory Carmichael, Brooke Chan, Che Chang, Fotis Chantzis, Derek Chen, Sully Chen, Ruby Chen, Jason Chen, Mark Chen, Ben Chess, Chester Cho, Casey Chu, Hyung Won Chung, Dave Cummings, Jeremiah Currier, Yunxing Dai, Cory Decareaux, Thomas Degry, Noah Deutsch, Damien Deville, Arka Dhar, David Dohan, Steve Dowling, Sheila Dunning, Adrien Ecoffet, Atty Eleti, Tyna Eloundou, David Farhi, Liam Fedus, Niko Felix, Simón Posada Fishman, Juston Forte, Isabella Fulford, Leo Gao, Elie Georges, Christian Gibson, Vik Goel, Tarun Gogineni, Gabriel Goh, Rapha Gontijo-Lopes, Jonathan Gordon, Morgan Grafstein, Scott

Gray, Ryan Greene, Joshua Gross, Shixiang Shane Gu, Yufei Guo, Chris Hallacy, Jesse Han, Jeff Harris, Yuchen He, Mike Heaton, Johannes Heidecke, Chris Hesse, Alan Hickey, Wade Hickey, Peter Hoeschele, Brandon Houghton, Kenny Hsu, Shengli Hu, Xin Hu, Joost Huizinga, Shantanu Jain, Shawn Jain, Joanne Jang, Angela Jiang, Roger Jiang, Haozhun Jin, Denny Jin, Shino Jomoto, Billie Jonn, Heewoo Jun, Tomer Kaftan, Łukasz Kaiser, Ali Kamali, Ingmar Kanitscheider, Nitish Shirish Keskar, Tabarak Khan, Logan Kilpatrick, Jong Wook Kim, Christina Kim, Yongjik Kim, Jan Hendrik Kirchner, Jamie Kiros, Matt Knight, Daniel Kokotajlo, Łukasz Kondraciuk, Andrew Kondrich, Aris Konstantinidis, Kyle Kosic, Gretchen Krueger, Vishal Kuo, Michael Lampe, Ikai Lan, Teddy Lee, Jan Leike, Jade Leung, Daniel Levy, Chak Ming Li, Rachel Lim, Molly Lin, Stephanie Lin, Mateusz Litwin, Theresa Lopez, Ryan Lowe, Patricia Lue, Anna Makanju, Kim Malfacini, Sam Manning, Todor Markov, Yaniv Markovski, Bianca Martin, Katie Mayer, Andrew Mayne, Bob McGrew, Scott Mayer McKinney, Christine McLeavey, Paul McMillan, Jake McNeil, David Medina, Aalok Mehta, Jacob Menick, Luke Metz, Andrey Mishchenko, Pamela Mishkin, Vinnie Monaco, Evan Morikawa, Daniel Mossing, Tong Mu, Mira Murati, Oleg Murk, David Mély, Ashvin Nair, Reiichiro Nakano, Rajeev Nayak, Arvind Neelakantan, Richard Ngo, Hyeonwoo Noh, Long Ouyang, Cullen O'Keefe, Jakub Pachocki, Alex Paino, Joe Palermo, Ashley Pantuliano, Giambattista Parascandolo, Joel Parish, Emy Parparita, Alex Passos, Mikhail Pavlov, Andrew Peng, Adam Perelman, Filipe de Avila Belbute Peres, Michael Petrov, Henrique Ponde de Oliveira Pinto, Michael, Pokorny, Michelle Pokrass, Vitchyr H. Pong, Tolly Powell, Alethea Power, Boris Power, Elizabeth Proehl, Raul Puri, Alec Radford, Jack Rae, Aditya Ramesh, Cameron Raymond, Francis Real, Kendra Rimbach, Carl Ross, Bob Rotsted, Henri Roussez, Nick Ryder, Mario Saltarelli, Ted Sanders, Shibani Santurkar, Girish Sastry, Heather Schmidt, David Schnurr, John Schulman, Daniel Selsam, Kyla Sheppard, Toki Sherbakov, Jessica Shieh, Sarah Shoker, Pranav Shyam, Szymon Sidor, Eric Sigler, Maddie Simens, Jordan Sitkin, Katarina Slama, Ian Sohl, Benjamin Sokolowsky, Yang Song, Natalie Staudacher, Felipe Petroski Such, Natalie Summers, Ilya Sutskever, Jie Tang, Nikolas Tezak, Madeleine B. Thompson, Phil Tillet, Amin Tootoonchian, Elizabeth Tseng, Preston Tuggle, Nick Turley, Jerry Tworek, Juan Felipe Cerón Uribe, Andrea Vallone, Arun Vijayvergiya, Chelsea Voss, Carroll Wainwright, Justin Jay Wang, Alvin Wang, Ben Wang, Jonathan Ward, Jason Wei, CJ Weinmann, Akila Welihinda, Peter Welinder, Jiayi Weng, Lilian Weng, Matt Wiethoff, Dave Willner, Clemens Winter, Samuel Wolrich, Hannah Wong, Lauren Workman, Sherwin Wu, Jeff Wu, Michael Wu, Kai Xiao, Tao Xu, Sarah Yoo, Kevin Yu, Qiming Yuan, Wojciech Zaremba, Rowan Zellers, Chong Zhang, Marvin Zhang, Shengjia Zhao, Tianhao Zheng, Juntang Zhuang, William Zhuk, and Barret Zoph. 2024. Gpt-4 technical report. *Preprint*, arXiv:2303.08774.

Kishore Papineni, Salim Roukos, Todd Ward, and Wei-Jing Zhu. 2002. Bleu: a method for automatic evaluation of machine translation. In *Proceedings of the 40th Annual Meeting of the Association for Computational Linguistics*, Philadelphia, Pennsylvania, USA. Association for Computational Linguistics.

Joon Sung Park, Joseph C. O'Brien, Carrie J. Cai, Meredith Ringel Morris, Percy Liang, and Michael S. Bernstein. 2023. Generative agents: Interactive simulacra of human behavior. *Preprint*, arXiv:2304.03442.

Katrina L. Piercy, Richard P. Troiano, Rachel M. Ballard, Susan A. Carlson, Janet E. Fulton, Deborah A. Galuska, Stephanie M. George, and Richard D. Olson. 2018. The physical activity guidelines for americans. *JAMA*, 320(19):2020–2028.

Colin Raffel, Noam Shazeer, Adam Roberts, Katherine Lee, Sharan Narang, Michael Matena, Yanqi Zhou, Wei Li, and Peter J. Liu. 2020. Exploring the limits of transfer learning with a unified text-to-text transformer. *Journal of Machine Learning Research*, 21(140):1–67.

Oscar J. Romero, Antian Wang, John Zimmerman, Aaron Steinfeld, and Anthony Tomasic. 2021. A task-oriented dialogue architecture via transformer neural language models and symbolic injection. In *Proceedings of the 22nd Annual Meeting of the Special Interest Group on Discourse and Dialogue*, pages 438–444, Singapore and Online. Association for Computational Linguistics.

D. Salunke, A. Tayal, B. Di Eugenio, P. G. Allen-Meares, C. Dickens, O. Garcia, E. P. Abril, and A. D. Boyd. 2023. Assessing bias in chatgpt's simulated clinical responses. In *AMIA Annual Symposium*, New Orleans, LA, USA.

Karen Sparck Jones and Julia R Galliers. 1995. *Evaluating natural language processing systems: An analysis and review*. Springer Science & Business Media.

Yixuan Su, Lei Shu, Elman Mansimov, Arshit Gupta, Deng Cai, Yi-An Lai, and Yi Zhang. 2022. Multi-task pre-training for plug-and-play task-oriented dialogue system. In *Proceedings of the 60th Annual Meeting of the Association for Computational Linguistics (Volume 1: Long Papers)*, pages 4661–4676, Dublin, Ireland. Association for Computational Linguistics.

Anuja Tayal, Barbara Di Eugenio, Devika Salunke, Andrew D. Boyd, Carolyn A. Dickens, Eulalia P. Abril, Olga Garcia-Bedoya, and Paula G. Allen-Meares. 2024. A neuro-symbolic approach to monitoring salt content in food. In *Proceedings of the First Workshop on Patient-Oriented Language Processing (CL4Health) @ LREC-COLING 2024*, pages 93–103, Torino, Italia. ELRA and ICCL.

Anuja Tayal, Devika Salunke, Barbara Di Eugenio, Paula Allen-Meares, Eulalia Puig Abril, Olga Garcia, Carolyn Dickens, and Andrew Boyd. 2025a. Conversational assistants to support heart failure patients:

comparing a neurosymbolic architecture with chatgpt. *Preprint*, arXiv:2504.17753.

Anuja Tayal, Devika Salunke, Barbara Di Eugenio, Paula G Allen-Meares, Eulalia P Abril, Olga Garcia-Bedoya, Carolyn A Dickens, and Andrew D. Boyd. 2025b. Towards conversational assistants for health applications: using chatgpt to generate conversations about heart failure. *Preprint*, arXiv:2505.03675.

USFDC. 2022. Us food data central.

Mina Valizadeh and Natalie Parde. 2022. The AI doctor is in: A survey of task-oriented dialogue systems for healthcare applications. In *Proceedings of the 60th Annual Meeting of the Association for Computational Linguistics (Volume 1: Long Papers)*, pages 6638–6660, Dublin, Ireland. Association for Computational Linguistics.

Marilyn Walker and Steve Whittaker. 1990. Mixed initiative in dialogue: An investigation into discourse segmentation. In *28th Annual Meeting of the Association for Computational Linguistics*, pages 70–78, Pittsburgh, Pennsylvania, USA. Association for Computational Linguistics.

Marilyn A Walker, Diane J Litman, Candace A Kamm, and Alicia Abella. 1998. Evaluating spoken dialogue agents with paradise: Two case studies. *Computer Speech & Language*, 12(4):317–347.

Jinping Wang, Hyun Yang, Ruosi Shao, Saeed Abdullah, and S. Shyam Sundar. 2020. Alexa as coach: Leveraging smart speakers to build social agents that reduce public speaking anxiety. In *Proceedings of the 2020 CHI Conference on Human Factors in Computing Systems*, CHI '20, page 1–13, New York, NY, USA. Association for Computing Machinery.

Junda Wang, Zonghai Yao, Zhichao Yang, Huixue Zhou, Rumeng Li, Xun Wang, Yucheng Xu, and Hong Yu. 2024. Notechat: a dataset of synthetic patient-physician conversations conditioned on clinical notes. In *Findings of the Association for Computational Linguistics ACL 2024*, pages 15183–15201.

Xuewei Wang, Weiyan Shi, Richard Kim, Yoojung Oh, Sijia Yang, Jingwen Zhang, and Zhou Yu. 2019a. Persuasion for good: Towards a personalized persuasive dialogue system for social good. In *Proceedings of the 57th Annual Meeting of the Association for Computational Linguistics*, pages 5635–5649, Florence, Italy. Association for Computational Linguistics.

Yanshan Wang, Ahmad Tafti, Sunghwan Sohn, and Rui Zhang. 2019b. Applications of natural language processing in clinical research and practice. In *Proceedings of the 2019 Conference of the North American Chapter of the Association for Computational Linguistics: Tutorials*, pages 22–25, Minneapolis, Minnesota. Association for Computational Linguistics.

Jason Wei, Xuezhi Wang, Dale Schuurmans, Maarten Bosma, Fei Xia, Ed Chi, Quoc V Le, Denny Zhou, et al. 2022. Chain-of-thought prompting elicits reasoning in large language models. *Advances in Neural Information Processing Systems*, 35:24824–24837.

Zhongyu Wei, Qianlong Liu, Baolin Peng, Huaixiao Tou, Ting Chen, Xuanjing Huang, Kam-fai Wong, and Xiangying Dai. 2018. Task-oriented dialogue system for automatic diagnosis. In *Proceedings of the 56th Annual Meeting of the Association for Computational Linguistics (Volume 2: Short Papers)*, pages 201–207, Melbourne, Australia. Association for Computational Linguistics.

Joseph Weizenbaum. 1966. Eliza—a computer program for the study of natural language communication between man and machine. *Commun. ACM*, 9(1):36–45.

Fangzhi Xu, Zhiyong Wu, Qiushi Sun, Siyu Ren, Fei Yuan, Shuai Yuan, Qika Lin, Yu Qiao, and Jun Liu. 2024. Symbol-LLM: Towards foundational symbol-centric interface for large language models. In *Proceedings of the 62nd Annual Meeting of the Association for Computational Linguistics (Volume 1: Long Papers)*, pages 13091–13116, Bangkok, Thailand. Association for Computational Linguistics.

Yi-Ting Yeh, Maxine Eskenazi, and Shikib Mehri. 2021. A comprehensive assessment of dialog evaluation metrics. In *The First Workshop on Evaluations and Assessments of Neural Conversation Systems*, pages 15–33, Online. Association for Computational Linguistics.

Taedong Yun, Eric Yang, Mustafa Safdari, Jong Ha Lee, Vaishnavi Vinod Kumar, S. Sara Mahdavi, Jonathan Amar, Derek Peyton, Reut Aharony, Andreas Michaelides, Logan Schneider, Isaac Galatzer-Levy, Yugang Jia, John Canny, Arthur Gretton, and Maja Matarić. 2025. Sleepless nights, sugary days: Creating synthetic users with health conditions for realistic coaching agent interactions. *Preprint*, arXiv:2502.13135.

Yi Zeng, Hongpeng Lin, Jingwen Zhang, Diyi Yang, Ruoxi Jia, and Weiyan Shi. 2024. How johnny can persuade LLMs to jailbreak them: Rethinking persuasion to challenge AI safety by humanizing LLMs. In *Proceedings of the 62nd Annual Meeting of the Association for Computational Linguistics (Volume 1: Long Papers)*, pages 14322–14350, Bangkok, Thailand. Association for Computational Linguistics.

Xiaoying Zhang, Baolin Peng, Kun Li, Jingyan Zhou, and Helen Meng. 2023. SGP-TOD: Building task bots effortlessly via schema-guided LLM prompting. In *Findings of the Association for Computational Linguistics: EMNLP 2023*, pages 13348–13369, Singapore. Association for Computational Linguistics.

Jeffrey Zhao, Yuan Cao, Raghav Gupta, Harrison Lee, Abhinav Rastogi, Mingqiu Wang, Hagen Soltau, Izhak Shafran, and Yonghui Wu. 2023. AnyTOD:

A programmable task-oriented dialog system. In *Proceedings of the 2023 Conference on Empirical Methods in Natural Language Processing*, pages 16189–16204, Singapore. Association for Computational Linguistics.

Lianmin Zheng, Wei-Lin Chiang, Ying Sheng, Siyuan Zhuang, Zhanghao Wu, Yonghao Zhuang, Zi Lin, Zhuohan Li, Dacheng Li, Eric Xing, et al. 2023. Judging llm-as-a-judge with mt-bench and chatbot arena. *Advances in Neural Information Processing Systems*, 36:46595–46623.

Yue Zhou, Barbara Di Eugenio, Brian Ziebart, Lisa Sharp, Bing Liu, Ben Gerber, Nikolaos Agadakos, and Shweta Yadav. 2022. Towards enhancing health coaching dialogue in low-resource settings. In *Proceedings of the 29th International Conference on Computational Linguistics*, pages 694–706, Gyeongju, Republic of Korea. International Committee on Computational Linguistics.

Zhenpeng Zhou, Ahmad Beirami, Paul Crook, Pararth Shah, Rajen Subba, and Alborz Geramifard. 2020. Resource constrained dialog policy learning via differentiable inductive logic programming. In *Proceedings of the 28th International Conference on Computational Linguistics*, pages 6775–6787, Barcelona, Spain (Online). International Committee on Computational Linguistics.

A Appendix

Train Size	Epochs	Joint Accuracy	
		PPTOD	NS-PPTOD
100	6	55.56	73.08
300	4	51.92	72.8
500	6	58.75	83.2
1000	6	58.53	85.2

Table 3: Increase in Joint Accuracy when using the neuro-symbolic model (NS-PPTOD) compared to the fine-tuned model (PPTOD) across different training sizes.

Speaker	Turn
System	Thank you for specifying the preparation method. Now, could you please tell me the portion size of the **grilled turkey sausage in grams?**
User	**5 milligrams.**
System	It seems there might be a misunderstanding with the portion size. Typically, food portion sizes are measured in grams (g) and would be much larger than 5 milligrams (mg). Could you please provide the portion size again in grams? For reference, a common serving size for sausage might be around 50 to 150 grams.
User	**100 milligrams**
System	It looks like we're still not quite accurate on the portion size. When we're talking about turkey sausage, the realistic portion size is usually around 100 grams (g), not milligrams (mg). **One gram is equal to 1000 milligrams**, so a portion size of turkey sausage might be 100 grams (which is 100,000 milligrams), for instance. Could you clarify the portion size in grams for the turkey sausage?

Figure 4: Excerpt of an HFFood-GPT Conversation

Enriching the Low-Resource Neural Machine Translation with Large Language Model

Sachin Giri **Takashi Ninomiya** **Isao Goto**
Graduate School of Science and Engineering, Ehime University
sachin.giri.cs@gmail.com, {ninomiya.takashi.mk, goto.isao.fn}@ehime-u.ac.jp

Abstract

Improving the performance of neural machine translation for low-resource languages is challenging due to the limited availability of parallel corpora. However, recently available Large Language Models (LLM) have demonstrated superior performance in various natural language processing tasks, including translation. In this work, we propose to incorporate an LLM into a Machine Translation (MT) model as a prior distribution to leverage its translation capabilities. The LLM acts as a teacher, instructing the student MT model about the target language. We conducted an experiment in four language pairs: English ⇔ German and English ⇔ Hindi. This resulted in improved BLEU and COMET scores in a low-resource setting.

1 Introduction

Training Neural Machine Translation (NMT) (Sutskever, 2014; Bahdanau, 2014; Luong, 2015; Vaswani, 2017) requires a large number of parallel corpora (Koehn and Knowles, 2017) and careful hyperparameter tuning (Sennrich and Zhang, 2019). Low-Resource Language (LRL) pairs generally possess a relatively limited amount of parallel data. In order to address the data scarcity problem, a possible solution is to utilize monolingual corpora (Wu et al., 2019). Using monolingual data, techniques such as generating synthetic parallel data via prompting Large Language Model (LLM) (Li et al., 2024; Enis and Hopkins, 2024), data augmentation via back translation (Hoang et al., 2018), Language Model (LM) prior (Baziotis et al., 2020), Knowledge Distillation (KD) or feature fusion using BERT (Yang et al., 2020; Zhu et al., 2020) and fine-tuning mBART (Zheng et al., 2021; San et al., 2024) have demonstrated a notable degree of performance improvement. But these approaches require training or fine-tuning of an additional teacher-like model to acquire text generation and translation capabilities or generate parallel corpora, followed by the transfer of knowledge to the Machine Translation (MT) model. However, recently available LLMs such as Llama (Dubey et al., 2024) have demonstrated remarkable proficiency in the translation task, which can be used to guide the MT model.

LLMs for translation (Hendy et al., 2023; Peng et al., 2023; Jiao et al., 2023) have shown significant success in generating high-quality translations. The deployment of these LLMs incurs substantial computational costs. LMs have been used in NMT to rerank the predictions of the MT model, or as an additional context, via LM fusion (Stahlberg et al., 2018), but lead to computational overhead, since LM is required during inference. Baziotis et al. (2020) proposed adding LM only in training and not in inference as a regularization term. However, this approach does not incorporate the source language information into LM when determining the regularization term, thereby failing to fully leverage the effectiveness of LLM.

We propose a new regularization term with the source sentence included to provide more context and replace LM with LLM to use its translation capabilities. Our contributions are as follows: (i) To the best of our knowledge, this is the first approach to using an instruction-tuned LLM as a regularization term, as described in Section 3 where both the source and target sentences are provided to the LLM as translation prompts. (ii) We evaluated the effects of using LLM in a low-resource setting and obtained an improvement in four directions: English-German (EN-DE), German-English (DE-EN), English-Hindi (EN-HI) and Hindi-English (HI-EN) (Section 4.5). In addition, we show that the proposed LLM prior outperforms the LM prior and baseline models.

2 Related Work

Baziotis et al. (2020) put the LM out of the MT model and the LM is used as a prior over the MT

Proceedings of the IJCNLP-AACL 2025 Student Research Workshop, pages 184–192
December 20-24, 2025

model's decoder by implementing posterior regularization using the loss function (Ganchev et al., 2010) in Equation 1:

$$\mathcal{L} = \sum_{t=1}^{N} -\log\, p_{\mathrm{MT}}(y_t|y_{<t}, \boldsymbol{x}) + \lambda\tau^2 \times D_{\mathrm{KL}}(p_{\mathrm{MT}}(y_t|y_{<t}, \boldsymbol{x}; \tau) \,||\, p_{\mathrm{LM}}(y_t|y_{<t}; \tau)), \tag{1}$$

where D_{KL}, $\boldsymbol{x}$ and y represent the Kullback–Leibler divergence, the source sentence and the target sentence, respectively, and $\boldsymbol{y} = y_1 y_2 ... y_N$. The posterior regularization includes prior information by imposing soft constraints on a posterior distribution of MT model. For computing D_{KL} between the MT model and LM distributions, softmax temperature parameters $\tau \geq 1$ are used. The same value of τ is applied to both LM and MT model at the same time. τ controls the smoothness of the output distributions $p_i = \frac{\exp(s_i/\tau)}{\sum_j \exp(s_j/\tau)}$, where s_i refers to the score (i.e., logit) obtained from the model before normalization of each word ID i. The magnitude of D_{KL} is on scales of $1/\tau^2$, so it is necessary to multiply its output by τ^2 to make the scale of D_{KL} loss invariant.

3 Proposed Approach

We propose using instruction-tuned LLM with source $\boldsymbol{x}$ to provide additional knowledge about the source language.

3.1 Loss Function

We changed p_{LM} of the loss function in Equation 1 with p_{LLM} and added the source $\boldsymbol{x}$ to it, resulting in the following equation.

$$\mathcal{L} = \sum_{t=1}^{N} -\log\, p_{\mathrm{MT}}(y_t|y_{<t}, \boldsymbol{x}) + \lambda\tau^2 \times D_{\mathrm{KL}}(p_{\mathrm{MT}}(y_t|y_{<t}, \boldsymbol{x}; \tau) \,||\, p_{\mathrm{LLM}}(y_t|y_{<t}, \boldsymbol{x}; \tau)), \tag{2}$$

where p_{LLM} is the probability distribution of the LLM conditioned on the translation prompt as in Figure 2. In Equation 2, the first term is the standard translation objective $\mathcal{L}_{\mathrm{MT}}$. The second term is the regularization term $\mathcal{L}_{\mathrm{KL}}$ referred to as the Kullback-Leibler divergence between the target side distributions of the MT model and the LLM output, weighted by λ. p_{LLM} can be viewed as weakly informative prior to the MT model distributions p_{MT}. It conveys partial information about $\boldsymbol{y}$. The LLM is

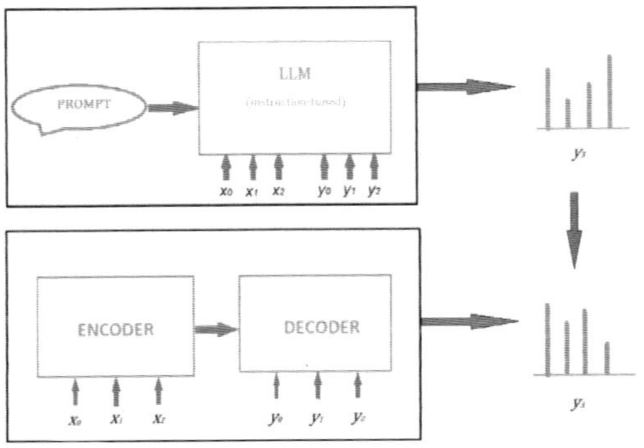

Figure 1: Distilling knowledge from LLM to MT model

```
prompt = [{ "role": "user",
            "content": "Translate the following from src_lang to
                        tgt_lang: 'x'"},
          { "role": "assistant",
            "content": "\n\nThe translation of the sentence \"x\"
            from src_lang to tgt_lang is: \n\n\"y\""}]
```

Figure 2: Translation prompt used

no longer a component of the MT model architecture, and inference is conducted exclusively using the MT model.

3.2 Relation to Knowledge Distillation

The regularization term present in Equation 2 signifies the use of KD where the output probabilities of a larger teacher model are used to train a small student model as illustrated in Figure 1, minimizing D_{KL}. In standard KD (Hinton, 2015; Ba and Caruana, 2014; Buciluă et al., 2006), the teacher model is required to be trained with the same task as the student model, such as KD for machine translation (Kim and Rush, 2016) and KD for LLM (Gu et al., 2023; Ko et al., 2024; Agarwal et al., 2024; Zhong et al., 2024). These KD approaches can be of LogitKD (Hinton, 2015; Tan et al., 2019; Gu et al., 2023; Ko et al., 2024; Agarwal et al., 2024; Zhong et al., 2024), which optimizes the student model to minimize the difference between its predictions and the predicted distribution of the teacher model and of sequence KD (SeqKD) (Kim and Rush, 2016; Wang et al., 2021; Li et al., 2024), in which the student model learns from a synthetic target sequence generated by the teacher model. The SeqKD approach requires the generation of large amounts of synthetic data, which might require additional large-scale monolingual data. Therefore, our method is based on LogitKD and uses an LLM as the teacher model and an MT model as the student model. sq

4 Experimental Setup

Zhu et al. (2024) have shown that current LLM are more effective in machine translation from XX to EN than from EN to XX. To use LLM as a teacher model, we opt for Llama3.2[1] with a vocabulary size of 128,256, which is publicly available and supports eight languages with parameter sizes of 1B and 3B. We then evaluated the effectiveness of the LLM in situations where the amount of available parallel data is limited for the languages it supports. Therefore, we also conducted evaluation experiments using the EN–DE and EN–HI language pairs supported by Llama3.2-1B and Llama3.2-3B.

4.1 Training Data

275K and 188K bitexts were collected in EN-DE and EN-HI, respectively. These were then also formatted into DE-EN and HI-EN directions. Taking into account these bitext counts and following Koishekenov et al. (2023); Costa-Jussà et al. (2022)[2], we assumed that the language pairs are low-resource as they have between 100K and 1M bitexts. Also, we randomly sampled 10K bitexts to perform the experiment in a very low resource setting. EN-DE was acquired from WMT18 News Commentary v13[3], EN-HI was acquired from Opus WikiMatrix v2[4]. The official WMT-2017 test set and the FLORES-200[5] dev set were used as the validation set, and the WMT 2018 test set and FLORES-200 devtest set were used as the test set for EN-DE and EN-HI respectively. Monolingual data sets containing 3M and 30M sentences for each language were collected. The data sets prepared by Baziotis et al. (2020) were used to train English and German LM, and the News Crawls 2024[6] dataset was used to train Hindi LM.

4.2 Pre-processing

Fairseq[7] was used to train all models. For source languages, the sentencepiece (Kudo and Richardson, 2018)[8] tokenizer was used to train the tokenizer with a vocabulary size of 16,000. To distill the knowledge of the Llama3.2 model on the decoder side of the MT model, the MT model and Llama3.2 must share the same vocabulary and output space. Therefore, for target languages, we used the Llama3.2 model AutoTokenizer from the Transformers library (Wolf et al., 2020)[9]. With Fairseq, the final vocabulary 16,000 was generated for the encoder and 128,260 was generated for the decoder of the MT model which includes four additional specials tokens <s>, </pad>, </s> and <unk>.

4.3 Model Configuration

MT models are the Transformer architecture (Vaswani, 2017). LMs have a decoder layer only as shown in the Appendix A. We used the pre-trained and instruction-tuned Llama3.2 models with the default settings, employing the AutoModelForCausalLM class from the Transformers library. At each training step, the target sentence $\boldsymbol{y}$ in the case of the pre-trained or the translation prompt in Figure 2 in the case of the instruction tuned is passed as input to the AutoModelForCausalLM object to obtain the LLM probability distribution. For optimization, the Adam optimizer was used with a learning rate of 0.0005. The batch size was 32 sentences and 50 epochs with patience limit up to 10 epochs; that is, if the validation loss does not update for 10 consecutive validation epochs, the training stops. We extended Baziotis et al. (2020) implementation of using LM prior[10] to LLM prior.

4.4 Training and Inference

Approaches used to train MT models:

- **LM-KD** (Baziotis et al., 2020): defined in Equation 1.
- **LLM-KD** our comparison method: replaced p_{LM} by p_{LLM} defined in Equation 1.
- **LLM-Ins-KD** our proposed method: defined in Equation 2.

The training server specification is defined in Appendix A. LM (142M-3M text) and LM (142M-30M text) were trained for the English, German, and Hindi languages with 3 million and 30 million sentences, respectively. The MT model "LLM-KD (1B)" in EN-DE with different values of λ and τ was trained and calculated the BLEU scores on the validation data set. We found that the best values were $\lambda = 0.5$ and $\tau = 2$, as indicated in Appendix A. These hyperparameter values were used during

[1]https://huggingface.co/collections/meta-llama/llama-32
[2]https://github.com/nllb/train-example-count
[3]https://www.statmt.org/wmt18/translation-task.html
[4]https://opus.nlpl.eu/WikiMatrix
[5]https://github.com/openlanguagedata/flores
[6]https://data.statmt.org/news-crawl/hi/
[7]https://github.com/facebookresearch/fairseq
[8]https://github.com/google/sentencepiece
[9]https://github.com/huggingface/transformers
[10]https://github.com/cbaziotis/lm-prior-for-nmt

model	EN-DE		DE-EN		EN-HI		HI-EN	
	BLEU	COMET	BLEU	COMET	BLEU	COMET	BLEU	COMET
10K train set								
base (118M)	2.0	0.3080	1.8	0.3611	1.3	0.3380	0.8	0.3972
LM-KD (142M-3M text)	3.9	0.3509	4.8	0.4011	1.5	0.3487	1.0	0.4029
LM-KD (142M-30M text)	3.8	0.3674	4.7	0.4024	1.7	0.3485	0.7	0.3961
LLM-KD (1B)	4.1	0.3682	3.0	0.3786	1.1	0.3393	0.9	0.4061
LLM-KD (3B)	4.2	0.3668	2.8	0.3776	1.5	0.3478	1.0	0.4055
LLM-Ins-KD (1B-Ins) (ours)	**5.2**	**0.3771**	**5.9**	**0.4376**	**1.8**	**0.3778**	**1.4**	**0.4198**
LLM-Ins-KD (3B-Ins) (ours)	4.1	0.3651	4.9	0.4156	1.6	**0.3779**	**1.4**	**0.4240**
full train set								
base (118M)	23.8	0.6703	24.3	0.6850	14.9	0.6042	12.7	0.6690
LM-KD (142M-3M text)	24.8	0.6894	24.7	0.6876	14.7	0.5803	15.0	0.6930
LM-KD (142M-30M text)	25.6	0.6953	26.9	0.7209	14.6	0.5914	15.6	0.7043
LLM-KD (1B)	25.9	0.7014	26.9	0.7256	15.2	0.5937	15.3	0.7027
LLM-KD (3B)	25.7	0.7044	27.0	0.7254	16.3	0.6053	15.3	0.7011
LLM-Ins-KD (1B-Ins) (ours)	**27.6**	**0.7240**	**28.8**	**0.7457**	**16.7**	**0.6195**	**17.3**	**0.7251**
LLM-Ins-KD (3B-Ins) (ours)	27.3	0.7189	28.7	0.7418	16.3	0.6188	17.1	0.7242
prompting								
1B-Ins	17.0	0.6925	25.5	0.7887	6.3	0.5517	13.6	0.7500
3B-Ins	23.0	0.7765	33.1	0.8291	12.7	0.6317	20.6	0.7880

Table 1: Comparison of BLEU and COMET scores of each MT model on test data-set. Bold scores denote highest gain score in each section.

training. The trained MT models were used to translate the test data set. In addition, we prepared script to automatically obtain the translation output of Llama3.2 Instruct models by prompting with the same prompt mentioned in Figure 2 without the target sentence y and temperature $= 1$. The translations obtained were detokenized and converted into sentences. We calculated the BLEU scores using SacreBLEU (Post, 2018)[11] with default tokenizer "13a" and the COMET scores (Rei et al., 2020)[12] with "Unbabel/wmt22-comet-da".

4.5 Results

Table 1 shows the experimental results. For reference, we have included some translation examples in Appendix A. We also present BLEU and COMET scores for the teacher model in the bottom section of Table 1.

As indicated in bold letter, the MT model "LLM-Ins-KD (1B-Ins)" yielded an improvement in the BLEU score as well as the COMET score across all language pairs compared to all models. Training each LM took approximately five days using 4 GPUs. However, using the pre-trained Llama3.2 model, no training is required. This suggests that using an instruction-tuned LLM rather than an LM for KD to an MT model is more effective, provides enriched translation, and yields better results.

The instruction-tuned LLM outperformed the pre-trained LLM. This corroborates our hypothesis that pretrained LLM has better text generation capabilities but is unaware of the source sentence, which can mislead the target side of the MT model due to which the LLM-KD approach has not resulted in improvement in few language pairs than LM-KD.

Training the "LLM-Ins-KD (3B-Ins)" model did not result in higher BLEU or COMET scores than the "LLM-Ins-KD (1B-Ins)" model. However, the scores were approximately the same, as shown in Table 1. We hypothesize that the scores did not improve further due to the small capacity of the student MT model used. Significant differences in the capacity of the teacher and student models can affect performance, as discussed in (Cho and Hariharan, 2019; Fan et al., 2024).

"LLM-Ins-KD (1B-Ins)" MT model scores are close to those of the teacher models. This shows that "LLM-Ins-KD" leads to effective learning, but has room for further improvement. Teacher models have up to 3B parameters, but our trained MT models only have 118M, as indicated in Appendix A, so we achieved 96 % reduction in parameters.

Since Llama3.2 models have 1B or 3B parameters, it takes little more time and memory to provide logits for the KD process. So, the training time for the LLM-Ins-KD and LLM-KD methods was 1.5 times that of the LM-KD method. Our hypothesis is that the training time cost can be reduced by storing LLM in memory that we leave for future work.

[11]https://github.com/mjpost/sacrebleu

[12]https://github.com/Unbabel/COMET

5 Conclusion

In this work, we proposed knowledge distillation from a pre-trained LLM to a NMT model. We used both the text generation and translation capabilities of the LLM. This approach is suitable because we do not need any monolingual data set or additional teacher model training. We also achieved improvement in BLEU and COMET scores for all language pairs compared to baselines in a low resource setting. We demonstrated that using the instruction-tuned LLM can be more effective than using the LM to distill knowledge to MT model.

Limitations

First, we used the lightweight open-source Llama 3.2 1B and 3B models for our experiment. We could have chosen larger LLMs, such as 8B or 70B, but we opted for the smaller models to perform the experiment quickly and with less computational cost. Second, we compared the BLEU and COMET scores of the translation model with the Llama3.2-1B-Instruct model. LLM return a translation output with extra description when inference is made with translation prompts. To automatically extract only the translation sentences, we wrote a program script. However, we believe that this approach might not be suitable. There may be a better way to obtain only the translated output from the LLM inference pipeline.

Acknowledgements

These research results were obtained from the commissioned research (No.22501) by National Institute of Information and Communications Technology (NICT), Japan. This work was supported by JSPS KAKENHI Grant Number JP24K15071.

References

Rishabh Agarwal, Nino Vieillard, Yongchao Zhou, Piotr Stanczyk, Sabela Ramos Garea, Matthieu Geist, and Olivier Bachem. 2024. On-policy distillation of language models: Learning from self-generated mistakes. In *The Twelfth International Conference on Learning Representations*.

Jimmy Ba and Rich Caruana. 2014. Do deep nets really need to be deep? *Advances in neural information processing systems*, 27.

Dzmitry Bahdanau. 2014. Neural machine translation by jointly learning to align and translate. *arXiv preprint arXiv:1409.0473*.

Christos Baziotis, Barry Haddow, and Alexandra Birch. 2020. Language model prior for low-resource neural machine translation. In *Proceedings of the 2020 Conference on Empirical Methods in Natural Language Processing (EMNLP)*, pages 7622–7634, Online. Association for Computational Linguistics.

Cristian Buciluă, Rich Caruana, and Alexandru Niculescu-Mizil. 2006. Model compression. In *Proceedings of the 12th ACM SIGKDD international conference on Knowledge discovery and data mining*, pages 535–541.

Jang Hyun Cho and Bharath Hariharan. 2019. On the efficacy of knowledge distillation. In *Proceedings of the IEEE/CVF international conference on computer vision*, pages 4794–4802.

Marta R Costa-Jussà, James Cross, Onur Çelebi, Maha Elbayad, Kenneth Heafield, Kevin Heffernan, Elahe Kalbassi, Janice Lam, Daniel Licht, Jean Maillard, and 1 others. 2022. No language left behind: Scaling human-centered machine translation. *arXiv preprint arXiv:2207.04672*.

Abhimanyu Dubey, Abhinav Jauhri, Abhinav Pandey, Abhishek Kadian, Ahmad Al-Dahle, Aiesha Letman, Akhil Mathur, Alan Schelten, Amy Yang, Angela Fan, and 1 others. 2024. The Llama 3 herd of models. *arXiv preprint arXiv:2407.21783*.

Maxim Enis and Mark Hopkins. 2024. From LLM to NMT: Advancing low-resource machine translation with claude. *arXiv preprint arXiv:2404.13813*.

Wen-Shu Fan, Xin-Chun Li, and De-Chuan Zhan. 2024. Exploring dark knowledge under various teacher capacities and addressing capacity mismatch. *arXiv preprint arXiv:2405.13078*.

Kuzman Ganchev, Joao Graça, Jennifer Gillenwater, and Ben Taskar. 2010. Posterior regularization for structured latent variable models. *The Journal of Machine Learning Research*, 11:2001–2049.

Yuxian Gu, Li Dong, Furu Wei, and Minlie Huang. 2023. Knowledge distillation of large language models. *arXiv preprint arXiv:2306.08543*.

Amr Hendy, Mohamed Abdelrehim, Amr Sharaf, Vikas Raunak, Mohamed Gabr, Hitokazu Matsushita, Young Jin Kim, Mohamed Afify, and Hany Hassan Awadalla. 2023. How good are GPT models at machine translation? a comprehensive evaluation. *arXiv preprint arXiv:2302.09210*.

Geoffrey Hinton. 2015. Distilling the knowledge in a neural network. *arXiv preprint arXiv:1503.02531*.

Cong Duy Vu Hoang, Philipp Koehn, Gholamreza Haffari, and Trevor Cohn. 2018. Iterative back-translation for neural machine translation. In *2nd Workshop on Neural Machine Translation and Generation*, pages 18–24. Association for Computational Linguistics.

Wenxiang Jiao, Wenxuan Wang, Jen-tse Huang, Xing Wang, Shuming Shi, and Zhaopeng Tu. 2023. Is ChatGPT a good translator? yes with GPT-4 as the engine. *arXiv preprint arXiv:2301.08745*.

Yoon Kim and Alexander M Rush. 2016. Sequence-level knowledge distillation. *arXiv preprint arXiv:1606.07947*.

Jongwoo Ko, Sungnyun Kim, Tianyi Chen, and Se-Young Yun. 2024. DistiLLM: Towards streamlined distillation for large language models. *arXiv preprint arXiv:2402.03898*.

Philipp Koehn and Rebecca Knowles. 2017. Six challenges for neural machine translation. *arXiv preprint arXiv:1706.03872*.

Yeskendir Koishekenov, Alexandre Berard, and Vassilina Nikoulina. 2023. Memory-efficient NLLB-200: Language-specific expert pruning of a massively multilingual machine translation model. In *Proceedings of the 61st Annual Meeting of the Association for Computational Linguistics (Volume 1: Long Papers)*, pages 3567–3585, Toronto, Canada. Association for Computational Linguistics.

Taku Kudo and John Richardson. 2018. SentencePiece: A simple and language independent subword tokenizer and detokenizer for neural text processing. In *Proceedings of the 2018 Conference on Empirical Methods in Natural Language Processing: System Demonstrations*, pages 66–71, Brussels, Belgium. Association for Computational Linguistics.

Jiahuan Li, Shanbo Cheng, Shujian Huang, and Jiajun Chen. 2024. MT-PATCHER: Selective and extendable knowledge distillation from large language models for machine translation. In *Proceedings of the 2024 Conference of the North American Chapter of the Association for Computational Linguistics: Human Language Technologies (Volume 1: Long Papers)*, pages 6445–6459, Mexico City, Mexico. Association for Computational Linguistics.

Minh-Thang Luong. 2015. Effective approaches to attention-based neural machine translation. *arXiv preprint arXiv:1508.04025*.

Keqin Peng, Liang Ding, Qihuang Zhong, Li Shen, Xuebo Liu, Min Zhang, Yuanxin Ouyang, and Dacheng Tao. 2023. Towards making the most of ChatGPT for machine translation. *arXiv preprint arXiv:2303.13780*.

Matt Post. 2018. A call for clarity in reporting BLEU scores. In *Proceedings of the Third Conference on Machine Translation: Research Papers*, pages 186–191, Brussels, Belgium. Association for Computational Linguistics.

Ricardo Rei, Craig Stewart, Ana C Farinha, and Alon Lavie. 2020. COMET: A neural framework for MT evaluation. In *Proceedings of the 2020 Conference on Empirical Methods in Natural Language Processing (EMNLP)*, pages 2685–2702, Online. Association for Computational Linguistics.

Mya Ei San, Sasiporn Usanavasin, Ye Kyaw Thu, and Manabu Okumura. 2024. A study for enhancing low-resource Thai-Myanmar-English neural machine translation. *ACM Transactions on Asian and Low-Resource Language Information Processing*, 23(4):1–24.

Rico Sennrich and Biao Zhang. 2019. Revisiting low-resource neural machine translation: A case study. *arXiv preprint arXiv:1905.11901*.

Felix Stahlberg, James Cross, and Veselin Stoyanov. 2018. Simple fusion: Return of the language model. *arXiv preprint arXiv:1809.00125*.

I Sutskever. 2014. Sequence to sequence learning with neural networks. *arXiv preprint arXiv:1409.3215*.

Xu Tan, Yi Ren, Di He, Tao Qin, Zhou Zhao, and Tie-Yan Liu. 2019. Multilingual neural machine translation with knowledge distillation. *arXiv preprint arXiv:1902.10461*.

A Vaswani. 2017. Attention is all you need. *Advances in Neural Information Processing Systems*.

Fusheng Wang, Jianhao Yan, Fandong Meng, and Jie Zhou. 2021. Selective knowledge distillation for neural machine translation. In *Proceedings of the 59th Annual Meeting of the Association for Computational Linguistics and the 11th International Joint Conference on Natural Language Processing (Volume 1: Long Papers)*, pages 6456–6466, Online. Association for Computational Linguistics.

Thomas Wolf, Lysandre Debut, Victor Sanh, Julien Chaumond, Clement Delangue, Anthony Moi, Pierric Cistac, Tim Rault, Remi Louf, Morgan Funtowicz, Joe Davison, Sam Shleifer, Patrick von Platen, Clara Ma, Yacine Jernite, Julien Plu, Canwen Xu, Teven Le Scao, Sylvain Gugger, and 3 others. 2020. Transformers: State-of-the-art natural language processing. In *Proceedings of the 2020 Conference on Empirical Methods in Natural Language Processing: System Demonstrations*, pages 38–45, Online. Association for Computational Linguistics.

Lijun Wu, Yiren Wang, Yingce Xia, Tao Qin, Jianhuang Lai, and Tie-Yan Liu. 2019. Exploiting monolingual data at scale for neural machine translation. In *Proceedings of the 2019 Conference on Empirical Methods in Natural Language Processing and the 9th International Joint Conference on Natural Language Processing (EMNLP-IJCNLP)*, pages 4207–4216.

Jiacheng Yang, Mingxuan Wang, Hao Zhou, Chengqi Zhao, Weinan Zhang, Yong Yu, and Lei Li. 2020. Towards making the most of BERT in neural machine translation. In *Proceedings of the AAAI conference on artificial intelligence*, volume 34, pages 9378–9385.

Francis Zheng, Machel Reid, Edison Marrese-Taylor, and Yutaka Matsuo. 2021. Low-resource machine translation using cross-lingual language model pretraining. In *Proceedings of the First Workshop on Natural Language Processing for Indigenous Languages of the Americas*, pages 234–240.

Qihuang Zhong, Liang Ding, Li Shen, Juhua Liu, Bo Du, and Dacheng Tao. 2024. Revisiting knowledge distillation for autoregressive language models. *arXiv preprint arXiv:2402.11890*.

Jinhua Zhu, Yingce Xia, Lijun Wu, Di He, Tao Qin, Wengang Zhou, Houqiang Li, and Tie-Yan Liu. 2020. Incorporating BERT into neural machine translation. *arXiv preprint arXiv:2002.06823*.

Wenhao Zhu, Hongyi Liu, Qingxiu Dong, Jingjing Xu, Shujian Huang, Lingpeng Kong, Jiajun Chen, and Lei Li. 2024. Multilingual machine translation with large language models: Empirical results and analysis. In *Findings of the Association for Computational Linguistics: NAACL 2024*, pages 2765–2781, Mexico City, Mexico. Association for Computational Linguistics.

A Appendix

A.1 Architecture of the Models

Table 2 shows the architecture of the different models used in these experiments along with the number of parameters.

component	value			
	MT	**LM**	**1B**	**3B**
parameters	118M	142M	1B	3B
Embedding	512	1024	2048	3072
Encoder layer	6	6	N/A	N/A
Decoder layer	6	6	16	28
Encoder head	8	8	N/A	N/A
Decoder head	8	16	N/A	N/A
Dropout (all)	0.3	0.3	N/A	N/A

Table 2: Architecture of each model used

A.2 Specification of Training Server

The specification of the training server for this experiment is shown in Table 3.

hardware	**capacity**
GPU	47GB
number of GPU	1-4
CPU	6-8 core
RAM	40-60 GB
total training time	15days

Table 3: Specification of training server

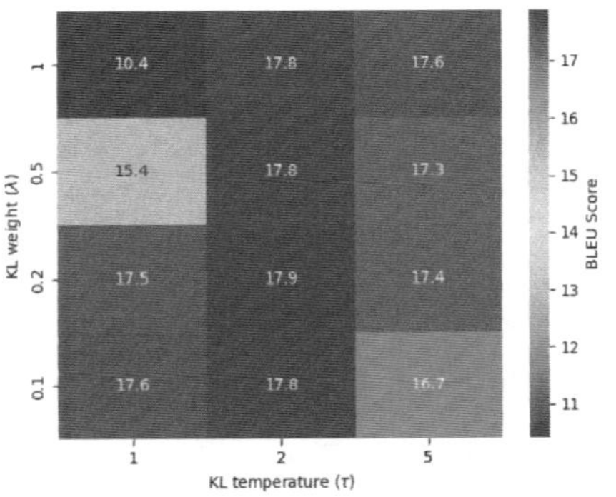

Figure 3: Valid set BLEU scores of "LLM-KD (1B)" in the EN-DE direction with different value of λ and τ

A.3 Hyperparameter Tuning

Figure 3 shows the heat map of the valid-set BLEU scores with different combinations of λ and τ in the EN-DE direction. This MT model trained with our comparison method: replaced p_{LM} by p_{LLM} defined in Equation 1.

Taking the baseline BLEU score of the MT model 16.8, we see the pattern as follows: Using $\tau = 2$ results in the MT model to acquire more dark knowledge encoded in the LLM logits, and at this stage, changing λ affects the performance of the MT model. So, we selected $\lambda = 0.5$ and $\tau = 2$ to train all models in our experiments.

A.4 Translation Examples

Table 7 provides some translation examples.

Source	Munich 1856: Four maps that will change your view of the city
Reference	München 1856: Vier Karten, die Ihren Blick auf die Stadt verändern
Trained with 10K train set	
base (118M)	Mushalt 2015: 2006 wird das Bürgerkrieg gegenüber den Vereinigten Staaten erwartet werden.
LM-KD (142M-3M text)	München: Im Jahr 1865 wird die Stadtkarte auf den Inseln gestoppt werden.
LM-KD (142M-30M text)	München: Im Jahr 1865 wird die Stadt von den Inseln gestohlen, um die Stadt zu den Inseln zu verfehlen.
LLM-KD (1B)	Menschen 1865 wird das Begrüßte angesichts der Stadt veränderten, dass die Stadtveränderung der Stadt erkannt werden.
LLM-KD (3B)	Menschen wird 1862 verfügt: Die Befürdigen der Stadt verändert werden.
LLM-Ins-KD (1B-Ins) (ours)	München 18. Dezember 1861 verfügt: Die Hoffnung der Stadt erfüllt.
LLM-Ins-KD (3B-Ins) (ours)	Menschen 1866 wird 1861 ein Südenkrieg beigetragen: Der Bürger der Stadt ziehen.
Trained with full train set	
base (118M)	München 1856: Vier Landkarten, die Ihre Sichtweise der Stadt ändern werden
LM-KD (142M-3M text)	München 1856: Vier Landkarten, die Ihre Sichtweise der Stadt ändern werden
LM-KD (142M-30M text)	München 1856: Vier Karten, die Ihre Sicht der Stadt ändern werden.
LLM-KD (1B)	München 1856: Vier Landkarten, die Ihre Sicht der Stadt verändern werden.
LLM-KD (3B)	München 1856: Vier Landkarten, die Ihre Sicht der Stadt verändern werden
LLM-Ins-KD (1B-Ins) (ours)	München 1856: Vier Karten werden Ihre Sicht der Stadt ändern
LLM-Ins-KD (3B-Ins) (ours)	München 1856: Vier Landkarten, die Ihre Ansicht in der Stadt verändern werden.

Table 4: EN-DE translation example

Source	München 1856: Vier Karten, die Ihren Blick auf die Stadt verändern
Reference	Munich 1856: Four maps that will change your view of the city
Trained with 10K train set	
base (118M)	meanwhile, 6.6% of your city are on the city of your city.
LM-KD (142M-3M text)	meanwhile, 6.6% of your city are on the city of your city.
LM-KD (142M-30M text)	after all, 6.6% of your books, you are changing the city of your city.
LLM-KD (1B)	the 1 of 1, 1,000 deaths on the city of the city.
LLM-KD (3B)	every year, 1, 1,000 I am on the city of the city of the city.
LLM-Ins-KD (1B-Ins) (ours)	Abba 1876,000 met the city of your city on your city to change.
LLM-Ins-KD (3B-Ins) (ours)	Copenhagen 18,000 die at the city of the city of the city to leave the city of the city.
Trained with full train set	
base (118M)	Munich 1856: Four Crises changing your eyes on the city
LM-KD (142M-3M text)	Munich, 1856: Four maps changing your eyes to the city
LM-KD (142M-30M text)	Munich, 1856: Four cards change your view of the city.
LLM-KD (1B)	Munich, 1856: Four maps changing your eyes to the city
LLM-KD (3B)	Munich, 1856: Four maps changing your eyes to the city
LLM-Ins-KD (1B-Ins) (ours)	Munich 1856: Four maps changing your eyes on the city
LLM-Ins-KD (3B-Ins) (ours)	Munich 1856: Four cards that change your eyes on the city

Table 5: DE-EN translation example

Source	"While one experimental vaccine appears able to reduce Ebola mortality
Reference	"जबकि एक प्रायोगिक वैक्सीन इबोला से मृत्यु दर में कमी हो सकती है
Trained with 10K train set	
base (118M)	" इस प्रकार के लिए बहुत कम हो जाता है।
LM-KD (142M-3M text)	"प्रत्येक व्यक्ति को कवर करने के लिए एक मूर्ति का प्रयास किया गया है।
LM-KD (142M-30M text)	"जो मात्मा को माता है कि मात्मा को मात्मा मिल जाता है।
LLM-KD (1B)	हालांकि का पूरा है।
LLM-KD (3B)	इसी मृत्यु का प्रयोग किया जा सकता है।
LLM-Ins-KD (1B-Ins) (ours)	बूगल को मृत्यु के लिए एक सप्ताह में खोला जाता है।
LLM-Ins-KD (3B-Ins) (ours)	" फिल्म का प्रयोग किया जाता है।
Trained with full train set	
base (118M)	"व्हील एक प्रयोगात्मक टीका ईबोला मृत्यु को कम करने में सक्षम है।
LM-KD (142M-3M text)	एक प्रयोगात्मक टीका इबोला मृत्यु दर कम करने में सक्षम होता है।
LM-KD (142M-30M text)	एक प्रायोगिक टीका एबोला मृत्यु दर को कम करने में सक्षम होता है।
LLM-KD (1B)	एक प्रयोगात्मक टीका ईबोला मृत्यु दर को कम करने में सक्षम है।
LLM-KD (3B)	एक प्रयोगात्मक वैक्सीन एबोला मृत्यु को कम करने में सक्षम दिखाई देता है।
LLM-Ins-KD (1B-Ins) (ours)	एक प्रयोगात्मक टीका मृत्यु मृत्यु को कम करने में सक्षम है।
LLM-Ins-KD (3B-Ins) (ours)	"एक प्रयोगात्मक वैक्सीन एबोला मृत्यु को कम करने में सक्षम लगता है।

Table 6: EN-HI translation example

Source	"जबकि एक प्रायोगिक वैक्सीन इबोला से मृत्यु दर में कमी हो सकती है
Reference	"While one experimental vaccine appears able to reduce Ebola mortality
Trained with 10K train set	
base (118M)	It is one of them to make it it it it to be in 10.
LM-KD (142M-3M text)	It can be one of an important time, but it can be used for a time.
LM-KD (142M-30M text)	It can be an important for an time.
LLM-KD (1B)	It is one of one of it is one person to be a matter of it.
LLM-KD (3B)	It is one of a person to be one of one person to be a matter of people.
LLM-Ins-KD (1B-Ins) (ours)	It can be one of one of a person to be about 1000.
LLM-Ins-KD (3B-Ins) (ours)	It is one of one of an reason, but is one of about 1000.
Trained with full train set	
base (118M)	As a result, an active vaccine may be decreased in the rate of death.
LM-KD (142M-3M text)	"Exposure to an experimental vaccine may reduce mortality rates from an outbreak.
LM-KD (142M-30M text)	"Currently an experimental vaccine may be reduced to death rates".
LLM-KD (1B)	"While one experimental vaccine appears able to reduce Ebola mortality
LLM-KD (3B)	"An experimental vaccine may be reduced to death rates".
LLM-Ins-KD (1B-Ins) (ours)	"Failure to reduce mortality rate by immunoscopy".
LLM-Ins-KD (3B-Ins) (ours)	A pilot vaccine may reduce mortality rate from the immunoglobulin.

Table 7: HI-EN translation example

Investigating Training and Generalization in Faithful Self-Explanations of Large Language Models

Tomoki Doi[1,2], **Masaru Isonuma**[1,2,3,4], **Hitomi Yanaka**[1,2,3]
[1]The University of Tokyo [2]Riken [3]Tohoku University [4]NII LLMC
{doi-tomoki701, hyanaka}@is.s.u-tokyo.ac.jp
isonuma@nii.ac.jp

Abstract

Large language models have the potential to generate explanations for their own predictions in a variety of styles based on user instructions. Recent research has examined whether these self-explanations faithfully reflect the models' actual behavior and has found that they often lack faithfulness. However, the question of how to improve faithfulness remains underexplored. Moreover, because different explanation styles have superficially distinct characteristics, it is unclear whether improvements observed in one style also arise when using other styles. This study analyzes the effects of training for faithful self-explanations and the extent to which these effects generalize, using three classification tasks and three explanation styles. We construct one-word constrained explanations that are likely to be faithful using a feature attribution method, and use these pseudo-faithful self-explanations for continual learning on instruction-tuned models. Our experiments demonstrate that training can improve self-explanation faithfulness across all classification tasks and explanation styles, and that these improvements also show signs of generalization to the multi-word settings and to unseen tasks. Furthermore, we find consistent cross-style generalization among three styles, suggesting that training may contribute to a broader improvement in faithful self-explanation ability.

1 Introduction

Instruction-tuned large language models (LLMs) appear capable of generating natural language explanations about their own decisions (i.e., self-explanations) in a variety of styles (Calderon and Reichart, 2025). Users can instruct the models to identify the key information in the input that drives their predictions or to construct counterfactual inputs that invert the original predictions. Self-explanations have the potential to give explainability to LLMs, converting their black-box processing into interpretable expressions.

Train - Attribution Style	
User:	Text: "I hate waking up early." What is the sentiment of the text?
Assistant:	Negative
User:	List the most important word for determining the sentiment.
Assistant:	**"hate"**
Test - Counterfactual Style	
User:	Text: "my room walls are boring" What is the sentiment of the text?
Assistant:	Negative
User:	Edit the text so that the predicted sentiment would change.
Assistant:	**"my room walls are exciting"**

Table 1: Training and test examples used to evaluate cross-style generalization. The training style instructs models to output *words* that strongly *support* their predictions, whereas the test style requires generating *sentences* that *contradicts* the predictions.

Recent studies have investigated the extent to which self-explanations faithfully reflect actual model behavior. They have designed evaluation protocols for each explanation style: checking the model's prediction change when editing the input according to the self-explanations (Atanasova et al., 2023; Siegel et al., 2024; Madsen et al., 2024), and checking whether the Chain-of-Thought reasoning steps accurately reflect their biases in predictions (Turpin et al., 2023; Chen et al., 2025). These studies show that self-explanations produced by LLMs are often unfaithful and unreliable across styles, underscoring the need for improvement.

However, it remains unclear how, and to what extent, the self-explanation faithfulness of LLMs can be improved. Because the faithfulness of a model's self-explanation should be evaluated based on observations of its own behavior (Jacovi and Goldberg, 2020), it is inherently challenging to provide general supervised signals of faithful self-explanations that can apply to any model. Moreover, explanation styles exhibit distinct surface

Proceedings of the IJCNLP-AACL 2025 Student Research Workshop, pages 193–208
December 20-24, 2025 ©2025 Association for Computational Linguistics

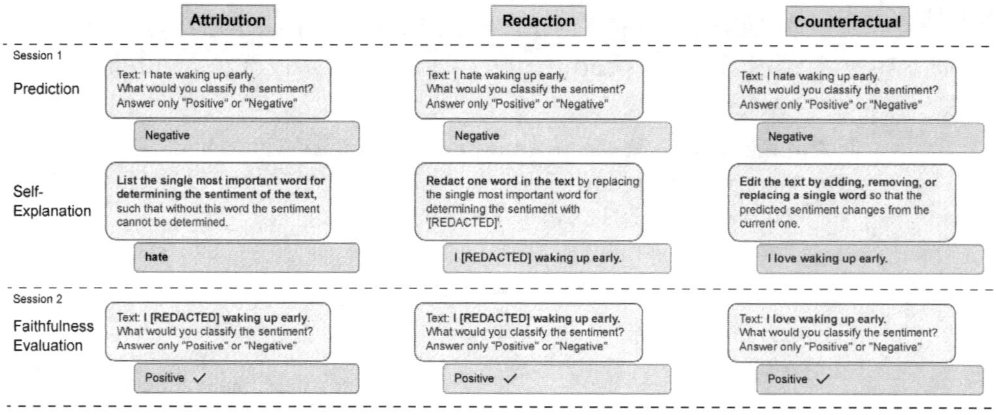

Figure 1: Examples of one-word-constrained self-explanations and faithfulness evaluation for each explanation style. Self-explanations are generated in the same session as the classification task: Attribution and Redaction require listing and redacting the most important input words affecting the prediction, respectively, while Counterfactual requires editing the input text so that the predicted label will flip. Faithfulness evaluation involves a separate session, in which a self-explanation is considered faithful if editing the input according to it indeed flips the prediction.

characteristics: an attribution-style self-explanation consists of words that support the model's prediction, whereas a counterfactual-style explanation is expressed through a sentence that contradicts the original prediction (Table 1). It remains an open question how the faithfulness of self-explanations in each explanation style can be effectively improved, and whether such improvements are transferable across styles.

In this paper, we construct pseudo-faithful self-explanations in three explanation styles (Figure 1) and examine how training LLMs on these constructed explanations affects their faithfulness. We further investigate how well the resulting improvements generalize along three dimensions: unconstrained multi-word settings (Section 4.2), unseen classification tasks (Section 4.3), and cross-style generalization (Section 4.4). We construct training datasets of pseudo-faithful self-explanations for three classification tasks using a feature attribution method under a one-word constrained setting. We then train the instruction-tuned models by mixing the constructed self-explanations with their original instruction tuning data, and evaluate the self-explanation faithfulness before and after training.

Our experimental results show that training improves faithfulness across almost all classification tasks and explanation styles. We also find that, for one explanation style, the improvement generalizes to unseen classification tasks and to unconstrained multi-word settings. Furthermore, we observe generalization of faithfulness improvements across distinct explanation styles. For example, a model trained to identify words that support its prediction can also modify the input sentence by deleting or replacing those words to invert the prediction. These findings suggest that training on pseudo-faithful self-explanations may improve self-explanation faithfulness across explanation styles, even without access to truly faithful self-explanations.

2 Explanation Styles and Faithfulness

Previous work has proposed a variety of explanation styles and corresponding protocols for assessing their faithfulness to model behavior. A common style requires models to produce self-explanations consisting of input words identified as contributing to predictions (Atanasova et al., 2023; Huang et al., 2023; Madsen et al., 2024), while more free-form explanations have also been explored (Siegel et al., 2024). Another line of research adopts a counterfactual style, in which explanations take the form of sentences similar to the original input but intended to induce different predictions (Singh et al., 2024; Calderon and Reichart, 2025). In this setting, faithfulness can be evaluated by checking whether the generated counterfactuals indeed produce the prediction change.

We focus on three styles of self-explanations, namely attribution, redaction, and counterfactual, and evaluate their faithfulness primarily through the self-consistency check protocol (Madsen et al.,

2024), as illustrated in Figure 1. We describe the details as follows:

Attribution In this style, the model lists input words that it considers important for its prediction, thereby simulating feature attribution methods. If the explanation is faithful, the listed words should have a substantial impact on the prediction being explained. Faithfulness is therefore assessed by examining whether the prediction changes when the listed words are removed from the original input. Following Madsen et al. (2024), we create such redacted inputs by automatically replacing the listed input words with the "[REDACTED]" tokens rather than deleting them, in order to preserve the grammatical structure.

Redaction In this style, the model directly generates a redacted version of the input in which the words it deems important for its prediction are replaced with "[REDACTED]". Unlike attribution, which requires the model to list important words, the redaction style requires the model to erase them while preserving the rest of the input sentence. We evaluate faithfulness by checking whether the model's prediction changes when it is given the redacted input sentence it produced.

Counterfactual This style requires the model to edit the input sentence such that the resulting sentence changes the model's original prediction. The model may add, remove, or replace input words, subject to editing-distance constraints specified in a prompt. To evaluate faithfulness, we feed the generated counterfactual sentences back into the model and test whether the predicted label changes accordingly.

It is important to note that these explanation styles differ substantially in their surface forms: whether a self-explanation is a sentence or a list of words, whether it involves adding new content beyond the original input, and whether it supports or contradicts the original prediction.

3 Training for Faithful Self-Explanations

Our goal is to analyze how training models with faithful self-explanations improves faithfulness and how these improvements generalize. We do not have access to the ground truth of truly faithful self-explanations as a principle (Jacovi and Goldberg, 2020); faithfulness is defined through the model's black-box behavior and evaluated by checking the consistency of generated self-explanations in a post-hoc manner. We therefore consider pseudo-faithful self-explanations that are more likely to be judged as faithful, rather than attempting to construct genuinely faithful ones. We first create datasets of pseudo-faithful self-explanations for each of the three styles, using influential words estimated via a feature attribution method. We then train models on these datasets in a continual learning setup and evaluate the effects using the faithfulness evaluation protocols for each style.

3.1 Training Dataset Construction

For all of our experiments, we construct training datasets of pseudo-faithful self-explanations using instruction-tuned Llama-2 (Touvron et al., 2023) models, specifically Tulu-2 (Ivison et al., 2023) 7B and 13B, and three classification tasks: Sentiment140 (Go et al., 2009), SNLI (Bowman et al., 2015), and AGNews[1]. We assume that faithful explanations, including attribution, redaction, and counterfactual styles, are generally expected to capture the causal influence of input words on model predictions. For this reason, we hypothesize that pseudo-faithful self-explanations can be constructed from the most influential input word identified by a feature attribution method.

Influential Word Estimation The influence of each input word is estimated using an erasure-based attribution method (Li et al., 2017). Let the input sentence be $x = (w_1, w_2, \ldots, w_m)$ and the model prediction be $\hat{y} = \arg\max_y p_\theta(y \mid x)$, where θ denotes the model. We compute the influence of an input word w on the prediction $\hat{y}$:

$$I_\theta(w \mid x) = p_\theta(\hat{y} \mid x) - p_\theta(\hat{y} \mid x_{-w}), \quad (1)$$

where x_{-w} is obtained by replacing w with the "[REDACTED]" token. We then identify the word w^* with the highest value as the most influential word on their prediction:

$$w^* = \arg\max_{w \in x} I_\theta(w \mid x). \quad (2)$$

Construction of Pseudo-Ground Truth Using the identified influential word w^*, we construct pseudo-ground truth of faithful self-explanations for each style. For all styles, we constrain the self-explanations to a one-word setting (Figure 1). The construction procedure is as follows:

[1] https://www.kaggle.com/datasets/amananandrai/ag-news-classification-dataset

User:	Text: {input x} What is the sentiment of text?
Assistant:	{model prediction $\hat{y}$}
User:	{self-explanation instruction for style S}
Assistant:	**{constructed self-explanation}**

Table 2: Template of the training data. The loss is computed solely from **the responses of self-explanations**.

- **Attribution**: The pseudo-ground truth self-explanation is simply the influential word w^* corresponding to the model's prediction $\hat{y}$ (e.g., `hate`).
- **Redaction**: The pseudo-ground truth self-explanation is the redacted input x_{-w^*}, created by replacing w^* with "[REDACTED]" (e.g., `I [REDACTED] waking up early.`).
- **Counterfactual**: The pseudo-ground truth self-explanation is constructed by replacing w^* with another word $w_{\bar{y}}$ associated with the second most probable prediction $\bar{y}$ (e.g., `I love waking up early.`). We obtain $w_{\bar{y}}$ by prompting the Tulu-2 models with the following instruction:

```
Redacted sentence: {x_{-w*}}
Replace "[REDACTED]" with exactly
one word that would make the
completed sentence very likely to
be predicted with the {ȳ}.
Output word:
```

We then convert the pseudo-ground truth self-explanations for each style into training examples using a template exemplified in Table 2. Self-explanation instructions follow the format shown in Figure 1, with additional details provided in Appendix B.

Our dataset construction procedure aims to generate pseudo-ground truth self-explanations that are more faithful than originally produced self-explanations, rather than attempting to obtain fully faithful explanations, which are unavailable. As shown in Table 3, we validate the quality of our constructed datasets by ensuring that the faithfulness scores (Section 3.3) of the training samples exceed those of the originally generated ones[2].

[2]The constructed self-explanations for the attribution and redaction styles are expected to yield the same faithfulness scores, as they are evaluated using the same redacted inputs.

	Attribution One-word	Redaction One-word	Counterfact One-word
Tulu-2 7B			
Original	0.124	0.124	0.186
Constructed	**0.342**	**0.342**	**0.331**
Tulu-2 13B			
Original	0.134	0.090	0.335
Constructed	**0.304**	**0.304**	**0.435**

Table 3: Comparison of faithfulness scores between self-explanations originally generated by the models and constructed ones included in the training dataset, each evaluated on 1,000 samples from Sentiment140.

3.2 Continual Learning

We train the Tulu-2 7B and 13B models using the constructed self-explanation datasets in a continual learning setting. Preventing catastrophic forgetting (Luo et al., 2023) is particularly important in our experiments, as the faithfulness evaluation and our analysis of generalization require the models to maintain performance on multiple tasks beyond the training setting. To mitigate forgetting, we mix the instruction-tuning data originally used for training the Tulu-2 models during continual learning (Scialom et al., 2022). We apply Low-Rank Adaptation (LoRA; Hu et al., 2021), training for one epoch with 50,000 samples from the constructed self-explanation dataset and 10,000 samples from the instruction-tuning data.

3.3 Evaluation

We evaluate the faithfulness of the models' self-explanations before and after training as the proportion of self-explanations judged faithful using the self-consistency check (Section 2). Specifically, we first collect the model's predictions on 5,000 samples that do not overlap with the training data, together with self-explanations for each style. For each style, we then edit the inputs according to the generated self-explanations and compute faithfulness as the proportion of cases in which the model's prediction changes.

We exclude instances that violate either the style condition or the number-of-word condition[3]. The style condition requires that self-explanations: (i) list only the input words in the attribution style, (ii) include the "[REDACTED]" tokens without altering the remaining input in the redaction style, and (iii) edit the input without using "[REDACTED]" tokens or the classification label itself (e.g., "Pos-

[3]The number of evaluation instances retained for each experiment is reported in Table 10

	Attribution One-word			Redaction One-word			Counterfactual One-word		
	Sent140	SNLI	AGNews	Sent140	SNLI	AGNews	Sent140	SNLI	AGNews
Tulu-2 7B									
No-Training	0.120	0.199	**0.248**	0.102	0.244	0.237	0.173	0.076	0.087
w/ Predictions	0.126	0.161	0.127	0.099	0.282	0.136	0.129	0.079	0.035
w/ Explanations	**0.300**	**0.457**	0.199	**0.271**	**0.355**	**0.323**	**0.241**	**0.170**	**0.249**
Tulu-2 13B									
No-Training	0.140	0.177	0.185	0.110	0.317	0.149	0.303	**0.243**	0.049
w/ Predictions	0.141	0.182	0.099	0.080	**0.335**	0.077	0.270	0.216	0.027
w/ Explanations	**0.255**	**0.299**	**0.281**	**0.204**	0.306	**0.265**	**0.595**	0.192	**0.417**

Table 4: Faithfulness scores, measured as the proportion of faithful self-explanations (Section 3.3) before and after training. "No-Training" refers to the off-the-shelf model before training, "w/ Predictions" refers to models trained with ground-truth predictions for the classification tasks, and "w/ Explanations" refers to models trained with the constructed pseudo-faithful self-explanations for each style conditioned on their own predictions.

itive") in the counterfactual style. Because the prompts explicitly instructed the models to satisfy these requirements, violations indicate failures in instruction following rather than evidence of unfaithfulness. The number-of-word condition retains only the self-explanations in which the model lists N words in the attribution style, redacts N words in the redaction style, and modifies the input with an edit distance of N in the counterfactual style ($N = 1, 2, 3, 4, 5$). This condition ensures fair comparison; for example, if a model lists, redacts, or edits an excessively large number of words in its self-explanation, it may be judged faithful in an unfair manner. We set $N = 1$ in most experiments, instructing the model to produce one-word constrained self-explanations for each style to match the training setup. In Section 4.2, we also evaluate faithfulness for $N = 2, 3, 4, 5$ in a generalized multi-word setting, using prompts that instruct the model to list, redact, or edit any number of input words for each style.

4 Results

4.1 Training Effects

We first examine the interpolation effects of training by evaluating the faithfulness of the models before and after training under the same settings used during training. In addition to the off-the-shelf models, we include a baseline in which models are trained using the ground-truth predictions for the classification tasks.

Table 4 shows that models trained with the constructed self-explanation datasets produce more faithful self-explanations than the off-the-shelf models in most settings. For example, the 13B models trained with self-explanations improve by 0.115, 0.094, and 0.292 points in the attribution,

	Attribution Multi-word	Redaction Multi-word	Counterfactual Multi-word
Tulu-2 7B			
No Training	0.216	0.074	**0.246**
w/ Explanations	**0.451**	**0.154**	0.231
Tulu-2 13B			
No Training	0.234	0.125	0.345
w/ Explanations	**0.435**	**0.174**	**0.497**

Table 5: Faithfulness scores for the Sentiment140 dataset in the unconstrained multi-word setting. "w/ Explanations" models are trained using one-word constrained self-explanations for each style.

redaction, and counterfactual styles, respectively, on the sentiment analysis task (Sentiment140). These results empirically confirm that training with pseudo-faithful self-explanations can enhance self-explanation faithfulness, even without access to true "ground-truth" faithful explanations.

By contrast, models trained with the ground-truth predictions for the classification tasks often show improvements of less than 0.01 or even a decrease in self-explanation faithfulness. This demonstrates that faithfulness is improved specifically by training on the constructed self-explanations conditioned on the models' own predictions, rather than by training on ground-truth predictions for the classification tasks[4].

4.2 Generalization to Multi-Word Setting

During training, the models learn to generate self-explanations in the one-word setting, where they are permitted to list, redact, or edit only a single input word. However, self-explanations in practice are not necessarily restricted to a single word, since interactions among multiple words may be

[4]The performance on the classification task is reported in Appendix D, and is not significantly changed after training.

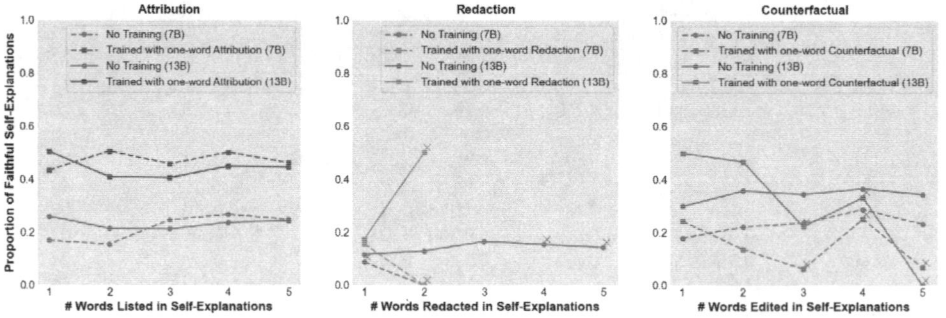

Figure 2: Evaluation of the generalization to the multi-word setting (Section 4.2) on the Sentiment140 dataset. We report the proportion of faithful self-explanations for each number of words that are used in the self-explanations for each style. Data plots marked with "×" indicate that the number of evaluation instances is less than 50.

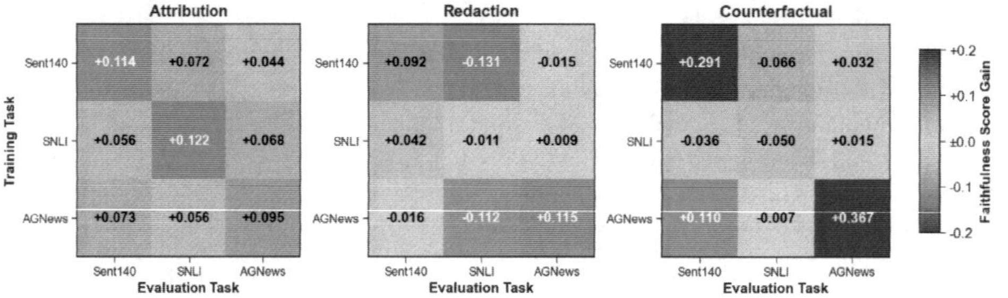

Figure 3: Evaluation of the generalization across different classification tasks. For each training-evaluation task pair, we measure the faithfulness score gain before and after training with self-explanations, defined as the increase or decrease in the proportion of faithful self-explanations. Results are reported using the Tulu-2 13B model.

required to express certain meanings. We therefore introduce a multi-word setting using prompts that permit the model to use any number of words in its self-explanations, rather than enforcing a one-word constraint, as illustrated below:

```
List all and only the most
important words for determining the
sentiment.
```

We focus on the Sentiment140 dataset because the trained models consistently exhibit improvements across all three styles on this dataset.

We first measure faithfulness as the proportion of self-explanations that are judged as faithful (Section 2) and satisfy the style condition, while removing the number-of-word condition (Section 3.3). As shown in Table 5, the models trained with one-word self-explanations achieve higher faithfulness scores even when multi-word self-explanations are allowed. This suggests that their advantage is maintained beyond the one-word setting.

We further examine whether improvements in faithfulness occur for each word count that the model lists, redacts, or edits in its explanations ($N = 1, 2, 3, 4, 5$). Specifically, we group self-explanations by the number of words listed, redacted, or edited for each style, and compute the proportion of faithful self-explanations within each group. Figure 2 shows that, only in the attribution style, models trained with one-word self-explanations consistently generate more faithful explanations across different numbers of used words. These findings indicate that generalization to multi-word settings depends on the style and may emerge exclusively in the attribution style.

4.3 Generalization across Classification Tasks

We have observed that, for a given classification task, training improves the faithfulness of the model's self-explanations for each style. A natural question is whether such training also improves faithfulness on unseen classification tasks.

Figure 3 reports the gains in faithfulness scores relative to the off-the-shelf models, evaluated across different combinations of training and evaluation tasks. We find consistent faithfulness improvements in the attribution style: for example,

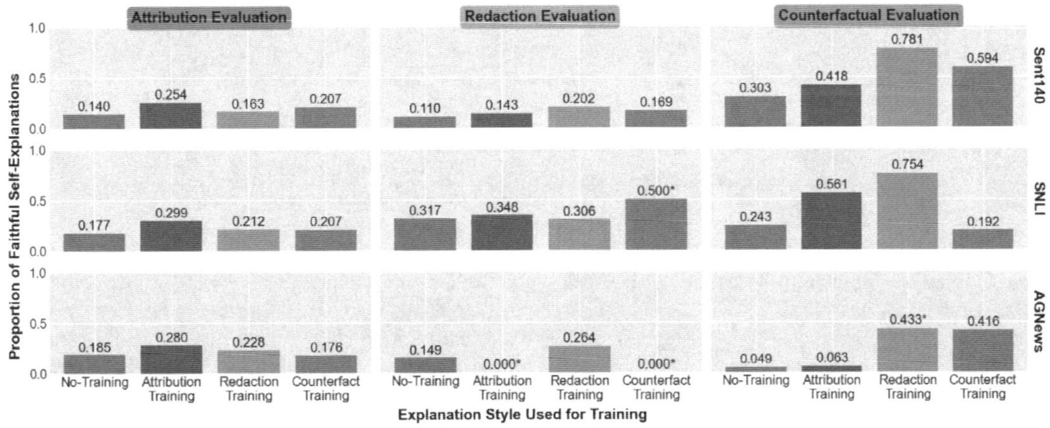

Figure 4: Evaluation of generalization across explanation styles. Each value represents the faithfulness score obtained under a given evaluation style, and each training condition specifies the explanation style used for training. Values marked with "*" indicate that the number of evaluation instances is less than 50. Results are reported using the Tulu-2 13B model.

models trained with attribution-style explanations on the Sentiment140 dataset achieve increases of 0.072 points on SNLI and 0.044 points on AGNews. In contrast, under the redaction and counterfactual styles, the models struggle to generate faithful self-explanations for unseen classification tasks. These results indicate that, mirroring the trend observed in the multi-word setting, whether the training effects generalize across classification tasks depends on the explanation style; generalization is most reliably observed in the attribution style.

4.4 Generalization across Explanation Styles

We have examined the effects of training and its generalization within each explanation style. We next investigate whether training generalizes across explanation styles. Such cross-style generalization is practically important, as real-world explanation styles are often more diverse and more free-form than those included in our experiments.

We evaluate self-explanation faithfulness using styles that the models did not encounter during training. As before, faithfulness is measured as the proportion of self-explanations that are judged faithful and that satisfy the conditions; for instance, if a model trained on the redaction style produces a self-explanation containing the "[REDACTED]" token in the counterfactual style, that instance is excluded because it violates the prompt instructions.

Figure 4 shows the proportion of faithful self-explanations for each training–evaluation style pair, comparing the results before and after training. We observe improvements in faithfulness even when the training and evaluation styles differ. For instance, on the Sentiment140 dataset (top row), models trained using attribution-style explanations (blue bars) generate more faithful self-explanations than the untrained models (black bars) even when evaluated using the redaction or counterfactual styles, which were unseen during training. These improvements are notable given that the attribution style requires the model to output input words that support their predictions, whereas the redaction and counterfactual styles require the model to generate sentences that contradict them. This suggests that the training effects can transfer across different styles, rather than being confined to the style used during training.

5 Discussion

We observe that the improvements from training can generalize across classification tasks and across explanation styles. However, one might suspect that models simply acquire heuristics tailored to the evaluation protocol and therefore behave consistently across different evaluation settings. Although a truly faithful self-explanation cannot be predefined in principle, trained models are not expected to produce self-explanations in a uniform manner across conditions, even when these explanations are judged as faithful. This raises a question: do the trained models rely on fixed heuristics regardless of the setting, or do they acquire a more general capability for generating faithful explanations across different conditions?

Explanation Style	Classification Task	Top-10 Frequent Words in Faithful Self-Explanations
Attribution	Sentiment140	not, no, good, don't, miss, hate, sad, can't, love, bad
Attribution	AGNews	Iraq, Afghan, Arafat, Iran, Oracle, Putin, Google, Baghdad, Microsoft, Stocks
Counterfactual	Sentiment140	DELETION*, happy, hate, good, bad, love, terrible, worse, great

Table 6: Examples of the most frequent words appearing in faithful self-explanations for each setting, generated by the Tulu-2 13B model trained with attribution-style self-explanations on the Sentiment140 dataset. For the counterfactual style, the listed words correspond to words replaced or added relative to the original input, and "DELETION*" indicates that a certain word is removed from the input.

To answer this question, we qualitatively analyze the generated self-explanations that are judged as faithful during evaluation. Table 6 reports the lemmatized words generated in self-explanations from the Tulu-2 13B model trained with attribution-style explanations on the sentiment analysis task (Sentiment140). In the training setting of attribution-style explanations for sentiment analysis, the model tends to generate negation expressions (e.g., "no", "can't"), as well as words associated with emotions (e.g., "hate", "love"). In self-explanations for the unseen topic classification task (AGNews), however, the same model generates different types of words, including proper nouns (e.g., "Iraq", "Google") and business words (e.g., "Stocks"). We also observe such vocabulary differences across explanation styles. In unseen counterfactual-style explanations for sentiment analysis, the model frequently produces sentiment-bearing words (e.g., "hate", "terrible") as expected; however, it does not use negation expressions, which are common in the attribution-style setting used during training. These observations may suggest that the models after training could generate faithful self-explanations generally to the given classification tasks and styles, rather than depending on fixed heuristics tailored to the evaluation protocol of the training style.

6 Related Work

Researchers have investigated how faithfully the intermediate reasoning chains generated by LLMs reflect their final decisions under Chain-of-Thought prompting (Turpin et al., 2023; Chen et al., 2025). In evaluations of CoT faithfulness, prior work introduces typical forms of bias that alter the model's prediction, such as inserting phrases like "I think the answer is (A)," and shows that the resulting CoT reasoning steps often fail to reflect these inserted biases (Turpin et al., 2023; Matton and Kiciman, 2024). Recent studies have suggested that reasoning models, which are trained via reinforcement learning to improve general CoT performance, exhibit higher CoT faithfulness than non-reasoning models, though there remains room for improvement. (Chen et al., 2025; Chua and Evans, 2025).

Our study focuses on three explanation styles other than CoT and examines both the training effects and their generalization when using supervised signals explicitly designed to promote faithful self-explanations. It is worth noting that constructing pseudo-faithful CoT reasoning steps is inherently difficult, because each intermediate reasoning step must influence subsequent steps as well as the final prediction.

7 Conclusion

We investigated how training affects the faithfulness of LLM self-explanations and the extent to which these effects generalize. To address the lack of access to truly faithful explanations, we constructed pseudo-ground truth data of faithful self-explanations under a one-word constrained setting using an attribution method. Our experiments demonstrated that training generally improves self-explanation faithfulness across classification tasks and explanation styles. We further found evidence that these improvements can generalize to the unconstrained multi-word setting and to unseen classification tasks. In addition, we observed consistent cross-style generalization, indicating that the benefits of training extend beyond individual explanation styles. We believe that our findings on faithfulness contribute to advancing the understanding and improvement of LLM trustworthiness.

Limitations

The training procedure in our experiments requires access to the trained model's instruction-tuning data. This requirement limits the applicability of similar investigations to models for which such training data is publicly available. Although we incorporate multiple classification tasks commonly used in the faithfulness evaluation literature, the scope of tasks remains limited, excluding more complex settings such as generative tasks. Moreover, our training and evaluation primarily focus on simple explanations involving single-word operations, with existing but only limited assessment of generalization to more complex, freer-format setups. Finally, as our primary scope is the evaluation of self-explanation faithfulness, we leave other evaluation perspectives for future work, particularly examining whether the observed improvements contribute to human-centered explainability, such as simulatability (Hase and Bansal, 2020).

Ethics Statement

Although our procedures for constructing the self-explanation dataset do not involve any explicit gender bias or abusive language, there remains the possibility that such biases could be inherited from the models or datasets used in our experiments. We caution that users of LLMs should not place unwarranted trust in a model's self-explanations without careful consideration, regardless of whether the model was trained following our procedures. We hope that this work will contribute to future research aimed at analyzing and enhancing the trustworthiness of LLMs, thereby supporting sound and responsible human decision-making.

Acknowledgements

We thank the three anonymous reviewers for their helpful comments and feedback. This work was partially supported by JSPS KAKENHI Grant Number JP24H00809, JST BOOST Grant Number JPMJBY24H5, and JST SPRING Grant Number JPMJSP2108.

References

Pepa Atanasova, Oana-Maria Camburu, Christina Lioma, Thomas Lukasiewicz, Jakob Grue Simonsen, and Isabelle Augenstein. 2023. Faithfulness tests for natural language explanations. In *Proceedings of the 61st Annual Meeting of the Association for Computational Linguistics (Volume 2: Short Papers)*, pages 283–294, Toronto, Canada. Association for Computational Linguistics.

Steven Bird, Ewan Klein, and Edward Loper. 2009. *Natural language processing with Python: analyzing text with the natural language toolkit.* " O'Reilly Media, Inc.".

Samuel R. Bowman, Gabor Angeli, Christopher Potts, and Christopher D. Manning. 2015. A large annotated corpus for learning natural language inference. In *Proceedings of the 2015 Conference on Empirical Methods in Natural Language Processing*, pages 632–642, Lisbon, Portugal. Association for Computational Linguistics.

Nitay Calderon and Roi Reichart. 2025. On behalf of the stakeholders: Trends in NLP model interpretability in the era of llms. In *Proceedings of the 2025 Conference of the Nations of the Americas Chapter of the Association for Computational Linguistics: Human Language Technologies, NAACL 2025 - Volume 1: Long Papers, Albuquerque, New Mexico, USA, April 29 - May 4, 2025*, pages 656–693. Association for Computational Linguistics.

Yanda Chen, Joe Benton, Ansh Radhakrishnan, Jonathan Uesato, Carson Denison, John Schulman, Arushi Somani, Peter Hase, Misha Wagner, Fabien Roger, Vlad Mikulik, Samuel R. Bowman, Jan Leike, Jared Kaplan, and Ethan Perez. 2025. Reasoning models don't always say what they think. *Computing Research Repository*, arXiv:2505.05410. Version 1.

James Chua and Owain Evans. 2025. Are deepseek r1 and other reasoning models more faithful? *Computing Research Repository*, arXiv:2501.08156. Version 5.

Alec Go, Richa Bhayani, and Lei Huang. 2009. Twitter sentiment classification using distant supervision. *CS224N project report, Stanford*, 1(12):2009.

Peter Hase and Mohit Bansal. 2020. Evaluating explainable AI: Which algorithmic explanations help users predict model behavior? In *Proceedings of the 58th Annual Meeting of the Association for Computational Linguistics*, pages 5540–5552, Online. Association for Computational Linguistics.

Edward J. Hu, Yelong Shen, Phillip Wallis, Zeyuan Allen-Zhu, Yuanzhi Li, Shean Wang, Lu Wang, and Weizhu Chen. 2021. Lora: Low-rank adaptation of large language models. *arXiv preprint arXiv:2106.09685*.

Shiyuan Huang, Siddarth Mamidanna, Shreedhar Jangam, Yilun Zhou, and Leilani H. Gilpin. 2023. Can large language models explain themselves? a study of llm-generated self-explanations. *Computing Research Repository*, arXiv:2310.11207. Version 1.

Hamish Ivison, Yizhong Wang, Valentina Pyatkin, Nathan Lambert, Matthew Peters, Pradeep Dasigi, Joel Jang, David Wadden, Noah A. Smith, Iz Beltagy, and Hannaneh Hajishirzi. 2023. Camels in a changing climate: Enhancing lm adaptation with tulu 2. *arXiv preprint arXiv:2311.10702*.

Alon Jacovi and Yoav Goldberg. 2020. Towards faithfully interpretable NLP systems: How should we define and evaluate faithfulness? In *Proceedings of the 58th Annual Meeting of the Association for Computational Linguistics*, pages 4198–4205, Online. Association for Computational Linguistics.

Jiwei Li, Will Monroe, and Dan Jurafsky. 2017. Understanding neural networks through representation erasure. *Computing Research Repository*, arXiv:1612.08220. Version 3.

Yun Luo, Zhen Yang, Fandong Meng, Yafu Li, Jie Zhou, and Yue Zhang. 2023. An empirical study of catastrophic forgetting in large language models during continual fine-tuning. *arXiv preprint arXiv:2308.08747*.

Andreas Madsen, Sarath Chandar, and Siva Reddy. 2024. Are self-explanations from large language models faithful? In *Findings of the Association for Computational Linguistics: ACL 2024*, pages 295–337, Bangkok, Thailand. Association for Computational Linguistics.

Katie Matton and Robert Ness & Emre Kiciman. 2024. Walk the talk? measuring the faithfulness of large language model explanations. In *ICLR 2024 Workshop on Secure and Trustworthy Large Language Models*.

Adam Paszke, Sam Gross, Francisco Massa, Adam Lerer, James Bradbury, Gregory Chanan, Trevor Killeen, Zeming Lin, Natalia Gimelshein, Luca Antiga, Alban Desmaison, Andreas Köpf, Edward Yang, Zach DeVito, Martin Raison, Alykhan Tejani, Sasank Chilamkurthy, Benoit Steiner, Lu Fang, and 2 others. 2019. Pytorch: an imperative style, high-performance deep learning library. In *Proceedings of the 33rd International Conference on Neural Information Processing Systems*, Red Hook, NY, USA. Curran Associates Inc.

Thomas Scialom, Tuhin Chakrabarty, and Smaranda Muresan. 2022. Fine-tuned language models are continual learners. In *Proceedings of the 2022 Conference on Empirical Methods in Natural Language Processing*, pages 6107–6122, Abu Dhabi, United Arab Emirates. Association for Computational Linguistics.

Noah Siegel, Oana-Maria Camburu, Nicolas Heess, and Maria Perez-Ortiz. 2024. The probabilities also matter: A more faithful metric for faithfulness of free-text explanations in large language models. In *Proceedings of the 62nd Annual Meeting of the Association for Computational Linguistics (Volume 2: Short Papers)*, pages 530–546, Bangkok, Thailand. Association for Computational Linguistics.

Chandan Singh, Jeevana Priya Inala, Michel Galley, Rich Caruana, and Jianfeng Gao. 2024. Rethinking interpretability in the era of large language models. Version 1.

Hugo Touvron, Louis Martin, Kevin Stone, Peter Albert, Amjad Almahairi, Yasmine Babaei, Nikolay Bashlykov, Soumya Batra, Prajjwal Bhargava, Shruti Bhosale, Dan Bikel, Lukas Blecher, Cristian Canton Ferrer, Moya Chen, Guillem Cucurull, David Esiobu, Jude Fernandes, Jeremy Fu, Wenyin Fu, and 49 others. 2023. Llama 2: Open foundation and fine-tuned chat models. *arXiv preprint arXiv:2307.09288*.

Miles Turpin, Julian Michael, Ethan Perez, and Samuel Bowman. 2023. Language models don't always say what they think: Unfaithful explanations in chain-of-thought prompting. In *Advances in Neural Information Processing Systems*.

Thomas Wolf, Lysandre Debut, Victor Sanh, Julien Chaumond, Clement Delangue, Anthony Moi, Pierric Cistac, Tim Rault, Remi Louf, Morgan Funtowicz, Joe Davison, Sam Shleifer, Patrick von Platen, Clara Ma, Yacine Jernite, Julien Plu, Canwen Xu, Teven Le Scao, Sylvain Gugger, and 3 others. 2020. Transformers: State-of-the-art natural language processing. In *Proceedings of the 2020 Conference on Empirical Methods in Natural Language Processing: System Demonstrations*, pages 38–45, Online. Association for Computational Linguistics.

A Dataset

We employ three classification datasets in Table 8: Sentiment140 for the binary sentiment analysis, SNLI for the ternary NLI task, and AGNews for the quaternary topic classification. For our experiments, we sample almost 50,000 examples for training and nearly 5,000 samples for evaluation from each dataset, ensuring that the class labels are balanced. The statistics of these examples are shown in Table 9.

B Prompt

We present prompt templates for classification and self-explanation tasks on Sentiment140 in Table 11, and those for SNLI and AGNews in Table 12. Although all prompt designs largely follow those introduced by Madsen et al. (2024), we include additional instructions for the response format in the self-explanation tasks, such as "one word following Answer:" and "answer in JSON format." The Tulu-2 models sufficiently adhere to these format instructions in the experiments, enabling a fair evaluation of their performance in the self-explanation task without major formatting issues.

In Table 13, we show the prompts used for obtaining the word $w_{\bar{y}}$, which is expected to be associated with the second probable prediction $\bar{y}$, to construct the counterfactual self-explanation datasets. The instruction includes prohibiting the use of the prediction label itself or the "[REDACTED]" token, to prevent a skeptical shortcut for the counterfactual self-explanations. We also automatically filter out such instances to ensure exclusion.

C Hyperparamters

For text generation, the temperature is set to 0, and the number of beam searches is 1, enabling the Tulu-2 models to generate tokens one by one in a deterministic greedy manner. This setting ensures reproducibility without any randomness; we conduct the experiments only once. For continual learning, we mainly adopt the setting used for instruction tuning with LoRA in the Tulu-2 models. Specifically, the learning rate is set to 1e-4, the LoRA rank is set to 64, the value of α is set to 16, and the dropout rate is set to 0.1. All attention layers are designated as trainable modules, and the model is trained for one epoch.

	Sent140	SNLI	AGNews
Tulu-2 7B			
No Training	0.737	0.760	0.750
w/ Predictions	**0.896**	**0.911**	**0.904**
w/ Attribution	0.804	0.685	0.532
w/ Redaction	0.780	0.706	0.743
w/ Counterfactual	0.700	0.740	0.634
Tulu-2 13B			
No Training	0.712	0.814	0.815
w/ Predictions	**0.901**	**0.918**	**0.905**
w/ Attribution	0.788	0.653	0.597
w/ Redaction	0.773	0.703	0.807
w/ Counterfactual	0.795	0.698	0.818
Chance Rate	0.500	0.333	0.250

Table 7: Classification accuracy before and after training. "No-Training" and "w/ Predictions" refer to the off-the-shelf models and those trained with ground-truth predictions, respectively. "w/ Attribution", "w/ Redaction" and "w/ Counterfactual" refer to models trained with self-explanations constructed for each style.

D Classification Task Performance

Before evaluating self-explanation faithfulness, we validate whether the models used in the experiments could perform a classification task, for which they are required to generate self-explanations.

Table 7 reports classification accuracy of the models before and after training, including those trained with the ground-truth predictions introduced in Section 4.1. The off-the-shelf Tulu-2 models score around $0.7 \sim 0.8$, while the prediction-trained models perform the best as expected, scoring around 0.9. As for the models after training with the constructed self-explanations, we do not observe a significant drop in their prediction accuracies regardless of style, maintaining their classification performances sufficiently for faithfulness evaluation without serious catastrophic forgetting.

E Implementation Details

We implemented the codes for the experiments using Python v3.10.12, Py-Torch v2.5.1 (Paszke et al., 2019), and Transformers v4.44.2 (Wolf et al., 2020). For word lemmatization, we used NLTK v3.9.1 (Bird et al., 2009). Our study was conducted under the licenses and terms of the scientific artifacts.

We conducted the experiments with eight NVIDIA A100 (40GB) GPUs for dataset construction and training, and a single NVIDIA A100 (40GB) GPU for evaluation. The construction of training datasets took approximately 21 GPU hours with Tulu-2 7B, and 30 GPU hours with Tulu-2

13B. Training with instruction-tuning data combined with either ground-truth prediction responses or a self-explanation dataset takes approximately 8.19 GPU hours for Tulu-2 7B and 12.9 GPU hours for Tulu-2 13B. Evaluation in each explanation style takes approximately 0,02 GPU hours for Tulu-2 7B, and 0.03 GPU hours for Tulu-2 13B, regardless of whether the model has been trained or not.

	Input	Second Input	Ground Truth Predicton
Sentiment140	@cocodkr Not even superman can save me now	-	Positive Negative ✓
SNLI	A fisherman using a cellphone on a boat.	A fisherman is sleeping on his boat.	Entailment Contradiction ✓ Neutral
AGNews	Next space station crew to launch	-	World politics Sports Business Science and technology ✓

Table 8: Examples of each prediction dataset. "Input" refers to social networking posts in Sentiment140, premise sentences in SNLI, and news titles in AGNews, respectively. SNLI also includes hypothesis sentences as the second input.

	Split	# of Examples	Input Avg. Length	Second Input Avg. Length
Sentiment140	Train	50,000	13.17	-
	Test	5,000	13.09	-
SNLI	Train	49,998	12.84	7.43
	Test	4,998	13.88	7.53
AGNews	Train	50,000	6.78	-
	Test	5,000	6.76	-

Table 9: Statistics of the classification datasets used for our experiments.

	Attribution			Redaction			Counterfactual		
	Sent140	SNLI	AGNews	Sent140	SNLI	AGNews	Sent140	SNLI	AGNews
No Training	4600	4925	4528	886	1330	1743	529	659	691
w/ Explanations	4952	4992	4980	4706	4984	4978	4215	4834	4895

(a) Tulu-2 7B

		Attribution			Redaction			Counterfactual		
		Sent140	SNLI	AGNews	Sent140	SNLI	AGNews	Sent140	SNLI	AGNews
No Training	No Training	4618	4865	4204	1291	685	2743	1072	536	1094
w/ Attribution	Sent140	4964	4773	4908	175	-	-	1069	-	-
	SNLI	4861	4991	4901	-	1382	-	-	783	-
	AGNews	4927	4971	4978	-	-	1	-	-	622
w/ Redaction	Sent140	3293	-	-	4719	3454	4599	96	-	-
	SNLI	-	3371	-	4032	4983	4443	-	410	-
	AGNews	-	-	4776	4197	4589	4972	-	-	30
w/ Counterfactual	Sent140	4793	-	-	617	-	-	4516	1579	3272
	SNLI	-	4266	-	-	46	-	2096	4874	2254
	AGNews	-	-	4683	-	-	1	3200	1253	4867

(b) Tulu-2 13B

Table 10: The number of evaluation instances used for faithfulness assessment of Tulu-2 7B and 13B. Instances in which generated self-explanations did not meet the requirements specified in the prompts were excluded from evaluation (see Section 3.3).

Dataset	Task	Prompt
Sentiment140	Classification	Text: {input}\n\n Question: What would you classify the sentiment of the text as? The text can contain redacted words marked with [REDACTED]. Answer either ‘Positive’ or ‘Negative’ in a single word. Do not explain the answer.
	Attribution (one-word)	Question: List the single most important word for determining the sentiment of the text, such that without this word the sentiment cannot be determined. Answer one word following ‘Answer:’. Do not explain the answer.
	Attribution (multi-word)	Question: List all and only the most important words for determining the sentiment of the text, such that without these words the sentiment cannot be determined. Answer in JSON format as {“words”: [“word1”, “word2”, ..., “wordN”]}.
	Redaction (one-word)	Question: Redact one word in the text by replacing the single most important word for determining the sentiment with ’[REDACTED]’. Answer with the new redacted text following ’Answer:’. Do not explain your answer.
	Redaction (multi-word)	Question: Replace all and only the most important words in the text with ’[REDACTED]’, such as changing “AAA BBB CCC” into “AAA [REDACTED] [REDACTED]”. Answer in JSON format as {“redacted_text”: “<text with words replaced by [REDACTED]>”}.
	Counterfactual (one-word)	Question: Edit the text by adding, removing, or replacing a single word so that the predicted sentiment changes from the current one. Do not use either ’[REDACTED]’ or the sentiment label itself. Answer with the new edited text following ’Answer:’. Do not explain your answer.
	Counterfactual (multi-word)	Question: Edit the text by adding, removing, or replacing words, making sure to change all and only the words necessary so that the predicted sentiment changes from the current one. Do not use either ’[REDACTED]’ or the sentiment label itself. Answer in JSON format as {“edited_text”: “<text with exactly two words edited>”}

Table 11: Prompt templates we use for Sentiment140 in the experiments. The placeholders of {input} is replaced with the appropriate strings for each instance.

Dataset	Task	Prompt
SNLI	Classification	Sentence: {input}\n\n Question: Does this sentence imply that '{second input}'? The sentence can contain redacted words marked with [REDACTED]. Answer either 'Yes', 'No', or 'Maybe' in a single word. Do not explain the answer.
	Attribution (one-word)	Question: List the single most important word in the sentence, for determining the implication. Answer one word following 'Answer:'. Do not explain the answer.
	Redaction (one-word)	Question: Redact one word in the sentence by replacing the single most important word for determining whether it entails '{second input}' with '[REDACTED]'. Answer with the new redacted sentence following 'Answer:'. Do not explain your answer.
	Counterfactual (one-word)	Question: Edit the sentence by adding, removing, or replacing a single word so that the predicted NLI relationship to '{second input}' changes from the current one. Do not use either '[REDACTED]' or the NLI label itself. Answer with the new edited sentence following 'Answer:'. Do not explain your answer.
AGnews	Classification	Title: {input}\n\n Question: What label best describes this news title? The title can contain redacted words marked with [REDACTED]. Respond with one of the following single words: 'World', 'Sport', 'Business', or 'Tech'. Do not explain the answer.
	Attribution (one-word)	Question: List the single most important word in the title for determining its topic label. Answer one word following 'Answer:'. Do not explain the answer.
	Redaction (one-word)	Question: Redact one word in the title by replacing the single most important word for determining the topic label with '[REDACTED]'. Answer with the new redacted title following 'Answer:'. Do not explain your answer.
	Counterfactual (one-word)	Question: Edit the title by adding, removing, or replacing a single word so that the predicted topic label changes from the current one. Do not use either '[REDACTED]' or the topic label itself. Answer with the new edited title following 'Answer:'. Do not explain your answer.

Table 12: Prompt templates we use for SNLI and AGNews in the experiments. The placeholders of {input} and {second input} are replaced with the appropriate strings for each instance.

Dataset	Prompt
Sentiment140	You are given an English sentence with one redacted part, represented as [REDACTED], and a target sentiment prediction ('Positive' or 'Negative'). Replace [REDACTED] with exactly one word that would make the completed sentence very likely to be predicted with the target sentiment. Keep the sentence natural and fluent, do not mention the sentiment label itself. Output only the replacement word. Do not explain the answer.\n\nSentence with redaction: {redacted_input}\nTarget label: {target_label}\nOutput word:
SNLI	You are given a premise–hypothesis pair in English. The premise contains one redacted part, represented as [REDACTED], and a target NLI prediction ('Yes,' 'No,' or 'Maybe'). Replace [REDACTED] with exactly one word that would make the completed premise–hypothesis pair very likely to be predicted with the target answer. Keep both sentences natural and fluent, and do not mention the answer itself. Output only the replacement word. Do not explain the answer.\n\nPremise with redaction: {redacted_input}\nHypothesis: {second_input}\nTarget label: {target_label}\nOutput word:
AGNews	You are given an English news title with one redacted part, represented as [REDACTED], and a target topic prediction ('World', 'Sport', 'Business', or 'Tech'). Replace [REDACTED] with exactly one word that would make the completed title very likely to be predicted with the target topic. Keep the title natural and fluent, and do not mention the topic label itself. Output only the replacement word. Do not explain the answer.\n\nTitle with redaction: {redacted_input}\nTarget label: {target_label}\nOutput word:

Table 13: Prompt templates we use for obtaining the word $w_{\bar{y}}$ during the construction of the counterfactual self-explanation datasets. The placeholders of {redacted_input} and {target_label} are replaced with the appropriate strings of the redacted input x_{-w*} and $\bar{y}$, respectively, for each instance. In SNLI, {second_input} is also replaced with adequate strings for each instance. See Section 3 for the details.

Thesis Proposal: Efficient Methods for Natural Language Generation/Understanding Systems

Nalin Kumar
Charles University, Faculty of Mathematics and Physics
Institute of Formal and Applied Linguistics
Prague, Czechia
nkumar@ufal.mff.cuni.cz

Abstract

While Large Language Models (LLMs) have shown remarkable performance in various Natural Language Processing (NLP) tasks, their effectiveness seems to be heavily biased toward high-resource languages. This proposal aims to address this gap by developing efficient training strategies for low-resource languages. We propose various techniques for efficient learning in simulated low-resource settings for English. We then plan to adapt these methods for low-resource languages. We plan to experiment with both natural language generation and understanding models. We evaluate the models on similar benchmarks as the BabyLM challenge for English. For other languages, we plan to use treebanks and translation techniques to create our own silver test set to evaluate the low-resource LMs.

1 Introduction

General-purpose Large Language Models (LLMs) have shown exceptional performance in various Natural Language Processing (NLP) tasks (Achiam et al., 2023; Team et al., 2023; Dubey et al., 2024; Team et al., 2024). This is made possible using an extensive amount of data and computational resources to train the model, and then further finetuning or prompt tuning on the specific task. However, many such models have huge numbers of parameters and are closed-source (FitzGerald et al., 2022; Li et al., 2024). To counter this, many open-source LLMs have been released with comparable performance. However, the performance of current LLMs has largely been restricted to high-resource languages, even more so only for English, as they are predominantly trained on English and other high-resource languages (Li et al., 2024).

The availability of an adequate pretraining dataset plays the most important role in developing any LLM. Cleaning and processing web-crawled data is a common way of getting monolingual and parallel datasets (Conneau et al., 2020; De Gibert et al., 2024; Tiedemann, 2009). However, getting such data can be quite challenging for languages with minimal web presence, especially for a specific domain or task. Recent works alleviate the issue by creating synthetic data using zero-shot NMT systems. These works mainly involve using English as a pivot language and transferring the knowledge to the target language. Although there tends to be a performance improvement using such noisy data in contrast to a zero-shot setting, the models' applicability is still debatable (Maheshwari et al., 2024) simply due to the lack of ground truth. To counter this, various challenges have been organized (Cripwell et al., 2023). There has also been an effort to create linguistically rich datasets (Nivre et al., 2016). However, creating such corpora is too costly, which limits the amount of available data instances. Consequently, challenges such as BabyLM (Warstadt et al., 2023) focus on efficient training with the least training instances but are English-only.

Thesis objectives The performance of the current LLMs is mainly limited to high- and moderate-resource languages. The primary objective is to develop new methods for training models for low-resource languages. To achieve this, we will develop general approaches to training LLMs in a low-resource setting, which will first be tested on English for ease of evaluation. We will then work on exploring ways to transfer the data knowledge and tuning strategies to any low-resource language. The thesis will cover both theoretical and experimental aspects of the problem while keeping the solutions linguistically oriented. The secondary goal of this thesis is to release data and produce models for several languages. Using the thesis output, we can work on various NLP tasks for non-English languages. The contribution of this thesis will be three-fold: (1) we will develop efficient pretraining

Proceedings of the IJCNLP-AACL 2025 Student Research Workshop, pages 209–217
December 20-24, 2025 ©2025 Association for Computational Linguistics

strategies with limited data, (2) we will release the intermediate synthetic silver data, and (3) we will release the created models.

Thesis Structure The thesis is structured into two main halves. The first half is focused on experiments with English in a low-resource setting (Section 3.1). We propose various approaches suitable for low-resource language modeling. We will evaluate these approaches based on the evaluation metrics used by the BabyLM challenge. These approaches will then be adapted to actual low-resource languages, which constitute the other half. One major challenge is finding ways to evaluate such LMs. We use state-of-the-art NMT systems and existing dataset resources to tackle it. We discuss more about the datasets and evaluation in Section 4. We finally conclude the proposal in Section 5.

Research Questions To summarize we aim to answer our following primary research questions:

- How can we design efficient pretraining strategies that maximize performance with minimal data for low-resource languages?
- Can modular approaches be shown to work better than end-to-end training? How significant a role do the embeddings play?
- Does introducing semantics and syntax knowledge separately help with model training?
- Does delexicalized pretraining improve robustness to sparsity in named entities and rare words?
- How effective are Reinforcement Learning from Human Feedback (RLHF) methods in aligning outputs with human preferences when training data is scarce?

2 Background

2.1 Token Representation

The efficiency of token-level representation plays a significant role in model's performance. Since languages have different scripts, converting them to a common script can make the representation more efficient. There have been various works to study the effectiveness of transliteration in the context of low-resource languages. While transliteration can lead to loss of phonological and morphological accuracy along with other ambiguities, romanization of languages has been shown to improve cross-lingual alignment (Amrhein and Sennrich, 2020; Purkayastha et al., 2023; Liu et al., 2024), as the base models usually are primarily trained on Roman script. However, the performance of such methods is mainly dependent on the tasks, model size, and target languages (Ma et al., 2024).

2.2 Multilingual LLMs

Multilingual LLMs (MLLMs) are trained on almost all available data in various languages with the hypothesis that a deprived language would benefit from the cross-lingual transfer with the higher-resourced ones (Lin et al., 2024; Üstün et al., 2024). However, Wang et al. (2020) show a negative interference for both high and low-resource languages because of the presence of language-specific parameters. The sub-par performance of lower-resourced languages can mainly be attributed to the huge training data imbalance and inefficient vocabulary and tokenization. Consequently, monolingual models, or models trained on better-sampled data, often capture richer linguistic features, especially for lower-resourced languages (Feijo and Moreira, 2020; Xue et al., 2021; Armengol-Estapé et al., 2021; Huang et al., 2023). Furthermore, multilingual models may lack cultural awareness for the under-represented languages (Hämmerl et al., 2022; Zhang et al., 2024).

2.3 Vocabulary Extension

Another way to extrapolate the performance of higher-resourced languages is through vocabulary extension and further pretraining on specific languages. Zhao et al. (2024) show that further pretraining, or pre-finetuning, on merely 1% of the pretraining data for non-English significantly improves the performance. However, tuning the model parameters entirely on new data often leads to catastrophic forgetting (Luo et al., 2023). To alleviate the issue, Marchisio et al. (2023) considered extending the vocabulary and proposed data mixing strategies. Kim et al. (2024) shows that expanding vocabulary along with several steps of training strategies to tune the model parameters can efficiently improve the model performance on non-English languages. However, the improvement is often limited to closely related languages. As most of the current works on low-resource languages focus on cross-lingual transfer instead of efficient training strategies, we try to bridge this gap with our work by focusing more on the latter.

2.4 Instruction Tuning and RLHF

There have been numerous works that include instruction tuning and training on human feedback to generate outputs better aligned with human preference (Ouyang et al., 2022; Achiam et al., 2023; Touvron et al., 2023), the current multilingual setups are typically not instruction-tuned due to data scarcity, which limits their performance. Direct Preference Optimization (DPO) (Rafailov et al., 2024) is among the recent frameworks that optimize directly on user preference data without the need for a separate reward model. It has proved to be effective for high-resource languages, but its applicability to low-resource ones is still unknown.

3 Proposed Approaches

Following state-of-the-art approaches for LLM training, we will use the standard transformer architecture for our experiments while focusing primarily on data and training improvements. Specifically, we try to use the data more efficiently by leveraging linguistic annotation. We design our experiments in two steps: (1) we will first benchmark several methods on English, (2) we will transfer those strategies to low-resource languages. Additionally, we will also experiment with several other methods.

3.1 Experiments in English

For simpler evaluation, we will begin with working with the English language in a simulated low-resource setting. The primary goal is to optimize the amount of pretraining tokens used. Specifically, we will experiment with the following strategies for efficient training of English LMs:

1. **Curriculum Learning:** We will use various linguistic features to measure the complexity of the training instances and consequently feed the model simpler instances first, then gradually increase complexity (i.e. build the curriculum). This approach has widely been used in the submitted works at the BabyLM challenge (Chobey et al., 2023; Nguyen et al., 2024; Salhan et al., 2024; Saha et al., 2024). However, the majority of them only categorize the complexity on the dataset-level, due to which potential outliers can get overlooked, whereas in the thesis proposal, we plan to step up to a more fine-grained instance-level curriculum. Specifically, we calculate the complexity for each training instance on various linguistic levels, e.g., height/number of edges of the dependency tree, etc.

2. **Lexical learning using WordNet:** WordNet provides a hierarchical, lexically rich database of words and synonyms, enabling embedding training focused on word relationships. To boost the initial training stage of our models without using large-scale plain text data, we will first initialize the subword embeddings of the model using the WordNet embeddings as ground truth (Saedi et al., 2018). We then employ different strategies using the WordNet dataset to tune the embeddings further. For example, given a sentence, we replace one of the words using WordNet and further train the model to predict if the two sentences are similar or not.

3. **Syntactic learning using UD treebanks:** We plan to train the encoder on syntactic tasks like Parts-Of-Speech (POS) tagging, using a dataset like the UD treebanks (de Marneffe et al., 2021), which supports syntactically rich and structured text. We will explore syntactically relevant pretraining objectives, such as part-of-speech tagging or masked prediction. Two such examples are given below:
    - Predict POS tags from text, building a foundation in syntactic structure.
    - Predict masked POS tags (sequence-to-sequence of POS tags), focusing on syntactic dependencies.

4. **Delexicalized Pretraining:** Named entities in the training data can lead to sparsity problems in the input data. Consequently, lower-resource language models often struggle with named entities and numbers. To mitigate this issue, we delexicalise the named entities by replacing them with placeholders, focusing instead on the syntactic structure and grammatical relationships.

3.2 Experiments in low-resource languages

We adapt the tuning strategies from English to the low-resource languages. We also propose additional methods to train the models more efficiently. We plan to experiment with the following strategies:

1. **Shuffling:** We plan to experiment with more sophisticated sentence-level shuffling as our pretraining technique. We will propose a self-supervised method that focuses on reconstructing a shuffled input without altering the subject-verb-object order, akin to BART's objective (Lewis et al., 2019) but adapted for linguistic nuances. Additionally, we experiment with instruction-tuning as well.

2. **Transliteration:** Romanized transliteration has shown better transfer between related languages (Amrhein and Sennrich, 2020). However, it might lead to a loss of information on the morphological level. (Micallef et al., 2023) demonstrated that transliterating to the original script might improve the performance for that language. Thus, we will also experiment on the effect of transliteration for the selected low-resource languages.

3. **Lexical and Syntactic Learning:** If WordNet-enhanced embeddings and syntactic learning prove effective in English, we plan to extend the approach to other languages. Training data for syntactic learning (UD treebank) already exists for the considered languages. For lexical learning, we plan to use NMT systems to generate the candidates for each lexicon in the training data.

4. **Using encoder as assistant for efficient finetuning:** The current LLMs perform significantly well on English language. Using this to our advantage, we plan to use a multi-encoder for faster finetuning on a downstream task. Specifically, we use an additional English encoder to assist the model in finetuning on downstream tasks. We use NMT system for generating the input for the English encoder. Additionally, during the tuning process, we plan to gradually decrease the dependence on the assistant encoder.

5. **Multilingual LMs with language-specific word embeddings:** We also plan to train the embeddings agnostic of other model parameters and vice versa. We aim to get language-specific embeddings while the model parameters serving as a universal grammatical representation. To check the effectiveness, we plan to experiment with different number and combinations of languages, e.g., languages from the same family. Previous works have shown that the embeddings generated from similar techniques are isomorphic across languages (Vulić et al., 2020). Consequently, we plan to swap embeddings along with further small finetuning to build a low-resource LM.

6. **Direct Preference Optimization (DPO):** DPO has emerged as an alternative to RLHF. It aims to align the outputs to the human-preferred generations. This method can be applied to various sequence-to-sequence tasks, such as summarization, question answering, paraphrasing, and machine translation. We will create substandard samples using back-translation with English as the pivot language. We plan to apply this method for finetuning and instruction-tuning on downstream tasks. We investigate its applicability by integrating it with previously discussed methods.

7. **Curriculum Learning and Delexicalised Pretraining:** We will adopt similar strategies from the English language for the other low-resource languages.

We will consider Aya (Üstün et al., 2024) and mT5 (Xue et al., 2021) as our baseline models, both of which contain the considered languages in their pretraining data. Aya, with 13B parameters, serves as a strong baseline performing well on a wide range of language understanding and generation tasks. We will also train a vanilla language model for each considered language using BART-inspired self-supervised pretraining techniques.

4 Training Dataset, Evaluation and Early Experiments

We will work with English in a limited data setting and 5 other diverse low-resource languages. We consider 2 European languages Irish (ga) and Scottish Gaelic (gd), a Semitic language, Maltese (mt), an Indic language, Urdu (ur), and an African language, Swahili (sw), for our experiments. The choice of languages is motivated by the existence of appropriate evaluation datasets. We will use *CC-100*[1](Wenzek et al., 2020) corpus for getting the monolingual data. To get parallel data for our experiments using English as the pivot language, we will be using the *OPUS*[2] corpus. Additionally,

[1]https://data.statmt.org/cc-100/

[2]https://opus.nlpl.eu/

		BERT				mBERT			
Training →		full		non-emb		full		non-emb	
emb ↓	vocab →	model	custom	model	custom	model	custom	model	custom
model		0.1520	0.3642	0.2180	0.5220	0.2446	0.4392	0.3160	0.5454
fasttext		-	0.4356	-	0.5288	-	0.3570	-	**0.5588**
random		0.1976	0.4000	0.2094	0.5004	0.2011	0.3430	0.2047	0.5341

Table 1: Evaluation results of BERT and mBERT trained for the Scottish Gaelic language with different training settings (Training), embedding initializations (emb.) and vocabularies (vocab.).

we will use the *UD treebanks* (available for all the considered languages) (Nivre et al., 2020) and *WordNet* (Miller, 1995) for English.

4.1 Evaluation

We plan to test our English models on the BLiMP benchmark to evaluate grammatical competence, especially in minimal token usage, which stresses the model's syntactic and semantic efficiency.

Evaluating low-resource LMs gets tricky due to the nonavailability of appropriate evaluation sets. We use zero-shot NMT systems to address this challenge. For most of our evaluation in low-resource, we use English as our pivot language to generate test sets from the available monolingual corpora. Previous work (Kumar et al., 2023) has shown that generating via English has better performance than direct generation. Thus, to evaluate the applicability of our general-purpose LMs in low-resource languages, we will perform evaluation on three types of tasks:

Generation tasks We choose *paraphrasing* and *summarization* tasks to evaluate the models on their language generation capability. Since there is no gold data available, we plan to create silver test data using the NMT system and the available monolingual corpora. Specifically, for each data instance in the monolingual corpus, we will create its corresponding synthetic input using NMT systems and state-of-the-art English LLMs, depending on the downstream task. Specifically, for a given data instance y_l in language l, we first translate y_l to English y_{en}. We use current English-centric LLMs to generate corresponding synthetic input (for summarization - longer sentence) in English (x_{en}). We translate it back to the target language l (x_l) to get a silver parallel data, while preserving the naturalness of the task outputs. Additionally, we will test our methods on the WebNLG dataset for *data-to-text* generation for the Irish language.

Single-input Understanding Tasks We will use UD treebanks for training and testing on the *POS tagging* task for all the languages. We will also create silver test data for *NER*. We follow a similar approach as the previous paragraph. We translate the sentences into English, classify the named entities, and transfer the labels back to the target language using cross-attention scores.

Input-pair tasks We will use *XNLI* to evaluate Swahili and Urdu models. For the other three languages, we evaluate them again on the synthetic test data using English as a pivot language.

4.2 Early Experiments and Results

To start off, we hypothesize that full model tuning is often unnecessary and propose a more modular approach. Specifically, our method involves first training a language-specific tokenizer and creating corresponding embeddings, followed by tuning only the non-embedding parameters. We perform a comprehensive analysis across multiple scenarios, including multilingual-to-monolingual transfer and adaptation from high-resource to low-resource monolingual models. When applied to multilingual models, our method significantly reduces the number of tunable parameters and the overall training time. We further evaluate the natural language understanding (NLU) models on the mask-filling task. We present the accuracy scores in Table 1. Training only the non-embedding parameters consistently yields better results, while using a custom tokenizer provides a significant performance boost. Additionally, mBERT performs slightly better than BERT, and FastText embeddings offer only minimal improvement.

We also experiment with parameter-efficient training methods through artificial language-based pretraining strategies. Prior studies (Papadimitriou and Jurafsky, 2020; Chiang and yi Lee, 2022) demonstrate that models pretrained on non-linguistic data can achieve performance comparable to those trained on English sentences. We adapt the best performing approach followed by a parameter-efficient *pretraining* for language acquisition from limited data. Our method initializes the model using token embeddings trained with a shallow model, followed by tuning only the non-embedding parameters on non-linguistic data to introduce structural biases. Subsequently, the model is frozen and further pretrained on the 10M-token BabyLM corpus using LoRA adapters. Experiments on small-scale dataset show that this approach leads to performance comparable to classic full-model pretraining.

5 Conclusion

The thesis proposal outlines various approaches to tune the models efficiently. We discuss related literature and current challenges specific to language modeling for low-resource languages.

We propose several techniques for efficient tuning in a simulated low-resource setting for English. Specifically, we plan to use curriculum learning at both the instance and dataset levels. We also plan to evaluate the role of grammar-rich datasets in model training. Furthermore, we also propose a delexicalised pretraining method to address the challenge of data sparsity in low-resource scenarios. We plan to train and evaluate the models for both generation and understanding tasks.

We further extend these approaches to actual low-resource languages. Additionally, we also try modular approaches to train the model separately on different linguistic levels. We also propose an encoder-assisted finetuning method for faster convergence and better knowledge transfer from higher-resource languages. We also plan to use DPO for generating better-aligned outputs to humans for low-resource languages. We evaluate our proposed approaches on various tasks, depending on the availability of test sets. We also plan to generate silver test sets using NMT systems on evaluation sets from higher-resource languages.

Challenges

We identify the following challenges and possible alternatives for the proposed approaches:

- Failing to adapt WordNet dataset for low-resource languages: Since this method depends on the chosen NMT system (NLLB, in this case), the quality of the generated data can be inadequate. We mitigate this issue by checking with several other NMT systems (Üstün et al., 2024; Fan et al., 2021; Zhang et al., 2020); if nothing works, we plan to use the Wiki dataset for lexical training.
- Curriculum learning on data instance level could prove ineffective: While this is a low-level risk, curriculum learning has proven to be effective on the dataset level for English (Mi, 2023). Thus, we can alleviate the issue by applying similar techniques to non-English languages.
- Delexicalised Pretraining may prove ineffective: In case this doesn't work out, we plan to delexicalise only during the inference, as this has been proven beneficial for end-to-end task-oriented dialogue systems (Kulhánek et al., 2021).
- Failure of language-specific embeddings for multilingual LMs: We permanently integrate the additional encoder into the model instead of relying on its assistance only during finetuning.

Acknowledgments

This work was supported by the European Research Council (Grant agreement No. 101039303, NG-NLG) and Grant Agency of Charles University (Grant No. 302425), and used resources of the LINDAT/CLARIAH-CZ Research Infrastructure (Czech Ministry of Education, Youth, and Sports project No. LM2018101).

References

Josh Achiam, Steven Adler, Sandhini Agarwal, Lama Ahmad, Ilge Akkaya, Florencia Leoni Aleman, Diogo Almeida, Janko Altenschmidt, Sam Altman, Shyamal Anadkat, and 1 others. 2023. Gpt-4 technical report. *arXiv preprint arXiv:2303.08774*.

Chantal Amrhein and Rico Sennrich. 2020. On Romanization for model transfer between scripts in neural machine translation. In *Findings of the Association for Computational Linguistics: EMNLP 2020*, pages 2461–2469, Online. Association for Computational Linguistics.

Jordi Armengol-Estapé, Casimiro Pio Carrino, Carlos Rodriguez-Penagos, Ona de Gibert Bonet, Carme Armentano-Oller, Aitor Gonzalez-Agirre, Maite Melero, and Marta Villegas. 2021. Are multilingual models the best choice for moderately under-resourced languages? A comprehensive assessment for Catalan. In *Findings of the Association for Computational Linguistics: ACL-IJCNLP 2021*, pages 4933–4946, Online. Association for Computational Linguistics.

Cheng-Han Chiang and Hung yi Lee. 2022. On the transferability of pre-trained language models: A study from artificial datasets. *Preprint*, arXiv:2109.03537.

Aryaman Chobey, Oliver Smith, Anzi Wang, and Grusha Prasad. 2023. Can training neural language models on a curriculum with developmentally plausible data improve alignment with human reading behavior? In *Proceedings of the BabyLM Challenge at the 27th Conference on Computational Natural Language Learning*, pages 98–111, Singapore. Association for Computational Linguistics.

Alexis Conneau, Kartikay Khandelwal, Naman Goyal, Vishrav Chaudhary, Guillaume Wenzek, Francisco Guzmán, Edouard Grave, Myle Ott, Luke Zettlemoyer, and Veselin Stoyanov. 2020. Unsupervised cross-lingual representation learning at scale. In *Proceedings of the 58th Annual Meeting of the Association for Computational Linguistics*, pages 8440–8451, Online. Association for Computational Linguistics.

Liam Cripwell, Anya Belz, Claire Gardent, Albert Gatt, Claudia Borg, Marthese Borg, John Judge, Michela Lorandi, Anna Nikiforovskaya, and William Soto Martinez. 2023. The 2023 WebNLG shared task on low resource languages. overview and evaluation results (WebNLG 2023). In *Proceedings of the Workshop on Multimodal, Multilingual Natural Language Generation and Multilingual WebNLG Challenge (MM-NLG 2023)*, pages 55–66, Prague, Czech Republic. Association for Computational Linguistics.

Ona De Gibert, Graeme Nail, Nikolay Arefyev, Marta Bañón, Jelmer Van Der Linde, Shaoxiong Ji, Jaume Zaragoza-Bernabeu, Mikko Aulamo, Gema Ramírez-Sánchez, Andrey Kutuzov, and 1 others. 2024. A new massive multilingual dataset for high-performance language technologies. In *Proceedings of the 2024 Joint International Conference on Computational Linguistics, Language Resources and Evaluation (LREC-COLING 2024)*, pages 1116–1128.

Marie-Catherine de Marneffe, Christopher D. Manning, Joakim Nivre, and Daniel Zeman. 2021. Universal dependencies. *Computational Linguistics*, 47(2):255–308.

Abhimanyu Dubey, Abhinav Jauhri, Abhinav Pandey, Abhishek Kadian, Ahmad Al-Dahle, Aiesha Letman, Akhil Mathur, Alan Schelten, Amy Yang, Angela Fan, and 1 others. 2024. The llama 3 herd of models. *arXiv preprint arXiv:2407.21783*.

Angela Fan, Shruti Bhosale, Holger Schwenk, Zhiyi Ma, Ahmed El-Kishky, Siddharth Goyal, Mandeep Baines, Onur Celebi, Guillaume Wenzek, Vishrav Chaudhary, and 1 others. 2021. Beyond english-centric multilingual machine translation. *Journal of Machine Learning Research*, 22(107):1–48.

Diego de Vargas Feijo and Viviane Pereira Moreira. 2020. Mono vs multilingual transformer-based models: a comparison across several language tasks. *arXiv preprint arXiv:2007.09757*.

Jack FitzGerald, Shankar Ananthakrishnan, Konstantine Arkoudas, Davide Bernardi, Abhishek Bhagia, Claudio Delli Bovi, Jin Cao, Rakesh Chada, Amit Chauhan, Luoxin Chen, and 1 others. 2022. Alexa teacher model: Pretraining and distilling multi-billion-parameter encoders for natural language understanding systems. In *Proceedings of the 28th ACM SIGKDD Conference on Knowledge Discovery and Data Mining*, pages 2893–2902.

Katharina Hämmerl, Björn Deiseroth, Patrick Schramowski, Jindřich Libovický, Alexander Fraser, and Kristian Kersting. 2022. Do multilingual language models capture differing moral norms? *arXiv preprint arXiv:2203.09904*.

Zhiqi Huang, Puxuan Yu, and James Allan. 2023. Improving cross-lingual information retrieval on low-resource languages via optimal transport distillation. In *Proceedings of the Sixteenth ACM International Conference on Web Search and Data Mining*, pages 1048–1056.

Seungduk Kim, Seungtaek Choi, and Myeongho Jeong. 2024. Efficient and effective vocabulary expansion towards multilingual large language models. *arXiv preprint arXiv:2402.14714*.

Jonáš Kulhánek, Vojtěch Hudeček, Tomáš Nekvinda, and Ondřej Dušek. 2021. AuGPT: Auxiliary tasks and data augmentation for end-to-end dialogue with pre-trained language models. In *Proceedings of the 3rd Workshop on Natural Language Processing for Conversational AI*, pages 198–210, Online. Association for Computational Linguistics.

Nalin Kumar, Saad Obaid Ul Islam, and Ondřej Dušek. 2023. Better translation+ split and generate for multilingual rdf-to-text (webnlg 2023). In *Proceedings of the Workshop on Multimodal, Multilingual Natural Language Generation and Multilingual WebNLG Challenge (MM-NLG 2023)*, pages 73–79.

Mike Lewis, Yinhan Liu, Naman Goyal, Marjan Ghazvininejad, Abdelrahman Mohamed, Omer Levy, Ves Stoyanov, and Luke Zettlemoyer. 2019. Bart: Denoising sequence-to-sequence pre-training for natural language generation, translation, and comprehension. *arXiv preprint arXiv:1910.13461*.

Zihao Li, Yucheng Shi, Zirui Liu, Fan Yang, Ninghao Liu, and Mengnan Du. 2024. Quantifying multilingual performance of large language models across languages. *arXiv preprint arXiv:2404.11553*.

Peiqin Lin, Shaoxiong Ji, Jörg Tiedemann, André FT Martins, and Hinrich Schütze. 2024. Mala-500: Massive language adaptation of large language models. *arXiv preprint arXiv:2401.13303*.

Yihong Liu, Mingyang Wang, Amir Hossein Kargaran, Ayyoob Imani, Orgest Xhelili, Haotian Ye, Chunlan Ma, François Yvon, and Hinrich Schütze. 2024. How transliterations improve crosslingual alignment. *arXiv preprint arXiv:2409.17326*.

Yun Luo, Zhen Yang, Fandong Meng, Yafu Li, Jie Zhou, and Yue Zhang. 2023. An empirical study of catastrophic forgetting in large language models during continual fine-tuning. *arXiv preprint arXiv:2308.08747*.

Chunlan Ma, Yihong Liu, Haotian Ye, and Hinrich Schütze. 2024. Exploring the role of transliteration in in-context learning for low-resource languages written in non-latin scripts. *arXiv preprint arXiv:2407.02320*.

Gaurav Maheshwari, Dmitry Ivanov, and Kevin El Haddad. 2024. Efficacy of synthetic data as a benchmark. *arXiv preprint arXiv:2409.11968*.

Kelly Marchisio, Patrick Lewis, Yihong Chen, and Mikel Artetxe. 2023. Mini-model adaptation: Efficiently extending pretrained models to new languages via aligned shallow training. In *Findings of the Association for Computational Linguistics: ACL 2023*, pages 5474–5490, Toronto, Canada. Association for Computational Linguistics.

Maggie Mi. 2023. Mmi01 at the BabyLM challenge: Linguistically motivated curriculum learning for pretraining in low-resource settings. In *Proceedings of the BabyLM Challenge at the 27th Conference on Computational Natural Language Learning*, pages 269–278, Singapore. Association for Computational Linguistics.

Kurt Micallef, Fadhl Eryani, Nizar Habash, Houda Bouamor, and Claudia Borg. 2023. Exploring the impact of transliteration on NLP performance: Treating Maltese as an Arabic dialect. In *Proceedings of the Workshop on Computation and Written Language (CAWL 2023)*, pages 22–32, Toronto, Canada. Association for Computational Linguistics.

George A. Miller. 1995. Wordnet: a lexical database for english. *Commun. ACM*, 38(11):39–41.

Hiep Nguyen, Lynn Yip, and Justin DeBenedetto. 2024. Automatic quality estimation for data selection and curriculum learning. In *The 2nd BabyLM Challenge at the 28th Conference on Computational Natural Language Learning*, pages 212–220, Miami, FL, USA. Association for Computational Linguistics.

Joakim Nivre, Marie-Catherine de Marneffe, Filip Ginter, Yoav Goldberg, Jan Hajič, Christopher D. Manning, Ryan McDonald, Slav Petrov, Sampo Pyysalo, Natalia Silveira, Reut Tsarfaty, and Daniel Zeman. 2016. Universal Dependencies v1: A multilingual treebank collection. In *Proceedings of the Tenth International Conference on Language Resources and Evaluation (LREC'16)*, pages 1659–1666, Portorož, Slovenia. European Language Resources Association (ELRA).

Joakim Nivre, Marie-Catherine de Marneffe, Filip Ginter, Jan Hajič, Christopher D. Manning, Sampo Pyysalo, Sebastian Schuster, Francis Tyers, and Daniel Zeman. 2020. Universal Dependencies v2: An evergrowing multilingual treebank collection. In *Proceedings of the Twelfth Language Resources and Evaluation Conference*, pages 4034–4043, Marseille, France. European Language Resources Association.

Long Ouyang, Jeffrey Wu, Xu Jiang, Diogo Almeida, Carroll Wainwright, Pamela Mishkin, Chong Zhang, Sandhini Agarwal, Katarina Slama, Alex Ray, and 1 others. 2022. Training language models to follow instructions with human feedback. *Advances in neural information processing systems*, 35:27730–27744.

Isabel Papadimitriou and Dan Jurafsky. 2020. Learning Music Helps You Read: Using transfer to study linguistic structure in language models. In *Proceedings of the 2020 Conference on Empirical Methods in Natural Language Processing (EMNLP)*, pages 6829–6839, Online. Association for Computational Linguistics.

Sukannya Purkayastha, Sebastian Ruder, Jonas Pfeiffer, Iryna Gurevych, and Ivan Vulić. 2023. Romanization-based large-scale adaptation of multilingual language models. In *Findings of the Association for Computational Linguistics: EMNLP 2023*, pages 7996–8005.

Rafael Rafailov, Archit Sharma, Eric Mitchell, Christopher D Manning, Stefano Ermon, and Chelsea Finn. 2024. Direct preference optimization: Your language model is secretly a reward model. *Advances in Neural Information Processing Systems*, 36.

Chakaveh Saedi, António Branco, João António Rodrigues, and João Silva. 2018. WordNet embeddings. In *Proceedings of the Third Workshop on Representation Learning for NLP*, pages 122–131, Melbourne, Australia. Association for Computational Linguistics.

Rohan Saha, Abrar Fahim, Alona Fyshe, and Alex Murphy. 2024. Exploring curriculum learning for vision-language tasks: A study on small-scale multimodal training. In *The 2nd BabyLM Challenge at the 28th Conference on Computational Natural Language Learning*, pages 65–81, Miami, FL, USA. Association for Computational Linguistics.

Suchir Salhan, Richard Diehl Martinez, Zébulon Goriely, and Paula Buttery. 2024. Less is more: Pretraining cross-lingual small-scale language models with cognitively-plausible curriculum learning strategies. In *The 2nd BabyLM Challenge at the 28th Conference on Computational Natural Language Learning*, pages 174–188, Miami, FL, USA. Association for Computational Linguistics.

Gemini Team, Rohan Anil, Sebastian Borgeaud, Jean-Baptiste Alayrac, Jiahui Yu, Radu Soricut, Johan Schalkwyk, Andrew M Dai, Anja Hauth, Katie Millican, and 1 others. 2023. Gemini: a family of highly capable multimodal models. *arXiv preprint arXiv:2312.11805*.

Gemma Team, Morgane Riviere, Shreya Pathak, Pier Giuseppe Sessa, Cassidy Hardin, Surya Bhupatiraju, Léonard Hussenot, Thomas Mesnard, Bobak Shahriari, Alexandre Ramé, and 1 others. 2024. Gemma 2: Improving open language models at a practical size. *arXiv preprint arXiv:2408.00118*.

Jörg Tiedemann. 2009. *News from OPUS - A Collection of Multilingual Parallel Corpora with Tools and Interfaces*, volume V, pages 237–248.

Hugo Touvron, Louis Martin, Kevin Stone, Peter Albert, Amjad Almahairi, Yasmine Babaei, Nikolay Bashlykov, Soumya Batra, Prajjwal Bhargava, Shruti Bhosale, and 1 others. 2023. Llama 2: Open foundation and fine-tuned chat models. *arXiv preprint arXiv:2307.09288*.

Ahmet Üstün, Viraat Aryabumi, Zheng-Xin Yong, Wei-Yin Ko, Daniel D'souza, Gbemileke Onilude, Neel Bhandari, Shivalika Singh, Hui-Lee Ooi, Amr Kayid, and 1 others. 2024. Aya model: An instruction finetuned open-access multilingual language model. *arXiv preprint arXiv:2402.07827*.

Ivan Vulić, Sebastian Ruder, and Anders Søgaard. 2020. Are all good word vector spaces isomorphic? In *Proceedings of the 2020 Conference on Empirical Methods in Natural Language Processing (EMNLP)*, pages 3178–3192, Online. Association for Computational Linguistics.

Zirui Wang, Zachary C. Lipton, and Yulia Tsvetkov. 2020. On negative interference in multilingual models: Findings and a meta-learning treatment. In *Proceedings of the 2020 Conference on Empirical Methods in Natural Language Processing (EMNLP)*, pages 4438–4450, Online. Association for Computational Linguistics.

Alex Warstadt, Aaron Mueller, Leshem Choshen, Ethan Wilcox, Chengxu Zhuang, Juan Ciro, Rafael Mosquera, Bhargavi Paranjabe, Adina Williams, Tal Linzen, and Ryan Cotterell, editors. 2023. *Proceedings of the BabyLM Challenge at the 27th Conference on Computational Natural Language Learning*. Association for Computational Linguistics, Singapore.

Guillaume Wenzek, Marie-Anne Lachaux, Alexis Conneau, Vishrav Chaudhary, Francisco Guzmán, Armand Joulin, and Edouard Grave. 2020. CCNet: Extracting high quality monolingual datasets from web crawl data. In *Proceedings of the Twelfth Language Resources and Evaluation Conference*, pages 4003–4012, Marseille, France. European Language Resources Association.

Linting Xue, Noah Constant, Adam Roberts, Mihir Kale, Rami Al-Rfou, Aditya Siddhant, Aditya Barua, and Colin Raffel. 2021. mT5: A massively multilingual pre-trained text-to-text transformer. In *Proceedings of the 2021 Conference of the North American Chapter of the Association for Computational Linguistics: Human Language Technologies*, pages 483–498, Online. Association for Computational Linguistics.

Biao Zhang, Philip Williams, Ivan Titov, and Rico Sennrich. 2020. Improving massively multilingual neural machine translation and zero-shot translation. In *Proceedings of the 58th Annual Meeting of the Association for Computational Linguistics*, pages 1628–1639.

Chen Zhang, Mingxu Tao, Quzhe Huang, Jiuheng Lin, Zhibin Chen, and Yansong Feng. 2024. MC^2: Towards transparent and culturally-aware NLP for minority languages in China. In *Proceedings of the 62nd Annual Meeting of the Association for Computational Linguistics (Volume 1: Long Papers)*, pages 8832–8850, Bangkok, Thailand. Association for Computational Linguistics.

Jun Zhao, Zhihao Zhang, Luhui Gao, Qi Zhang, Tao Gui, and Xuanjing Huang. 2024. Llama beyond english: An empirical study on language capability transfer. *arXiv preprint arXiv:2401.01055*.

A Example Appendix

This is an appendix.

Two Step Automatic Post Editing of Patent Machine Translation based on Pre-trained Encoder Models and LLMs

Kosei Buma[1] **Takehito Utsuro**[1] **Masaaki Nagata**[2]
[1]University of Tsukuba [2]NTT, Inc.
s2520812_@_u.tsukuba.ac.jp utsuro_@_iit.tsukuba.ac.jp
masaaki.nagata_@_ntt.com

Abstract

We study automatic post-editing for patent translation, where accuracy and traceability are critical, and propose a two-step pipeline that combines a multilingual encoder for token-level error detection with an LLM for targeted correction. As no word-level annotations exist for Japanese–English patents, we create supervised data by injecting synthetic errors into parallel patent sentences and fine-tune mBERT, XLM-RoBERTa, and mDeBERTa as detectors. In the second stage, GPT-4o is prompted to revise translations either freely or under a restricted policy that allows edits only on detector-marked spans. For error detection, evaluation on synthetic errors shows that encoder-based detectors outperform LLMs in both F1 and MCC. For error correction, tests on synthetic, repetition, and omission datasets demonstrate statistically significant BLEU gains over LLM methods for synthetic and repetition errors, while omission errors remain challenging. Overall, pairing compact encoders with an LLM enables more accurate and controllable post-editing for key patent error types, reducing unnecessary rewrites via restricted edits. Future work will focus on strengthening omission modeling to better detect and correct missing content.

1 Introduction

Recent advances in large language models (LLMs) have enabled powerful multi-step reasoning approaches, such as LLMRefine (Xu et al., 2024), which iteratively refine translation outputs through repeated analysis and correction. More ambitious designs, like Google's recent multi-stage pipeline (Briakou et al., 2024), extend this paradigm even further. However, not all components of a machine translation pipeline need to rely exclusively on LLMs. In particular, error detection can often be performed more accurately and with far lower computational cost using pre-trained transformer encoders (Obeidat et al., 2025). Lukito et al. (2024) demonstrate that, in a classification task detecting connective language—defined as language that facilitates engagement, understanding, and conversation—across social media platforms, a BERT-based classifier significantly outperforms GPT-3.5 Turbo in precision, recall, and F1-score.

In this paper, we present a two-stage translation refinement method (Figure 1) that combines token-level error detection with LLM-based correction. In the first stage, we fine-tune a pre-trained multilingual transformer encoder to identify token-level errors. Because no error-annotated dataset exists for Japanese–English patent translation, we construct a synthetic training set by injecting artificial errors into target-side sentences of parallel patent data. This enables the encoder to learn how to detect mistranslations at the token level. In the second stage, an LLM (GPT-4o[1]) (OpenAI et al., 2024) corrects the translations based on the detected error tags.

We evaluate our method in the patent domain, where translation accuracy has particularly high stakes due to legal and technical requirements, making post-editing especially important. For error detection, we evaluated the fine-tuned multilingual transformer encoder on Japanese–English and English–Japanese patent datasets. The model achieved higher F1 and Matthews correlation coefficient (MCC) scores than an LLM-based approach, demonstrating its superior capability in identifying mistranslations at the token level. For translation correction, experiments on three dataset types—artificially corrupted sentences, repetitive-error sets, and omission scenarios—show that our hybrid strategy, using a compact transformer encoder for detection followed by LLM-based targeted correction, outperforms purely LLM-based

[1]All GPT-4o results are obtained using the gpt-4o-2024-08-06 model version.

Proceedings of the IJCNLP-AACL 2025 Student Research Workshop, pages 218–231
December 20-24, 2025 ©2025 Association for Computational Linguistics

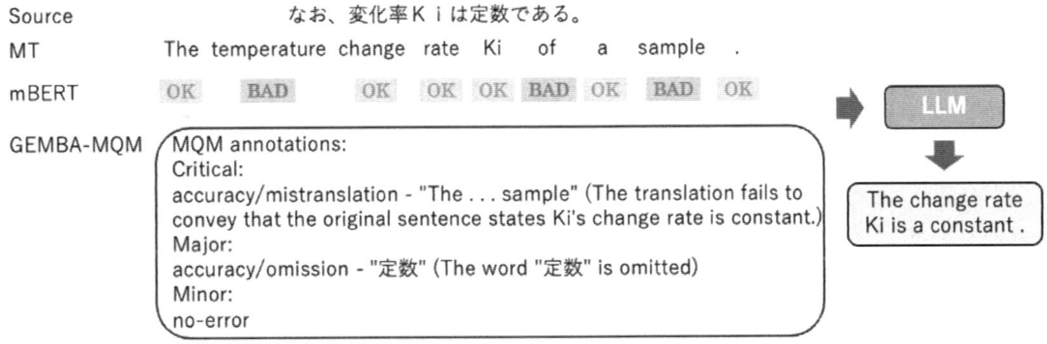

Figure 1: Overview of the Proposed Method.The first stage performs mistranslation detection, and the second stage conducts mistranslation correction.

approaches in BLEU (Papineni et al., 2002) scores. However, omission errors remain difficult to detect and correct, indicating that future work should explore more effective integration of LLM reasoning with dedicated detection modules. We conclude that while multi-step LLM reasoning is powerful, selectively integrating compact transformer encoders can yield more accurate and efficient solutions for machine translation error detection and correction. In summary, our contributions are threefold:

- By fine-tuning encoder models, we achieved higher accuracy than a state-of-the-art LLM on the error detection task, despite LLMs generally showing strong performance across tasks.
- By creating synthetic error-injected patent sentence data, we enabled supervised training of an error detection model without the need for manually annotated datasets.
- Our proposed encoder–LLM hybrid method achieved statistically significant improvements in translation quality compared to LLM-only baselines.

2 Related Work

2.1 Word-Level Quality Estimation in Translation

Word-level QE is commonly formulated as tagging each MT token (and gap positions) with OK/BAD labels, a setup consolidated through the WMT shared tasks and their findings reports over multiple years (Specia et al., 2018; Fonseca et al., 2019; Zerva et al., 2022). This formulation has catalyzed neural approaches and standardized evaluation at the token/gap level without reference translations.

Among early neural architectures, the Predictor–Estimator framework explicitly separates a word predictor trained on large parallel data from a QE estimator trained on annotated QE data, achieving top performance at WMT17 (Kim et al., 2017). Its design influenced subsequent open-source toolkits such as OpenKiwi, which implements state-of-the-art QE systems for word- and sentence-level tasks in a unified PyTorch framework (Kepler et al., 2019). Building on cross-lingual pretrained encoders, Ranasinghe et al. (2020) proposed TransQuest, which attained state-of-the-art results in WMT20 and demonstrated strong cross-lingual transfer.

Closer to our setting, Wei et al. (2022) propose a supervised word-level QE model based on `bert-base-multilingual-cased` (mBERT): given the concatenation of source and MT, a regression head estimates the probability that each MT token is tagged as BAD. We adopt this supervised, token-level formulation for the patent domain, where terminology and style diverge from general-domain WMT data. Beyond a single language pair, multilingual transformer encoders have also shown promising cross-lingual generalization for word-level QE (Ranasinghe et al., 2021).

In parallel, learned MT metrics have moved from sentence-level scores toward span-level feedback. Rei et al. (2022) introduce COMET, while Guerreiro et al. (2024) extend it to xCOMET, which provides sentence-level evaluation and error-span attribution with strong WMT performance. For robustness analysis, Alves et al. (2022) propose SMAUG, a synthetic error generator introducing controlled perturbations (e.g., hallucinations, deletions, mistranslations) to stress-test metrics. Unlike xCOMET, which uses synthetic errors primarily for metric robustness, we leverage synthetic errors as supervision to train a token-level detector that subsequently guides LLM-based correction.

2.2 LLM-based Quality Evaluation

Large language models (LLMs) have recently been adopted as reference-free, span-level evaluators for machine translation (MT). Kocmi and Federmann (2023) introduce GEMBA-MQM, a GPT-4–based evaluation method that uses a fixed 3-shot prompt to identify error spans and types following the MQM framework (Lommel et al., 2013), without requiring reference translations; their results show strong correlations with human MQM judgments at system and segment levels in WMT23 settings.

At the same time, recent meta-evaluations highlight limitations of LLM-based evaluators. LLM-based metrics show limited robustness; this raises concerns about bias and stability. Broader analyses caution that LLM judges can be sensitive to prompt choices and sometimes conflate evaluation criteria, affecting reliability (Bavaresco et al., 2025). These findings motivate using LLM-based evaluation with care and, when possible, complementing it with interpretable span-level feedback or learned metrics.

In our study we employ LLMs primarily as detectors/correctors rather than as final evaluators: we use GEMBA-MQM–style prompting as one of the error detectors and then perform post-editing with an LLM, while reporting standard automatic metrics (e.g., BLEU) for quantitative evaluation. This design choice balances the interpretability and flexibility of LLMs with established, reproducible evaluation protocols.

2.3 Post-Editing in Machine Translation

Deguchi et al. (2024) propose a Detector–Corrector framework that decomposes Automatic Post-Editing (APE) into two interpretable stages: an XLM-RoBERTa detector performing three binary tagging tasks—MT-tag, MT-gap, and SRC-tag—to localize error spans, followed by a corrector which edits only the detected spans. Their edit-based pipeline improves TER and enhances explainability by tying edits to explicit detector rationales. Our work adopts the same two-stage intuition but replaces the detector with multilingual transformer encoders fine-tuned on patent-domain supervision and couples them with an LLM corrector instructed to modify only detector-marked spans.

In parallel, LLM-based post-editing has emerged. Ki and Carpuat (2024) guide an LLM with external MQM-style feedback—at varying granularities from generic scores to fine-grained span/type annotations—and show consistent improvements in TER, BLEU, and COMET on Zh–En, En–De, and En–Ru, with fine-grained feedback yielding the strongest gains. Orthogonally, Xu et al. (2024) introduce LLMRefine, which iteratively pinpoints defects with a learned feedback model and refines hypotheses, improving translation quality.

3 Mistranslation Detection

3.1 Mistranslation Detection Using Encoders

In this study, we utilize mBERT[2], XLM-RoBERTa[3], mDeBERTa[4] (He et al., 2023), which are pre-trained multilingual transformer encoders, to perform token-level quality estimation in machine translation. Specifically, we leverage the pre-trained knowledge of encoder models to detect translation errors and assign appropriate error labels to each token.

For training encoder models, we follow the data augmentation method proposed by Deguchi et al. (2024) and generate synthetic error data by sampling 10,000 sentences from the NTCIR-7 (Fujii et al., 2008) (1,798,571 sentence pairs) and NTCIR-8 (Fujii et al., 2010) (3,186,284 sentence pairs) patent parallel corpora. We sample 10,000 sentence pairs and generate synthetic errors for both translation directions. The same 10,000 pairs are split into 8,000 for training, 1,000 for development, and 1,000 for testing, before applying the following operations:

- Deletion: Delete tokens with a probability of 5%
- Insertion: Insert tokens with a probability of 10%
- Replacement: Replace tokens with a probability of 30%

The probabilities of these operations are determined in accordance with Deguchi et al. (2024). For insertion and replacement, we adopt a mask-filling approach using mBERT. We insert [MASK]

[2]https://huggingface.co/google-bert/bert-base-multilingual-cased

[3]https://huggingface.co/FacebookAI/xlm-roberta-base

[4]https://huggingface.co/microsoft/mdeberta-v3-base

tokens at the target positions and let mBERT generate candidate substitutions using the fill-mask prediction head. From the top-k predictions returned by the model (we set $k = 5$), we intentionally choose the token with the *lowest* predicted probability so as to maximize the divergence from the original token. This token is then inserted or substituted to produce an artificial error. After generating the corrupted sentence, we annotate the manipulated tokens with the BAD tag and all other tokens with the OK tag to construct supervised training dataset.

Using this method, we generate 8,000 annotated sentences for training encoder models. Training uses the Hugging Face Trainer[5] with `num_train_epochs` = 10 and `per_device_train_batch_size` = 2. Unless otherwise specified, we keep the Hugging Face defaults for optimizer and scheduler (AdamW, learning rate = 5×10^{-5}, $\beta_1 = 0.9$, $\beta_2 = 0.999$, linear scheduler).

To assess the effectiveness of the constructed training data, we conducted additional experiments with mBERT under different dataset conditions. Details are provided in Appendix A.

3.2 Mistranslation Detection Using LLM

We adopt GEMBA-MQM, a GPT-based evaluation method proposed by Kocmi and Federmann (2023), for mistranslation detection using large language models (LLMs). Based on the GEMBA-MQM framework, we perform error detection under the following two settings:

- 0-shot: Error detection is performed without any prior examples.
- 3-shot: Error detection is performed using three language-independent examples, following exactly the same examples provided by Kocmi and Federmann (2023).

Among these (Kocmi and Federmann, 2023), the 3-shot setting has been reported to achieve the highest error detection accuracy using GPT-4.

The mistranslation detection using encoder models and LLM serves as a preprocessing step for the subsequent translation correction. By utilizing the detection results, we aim to enhance the accuracy of the translation correction process.

[5] https://huggingface.co/docs/transformers/main_classes/trainer

4 Mistranslation Correction Using LLM

By providing both the source sentence and its translation as input, the LLM analyzes translation errors and generates appropriate corrections. Specifically, the LLM closely analyzes the detected erroneous parts, explains the nature of the errors and their locations, and generates corrected translations based on this analysis. By explicitly stating the reasoning behind each correction, the LLM enhances the transparency of the correction process and makes the translation refinement more interpretable.

Furthermore, in this study, we propose a method that utilizes the mistranslation detection results obtained from the encoder described in the previous section as input for translation correction using an LLM. In this experiment, we tested two types of prompts: one instructing the LLM to perform translation correction with reference to the first-stage error detection results, and another instructing it to correct only the segments identified as erroneous in the first stage, leaving all other parts unchanged. By incorporating the detection outputs from either the LLM or encoder model, we aim to further improve the accuracy of translation correction.

The prompt for the proposed method is provided in Appendix B.

5 Evaluation

5.1 Dataset

In this study, we focus on mistranslations, repetitions, and omissions. These error types are not only frequently observed in patent translations but also critically impact semantic fidelity, which is of utmost importance in the context of patent documents. we evaluate our proposed method using the following three types of datasets:

- Mistranslation patent dataset (Synthetic)
- Repetition error patent claim dataset (Non-Synthetic)
- Omission error patent claim dataset (Non-Synthetic)

The synthetic error patent data is generated by introducing artificial errors into Japanese-English parallel patent sentences from NTCIR-7 and NTCIR-8 using the method described in Section 3.1. We evaluate the detection and correction capabilities of our method using 200 sentences from the synthetic error patent dataset.

Model	Label	Precision	Recall	F1
GPT-4o (0-shot)	OK	0.843	0.077	0.142
	BAD	0.389	0.976	0.556
	TOTAL	F1: 0.298, MCC: 0.111		
GPT-4o (3-shot)	OK	0.755	0.268	0.395
	BAD	0.409	0.853	0.553
	TOTAL	F1: 0.454, MCC: 0.141		
mBERT	OK	0.855	0.883	0.869
	BAD	0.785	0.740	0.762
	TOTAL	F1: 0.830*, MCC: 0.631*		
XLM-RoBERTa	OK	0.924	0.924	0.924
	BAD	0.868	0.868	0.868
	TOTAL	F1: 0.903*, MCC: 0.792*		
mDeBERTa	OK	0.935	0.944	**0.940**
	BAD	0.901	0.887	**0.894**
	TOTAL	F1: **0.923***, MCC: **0.834***		

(a) Japanese-English Translation

Model	Label	Precision	Recall	F1
GPT-4o (0-shot)	OK	0.804	0.287	0.423
	BAD	0.415	0.879	0.563
	TOTAL	F1: 0.474, MCC: 0.190		
GPT-4o (3-shot)	OK	0.709	0.503	0.588
	BAD	0.419	0.634	0.504
	TOTAL	F1: 0.558, MCC: 0.132		
mBERT	OK	0.870	0.880	0.875
	BAD	0.784	0.769	0.776
	TOTAL	F1: 0.839*, MCC: 0.655*		
XLM-RoBERTa	OK	0.918	0.935	0.926
	BAD	0.881	0.852	0.866
	TOTAL	F1: 0.904*, MCC: 0.792*		
mDeBERTa	OK	0.936	0.946	**0.941**
	BAD	0.903	0.885	**0.894**
	TOTAL	F1: **0.924***, MCC: **0.835***		

(b) English-Japanese Translation

Table 1: Mistranslation Detection Evaluation on Synthetic Errors. $*$ indicates a statistically significant difference from the GPT-4o(3-shot) ($p < 0.05$).

In addition, to assess correction accuracy for repetition and omission errors, we extract sentences from Japanese–English translations of patent claims generated by a Transformer (Vaswani et al., 2023) based on the following criteria:

- Repetition error sentences: Translated sentences that are more than twice as long as the reference translation
- Omission error sentences: Translated sentences that are less than half the length of the reference translation

We then evaluate the correction performance using patent claims extracted from patent documents published in 2021. To ensure the quality of the parallel data, we compute sentence similarity between the source and reference translations using LaBSE embeddings (Feng et al., 2022), and extract only those pairs with similarity scores between 0.8 and 0.98. As a result, we use 200 repetition error sentences and omission error sentences for evaluation.

Further details of the datasets, including the number of sentences, tokens, and other statistics, are provided in Appendix C.

5.2 Evaluation Procedure

5.2.1 Mistranslation Detection

Each token in the translated sentence is labeled with a BAD tag at erroneous positions, allowing for token-level evaluation. Both encoder models and the LLM perform tagging in the same manner as illustrated on the left side of Figure 1. For Japanese tokenization, we employed MeCab[6] together with the UniDic dictionary[7].

We evaluate translation error detection using the following models:

1. LLM(GPT-4o) - 0-shot
2. LLM(GPT-4o) - 3-shot
3. mBERT
4. XLM-RoBERTa
5. mDeBERTa

All experiments involving GPT-4o—both in detection and correction—use greedy decoding (temperature = 0.0), with all other parameters kept at their provider defaults.

We report F1 score and Matthews Correlation Coefficient (MCC) as our evaluation metrics.

5.2.2 Mistranslation Correction

For the evaluation of error correction, we use three types of data: patent sentences with artificially introduced errors, patent claim sentences of repetition errors and patent claim sentences of omission errors. Error correction is performed using an LLM, where the input consists of the source sentence, the translated sentence, and the error detection results from encoder model or LLM.

The combinations of models used in the evaluation are as follows:

1. **No Correction**: The raw MT output is evaluated without any post-editing.

[6] https://taku910.github.io/mecab/

[7] https://clrd.ninjal.ac.jp/unidic/

	Method	Synthetic (Ja→En)		Synthetic (En→Ja)		Repetition		Omission	
		BLEU	Δ	BLEU	Δ	BLEU	Δ	BLEU	Δ
1	No Correction	31.69	−14.72	32.63	−6.46	21.49	−4.79	19.09	−45.40
2	LLM-only Correction	47.25	+0.84	**40.35**	+1.26*	26.70	+0.42	62.50	−1.99
3	LLM Detection (GEMBA-MQM, 0-shot) + LLM Correction	43.88	−2.53	37.58	−1.51	26.16	−0.12	62.31	−2.18
4	**Baseline**: LLM Detection (GEMBA-MQM, 3-shot) + LLM Correction	46.41	–	39.09	–	26.28	–	**64.49**	–
5	**Proposed**: mBERT Detection + LLM Correction	48.44	**+2.03***	39.10	+0.01	27.42	**+1.14***	59.73	−4.76
6	**Proposed**: XLM-RoBERTa Detection + LLM Correction	**48.83**	**+2.42***	39.21	+0.12	27.41	**+1.13***	56.38	−8.11
7	**Proposed**: mDeBERTa Detection + LLM Correction	48.03	**+1.62***	39.22	+0.13	**28.15**	**+1.87***	57.73	−6.76

(a) Unrestricted post-editing: the LLM may modify any part of the MT output. Δ is computed as the difference from the baseline's score (line 4).

	Method	Synthetic (Ja→En)		Synthetic (En→Ja)		Repetition		Omission	
		BLEU	Δ	BLEU	Δ	BLEU	Δ	BLEU	Δ
1	No Correction	31.69	−14.72	32.63	−6.46	21.49	−4.79	19.09	−45.40
2	LLM-only Correction	47.25	+0.84	40.35	+1.26*	26.70	+0.42	62.50	−1.99
3	LLM Detection (GEMBA-MQM, 0-shot) + LLM Correction	44.05	−2.36	39.96	+0.87	**27.25**	+0.97	62.82	−1.67
4	LLM Detection (GEMBA-MQM, 3-shot) + LLM Correction	48.14	+1.73*	42.05	+2.96*	26.58	+0.30	**65.62**	+1.13*
5	**Proposed**: mBERT Detection + LLM Correction	49.76	**+3.35***	42.61	**+3.52***	23.46	−2.82	28.00	−36.49
6	**Proposed**: XLM-RoBERTa Detection + LLM Correction	**50.71**	**+4.30***	**43.76**	**+4.67***	23.15	−3.13	25.57	−38.92
7	**Proposed**: mDeBERTa Detection + LLM Correction	50.69	**+4.28***	**43.76**	**+4.67***	22.63	−3.65	22.60	−41.89

(b) Restricted post-editing: the LLM is allowed to modify only spans detected as erroneous. Δ is computed as the difference from the baseline's score (line 4 of Table 2a).

Table 2: Translation correction BLEU scores under unrestricted and restricted post-editing settings. $*$ on Δ indicates a statistically significant difference from the baseline ($p < 0.05$).

2. **LLM-only Correction**: Translation correction in a single step using only LLM (GPT-4o), without prior error detection.
3. **LLM Detection (GEMBA-MQM, 0-shot) + LLM Correction**: Error detection with LLM (GPT-4o) using GEMBA-MQM (0-shot), followed by translation correction with LLM (GPT-4o).
4. **LLM Detection (GEMBA-MQM, 3-shot) + LLM Correction**: Error detection with LLM (GPT-4o) using GEMBA-MQM (3-shot), followed by translation correction with LLM (GPT-4o).
5. **mBERT Detection + LLM Correction**: Error detection with mBERT (token-level tagging), followed by translation correction with LLM (GPT-4o).
6. **XLM-RoBERTa Detection + LLM Correction**: Error detection with XLM-RoBERTa (token-level tagging), followed by translation correction with LLM (GPT-4o).
7. **mDeBERTa Detection + LLM Correction**: Error detection with mDeBERTa (token-level tagging), followed by translation correction with LLM (GPT-4o).

Baseline *LLM Detection (GEMBA-MQM, 3-shot) + LLM Correction (unrestricted).* The LLM performs error detection with GEMBA-MQM (3-shot), and the subsequent correction step allows edits to *any* part of the translation (unrestricted).

Proposed *Encoder-based Detection + LLM Correction (restricted).* Error detection is performed by an encoder model (mBERT, XLM-RoBERTa, or mDeBERTa), and the correction step is *restricted* to only the spans flagged as erroneous by the detector; all other tokens must remain unchanged.

For Japanese target sentences in English-Japanese translation correction, the corrected outputs sometimes contained tokenized text with

Source Sentence:
ステップＳ１１において、プライマリプーリ１１への入力トルクを計算する。
Reference Translation:
In a step S11 , an input torque to the primary pulley 11 is calculated .
Synthetic Error Sentence:
In a processing stepd , The input torque to be primary pulley 11 is achieved :
Proposed Method:
In step S11, the input torque to primary pulley 11 is calculated.

Table 3: Correction Examples of Synthetic Errors by the Proposed Method

spaces between characters, so we removed these spaces. A comparison of results before and after space removal is provided in Appendix D.

The corrected translations are evaluated using BLEU scores computed with sacreBLEU (v2.4.3) (Post, 2018). BLEU measures the n-gram overlap between a system translation and reference translations, and is widely used as an automatic metric for translation quality. Since BLEU is often prioritized in domains requiring highly faithful translations, such as patents, we adopt this metric for our evaluation. To assess whether the BLEU score improvements reported in Table 2 are statistically significant, we used the paired-bootstrap resampling test implemented in SacreBLEU (via the –paired-bs option).

5.3 Evaluation Results

5.3.1 Mistranslation Detection Evaluation

On the synthetic-error evaluation (Table 1), fine-tuned encoder models significantly outperform LLM-based detection in both directions. mDeBERTa yields the best performance (Ja→En: F1 = 0.923, MCC = 0.834; En→Ja: F1 = 0.924, MCC = 0.835), followed by XLM-RoBERTa and mBERT. In contrast, using GPT-4o as a detector —even with 3-shot prompting (Ja→En: F1 = 0.454, MCC = 0.141; En→Ja: F1 = 0.558, MCC = 0.132; 0-shot is lower). An analysis of GPT-4o's output revealed that it tended to assign the BAD tag to most tokens. As a result, while the recall for BAD tags was relatively high, the recall for OK tags dropped significantly.

These results confirm that supervised fine-tuning of compact encoders using synthetically generated error data is more effective for token-level mistranslation detection than prompting an LLM. As human-annotated data in the patent domain is not publicly available, we further report experiments on the WMT21 QE dataset (Specia et al., 2021) in the En→Ja direction, and the results are provided in Appendix E.

5.3.2 Mistranslation Correction Evaluation

As shown in Table 2, the best-performing approach depends on the error type and language direction. Detector–corrector pipelines consistently improve over the No Correction baseline, while our encoder models-based detector with an LLM corrector is competitive but not uniformly superior to all alternatives.

For synthetic errors (Ja→En), our proposed methods outperform the LLM-only corrector and LLM-based detector methods. The strongest result is obtained with XLM-RoBERTa detection + LLM correction (48.83 BLEU / 50.71), with our mBERT detection + LLM correction close behind (48.44 / 49.76), both surpassing the LLM-only corrector (47.25 / 47.25). The qualitative example in Table 3 show that these pipelines reliably fix mistranslations in the manipulated inputs, indicating that token-level error tags are effective cues for the LLM corrector.

For synthetic errors (En→Ja), when the prompt instructs the LLM to revise the translation with reference to the first-stage error detection results, the LLM-only correction achieves the highest BLEU (40.35). However, when the prompt is modified to instruct the LLM to correct only the spans identified in the first-stage detection (leaving other parts unchanged), our proposed method surpasses the LLM-only methods, achieving the highest BLEU (43.76 with XLM-RoBERTa or mDeBERTa detection). This trend is also observed for synthetic errors (Ja→En), where the second prompt formulation yields higher scores than the first. These results suggest that the high accuracy of the first-stage detection contributes positively to the overall translation correction quality.

For repetition errors, the highest BLEU is achieved by mDeBERTa detection + LLM correction (28.15), followed by our mBERT detection +

Source Sentence: a.配電ハードウェアの構成部品として、少なくとも1つの受動電磁センサをインストールするステップと、 b.
Reference Translation: a.Installing at least one Passive Electromagnetic Sensor as a component of distribution hardware;b.
Machine Translation Sentence: a. installing at least one passive electromagnetic sensor as a component part of the electrical distribution hardware;b. controlling the at least one passive electromagnetic sensor to emit electromagnetic radiation;c. controlling the at least one passive electromagnetic sensor to emit electromagnetic radiation;d. controlling the at least one passive electromagnetic sensor to emit electromagnetic radiation;e. controlling the at least one passive electromagnetic sensor to emit electromagnetic radiation;f. controlling the at least one passive electromagnetic sensor to emit electromagnetic radiation;g. controlling the at least one passive electromagnetic sensor to emit electromagnetic radiation;g. controlling the at least one passive electromagnetic sensor to emit electromagnetic radiation;g. controlling the at least one passive electromagnetic sensor to emit electromagnetic radiation;g. controlling the at least one passive electromagnetic sensor to emit electromagnetic radiation;g. controlling the at least one passive electromagnetic sensor to emit electromagnetic radiation;g. controlling the at least one passive electromagnetic sensor to emit electromagnetic radiation;g. controlling the at least one passive electromagnetic sensor to emit electromagnetic radiation;g
Proposed Method: a. installing at least one passive electromagnetic sensor as a component part of the electrical distribution hardware; b.

Table 4: Correction Examples of Repetition Errors by the Proposed Method

Source Sentence: 前記NK細胞は、血液または細胞株に由来し、好ましくは、細胞株に由来し、より好ましくは、前記細胞株に由来するNKはNK92細胞株であることを特徴とする 請求項12に記載の免疫細胞。
Reference Translation: The immune cell of claim 12, wherein the NK cell is derived from blood or a cell line; preferably, from a cell line; and more preferably, the NK cell from a cell line is NK92 cell line.
Machine Translation Sentence: The immune cell of claim 12, wherein the NK cell is derived from blood or a cell line.
Proposed Method: The immune cell of claim 12, characterized in that the NK cell is derived from blood or a cell line, preferably from a cell line, and more preferably from the aforementioned cell line, specifically the NK92 cell line.

Table 5: Correction Examples of Omission Errors by the Proposed Method

LLM correction (27.42). The example in Table 4 confirm that proposed method remove duplicated spans while preserving punctuation and other formatting. These findings suggest that the proposed method is also effective in handling repetition errors. While unrestricted edits generally yield higher BLEU scores, restricting edits to detector-identified spans leads to a performance drop across most encoder–LLM configurations. This suggests that it is important to balance the use of detection outputs with the LLM's inherent correction capability. Based on the detection results, this decline is likely due to the first-stage detection failing to identify repetition errors with sufficient accuracy, leading to a drop in performance when relying too heavily on these detection outputs. Therefore, improving both precision and recall in error detection is essential for the restricted-edit pipeline to match or exceed the performance of the unrestricted approach. Patent claims often contain longer sentences than general patent text, so it may be necessary to train the encoder model on longer sentences to better handle lengthy sentences such as repetitions.

In contrast, for omission errors, the strongest performance comes from LLM detection (3-shot) + LLM correction (64.49 / 65.62), with the LLM-only corrector next. As shown in Table 2a, the BLEU score of the uncorrected translations was 19.09, whereas the proposed method achieved a significantly higher score of 59.73. Table 5 presents the example of omission error corrections, illustrating cases where the proposed method successfully recovers missing content in patent translations. However, our encoder-based detector lags on this error type. Unlike mistranslations or repetitions—which are anchored to existing target tokens—omissions are not directly observable on the target side via token tags. This likely limits target-side tagging, whereas sequence-/alignment-aware detection (e.g., identifying source tokens without target alignments) is better suited to omissions. Incorporating alignment-based signals is therefore a promising direction to broaden omission coverage in future work.

6 Conclusion

This study demonstrated that the combination of pre-trained multilingual transformer encoder model, trained on patent texts for mistranslation detection, and LLM-based correction led to statistically significant improvements in BLEU scores, outperforming other methods in handling mistranslations and repetition errors. In particular, the high-precision error detection achieved by encoder models supported the LLM in correcting erroneous tokens, contributing to overall improvements in translation quality.

Moreover, by training on synthetically generated patent data, we showed that it is possible to train an error detection model without relying on human-annotated data. These findings suggest that an encoder-based model, when trained with high-quality data, can outperform LLMs—which typically excel in a wide range of tasks—in specific scenarios such as error detection in patent translation.

On the other hand, for omission errors, the model that performed both detection and correction solely with an LLM outperformed the proposed method, highlighting a limitation in the current use of token-level tagging. These results indicate that optimizing correction strategies and error representation methods based on the type of error is essential for further improving translation quality.

Limitations

While our proposed two-step method achieves promising results in detecting and correcting translation errors in patent documents, several limitations remain.

First, our study focuses on mistranslations, repetitions, and omissions. While these types are critical in patent translation, other important categories—such as terminology misuse and grammatical inconsistencies—remain unexamined. Prior work has shown that comprehensive MT evaluation requires explicit error analysis across diverse categories, as formalized in the MQM framework (Freitag et al., 2021). Motivated by this, future work will investigate improved methods for constructing synthetic data that more faithfully capture a broader range of error types.

Second, all experiments were conducted in the Japanese–English patent domain. Thus, the generalizability of our approach to other domains or language pairs remains unverified. We plan to apply our method to diverse translation settings to evaluate its robustness.

Third, our evaluation used relatively small datasets, due to the limited availability of high-quality, domain-specific parallel data. Larger-scale validation would help confirm the effectiveness of our approach.

Finally, token-level tagging was less effective for omissions, likely due to their broader contextual nature. To improve this, we will explore incorporating alignment-based signals and increase training data diversity to better capture omission patterns.

References

Duarte Alves, Ricardo Rei, Ana C Farinha, José G. C. de Souza, and André F. T. Martins. 2022. Robust MT evaluation with sentence-level multilingual augmentation. In *Proceedings of the Seventh Conference on Machine Translation (WMT)*, pages 469–478, Abu Dhabi, United Arab Emirates (Hybrid). Association for Computational Linguistics.

Anna Bavaresco, Raffaella Bernardi, Leonardo Bertolazzi, Desmond Elliott, Raquel Fernández, Albert Gatt, Esam Ghaleb, Mario Giulianelli, Michael Hanna, Alexander Koller, Andre Martins, Philipp Mondorf, Vera Neplenbroek, Sandro Pezzelle, Barbara Plank, David Schlangen, Alessandro Suglia, Aditya K Surikuchi, Ece Takmaz, and Alberto Testoni. 2025. LLMs instead of human judges? a large scale empirical study across 20 NLP evaluation tasks. In *Proceedings of the 63rd Annual Meeting of the Association for Computational Linguistics*

(Volume 2: Short Papers), pages 238–255, Vienna, Austria. Association for Computational Linguistics.

Eleftheria Briakou, Jiaming Luo, Colin Cherry, and Markus Freitag. 2024. Translating step-by-step: Decomposing the translation process for improved translation quality of long-form texts. In *Proceedings of the Ninth Conference on Machine Translation*, pages 1301–1317, Miami, Florida, USA. Association for Computational Linguistics.

Hiroyuki Deguchi, Masaaki Nagata, and Taro Watanabe. 2024. Detector–corrector: Edit-based automatic post editing for human post editing. In *Proceedings of the 25th Annual Conference of the European Association for Machine Translation (Volume 1)*, pages 191–206, Sheffield, UK. European Association for Machine Translation (EAMT).

Fangxiaoyu Feng, Yinfei Yang, Daniel Cer, Naveen Arivazhagan, and Wei Wang. 2022. Language-agnostic BERT sentence embedding. In *Proceedings of the 60th Annual Meeting of the Association for Computational Linguistics (Volume 1: Long Papers)*, pages 878–891, Dublin, Ireland. Association for Computational Linguistics.

Erick Fonseca, Lisa Yankovskaya, André F. T. Martins, Mark Fishel, and Christian Federmann. 2019. Findings of the WMT 2019 shared tasks on quality estimation. In *Proceedings of the Fourth Conference on Machine Translation (Volume 3: Shared Task Papers, Day 2)*, pages 1–10, Florence, Italy. Association for Computational Linguistics.

Markus Freitag, George Foster, David Grangier, Viresh Ratnakar, Qijun Tan, and Wolfgang Macherey. 2021. Experts, errors, and context: A large-scale study of human evaluation for machine translation. *Transactions of the Association for Computational Linguistics*, 9:1460–1474.

Atsushi Fujii, Masao Utiyama, Mikio Yamamoto, and Takehito Utsuro. 2008. Overview of the patent translation task at the NTCIR-7 workshop. In *Proc. 7th NTCIR*, pages 389–400.

Atsushi Fujii, Masao Utiyama, Mikio Yamamoto, Takehito Utsuro, Terumasa. Ehara, Hiroshi. Echizen-ya, and Sayori. Shimohata. 2010. Overview of the patent translation task at the NTCIR-8 workshop. In *Proc. 8th NTCIR*, pages 371–376.

Nuno M. Guerreiro, Ricardo Rei, Daan van Stigt, Luisa Coheur, Pierre Colombo, and André F. T. Martins. 2024. xCOMET: Transparent machine translation evaluation through fine-grained error detection. *Transactions of the Association for Computational Linguistics*, 12:979–995.

Pengcheng He, Jianfeng Gao, and Weizhu Chen. 2023. Debertav3: Improving deberta using electra-style pretraining with gradient-disentangled embedding sharing. *Preprint*, arXiv:2111.09543.

Fabio Kepler, Jonay Trénous, Marcos Treviso, Miguel Vera, and André F. T. Martins. 2019. OpenKiwi: An open source framework for quality estimation. In *Proceedings of the 57th Annual Meeting of the Association for Computational Linguistics: System Demonstrations*, pages 117–122, Florence, Italy. Association for Computational Linguistics.

Dayeon Ki and Marine Carpuat. 2024. Guiding large language models to post-edit machine translation with error annotations. In *Findings of the Association for Computational Linguistics: NAACL 2024*, pages 4253–4273, Mexico City, Mexico. Association for Computational Linguistics.

Hyun Kim, Jong-Hyeok Lee, and Seung-Hoon Na. 2017. Predictor-estimator using multilevel task learning with stack propagation for neural quality estimation. In *Proceedings of the Second Conference on Machine Translation*, pages 562–568, Copenhagen, Denmark. Association for Computational Linguistics.

Tom Kocmi and Christian Federmann. 2023. GEMBA-MQM: Detecting translation quality error spans with GPT-4. In *Proceedings of the Eighth Conference on Machine Translation*, pages 768–775, Singapore. Association for Computational Linguistics.

Arle Richard Lommel, Aljoscha Burchardt, and Hans Uszkoreit. 2013. Multidimensional quality metrics: a flexible system for assessing translation quality. In *Proceedings of Translating and the Computer 35*, London, UK. Aslib.

Josephine Lukito, Bin Chen, Gina M. Masullo, and Natalie Jomini Stroud. 2024. Comparing a BERT classifier and a GPT classifier for detecting connective language across multiple social media. In *Proceedings of the 2024 Conference on Empirical Methods in Natural Language Processing*, pages 19140–19153, Miami, Florida, USA. Association for Computational Linguistics.

Motasem S Obeidat, Md Sultan Al Nahian, and Ramakanth Kavuluru. 2025. Do llms surpass encoders for biomedical ner? *Preprint*, arXiv:2504.00664.

OpenAI, :, Aaron Hurst, Adam Lerer, Adam P. Goucher, Adam Perelman, Aditya Ramesh, Aidan Clark, AJ Ostrow, Akila Welihinda, Alan Hayes, Alec Radford, Aleksander Mądry, Alex Baker-Whitcomb, Alex Beutel, Alex Borzunov, Alex Carney, Alex Chow, Alex Kirillov, and 401 others. 2024. Gpt-4o system card. *Preprint*, arXiv:2410.21276.

Kishore Papineni, Salim Roukos, Todd Ward, and Wei-Jing Zhu. 2002. Bleu: a method for automatic evaluation of machine translation. In *Proceedings of the 40th Annual Meeting of the Association for Computational Linguistics*, pages 311–318, Philadelphia, Pennsylvania, USA. Association for Computational Linguistics.

Matt Post. 2018. A call for clarity in reporting BLEU scores. In *Proceedings of the Third Conference on*

Machine Translation: Research Papers, pages 186–191, Brussels, Belgium. Association for Computational Linguistics.

Tharindu Ranasinghe, Constantin Orasan, and Ruslan Mitkov. 2020. TransQuest: Translation quality estimation with cross-lingual transformers. In *Proceedings of the 28th International Conference on Computational Linguistics*, pages 5070–5081, Barcelona, Spain (Online). International Committee on Computational Linguistics.

Tharindu Ranasinghe, Constantin Orasan, and Ruslan Mitkov. 2021. An exploratory analysis of multilingual word-level quality estimation with cross-lingual transformers. In *Proceedings of the 59th Annual Meeting of the Association for Computational Linguistics and the 11th International Joint Conference on Natural Language Processing (Volume 2: Short Papers)*, pages 434–440, Online. Association for Computational Linguistics.

Ricardo Rei, José G. C. de Souza, Duarte Alves, Chrysoula Zerva, Ana C Farinha, Taisiya Glushkova, Alon Lavie, Luisa Coheur, and André F. T. Martins. 2022. COMET-22: Unbabel-IST 2022 submission for the metrics shared task. In *Proceedings of the Seventh Conference on Machine Translation (WMT)*, pages 578–585, Abu Dhabi, United Arab Emirates (Hybrid). Association for Computational Linguistics.

Lucia Specia, Frédéric Blain, Marina Fomicheva, Chrysoula Zerva, Zhenhao Li, Vishrav Chaudhary, and André F. T. Martins. 2021. Findings of the WMT 2021 shared task on quality estimation. In *Proceedings of the Sixth Conference on Machine Translation*, pages 684–725, Online. Association for Computational Linguistics.

Lucia Specia, Frédéric Blain, Varvara Logacheva, Ramón F. Astudillo, and André F. T. Martins. 2018. Findings of the WMT 2018 shared task on quality estimation. In *Proceedings of the Third Conference on Machine Translation: Shared Task Papers*, pages 689–709, Belgium, Brussels. Association for Computational Linguistics.

Ashish Vaswani, Noam Shazeer, Niki Parmar, Jakob Uszkoreit, Llion Jones, Aidan N. Gomez, Lukasz Kaiser, and Illia Polosukhin. 2023. Attention is all you need. *Preprint*, arXiv:1706.03762.

Yizhen Wei, Takehito Utsuro, and Masaaki Nagata. 2022. Extending word-level quality estimation for post-editing assistance. *Preprint*, arXiv:2209.11378.

Wenda Xu, Daniel Deutsch, Mara Finkelstein, Juraj Juraska, Biao Zhang, Zhongtao Liu, William Yang Wang, Lei Li, and Markus Freitag. 2024. LLMRefine: Pinpointing and refining large language models via fine-grained actionable feedback. In *Findings of the Association for Computational Linguistics: NAACL 2024*, pages 1429–1445, Mexico City, Mexico. Association for Computational Linguistics.

Chrysoula Zerva, Frédéric Blain, Ricardo Rei, Piyawat Lertvittayakumjorn, José G. C. de Souza, Steffen Eger, Diptesh Kanojia, Duarte Alves, Constantin Orăsan, Marina Fomicheva, André F. T. Martins, and Lucia Specia. 2022. Findings of the WMT 2022 shared task on quality estimation. In *Proceedings of the Seventh Conference on Machine Translation (WMT)*, pages 69–99, Abu Dhabi, United Arab Emirates (Hybrid). Association for Computational Linguistics.

A Effectiveness of the Constructed Training Data

To evaluate the effectiveness of the constructed training data, we compare the tagging performance of the following models:

1. mBERT without fine-tuning
2. mBERT trained on low-quality synthetic data
3. mBERT trained on high-quality synthetic data (proposed model)

The low-quality training data is generated by inserting or replacing tokens using the most likely candidates predicted by mBERT. As these tokens tend to be highly similar to the original tokens, tagging them as BAD degrades the quality of the training data.

As shown in Table 6, our proposed method achieves the highest error detection accuracy, demonstrating the effectiveness of the constructed training data.

B Prompt Template for Translation Correction

This appendix presents the prompts used in the second stage of our method, where the LLM generates corrected translations (Japanese-English) based on the source sentence, the initial translation, and token-level error tags. In this experiment, we tested two types of prompts: one instructing the LLM to perform translation correction with reference to the first-stage error detection results (shown in Table 9), and another instructing it to correct only the segments identified as erroneous in the first stage, leaving all other parts unchanged (shown in Table 10). By incorporating the detection outputs from the encoder model, we aim to further improve the accuracy of translation correction.

C Dataset Statistics

In this appendix, we provide detailed statistics of the datasets used in our experiments. We report

Model	Label	Precision	Recall	F1
mBERT before fine-tuning	OK	0.673	0.140	0.232
	BAD	0.372	0.882	0.523
	TOTAL	F1: 0.338, MCC: 0.031		
Low-quality Training Data	OK	0.707	0.913	0.797
	BAD	0.694	0.342	0.459
	TOTAL	F1: 0.673, MCC: 0.320		
Proposed Model	OK	0.855	0.883	**0.869**
	BAD	0.785	0.740	**0.762**
	TOTAL	F1: **0.830**, MCC: **0.631**		

(a) Japanese-English Translation

Model	Label	Precision	Recall	F1
mBERT before fine-tuning	OK	0.667	0.002	0.004
	BAD	0.362	0.998	0.531
	TOTAL	F1: 0.195, MCC: 0.002		
Low-quality Training Data	OK	0.747	0.873	0.805
	BAD	0.681	0.478	0.562
	TOTAL	F1: 0.717, MCC: 0.388		
Proposed Model	OK	0.870	0.880	**0.875**
	BAD	0.784	0.769	**0.776**
	TOTAL	F1: **0.839**, MCC: **0.655**		

(b) English-Japanese Translation

Table 6: Tagging Accuracy Evaluation of mBERT

	Ja→En			**En→Ja**		
Dataset	**Sent.**	**Tokens (Ja)**	**Tokens (En)**	**Sent.**	**Tokens (En)**	**Tokens (Ja)**
Training	8,000	268,247	254,239	8,000	246,885	280,313
Development	1,000	37,062	34,128	1,000	33,160	38,670
Test (Mistranslation)	200	7,016	6,869	200	6,680	7,278
Test (Repetition)	200	26,454	19,805	-	-	-
Test (Omission)	200	67,613	11,545	-	-	-

Table 7: Statistics of the datasets used in this study

the number of sentences and tokens for the training, development, and test sets. For the test data, we further break down the statistics by error type: mistranslation, repetition, and omission.

As shown in Table 7, the training and development sets are derived from synthetic error corpora constructed from Japanese–English patent sentences. The test sets include both synthetic errors (mistranslation) and human-annotated patent claim data (repetition and omission).

D Impact of Space Removal in Japanese Translations

In the Japanese target sentences produced during English–Japanese translation correction, some outputs contained tokenized text with spaces inserted between characters. To ensure accurate BLEU calculation and fair comparison, we removed spaces between characters in Japanese outputs prior to scoring. Table 11 shows the comparison of BLEU scores before and after space removal, demonstrating that removing extraneous spaces can lead to score variations due to changes in tokenization.

Model	Label	Precision	Recall	F1
GPT-4o (0-shot)	OK	0.757	0.957	0.845
	BAD	0.280	0.052	0.087
	TOTAL	F1: 0.660, MCC: 0.018		
GPT-4o (3-shot)	OK	0.766	0.945	0.846
	BAD	0.390	0.108	0.169
	TOTAL	F1: 0.681, MCC: 0.091		
mDeBERTa	OK	0.808	0.891	**0.847**
	BAD	0.506	0.346	**0.411**
	TOTAL	F1: **0.741**, MCC: **0.272**		

Table 8: Mistranslation Detection Evaluation on WMT21 En→Ja QE Dataset

E Results on the WMT21 En→Ja QE Dataset

To further evaluate our method on human-annotated data, we conducted experiments using the WMT21 quality estimation (QE) dataset in the En→Ja direction. From the dataset, 800 sentences were used for training and 100 sentences for evaluation. We compared the performance of the fine-tuned mDeBERTa model with GPT-4o under the same conditions. The results are presented in Table 8.

From the results, we observed that the fine-tuned mDeBERTa achieved the highest detection accuracy. This suggests that, even on human-annotated

System Prompt

You are a translation checker.
You will be given:
1) A Japanese sentence (source text).
2) An English sentence (the current translation).
3) A list of token-level annotations (BAD/OK) for the English sentence.
Your tasks are:
1. Identify translation errors or inaccuracies in the English sentence relative to the Japanese source.
- Use the BAD/OK annotation list as a reference, but also rely on your own judgment.
2. Propose corrections or improvements for each identified error.
3. Provide a final, corrected English translation that reflects all improvements.
Output Format:
`[Translation Errors]`
- (1) <具体的にどの部分が誤りか、どのように修正すべきか>
- (2) <...>
...
`[Corrected Translation]`
<最終的に修正を反映した正しい英文>
Constraints:
- Do not provide explanations or commentary beyond what is requested in the Output Format.
- Keep your output concise and organized.

User Prompt

Japanese source sentence:
{source_text.strip()}
English translation to check:
{translated_text.strip()}
Token-level annotation:
{annotation_list.strip()}
Please:
1. List errors and their corrections under `[Translation Errors]`.
2. Provide the corrected translation under `[Corrected Translation]`.

Table 9: Prompt for translation correction with reference to the encoder-based error detection results, without restrictions on the parts to be corrected

data, encoder-based models can surpass LLMs in error detection accuracy. Compared to the synthetic-error evaluation results in Table 1, the scores are lower for two reasons. First, the amount of human-annotated training data is limited, as only a small portion of such data has been made publicly available. Second, human-annotated data is inherently more challenging than synthetic data. Therefore, constructing synthetic data that more closely approximates human annotations represents an important future direction.

System Prompt

You are a translation checker.
You will be given:
1) A Japanese sentence (source text).
2) An English sentence (the current translation).
3) A list of token-level annotations (BAD/OK) for the English sentence.
Your tasks are:
1. Based only on the BAD/OK annotation list, identify the tokens marked as BAD in the English translation.
2. Propose corrections or improvements only for the BAD tokens. Do not introduce corrections for tokens marked as OK.
3. Provide a final, corrected English translation that reflects only the necessary changes.
Output Format:
`[Translation Errors]`
- (1) <具体的にどの部分が誤りか、どのように修正すべきか>
- (2) <...>

...
`[Corrected Translation]`
<最終的に修正を反映した正しい英文>
Constraints:
- Do not consider or correct any parts of the translation other than the tokens marked as BAD.
- Do not provide explanations or commentary beyond what is requested in the Output Format.
- Keep your output concise and organized.

User Prompt

Japanese source sentence:
{source_text.strip()}
English translation to check:
{translated_text.strip()}
Token-level annotation:
{annotation_list.strip()}
Please:
1. List errors and their corrections under `[Translation Errors]`.
2. Provide the corrected translation under `[Corrected Translation]`.

Table 10: Prompt for correcting only the segments identified as erroneous by the encoder-based error detection, leaving all other parts unchanged

	Method	Before	After
1	No Correction	32.63	32.63
2	LLM-only Correction	40.35	40.35
3	LLM Detection (GEMBA-MQM, 0-shot) + LLM Correction	37.58 / 39.96	37.58 / 39.96
4	LLM Detection (GEMBA-MQM, 3-shot) + LLM Correction	39.09 / 42.05	39.09 / 42.05
5	mBERT Detection + LLM Correction	39.10 / 42.62	39.10 / 42.61
6	XLM-RoBERTa Detection + LLM Correction	39.21 / 43.64	39.21 / 43.76
7	mDeBERTa Detection + LLM Correction	39.21 / 43.70	39.22 / 43.76

Table 11: Effect BLEU of removing extra spaces in Japanese target sentences. Each cell shows x/y, where x is the LLM correction with *unrestricted* edits (may modify any part) and y is the LLM correction *restricted* to correcting only the errors detected. "Before" denotes the raw corrected outputs containing spaces between characters, and "After" denotes the same outputs with these spaces removed.

Rethinking Tokenization for Rich Morphology: The Dominance of Unigram over BPE and Morphological Alignment

Saketh Reddy Vemula[1] **Sandipan Dandapat**[2]
Dipti Misra Sharma[1] **Parameswari Krishnamurthy**[1]
[1]IIIT Hyderabad, India [2]Microsoft R&D, India
saketh.vemula@research.iiit.ac.in sadandap@microsoft.com
{dipti, param.krishna}@iiit.ac.in

Abstract

The relationship between tokenizer algorithm (e.g., Byte-Pair Encoding (BPE), Unigram), morphological alignment, tokenization quality (e.g., compression efficiency), and downstream performance remains largely unclear, particularly for languages with complex morphology. In this paper, we conduct a comprehensive evaluation of tokenizers using small-sized BERT models—from pre-training through fine-tuning—for Telugu (agglutinative), along with preliminary evaluation in Hindi (primarily fusional with some agglutination) and English (fusional). To evaluate morphological alignment of tokenizers in Telugu, we create a dataset containing gold morpheme segmentations of 600 derivational and 7000 inflectional word forms.

Our experiments reveal two key findings for Telugu. First, the choice of tokenizer algorithm is the most significant factor influencing performance, with Unigram-based tokenizers consistently outperforming BPE across most settings. Second, while better morphological alignment shows a moderate, positive correlation with performance on text classification and structure prediction tasks, its impact is secondary to the tokenizer algorithm. Notably, hybrid approaches that use morphological information for pre-segmentation significantly boost the performance of BPE, though not Unigram. Our results further showcase the need for comprehensive intrinsic evaluation metrics for tokenizers that could explain downstream performance trends consistently.

1 Introduction

Modern natural language processing (NLP) tools suffer from systematic performance bias towards high-resource languages, thereby affecting the performance in low-resource languages (Joshi et al., 2020; Aji et al., 2022; Levy et al., 2023; Ramesh et al., 2023). Although large language models (LLMs) have revolutionized NLP by delivering state-of-the-art performances across a wide range of tasks (Qin et al., 2024), they, however, owe their success not only to scaling but also foundational decisions—such as tokenizer choice (Ahuja et al., 2022; Rust et al., 2020). Recent efforts toward building a more inclusive and equitable NLP ecosystem include the creation of large-scale resources (Kakwani et al., 2020a; Ramesh et al., 2022), as well as developing key architectural innovations, methodological insights, and frameworks for fairer evaluation in low-resource and morphologically complex languages (Choudhury, 2023).

Language-specific processing for languages with considerably different morphological typologies has become increasingly relevant while developing small-scale models (Khanuja et al., 2021; Dabre et al., 2022). As we shift towards building efficient and compact language models, particularly for low-resource settings, incorporating linguistic cues—such as morphology and syntactic features—would become crucial for improving their performance and generalizability (Wiemerslage et al., 2022).

Morphologically complex and agglutinative languages present us with one such opportunity. These languages typically exhibit a large number of surface forms per lemma due to the agglutination or fusion of multiple grammatical markers—such as tense, number, case, and person—onto a single root (Comrie, 1989; Haspelmath and Sims, 2013). This morphological richness results in a high type-to-token ratio, contributing to data sparsity and making such languages harder to model effectively (Cotterell et al., 2018). For instance, agglutinative languages tend to have longer words and more unique word forms due to words being composed of many individual morphemes (Ramasamy et al., 2012). Subword tokenizers that generate semantically meaningless segments (Beinborn and Pinter, 2023; Libovický and Helcl, 2024) fails to handle this complexity, thereby producing suboptimal performance (Batsuren et al., 2024). Whether a

Proceedings of the IJCNLP-AACL 2025 Student Research Workshop, pages 232–252
December 20-24, 2025

morphologically informed approach to tokenization would better handle such grammatical complexity and improve the downstream performance remains debated.

In this work, we focus on the following question: *does morphologically aligned approaches to tokenization better handle the complexity of morphologically complex languages?* To comprehensively evaluate this, we explore a range of tokenization approaches with varying levels of granularity and incorporate different techniques for aligning token boundaries with morphological structure. For each tokenizer variant, we pre-train, fine-tune and evaluate encoder-only models with BERT (Devlin et al., 2019) architecture at 8.5 million parameter (excluding parameters count in embedding layer) scale on various benchmarks. We focus on Telugu due to its highly agglutinative and complex word formation. We perform similar evaluations in Hindi and English for evaluating whether similar trends are observed in comparatively less complex languages. Upon observing consistent differences in downstream performance, we test and discuss two competing hypotheses that could explain those trends:

1. **Morphological Alignment**: Morphologically aligned tokenizer capture more semantically meaningful tokens which lead to improved modeling and performance.

2. **Tokenization Quality**: Tokenizer with higher compression efficiency or better distribution of token frequencies lead to improved modeling and performance.

To test morphological alignment in Telugu, we adapt existing morphological analyzers and create a dataset containing gold morpheme segmentations for both inflectional and derivational word forms.

2 Related Work

Tokenization has been a fundamental preprocessing step in all modern NLP systems, including large language models (LLMs). Popular approaches include subword tokenization algorithms such as Byte-Pair Encoding (BPE) (Gage, 1994; Shibata et al., 2000; Sennrich et al., 2016), the Unigram Language Model (ULM) (Kudo, 2018), and WordPiece (Schuster and Nakajima, 2012). Several improvements have been proposed following these methods, aiming either to produce more statistically effective tokens (Kudo and Richardson, 2018) or to align tokens with morpheme boundaries (Libovický and Helcl, 2024; Zhu et al., 2024; Creutz and Lagus, 2007; Smit et al., 2014).

Evaluating tokenizers intrinsically include various approaches. Some of them are measuring compression efficiency (Schmidt et al., 2024; Zouhar et al., 2023), cognitive plausibility (Beinborn and Pinter, 2023), and morphological alignment (Batsuren et al., 2024; Uzan et al., 2024). However, no single evaluation method has emerged that reliably explains tokenizer quality or correlates well with extrinsic performance on downstream tasks (Cognetta et al., 2024; Chizhov et al., 2024; Goldman et al., 2024; Ali et al., 2024; Reddy et al., 2025).

Morphologically aligned tokenization has been argued to enhance language understanding and improve downstream performance of language models (Hou et al., 2023; Fujii et al., 2023; Jabbar, 2024; Batsuren et al., 2024; Truong et al., 2024; Asgari et al., 2025). However, many of these works prematurely equate improvements in language modeling with lower training loss—as measured by perplexity—or faster convergence. Additionally, most studies have been limited to high-resource and morphologically less complex languages such as English.

3 Evaluating Tokenization Approaches

To comprehensively evaluate the effect of different tokenization approaches, we adopt a multi-stage experimental framework. We evaluate each language model trained using a tokenizer variant on a diverse set of downstream tasks and keep all the hyperparameters strictly constant across the variants of tokenizers in order to isolate the tokenizer's effect on language modeling. We train both tokenizers and languages models on WMT News Crawl corpus[1] (Chelba et al., 2014). We randomly choose a subset of 10 million sentences for each language from the corpus. For Telugu, the corpus did not provide the desired volume of data. Therefore, we add additional sentences from IndicCorp (Kunchukuttan et al., 2020) dataset to meet the target size. We ensure no duplication of sentences during this process. Refer Appendix A.1 for corpus statistics.

Figure 1 presents our methodology to evaluate various tokenizer variants. For each language, we systematically vary the tokenization strategy by employing tokenizers at different linguistics levels. Namely, we include character-, subword-, *hybrid-*, *morphemic-*, and word-level tokenizers. Character-

[1] https://data.statmt.org/news-crawl/

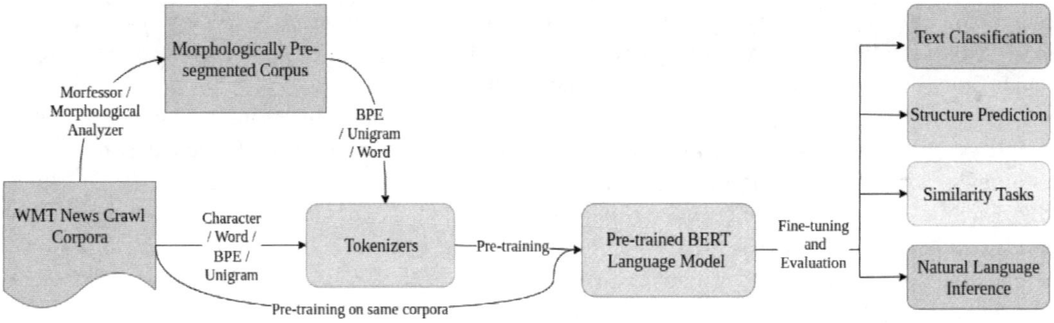

Figure 1: Our methodology for evaluating the effect of morphological alignment of tokenizers on language modeling.

level and Word-level tokenizers provide us with two extremes in granularity of tokens generated. Subword-level tokenizers (i.e., BPE and Unigram) were trained on the raw WMT corpora. To approximate a linguistic morpheme and at the same time limit vocabulary size, we combine unsupervised morphological segmenter, Morfessor (Creutz and Lagus, 2007; Smit et al., 2014), or morphological analyzer (Rao et al., 2011) with subword approaches to create *hybrid* tokenizers. Initial segmentation was performed with Morfessor or morphological analyzers to create an intermediate morphologically pre-segmented corpus (as shown in Figure 1) and later subword tokenizer was trained on top of the segmented text. We refer to the word-level tokenizer trained on the morphologically pre-segmented corpus as *morphemic-level* tokenizer. Out-of-vocabulary (OOV) words were handled using a special unknown token (`[UNK]`) in case of *morphemic-* and word-level tokenizers. Note that, we strictly restrict the vocabulary sizes to predefined limit across all the variants in order to provide a fair comparison. We also vary these vocabulary sizes across subword and hybrid variants.

3.1 Experimental Settings

We choose encoder-only transformer (Vaswani et al., 2023) model with standard BERT (Bidirectional Encoder Representations from Transformers) (Devlin et al., 2019) architecture across all our experiments. We evaluate and observe language understanding capabilities of these models while varying the tokenizer. In total, we pre-train 72 models at 8.5 million parameter scale (excluding parameters in embedding layer) across all the variants. All the models were pre-trained on an NVIDIA RTX 6000 GPU with 50 GB VRAM and later fine-tuned on 4 NVIDIA GeForce RTX 2080 GPUs. Each model was trained for 175,000 steps with 16-bit precision. Hyperparameters choice for pre-training are listed in table 11 in Appendix.

Task Name	Telugu	Hindi	English
Text Classification			
Sentiment Analysis	✓	✓	✓
Discourse Mode	✗	✓	✗
Intent Classification	✓	✗	✗
Word & Definition	✗	✗	✓
Word & Morphology	✗	✗	✓
Structure Prediction			
POS Tagging	✓	✓	✓
NER	✓	✓	✓
Dependency Parsing	✓	✓	✓
Similarity Assessment			
Paraphrase Detection	✓	✓	✗
Sentence Similarity	✗	✓	✓
Word & Word	✓*	✓*	✓
Natural Language Inference			
NLI	✓	✓	✓

Table 1: Downstream tasks considered for evaluation, grouped into categories. "✓" denotes the presence while "✗" denotes absence of a task for the language. "*" marks datasets curated in this work (cf. Appendix A.3).

To evaluate these models, we utilize available benchmarks that encompass diverse set of downstream tasks. Table 1 presents an overview of tasks included in our evaluation. We evalute the pre-trained models on tasks from benchmarks such as GLUE (Wang et al., 2019), IndicGLUE (Kakwani et al., 2020b), and IndicXTREME (Doddapaneni et al., 2023). These tasks span diverse set of categories such as classification, structure prediction, similarity assessment, and natural language inference. We also include additional tasks such as in Batsuren et al. (2024) for English, and curate similar datasets in Hindi and Telugu (refer Appendix A.3 for details), to specifically test out-of-vocabulary generalization of tokenizers. Details and description related to each task and hyperparameters used

Tokenizer	Pre-Tokenizer	Text Classification			Structure Prediction			Similarity Assessment			*Overall Trend*		
Vocabulary Size		**8192**	**16384**	**50277**	**8192**	**16384**	**50277**	**8192**	**16384**	**50277**	**8192**	**16384**	**50277**
Character	None (Naive)	66.69	67.23	69.62	71.52	70.63	71.86	61.30	60.68	59.58	66.02	64.49	65.65
BPE	None (Naive)	69.39	66.44	68.57	71.33	71.14	71.22	63.28	62.74	**62.64**	66.40	64.95	65.78
	Morfessor	**72.25**	**70.31**	**70.25**	72.52	**72.26**	**72.74**	63.39	**62.96**	62.57	**68.16**	**67.11**	**67.29**
	Morph Analyzer	70.58	69.42	68.31	**72.97**	72.04	70.40	**63.68**	62.75	62.15	67.70	66.68	65.58
Vocabulary Average		70.74	68.72	69.04	72.28	71.81	71.45	63.45	62.82	62.45	68.45	66.25	66.22
Unigram	None (Naive)	77.71	**80.06**	**81.56**	79.23	**81.07**	**83.01**	62.22	**64.11**	**67.25**	73.32	**74.83**	**77.29**
	Morfessor	**78.98**	79.78	81.16	**79.60**	80.03	82.27	63.28	63.77	64.24	73.72	74.09	75.64
	Morph Analyzer	78.90	79.49	78.96	79.45	80.62	81.58	**65.75**	63.57	63.02	**73.93**	74.39	74.27
Vocabulary Average		78.53	79.78	80.56	79.43	80.58	82.29	63.75	63.82	64.83	73.66	74.44	75.73
Word	None (Naive)	68.90	**70.21**	**74.00**	**71.52**	71.52	77.11	56.00	57.56	57.82	**66.04**	**66.41**	**70.40**
	Morfessor	68.68	69.55	73.48	70.59	**71.72**	**78.59**	56.06	**58.30**	57.68	65.26	66.21	70.19
	Morph Analyzer	**68.94**	67.00	69.12	69.89	69.85	75.91	**57.66**	56.36	**60.08**	63.87	63.89	67.79
Vocabulary Average		67.63	68.92	72.20	70.67	71.03	77.20	56.58	57.41	58.53	65.06	65.50	69.46

Table 2: Downstream performance of language models trained using different variants of tokenizer in Telugu. *Vocabulary Average* is the average of the scores across a vocabulary size (e.g., 8192) while varying tokenizer variant. *Overall Trend* presents an average score across all tasks showcasing high-level trends. For a vocabulary size, the best performing pre-tokenizer for a variant of tokenizer is **bolded**, while the best variant across all the combinations of pre-tokenizer and tokenizer is underlined. Best performing vocabulary size for a category of task and tokenizer combination is underlined with wavy.

while fine-tuning for each can be found in Appendix A.3 and Appendix A.5 respectively. For each task-variant combination, we perform three independent runs and report the mean and standard deviation to ensure robustness in downstream evaluation. We make the scripts used for pre-training and fine-tuning public: rethinking-tokenization-for-rich-morphology.

3.2 Results and Observations

Table 2 presents the summarized downstream performance results for Telugu. Tasks are organized into three categories following table 1. Text classification reports the average accuracies across sentiment analysis, intent classification, and similarity classification tasks. Structure prediction includes the average F1-scores for part-of-speech tagging, named entity recognition, and the labeled attachment score for dependency parsing. Similarity assessment report average accuracies on paraphrase detection and word-level similarity classification. Detailed results for all languages and individual task scores are presented in Appendix A.6.

We observe that the naive[2] Unigram tokenizers consistently delivers the best overall performance with significant margins across most tokenizer variants and downstream tasks. Interestingly, the performance gains from naive BPE tokenizer were marginal compared to character- or word-level tokenizers. For text classification, naive BPE tokenizer performed worse than other approaches at larger vocabulary sizes. However, incorporating linguistically motivated strategies—particularly pre-segmentation using Morfessor—led to substantial improvements within the BPE framework. Hybrid approaches combining Morfessor and BPE outperformed their naive counterparts, with significant gains in both text classification and structure prediction tasks. Similar gains were not observed across vocabulary sizes in case of hybrid tokenizers involving Unigram framework. Only at smaller vocabulary sizes, do these tokenizers outperform their naive counterparts.

Furthermore, we observe consistent patterns with the optimal vocabulary sizes for different tokenizers. BPE performed best at lower vocabulary sizes, whereas Unigram achieved peak performance at higher vocabulary sizes. Additionally, the improvements from linguistically informed approaches were more consistent at smaller vocabulary sizes for tokenizers involving BPE and Unigram framework.

Following the analysis in Arnett and Bergen (2024), we test two competing hypothesis that could explain our observations: Morphological Alignment and Tokenization Quality. Note that since we did not include tokenizer variants involving morphological analyzers as pre-tokenizer for Hindi and English, we had only 12 data points (as compared to 18 data points in Telugu), thereby compromising the statistical power of many complex tests for

[2]We refer to tokenizers trained directly on the corpus without morphological pre-segmentation or pre-tokenization as "naive".

Word	Pre-tokenizer	Tok	Segmentation	Gold	Pred	Recall	Precision
ఆధారపడతాము	*gold reference*		ఆధారపడ + తా + ము				
	-	BPE	ఆధార + పడ + తాము	[6, 8]	[4, 6]	0.5	0.5
	Morfessor	BPE	ఆధారపడ + తాము	[6, 8]	[6]	0.5	1.0
	Morph Analyzer	BPE	ఆధార + పడ + తాము	[6, 8]	[4, 6]	0.5	0.5
	-	UNI	ఆధారపడ + తాము	[6, 8]	[6]	0.5	1.0
	Morfessor	UNI	ఆధారపడ + తాము	[6, 8]	[6]	0.5	1.0
	Morph Analyzer	UNI	ఆధారపడ + తాము	[6, 8]	[6]	0.5	1.0
ఆర్థికాభివృద్ధికి	*gold reference*		ఆర్థికాభివృద్ధి + కి				
	-	BPE	ఆర్థి + కా + భివృద్ధి + కి	[15]	[5, 7, 15]	1.0	0.33
	Morfessor	BPE	ఆర్థ + ి+ కా + భివృద్ధి + కి	[15]	[4, 5, 7, 15]	1.0	0.25
	Morph Analyzer	BPE	ఆర్థి + కా + భివృద్ధి + కి	[15]	[5, 7, 15]	1.0	0.33
	-	UNI	ఆర్థిక +ాభివృద్ధి + కి	[15]	[6, 15]	1.0	0.5
	Morfessor	UNI	ఆర్థిక +ాభివృద్ధి + క + ి	[15]	[6, 15, 16]	1.0	0.33
	Morph Analyzer	UNI	ఆర్థిక +ాభివృద్ధి + కి	[15]	[6, 15]	1.0	0.5

Table 3: Example word forms in Telugu along with their MorphScores and segmentations produced by different tokenizers. "Gold" indicates the character-level morpheme boundary positions from the ground-truth annotations, while "Pred" shows the corresponding predicted boundary positions generated by each tokenizer variant. BPE denotes Byte-Pair Encoding tokenizer and UNI denotes Unigram tokenizer.

those languages. For instance, we could perform correlation tests using fixed effects models only for Telugu. Therefore, the findings involving fixed effects models in further sections are only in Telugu and must be treated as exploratory and preliminary, not conclusive.

4 Morphological Alignment

One possible explanation for our observations is that morphologically aligned tokenization produced more meaningful tokens, which ultimately lead to improved language modeling and downstream performance. This explanation becomes even more compelling in the case of morphologically rich languages. In such languages, words are often formed by combining multiple morphemes, each carrying a distinct grammatical feature. It is therefore intuitive to assume that a tokenizer which explicitly segments these morphemes can generate more meaningful embeddings, thereby enhancing language modeling performance.

To evaluate this hypothesis, we utilize the existing boundary-based evaluation metric—MorphScore (Arnett and Bergen, 2024; Arnett et al., 2025)—for evaluating morphological alignment. Refer Appendix A.2 for detailed description of MorphScore. For Telugu, we create a dataset containing gold morpheme segmentations for approximately 600 derivational and 7000 inflectional words. To the best of our knowledge, this is the first dataset containing gold morpheme segmentations in Telugu. For Hindi and English, we utilize the existing dataset created in Arnett et al. (2025).

4.1 Morpheme Segmentations in Telugu

To evaluate morphological alignment in Telugu, we required gold morpheme segmentations that represent the ground-truth for a morphemic-segmentation (i.e., segmentation of a complex word form where each segment is semantically meaningful). We utilize existing Telugu morphological analyzer (Rao et al., 2011) and extract word forms that contain derivational and inflectional suffixes from paradigms. In total, we could extract 1297 derivational and 9275 inflectional unique word forms. We filter out word forms for which the segments, as analyzed by the morphological analyzer, do not combine to form the original word form. This is crucial as tokenizers simply segments complex words and does not transform the existing stem into its lemma. 634 derivational and 7458 inflectional unique word forms remained after filtering. These word forms along with their segmented outputs serve as our gold morpheme segmentations. We further validate the correctness of the segmentations manually and found no considerable errors. We make the dataset public: TeluguMorphScore.

4.2 Evaluation

MorphScore assesses how well segmentations from tokenizer correspond to ground-truth morphological boundaries. The algorithm operates by comparing character-level boundary positions between gold morphological segmentations and tokenizer

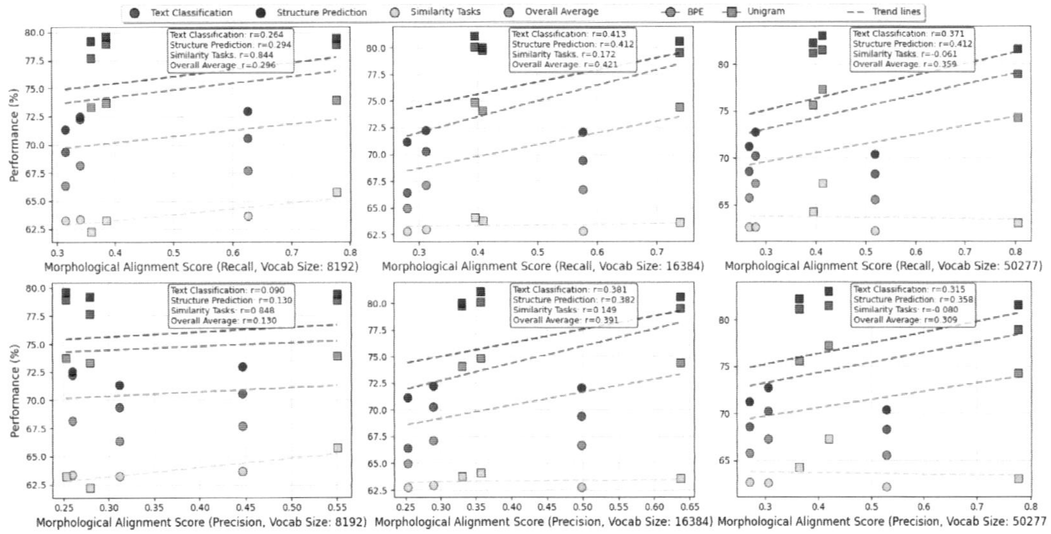

Figure 2: Variation in Downstream Performance with Morphological Alignment Scores for different tokenizer variants in Telugu, grouped by Vocabulary Size.

outputs, computing recall and precision metrics to quantify morphological alignment. Refer Appendix A.2 for an example walkthrough. Words tokenized as a single token are excluded from the evaluation in order to consider only complex word forms into the final score. Similarly, words with no ground-truth morpheme boundaries (i.e., word consisting of a single morpheme) are also excluded. The inclusion of both recall and precision metrics offers insights into whether a tokenizer tend toward over-segmentation or under-segmentation relative to morphological boundaries. Approximately 2000 word forms were evaluated consistently across all variants of tokenizers after all exclusions. Table 3 lists out few example word forms in Telugu along with the morphological alignment scores calculated for each variant of tokenizer at vocabulary size of 16384.

Figure 2 presents dot plots grouped by vocabulary sizes illustrating the relationship between morphological alignment scores and downstream performance for Telugu. Figure 5 in Appendix A.2 shows comprehensive plot combining all vocabulary sizes. The corresponding plots for Hindi (Figure 6) and English (Figure 7) are also included in Appendix A.2. Tables 5, 6 and 7 includes detailed morphscores for each language in Appendix A.2.

4.3 Results & Discussion

Based on our analysis, we found that there is a statistically significant but moderate positive correlation between the morphological alignment of a tokenizer and its performance on downstream tasks. However, we observe that the choice of tokenizer algorithm (BPE vs. Unigram) has a much stronger impact on performance than morphological alignment alone.

Initially, we explored the direct relationship between morphological metrics (such as recall, precision, and F1-score) and downstream task performance. Pearson correlation to account for linear relationship showed weak to moderate positive correlations. For example, the correlation between the overall trend and morphological F1-score was not statistically significant ($r = 0.332$, $p = 0.179$). This indicates the absence of a strong linear relationship. Spearman correlation, on the other hand, which accounts for monotonic relationship, revealed a stronger and more significant relationship. For instance, correlation between overall trend and recall was 0.486 ($p = 0.041$), and with F1-score it was 0.474 ($p = 0.047$). The strongest correlation among task categories was observed with structure prediction ($r = 0.478$, $p = 0.045$ for recall).

We performed ANOVA (Analysis of Variance) and ANCOVA (Analysis of Covariance) tests to disentangle the effects of different factors. Across almost all tasks, tokenizer (BPE vs. Unigram) had a very large and statistically significant effect on performance. For instance, in the two-way ANOVA for text classification, the F-statistic for C(Tokenizer) was 276.82 ($p < 0.001$), indicating that it is a pri-

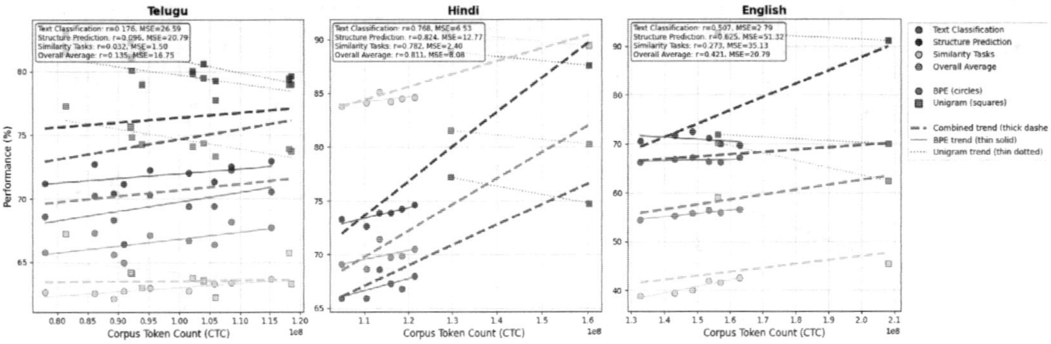

Figure 3: Variation in Downstream Performance with Corpus Token Count (CTC) for different tokenizer variants in Telugu, Hindi, and English.

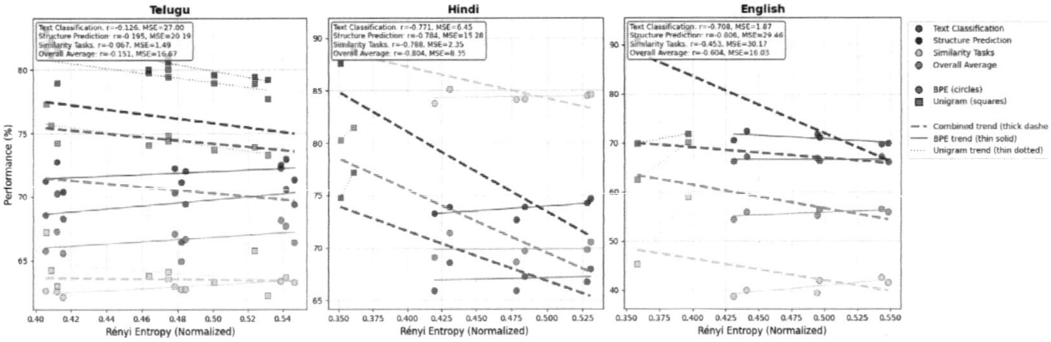

Figure 4: Variation in Downstream Performance with Rényi Entropy (normalized) for different tokenizer variants in Telugu, Hindi, and English.

mary driver of performance difference. On the other hand, the pre-tokenizer showed no significant effect on performance. When ANCOVA test introduced the F1-score (from MorphScores) as a covariate, for structure prediction, even after accounting for the powerful effects of the pre-tokenizer and tokenizer, it remained a statistically significant predictor of performance ($F = 5.71$, $p = 0.033$). Thus better morphological alignment independently contributes to better performance on syntax-based tasks. This effect was not significant for other tasks once tokenizer choice was factored in.

We also tested the correlation using fixed effects model in order to account for group-level variations. The model included tokenizer and pre-tokenizer as categorical predictors. For structure prediction tasks, both precision (coefficient $= 9.182$, $p = 0.046$) and F1-score (coefficient $= 13.148$, $p = 0.033$) were statistically significant predictors. This implies that after controlling for the choice of tokenizer, a higher morphological precision and F1-score is significantly associated with better performance on structure prediction tasks. For all other tasks, none of the morphological scores show a significant effect once the tokenizer and pre-tokenizer were included in the model.

Since morphological alignment alone cannot account for the large performance differences across all tasks, particularly the consistent success of Unigram tokenizers, we next investigate our second hypothesis, i.e., whether tokenization quality explains the observed trends.

5 Tokenization Quality

Another explanation for the observed trend can be that certain tokenizers are inherently more efficient at compressing large data, or they have more efficient distribution of token frequency which helps in better modeling by language model's architecture. We measure compression efficiency using Corpus Token Count (CTC) (Schmidt et al., 2024) and evaluate token frequency distribution using Rényi Entropy (Zouhar et al., 2023).

5.1 Corpus Token Count (CTC)

Corpus Token Count (CTC) (Schmidt et al., 2024) is defined as the number of tokens required to encode a given text. It has been argued that better compression leads to improved performance (Gallé, 2019; Goldman et al., 2024). Intuitively, if a tokenizer can represent a text using fewer tokens, it suggests more efficient compression. Thus, a lower CTC is often assumed to indicate better compression and, by extension, better downstream performance. However, our analysis in Telugu, Hindi and English shows that this is not the case for small-sized BERT models at 8.5M scale. Figure 3 shows a plot showing variation in performance with varying CTC. This finding supports previous conclusions by Schmidt et al. (2024); Ali et al. (2024), indicating that compression measured using CTC does not account for the observed variations in downstream task performance across different tokenization settings. We find no statistically significant correlation between CTC and performance on any task. Pearson and Spearman correlations between CTC and performance across all tasks were very weak and not statistically significant. For instance, the pearson correlation between CTC and overall average performance was only $r = 0.135$ ($p = 0.594$), indicating no meaningful linear relationship. We also perform analysis using fixed effects model and found that the coefficient for the logarithm of CTC was not statistically significant. This shows that compression efficiency, atleast as measured using CTC, fails to explain our observed trends in section 3.2.

5.2 Rényi Entropy

Zouhar et al. (2023) proposed using an information theoretic measure called Rényi entropy to characterize a good tokenization schema and measure tokenization quality. They contend that Rényi efficiency of the unigram distribution, that a tokenization schema produces, to be the principal measure of tokenization quality. This may also explain the observed performance differences in section 3.2.

We evaluate Rényi entropy for each tokenization variant on a subset of 5 million sentences of our pre-training corpora for corresponding language. Figure 4 shows variation in performance with varying Rényi entropy. We set the parameter $\alpha = 2.5$ as this setting has been found to be the most correlated in Zouhar et al. (2023) with performance. However, we found no statistically significant direct correlation between Rényi entropy and the downstream performance for our small-sized models. While the tokenizer type itself has a major impact on performance, Rényi entropy alone fails to explain the observed trends. Initial correlation tests (both Pearson and Spearman) showed very weak and statistically insignificant relationships between Rényi entropy and performance across all tasks. For instance, the Pearson correlations between Rényi entropy and overall average performance was negligible ($r = -0.151$). Similar to that in section 4.3, ANOVA tests revealed that tokenizer (BPE vs. Unigram) itself has significant effect. The fixed effects models also confirmed these findings. The coefficient of Rényi entropy was consistently not statistically significant across the performance of all tasks. For example, in predicting overall trend, the p-value for the Rényi entropy coefficient was 0.661.

6 Discussion

Our findings consistently reveal that Unigram-based tokenizers outperform BPE for small-scale encoder-only BERT models. While successfully demonstrating that this advantage is not explained by intrinsic metrics like Corpus Token Count and Rényi Entropy, the precise reasons for Unigram's success remains unclear. Morphologically-informed pre-tokenization significantly boosted the performance of BPE-based tokenizers, but a similar benefit is not observed for Unigram-based tokenizers.

While morphological alignment showed a moderate yet statistically significant correlation with text classification and structure prediction tasks, it did not fully explain the performance variance across all tasks. Taken together, our results suggest that while linguistic alignment can aid performance, particularly in morphologically rich settings, algorithmic design and vocabulary configuration play a significant role. Designing intrinsic metrics that could consistently explain the performance variations is necessary, and it is important to consider different trade-offs such as between statistical efficiency and linguistic alignment while designing such metrics.

7 Conclusion

In this work, we conducted a systematic evaluation of tokenization strategies for languages—Telugu, Hindi and English, with a particular emphasis on agglutinative language—Telugu. Our results shows that morphological alignment have positive correlation with downstream effectiveness of tokenizers, while also highlighting the need for more comprehensive intrinsic evaluation of tokenizers which account for various trade-offs.

Limitations

Our experiments were constrained to encoder-only model and specific to models based on BERT architecture. Therefore there is a potential risk in considering our results generalizable to other architectures. Moreover, we limited our models to 8.5 million parameters. It is not conclusive how our results would scale to larger models. We limited our experiments to three languages with varying degree of morphological complexity. Our conclusion might not be generalizable to all morphologically complex languages, especially given large diversity in morphology across languages. Our evaluations were restricted to natural language understanding (NLU) tasks. Tokenization choices can have different effects on generative tasks (e.g., text summarization, machine translation). Replicating our experiments on other tasks and using models with different architecture might produce considerably different results.

Ethical considerations

This research was conducted with careful consideration of its ethical dimensions. The models were trained on publicly available corpora, and we acknowledge that these datasets may contain biases from their web-based sources. The primary goal of our work is to positively impact the NLP field by providing a foundation for more equitable and effective models for morphologically complex and under-resourced languages. The new gold-standard morphological dataset created for Telugu is intended for linguistic analysis and is free of any personally identifiable information. As our experiments focus on NLU tasks rather than free-form text generation, the risk of producing harmful content is minimal, though we recognize that the models may still reflect biases from the training data.

In line with our commitment to transparent and reproducible research, we will make all created resources—including the Telugu dataset and all scripts for tokenizer and model training—publicly available. We also acknowledge the significant computational and environmental cost of this work, which involved pre-training 72 models and conducting over 2,160 fine-tuning runs on multiple GPUs. This extensive experimentation was a necessary trade-off to ensure the robustness and validity of our findings.

Acknowledgments

We would like to express our sincere gratitude to Vandan Mujadia at IIIT Hyderabad for his invaluable guidance and support throughout the various phases of this work. We also thank Nagaraju Vuppala and the language experts at Language Technologies Research Centre (LTRC), IIIT Hyderabad, for their assistance in developing the morphological segmentation tool and also validating the datasets curated in this work.

References

Divyanshu Aggarwal, Vivek Gupta, and Anoop Kunchukuttan. 2022. Indicxnli: Evaluating multilingual inference for indian languages. *Preprint*, arXiv:2204.08776.

Kabir Ahuja, Shanu Kumar, Sandipan Dandapat, and Monojit Choudhury. 2022. Multi task learning for zero shot performance prediction of multilingual models. *arXiv preprint arXiv:2205.06130*.

Alham Fikri Aji, Genta Indra Winata, Fajri Koto, Samuel Cahyawijaya, Ade Romadhony, Rahmad Mahendra, Kemal Kurniawan, David Moeljadi, Radityo Eko Prasojo, Timothy Baldwin, Jey Han Lau, and Sebastian Ruder. 2022. One country, 700+ languages: NLP challenges for underrepresented languages and dialects in Indonesia. In *Proceedings of the 60th Annual Meeting of the Association for Computational Linguistics (Volume 1: Long Papers)*, pages 7226–7249, Dublin, Ireland. Association for Computational Linguistics.

Md Shad Akhtar, Ayush Kumar, Asif Ekbal, and Pushpak Bhattacharyya. 2016. A hybrid deep learning architecture for sentiment analysis. In *Proceedings of COLING 2016, the 26th International Conference on Computational Linguistics: Technical Papers*, pages 482–493, Osaka, Japan. The COLING 2016 Organizing Committee.

Mehdi Ali, Michael Fromm, Klaudia Thellmann, Richard Rutmann, Max Lübbering, Johannes Leveling, Katrin Klug, Jan Ebert, Niclas Doll, Jasper Schulze Buschhoff, Charvi Jain, Alexander Arno Weber, Lena Jurkschat, Hammam Abdelwahab, Chelsea John, Pedro Ortiz Suarez, Malte Ostendorff, Samuel Weinbach, Rafet Sifa, Stefan Kesselheim, and Nicolas Flores-Herr. 2024. Tokenizer choice for llm training: Negligible or crucial? *Preprint*, arXiv:2310.08754.

Catherine Arnett and Benjamin K. Bergen. 2024. Why do language models perform worse for morphologically complex languages? *Preprint*, arXiv:2411.14198.

Catherine Arnett, Marisa Hudspeth, and Brendan O'Connor. 2025. Evaluating morphological alignment of tokenizers in 70 languages. *Preprint*, arXiv:2507.06378.

Ehsaneddin Asgari, Yassine El Kheir, and Mohammad Ali Sadraei Javaheri. 2025. Morphbpe: A morpho-aware tokenizer bridging linguistic complexity for efficient llm training across morphologies. *Preprint*, arXiv:2502.00894.

Khuyagbaatar Batsuren, Ekaterina Vylomova, Verna Dankers, Tsetsuukhei Delgerbaatar, Omri Uzan, Yuval Pinter, and Gábor Bella. 2024. Evaluating subword tokenization: Alien subword composition and oov generalization challenge. *Preprint*, arXiv:2404.13292.

Lisa Beinborn and Yuval Pinter. 2023. Analyzing cognitive plausibility of subword tokenization. In *Proceedings of the 2023 Conference on Empirical Methods in Natural Language Processing*, pages 4478–4486, Singapore. Association for Computational Linguistics.

Daniel Cer, Mona Diab, Eneko Agirre, Inigo Lopez-Gazpio, and Lucia Specia. 2017. Semeval-2017 task 1: Semantic textual similarity multilingual and crosslingual focused evaluation. In *Proceedings of the 11th International Workshop on Semantic Evaluation (SemEval-2017)*. Association for Computational Linguistics.

Ciprian Chelba, Tomas Mikolov, Mike Schuster, Qi Ge, Thorsten Brants, Phillipp Koehn, and Tony Robinson. 2014. One billion word benchmark for measuring progress in statistical language modeling. *Preprint*, arXiv:1312.3005.

Pavel Chizhov, Catherine Arnett, Elizaveta Korotkova, and Ivan P. Yamshchikov. 2024. Bpe gets picky: Efficient vocabulary refinement during tokenizer training. *Preprint*, arXiv:2409.04599.

Monojit Choudhury. 2023. Generative ai has a language problem. *Nature Human Behaviour*, 7(11):1802–1803. Letter.

Marco Cognetta, Vilém Zouhar, Sangwhan Moon, and Naoaki Okazaki. 2024. Two counterexamples to tokenization and the noiseless channel. *Preprint*, arXiv:2402.14614.

B. Comrie. 1989. *Language Universals and Linguistic Typology: Syntax and Morphology*. University of Chicago Press.

Alexis Conneau, Guillaume Lample, Ruty Rinott, Adina Williams, Samuel R. Bowman, Holger Schwenk, and Veselin Stoyanov. 2018. Xnli: Evaluating cross-lingual sentence representations. *Preprint*, arXiv:1809.05053.

Ryan Cotterell, Sabrina J. Mielke, Jason Eisner, and Brian Roark. 2018. Are all languages equally hard to language-model? In *Proceedings of the 2018 Conference of the North American Chapter of the Association for Computational Linguistics: Human Language Technologies, Volume 2 (Short Papers)*, pages 536–541, New Orleans, Louisiana. Association for Computational Linguistics.

Mathias Creutz and Krista Lagus. 2007. Unsupervised models for morpheme segmentation and morphology learning. *ACM Trans. Speech Lang. Process.*, 4(1).

Raj Dabre, Himani Shrotriya, Anoop Kunchukuttan, Ratish Puduppully, Mitesh Khapra, and Pratyush Kumar. 2022. Indicbart: A pre-trained model for indic natural language generation. In *Findings of the Association for Computational Linguistics: ACL 2022*. Association for Computational Linguistics.

Jacob Devlin, Ming-Wei Chang, Kenton Lee, and Kristina Toutanova. 2019. Bert: Pre-training of deep bidirectional transformers for language understanding. *Preprint*, arXiv:1810.04805.

Swapnil Dhanwal, Hritwik Dutta, Hitesh Nankani, Nilay Shrivastava, Yaman Kumar, Junyi Jessy Li, Debanjan Mahata, Rakesh Gosangi, Haimin Zhang, Rajiv Ratn Shah, and Amanda Stent. 2020. An annotated dataset of discourse modes in Hindi stories. In *Proceedings of the Twelfth Language Resources and Evaluation Conference*, pages 1191–1196, Marseille, France. European Language Resources Association.

Sumanth Doddapaneni, Rahul Aralikatte, Gowtham Ramesh, Shreya Goyal, Mitesh M. Khapra, Anoop Kunchukuttan, and Pratyush Kumar. 2023. Towards leaving no indic language behind: Building monolingual corpora, benchmark and models for indic languages. *Preprint*, arXiv:2212.05409.

Jack FitzGerald, Christopher Hench, Charith Peris, Scott Mackie, Kay Rottmann, Ana Sanchez, Aaron Nash, Liam Urbach, Vishesh Kakarala, Richa Singh, Swetha Ranganath, Laurie Crist, Misha Britan, Wouter Leeuwis, Gokhan Tur, and Prem Natarajan. 2023. MASSIVE: A 1M-example multilingual natural language understanding dataset with 51 typologically-diverse languages. In *Proceedings of the 61st Annual Meeting of the Association for Computational Linguistics (Volume 1: Long Papers)*, pages 4277–4302, Toronto, Canada. Association for Computational Linguistics.

Takuro Fujii, Koki Shibata, Atsuki Yamaguchi, Terufumi Morishita, and Yasuhiro Sogawa. 2023. How do different tokenizers perform on downstream tasks in scriptio continua languages?: A case study in Japanese. In *Proceedings of the 61st Annual Meeting of the Association for Computational Linguistics (Volume 4: Student Research Workshop)*, pages 39–49, Toronto, Canada. Association for Computational Linguistics.

Philip Gage. 1994. A new algorithm for data compression. *C Users J.*, 12(2):23–38.

Matthias Gallé. 2019. Investigating the effectiveness of BPE: The power of shorter sequences. In *Proceedings of the 2019 Conference on Empirical Methods in Natural Language Processing and the 9th International Joint Conference on Natural Language Processing (EMNLP-IJCNLP)*, pages 1375–1381, Hong Kong, China. Association for Computational Linguistics.

Omer Goldman, Avi Caciularu, Matan Eyal, Kris Cao, Idan Szpektor, and Reut Tsarfaty. 2024. Unpacking tokenization: Evaluating text compression and its correlation with model performance. *Preprint*, arXiv:2403.06265.

Martin Haspelmath and Andrea Sims. 2013. *Understanding morphology*. Routledge.

Jue Hou, Anisia Katinskaia, Anh-Duc Vu, and Roman Yangarber. 2023. Effects of sub-word segmentation on performance of transformer language models. In *Proceedings of the 2023 Conference on Empirical Methods in Natural Language Processing*, pages 7413–7425, Singapore. Association for Computational Linguistics.

Haris Jabbar. 2024. Morphpiece : A linguistic tokenizer for large language models. *Preprint*, arXiv:2307.07262.

Pratik Joshi, Sebastin Santy, Amar Budhiraja, Kalika Bali, and Monojit Choudhury. 2020. The state and fate of linguistic diversity and inclusion in the NLP world. In *Proceedings of the 58th Annual Meeting of the Association for Computational Linguistics*, pages 6282–6293, Online. Association for Computational Linguistics.

Divyanshu Kakwani, Anoop Kunchukuttan, Satish Golla, Gokul N.C., Avik Bhattacharyya, Mitesh M. Khapra, and Pratyush Kumar. 2020a. IndicNLPSuite: Monolingual corpora, evaluation benchmarks and pre-trained multilingual language models for Indian languages. In *Findings of the Association for Computational Linguistics: EMNLP 2020*, pages 4948–4961, Online. Association for Computational Linguistics.

Divyanshu Kakwani, Anoop Kunchukuttan, Satish Golla, Gokul N.C., Avik Bhattacharyya, Mitesh M. Khapra, and Pratyush Kumar. 2020b. IndicNLPSuite: Monolingual corpora, evaluation benchmarks and pre-trained multilingual language models for Indian languages. In *Findings of the Association for Computational Linguistics: EMNLP 2020*, pages 4948–4961, Online. Association for Computational Linguistics.

Diptesh Kanojia, Kevin Patel, and Pushpak Bhattacharyya. 2022. Indian language wordnets and their linkages with princeton wordnet. *Preprint*, arXiv:2201.02977.

Simran Khanuja, Diksha Bansal, Sarvesh Mehtani, Savya Khosla, Atreyee Dey, Balaji Gopalan, Dilip Kumar Margam, Pooja Aggarwal, Rajiv Teja Nagipogu, Shachi Dave, Shruti Gupta, Subhash Chandra Bose Gali, Vish Subramanian, and Partha Talukdar. 2021. Muril: Multilingual representations for indian languages. *Preprint*, arXiv:2103.10730.

Taku Kudo. 2018. Subword regularization: Improving neural network translation models with multiple subword candidates. *Preprint*, arXiv:1804.10959.

Taku Kudo and John Richardson. 2018. Sentencepiece: A simple and language independent subword tokenizer and detokenizer for neural text processing. *Preprint*, arXiv:1808.06226.

Aman Kumar, Himani Shrotriya, Prachi Sahu, Raj Dabre, Ratish Puduppully, Anoop Kunchukuttan, Amogh Mishra, Mitesh M. Khapra, and Pratyush Kumar. 2022. Indicnlg benchmark: Multilingual datasets for diverse nlg tasks in indic languages. *Preprint*, arXiv:2203.05437.

Anoop Kunchukuttan, Divyanshu Kakwani, Satish Golla, Gokul N.C., Avik Bhattacharyya, Mitesh M. Khapra, and Pratyush Kumar. 2020. Ai4bharat-indicnlp corpus: Monolingual corpora and word embeddings for indic languages. *arXiv preprint arXiv:2005.00085*.

Sharon Levy, Neha John, Ling Liu, Yogarshi Vyas, Jie Ma, Yoshinari Fujinuma, Miguel Ballesteros, Vittorio Castelli, and Dan Roth. 2023. Comparing biases and the impact of multilingual training across multiple languages. In *Proceedings of the 2023 Conference on Empirical Methods in Natural Language Processing*, pages 10260–10280, Singapore. Association for Computational Linguistics.

Jindřich Libovický and Jindřich Helcl. 2024. Lexically grounded subword segmentation. In *Proceedings of the 2024 Conference on Empirical Methods in Natural Language Processing*, pages 7403–7420, Miami, Florida, USA. Association for Computational Linguistics.

Sandeep Sricharan Mukku and Radhika Mamidi. 2017. ACTSA: Annotated corpus for Telugu sentiment analysis. In *Proceedings of the First Workshop on Building Linguistically Generalizable NLP Systems*, pages 54–58, Copenhagen, Denmark. Association for Computational Linguistics.

Joakim Nivre, Marie-Catherine de Marneffe, Filip Ginter, Jan Hajič, Christopher D. Manning, Sampo Pyysalo, Sebastian Schuster, Francis Tyers, and Daniel Zeman. 2020. Universal Dependencies v2: An evergrowing multilingual treebank collection. In *Proceedings of the Twelfth Language Resources and Evaluation Conference*, pages 4034–4043, Marseille, France. European Language Resources Association.

Joakim Nivre and Chiao-Ting Fang. 2017. Universal Dependency evaluation. In *Proceedings of the NoDaLiDa 2017 Workshop on Universal Dependencies (UDW 2017)*, pages 86–95, Gothenburg, Sweden. Association for Computational Linguistics.

Xiaoman Pan, Boliang Zhang, Jonathan May, Joel Nothman, Kevin Knight, and Heng Ji. 2017. Cross-lingual name tagging and linking for 282 languages. In *Proceedings of the 55th Annual Meeting of the Association for Computational Linguistics (Volume 1: Long*

Papers), pages 1946–1958, Vancouver, Canada. Association for Computational Linguistics.

Ritesh Panjwani, Diptesh Kanojia, and Pushpak Bhattacharyya. 2018. pyiwn: A python based API to access Indian language WordNets. In *Proceedings of the 9th Global Wordnet Conference*, pages 378–383, Nanyang Technological University (NTU), Singapore. Global Wordnet Association.

Libo Qin, Qiguang Chen, Xiachong Feng, Yang Wu, Yongheng Zhang, Yinghui Li, Min Li, Wanxiang Che, and Philip S Yu. 2024. Large language models meet nlp: A survey. *arXiv preprint arXiv:2405.12819*.

Loganathan Ramasamy, Zdeněk Žabokrtský, and Sowmya Vajjala. 2012. The study of effect of length in morphological segmentation of agglutinative languages. In *Proceedings of the First Workshop on Multilingual Modeling*, pages 18–24, Jeju, Republic of Korea. Association for Computational Linguistics.

Gowtham Ramesh, Sumanth Doddapaneni, Aravinth Bheemaraj, Mayank Jobanputra, Raghavan AK, Ajitesh Sharma, Sujit Sahoo, Harshita Diddee, Mahalakshmi J, Divyanshu Kakwani, Navneet Kumar, Aswin Pradeep, Srihari Nagaraj, Kumar Deepak, Vivek Raghavan, Anoop Kunchukuttan, Pratyush Kumar, and Mitesh Shantadevi Khapra. 2022. Samanantar: The largest publicly available parallel corpora collection for 11 Indic languages. *Transactions of the Association for Computational Linguistics*, 10:145–162.

Krithika Ramesh, Sunayana Sitaram, and Monojit Choudhury. 2023. Fairness in language models beyond English: Gaps and challenges. In *Findings of the Association for Computational Linguistics: EACL 2023*, pages 2106–2119, Dubrovnik, Croatia. Association for Computational Linguistics.

G. Uma Maheshwar Rao, Amba P. Kulkarni, and Christopher M. 2011. A telugu morphological analyzer. *International Telugu Internet Conference Proceedings*.

Varshini Reddy, Craig W. Schmidt, Yuval Pinter, and Chris Tanner. 2025. How much is enough? the diminishing returns of tokenization training data. *Preprint*, arXiv:2502.20273.

Phillip Rust, Jonas Pfeiffer, Ivan Vulić, Sebastian Ruder, and Iryna Gurevych. 2020. How good is your tokenizer? on the monolingual performance of multilingual language models. *arXiv preprint arXiv:2012.15613*.

Erik F. Tjong Kim Sang and Fien De Meulder. 2003. Introduction to the conll-2003 shared task: Language-independent named entity recognition. *Preprint*, arXiv:cs/0306050.

Craig W. Schmidt, Varshini Reddy, Haoran Zhang, Alec Alameddine, Omri Uzan, Yuval Pinter, and Chris Tanner. 2024. Tokenization is more than compression. *Preprint*, arXiv:2402.18376.

Mike Schuster and Kaisuke Nakajima. 2012. Japanese and korean voice search. In *2012 IEEE International Conference on Acoustics, Speech and Signal Processing (ICASSP)*, pages 5149–5152.

Rico Sennrich, Barry Haddow, and Alexandra Birch. 2016. Neural machine translation of rare words with subword units. In *Proceedings of the 54th Annual Meeting of the Association for Computational Linguistics (Volume 1: Long Papers)*, pages 1715–1725, Berlin, Germany. Association for Computational Linguistics.

Yusuke Shibata, Takuya Kida, Shuichi Fukamachi, Masayuki Takeda, Ayumi Shinohara, Takeshi Shinohara, and Setsuo Arikawa. 2000. Speeding up pattern matching by text compression. In *Algorithms and Complexity*, pages 306–315, Berlin, Heidelberg. Springer Berlin Heidelberg.

Peter Smit, Sami Virpioja, Stig-Arne Grönroos, and Mikko Kurimo. 2014. Morfessor 2.0: Toolkit for statistical morphological segmentation. In *Proceedings of the Demonstrations at the 14th Conference of the European Chapter of the Association for Computational Linguistics*, pages 21–24, Gothenburg, Sweden. Association for Computational Linguistics.

Thinh Truong, Yulia Otmakhova, Karin Verspoor, Trevor Cohn, and Timothy Baldwin. 2024. Revisiting subword tokenization: A case study on affixal negation in large language models. In *Proceedings of the 2024 Conference of the North American Chapter of the Association for Computational Linguistics: Human Language Technologies (Volume 1: Long Papers)*, pages 5082–5095, Mexico City, Mexico. Association for Computational Linguistics.

Omri Uzan, Craig W. Schmidt, Chris Tanner, and Yuval Pinter. 2024. Greed is all you need: An evaluation of tokenizer inference methods. In *Proceedings of the 62nd Annual Meeting of the Association for Computational Linguistics (Volume 2: Short Papers)*, pages 813–822, Bangkok, Thailand. Association for Computational Linguistics.

Ashish Vaswani, Noam Shazeer, Niki Parmar, Jakob Uszkoreit, Llion Jones, Aidan N. Gomez, Lukasz Kaiser, and Illia Polosukhin. 2023. Attention is all you need. *Preprint*, arXiv:1706.03762.

Alex Wang, Amanpreet Singh, Julian Michael, Felix Hill, Omer Levy, and Samuel R. Bowman. 2019. Glue: A multi-task benchmark and analysis platform for natural language understanding. *Preprint*, arXiv:1804.07461.

Adam Wiemerslage, Miikka Silfverberg, Changbing Yang, Arya McCarthy, Garrett Nicolai, Eliana Colunga, and Katharina Kann. 2022. Morphological processing of low-resource languages: Where we are and what's next. In *Findings of the Association for Computational Linguistics: ACL 2022*, pages 988–1007, Dublin, Ireland. Association for Computational Linguistics.

Qingyang Zhu, Xiang Hu, Pengyu Ji, Wei Wu, and Kewei Tu. 2024. Unsupervised morphological tree tokenizer. *Preprint*, arXiv:2406.15245.

Vilém Zouhar, Clara Meister, Juan Luis Gastaldi, Li Du, Mrinmaya Sachan, and Ryan Cotterell. 2023. Tokenization and the noiseless channel. *Preprint*, arXiv:2306.16842.

A Appendix

A.1 Pre-training Corpus Statistics

Table 4 presents the detailed statistics of the corpus used in this study. TTR represents Type-Token Ratio, MATTR represent Mean-Average Type-Token Ratio and MLW represent Mean Length of Word across the corpus.

Metrics	English	Hindi	Telugu
#Sentences	10,000,000	10,095,405	6,721,543 + 3,278,457* = 10,000,000
#Tokens	198,637,872	169,127,701	95,063,928
#Types	2,499,750	1,462,501	4,206,880
TTR	0.012584	0.008647	0.0442531
MLW	4.7760	4.0329	6.8989
MATTR†	0.8051	0.4674	0.4167

Table 4: Corpus statistics of different languages used for training tokenizers and pretraining the language models. * indicates data from the IndicCorp dataset. Metrics marked with † are calculated on 100 million character subset of the corpus.

A.2 Morphological Alignment

Figures 5, 6 and 7 shows downstream performance vs. morphological alignment trends for Telugu, Hindi, and English respectively. Tables 5, 6 and 7 presents detailed MorphScores for each tokenization variant across Telugu, Hindi and English respectively.

To quantify the degree to which a tokenizer's segmentations align with linguistic morpheme boundaries, we employ the **MorphScore** evaluation metric (Arnett and Bergen, 2024; Arnett et al., 2025). This is a boundary-based method that compares the segmentation points produced by a tokenizer against a gold standard set of morpheme boundaries for a given list of words. The evaluation proceeds as follows for each word in the test set:

1. **Boundary Identification:** Both the gold-standard morphemic segmentation and the tokenizer's output are converted into sets of character-level boundary indices. For a word of length N, a boundary is an integer index i (from 1 to $N-1$) that marks the end of a segment. This results in a gold set, B_{gold}, and a predicted set, B_{pred}.
2. **Metric Calculation:** Using these sets, we calculate True Positives (TP), False Positives (FP), and False Negatives (FN) to assess the alignment:
   - **True Positives (TP):** The number of boundaries correctly identified by the tokenizer. This corresponds to the size of the intersection of the two sets.

     $$\text{TP} = |B_{gold} \cap B_{pred}|$$

   - **False Positives (FP):** The number of boundaries predicted by the tokenizer that do not exist in the gold standard. This indicates over-segmentation.

     $$\text{FP} = |B_{pred} - B_{gold}|$$

   - **False Negatives (FN):** The number of gold-standard boundaries missed by the tokenizer. This indicates under-segmentation.

     $$\text{FN} = |B_{gold} - B_{pred}|$$

   From these counts, we compute **Precision, Recall**, and the **F1-score** for each word:

   $$\text{Precision} = \frac{\text{TP}}{\text{TP} + \text{FP}}$$

   $$\text{Recall} = \frac{\text{TP}}{\text{TP} + \text{FN}}$$

   $$\text{F1} = 2 \cdot \frac{\text{Precision} * \text{Recall}}{\text{Precision} + \text{Recall}}$$

3. **Exclusion Criteria:** To ensure a fair evaluation focused on complex word forms, certain words are excluded from the calculation:
   - Words that the tokenizer outputs as a single token (i.e., where B_{pred} is empty).
   - Words that consist of a single morpheme in the gold standard (i.e., where B_{gold} is empty).
4. **Final Score Aggregation:** The final Recall, Precision, and F1-score for a given tokenizer are the micro-averages of these metrics calculated over all non-excluded words in the evaluation dataset.

Example Calculation

Consider the Telugu word ఆధారపడతాము (length 11).

- **Gold Segmentation:** ఆధారపడ + త + ము
  The morpheme boundaries are after the 6th character ('డ') and the 8th character ('త').

$$B_{gold} = \{6, 8\}$$

- **Tokenizer Output (Morfessor + BPE):** ఆధారపడ + తాము
  The tokenizer places one boundary after the 6th character ('డ').

$$B_{pred} = \{6\}$$

The metrics are then calculated as follows:

- TP $= |\{6, 8\} \cap \{6\}| = 1$
- FP $= |\{6\} - \{6, 8\}| = 0$
- FN $= |\{6, 8\} - \{6\}| = 1$

$$\text{Recall} = \frac{1}{1+1} = 0.5$$

$$\text{Precision} = \frac{1}{1+0} = 1.0$$

This indicates that while every boundary the tokenizer predicted was correct (high precision), it only found half of the true morpheme boundaries (lower recall).

A.3 Downstream Tasks Description

To assess the performance across tokenization variants, we utilize an extensive set of downstream tasks, verified and suitable for each language. These tasks span diverse categories including Classification, Structure Prediction, Question Answering, and Natural Language Inference. We provide details below, organized by language, with overlapping tasks clearly indicated.

A.3.1 Tasks Description

Word & Definition (WaD): Classify whether a given word and a given definition match semantically (Batsuren et al., 2024).

word	definition	label
clerking	the activity of recording business transactions	1
ammo	alternatively placed in genus Martynia	0
enforced	forced or compelled or put in force	1
snowline	a fishing line managed principally by hand	0

Table 8: Example data points in Word and Definition task.

Word & Morphology (WaM): Classify whether a given word contains inflection, derivation, or compounding (Batsuren et al., 2024).

word	morphology	label
leaderboard	derivation	1
overpressing	compound	0
coteaches	inflection	1
sharemarkets	derivation	0

Table 9: Example data points in Word and Morphology task.

Word & Word (WaW): Classify whether two given words are semantically related (Batsuren et al., 2024). For Telugu and Hindi, we utilize IndicWordNet[3] (Kanojia et al., 2022), accessing through API[4] (Panjwani et al., 2018). We follow similar steps as mentioned in Batsuren et al. (2024) while curating the data. The resulting dataset is further manually validated by language experts to ensure correctness.

For each synset in IndicWordNet, we extract the *head word* and collect words connected through semantic relations such as SIMILAR, HYPERNYMY, and HYPONYMY. Word pairs are then formed between the head word and each related word. Pairs containing special characters or identical words are discarded, and duplicates are removed. The resulting pairs are assigned the label **1 (related)**.

Negative pairs are generated to ensure semantic unrelatedness. For each positive pair, a random candidate pair is sampled from the vocabulary, subject to strict constraints: (i) the two words must not be identical, (ii) the pair or its reverse must not exist among positive samples, (iii) the words must not share neighbors in the semantic graph, (iv) the words must not share hypernyms, and (v) the words must not be connected by entailment. A maximum attempt limit is enforced to prevent infinite loops. All validated pairs are labeled **0 (unrelated)**.

The curated dataset is stored in TSV format with columns: `index`, `word_a`, `word_b`, and `label`. Finally, the dataset is manually validated by language experts to ensure correctness. The dataset can be found here: IndicSigmorphon-Dataset.

Parts of Speech Tagging (POS): Assigning grammatical category (such as noun, verb, adjective, etc.) to each word in a sentence based on both its definition and its context within the sentence (Nivre et al., 2020). For deciding the

[3] https://www.cfilt.iitb.ac.in/indowordnet/
[4] https://github.com/cfiltnlp/pyiwn

Pre-tokenizer	Tokenizer	Vocabulary Size	Recall	Precision	F1-score
-	Character	-	1.0000	0.145931	0.254695
	BPE	8192	0.3118	0.3118	0.313208
-	BPE	16384	0.2789	0.2527	0.265214
	BPE	50277	0.2661	0.2707	0.268367
	BPE	8192	0.3406	0.2599	0.294857
Morfessor	BPE	16384	0.3111	0.2896	0.300285
	BPE	50277	0.2785	0.3053	0.291013
	BPE	8192	0.6257	0.4463	0.521033
Morph Analyzer	BPE	16384	0.5757	0.4983	0.534195
	BPE	50277	0.5190	0.5291	0.523997
	Unigram	8192	0.3924	0.3544	0.372837
-	Unigram	16384	0.3950	0.3572	0.375818
	Unigram	50277	0.4146	0.4211	0.417517
	Unigram	8192	0.3852	0.2526	0.305000
Morfessor	Unigram	16384	0.4079	0.3307	0.364393
	Unigram	50277	0.3949	0.3674	0.380777
	Unigram	8192	0.7774	0.5505	0.644564
Morph Analyzer	Unigram	16384	0.7385	0.6368	0.683873
	Unigram	50277	0.8046	0.7769	0.790517

Table 5: MorphScores of various tokenization strategies using different tokenizer variants across various vocabulary sizes in Telugu.

class of a word given subword classes, we report both results considering first token class and max-pooling of the classes of each token. We refer first token class based classification as POS, while max-pooling as POS-Pooled in all our results.

ACTSA (Annotated Corpus for Telugu Sentiment Analysis): Determine the sentiment associated with a sentence (sentiment analysis) (Mukku and Mamidi, 2017). This task is specifically curated for Telugu by native Telugu speakers.

IndicSentiment: Sentiment analysis on synthetically created product reviews introduced in Doddapaneni et al. (2023). This task presents a 13-way parallel dataset, with sentences synthetically created for English and later translated to Indian languages. This dataset claims to avoid one-dimensional and highly polarized product reviews (makes classification easier).

IIT-Patna Movie Reviews & Product Reviews: Includes sentiment analysis task with dataset specifically curated by using reviews posted in Hindi (Akhtar et al., 2016). These datasets has 4 classes namely positive, negative, neutral, and conflict.

MASSIVE Intent Classification: Multilingual Amazon Slu resource package for Intent Classification. This dataset was introduced in FitzGerald et al. (2023) and was created using user queries collected by Amazon Alexa. The dataset contains 60 intents.

Named Entity Recognition (NER): Involves identifying and classifying named entities in text into predefined categories such as persons, organizations, locations, dates and other proper nouns. For Telugu and Hindi, we use dataset from WikiAnn[5] (Pan et al., 2017; Doddapaneni et al., 2023). The dataset consists of coarse grained labels: Person (PER), Organization (ORG) and Location (LOC). While for English, we use CoNLL NER dataset (Sang and Meulder, 2003). It contains predefined categories such as Person (PER), Organization (ORG), Location (LOC), and Miscellaneous (MISC).

IndicXParaphrase: This task involves classifying whether a pair of sentences are paraphrased or not (Kumar et al., 2022; Doddapaneni et al., 2023)[6]. Each entry in the dataset is a tuple

[5] https://elisa-ie.github.io/wikiann/

[6] https://huggingface.co/datasets/ai4bharat/IndicXParaphrase

Pre-tokenizer	Tokenizer	Vocabulary Size	Recall	Precision	F1-score
-	Character	-	1.0000	0.1414	0.247791
	BPE	8192	0.7312	0.1484	0.246745
-	BPE	16384	0.6659	0.1538	0.249938
	BPE	50277	0.5247	0.1519	0.235697
	BPE	8192	0.7667	0.1571	0.257695
Morfessor	BPE	16384	0.6824	0.1653	0.266085
	BPE	50277	0.4862	0.1707	0.252684
	Unigram	8192	0.8099	0.1748	0.287547
-	Unigram	16384	0.7657	0.1929	0.301085
	Unigram	50277	0.6759	0.2286	0.341597
	Unigram	8192	0.8155	0.1902	0.308457
Morfessor	Unigram	16384	0.6549	0.2026	0.309463
	Unigram	50277	0.5237	0.1907	0.279579

Table 6: MorphScores of various tokenization strategies using different tokenizer variants across various vocabulary sizes in Hindi.

Pre-tokenizer	Tokenizer	Vocabulary Size	Recall	Precision	F1-score
-	Character	-	1.0000	0.1414	0.247791
	BPE	8192	0.3049	0.1299	0.18226
-	BPE	16384	0.2483	0.1105	0.15295
	BPE	50277	0.2163	0.0975	0.134405
	BPE	8192	0.5238	0.2241	0.313355
Morfessor	BPE	16384	0.5078	0.2356	0.321848
	BPE	50277	0.4916	0.2378	0.32052
	Unigram	8192	0.8929	0.3351	0.487372
-	Unigram	16384	0.8515	0.3541	0.500189
	Unigram	50277	0.8146	0.3732	0.517995
	Unigram	8192	0.9209	0.3115	0.465555
Morfessor	Unigram	16384	0.9111	0.3222	0.476074
	Unigram	50277	0.9063	0.3229	0.476204

Table 7: MorphScores of various tokenization strategies using different tokenizer variants across various vocabulary sizes in English.

word	word	label
visitor	traveler	1
shopper	earless	0
photocopy	mosaic	1
bleed	medicine	1

Table 10: Example datapoints in Word and Word task.

<English_sentence, sentence-1, sentence-2>, where sentence-1 and sentence-2 refer to pairs of sentences.

Natural Language Inference (NLI): Includes multilingual natural language inference benchmark that evaluates a model's ability to determine the logical relationship-entailment, contradictions, or neutrality-between pairs of sentences, called premise and hypothesis. (Aggarwal et al., 2022; Conneau et al., 2018).

Discourse Mode Classification (DM): Identifying the discourse mode or textual function of a given Hindi sentence or paragraph. A discourse mode represents the communicative purpose or rhetorical function of a segment of text. The dataset contains five different discourse modes: *argumentative, narrative, descriptive, dialogic, and informative* (Dhanwal et al., 2020).

STS-B: The Semantic Textual Similarity task (Cer et al., 2017) is a collection of sentence pairs drawn from news headlines, video and image captions, and natural language inference data. Each pair is

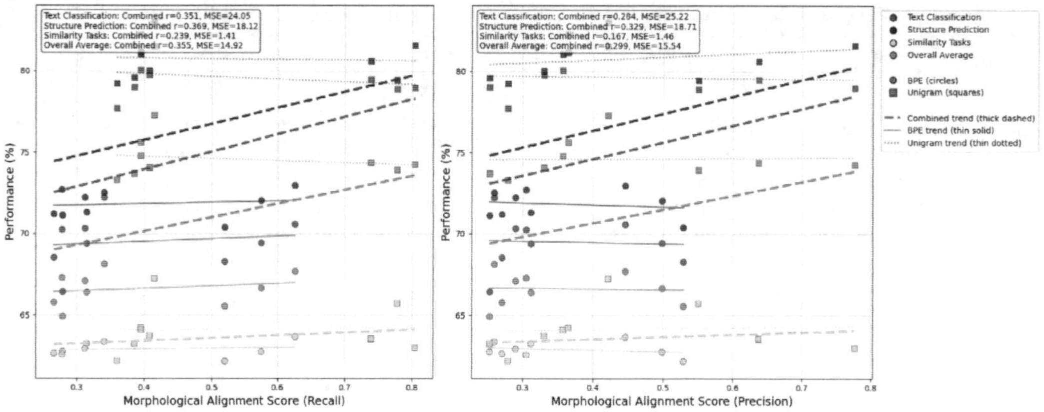

Figure 5: Variation in Downstream Performance with Morphological Alignment Scores for different tokenizer variants in Telugu.

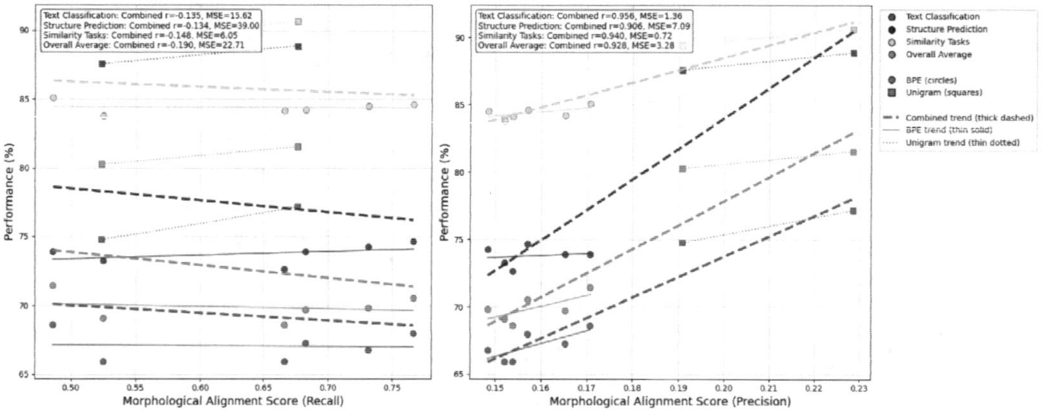

Figure 6: Variation in Downstream Performance with Morphological Alignment Scores for different tokenizer variants in Hindi.

human-annotated with a similarity score from 1 to 5. The task involves predicting these scores. Evaluation metrics includes Pearson and Spearman correlation coefficients. (Wang et al., 2019)

Dependency Parsing: Involved analyzing the grammatical structure of a sentence by identifying relationships between "head" words and their dependents. We used Universal Dependencies (UD) Treebank dataset (Nivre et al., 2020) to perform dependency parsing. The model was adapted to predict both the syntactic head of each word and the type of dependency relation. Performance was evaluated using standard metrics: Unlabeled Attachment Score (UAS) and Labeled Attachment Score (LAS) (Nivre and Fang, 2017).

A.4 Pre-training Hyperparameters

Hyperparameters settings of BERT models in our experiments are shown in Table 11. Each model contained approximately 8.5 million parameters excluding the parameters in embedding layer.

A.5 Fine-tuning Hyperparameters

We adopt hyperparameter settings from prior work, as our experiments focus solely on comparative evaluation. Consequently, we did not find it necessary to perform additional hyperparameter tuning. Details regarding specific hyperparameter for each task can be found in table 12.

A.6 Downstream Performance

We evaluated performance of languages models on extensive set of downstream tasks ranging from Sequence Classification, Parts-of-Speech Tagging

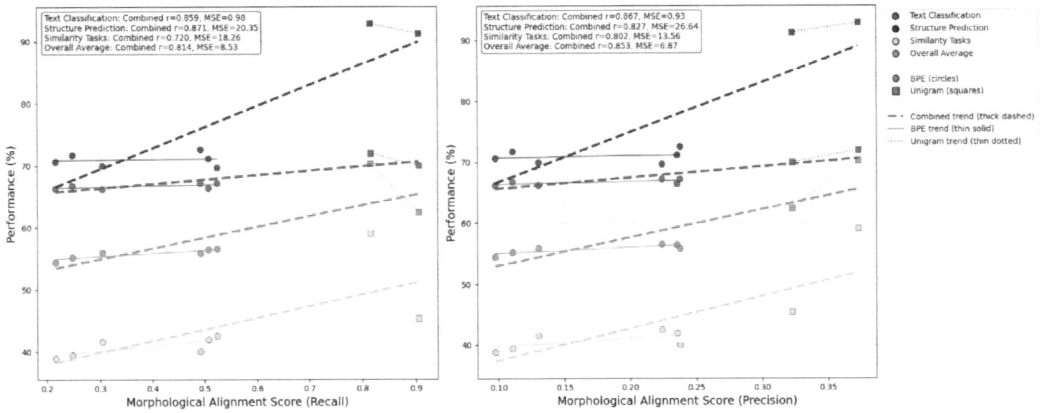

Figure 7: Variation in Downstream Performance with Morphological Alignment Scores for different tokenizer variants in English.

Hyperparameter	Value
Batch size	128
Total training steps	175,000
Adam ϵ	1×10^{-6}
Adam β_1	0.9
Adam β_2	0.999
Sequence length	128
Learning rate	1×10^{-4}
Learning rate schedule	Linear warmup
Warmup steps	3,750
Weight decay	0.01
Attention dropout	0.1
Dropout	0.1
Hidden Size	384
Number of Attention Heads	6
Number of Hidden Layers	6

Table 11: Hyperparameters choices of the BERT language models pre-trained for our evaluations.

to Natural Language Inference Tasks such as IndicXNLI. Tables 13, 14, and 15 show performance across various languages and downstream tasks.

Hyperparameter	Value
Train Batch size	16 for POS, IndicXNLI, STS-B, Dependency Parsing 32 for WaD, WaM, WaW, ACTSA, IndicSentiment, IITP-MR, IITP-PR, MASSIVE, IndicX-Para, DM
Eval Batch size	16 for POS, IndicXNLI, STS-B, Dependency Parsing 32 for WaD, WaM, WaW, ACTSA, IndicSentiment, IITP-MR, IITP-PR, Wiki-NER, IndicX-Para, DM 64 for MASSIVE
Epochs	5 for WaD, WaM, WaW, POS, IndicXNLI 10 for ACTSA, IndicSentiment, IITP-MR, IITP-PR, MASSIVE, Wiki-NER, DM, STS-B 20 for IndicXPara
Adam ϵ	1e-8
Adam β_1	0.9
Adam β_2	0.999
Learning rate	2e-5 for ACTSA, IndicSentiment, IITP-MR, IITP-PR, IndicXPara, DM 3e-5 for WaD, WaM, WaW, IndicXNLI, STS-B 5e-5 for MASSIVE, Wiki-NER
Learning rate schedule	Linear warmup
Warmup steps	10% of steps
Weight decay	0.01
Attention dropout	0.1
Dropout	0.1
Sequence Length	128

Table 12: Hyperparameters used for fine-tuning for each downstream task.

Pre-tokenizer	Tokenizer	Vocab Size	Downstream Tasks				
			WaW Accuracy	**POS** F1	**POS-Pooled** F1	**ACTSA** Accuracy	**IndicSentiment** Accuracy
None (Naive)	Character	-	78.54±0.60	83.63±0.11	84.44±0.10	55.41±1.55	69.23±2.93
None (Naive)	BPE	8192	78.92±0.58	78.72±0.11	86.18±0.04	53.61±0.00	72.44±0.00
		16384	77.86±0.47	77.52±0.06	85.37±0.08	54.16±0.00	62.18±0.00
		50277	77.64±0.31	78.24±0.36	85.86±0.16	53.23±0.00	72.44±0.00
Morfessor	BPE	8192	79.15±0.39	79.94±0.18	86.40±0.26	56.26±0.00	78.85±0.00
		16384	78.28±0.20	78.38±0.28	85.74±0.02	54.16±0.00	76.28±0.00
		50277	77.51±0.17	79.43±0.58	86.26±0.25	54.53±0.00	75.64±0.00
Morph Analyzer	BPE	8192	79.72±0.21	80.69±0.06	86.28±0.20	56.38±0.00	73.72±0.00
		16384	77.88±0.26	79.27±0.25	85.49±0.18	53.97±0.00	73.72±0.00
		50277	76.66±0.18	77.87±0.17	84.96±0.05	56.01±0.00	69.87±0.00
None (Naive)	Unigram	8192	84.53±0.24	83.62±0.28	86.16±0.11	64.51±0.00	85.26±0.00
		16384	86.33±0.25	84.20±0.28	85.32±0.00	67.10±0.00	85.26±0.00
		50277	89.36±0.13	87.76±0.22	86.99±0.20	66.54±0.00	87.18±0.00
Morfessor	Unigram	8192	84.91±0.32	84.07±0.14	86.28±0.17	65.80±-0.00	84.62±0.00
		16384	86.90±0.15	85.02±0.10	85.55±0.00	67.47±0.00	82.69±0.00
		50277	88.82±0.09	88.71±0.18	86.95±0.55	65.80±0.00	87.18±0.00
Morph Analyzer	Unigram	8192	84.87±0.15	81.73±0.15	86.21±0.05	64.51±0.00	85.26±0.00
		16384	77.88±0.26	80.00±0.20	85.49±0.18	53.97±0.00	73.72±0.00
		50277	87.63±0.06	83.52±0.10	85.64±0.20	64.14±0.00	82.69±0.00
Morph Analyzer	Word	8192	72.19±0.07	34.22±0.11	34.66±0.29	58.23±0.00	75.00±0.00
		16384	74.07±0.06	34.17±0.20	34.92±0.12	57.86±0.00	75.64±0.00
		50277	76.53±0.19	34.57±0.04	57.90±0.03	58.60±0.00	75.64±0.00
Morfessor	Word	8192	70.98±0.11	44.14±0.05	35.04±0.24	63.50±0.00	78.20±0.00
		16384	75.19±0.14	59.46±0.07	34.88±0.08	62.48±0.00	76.28±0.00
		50277	79.45±0.09	72.50±0.03	59.46±0.06	63.96±0.00	82.05±0.00
None (Naive)	Word	8192	70.36±0.14	38.82±0.04	34.97±0.21	65.06±0.00	76.28±0.00
		16384	74.98±0.09	55.17±0.06	34.95±0.23	60.63±0.00	79.49±0.00
		50277	77.97±0.08	64.16±0.02	54.46±0.09	63.77±0.00	82.05±0.00

Pre-tokenizer	Tokenizer	Vocab Size	Downstream Tasks				
			Massive Intent Accuracy	**Wiki-NER** F1	**IndicXPara** Accuracy	**IndicXNLI** F1	**Dependency Parsing** LAS/UAS
None (Naive)	Character	-	75.42±0.71	88.75±0.05	44.06±3.25	51.45±1.03	50.82±1.03/62.09±1.72
None (Naive)	BPE	8192	73.00±0.00	87.97±0.29	47.63±0.00	53.15±0.47	48.82±0.47/62.34±0.53
		16384	71.57±0.00	86.72±0.23	47.63±0.00	51.59±0.16	49.84±0.94/62.60±0.99
		50277	70.98±0.00	86.69±0.10	47.63±0.00	51.03±0.56	49.74±0.32/62.60±0.99
Morfessor	BPE	8192	74.96±0.00	87.96±0.09	47.63±0.00	54.62±0.06	51.75±0.73/63.99±0.89
		16384	72.50±0.00	87.67±0.08	47.63±0.00	53.20±0.36	50.87±0.79/64.76±0.44
		50277	73.34±0.00	88.00±0.16	47.63±0.00	53.24±0.34	51.29±0.58/65.43±0.46
Morph Analyzer	BPE	8192	73.09±0.00	88.59±0.25	47.63±0.00	54.59±0.48	51.75±0.62/65.28±0.86
		16384	72.11±0.00	87.12±0.12	47.63±0.00	53.34±0.40	50.82±0.73/64.71±1.25
		50277	70.68±0.00	86.33±0.16	47.63±0.00	53.38±0.38	48.51±0.70/61.78±0.76
None (Naive)	Unigram	8192	81.36±0.00	94.01±0.16	39.90±0.00	60.68±0.28	63.39±0.30/73.37±1.09
		16384	81.55±0.00	94.58±0.06	41.90±0.00	61.90±0.06	67.07±1.23/77.32±1.18
		50277	83.18±0.00	95.78±0.04	45.14±0.00	69.51±0.22	70.46±1.15/78.81±1.23
Morfessor	Unigram	8192	80.96±0.00	94.16±0.14	41.65±0.00	60.93±0.06	63.99±0.76/73.95±0.61
		16384	82.05±0.00	94.42±0.06	40.65±0.00	61.08±0.04	65.29±0.35/74.86±0.75
		50277	82.83±0.00	95.50±0.14	39.65±0.00	62.98±0.68	68.89±0.40/77.74±0.38
Morph Analyzer	Unigram	8192	80.92±0.00	94.42±0.08	46.63±0.00	59.31±0.12	63.78±0.78/73.40±0.40
		16384	72.11±0.00	94.91±0.15	41.15±0.00	62.36±0.15	66.16±1.30/75.66±1.02
		50277	81.36±0.00	95.14±0.12	38.40±0.00	62.15±0.28	67.94±1.55/77.59±1.59
Morph Analyzer	Word	8192	57.65±0.00	90.59±0.18	43.14±0.00	52.90±0.03	69.52±1.20/84.79±0.47
		16384	60.45±0.00	91.78±0.09	38.65±0.00	52.88±0.02	69.12±0.32/83.56±0.09
		50277	65.72±0.00	93.27±0.13	43.64±0.00	54.18±0.13	69.06±0.55/83.41±0.69
Morfessor	Word	8192	60.85±0.00	91.21±0.06	41.15±0.00	55.54±0.34	71.36±0.80/84.74±0.62
		16384	64.24±0.00	92.27±0.03	41.40±0.00	55.62±0.29	73.81±0.55/85.91±0.85
		50277	68.47±0.00	93.84±0.18	35.91±0.00	57.73±0.50	74.94±0.69/86.12±0.35
None (Naive)	Word	8192	63.26±0.00	91.75±0.08	41.65±0.00	57.73±0.06	73.81±0.55/85.55±0.64
		16384	65.76±0.00	92.87±0.076	40.15±0.00	57.03±0.60	73.81±1.53/84.43±0.87
		50277	72.21±0.00	94.43±0.051	37.66±0.00	61.86±0.03	74.27±0.67/85.30±0.26

Table 13: Comparison of downstream performances across tokenizers in Telugu.

Pre-tokenizer	Tokenizer	Vocab Size	Downstream Tasks				
			WaW Accuracy	POS F1	POS-Pooled F1	IITP-MR Accuracy	IITP-PR Accuracy
None (Naive)	Character	-	85.36±0.28	83.35±0.21	79.32±0.87	47.96±0.19	67.11±0.33
None (Naive)	BPE	8192	84.50±0.10	81.01±0.27	83.71±0.27	47.10±0.00	61.76±0.00
		16384	84.13±0.71	80.03±0.21	82.58±0.14	43.55±0.00	62.14±0.00
		50277	83.81±0.34	81.28±0.53	82.35±0.31	44.52±0.00	62.14±0.00
Morfessor	BPE	8192	84.62±0.13	80.68±0.50	83.93±0.10	48.39±0.00	64.63±0.00
		16384	84.21±0.01	80.88±0.09	83.20±0.11	46.45±0.00	64.44±0.00
		50277	85.11±0.07	82.24±0.26	84.40±0.24	49.03±0.00	64.82±0.00
None (Naive)	Unigram	8192	-±-	-±-	-±-	-±-	-±-
		16384	-±-	-±-	-±-	-±-	-±-
		50277	90.64±0.06	89.50±0.09	96.82±0.00	62.26±0.00	77.06±0.00
Morfessor	Unigram	8192	-±-	-±-	-±-	-±-	-±-
		16384	-±-	-±-	-±-	-±-	-±-
		50277	89.43±0.20	89.80±0.05	95.67±0.05	57.42±0.00	74.19±0.00
Morfessor	Word	8192	78.84±0.02	48.19±0.11	94.21±0.12	59.36±0.00	73.04±0.00
		16384	82.73±0.05	64.20±0.12	92.65±0.11	59.68±0.00	73.23±0.00
		50277	-±-	-±-	-±-	-±-	-±-
None (Naive)	Word	8192	77.87±0.03	38.38±0.06	95.42±0.03	57.10±0.00	74.00±0.00
		16384	83.44±0.05	54.53±0.07	93.83±0.04	61.29±0.00	76.86±0.00
		50277	87.25±0.03	71.12±0.02	97.16±0.02	60.64±0.00	78.78±0.00

Pre-tokenizer	Tokenizer	Vocab Size	Downstream Tasks				
			DM Accuracy	Wiki-NER F1	IndicXPara Accuracy	IndicXNLI F1	Dependency Parsing LAS/UAS
None (Naive)	Character	-	74.36±0.12	86.60±0.28	47.13±1.95	51.49±-	58.83±0.74/66.71±0.62
None (Naive)	BPE	8192	73.72±0.00	86.08±0.29	62.84±0.00	53.26±-	59.44±0.33/67.74±0.31
		16384	73.92±0.00	84.13±0.42	46.88±0.00	51.87±-	57.86±0.31/65.99±0.36
		50277	73.22±0.00	84.59±0.62	63.84±0.00	52.86±-	58.89±0.29/67.18±0.23
Morfessor	BPE	8192	74.32±0.00	86.20±0.40	61.84±0.00	53.93±-	60.18±0.08/68.28±0.10
		16384	74.02±0.00	85.50±0.64	62.34±0.00	51.65±-	59.38±0.39/67.51±0.37
		50277	75.43±0.00	86.66±0.21	61.10±0.00	53.77±-	62.59±0.13/70.43±0.14
None (Naive)	Unigram	8192	-±-	-±-	-±-	-±-	-±-/-±-
		16384	-±-	-±-	-±-	-±-	-±-/-±-
		50277	90.64±0.06	83.22±0.21	-±-	61.64±-	85.83±0.08/89.66±0.02
Morfessor	Unigram	8192	-±-	-±-	-±-	-±-	-±-/-±-
		16384	-±-	-±-	-±-	-±-	-±-/-±-
		50277	89.43±0.20	83.65±0.24	-±-	63.44±-	83.37±0.05/87.69±0.04
Morfessor	Word	8192	77.53±0.00	87.37±0.22	81.30±0.00	60.61±-	83.54±0.07/88.67±0.05
		16384	76.93±0.00	88.43±0.22	82.29±0.00	60.25±-	83.86±0.05/88.82±0.02
		50277	-±-	-±-	-±-	-±-	-±-/-±-
None (Naive)	Word	8192	77.33±0.00	85.73±0.14	84.04±0.00	60.51±-	85.30±0.08/89.65±0.06
		16384	77.53±0.00	87.92±0.19	84.29±0.00	62.18±-	86.16±0.07/90.11±0.09
		50277	78.34±0.00	91.04±0.29	84.29±0.00	65.15±-	87.64±0.08/91.31±0.05

Table 14: Comparison of downstream performances across tokenizers in Hindi.

Pre-tokenizer	Tokenizer	Vocab Size	Downstream Tasks				
			WaW Accuracy	**WaM** Accuracy	**WaW** Accuracy	**POS** F1	**POS-Pooled** F1
None (Naive)	Character	-	54.18±0.57	73.54±1.36	58.78±1.46	66.36±0.54	41.96±0.36
None (Naive)	BPE	8192	54.47±0.24	74.51±0.17	63.01±0.98	76.57±0.22	21.12±1.67
		16384	55.20±0.44	75.84±0.17	64.21±0.55	74.64±0.30	32.46±1.55
		50277	55.49±0.14	74.32±1.29	63.46±0.34	73.86±0.94	42.13±0.19
Morfessor	BPE	8192	56.04±0.54	76.10±0.74	64.55±0.86	76.37±0.56	41.86±0.79
		16384	55.31±0.25	75.84±0.81	62.78±0.78	74.30±0.50	41.36±1.62
		50277	55.11±0.69	74.88±0.50	64.84±0.52	74.86±0.91	42.64±0.20
None (Naive)	Unigram	8192	-±-	-±-	-±-	-±-	-±-
		16384	-±-	-±-	-±-	-±-	-±-
		50277	66.64±0.38	80.82±0.29	68.27±1.57	94.34±0.11	34.52±0.16
Morfessor	Unigram	8192	-±-	-±-	-±-	-±-	-±-
		16384	-±-	-±-	-±-	-±-	-±-
		50277	60.13±0.53	82.05±0.22	67.75±1.24	93.37±0.01	34.70±0.09
Morfessor	Word	8192	54.40±0.70	51.91±0.13	58.60±0.10	89.96±0.01	34.37±0.35
		16384	54.09±0.14	53.62±0.00	59.18±0.30	90.71±0.05	34.88±0.09
		50277	-±-	-±-	-±-	-±-	-±-
None (Naive)	Word	8192	54.38±0.31	51.47±0.28	58.60±0.20	92.10±0.04	34.09±0.20
		16384	54.24±0.52	55.15±1.17	60.26±0.26	93.21±0.04	33.92±0.03
		50277	60.82±0.28	60.20±0.51	61.18±0.86	94.63±0.12	33.86±0.52

Pre-tokenizer	Tokenizer	Vocab Size	Downstream Tasks				
			DM Accuracy	**STS-B** Pearson/Spearman	**NER-CoNLL** F1	**SST-2** Accuracy	**Dependency Parsing** LAS/UAS
None (Naive)	Character	-	55.99±0.39	16.05±3.40/14.76±3.62	57.44±0.25	71.10±1.40	21.68±1.82
None (Naive)	BPE	8192	59.73±0.81	20.09±0.18/18.79±0.49	63.37±0.26	72.86±0.29	30.20±0.78
		16384	59.15±0.18	14.57±0.57/12.46±0.84	68.78±0.36	72.02±0.41	27.71±0.12
		50277	57.22±0.48	14.14±0.72/11.96±0.46	67.38±0.31	71.86±0.63	29.73±0.08
Morfessor	BPE	8192	59.97±0.51	20.56±0.47/20.04±0.61	63.06±0.27	72.10±0.18	28.68±0.12
		16384	58.28±0.18	21.17±2.83/20.21±3.12	68.05±0.11	71.75±0.76	27.97±0.08
		50277	60.40±0.17	15.10±2.06/13.28±2.20	70.21±0.52	74.01±0.63	31.05±0.16
None (Naive)	Unigram	8192	-±-	-±-	-±-	-±-	-±-/-±-
		16384	-±-	-±-	-±-	-±-	-±-/-±-
		50277	62.10±0.29	49.83±0.74/48.39±1.03	91.37±0.08	-±-	69.60±0.32
Morfessor	Unigram	8192	-±-	-±-	-±-	-±-	-±-/-±-
		16384	-±-	-±-	-±-	-±-	-±-/-±-
		50277	61.93±0.31	22.97±0.63/22.09±1.08	89.06±0.15	-±-	64.88±0.07
Morfessor	Word	8192	68.55±0.21	24.95±0.89/25.19±0.95	75.60±0.04	79.85±0.24	66.64±0.00
		16384	68.11±0.28	28.15±2.24/28.09±2.68	80.10±0.15	81.00±0.54	66.49±0.40
		50277	-±-	-±-	-±-	-±-	-±-/-±-
None (Naive)	Word	8192	71.34±0.37	22.06±1.28/23.60±1.38	79.45±0.45	80.70±0.56	68.88±0.25
		16384	72.01±0.32	27.53±1.77/27.48±1.91	85.35±0.22	83.94±0.23	70.96±0.05
		50277	72.59±0.42	45.33±0.63/44.87±1.06	90.40±0.26	87.27±0.11	69.73±0.42

Table 15: Comparison of downstream performances across tokenizers in English.

Are LLMs Good for Semantic Role Labeling via Question Answering?: A Preliminary Analysis

Ritwik Raghav, Abhik Jana
IIT Bhubaneswar, India
{a23cs09001, abhikjana}@iitbbs.ac.in

Abstract

Semantic role labeling (SRL) is a fundamental task in natural language processing that is crucial for achieving deep semantic understanding. Despite the success of large language models (LLMs) in several downstream NLP tasks, key tasks such as SRL remain a challenge for LLMs. Hence, in this study, we attempt to instantiate the efficacy of LLMs for the task of SRL via Question answering. Toward that goal, we investigate the effectiveness of five different LLMs (Llama, Mistral, Qwen, OpenChat, Gemini) using zero-shot and few-shot prompting. Our findings indicate that few-shot prompting enhances the performance of all models. Although Gemini outperformed others by a margin of 11%, Qwen and Llama are not too far behind. Additionally, we conduct a comprehensive error analysis to shed light on the cases where LLMs fail. This study offers valuable insights into the performance of LLMs for structured prediction and the effectiveness of simple prompting techniques in the Question-Answering framework for SRL.

1 Introduction

Semantic Role Labeling (SRL) involves determining "who did what to whom, when, where, and how" to effectively extract the predicate-argument structure of a sentence (Gildea and Jurafsky, 2002).While early SRL systems relied heavily on syntactic parsers and task-specific models trained on datasets such as 'PropBank' (Palmer et al., 2005) or 'FrameNet' (Baker et al., 1998), the domain of Natural Language Processing (NLP) itself has witnessed remarkable advancements in recent years, primarily driven by the sophisticated neural architectures.

The advent of Large Language Models (LLMs) has revolutionized NLP, pushing the boundaries of possibilities in the field of language understanding and generation (Brown et al., 2020). Models such as GPT (Brown et al., 2020), Llama (Weerawardhena et al., 2025), and Gemini (Pichai et al., 2024), trained on massive corpora of textual data, have shown unprecedented capabilities that could be accessed using various prompting techniques. However, understanding the inherent capabilities of LLMs for complex structured prediction tasks without extensive fine-tuning has become vital for more efficient, scalable, and generalizable NLP systems.

SRL has long been studied through supervised methods using syntactic and dependency features (Palmer et al., 2005; Baker et al., 1998; Roth and Lapata, 2016). The QA-SRL framework (He et al., 2015; FitzGerald et al., 2018) reformulates SRL as a question-answering (QA) task, lowering annotation costs and aligning more closely with natural language understanding. Meanwhile, transformer-based LLMs such as BERT (Devlin et al., 2019), GPT (Radford et al., 2018), and T5 (Raffel et al., 2020) shift NLP from fine-tuning approaches to in-context learning (Brown et al., 2020; Min et al., 2022). Despite progress in both areas, systematic evaluations of pre-trained LLMs on QA-SRL have not been done, to the best of our knowledge.

Addressing this gap, this work evaluates five widely used LLMs — Llama (Weerawardhena et al., 2025), OpenChat (Wang et al., 2023), Mistral (Jiang et al., 2023), Qwen (Yang et al., 2025), and Gemini (Pichai et al., 2024)—on the QA-SRL benchmark.

The contributions of this paper are twofold.

- A comprehensive empirical evaluation of Llama 3.1 8B, Openchat 3.5, Qwen3-8B, Mistral-7B, and Gemini 2.0 Flash on QA-SRL 2.0 dataset (FitzGerald et al., 2018), assessing their performance in zero-shot and three-shot prompting settings without any model refinement or pretraining.
- A qualitative error analysis, identifying com-

Proceedings of the IJCNLP-AACL 2025 Student Research Workshop, pages 253–258
December 20-24, 2025 ©2025 Association for Computational Linguistics

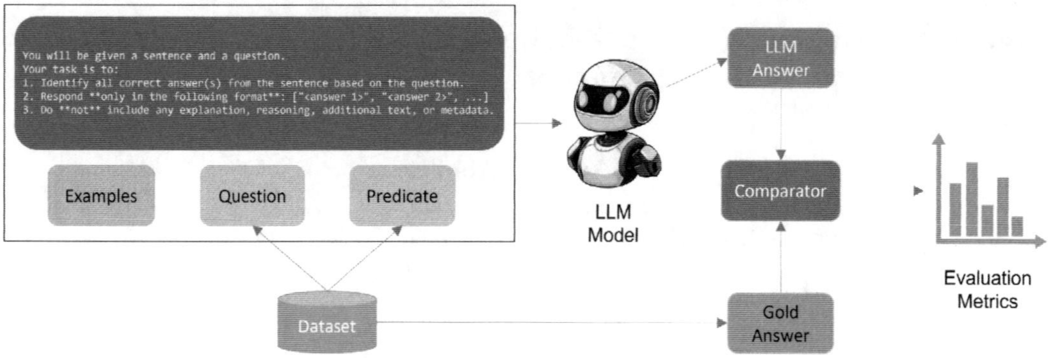

Figure 1: End-to-end pipeline for evaluating a large language model (LLM) on semantic role labeling (SRL) using the QA-SRL dataset. The process includes prompt creation, model inference with zero-shot or few-shot prompting, and quantitative evaluation of the generated semantic roles based on Precision, Recall, and F1-score metrics.

mon failure modes and describing the challenges faced by LLMs when performing structured SRL through in-context learning (Min et al., 2022)

The code for reproducing our experiments is available at: `https://github.com/ritwikraghav14/Benchmarking-LLMs-QA-SRL`.

2 Task Formulation

We formulate our study around the Question Answering-based Semantic Role Labeling (QA-SRL) framework introduced by He et al. (2015) and later extended by FitzGerald et al. (2018).Instead of requiring annotators to assign argument labels such as ARG0 or ARG1, QA-SRL generates natural language questions for each predicate in a sentence. Answers to these questions are contiguous spans extracted directly from the sentence, making the task intuitive and cost-effective.
In QA-SRL, each predicate anchors a set of questions targeting possible semantic roles such as agent, theme/object, or purpose. Sentences may contain multiple predicates, each generating distinct question–answer pairs.

To illustrate, consider the following example:
Sentence: As we test our ideas, we may come up with more questions.
Predicate 1: come
Question: who might come up something?
Answer: we
Question: what might someone come up?
Answer: with more questions

Here, the predicate *come* highlights the agent (we) and the object (with more questions). This demonstrates how a single sentence can support multiple semantic frames, each contributing to a richer representation of meaning.

In this study we use the publicly available QA-SRL 2.0 dataset (FitzGerald et al., 2018), which is a large-scale corpus consisting of over 64,000 sentences and over 250,000 question-answer pairs that model the verbal predicate-argument structure of a sentence. This size provides large-scale annotations of sentence-predicate-question-answer triples that instantiate this problem.

To better understand the performance of the LLMs, it is important to note that the QA-SRL task shows high consistency among human annotators. On the densely annotated subset, the agreement on answer spans reached an 83.1% exact match rate, showing strong human consensus on the expected output format of contiguous spans. The best-performing fine-tuned QA-SRL model reported by FitzGerald et al. (2018) achieved a 77.6% span-level accuracy. These figures represent the upper bound of human agreement and the benchmark performance of specialized systems, providing the necessary context for evaluating our zero-shot and few-shot LLM results.

3 Methodology

We investigate the efficacy of large language models (LLMs) for the task of SRL using the QA-SRL dataset (FitzGerald et al., 2018), in both zero-shot and three-shot settings. We create a structured prompt that explicitly instructs the model to extract all valid responses. It contains the task instructions, the sentence, the predicate, and the required output format. Figure 2 demonstrates the zero-shot and three-shot prompt structures we use for this study. While zero-shot prompting uses the structured prompt without any examples for in-context learning, three example question-answer pairs are added to this prompt for three-shot settings. These illustrative examples are selected to be representative of common semantic roles (agent, patient, temporal modifier) and reflect the natural question style in QA-SRL. These are selected from the dataset partition different from the sentences under evaluation. Figure 1 demonstrates the entire pipeline that we follow in this work.

3.1 Models

Five LLMs are used for this comparative study, representing both open-source and proprietary advancements in this field:

Llama 3.1 8B (Weerawardhena et al., 2025): An accessible open-source LLM from Meta with 8 billion parameters.

Mistral-7B (Jiang et al., 2023): A competitive open-source LLM from Mistral AI featuring 7 billion parameters.

Qwen3-8B (Yang et al., 2025): A high-performance open-source LLM from Alibaba with 8 billion parameters.

OpenChat-3.5 (Wang et al., 2023): An instruction-tuned open-source LLM built upon Mistral architecture.

Gemini 2.0 Flash (Pichai et al., 2024): A proprietary model from Google optimized for language understanding and generation tasks.

3.2 Prompting and Evaluation Framework

We evaluate all models within a unified prompting and evaluation framework to ensure reproducibility. Two prompting configurations are used:

In the **zero-shot prompting**, models are provided only with structured task instructions, which contain the guidelines, the input sentence, and the question (see Figure 2). No examples are provided.

In the **three-shot prompting**, the same instructions are augmented with three illustrative input–output examples (see Figure 2). To avoid data leakage, the few-shot examples were drawn from dataset partitions distinct from the sentences under evaluation. Thus, the three illustrative question–answer pairs used in the few-shot prompts were not identical across all evaluations, as each evaluation batch used examples sampled from a separate partition. This ensures fairness while preventing overlap between the illustrative examples and the test instances.

```
You are an intelligent system. You will be
    given a sentence and a question.
Your task is to:

1. Identify all correct answer(s) from the
    sentence based on the question.

2. Respond only in the following format:
   ["answer 1", "answer 2", ...]
3. Do not include any explanation,
   reasoning, additional text, or
   metadata.

---

Example 1:
Sentence: In 2002, The Global Fund
    to Fight AIDS, Tuberculosis
    and Malaria was drawn up to
    improve the resources
    available.
Question: what was improved?
['the resources available', '
    Tuberculosis and Malaria']

Example 2:
Sentence: Soil type also influences
     the type of vegetation that
    can grow in the region.
Question: what influences something
    ?
['Soil type']

Example 3:
Sentence: He decided, on his twenty
    -second birthday, to revise
    the story into a novel he
    called Stephen Hero.
Question: who decided to do
    something?
['He']

---

Now, process the following:
Sentence: {sentence}
Question: {q}
```

Figure 2: The prompt structure used in our experiments. The highlighted section appears only in the three-shot setting, while its absence corresponds to the zero-shot.

Outputs are post-processed to standardize spans (e.g., stripping whitespace, resolving duplicates), and are evaluated using standard metrics (span-level precision, recall, and F1 score) (Carreras and Màrquez, 2005; Surdeanu et al., 2008). A prediction is considered correct only if the answer span exactly matches the gold annotation; partial overlaps do not receive credit. In cases where multiple answers are possible for a single question, the model must provide all of them to be considered entirely correct. Our setup tests the models' ability to identify all valid argument spans for a given sentence-predicate-question triple.

4 Experimental Setup

We evaluate the five LLMs under both zero-shot and three-shot setups, as described in Section 3.2. Here, we outline how these setups are applied in our experiments. The dataset is partitioned into ten parts to facilitate controlled comparison. For three-shot prompting, examples are always drawn from partitions other than the one under evaluation, ensuring that no overlap occurs between illustrative examples and test instances.

Zero-shot setup Models are evaluated using the zero-shot prompt described in Section 3.2, which provides only structured task instructions.

Three-shot setup Models are evaluated using the three-shot prompt described in Section 3.2, augmented with three examples drawn from non-overlapping dataset partitions.

5 Results and Analysis

This section presents the quantitative and qualitative results of our experiments, providing a detailed analysis of the performance of each model and the effects of various prompting strategies.

5.1 Quantitative Analysis

The performance of each model on the Semantic Role Labeling (SRL) task, under both zero-shot and three-shot prompting setups, is summarized in Table 1a, and Table 1b.

Model-Specific Performance The quantitative results consistently demonstrate the significant dominance of Gemini 2.0 Flash in all tasks and prompting strategies. For instance, on the three-shot setting (Table 1b), Gemini 2.0 Flash achieves an F1-score of 0.5702, which is 11% more than Llama's 0.4556 and 8% more than Qwen's 0.4826. Qwen outperforms Llama by a small margin in both prompting setups, while OpenChat is the weakest model in both cases, followed by Mistral.

Impact of Few-Shot Prompting The inclusion of examples in the 3-shot prompting strategy generally yields a positive impact on performance. All five models exhibit F1-score improvements from 0-shot to 3-shot on this task, with the most significant gain shown by Gemini-2.0-Flash, which increases its F1-score from 0.5022 to 0.5702, a growth of about 7%. Mistral shows a growth of about 6%, OpenChat about 5%, and Llama shows the least growth among all models — a mere half percent.

Model	Precision	Recall	F1-Score
Llama 3.1 8B	0.5753	0.3683	0.4491
Qwen3-8B	0.5606	0.3892	0.4594
Mistral-7B	0.5532	0.2611	0.3547
Openchat-3.5	0.5809	0.2491	0.3486
Gemini 2.0 Flash	**0.6854**	**0.3963**	**0.5022**

(a) Performance of Zero-shot Prompting

Model	Precision	Recall	F1-Score
Llama 3.1 8B	0.5525	0.3877	0.4556
Qwen3-8B	0.5409	0.4357	0.4826
Mistral-7B	0.476	0.3635	0.4122
Openchat-3.5	0.59	0.298	0.3959
Gemini 2.0 Flash	**0.6928**	**0.4844**	**0.5702**

(b) Performance of Three-shot Prompting

Table 1: Performance of both the prompting techniques on QA-SRL dataset for Semantic Role Labeling

5.2 Qualitative Analysis

A closer examination of model output reveals recurring error patterns. Most common errors are:

Imprecise Spans: Models frequently struggle to identify the exact span, often including extraneous words or omitting critical components. An example of this error type is:

Sentence: Cody makes an observation that raises a question.

Question: what was raised?

Gold Answer: 'a question'

LLM Generated Answer: 'question'

Inaccurate Extraction In some cases, extracted phrases are semantically related but do not constitute the correct answer, indicating a subtle misinterpretation of the prompt. An example of this error type is:

Sentence: Off-road vehicles disturb the landscape, and the area eventually develops bare spots where no plants can grow.

Question: what develops something?

Gold Answer: 'the area', 'area'

LLM Generated Answer: 'bare spots'

Formatting Deviation: Despite explicit instructions, models occasionally deviate from the required format, sometimes including extraneous explanations. An example of this error type is:

Sentence: In the example, the farmer chooses two fields and then changes only one thing between them.

Question: When does someone choose something?

Gold Answer: 'In the example'

LLM Generated Answer: '</think>'

To quantify these observations, we manually inspected 100 randomly sampled erroneous predictions (excluding all correct ones) across the five models. Each instance was assigned to one of three categories: Imprecise Span, Inaccurate Extraction, or Formatting Deviation. The distribution of these errors is shown in Table 2.

Error Type	Percentage
Imprecise Span	44%
Inaccurate Extraction	40%
Formatting Deviation	16%

Table 2: Frequency distribution of qualitative error types based on manual inspection of 100 erroneous predictions

These qualitative observations show that while LLMs demonstrate potential for QA-SRL evaluation through prompting, their performance heavily depends on the task format and the quality of in-context examples. Although they gain from in-context examples, the question-answer structure seems intuitive enough to show good performance for zero-shot prompts as well.

5.3 Baseline Comparison

To contextualize our results, we compare them with earlier fine-tuned SRL systems on the same dataset. The original QA-SRL parser by FitzGerald et al. (2018) achieved a span-level accuracy of 77.6% and a question-level accuracy of 82.6% on QA-SRL 2.0.

In contrast, our best few-shot LLM result (Gemini 2.0 Flash: 0.57 F1) remains below these supervised baselines, showing that current LLMs, when used purely via prompting, cannot yet match the performance of task-specific SRL models. However, our evaluation provides a useful zero-shot and few-shot benchmark for understanding how much semantic structure LLMs can recover without any fine-tuning, which is particularly relevant for low-resource or cross-lingual SRL scenarios.

6 Conclusion

In this study, we evaluate LLMs on Semantic Role Labeling (SRL), focusing on QA-SRL, which frames the task as natural language question-answering. LLMs show strong performance on QA-SRL in zero-shot setting, and few-shot prompting further enhances results, demonstrating the power of in-context learning. The findings highlight QA-SRL's suitability for LLMs and set a solid baseline for future research and prompt engineering. Immediate future work would be to apply fine-tuning with small amounts of annotated data, which could provide a better understanding of model adaptability for SRL tasks. Additionally, exploring advanced prompting strategies and integrating human-in-the-loop correction could further improve performance and reliability.

7 Limitations

This study establishes a benchmark for evaluating Large Language Models (LLMs) on Semantic Role Labeling (SRL), but it has several limitations. The evaluation is restricted to the English language, leaving the performance of LLMs on other languages unexplored. It also focuses solely on zero-shot and few-shot prompting without investigating fine-tuning, which may limit insights into the models' full potential. Furthermore, the study considers only a limited set of five widely-used LLMs and a small range of few-shot settings, which may not capture the full variability in model behavior.

References

Collin F Baker, Charles J Fillmore, and John B Lowe. 1998. The berkeley framenet project. In *COLING 1998 Volume 1: The 17th International Conference on Computational Linguistics*.

Tom Brown, Benjamin Mann, Nick Ryder, Melanie Subbiah, Jared D Kaplan, Prafulla Dhariwal, Arvind Neelakantan, Pranav Shyam, Girish Sastry, Amanda Askell, and 1 others. 2020. Language models are few-shot learners. *Advances in neural information processing systems*, 33:1877–1901.

Xavier Carreras and Lluís Màrquez. 2005. Introduction to the conll-2005 shared task: Semantic role labeling. In *Proceedings of the ninth conference on computational natural language learning (CoNLL-2005)*, pages 152–164.

Jacob Devlin, Ming-Wei Chang, Kenton Lee, and Kristina Toutanova. 2019. Bert: Pre-training of deep bidirectional transformers for language understanding. In *Proceedings of the 2019 conference of the North American chapter of the association for computational linguistics: human language technologies, volume 1 (long and short papers)*, pages 4171–4186.

Nicholas FitzGerald, Julian Michael, Luheng He, and Luke Zettlemoyer. 2018. Large-scale qa-srl parsing. In *Proceedings of the 56th Annual Meeting of the Association for Computational Linguistics (Volume*

1: Long Papers), pages 2051–2060. Association for Computational Linguistics.

Daniel Gildea and Daniel Jurafsky. 2002. Automatic labeling of semantic roles. *Computational linguistics*, 28(3):245–288.

Luheng He, Mike Lewis, and Luke Zettlemoyer. 2015. Question-answer driven semantic role labeling: Using natural language to annotate natural language. In *Proceedings of the 2015 conference on empirical methods in natural language processing*, pages 643–653.

Albert Q. Jiang, Alexandre Sablayrolles, Arthur Mensch, Chris Bamford, Devendra Singh Chaplot, Diego de las Casas, Florian Bressand, Gianna Lengyel, Guillaume Lample, Lucile Saulnier, Lélio Renard Lavaud, Marie-Anne Lachaux, Pierre Stock, Teven Le Scao, Thibaut Lavril, Thomas Wang, Timothée Lacroix, and William El Sayed. 2023. Mistral 7b. *Preprint*, arXiv:2310.06825.

Sewon Min, Xinxi Lyu, Ari Holtzman, Mikel Artetxe, Mike Lewis, Hannaneh Hajishirzi, and Luke Zettlemoyer. 2022. Rethinking the role of demonstrations: What makes in-context learning work? In *Proceedings of the 2022 Conference on Empirical Methods in Natural Language Processing*, pages 11048–11064. Association for Computational Linguistics.

Martha Palmer, Daniel Gildea, and Paul Kingsbury. 2005. The proposition bank: An annotated corpus of semantic roles. *Computational linguistics*, 31(1):71–106.

Sundar Pichai, Demis Hassabis, Kent Walker, James Manyika, Ruth Porat, Koray Kavukcuoglu, and the Gemini team. 2024. Introducing gemini 2.0: our new ai model for the agentic era. Google/DeepMind blog.

Alec Radford, Karthik Narasimhan, Tim Salimans, and Ilya Sutskever. 2018. Improving language understanding by generative pre-training. Technical report, OpenAI.

Colin Raffel, Noam Shazeer, Adam Roberts, Katherine Lee, Sharan Narang, Michael Matena, Yanqi Zhou, Wei Li, and Peter J Liu. 2020. Exploring the limits of transfer learning with a unified text-to-text transformer. *Journal of machine learning research*, 21(140):1–67.

Michael Roth and Mirella Lapata. 2016. Neural semantic role labeling with dependency path embeddings. In *Proceedings of the 54th Annual Meeting of the Association for Computational Linguistics (Volume 1: Long Papers)*, pages 1192–1202. Association for Computational Linguistics.

Mihai Surdeanu, Richard Johansson, Adam Meyers, Lluís Màrquez, and Joakim Nivre. 2008. The conll 2008 shared task on joint parsing of syntactic and semantic dependencies. In *CoNLL 2008: Proceedings of the Twelfth Conference on Computational Natural Language Learning*, pages 159–177.

Guan Wang, Sijie Cheng, Xianyuan Zhan, Xiangang Li, Sen Song, and Yang Liu. 2023. Openchat: Advancing open-source language models with mixed-quality data. *arXiv preprint arXiv:2309.11235*.

Sajana Weerawardhena, Paul Kassianik, Blaine Nelson, Baturay Saglam, Anu Vellore, Aman Priyanshu, Supriti Vijay, Massimo Aufiero, Arthur Goldblatt, Fraser Burch, and 1 others. 2025. Llama-3.1-foundationai-securityllm-8b-instruct technical report. *arXiv preprint arXiv:2508.01059*.

An Yang, Anfeng Li, Baosong Yang, Beichen Zhang, Binyuan Hui, Bo Zheng, Bowen Yu, Chang Gao, Chengen Huang, Chenxu Lv, and 1 others. 2025. Qwen3 technical report. *arXiv preprint arXiv:2505.09388*.

Could you BE more sarcastic? A Cognitive Approach to Bidirectional Sarcasm Understanding in Language Models

Veer Chheda[1] **Avantika Sankhe**[1] **Atharva Sankhe**[2]

[1] Dwarkadas J. Sanghvi College of Engineering, Mumbai, India
[2] Sardar Patel Institute of Technology, Mumbai, India
{veerchheda3525, avantikasankhe1, atharvasankhe984}@gmail.com

Abstract

Sarcasm is a specific form of ironic speech which can often be hard to understand for language models due to its nuanced nature. Recent improvements in the ability of such models to detect and generate sarcasm motivate us to try a new approach to help language models perceive sarcasm as a speech style, through a human cognitive perspective. In this work, we propose a multi-hop Chain of Thought (CoT) methodology to understand the context of an utterance that follows a dialogue and to perform bidirectional style transfer on that utterance, leveraging the Theory of Mind. We use small language models (SLMs) due to their cost-efficiency and fast response-time. The generated utterances are evaluated using both LLM-as-a-judge and human evaluation, suitable to the open-ended and stylistic nature of the generations. We also evaluate scores of automated metrics such as DialogRPT, BLEU and SBERT; drawing valuable insights from them that support our evidence. Based on this, we find that our cognitive approach to sarcasm is an effective way for language models to stylistically understand and generate sarcasm with better authenticity.

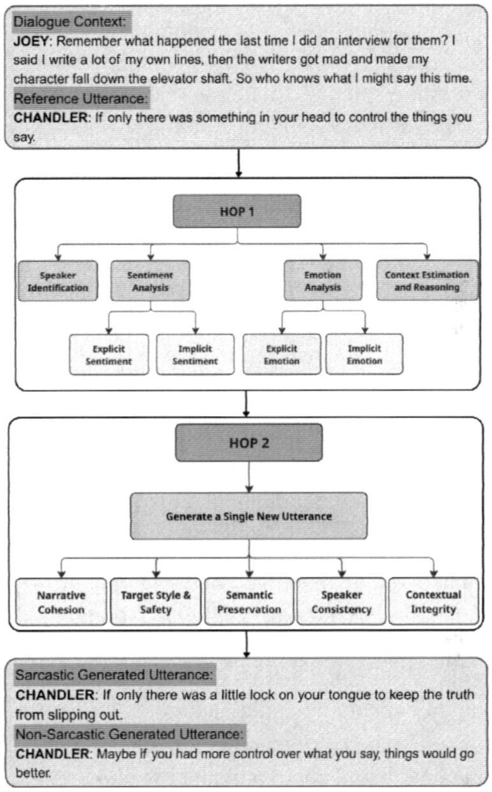

Figure 1: Illustration of our framework for bidirectional sarcasm understanding.

1 Introduction

Sarcasm is a form of verbal irony used to mock or convey contempt toward a person or subject. It is often used as a form of aggressive humour critical in tone indicating playful teasing (Pexman and Olineck, 2002; Frenda et al., 2022). Sarcasm is a communicative act rooted in social cognition and emotional intelligence. It heavily relies on contextual and linguistic cues, including preceding discourse (Campbell, 2012), conversational tone, and linguistic markers such as negation or inversion of literal meaning and use of interjections like 'gee' or 'yeah, right.'

Since sarcasm relies on implied meaning and situational cues, it can often be structurally indistinguishable from non-sarcastic speech, having the same or similar forms (Campbell, 2012). It is observed that language models can often struggle to understand the exact nuances that characterize sarcastic speech (Sharma et al., 2022), such as incongruity between the literal and intended meaning of a statement which particularly marks the presence of sarcasm (Kader et al., 2023; Mishra et al., 2019). Addressing these difficulties and helping language models overcome them is important to improve the natural, human-like quality of text generated by them. This would benefit the ability of language

Proceedings of the IJCNLP-AACL 2025 Student Research Workshop, pages 259–276
December 20-24, 2025 ©2025 Association for Computational Linguistics

models to generate and understand humour and double entendres in speech, useful to chatbots, social media analytics and content moderation.

Recent advancements have been made in helping language models detect the presence or absence of sarcasm as a stepping stone towards developing this understanding (Jang and Frassinelli, 2024). The emergence of datasets specifically annotated for sarcasm detection, (Oraby et al., 2016; Jang and Frassinelli, 2024; Oprea and Magdy, 2020; Castro et al., 2019), coupled with improvement in the ability of language models to reason and understand broader contexts (Srivastava et al., 2025) has made it possible to consider helping language models comprehend the nature of sarcasm from a human cognitive perspective. It is interpreted as a dynamic communicative act rather than a speech label, drawing from Theory of Mind (Shamay-Tsoory et al., 2005; Zhu and Wang, 2020).

We approach the task of perceiving sarcasm as a two-step process: 1) the ability of language models to comprehend sarcasm, and 2) to perform bidirectional transformation on the utterance to generate sarcastic or non-sarcastic utterances within an existing context. Using the MUStARD dataset (Castro et al., 2019), we prompt six small language models (SLMs) to generate both sarcastic and non-sarcastic utterances when given the preceding dialogue as context. We use three different prompting methods: 1) zero-shot prompting, 2) few-shot prompting, and 3) Chain of Thought (CoT) prompting. The utterances are generated as alternatives to existing utterances in the MUStARD dataset.

The remainder of this paper is structured as follows: Section 2 reviews related work; Section 3 details on our task; Section 4 describes our methodology; Section 5 covers experimental setup and evaluation; Section 6 delineates human evaluation; Section 7 presents results.

2 Related Works

While there has been significant breakthrough in sarcasm detection tasks (Castro et al., 2019; Oprea and Magdy, 2020; Gole et al., 2024), sarcasm generation remains an underexplored task. Recent works focus on highlighting the importance of context (Lunando and Purwarianti, 2013). One such work proposed an unsupervised, modular framework for generating sarcastic outputs by introducing contextual incongruity, setting a benchmark for style transfer techniques without paired data (Mishra et al., 2019). 'Chandler' is not only a sarcasm response generator but also provides explanations for why each response is sarcastic (Oprea et al., 2021). Evaluation of large language models (LLMs) and smaller 7B/8B models on the emerging Sarcasm Explanation in Dialogue (SED) task shows that larger parameter size is an effective factor for superior human language comprehension and reasoning capabilities (Zhang et al., 2024). Investigation of people's preferences on generated sarcasm showed that even when sarcasm was considered highly appropriate, non-sarcastic responses were still preferred (Oprea et al., 2022), which provided a backbone to the concept of sarcasm style transfer according to user preference.

While existing works either focus on detection or one-directional generation, our work stands out as the first to explore bidirectional sarcasm style transfer and incorporating contextual incongruity. We also direct our focus on evaluating our approach on lightweight SLMs.

3 Sarcasm Understanding

From a cognitive perspective, research has shown that sarcasm comprehension engages additional inferential processes compared to literal language (Fanari et al., 2023; McDonald, 1999). Prior work in sarcasm detection highlighted the importance of sarcastic cues for detection, but they don't assess whether a model actually understands sarcasm beyond recognition. To comprehend sarcasm, one must grasp the incongruity between literal meaning and intended meaning, drawing on contextual knowledge and theory of mind (Shamay-Tsoory et al., 2005; Zhu and Wang, 2020). Similarly, production of sarcasm requires speakers to manipulate linguistic cues to insert an incongruity while ensuring the underlying context remains interpretable (Ghosh et al., 2018; Ghosh and Veale, 2017). Motivated by this, we suggest a bidirectional framework with complementary tasks of comprehension and production, related but distinct cognitive processes that are necessary for demonstrating sarcasm perception.

3.1 Sarcasm Generation

Given a dialogue, the model must generate a sarcastic counterpart that retains the context while introducing pragmatic cues such as exaggeration, polarity reversal or context-dependent irony (Chakrabarty et al., 2020). This task reflects a

Model	Method	BLEU	SBERT	DialogRPT	Accuracy
Gemma 3 1B	Zero-shot	0.017 ± 0.001	0.439 ± 0.002	0.596 ± 0.001	0.902 ± 0.093
	Few-shot	0.046 ± 0.001	0.453 ± 0.001	0.634 ± 0.001	0.862 ± 0.087
	Ours	$\mathbf{0.057 \pm 0.001}$	0.462 ± 0.003	$\mathbf{0.651 \pm 0.001}$	$\mathbf{0.930 \pm 0.060}$
	Few-shot + Ours	0.052 ± 0.003	$\mathbf{0.469 \pm 0.001}$	0.642 ± 0.002	0.906 ± 0.068
Gemma 3 4B	Zero-shot	0.109 ± 0.002	0.443 ± 0.001	0.636 ± 0.001	0.924 ± 0.061
	Few-shot	0.150 ± 0.002	0.451 ± 0.001	0.638 ± 0.001	0.937 ± 0.045
	Ours	$\mathbf{0.189 \pm 0.003}$	0.466 ± 0.001	$\mathbf{0.643 \pm 0.001}$	$\mathbf{0.945 \pm 0.039}$
	Few-shot + Ours	0.167 ± 0.003	$\mathbf{0.467 \pm 0.001}$	0.640 ± 0.002	0.934 ± 0.035
LlaMa 3.2 1B	Zero-shot	0.047 ± 0.004	0.411 ± 0.004	0.602 ± 0.005	$\mathbf{0.839 \pm 0.103}$
	Few-shot	0.052 ± 0.004	0.407 ± 0.004	0.616 ± 0.010	0.706 ± 0.324
	Ours	0.057 ± 0.004	$\mathbf{0.435 \pm 0.003}$	$\mathbf{0.630 \pm 0.013}$	0.723 ± 0.224
	Few-shot + Ours	$\mathbf{0.059 \pm 0.008}$	0.412 ± 0.003	0.598 ± 0.017	0.592 ± 0.397
LlaMa 3.2 3B	Zero-shot	0.044 ± 0.003	0.424 ± 0.003	0.637 ± 0.002	0.906 ± 0.071
	Few-shot	0.072 ± 0.002	$\mathbf{0.453 \pm 0.001}$	0.646 ± 0.002	0.895 ± 0.051
	Ours	0.075 ± 0.002	0.437 ± 0.001	$\mathbf{0.648 \pm 0.001}$	$\mathbf{0.921 \pm 0.052}$
	Few-shot + Ours	$\mathbf{0.094 \pm 0.002}$	0.438 ± 0.002	0.646 ± 0.003	0.899 ± 0.061
Qwen 3 1.7B	Zero-shot	0.250 ± 0.005	0.417 ± 0.002	0.638 ± 0.001	0.773 ± 0.127
	Few-shot	0.271 ± 0.007	$\mathbf{0.432 \pm 0.001}$	0.640 ± 0.001	$\mathbf{0.786 \pm 0.095}$
	Ours	0.224 ± 0.008	0.425 ± 0.001	$\mathbf{0.653 \pm 0.002}$	0.781 ± 0.098
	Few-shot + Ours	$\mathbf{0.291 \pm 0.012}$	0.422 ± 0.001	0.642 ± 0.002	0.752 ± 0.080
Qwen 3 4B	Zero-shot	0.144 ± 0.004	0.424 ± 0.002	0.659 ± 0.001	0.933 ± 0.045
	Few-shot	0.153 ± 0.002	0.438 ± 0.001	0.648 ± 0.001	0.973 ± 0.018
	Ours	0.147 ± 0.004	$\mathbf{0.449 \pm 0.001}$	$\mathbf{0.664 \pm 0.001}$	$\mathbf{0.975 \pm 0.025}$
	Few-shot + Ours	$\mathbf{0.162 \pm 0.004}$	0.436 ± 0.002	0.650 ± 0.002	0.972 ± 0.019
GPT-4o	Zero-shot	0.019 ± 0.001	0.411 ± 0.000	0.671 ± 0.000	0.984 ± 0.017
	Few-shot	0.020 ± 0.001	0.413 ± 0.000	0.672 ± 0.000	0.988 ± 0.006
	Ours	0.020 ± 0.001	$\mathbf{0.423 \pm 0.000}$	$\mathbf{0.675 \pm 0.000}$	0.994 ± 0.006
	Few-shot + Ours	$\mathbf{0.021 \pm 0.002}$	0.422 ± 0.000	0.674 ± 0.000	$\mathbf{0.996 \pm 0.004}$

Table 1: Comparison of different models and methods across automatic evaluation metrics. Scores are reported as mean $\pm$ standard deviation over 5 runs. Best performing scores are highlighted in bold.

model's ability not only to recognize sarcastic cues but also to recreate it intentionally by understanding the inherent context. This includes both stylistic paraphrasing (sarcastic to sarcastic) and style transfer (non-sarcastic to sarcastic).

3.2 Sarcasm Removal

The model must produce a non-sarcastic utterance for a dialogue that retains the intended meaning by recognizing cues and resolving incongruity to recover the reader's intent (Pexman and Olineck, 2002). This includes both style neutralization (sarcastic to non-sarcastic) as it evaluates the model's ability to disentangle the core semantic content of an utterance from its style and factual paraphrasing (non-sarcastic to non-sarcastic) as an anchor point of literal communication for complete bidirectionality. A comprehensive understanding of sarcasm necessarily requires an equally robust understanding of non-sarcasm, since the recognition of irony depends on contrasting it with cases where intent and expression remain aligned.

4 Proposed Methodology

To model bidirectional understanding of sarcasm as a style, we propose a multi-hop framework to decompose the task into sequential stages of contextual understanding for intent and incongruity,

Model	Method	Context	Creativity	Meaning	Rank	Sarcasticness
Gemma 3 1B	Zero-shot	2.9541 ± 0.0608	2.2189 ± 0.0175	2.4931 ± 0.0777	3.0061 ± 0.0468	2.0257 ± 0.0468
	Few-shot	3.9237 ± 0.1063	2.5157 ± 0.0851	3.4439 ± 0.0631	2.4160 ± 0.1028	2.5942 ± 0.0761
	Ours	$\mathbf{3.9526 \pm 0.1119}$	$\mathbf{2.9104 \pm 0.0776}$	$\mathbf{3.4686 \pm 0.0387}$	$\mathbf{2.1986 \pm 0.0559}$	$\mathbf{3.0318 \pm 0.1428}$
	Few-shot + Ours	3.6230 ± 0.0996	2.4063 ± 0.0546	3.2265 ± 0.1106	2.5144 ± 0.0825	2.6474 ± 0.0677
Gemma 3 4B	Zero-shot	4.3400 ± 0.0494	2.9900 ± 0.0703	3.6700 ± 0.0650	2.7433 ± 0.0917	2.8700 ± 0.1139
	Few-shot	4.4033 ± 0.0845	2.8800 ± 0.0628	$\mathbf{4.0867 \pm 0.0639}$	2.3667 ± 0.1130	2.7667 ± 0.1196
	Ours	$\mathbf{4.5133 \pm 0.0681}$	$\mathbf{3.0133 \pm 0.1959}$	3.9010 ± 0.1014	$\mathbf{2.2267 \pm 0.1782}$	$\mathbf{3.0200 \pm 0.2253}$
	Few-shot + Ours	3.7067 ± 0.1475	2.6033 ± 0.1102	3.4767 ± 0.0535	2.9633 ± 0.0893	2.7333 ± 0.0825
LlaMa 3.2 1B	Zero-shot	3.1867 ± 0.1070	2.3333 ± 0.1359	2.7200 ± 0.0820	2.9167 ± 0.0577	2.0667 ± 0.1173
	Few-shot	$\mathbf{3.6333 \pm 0.1541}$	2.4767 ± 0.0962	3.2467 ± 0.1221	2.5200 ± 0.1023	2.4400 ± 0.1045
	Ours	3.6281 ± 0.1219	$\mathbf{2.8429 \pm 0.1756}$	$\mathbf{3.2742 \pm 0.1291}$	$\mathbf{2.2791 \pm 0.0807}$	$\mathbf{2.6605 \pm 0.2488}$
	Few-shot + Ours	2.6391 ± 0.2746	2.2533 ± 0.1958	2.4104 ± 0.2521	2.7238 ± 0.1469	2.3158 ± 0.2385
LlaMa 3.2 3B	Zero-shot	4.2267 ± 0.1116	2.9467 ± 0.0691	3.3933 ± 0.0673	2.3067 ± 0.1134	2.7767 ± 0.0894
	Few-shot	$\mathbf{4.3833 \pm 0.1646}$	3.0500 ± 0.1419	3.3067 ± 0.1489	2.5901 ± 0.1038	2.8300 ± 0.2053
	Ours	4.3331 ± 0.0987	$\mathbf{3.1759 \pm 0.1598}$	$\mathbf{3.5788 \pm 0.1013}$	$\mathbf{2.0888 \pm 0.1127}$	$\mathbf{2.8526 \pm 0.1108}$
	Few-shot + Ours	4.1644 ± 0.1336	3.0356 ± 0.1071	3.2875 ± 0.0879	3.0099 ± 0.0839	2.4581 ± 0.1302
Qwen 3 1.7B	Zero-shot	4.2400 ± 0.0596	2.6933 ± 0.0418	4.0300 ± 0.0861	2.3342 ± 0.0877	2.8767 ± 0.0723
	Few-shot	4.0700 ± 0.0606	2.6767 ± 0.0976	3.6167 ± 0.0850	2.4333 ± 0.0920	2.5900 ± 0.1294
	Ours	$\mathbf{4.3633 \pm 0.0869}$	$\mathbf{2.7467 \pm 0.0938}$	$\mathbf{4.2167 \pm 0.1550}$	$\mathbf{2.1333 \pm 0.0717}$	$\mathbf{2.9500 \pm 0.2062}$
	Few-shot + Ours	3.7225 ± 0.0736	2.4018 ± 0.2033	3.5190 ± 0.2180	2.9028 ± 0.0410	2.6254 ± 0.1585
Qwen 3 4B	Zero-shot	4.2633 ± 0.0861	2.9533 ± 0.0691	3.7633 ± 0.0477	2.3167 ± 0.1034	2.6900 ± 0.0450
	Few-shot	4.2433 ± 0.0855	$\mathbf{3.0600 \pm 0.1090}$	3.8200 ± 0.0811	2.2733 ± 0.1234	2.8700 ± 0.1431
	Ours	$\mathbf{4.2933 \pm 0.1090}$	2.9967 ± 0.1330	$\mathbf{4.2667 \pm 0.0565}$	$\mathbf{2.1910 \pm 0.0723}$	$\mathbf{2.9233 \pm 0.0703}$
	Few-shot + Ours	3.6667 ± 0.1523	2.8433 ± 0.0917	3.3700 ± 0.1293	3.0100 ± 0.2084	2.8200 ± 0.0545
GPT-4o	Zero-shot	4.1500 ± 0.0214	2.9333 ± 0.0834	3.4500 ± 0.1112	2.7598 ± 0.0128	2.6000 ± 0.0121
	Few-shot	4.2833 ± 0.1392	3.2167 ± 0.0323	4.0000 ± 0.1437	$\mathbf{2.4350 \pm 0.0548}$	$\mathbf{2.9032 \pm 0.1034}$
	Ours	$\mathbf{4.3167 \pm 0.2275}$	$\mathbf{3.3667 \pm 0.0288}$	$\mathbf{4.2833 \pm 0.0233}$	2.5062 ± 0.0832	2.6833 ± 0.0947
	Few-shot + Ours	3.9833 ± 0.1210	3.1000 ± 0.0955	3.5667 ± 0.0935	2.9899 ± 0.0754	2.8000 ± 0.0838

Table 2: Comparison of different models and different methods across LLM metrics over 5 runs. Scores are reported as mean $\pm$ standard deviation. Best performing scores are highlighted in bold.

and transformation for production of sarcastic or non-sarcastic style.

In the first hop, the language model extracts the implicit and explicit emotions and sentiment from each utterance in the dialogue. Explicit emotions and sentiment reflect the surface level state of the conversation while implicit ones are inferred from the linguistic cues, tone and context of the conversation (Chauhan et al., 2020). Disparities between the explicit and implicit emotions and between sentiments of the utterances lead to an incongruity which indicates possibility of sarcasm (Joshi et al., 2017). Utilizing chain-of-thought for reasoning, the model then deduces the underlying rationale and constructs the dialogue context.

This contextual representation of the dialogue is then leveraged to generate a sarcastic or a non-sarcastic conditioned utterance for the dialogue in the second hop (Lee et al., 2025). This hop preserves the speaker's original tone, emotional state and conversational dynamics using chain-of-thought, using the contextual presence or absence of incongruity to accordingly produce the specific style. Figure 1 illustrates the working of our methodology using an example from the MUStARD dataset.

5 Experimentation

5.1 Dataset

We use the publicly available MUStARD dataset (Castro et al., 2019) for our experimentation. It is a multi-modal dataset comprising of 690 audiovisual utterances and dialogue contexts with an even number of annotated sarcastic and non-sarcastic labels. Although, we only use the textual data which is appropriate to our methodology. Initially developed for sarcasm detection, we utilize the 690 dialogue long dataset for sarcasm generation and removal. Each dialogue has an utterance with a label for sarcasm. To achieve complete bi-directionality, we generate both sarcastic and non-sarcastic utterances for each dialogue irrespective of its label.

Model	Type	Zero-shot	Few-shot	Ours	Few-shot+Ours
Gemma-1B	Sarcastic	258.2 ± 5.8	81.8 ± 2.5	$\mathbf{61.4 \pm 8.2}$	71.8 ± 5.4
	Non-Sarcastic	194.0 ± 9.1	97.2 ± 3.6	$\mathbf{53.8 \pm 6.1}$	61.8 ± 2.4
Gemma-4B	Sarcastic	23.4 ± 1.1	31.4 ± 0.5	$\mathbf{15.2 \pm 3.5}$	20.0 ± 1.0
	Non-Sarcastic	24.6 ± 0.9	34.8 ± 0.8	$\mathbf{18.0 \pm 5.4}$	35.4 ± 4.7
LLaMA-1B	Sarcastic	228.4 ± 24.1	82.6 ± 16.4	$\mathbf{61.8 \pm 48.2}$	341.6 ± 78.4
	Non-Sarcastic	122.0 ± 18.3	$\mathbf{74.2 \pm 19.4}$	85.2 ± 27.8	251.6 ± 63.1
LLaMA-3B	Sarcastic	13.6 ± 1.7	9.8 ± 1.3	$\mathbf{9.6 \pm 1.9}$	13.4 ± 3.8
	Non-Sarcastic	10.8 ± 1.5	8.8 ± 1.3	$\mathbf{8.3 \pm 1.9}$	15.4 ± 4.3
Qwen-1B	Sarcastic	10.6 ± 0.5	16.8 ± 0.8	$\mathbf{8.2 \pm 2.3}$	13.8 ± 3.9
	Non-Sarcastic	12.8 ± 0.4	18.0 ± 0.7	$\mathbf{11.0 \pm 2.0}$	13.2 ± 4.4
Qwen-4B	Sarcastic	10.8 ± 1.3	2.2 ± 0.4	$\mathbf{1.2 \pm 0.8}$	1.4 ± 0.9
	Non-Sarcastic	6.8 ± 1.3	1.8 ± 0.9	$\mathbf{0.2 \pm 0.4}$	1.6 ± 1.3

Table 3: Failures (mean $\pm$ std) per model across settings (Zero-shot, Few-shot, Ours, Few-shot+Ours) over 5 runs. Rows report sarcastic and non-sarcastic utterances separately. Best performing scores are highlighted in bold.

5.2 Setup

All tests were run on 2 NVIDIA Tesla T4 GPUs. We report the inference time and memory usage of models in Appendix. We used 4-bit quantization via the Unsloth framework (Han and team, 2023), significantly reducing memory and computation needs, allowing for scalable experimentation. We also use zero-shot and few-shot as baselines along with an ablation of few-shot in our methodology to compare results and efficacy of our strategy.

5.3 Models

We focus primarily on open-weight smaller language models (SLMs) because they can be efficiently deployed on local, on-premises GPUs, enabling cost-effective fine-tuning on configurable sarcastic styles. We use LlaMa 3.2's 1B and 3B variants (Van Der Maaten et al., 2024) , Gemma3's 1B and 4B variants (Kamath and team, 2025), Qwen-3 1.7B and 4B variants(Yang and Qwen Team, 2025) and GPT-4o as a state-of-the-art (SOTA) baseline and LLM-as-a-judge due to its strong reasoning abilities and intelligence (Hurst and Team, 2024).

5.4 Metrics

To evaluate the effectiveness of the proposed multi-hop inference strategy for sarcasm understanding, we employed a combination of automated, LLM and human evaluated metrics.

5.4.1 Automated Metrics

We employed a suite of automatic metrics with sarcasm classification for detecting sarcasm in generated utterances, BLEU-4 for lexical overlap with the reference utterance (Papineni et al., 2002), semantic similarity with the dialogue using Sentence-BERT [1] (Reimers and Gurevych, 2019) and DialogRPT Updown [2] as a dialog-level appropriateness and relevance measure for generated utterances (Gao et al., 2020). We used GPT-4o as a classifier due to its ability to capture context-sensitive pragmatic cues. For every utterance, the dialogue was embedded as context for sarcasm detection.

5.4.2 LLM Metrics

We employed GPT-4o as our LLM-as-a-judge (Gu et al., 2025) to assess the quality of the utterances generated through our multi-hop inference framework on the dimensions mentioned in Table 4. The temperature was set to zero to ensure deterministic and reproducible judgments across all generated outputs.

6 Human Evaluation

We recruited 5 annotators on a volunteer basis from the general public to evaluate a total of 60 cases from the multimodal MUStARD dataset (Castro et al., 2019) in the survey. The annotators were chosen from a pool of volunteers with a minimum of a 4-year bachelor's degree from a program taught strictly in English, ensuring they were proficient

[1] Huggingface: sentence-transformers/all-MiniLM-L6-v2
[2] Huggingface: microsoft:DialogRPT-updown

in the language. Our aim with conducting this human survey was to measure multiple linguistic and stylistic dimensions, giving a deeper insight of how humans comprehend machine-generated sarcastic responses. All evaluations, including human evaluation, are conducted using only the dialogue transcripts and context provided in the dataset, without incorporating visual or audio signals.

6.1 Experimental Setup

The survey presents the participants with 60 distinct, randomly selected cases from the MUStARD dataset (Castro et al., 2019). Each case featured the following:

1. Dialogue context with respective speakers.
2. Four generated candidate utterances, each produced by one of the distinct prompting strategies up for comparison:
   - Using **zero-shot methodology**.
   - Using **few-shot methodology**.
   - Using **our novel methodology**.
   - Using **our novel methodology with few-shot**.

To further reduce order effects and anchoring bias, both the case order and the sequence in which candidate utterances appeared were randomized for every participant. For each set, the annotators were asked to perform two tasks:

1. **Comparative Ranking:** Participants were to rank each utterance from best (1) to worst (4) based on their overall subjective preference.
2. **Likert Scale Rating:** Participants were to rate each of the four generated utterances on a 5-point Likert scale (where 1 = poor quality and 5 = excellent quality) according to the four criteria detailed in Table 4.

Criterion	Description
Sarcasticness	How well does each utterance convey sarcasm?
Creativity	How well does the utterance avoid formulaic or repetitive patterns? How stylistically flexible is it?
Contextual Appropriateness	How fitting is the utterance to the provided dialogue context?
Meaning Preservation	How well does each generated utterance preserve the meaning of the original reference?

Table 4: Evaluation criteria for assessing the quality of generated utterances.

6.2 Justifying Evaluation Criteria

Implicit Display Theory (IDT) (Utsumi, 2005) distinguishes sarcasm from non-sarcasm, and portrays it as a dynamic communicative act with cognitive preconditions such as shared context, emotional intelligence, and the ability to navigate the incongruity between literal and intended meaning. A model could, in theory, detect sarcasm with high accuracy yet fail completely at generating an appropriate sarcastic utterance. In fact, people tend to prefer non-sarcastic responses over incoherent, overly specific sarcastic responses (Oprea et al., 2022). Thus, the evaluation of sarcasm generation must mirror the complexity and nuances of human judgment. Drawing inspiration from above, we rely on human-centric evaluation criteria as automated metrics are often blind to the very pragmatic and contextual nuances. Significance of each criterion is detailed below:

1. **Sarcasticness:** From a *theoretical* point of view, it is a direct application of IDT's concept of the "degree of ironicalness". This criterion measures how effectively an utterance conveys implicit irony. From an *empirical* standpoint, it measures if the model has successfully employed cognitive criteria like pragmatic insincerity and emotional markers. It is also the primary measure of style transfer accuracy.
2. **Creativity:** This criterion measures stylistic expression of the generated utterances. Sarcasm was typically preferred by users only when it was also considered "funny" (Oprea et al., 2022). Creativity includes 'humor' and 'originality', proving to be very valuable. It evaluates the quality of style transfer, assessing if the generated sarcasm is not just recognizable but also potentially preferable to a literal alternative.
3. **Contextual Appropriateness:** This metric directly assesses whether the model has correctly identified a valid context for sarcasm. An utterance cannot be sarcastic in the absence of "ironic environment" (Utsumi, 2005), and inappropriateness in general leads to negative reception of machine-generated sarcasm (Oprea et al., 2021). Measure of contextual incongruity is crucial for evaluating the model's pragmatic and social intelligence.

4. **Meaning Preservation:** It is a cornerstone of any text style transfer task, becoming more nuanced in the specific case of sarcasm. Sarcasm often works by inverting the literal meaning or valence of a statement. This metric ensures that the stylistic transformation does not generate an off-topic utterance that discards the original meaning. Particularly critical for evaluating our bidirectional methodology, it is used to confirm that stylistic neutralization retains semantics.

The evaluation framework required for our task cannot be limited to measuring classification accuracy as a binary evaluation, as it is fundamentally misaligned with the nature of the phenomenon it seeks to measure. Hence, we use 5-point Likert scale to capture the nuances of sarcasm. It is perfect to evaluate 'Sarcasticness' as it explicitly asks the evaluator to place the generated utterance on a continuum, judging not just *if* it is sarcastic, but *how* sarcastic it is. This allows for a much more fine-grained assessment of stylistic success. Ranking the generations according to reader's preference forces a comparative judgment, acknowledging that even among several "sarcastic" outputs, some will simply be better than others. Results are discussed in 7.4.

7 Results

The results of our human survey are summarized in Table 5; the results of automated evaluation metrics are presented in Table 1; Table 2 shows the results of LLM evaluation metrics.

7.1 Need for semantically-aware metrics

It is worthwhile to note that even though BLEU is a widely applied metric for style transfer and generation tasks, it does not lead to any significant trends in our task. In fact, the relatively low BLEU scores observed in our experiments can be attributed to the inherent limitations of lexical overlap metrics in capturing sarcasm and pragmatic nuances. Further, semantic similarity using transformers also fails to capture the shifts in context, style and expression in sarcasm generation. While DialogRPT provides a suitable metric for assessing dialogue quality, it also does not account for subtle changes in pragmatic nuance and sarcastic intent (Gao et al., 2020).

7.2 Limitations in using few shot for multi-hop reasoning

Our methodology shows consistent increases in human, LLM and automated metrics over the baselines and its few-shot counterpart. Incorporating few-shot examples into our strategy showed some improvement over baselines in automated metrics but perform sub-optimally in case of LLM and human evaluated metrics, which again calls for metrics that can capture more than surface-level cues. This is likely because few-shot prompting introduces fixed exemplar biases that may constrain the small language model's reasoning pathways, limiting its ability to explore alternative interpretations to leverage the dialogue context. Further, we also observed formulaic patterns in sarcastic generations like "Oh, absolutely!" or "Oh, really?" and non-sarcastic generations like "That's a bummer" or "I'm sorry to hear that". We theorize these generations were likely due to model's limited reasoning capabilities as utterances became more creative as model-size increased.

7.3 Punts and Failures

SLMs are known to have limited reasoning which leads to failures like punts, text degeneration, text repetition, etc. A primary example is a punt, which is a response where the model explicitly avoids or refuses to fulfill the prompt (e.g., "I'm sorry, I cannot help with that"). Other failures include text degeneration, text repetition and so on. We analyzed our generations for these failures along with our task specific failures such as wrong speaker name and empty generation ('<your generated line>'). We enumerate these errors in Table 3. Our methodology demonstrates an improvement in reasoning over the other methods by giving fewer punts. We do not include GPT-4o in the table as it did not lead to failures.

7.4 Result Analysis

Across all four bidirectional style transfer tasks, our method was consistently preferred by human annotators over the zero-shot and few-shot baselines. The inter-annotator agreement was calculated using Krippendorff's alpha which yielded a score of 0.4536. This depicts a moderate level of agreement which seems reasonable due to the highly subjective and nuanced nature of the task, where individual interpretations tend to vary. Our method achieved the best performance in Sarcasm Genera-

Category	Method	Context	Creativity	Meaning	Rank	Sarcasticness.
S→ S	ZS	3.45	3.23	3.32	2.79	3.57
	FS	3.59	3.19	3.13	2.65	3.44
	Ours	3.68	**3.68**	**3.38**	**2.50**	3.70
	Ours+FS	**3.80**	3.64	3.29	2.63	**3.76**
S→ NS	ZS	4.11	2.78	3.57	2.75	**3.15**
	FS	3.83	2.41	3.01	2.60	2.88
	Ours	**4.24**	**2.98**	**3.91**	**2.17**	2.48
	Ours+FS	4.07	2.85	3.68	2.48	2.84
NS→ S	ZS	3.73	3.39	3.01	2.73	2.96
	FS	3.71	3.61	2.80	2.60	3.34
	Ours	**4.01**	**3.81**	**3.51**	**2.21**	3.56
	Ours+FS	3.96	3.69	3.28	2.41	**3.60**
NS→ NS	ZS	3.71	2.55	3.25	2.48	**1.84**
	FS	3.79	2.61	3.17	2.45	1.76
	Ours	**4.17**	**2.77**	**3.97**	**2.11**	1.65
	Ours+FS	3.87	2.61	3.47	2.16	1.79

Table 5: Direction-wise Human Evaluation Metrics. Sarcastic (S), Non-sarcastic (NS). Best performing scores are highlighted in bold.

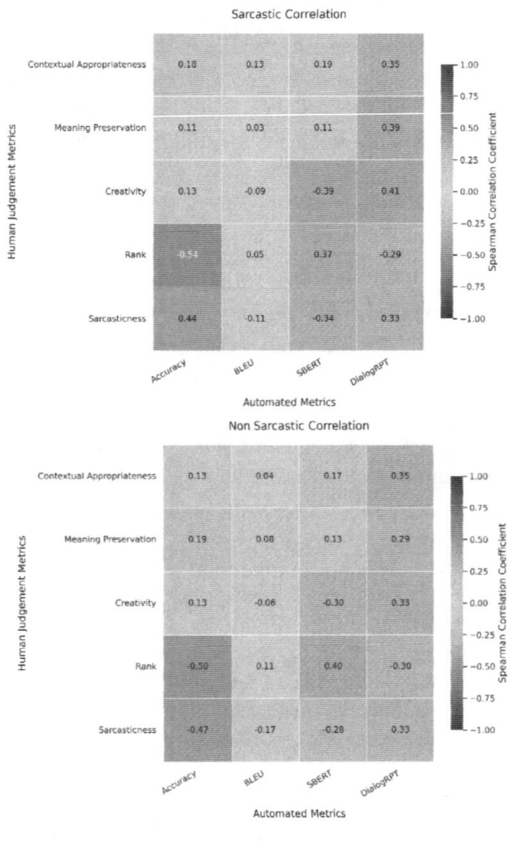

Figure 2: Spearman correlation between human and automated metrics across sarcastic and non-sarcastic cases.

tion, demonstrating that cognitive reasoning of the first hop enables the model to generate sarcastic utterances that are not only stylistically accurate but also fit naturally in the context. Our method also excelled in Sarcasm Removal and style maintenance tasks.

Our methodology shows consistent improvements over baselines in LLM evaluations and automated metrics as well. While Qwen Models show higher BLEU scores, they also show relatively lower Creativity scores in LLM evaluations. Tables in the Appendix display direction-wise LLM metrics and direction-wise automated metrics. Sarcasm Removal reports lower Creativity and Meaning Preservation scores indicating a loss in creativity and change of meaning, when going from sarcastic to non-sarcastic. However, Sarcasm Generation shows improvements in creativity while inducing sarcasm in utterances over their counterparts. Figures 2 show correlation of human and automated metrics for our task. Accuracy shows a positive and negative correlation with Sarcasticness for sarcastic and non-sarcastic generation respectively. Further, DialogRPT proves to be a good metric for nuanced communication analysis of human metrics. SBERT has a poor correlation demonstrating that higher semantic similarity with the original context doesn't lead to better generations.

8 Conclusion and Future Work

We have performed bidirectional transformation to approach the novel task of understanding of sarcasm as a style using a multi-hop CoT-based framework, helping SLMs generate utterances of specific styles with authenticity while maintaining their contextual relevance. By including a hop to first understand the context and perform reasoning to gain insight into its stylistic nature, in accordance with the Theory of Mind; we were able to generate new utterances in the next hop that preserved the original intent while being expressed creatively to suit the target style. Our experimentation was performed on the textual data of the MUStARD dataset with models taken from across three SLM families, as well as GPT-4o, a SOTA LLM model. Along with automated metrics, we employed human assessment and LLM-as-a-judge for evaluating these generations. We supplemented the results of our methodology with experimentation using other methods such as zero-shot and few-shot. The insights gained highlight the effectiveness of our strategy which approaches sarcasm inspired by principles of human cognition. In the future, we would like to improve the ability of small language models to perform reasoning for sarcasm using Implicit Display Theory (IDT) (Utsumi, 2005) and reinforcement learning, making use of the multimodal features of the MUStARD dataset, as well as employing newer datasets such as SE-MUStARD (Chauhan et al., 2020) with sentiment and emotion annotations.

Limitations

Our human evaluation process involved only 5 human annotators. While this added a valuable source to verify our generations, the paucity of our annotators limits the degree of diversity in insights that could have helped observe trends of human preference for various directions of style transfer. Furthermore, since we have only used the textual data presented within the MUStARD dataset, we were limited to experiment with 690 dialogue cases. We were also limited in the design of our prompts, since our experimentation did not involve the multimodal features of MUStARD which add further context to each dialogue case. We also found automated metrics such as BLEU and SBERT to show inconsistent alignment with human judgments of sarcasm, with only DialogRPT demonstrating robust correspondence, thus highlighting the scarcity of automated metrics for evaluating stylistic generations.

Ethics Statement

This work only uses public domain datasets and does not use any personal data. We appointed all of our human evaluators on volunteer-basis. Our system is intended solely for informational and research purposes.

Acknowledgments

We would like to express our sincere appreciation to Unsloth for providing an efficient and accessible framework that enabled low-resource conditioning and generation from large language models. Their contributions were instrumental in scaling our experiments across different model sizes while maintaining computational feasibility. We would also like to acknowledge the importance of MUStARD dataset in helping make the task of cognitively understanding sarcasm approachable. Furthermore, we also extend our gratitude to the human annotators who participated in our survey.

References

John D. Campbell. 2012. Investigating components of sarcastic context. *Electronic Thesis and Dissertation Repository*.

Santiago Castro, Devamanyu Hazarika, Verónica Pérez-Rosas, Roger Zimmermann, Rada Mihalcea, and Soujanya Poria. 2019. Towards multimodal sarcasm detection (an _Obviously_ perfect paper). In *Proceedings of the 57th Annual Meeting of the Association for Computational Linguistics*, pages 4619–4629, Florence, Italy. Association for Computational Linguistics.

Tuhin Chakrabarty, Debanjan Ghosh, Smaranda Muresan, and Nanyun Peng. 2020. R^3: Reverse, retrieve, and rank for sarcasm generation with commonsense knowledge. In *Proceedings of the 58th Annual Meeting of the Association for Computational Linguistics*, pages 7976–7986, Online. Association for Computational Linguistics.

Dushyant Singh Chauhan, Dhanush S R, Asif Ekbal, and Pushpak Bhattacharyya. 2020. Sentiment and emotion help sarcasm? a multi-task learning framework for multi-modal sarcasm, sentiment and emotion analysis. In *Proceedings of the 58th Annual Meeting of the Association for Computational Linguistics*, pages 4351–4360, Online. Association for Computational Linguistics.

Rachele Fanari, Sergio Melogno, and Roberta Fadda. 2023. An experimental study on sarcasm comprehension in school children: The possible role of contextual, linguistics and meta-representative factors. *Brain Sciences*, 13:863.

Simona Frenda, Alessandra Cignarella, Valerio Basile, Cristina Bosco, Viviana Patti, and Paolo Rosso. 2022. The unbearable hurtfulness of sarcasm. *Expert Systems with Applications*, 193:116398.

Xiang Gao, Yizhe Zhang, Michel Galley, Chris Brockett, and Bill Dolan. 2020. Dialogue response ranking training with large-scale human feedback data. In *Proceedings of the 2020 Conference on Empirical Methods in Natural Language Processing (EMNLP)*, pages 386–395, Online. Association for Computational Linguistics.

Aniruddha Ghosh and Tony Veale. 2017. Magnets for sarcasm: Making sarcasm detection timely, contextual and very personal. In *Proceedings of the 2017 Conference on Empirical Methods in Natural Language Processing*, pages 482–491, Copenhagen, Denmark. Association for Computational Linguistics.

Debanjan Ghosh, Alexander R. Fabbri, and Smaranda Muresan. 2018. Sarcasm analysis using conversation context. *Computational Linguistics*, 44(4):755–792.

Montgomery Gole, Williams-Paul Nwadiugwu, and Andriy Miranskyy. 2024. On sarcasm detection with openai gpt-based models. In *2024 34th International Conference on Collaborative Advances in Software and COmputiNg (CASCON)*, pages 1–6.

Jiawei Gu, Xuhui Jiang, Zhichao Shi, Hexiang Tan, Xuehao Zhai, Chengjin Xu, Wei Li, Yinghan Shen, Shengjie Ma, Honghao Liu, Saizhuo Wang, Kun Zhang, Yuanzhuo Wang, Wen Gao, Lionel Ni, and Jian Guo. 2025. A survey on llm-as-a-judge. *Preprint*, arXiv:2411.15594.

Han and Unsloth team. 2023. Unsloth.

Hurst and OpenAI Team. 2024. Gpt-4o system card. *Preprint*, arXiv:2410.21276.

Hyewon Jang and Diego Frassinelli. 2024. Generalizable sarcasm detection is just around the corner, of course! In *Proceedings of the 2024 Conference of the North American Chapter of the Association for Computational Linguistics: Human Language Technologies (Volume 1: Long Papers)*, pages 4238–4249, Mexico City, Mexico. Association for Computational Linguistics.

Aditya Joshi, Pushpak Bhattacharyya, and Mark J. Carman. 2017. Automatic sarcasm detection: A survey. *ACM Comput. Surv.*, 50(5).

Faria Binte Kader, Nafisa Hossain Nujat, Tasmia Binte Sogir, Mohsinul Kabir, Hasan Mahmud, and Md Kamrul Hasan. 2023. "when words fail, emojis prevail": A novel architecture for generating sarcastic sentences with emoji using valence reversal and semantic incongruity. In *Proceedings of the 61st Annual Meeting of the Association for Computational Linguistics (Volume 4: Student Research Workshop)*, pages 334–351, Toronto, Canada. Association for Computational Linguistics.

Kamath and Gemma team. 2025. Gemma 3: Technical Report. *arXiv preprint arXiv:2503.19786*. Published Mar 12 2025.

Joshua Lee, Wyatt Fong, Alexander Le, Sur Shah, Kevin Han, and Kevin Zhu. 2025. Pragmatic metacognitive prompting improves LLM performance on sarcasm detection. In *Proceedings of the 1st Workshop on Computational Humor (CHum)*, pages 63–70, Online. Association for Computational Linguistics.

Edwin Lunando and Ayu Purwarianti. 2013. Indonesian social media sentiment analysis with sarcasm detection. In *2013 International Conference on Advanced Computer Science and Information Systems (ICACSIS)*, pages 195–198.

Skye McDonald. 1999. Exploring the process of inference generation in sarcasm: A review of normal and clinical studies. *Brain and Language*, 68(3):486–506.

Abhijit Mishra, Tarun Tater, and Karthik Sankaranarayanan. 2019. A modular architecture for unsupervised sarcasm generation. In *Proceedings of the 2019 Conference on Empirical Methods in Natural Language Processing and the 9th International Joint Conference on Natural Language Processing (EMNLP-IJCNLP)*, pages 6144–6154, Hong Kong, China. Association for Computational Linguistics.

Silviu Oprea and Walid Magdy. 2020. iSarcasm: A dataset of intended sarcasm. In *Proceedings of the 58th Annual Meeting of the Association for Computational Linguistics*, pages 1279–1289, Online. Association for Computational Linguistics.

Silviu Oprea, Steven Wilson, and Walid Magdy. 2021. Chandler: An explainable sarcastic response generator. In *Proceedings of the 2021 Conference on Empirical Methods in Natural Language Processing: System Demonstrations*, pages 339–349, Online and Punta Cana, Dominican Republic. Association for Computational Linguistics.

Silviu Vlad Oprea, Steven Wilson, and Walid Magdy. 2022. Should a chatbot be sarcastic? understanding user preferences towards sarcasm generation. In *Proceedings of the 60th Annual Meeting of the Association for Computational Linguistics (Volume 1: Long Papers)*, pages 7686–7700, Dublin, Ireland. Association for Computational Linguistics.

Shereen Oraby, Vrindavan Harrison, Lena Reed, Ernesto Hernandez, Ellen Riloff, and Marilyn Walker. 2016. Creating and characterizing a diverse corpus of sarcasm in dialogue. In *Proceedings of the 17th Annual Meeting of the Special Interest Group on Discourse and Dialogue*, pages 31–41, Los Angeles. Association for Computational Linguistics.

Kishore Papineni, Salim Roukos, Todd Ward, and Wei-Jing Zhu. 2002. Bleu: a method for automatic evaluation of machine translation. In *Proceedings of the 40th Annual Meeting of the Association for Computational Linguistics*, pages 311–318, Philadelphia, Pennsylvania, USA. Association for Computational Linguistics.

Penny Pexman and Kara Olineck. 2002. Does sarcasm always sting? investigating the impact of ironic insults and ironic compliments. *Discourse Processes*, 33:199–218.

Nils Reimers and Iryna Gurevych. 2019. Sentence-BERT: Sentence embeddings using Siamese BERT-networks. In *Proceedings of the 2019 Conference on Empirical Methods in Natural Language Processing and the 9th International Joint Conference on Natural Language Processing (EMNLP-IJCNLP)*, pages 3982–3992, Hong Kong, China. Association for Computational Linguistics.

Simone Shamay-Tsoory, Rachel Tomer, and Judith Aharon-Peretz. 2005. The neuroanatomical basis of understanding sarcasm and its relationship to social cognition. *Neuropsychology*, 19:288–300.

Mayukh Sharma, Ilanthenral Kandasamy, and Vasantha W B. 2022. R2D2 at SemEval-2022 task 6: Are language models sarcastic enough? finetuning pre-trained language models to identify sarcasm. In *Proceedings of the 16th International Workshop on Semantic Evaluation (SemEval-2022)*, pages 1018–1024, Seattle, United States. Association for Computational Linguistics.

Gaurav Srivastava, Shuxiang Cao, and Xuan Wang. 2025. ThinkSLM: Towards reasoning in small language models. In *Proceedings of the 2025 Conference on Empirical Methods in Natural Language Processing*, pages 32600–32650, Suzhou, China. Association for Computational Linguistics.

Akira Utsumi. 2005. Implicit display theory of verbal irony : Towards a computational model of irony.

Laurens Van Der Maaten and 1 others. 2024. The llama 3 herd of models. *arXiv preprint arXiv:2407.21783*.

Yang and Qwen Team. 2025. Qwen3 technical report. *Preprint*, arXiv:2505.09388.

Yazhou Zhang, Chunwang Zou, Zheng Lian, Prayag Tiwari, and Jing Qin. 2024. Sarcasmbench: Towards evaluating large language models on sarcasm understanding. *Preprint*, arXiv:2408.11319.

Ning Zhu and Zhenlin Wang. 2020. The paradox of sarcasm: Theory of mind and sarcasm use in adults. *Personality and Individual Differences*, 163:110035.

A Appendix

A.1 Implementation Details

A.1.1 Model Cards

We have used six open-source small language models, with all converted by Unsloth's 4-bit quantization. These are the links to the official model cards for each model:

- unsloth/LlaMa-3.2-1B-Instruct-unsloth-bnb-523-4bit
- unsloth/LlaMa-3.2-3B-Instruct-unsloth-bnb-525-4bit
- unsloth/Qwen3-1.7B-unsloth-bnb-4bit
- unsloth/Qwen3-4B-unsloth-bnb-4bit
- unsloth/gemma-3-1b-it-unsloth-bnb-4bit
- unsloth/gemma-3-4b-it-unsloth-bnb-4bit

A.1.2 Inference Settings

Models were loaded with a maximum sequence length of 1024 tokens. Temperature was set to 0.7 for 5 validation runs for all models. For evaluation, since greedy decoding is not supported by OpenAI API, so we try using deterministic outputs by setting `temperature=0`.

A.1.3 Instruction Template

We follow a structured, instruction-based multihop prompting strategy to guide the model in generating new utterances of particular styles. In each prompt, the dialogue and utterance is specified followed by clear directions to help it understand the context in the first hop and then generate suitable utterances in the second hop. Additionally, we also provide the prompts used for few-shot and zero-shot strategies.

For the first hop which serves the purpose of contextual understanding, the model is prompted as follows:

```
Read the following dialogue.
Dialogue:
{dialogue}
{utterance}
For each line in the dialogue
as well as the utterance, do the following:
1. Identify the speaker.
2. Identify the **explicit sentiment**
(positive, neutral, negative) expressed
directly in what is said.
3. Identify the **implicit sentiment**
(positive, neutral, negative) inferred
from tone, choice of words, or context.
4. Name the **explicit emotion**
(anger, excited, fear, sad, surprised,
frustrated, happy, neutral, disgust).
5. Name the **implicit emotion**
(anger, excited, fear, sad, surprised,
frustrated, happy, neutral, disgust).
6. Briefly explain the reasoning for both
explicit and implicit sentiment/emotion.
7. Estimate the context based off of
the dialogue, identified implicit
and explicit sentiment, and emotion.
Format for each line:
Speaker: <name>
Explicit Sentiment:
<positive/neutral/negative/mixed>
Implicit Sentiment:
<positive/neutral/negative/mixed>
Explicit Emotion:
<emotion>
Implicit Emotion:
<emotion>
Reasoning:
<brief explanation>
Context: <context>
```

For the second hop which serves the purpose of generating utterances, the model is prompted as follows:

```
You are given a dialogue
and a detailed analysis of
explicit and implicit sentiment/emotion
for each line.
Previous sentiment analysis:
{hop1_output}
Original utterance:
{utterance}
Task:
Generate ONE new utterance that:
- Fits naturally after the dialogue.
- Is written in a {mode} style
that is not harmful.
- **Preserves the core meaning and intent**
of the original utterance.
- Matches the original speaker's tone,
emotional state, and relationship dynamics.
- Maintains the estimated
context of the conversation.

{example}

Format:
New utterance: {speaker_name}: <your
generated line>
```

For few-shot strategy, we used the following prompt:

```
Read the following dialogue.
Dialogue:
{dialogue}
Utterance:
{utterance}
Task:
Generate ONE new utterance that:
- Fits naturally after the dialogue.
- Is written in a {mode} style that is
not harmful.
- Preserves the core meaning and
intent of the original utterance.
- Matches the original speaker's tone,
emotional state, and relationship dynamics.
- Maintains the estimated context
of the conversation.
Example 1:
Input:
Dialogue:
Output:
{example_output_1}
Example 2:
Input:
Dialogue:
Output:
{example_output_2}
Format:
New utterance: {speaker_name}:
<your generated line>
"""
```

We evaluate the generated utterances using LLM by giving it the following prompt:

```
"You are evaluating multiple candidate
utterances for a dialogue.\n\n"
"Your evaluation must follow these steps:
\n\n"
"Step 1: Rank each utterance.\n"
"Rank the four generated utterances
in order from 1 (best) to 4 (worst) "
"based on their overall impression of
quality and effectiveness.\n\n"
"Step 2: Sarcasticness.\n"
"This dimension measures how well
each utterance conveys sarcasm. "
"Rate on a scale from 1 (not sarcastic
at all) to 5 (highly sarcastic). "
"\n\n"
"Step 3: Creativity.\n"
"Creativity assesses the originality
and inventiveness of the utterance. "
"A score of 1 means the utterance
is very plain or formulaic, "
"while 5 indicates a highly novel
and imaginative expression. "
"\n\n"
"Step 4: Contextual Appropriateness.
\n"
"This measures how well the utterance
fits within the dialogue context. "
"Rate on a scale from 1
(very inappropriate or off-topic)
to 5 (very natural and
contextually fitting).
\n\n"
"Step 5: Meaning Preservation
vs Reference.\n"
"How well does each generated utterance
preserve the meaning of the original
reference utterance? "
"Rate from 1 (completely different)
to 5 (very faithful).\n\n"
"Return your answer as a JSON object
mapping each 'utterance i'
```

```
to an object with:\n"
"{rank:int, sarcasticness:int,
creativity:int,
context:int, meaning:int}.\n\n"
"Example:\n"
"{\n"
"  \"utterance 1\": {\"rank\":2,
\"sarcasticness\":4, \"creativity\":3,
\"context\":5, \"meaning\":4},\n"
"  \"utterance 2\": {\"rank\":1,
\"sarcasticness\":2, \"creativity\":2,
\"context\":3, \"meaning\":3}\n"
"}\n\n"
f"Dialogue: {dialogue}\n"
f"Reference utterance (Label:
{label}): \"{reference}\"\n"
```

A.2 Examples

We have provided some examples of utterances generated from bidirectional style transfer according to our methodology. We cover six models across three SLM families that we conducted our experimentation on along with a SOTA LLM model, as listed below:

1. **LLaMA family:** LLaMA3.2 1B, LLaMA3.2 3B
2. **Qwen family:** Qwen3 1.7B, Qwen3 4B
3. **Gemma family:** Gemma3 1B, Gemma3 4B
4. **LLM model:** GPT-4o

In the following tables, we provide examples of generation performing style maintenance and style transfer performed on the utterance by each model. Table 10 shows generation performed over a sarcastic reference utterance, while Table 11 shows generation performed over a non-sarcastic reference utterance. The reference dialogue and utterances, both taken from the MUStARD dataset, are presented below:

1. **Sarcastic reference**:
   - PERSON: Leonard. Come, join us.
   - LEONARD: Hey, Dave.
     And Penny, what a surprise.
   - PENNY: Dave was just showing me around the university. This place is unbelievable!
   - LEONARD: I know, I've been offering to show you around for a year and a half. You always said you had yoga.
   - LEONARD: *Maybe I heard you wrong. A lot of words sound like "yoga."* (Reference utterance)
2. **Non-sarcastic reference**:
   - LEONARD: You'll never guess who they got to replace you at work.
   - SHELDON: Okay, I know what you're doing.
   - LEONARD: Really?
   - SHELDON: Yes, you're using chocolates as positive reinforcement for what you consider correct behaviour.
   - LEONARD: *Chocolate? - No, I don't want any chocolate!* (Reference utterance)

Model	Method	NS → NS				
		R	S	Cr	Cx	M
Gemma 3 1B	1	2.99 ± 0.32	1.49 ± 0.12	2.08 ± 0.14	2.99 ± 0.32	2.56 ± 0.34
	2	2.45 ± 0.17	1.75 ± 0.12	2.11 ± 0.09	3.87 ± 0.21	3.41 ± 0.09
	3	**2.31 ± 0.27**	**1.39 ± 0.26**	**2.48 ± 0.14**	**3.87 ± 0.30**	**3.61 ± 0.14**
	4	2.39 ± 0.25	1.53 ± 0.29	2.16 ± 0.14	3.63 ± 0.21	3.46 ± 0.19
Gemma 3 4B	1	2.56 ± 0.23	1.49 ± 0.06	2.41 ± 0.03	4.11 ± 0.12	3.75 ± 0.15
	2	2.37 ± 0.21	1.55 ± 0.14	2.53 ± 0.23	4.36 ± 0.14	3.95 ± 0.18
	3	**2.32 ± 0.10**	1.47 ± 0.16	**2.57 ± 0.23**	**4.44 ± 0.15**	**3.96 ± 0.21**
	4	2.75 ± 0.32	**1.42 ± 0.31**	2.19 ± 0.21	3.76 ± 0.40	3.64 ± 0.32
LlaMa 3.2 1B	1	2.80 ± 0.26	1.48 ± 0.29	2.19 ± 0.17	3.25 ± 0.20	2.85 ± 0.18
	2	2.43 ± 0.06	1.39 ± 0.17	2.12 ± 0.12	3.81 ± 0.14	3.44 ± 0.22
	3	**2.23 ± 0.12**	**1.29 ± 0.27**	**2.79 ± 0.17**	**3.91 ± 0.23**	**3.45 ± 0.24**
	4	2.55 ± 0.33	2.19 ± 0.14	2.48 ± 0.31	3.01 ± 0.44	2.75 ± 0.41
LlaMa 3.2 3B	1	2.30 ± 0.24	1.85 ± 0.18	2.49 ± 0.15	4.24 ± 0.17	3.77 ± 0.17
	2	2.24 ± 0.12	1.84 ± 0.41	2.60 ± 0.21	**4.35 ± 0.28**	3.91 ± 0.18
	3	**2.11 ± 0.14**	**1.61 ± 0.15**	**2.73 ± 0.20**	3.81 ± 0.24	**3.97 ± 0.21**
	4	2.18 ± 0.22	1.71 ± 0.34	2.25 ± 0.35	3.52 ± 0.31	3.81 ± 0.20
Qwen 3 1.7B	1	2.63 ± 0.13	1.79 ± 0.12	2.13 ± 0.08	**4.32 ± 0.06**	3.91 ± 0.13
	2	2.31 ± 0.10	1.57 ± 0.16	**2.28 ± 0.20**	4.20 ± 0.12	3.91 ± 0.19
	3	**2.19 ± 0.13**	**1.40 ± 0.15**	1.87 ± 0.17	4.28 ± 0.18	**4.12 ± 0.25**
	4	2.45 ± 0.22	1.68 ± 0.10	2.08 ± 0.18	3.69 ± 0.25	3.53 ± 0.37
Qwen 3 4B	1	2.60 ± 0.23	1.34 ± 0.12	2.13 ± 0.12	3.97 ± 0.25	3.71 ± 0.19
	2	2.35 ± 0.12	1.33 ± 0.09	2.39 ± 0.06	4.23 ± 0.06	3.99 ± 0.17
	3	**2.17 ± 0.28**	**1.19 ± 0.18**	2.43 ± 0.13	**4.44 ± 0.28**	**4.39 ± 0.28**
	4	2.84 ± 0.22	1.31 ± 0.26	**2.65 ± 0.26**	3.88 ± 0.32	3.79 ± 0.25
GPT-4o	1	3.20 ± 0.32	1.67 ± 0.11	2.33 ± 0.12	4.00 ± 0.18	3.53 ± 0.11
	2	2.53 ± 0.26	1.53 ± 0.14	2.80 ± 0.11	4.27 ± 0.09	3.80 ± 0.21
	3	**2.11 ± 0.17**	**1.30 ± 0.12**	**2.93 ± 0.19**	**4.67 ± 0.03**	**4.97 ± 0.09**
	4	2.13 ± 0.11	1.43 ± 0.31	2.73 ± 0.08	4.33 ± 0.12	4.87 ± 0.18

Table 6: LLM Evaluation Metrics for Models with Non-Sarcastic Source Text (NS → NS). Categories are NS (Non-Sarcastic) and S (Sarcastic). Parameters are R (Rank), S (Sarcasticness), Cr (Creativity), Cx (Context), and M (Meaning). Methods are 1 (zero-shot), 2 (few-shot), 3 (ours) and 4 (ours + few-shot).

Model	Method	NS → S				
		R	S	Cr	Cx	M
Gemma 3 1B	1	2.67 ± 0.15	2.75 ± 0.20	2.52 ± 0.14	3.08 ± 0.28	2.61 ± 0.17
	2	2.37 ± 0.16	2.73 ± 0.13	2.59 ± 0.16	3.64 ± 0.15	3.78 ± 0.13
	3	**2.27 ± 0.18**	**3.80 ± 0.39**	**3.19 ± 0.22**	**3.75 ± 0.28**	**3.94 ± 0.08**
	4	2.99 ± 0.13	2.92 ± 0.22	2.45 ± 0.18	3.56 ± 0.40	3.80 ± 0.48
Gemma 3 4B	1	2.79 ± 0.14	3.85 ± 0.13	**3.51 ± 0.13**	4.61 ± 0.09	3.53 ± 0.07
	2	2.37 ± 0.25	2.68 ± 0.14	2.83 ± 0.14	**4.69 ± 0.13**	**3.87 ± 0.08**
	3	**2.25 ± 0.23**	**4.15 ± 0.30**	3.32 ± 0.23	4.05 ± 0.21	3.81 ± 0.27
	4	3.12 ± 0.17	2.99 ± 0.25	2.48 ± 0.17	3.89 ± 0.12	3.68 ± 0.35
LlaMa 3.2 1B	1	2.85 ± 0.28	2.35 ± 0.26	2.47 ± 0.26	3.05 ± 0.47	2.69 ± 0.46
	2	**2.25 ± 0.22**	**3.32 ± 0.25**	**3.03 ± 0.18**	**3.87 ± 0.34**	**3.40 ± 0.39**
	3	2.46 ± 0.16	2.71 ± 0.38	2.76 ± 0.25	3.24 ± 0.12	3.02 ± 0.21
	4	3.10 ± 0.30	2.20 ± 0.40	1.92 ± 0.29	2.44 ± 0.37	2.24 ± 0.23
LlaMa 3.2 3B	1	2.17 ± 0.29	3.56 ± 0.28	3.29 ± 0.23	4.19 ± 0.25	3.48 ± 0.19
	2	**1.92 ± 0.27**	3.45 ± 0.36	**3.32 ± 0.34**	**4.51 ± 0.26**	**4.25 ± 0.18**
	3	2.57 ± 0.23	**3.67 ± 0.32**	2.97 ± 0.31	3.93 ± 0.32	3.52 ± 0.06
	4	3.33 ± 0.11	2.61 ± 0.24	2.43 ± 0.08	3.43 ± 0.28	3.44 ± 0.26
Qwen 3 1.7B	1	6.67 ± 0.21	2.66 ± 0.22	2.71 ± 0.08	4.24 ± 0.13	4.05 ± 0.13
	2	2.40 ± 0.31	2.68 ± 0.26	**2.81 ± 0.23**	**4.32 ± 0.13**	3.83 ± 0.08
	3	**2.23 ± 0.15**	**2.68 ± 0.28**	2.77 ± 0.34	4.25 ± 0.20	**4.20 ± 0.16**
	4	3.25 ± 0.19	2.43 ± 0.24	2.35 ± 0.21	3.76 ± 0.09	3.71 ± 0.24
Qwen 3 4B	1	2.41 ± 0.04	3.08 ± 0.11	3.31 ± 0.14	4.20 ± 0.08	3.53 ± 0.13
	2	2.32 ± 0.30	**4.07 ± 0.33**	3.63 ± 0.17	4.23 ± 0.17	3.93 ± 0.17
	3	**2.16 ± 0.27**	4.01 ± 0.25	**3.91 ± 0.26**	**4.29 ± 0.31**	**4.13 ± 0.18**
	4	3.15 ± 0.41	3.76 ± 0.35	3.23 ± 0.36	3.55 ± 0.17	3.11 ± 0.23
GPT-4o	1	2.67 ± 0.12	3.77 ± 0.11	3.42 ± 0.17	4.47 ± 0.11	3.51 ± 0.06
	2	2.56 ± 0.17	3.83 ± 0.02	3.53 ± 0.19	**4.83 ± 0.07**	3.83 ± 0.11
	3	**2.47 ± 0.06**	**3.91 ± 0.09**	**3.56 ± 0.12**	3.87 ± 0.12	**3.92 ± 0.12**
	4	2.90 ± 0.07	3.87 ± 0.04	3.48 ± 0.13	3.67 ± 0.08	3.75 ± 0.09

Table 7: LLM Evaluation Metrics for Models with Non-Sarcastic Source Text (NS → S). Categories are NS (Non-Sarcastic) and S (Sarcastic). Parameters are R (Rank), S (Sarcasticness), Cr (Creativity), Cx (Context), and M (Meaning). Methods are 1 (zero-shot), 2 (few-shot), 3 (ours) and 4 (ours + few-shot).

Model	Method	S → NS				
		R	S	Cr	Cx	M
Gemma 3 1B	1	3.60 ± 0.23	$\mathbf{1.43 \pm 0.28}$	1.91 ± 0.16	2.81 ± 0.30	2.28 ± 0.23
	2	2.39 ± 0.14	2.64 ± 0.19	2.60 ± 0.17	3.97 ± 0.15	3.41 ± 0.17
	3	2.32 ± 0.17	2.07 ± 0.39	2.52 ± 0.32	3.85 ± 0.09	3.19 ± 0.08
	4	$\mathbf{1.63 \pm 0.29}$	2.88 ± 0.39	$\mathbf{2.66 \pm 0.45}$	$\mathbf{4.02 \pm 0.24}$	$\mathbf{3.41 \pm 0.22}$
Gemma 3 4B	1	3.15 ± 0.10	2.19 ± 0.23	2.51 ± 0.14	$\mathbf{3.96 \pm 0.14}$	3.21 ± 0.20
	2	2.66 ± 0.19	2.96 ± 0.30	2.85 ± 0.16	3.85 ± 0.22	3.89 ± 0.20
	3	$\mathbf{2.60 \pm 0.25}$	$\mathbf{2.16 \pm 0.42}$	2.98 ± 0.17	3.63 ± 0.22	$\mathbf{3.92 \pm 0.23}$
	4	2.78 ± 0.17	3.20 ± 0.36	$\mathbf{3.09 \pm 0.22}$	3.65 ± 0.19	3.35 ± 0.18
LlaMa 3.2 1B	1	3.44 ± 0.35	$\mathbf{2.32 \pm 0.35}$	2.11 ± 0.23	2.96 ± 0.32	2.44 ± 0.33
	2	2.73 ± 0.15	2.91 ± 0.29	2.17 ± 0.13	3.33 ± 0.27	2.83 ± 0.25
	3	2.06 ± 0.21	2.60 ± 0.56	$\mathbf{2.88 \pm 0.36}$	$\mathbf{3.82 \pm 0.28}$	$\mathbf{3.28 \pm 0.30}$
	4	$\mathbf{2.02 \pm 0.22}$	2.89 ± 0.52	2.81 ± 0.38	2.90 ± 0.38	2.60 ± 0.40
LlaMa 3.2 3B	1	3.08 ± 0.26	2.99 ± 0.18	2.47 ± 0.24	3.76 ± 0.24	3.17 ± 0.22
	2	2.41 ± 0.24	2.87 ± 0.29	2.71 ± 0.18	$\mathbf{4.05 \pm 0.09}$	3.55 ± 0.21
	3	2.39 ± 0.29	$\mathbf{2.53 \pm 0.38}$	2.98 ± 0.27	3.96 ± 0.30	$\mathbf{3.55 \pm 0.38}$
	4	$\mathbf{2.12 \pm 0.31}$	2.83 ± 0.12	$\mathbf{3.14 \pm 0.19}$	3.68 ± 0.32	3.39 ± 0.26
Qwen 3 1.7B	1	2.57 ± 0.27	2.91 ± 0.31	2.64 ± 0.17	3.93 ± 0.17	3.60 ± 0.17
	2	2.71 ± 0.15	2.27 ± 0.28	2.40 ± 0.21	3.55 ± 0.06	3.04 ± 0.21
	3	$\mathbf{1.77 \pm 0.33}$	$\mathbf{2.21 \pm 0.47}$	$\mathbf{3.20 \pm 0.29}$	$\mathbf{4.57 \pm 0.25}$	$\mathbf{4.39 \pm 0.30}$
	4	2.32 ± 0.14	3.20 ± 0.21	2.53 ± 0.31	3.79 ± 0.20	3.47 ± 0.36
Qwen 3 4B	1	2.55 ± 0.27	2.60 ± 0.18	2.76 ± 0.27	4.09 ± 0.19	3.71 ± 0.18
	2	2.73 ± 0.18	2.41 ± 0.22	2.59 ± 0.28	3.88 ± 0.22	3.35 ± 0.21
	3	$\mathbf{1.89 \pm 0.24}$	$\mathbf{1.53 \pm 0.34}$	$\mathbf{3.37 \pm 0.30}$	$\mathbf{4.44 \pm 0.22}$	$\mathbf{4.21 \pm 0.29}$
	4	2.51 ± 0.44	2.71 ± 0.37	2.77 ± 0.20	3.80 ± 0.30	3.48 ± 0.27
GPT-4o	1	3.40 ± 0.13	2.42 ± 0.08	2.27 ± 0.13	3.47 ± 0.05	2.73 ± 0.15
	2	2.67 ± 0.14	2.13 ± 0.14	2.93 ± 0.18	4.13 ± 0.11	3.40 ± 0.13
	3	2.12 ± 0.11	$\mathbf{1.93 \pm 0.13}$	3.07 ± 0.21	4.40 ± 0.08	3.73 ± 0.11
	4	$\mathbf{1.87 \pm 0.38}$	2.87 ± 0.15	$\mathbf{3.80 \pm 0.03}$	$\mathbf{4.47 \pm 0.02}$	$\mathbf{4.00 \pm 0.03}$

Table 8: LLM Evaluation (S → NS). Parameters: R (Rank), S (Sarcasticness), Cr (Creativity), Cx (Context), M (Meaning). Best performing scores are highlighted in bold.

Model	Method	S → S				
		R	S	Cr	Cx	M
Gemma 3 1B	1	2.79 ± 0.14	2.41 ± 0.13	2.36 ± 0.17	2.94 ± 0.21	2.51 ± 0.22
	2	2.45 ± 0.28	3.21 ± 0.12	2.75 ± 0.18	3.97 ± 0.28	3.76 ± 0.13
	3	$\mathbf{1.82 \pm 0.15}$	$\mathbf{4.14 \pm 0.21}$	$\mathbf{3.40 \pm 0.25}$	$\mathbf{4.32 \pm 0.20}$	$\mathbf{3.98 \pm 0.25}$
	4	2.97 ± 0.18	2.85 ± 0.22	2.37 ± 0.13	3.33 ± 0.21	3.16 ± 0.14
Gemma 3 4B	1	2.18 ± 0.15	3.85 ± 0.25	$\mathbf{3.53 \pm 0.14}$	$\mathbf{4.68 \pm 0.09}$	3.99 ± 0.13
	2	2.26 ± 0.13	3.88 ± 0.20	3.31 ± 0.13	4.51 ± 0.15	$\mathbf{4.24 \pm 0.09}$
	3	$\mathbf{2.14 \pm 0.23}$	$\mathbf{3.91 \pm 0.38}$	3.48 ± 0.42	4.53 ± 0.12	4.03 ± 0.23
	4	3.23 ± 0.08	3.03 ± 0.14	2.65 ± 0.17	3.52 ± 0.13	3.24 ± 0.10
LlaMa 3.2 1B	1	2.57 ± 0.31	2.79 ± 0.36	2.57 ± 0.33	3.48 ± 0.36	2.89 ± 0.28
	2	2.67 ± 0.27	3.04 ± 0.32	2.59 ± 0.26	3.52 ± 0.31	3.32 ± 0.14
	3	$\mathbf{2.35 \pm 0.30}$	$\mathbf{3.32 \pm 0.38}$	$\mathbf{2.95 \pm 0.47}$	$\mathbf{3.55 \pm 0.36}$	$\mathbf{3.36 \pm 0.45}$
	4	3.22 ± 0.06	2.01 ± 0.22	1.81 ± 0.18	2.21 ± 0.22	2.07 ± 0.26
LlaMa 3.2 3B	1	2.77 ± 0.14	4.11 ± 0.10	3.53 ± 0.12	$\mathbf{4.72 \pm 0.17}$	3.95 ± 0.18
	2	2.43 ± 0.20	4.13 ± 0.37	3.57 ± 0.17	4.63 ± 0.16	$\mathbf{4.21 \pm 0.18}$
	3	$\mathbf{1.77 \pm 0.27}$	$\mathbf{4.23 \pm 0.35}$	$\mathbf{3.62 \pm 0.27}$	4.63 ± 0.23	4.17 ± 0.17
	4	2.98 ± 0.12	3.69 ± 0.24	2.33 ± 0.12	3.94 ± 0.19	3.01 ± 0.13
Qwen 3 1.7B	1	2.36 ± 0.08	3.25 ± 0.23	$\mathbf{3.29 \pm 0.23}$	4.17 ± 0.05	4.06 ± 0.09
	2	$\mathbf{2.32 \pm 0.14}$	3.74 ± 0.11	3.21 ± 0.21	4.21 ± 0.23	3.89 ± 0.14
	3	2.35 ± 0.15	$\mathbf{3.81 \pm 0.33}$	3.25 ± 0.28	$\mathbf{4.35 \pm 0.13}$	$\mathbf{4.16 \pm 0.11}$
	4	3.19 ± 0.17	3.20 ± 0.35	2.64 ± 0.51	3.65 ± 0.11	3.37 ± 0.25
Qwen 3 4B	1	2.83 ± 0.15	3.83 ± 0.05	3.61 ± 0.10	$\mathbf{4.79 \pm 0.07}$	4.11 ± 0.08
	2	$\mathbf{2.01 \pm 0.28}$	3.97 ± 0.14	3.64 ± 0.18	4.44 ± 0.17	4.01 ± 0.14
	3	2.23 ± 0.24	$\mathbf{4.05 \pm 0.15}$	$\mathbf{3.68 \pm 0.38}$	4.53 ± 0.36	$\mathbf{4.33 \pm 0.16}$
	4	3.55 ± 0.17	3.17 ± 0.33	2.72 ± 0.14	3.44 ± 0.08	3.11 ± 0.08
GPT-4o	1	2.83 ± 0.18	3.87 ± 0.09	3.60 ± 0.19	4.67 ± 0.09	3.93 ± 0.11
	2	2.62 ± 0.13	4.38 ± 0.05	4.20 ± 0.11	4.82 ± 0.02	4.27 ± 0.04
	3	$\mathbf{2.46 \pm 0.09}$	$\mathbf{4.56 \pm 0.03}$	$\mathbf{4.27 \pm 0.08}$	$\mathbf{4.88 \pm 0.04}$	$\mathbf{4.33 \pm 0.01}$
	4	3.12 ± 0.43	3.27 ± 0.19	3.17 ± 0.23	4.01 ± 0.07	3.90 ± 0.13

Table 9: LLM Evaluation (S → S). Methods are 1 (zero-shot), 2 (few-shot), 3 (ours) and 4 (ours + few-shot).

Model	Method	Non-Sarcastic → Sarcastic				Non-Sarcastic → Non-Sarcastic			
		BLEU	SBERT	DRPT	Acc.	BLEU	SBERT	DRPT	Acc.
Gemma 3 1B	1	0.019	0.455	0.616	0.902	0.020	0.424	0.607	0.880
	2	**0.074**	0.443	0.664	0.798	**0.065**	0.430	0.614	0.951
	3	0.040	**0.468**	0.669	**0.911**	0.038	**0.432**	**0.636**	0.968
	4	0.051	0.457	**0.670**	0.844	0.052	0.430	0.623	**0.978**
Gemma 3 4B	1	0.140	0.426	0.660	0.932	0.089	0.435	0.644	0.947
	2	**0.184**	0.427	0.661	0.908	**0.109**	0.433	0.636	0.956
	3	0.111	**0.432**	**0.670**	**0.952**	0.078	**0.444**	**0.647**	0.964
	4	0.144	0.429	0.665	0.923	0.091	0.438	0.638	**0.967**
LlaMa 3.2 1B	1	0.039	**0.510**	**0.643**	**0.626**	0.043	**0.487**	**0.656**	0.964
	2	**0.064**	0.417	0.612	0.409	**0.059**	0.411	0.634	0.986
	3	0.043	0.459	0.629	0.456	0.042	0.442	0.646	0.988
	4	0.048	0.424	0.594	0.194	0.056	0.415	0.619	**0.990**
LlaMa 3.2 3B	1	0.039	0.470	0.648	0.868	0.045	0.458	0.638	0.903
	2	0.082	0.471	0.657	0.837	0.070	0.460	0.637	0.947
	3	0.077	**0.496**	**0.670**	**0.920**	0.069	**0.462**	0.640	0.970
	4	**0.103**	0.477	0.668	0.905	**0.083**	0.461	**0.641**	**0.973**
Qwen 3 1.7B	1	**0.513**	**0.467**	0.661	0.722	**0.329**	**0.455**	0.637	0.759
	2	0.225	0.447	0.654	0.729	0.249	0.437	0.639	0.805
	3	0.321	0.437	**0.674**	**0.747**	0.280	0.432	**0.653**	0.819
	4	0.278	0.432	0.657	0.652	0.238	0.428	0.638	**0.841**
Qwen 3 4B	1	**0.177**	0.437	0.679	0.940	**0.170**	0.427	0.644	0.942
	2	0.073	0.450	0.673	0.959	0.084	0.439	0.642	0.965
	3	0.122	**0.469**	**0.695**	**0.986**	0.146	**0.456**	**0.655**	**0.976**
	4	0.084	0.468	0.685	0.979	0.102	0.442	0.645	0.974
GPT-4o	1	0.019	0.440	0.685	0.984	0.020	0.421	0.679	0.973
	2	0.019	0.430	0.686	0.995	**0.022**	0.412	0.683	0.993
	3	0.019	0.446	**0.712**	**0.998**	0.021	**0.431**	**0.685**	**0.997**
	4	**0.020**	**0.447**	0.701	0.996	**0.022**	0.429	0.684	0.995

Table 10: Automated metrics for transfers from a non-sarcastic source. The 'Method' column is abbreviated as: 1 (zero-shot), 2 (few-shot), 3 (ours) and 4 (ours + few-shot).

Model	Setting	Sarcastic → Sarcastic				Sarcastic → Non-Sarcastic			
		BLEU	**SBERT**	**DRPT**	**Acc.**	**BLEU**	**SBERT**	**DRPT**	**Acc.**
Gemma 3 1B	1	0.017	0.417	0.589	**0.985**	0.013	0.405	0.574	0.762
	2	**0.096**	0.412	0.655	0.785	**0.065**	0.407	0.601	0.912
	3	0.037	**0.420**	**0.669**	0.913	0.033	0.410	**0.630**	0.930
	4	0.053	0.418	0.666	0.837	0.052	**0.414**	0.611	**0.965**
Gemma 3 4B	1	0.132	**0.408**	0.656	0.953	0.075	0.425	0.625	0.845
	2	**0.198**	0.407	0.655	0.947	**0.109**	0.420	0.621	0.855
	3	0.110	0.404	0.663	**0.978**	0.059	0.425	**0.629**	**0.888**
	4	0.157	0.405	**0.665**	0.963	0.076	**0.426**	0.626	0.883
LlaMa 3.2 1B	1	0.057	0.427	0.610	**0.567**	0.050	0.421	**0.634**	0.902
	2	0.066	0.400	0.599	0.449	0.058	0.400	0.620	0.949
	3	0.052	**0.434**	**0.612**	0.476	0.045	**0.427**	0.631	0.973
	4	**0.067**	0.396	0.577	0.203	**0.061**	0.402	0.601	**0.982**
LlaMa 3.2 3B	1	0.045	0.431	0.665	0.904	0.049	0.415	**0.628**	0.808
	2	0.088	0.442	0.657	0.899	0.069	0.421	0.624	0.897
	3	0.087	**0.449**	**0.672**	**0.913**	0.066	**0.434**	0.625	0.920
	4	**0.111**	0.440	0.656	0.878	**0.080**	0.423	0.627	**0.930**
Qwen 3 1.7B	1	**0.601**	**0.435**	0.647	**0.944**	**0.356**	0.424	0.634	0.595
	2	0.297	0.426	0.638	0.882	0.313	0.420	0.628	0.726
	3	0.367	0.424	**0.659**	0.931	0.321	**0.427**	**0.636**	**0.768**
	4	0.349	0.421	0.642	0.812	0.299	0.415	0.631	0.705
Qwen 3 4B	1	**0.231**	**0.443**	0.660	0.982	**0.197**	**0.434**	0.629	0.866
	2	0.086	0.435	0.651	0.980	0.090	0.423	0.626	0.938
	3	0.157	0.430	**0.668**	0.976	0.162	0.429	**0.637**	0.942
	4	0.110	0.434	0.659	**0.988**	0.112	0.415	0.629	**0.945**
GPT-4o	1	0.017	**0.416**	0.667	0.981	0.019	0.413	0.655	0.962
	2	0.020	0.407	0.663	0.989	0.020	0.403	0.654	0.984
	3	0.020	0.396	**0.703**	**0.995**	0.020	**0.420**	**0.657**	0.988
	4	**0.021**	0.397	0.689	0.992	**0.021**	0.416	0.656	**0.990**

Table 11: Automated metrics for transfers from a sarcastic source. The 'Method' column is abbreviated as: 1 (zero-shot), 2 (few-shot), 3 (ours) and 4 (ours + few-shot).

Model	Sarcastic to Sarcastic	Sarcastic to Non-Sarcastic
Llama3.2 1B	Oh, great, just what I needed, another thing to add to my never-ending list of things I've been meaning to do for years.	I'm glad you're finally here, I've been looking forward to showing you around all morning.
Llama3.2 3B	Yeah, because nothing says "yoga" like a bunch of guys in their 30s doing downward-facing dog in the middle of a university building.	I'm glad you're here, though. I was just trying to figure out what you were saying.
Qwen3 1.7B	Maybe I heard you wrong. A lot of words sound like "yoga."	Maybe I heard you wrong. A lot of words sound like "yoga."
Qwen3 4B	Oh, I see. So it's not just the university that's unbelievable — it's the fact that I'm suddenly part of this conversation.	Maybe I heard you wrong. A lot of words sound like "yoga."
Gemma3 1B	Oh, really? You're really getting into the details of the campus layout, are you?	Don't worry, let's just take it slow. It's a lot to take in.
Gemma3 4B	Oh, *really*? You mean like, *actually* around the university?	Maybe I heard you wrong. A lot of words sound like "yoga." **I just meant, it's a really impressive place.**
GPT-4o	Sure, because "yoga" is definitely the first thing that comes to mind when you hear "unbelievable."	I just want to make sure we're on the same page here.

Table 12: Utterance generation from **sarcastic** reference utterance:
LEONARD: *Maybe I heard you wrong. A lot of words sound like "yoga."*

Model	Non-Sarcastic to Sarcastic	Non-Sarcastic to Non-Sarcastic
Llama3.2 1B	Oh, great, another thing you're using chocolates as positive reinforcement for your lack of effort.	Honestly, I'm not sure what to make of this chocolate as a reward for your good behavior.
Llama3.2 3B	Oh great, just what I always wanted, to be replaced by a chocolate fan.	I'm really disappointed that they replaced you with someone else.
Qwen3 1.7B	Chocolate? - No, I don't want any chocolate!	I'm not interested in chocolate. - Alright, fine.
Qwen3 4B	Oh, I see. You're not a fan of chocolate, but I'm sure you'd love a lifetime supply of it.	I don't want any chocolate. I'm not in the mood.
Gemma3 1B	Seriously? You're telling me you're rewarding *incorrect* behavior with chocolate?	Seriously?
Gemma3 4B	Really? Because that's *exactly* what I was hoping for.	I just thought you might be craving something sweet.
GPT-4o	Oh, right, because who wouldn't want a delicious distraction from reality?	Alright, I just thought it might lighten the mood a bit.

Table 13: Utterance generation from **non-sarcastic** reference utterance:
LEONARD: *Chocolate? - No, I don't want any chocolate!*

To What Extent Can In-Context Learning Solve Unseen Tasks?

Ryoma Shinto, Masashi Takeshita, Rzepka Rafal, Toshihiko Itoh
Hokkaido University
{shinto.ryoma, takeshita.masashi.68}@gmail.com
{rzepka, t-itoh}@ist.hokudai.ac.jp

Abstract

While Large Language Models (LLMs) are known for their In-Context Learning (ICL) capabilities, there is no consensus on the underlying mechanisms. A key point of debate is whether ICL allows models to adapt to unseen tasks without parameter updates—that is, whether they can extrapolate. In this study, we address this question by constructing an arithmetic dataset based on the bivariate linear function $z = ax + by$ to train a model and quantitatively evaluate its interpolation and extrapolation abilities through ICL. Our results show that while extrapolation was not achieved within our experimental design, tasks that were partially learned could be solved. We also found that the model acquires internal representations that can distinguish unseen tasks, and that greater task diversity in the training dataset improves ICL capabilities.

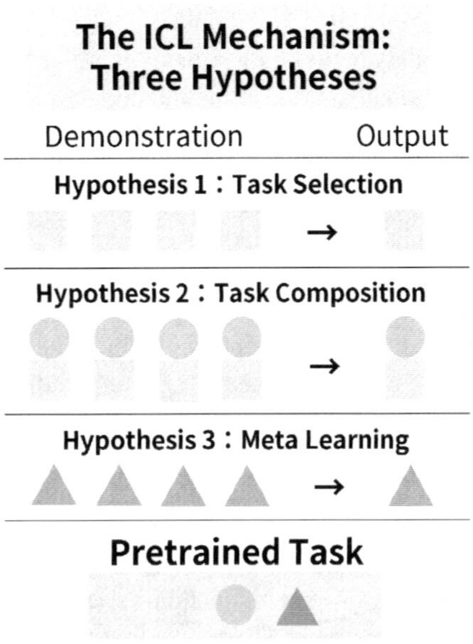

Figure 1: *A conceptual diagram of the three main hypotheses for the In-Context Learning (ICL) mechanism.* **Hypothesis (1) Task Selection**: The model selects and utilizes a single pre-trained task (e.g., blue squares) that matches the demonstration. **Hypothesis (2) Task Composition**: The model combines multiple pre-trained tasks to address the new task presented in the demonstration. **Hypothesis (3) Meta Learning**: The model learns and utilizes an unseen task (e.g., a green triangle), which does not exist in the pre-training data, on the fly from the context.

1 Introduction

Large Language Models (LLMs) are known to be capable of In-Context Learning (ICL) (Brown et al., 2020; Dong et al., 2024). ICL is a method that improves inference performance by presenting examples of a task within a prompt, without updating any parameters. This approach allows for efficient and flexible applications, as it does not require the preparation of training data or additional computational resources (Mosbach et al., 2023; Yin et al., 2024).

Regarding the mechanism of ICL, three main hypotheses have been proposed, as shown in Figure 1. One hypothesis is Task Selection, which posits that the model recognizes the characteristics of a task from in-context examples and then selects and applies a pre-trained task (Xie et al., 2022; Wies et al., 2023). Another is Task Composition, which suggests that the model can combine multiple pre-trained tasks to perform inference (Li et al., 2024). Furthermore, there is the Meta-learning hypothesis, which proposes that ICL enables the model to learn how to learn, adapting to unseen tasks based on in-context examples (Von Oswald et al., 2023; Akyurek et al., 2023). However, these hypotheses are not always consistent with subsequent experimental results (Kossen et al., 2024; Li et al., 2024), and a unified understanding of the ICL mechanism has not yet been achieved.

A key point of contention is whether ICL can

Proceedings of the IJCNLP-AACL 2025 Student Research Workshop, pages 277–288
December 20-24, 2025

be used to adapt to unseen tasks, as this could provide compelling evidence or counterexamples for these hypotheses (Garg et al., 2024; He et al., 2024). For instance, if a model can answer a task that it has not been pre-trained on simply by being shown examples in a prompt, it would imply that the model learned the task from the context alone without parameter updates. This would be evidence supporting the meta-learning hypothesis over the task selection and task composition hypotheses. However, when training on large-scale language data, it is not practical to clearly define the boundary between learned tasks (interpolation) and completely new tasks (extrapolation), making it difficult to rigorously evaluate the extrapolation capabilities of ICL.

Therefore, this research aims to provide important insights into the ICL mechanism by analyzing its extrapolation capabilities using arithmetic tasks. The advantage of arithmetic tasks is that, unlike language data, they allow for a clear separation between the domains of interpolation and extrapolation by controlling the number of digits and the range of variables.

In our experiments, we construct a total of 15 different datasets and analyze the extrapolation ability of ICL by evaluating the test data accuracy and internal representation vectors of models trained on each. The results revealed the following findings: (i) ICL can solve new tasks by combining previously learned tasks. (ii) Although the model cannot solve completely unseen tasks, it encodes internal representations that can identify them. (iii) The greater the diversity of tasks in the training dataset, the higher the ICL capability. The findings from this study are expected to make a significant contribution to the understanding of ICL mechanisms, for which a consensus has yet to be established.

2 Related Work

2.1 In-Context Learning

In-Context Learning (ICL) is one of the groundbreaking capabilities of Large Language Models (LLMs), enabling them to perform inference based on a few examples (Demonstrations) provided within a prompt, without any parameter updates. This ability, widely publicized by Brown et al. (2020) (Brown et al., 2020), allows a model to grasp the rules of a task on the fly from the examples in the prompt and adapt to new queries (Brown et al., 2020; Dong et al., 2024).

The emergence of ICL brought about a major paradigm shift in adapting models to specific tasks. Previously, the mainstream approach for adapting a model to a new task was Fine-Tuning (FT), which involved preparing high-quality annotated data to retrain all or part of the model's parameters (Devlin et al., 2019; Howard and Ruder, 2018). While this process had the advantage of requiring less computational cost and data compared to pre-training (Houlsby et al., 2019; Ben Zaken et al., 2022; Hu et al., 2022), it still necessitated parameter updates to adapt to new tasks.

In contrast, ICL uses natural language prompts as its interface and requires no additional training data or weight updates, enabling extremely low-cost and rapid task adaptation (Mosbach et al., 2023; Yin et al., 2024). Furthermore, whereas FT produces a task-specific model, ICL maintains a single, general-purpose model and demonstrates high versatility by flexibly handling a wide variety of tasks simply by rewriting the prompt (Brown et al., 2020; Wei et al., 2022; Ferber et al., 2024). Due to this efficiency and flexibility, ICL is considered a "new paradigm in natural language processing" and is recognized as a key characteristic of LLMs (Dong et al., 2024; Wies et al., 2023; Gu and Dao, 2024).

2.2 Hypotheses on the Mechanism of In-Context Learning

There is not yet a consensus on the mechanism by which ICL functions, and multiple hypotheses have been proposed. As mentioned in the introduction of this paper, these hypotheses can be broadly categorized into the following three.

The first is the "Task Selection" hypothesis, which posits that the model recognizes the characteristics of a task from in-context examples and then selects and applies an appropriate task from a set of tasks acquired during pre-training (Xie et al., 2022; Wies et al., 2023). This hypothesis formulates ICL as Bayesian inference, where the model infers a task conditioned on the input demonstrations.

The second is the "Task Composition" hypothesis, which suggests that the model performs inference by combining multiple learned tasks and knowledge (Li et al., 2024). This hypothesis explains that ICL can handle tasks that do not directly exist in the training data but can be derived by combining learned tasks.

The third is the "Meta-learning" hypothesis, which views ICL as a process of learning the solution to the task itself (Von Oswald et al., 2023; Akyurek et al., 2023). This perspective claims that a dynamic similar to gradient descent is driven internally during ICL, allowing the model to adapt to unknown tasks from contextual information. Therefore, it makes a fundamentally different claim from the "Task Selection" and "Task Composition" hypotheses in that it posits the model can handle tasks it has not pre-trained on, without parameter updates, based on contextual information.

In this study, based on these hypotheses, we design three corresponding types of experiments. Through quantitative analysis of their results, we aim to provide new insights into the mechanism of ICL.

3 Experimental Design

3.1 Dataset Construction

3.1.1 Data Representation Format

The dataset used in this study was constructed based on the bivariate linear function $z = ax + by$ to quantitatively evaluate the model's extrapolation capability in ICL (see Figure 2). The variables x and y are integers ranging from one to four digits, and the coefficients a and b are integers where $a, b \in \{0, 1, \ldots, 9\}$. The model is given a prompt consisting of k computational examples (Demonstrations) and one question (Query). A k-shot prompt is input as a concatenated sequence of k demonstrations, $D = \{(x_i, y_i, z_i)\}_{i=1}^{k}$, and a final query, $q = (x_{k+1}, y_{k+1})$. The coefficients (a, b) are common to all examples within a prompt, and x, y are randomly generated. The model is required to infer the common coefficients (a, b) from the given k examples and predict the corresponding z_{k+1} for the query.

Example of a 2-shot case with $a = 2, b = 1$

```
Demonstration 1: (132, 5532, 5796)
Demonstration 2: (355, 22, 732)
Query: (4412, 3356)
Target Output: 12180
```

As shown above, the coefficients a, b are not explicitly stated in the prompt. Therefore, the value of z cannot be uniquely determined from the query's x, y values alone. The model must use ICL to identify the common coefficients (a, b) from the k demonstrations to infer z. This design ensures

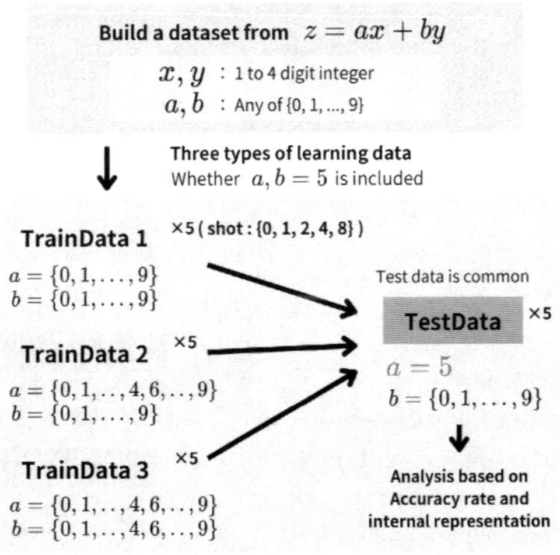

Figure 2: *Dataset construction and evaluation flow for analyzing the extrapolation capability of ICL.* The dataset is constructed based on $z = ax + by$. The training data is classified into three types based on whether they include coefficients $a, b = 5$. Since the test data involves tasks where $a = 5$, interpolation and extrapolation are defined by the range of a, b in the training data. Training datasets 1-3 are further subdivided by the number of shots into five types, for a total of 15 training datasets.

that a model properly trained on this dataset is performing ICL during inference.

Furthermore, all digits in the dataset are converted into unique symbols. This allows us to block the influence of the model's pre-existing arithmetic knowledge and purely analyze its reasoning ability through ICL[1].

Symbolic Representation of the Dataset

```
Demonstration 1: (%?{,«?{,<@$>)
Demonstration 2: (?«,{{,@?{)
Query: (!!%{,??<>)
Target Output: %{%;ˆ
```

Hereafter, we define a pair of coefficients (a, b) as a single "task." Since the coefficients a and b can each take 10 different values, the task space $\mathcal{T}$ in this study consists of 100 tasks, defined as follows:

$$\mathcal{T} = \{(a, b) \mid a, b \in \{0, 1, \ldots, 9\}\} \quad (1)$$

3.1.2 Dataset Composition

The training data consists of a total of 200,000 examples (train:validation = 8:2), and the test data

[1]See Appendix A.1 for the digit-to-symbol conversion mapping.

Table 1: Ranges of coefficients a, b in each dataset

Dataset	Range of a	Range of b
Training Data 1	$a \in \{0, .., 5, .., 9\}$	$b \in \{0, .., 5, .., 9\}$
Training Data 2	$a \in \{0, .., 4, 6, .., 9\}$	$b \in \{0, .., 5, .., 9\}$
Training Data 3	$a \in \{0, .., 4, 6, .., 9\}$	$b \in \{0, .., 4, 6, .., 9\}$
Test Data	$a = 5$	$b \in \{0, .., 5, .., 9\}$

consists of 1,000 examples.

In this study, to separately evaluate the interpolation and extrapolation capabilities of ICL, we establish three experimental settings based on the relationship between the set of tasks in the training data, $\mathcal{T}_{train}$, and the set of tasks in the test data, $\mathcal{T}_{test}$. Specifically, we define the datasets based on whether the coefficient '5' is included, as shown in Table 1.

The set of tasks used in the test data, $\mathcal{T}_{test}$, is fixed to tasks with the coefficient $a = 5$.

$$\mathcal{T}_{test} = \{(a, b) \in \mathcal{T} \mid a = 5\} \quad (2)$$

In contrast, the three types of training datasets each have the following task sets.

Setting 1: Interpolation The task set used in training data 1, $\mathcal{T}_{train1}$, is identical to the entire task space $\mathcal{T}$.

$$\mathcal{T}_{train1} = \mathcal{T} \quad (3)$$

In this setting, the condition $\mathcal{T}_{test} \subset \mathcal{T}_{train1}$ holds, meaning all tasks evaluated in the test set have been seen during training. Therefore, this setting evaluates the model's pure interpolation ability—whether it can correctly select and execute a learned task from the context.

Setting 2: Partial Interpolation The task set used in training data 2, $\mathcal{T}_{train2}$, consists only of tasks where the coefficient a does not include '5'.

$$\mathcal{T}_{train2} = \{(a, b) \in \mathcal{T} \mid a \neq 5\} \quad (4)$$

In this case, since the coefficient a in the test data is fixed to '5', $\mathcal{T}_{test} \cap \mathcal{T}_{train2} = \emptyset$, meaning the training data contains no tasks that perfectly match the test tasks. However, the task set $\mathcal{T}_{train2}$ does include the coefficient '5' for b. Therefore, this setting tests whether the model can solve tasks with coefficient $a = 5$ by leveraging its knowledge of tasks with coefficient $b = 5$ from training data 2.

Setting 3: Extrapolation The task set used in training data 3, $\mathcal{T}_{train3}$, consists only of tasks where neither coefficient a nor b includes '5'.

$$\mathcal{T}_{train3} = \{(a, b) \in \mathcal{T} \mid a \neq 5 \land b \neq 5\} \quad (5)$$

This is the most rigorous setting. The model is not trained on tasks with $a = 5$, nor even on tasks with $b = 5$. This means the model will observe the token for '5' for the first time in the test set's Demonstrations. This setting questions the model's true extrapolation ability—whether it can infer rules for a completely unseen domain from the context alone.

In addition to these three settings, each training dataset is further subdivided into five variations based on the number of examples in the prompt (number of shots): 0, 1, 2, 4, and 8-shot. This results in a total of 15 distinct training datasets for training and evaluation.

Note that in this study, we clearly distinguish between extrapolation and generalization. Extrapolation refers to the ability to handle unseen tasks $(a, b) \notin \mathcal{T}_{train}$, whereas generalization refers to the ability to correctly infer z from unseen inputs (x, y) within the scope of learned tasks $(a, b) \in \mathcal{T}_{train}$.

3.2 Model and Evaluation

For this research, we fine-tuned a pre-trained ByT5 base model (Xue et al., 2022). The Encoder-Decoder architecture adopted by ByT5 base has a clear separation between the roles of encoding the input sequence and decoding the output sequence. This makes it well-suited for analyzing the final hidden state of the encoder to understand how the model extracts task regularities from the context D and constructs internal representations. Furthermore, ByT5 tokenizes input symbol strings on a character-by-character basis, ensuring that multi-digit numbers are tokenized uniquely without being split. This guarantees a strict distinction between interpolation and extrapolation, regardless of the tokenizer.

The model is evaluated using the checkpoint that achieved the minimum loss on the validation dataset for each training setting. The primary evaluation metric is the accuracy on the test dataset. To visualize the acquisition process of the ICL capability during training, we recorded the accuracy trends for 1,000 samples each from the validation and test datasets every 1,000 steps during training[2].

[2]For experimental details such as training hyperparameters, see Appendix A.2

3.3 Probing Analysis

In this study, we anticipate that the model may sometimes be unable to solve unseen tasks. However, even in such cases, it is possible that the model internally captures the properties of the unseen task. To test this hypothesis, we conduct a probing experiment to verify whether the task (a, b) from the input prompt can be identified at the internal representation level. Probing is an analysis method that involves extracting a model's internal states (such as the activation vectors of hidden layers) and using a simple, external classifier (a probe) to test whether specific information (in this case, the task identifier) can be predicted from these vectors.

First, we create a new dataset for probing with 100,000 examples (train:validation = 9:1). The data format is the same as defined in Section 3.1. Each sample is assigned a unique integer label l based on the task (a, b) it belongs to, according to Equation 6.

$$l = 10a + b \quad (l \in \{0, 1, \ldots, 99\}) \tag{6}$$

This allows us to treat the 100 different tasks as a 100-class classification problem.

Next, using the encoder E of the fine-tuned ByT5 model, we extract an internal representation vector from each input prompt $P = (D, q)$. Specifically, we use the hidden state vector $h_{EOS} \in R^{1536}$ corresponding to the EOS (End-of-Sequence) token of the final encoder layer, which is considered to aggregate the contextual information of the entire prompt.

$$h_{EOS} = E(P) \tag{7}$$

Then, we train a linear classifier (a multi-class logistic regression model) f_{probe} to predict the task label l from this internal representation vector h_{EOS}.

$$\hat{l} = f_{probe}(h_{EOS}) \tag{8}$$

The classification accuracy in this probing task serves as an indicator of how well the model can internally distinguish the task (a, b). High accuracy would provide strong evidence that the task-identifying information is encoded in a linearly separable manner within the model's internal representations, suggesting that the model identifies tasks through ICL.

3.4 The Effect of Data Diversity on ICL

The three types of training datasets defined in Table 1 differ not only in their interpolation/extrapolation conditions but also in the total number of tasks, depending on whether they include $a, b = 5$. Specifically, the sizes of each training dataset's task set are as follows:

- Training Data 1: $|\mathcal{T}_{train1}| = 100$
- Training Data 2: $|\mathcal{T}_{train2}| = 90$
- Training Data 3: $|\mathcal{T}_{train3}| = 81$

This difference in the number of tasks could affect the acquisition of ICL capabilities and potentially confound the main analysis results. Therefore, we conduct an auxiliary experiment to independently evaluate the impact of task diversity within the training data on ICL performance.

3.4.1 Auxiliary Experiment Design

To evaluate the effect of task diversity, we created four new datasets with varying numbers of tasks by adjusting the range of coefficients a, b, based on Training Data 2. The task set for each dataset is defined as follows:

- **Training Data 2-1**: 30 tasks
  $\mathcal{T}_{train2-1} = \{(a, b) \mid a \in \{0, .., 4\}, b \in \{0, .., 5\}\}$
- **Training Data 2-2**: 42 tasks
  $\mathcal{T}_{train2-2} = \{(a, b) \mid a \in \{0, .., 4, 6\}, b \in \{0, .., 5, 6\}\}$
- **Training Data 2-3**: 56 tasks
  $\mathcal{T}_{train2-3} = \{(a, b) \mid a \in \{0, .., 4, 6, 7\}, b \in \{0, .., 5, 6, 7\}\}$
- **Training Data 2-4**: 90 tasks
  $\mathcal{T}_{train2-4} = \{(a, b) \mid a \in \{0, .., 4, 6, .., 9\}, b \in \{0, .., 5, .., 9\}\}$

Note that Training Data 2-4 is identical to Training Data 2 ($\mathcal{T}_{train2}$) from the main experiment. We train models on these datasets under the exact same settings as the main experiment and calculate the accuracy on the same test data (see Table 1) to compare and analyze the effect of task diversity on ICL capability. The number of demonstrations provided to the model is standardized to four (4-shot) for this verification.

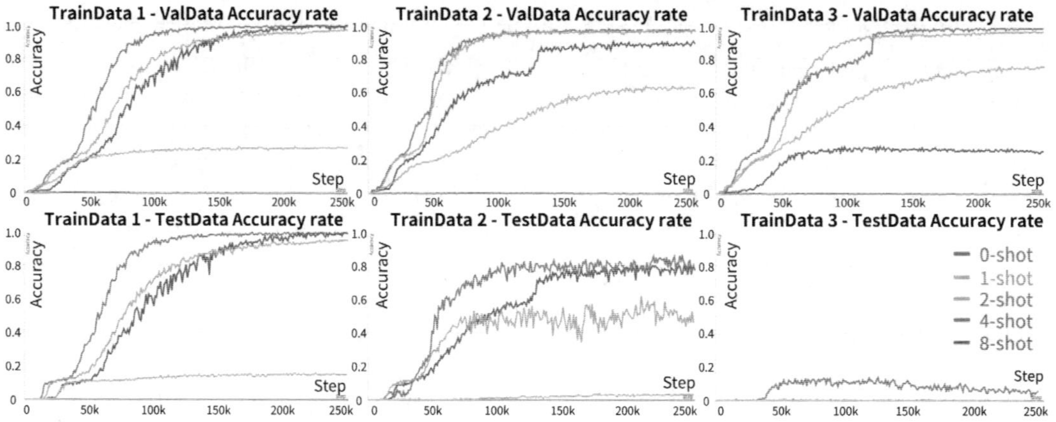

Figure 3: *Transition of accuracy on validation data (top) and test data (bottom) for models trained on each dataset.* Of particular note is the test data accuracy for TrainData 2 (bottom center), which only partially covers the test data task because it contains $b = 5$ but not $a = 5$. Nevertheless, the model achieved approximately 0.5 accuracy in the 2-shot setting and around 0.8 accuracy in both the 4-shot and 8-shot settings. In contrast, the test data accuracy for TrainData 3, which excludes $a, b = 5$ entirely, was nearly zero across all shot settings (bottom right).

4 Experimental Results

4.1 Accuracy Results

Figure 3 shows the accuracy trends for the validation data (top row) and test data (bottom row) for models trained on each dataset. It is important to note that, as explained in Section 3.1.2, the scope of the task sets for each of the validation datasets (three types) and the test dataset (one type) was intentionally manipulated (see Figure 2). Therefore, by confirming that the validation accuracy is nearly 1, we can ensure that training has completed successfully. This allows us to attribute the success or failure on the test data specifically to the model's in-context interpolation and extrapolation capabilities. Additionally, Table 2 shows the test data accuracy at the checkpoint with the lowest validation loss, which serves as the primary indicator for task success or failure.

Table 2: Test accuracy for each models

Dataset	0-shot	1-shot	2-shot	4-shot	8-shot
TrainData1	0.002	0.116	0.936	0.979	0.971
TrainData2	0.000	0.015	0.473	0.825	0.805
TrainData3	0.000	0.000	0.000	0.066	0.008

Validation Data Results A common trend in the validation accuracy plots (Figure 3, top row) is that while the accuracy for 0-shot and 1-shot models struggles to improve, the accuracy for 2-shot and 4-shot models approaches 1. For the 8-shot case, accuracy approached 1 for models trained on Training Data 1 and 2 (left and center columns), but it did not improve for the model trained on Training Data 3 (right column).[3] These results indicate that training was completed correctly for all datasets only in the 2- and 4-shot cases. Therefore, the analysis of ICL's interpolation and extrapolation capabilities will be based on the results of the 2- and 4-shot models.

Test Data Results - Training Data 1 The graph in the lower-left panel of Figure 3 shows that for the 2-, 4-, and 8-shot cases, the test accuracy converges to 1 during training. In contrast, the accuracy remained at 0.002 for the 0-shot case and 0.116 for the 1-shot case (see Table 2).

Test Data Results - Training Data 2 The graph in the lower-middle panel of Figure 3 shows that the accuracy converges to around 0.5 for the 2-shot case and around 0.8 for the 4- and 8-shot cases. In contrast, the accuracy for the 0- and 1-shot cases remained near zero (see Table 2).

Test Data Results - Training Data 3 As shown in Table 2, the accuracy was 0 for almost all shot counts. This indicates that, within our experimental setup, the model could not solve completely unseen tasks.

[3]The reason for this is discussed in Section 5.2 from the perspective of dataset diversity.

Table 3: Probing accuracy of each models

Dataset	0-shot	1-shot	2-shot	4-shot	8-shot
TrainData1	0.010	0.493	0.963	0.996	0.998
TrainData2	0.009	0.754	0.951	0.993	0.997
TrainData3	0.012	0.798	0.929	0.993	0.976

4.2 Probing Experiment Results

Table 3 shows the average accuracy for each model in the probing experiment, which classifies the task (a,b) from the internal representation of the input sequence. For the 2-, 4-, and 8-shot settings, the models trained on any of the training datasets achieved an accuracy of over 0.9, indicating that the classifier could properly linearly separate the tasks based on the internal representations of the input sequence. Notably, even for the model trained on Training Data 3, which had an accuracy of almost 0 in Table 2, the probing experiment recorded a high accuracy. On the other hand, the accuracy for the 0-shot case was nearly zero, and while the 1-shot case showed some variation depending on the training data, it did not reach a sufficient level of accuracy. The detailed results of the probing experiment for each model are visualized as confusion matrices in Appendix A.3.

4.3 Results of the Analysis of Dataset Diversity's Impact

Figure 4 shows the accuracy trends for the validation data (top) and test data (bottom) for models trained on the four types of datasets described in Section 3.4.1. The number of demonstrations was standardized to 4-shot. The accuracy on the validation data (top row) can be seen converging to 1 for all training datasets, indicating that training was completed successfully. On the other hand, the accuracy on the test data (bottom row) is observed to converge to higher levels as the diversity of the training data increases. Table 4 shows the test data accuracy at the checkpoint with the lowest validation data loss, and this table also demonstrates that increasing task diversity leads to significant changes in accuracy. Notably, for Training Data 2-1, although the validation accuracy converged to 1, the test accuracy remained at only 0.003, indicating that when the task diversity in the training data is low, the ICL capability cannot be properly generalized.

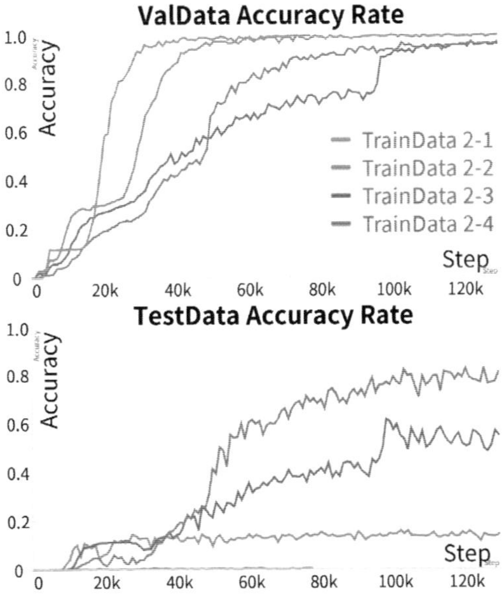

Figure 4: *Accuracy trends on the validation data (top row) and test data (bottom row) for each training dataset.*

Table 4: Test data accuracy for each training dataset

Dataset	Accuracy
Training Data 2-1	0.003
Training Data 2-2	0.158
Training Data 2-3	0.569
Training Data 2-4	0.825

5 Discussion

5.1 Extrapolation Capability of ICL from the Perspective of Accuracy and Probing Results

First, Figure 3 shows that for the 0- and 1-shot cases, the validation accuracy did not converge to 1 for any training dataset, and the test accuracy was also nearly 0. This is likely because the task was created from a bivariate function, which requires at least two demonstrations to identify the specific task (a, b).

Next, regarding Training Data 1, the models achieved approximately 100% accuracy on both the validation and test data for the 2-, 4-, and 8-shot cases (see Table 2). Since Training Data 1 includes the task scope of the test data (interpolation), this result suggests that the model can recognize the presented task via ICL and appropriately select and apply a task from its learned repertoire.

Subsequently, for Training Data 2, despite not

being trained on tasks with $a = 5$—i.e., tasks identical to the test data—the model achieved accuracies of 0.473 for 2-shot, 0.825 for 4-shot, and 0.805 for 8-shot on the test data (see Table 2). This suggests that ICL not only selects learned tasks but can also solve partially unseen tasks by composing them. Specifically, it is thought that the model solved the test tasks by combining the knowledge gained from learning tasks with $b = 5$ included in Training Data 2—i.e., tasks of the form $(a, b) = (k, 5)$ (where $k \in \{0, .., 4, 6, .., 9\}$)—with the demonstrations for the test tasks $(a, b) = (5, k)$ (where $k \in \{0, 1, .., 9\}$).

Finally, the test accuracy for the model trained on Training Data 3 was nearly 0 for all shot counts, providing no evidence that ICL enables extrapolation within the scope of this experiment. However, the results of the probing experiment (see Table 3) show that in the 2-shot and higher settings, the model trained on Training Data 3, similar to the models trained on other data, could linearly separate tasks from the input sequence. This suggests that in ICL, the model encodes internal representations from the input sequence in a way that enables it to separate each task, thereby distinguishing unseen tasks from learned ones. Therefore, while ICL allows the model to acquire internal representations that can identify completely new tasks, a failure to map these representations to the correct output—that is, a failure in the decoder's dynamics—is likely the cause of the extrapolation failure, warranting further investigation.

5.2 The Effect of Dataset Diversity on ICL Capability

As seen in Figure 4 and Table 4, while the validation accuracy (top row) converges to 1 for all training datasets, the test accuracy improves in line with the task diversity of the dataset. These results suggest that the diversity of tasks in the training data is crucial for acquiring ICL capability. This is likely because high task diversity enables the model to learn a general-purpose solution applicable to all tasks, rather than learning a specific solution for each individual task.

Based on this consideration, we can speculate on why only the 8-shot model for Training Data 3 failed to reach an accuracy of 1 on the validation data (top-right graph in Figure 3), unlike the models for Training Data 1 and 2. Specifically, since Training Data 3 has fewer total tasks compared to Training Data 1 and 2 (see Section 3.4), it is conceivable that a general-purpose ICL capability was not sufficiently acquired. It is important to note that this argument applies only to the 8-shot case, as the validation accuracies for the 2- and 4-shot models did converge to 1. Since it has been shown that ICL performance improves with more demonstrations (Brown et al., 2020; Dong et al., 2024), a significant challenge for further verifying extrapolation capability is to test with 8 or more shots. Therefore, to discuss the extrapolation capability of ICL in settings with 8 or more shots, it is necessary to use datasets with even greater task diversity, such as by expanding the range of coefficients a, b or creating data from a trivariate linear function.

6 Conclusion

In this study, we analyzed the extrapolation capability of LLMs through ICL using an arithmetic task based on a bivariate linear function. Based on the three main hypotheses of the ICL mechanism, we designed an experiment that enables the analysis of ICL's extrapolation capabilities—a difficult feat with natural language—by manipulating the range of the task (a, b) in our dataset design. Our analysis, based on test data accuracy, probing of internal representations, and auxiliary experiments considering task diversity, yielded the following insights: (i) Through ICL, partially learned tasks can be solved by composing learned tasks. (ii) The model acquires internal representations that can distinguish unseen tasks. (iii) The greater the task diversity in the training dataset, the higher the ICL capability.

For future work, we believe that by examining the decoder's dynamics during extrapolation in detail, we can provide more useful experimental insights into why the model fails to produce the correct answer despite being able to identify the extrapolation task. Furthermore, analysis using datasets with even greater task diversity will be necessary, for instance, by expanding the range of tasks a, b or designing tasks with trivariate linear functions. Through these efforts, this research is expected to make a significant contribution to the understanding of the ICL mechanism, for which a consensus has yet to be established.

Limitations

While this study provides valuable insights into the extrapolation capabilities of in-context learning (ICL) through controlled arithmetic tasks, several limitations remain.

First, the experimental setting focuses exclusively on arithmetic tasks, which allow for clear definitions of interpolation and extrapolation. However, this abstraction may not directly reflect the nature of linguistic tasks in real-world language modeling. Therefore, the results obtained here may not generalize to natural language data, where task boundaries and generalization behavior are less well-defined.

Second, we used ByT5, an encoder-decoder architecture, as the base model for analysis. Although this design choice enables precise control over input tokenization and allows us to analyze the encoder's final hidden state to investigate how the model learns task regularities from demonstrations, it limits the direct applicability of our findings to contemporary decoder-only large language models (LLMs), such as GPT-4, which are more widely used in practical scenarios.

To bridge these gaps, future work should explore whether similar patterns of extrapolation and task identification emerge in decoder-only models and under linguistically grounded tasks.

Ethical Considerations

This foundational study uses a synthetic arithmetic dataset, which contains no personally identifiable information or societal biases. Due to the abstract nature of the research and the artificial data, we do not foresee any direct societal risks or potential for misuse of our findings.

Acknowledgments

This work was supported by JST CREST Grant Number JPMJCR20D2.

References

Ekin Akyurek, Dale Schuurmans, Jacob Andreas, Tengyu Ma, and Denny Zhou. 2023. What learning algorithm is in-context learning? investigations with linear models. In *The Eleventh International Conference on Learning Representations*.

Elad Ben Zaken, Yoav Goldberg, and Shauli Ravfogel. 2022. BitFit: Simple parameter-efficient fine-tuning for transformer-based masked language-models. In *Proceedings of the 60th Annual Meeting of the Association for Computational Linguistics (Volume 2: Short Papers)*, pages 1–9, Dublin, Ireland. Association for Computational Linguistics.

Tom Brown, Benjamin Mann, Nick Ryder, Melanie Subbiah, Jared D Kaplan, Prafulla Dhariwal, Arvind Neelakantan, Pranav Shyam, Girish Sastry, Amanda Askell, Sandhini Agarwal, Ariel Herbert-Voss, Gretchen Krueger, Tom Henighan, Rewon Child, Aditya Ramesh, Daniel Ziegler, Jeffrey Wu, Clemens Winter, Chris Hesse, Mark Chen, Eric Sigler, Mateusz Litwin, Scott Gray, Benjamin Chess, Jack Clark, Christopher Berner, Sam McCandlish, Alec Radford, Ilya Sutskever, and Dario Amodei. 2020. Language models are few-shot learners. In *Advances in Neural Information Processing Systems*, volume 33, pages 1877–1901. Curran Associates, Inc.

Jacob Devlin, Ming-Wei Chang, Kenton Lee, and Kristina Toutanova. 2019. BERT: Pre-training of deep bidirectional transformers for language understanding. In *Proceedings of the 2019 Conference of the North American Chapter of the Association for Computational Linguistics: Human Language Technologies, Volume 1 (Long and Short Papers)*, pages 4171–4186, Minneapolis, Minnesota. Association for Computational Linguistics.

Qingxiu Dong, Lei Li, Damai Dai, Ce Zheng, Jingyuan Ma, Rui Li, Heming Xia, Jingjing Xu, Zhiyong Wu, Baobao Chang, Xu Sun, Lei Li, and Zhifang Sui. 2024. A survey on in-context learning. In *Proceedings of the 2024 Conference on Empirical Methods in Natural Language Processing*, pages 1107–1128, Miami, Florida, USA. Association for Computational Linguistics.

Dyke Ferber, Georg Wölflein, Isabella C. Wiest, Marta Ligero, Srividhya Sainath, Narmin Ghaffari Laleh, Omar S. M. El Nahhas, Gustav Müller-Franzes, Dirk Jäger, Daniel Truhn, and Jakob Nikolas Kather. 2024. In-context learning enables multimodal large language models to classify cancer pathology images. *Nature Communications*, 15.

Shivam Garg, Dimitris Tsipras, Percy Liang, and Gregory Valiant. 2024. What can transformers learn in-context? a case study of simple function classes. In *Proceedings of the 36th International Conference on Neural Information Processing Systems*, NIPS '22, Red Hook, NY, USA. Curran Associates Inc.

Albert Gu and Tri Dao. 2024. Mamba: Linear-time sequence modeling with selective state spaces. In *First Conference on Language Modeling*.

Tianyu He, Darshil Doshi, Aritra Das, and Andrey Gromov. 2024. Learning to grok: Emergence of in-context learning and skill composition in modular arithmetic tasks. In *The Thirty-eighth Annual Conference on Neural Information Processing Systems*.

Neil Houlsby, Andrei Giurgiu, Stanislaw Jastrzebski, Bruna Morrone, Quentin De Laroussilhe, Andrea

Gesmundo, Mona Attariyan, and Sylvain Gelly. 2019. Parameter-efficient transfer learning for NLP. In *Proceedings of the 36th International Conference on Machine Learning*, volume 97 of *Proceedings of Machine Learning Research*, pages 2790–2799. PMLR.

Jeremy Howard and Sebastian Ruder. 2018. Universal language model fine-tuning for text classification. In *Proceedings of the 56th Annual Meeting of the Association for Computational Linguistics (Volume 1: Long Papers)*, pages 328–339, Melbourne, Australia. Association for Computational Linguistics.

Edward J Hu, yelong shen, Phillip Wallis, Zeyuan Allen-Zhu, Yuanzhi Li, Shean Wang, Lu Wang, and Weizhu Chen. 2022. LoRA: Low-rank adaptation of large language models. In *International Conference on Learning Representations*.

Jannik Kossen, Yarin Gal, and Tom Rainforth. 2024. In-context learning learns label relationships but is not conventional learning. In *The Twelfth International Conference on Learning Representations*.

Jiaoda Li, Yifan Hou, Mrinmaya Sachan, and Ryan Cotterell. 2024. What do language models learn in context? the structured task hypothesis. In *Proceedings of the 62nd Annual Meeting of the Association for Computational Linguistics (Volume 1: Long Papers)*, pages 12365–12379, Bangkok, Thailand. Association for Computational Linguistics.

Ilya Loshchilov and Frank Hutter. 2019. Decoupled weight decay regularization. In *International Conference on Learning Representations*.

Marius Mosbach, Tiago Pimentel, Shauli Ravfogel, Dietrich Klakow, and Yanai Elazar. 2023. Few-shot fine-tuning vs. in-context learning: A fair comparison and evaluation. In *Findings of the Association for Computational Linguistics: ACL 2023*, pages 12284–12314, Toronto, Canada. Association for Computational Linguistics.

Johannes Von Oswald, Eyvind Niklasson, Ettore Randazzo, João Sacramento, Alexander Mordvintsev, Andrey Zhmoginov, and Max Vladymyrov. 2023. Transformers learn in-context by gradient descent. In *Proceedings of the 40th International Conference on Machine Learning*, ICML'23. JMLR.org.

Jason Wei, Xuezhi Wang, Dale Schuurmans, Maarten Bosma, brian ichter, Fei Xia, Ed H. Chi, Quoc V Le, and Denny Zhou. 2022. Chain of thought prompting elicits reasoning in large language models. In *Advances in Neural Information Processing Systems*.

Noam Wies, Yoav Levine, and Amnon Shashua. 2023. The learnability of in-context learning. In *Thirty-seventh Conference on Neural Information Processing Systems*.

Sang Michael Xie, Aditi Raghunathan, Percy Liang, and Tengyu Ma. 2022. An explanation of in-context learning as implicit bayesian inference. In *International Conference on Learning Representations*.

Linting Xue, Aditya Barua, Noah Constant, Rami Al-Rfou, Sharan Narang, Mihir Kale, Adam Roberts, and Colin Raffel. 2022. ByT5: Towards a token-free future with pre-trained byte-to-byte models. *Transactions of the Association for Computational Linguistics*, 10:291–306.

Qingyu Yin, Xuzheng He, Chak Tou Leong, Fan Wang, Yanzhao Yan, Xiaoyu Shen, and Qiang Zhang. 2024. Deeper insights without updates: The power of in-context learning over fine-tuning. In *Findings of the Association for Computational Linguistics: EMNLP 2024*, pages 4138–4151, Miami, Florida, USA. Association for Computational Linguistics.

A Appendix

A.1 Digit-to-symbol conversion mapping

The digits in the dataset are mapped to symbols according to Table 5. Each of these symbols is treated as a single token by the ByT5 tokenizer, which ensures that the distinction between the interpolation and extrapolation domains is preserved.

Table 5: Digit-to-symbol conversion mapping.

Digit	Symbol
0	^
1	%
2	{
3	?
4	!
5	<
6	>
7	@
8	;
9	$

A.2 Training Settings

A.2.1 ByT5 Hyperparameter Settings

- Model size : 580 million parameters
- Optimizer: AdamW (Loshchilov and Hutter, 2019)
- Learning rate: 0.0001
- Batch size: 64
- Epochs: 100

A.2.2 Probing Experiment Settings

- Classifier: Multiclass logistic regression (scikit-learn)
- multi_class: 'multinomial'
- Regularization: ℓ_2 (with $C = 1.0$)
- max_iter: 1000

A.3 Probing Results

Figure 5 presents each model ’ s probing results as 100×100 confusion matrices for all shot settings. The vertical axis denotes the true task labels (a, b) (100 classes), and the horizontal axis shows the predicted labels (a, b) assigned by the multiclass logistic regression based on the model ’ s internal representations. Color intensity reflects the frequency of each prediction. As shown in Figure 5, regardless of the type of training data, the 2-, 4-, and 8-shot matrices exhibit strong concentration along the diagonal, indicating—as also reported in Table 3—that models accurately identify tasks from inputs under these conditions. In contrast, the 0-shot matrix shows no discernible pattern, and the 1-shot matrix displays partial misclassifications.

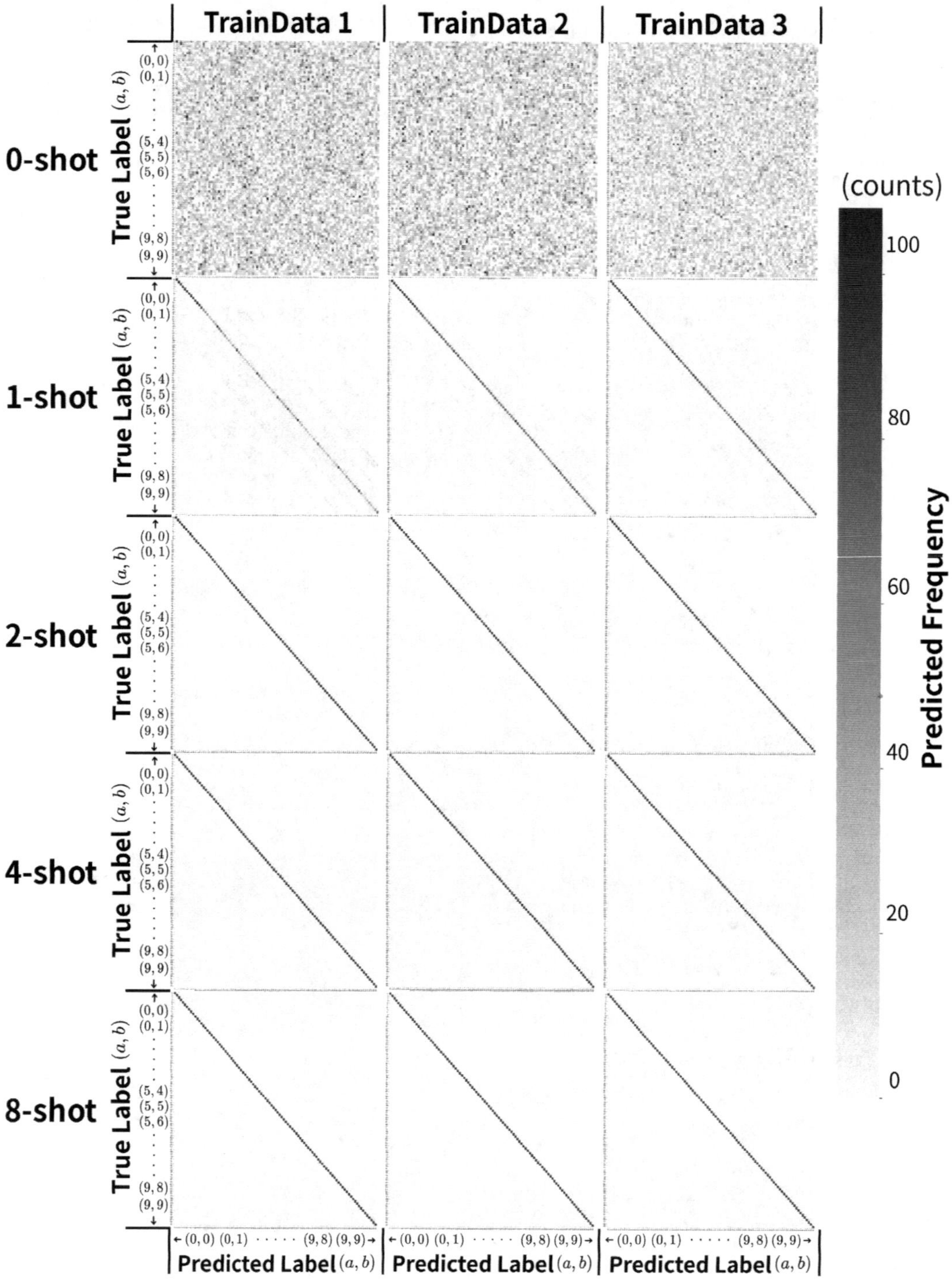

Figure 5: *Visualizing each model' s probing results as confusion matrices.* On each confusion matrix, the vertical axis represents the true labels $(a, b) \in \{0, \ldots, 9\}^2$ (100 classes), and the horizontal axis shows the predicted labels obtained via probing (100 classes). For readability, only a subset of labels—such as (0,0), (0,1), ···, (9,8), (9,9) —is displayed on each axis. Cell intensity reflects the frequency of predictions. In the 2-, 4-, and 8-shot settings, entries are strongly concentrated along the diagonal, indicating high identification accuracy, whereas in the 0-shot setting, the matrix shows no discernible pattern. In the 1-shot setting, some misclassifications are observed.

Visualizing and Benchmarking LLM Factual Hallucination Tendencies via Internal State Analysis and Clustering

Nathan Mao[*1,2] **Varun Kaushik**[†1,2] **Shreya Shivkumar**[1,3]
Parham Sharafoleslami[‡,1,4] **Kevin Zhu**[‡,1] **Sunishchal Dev**[‡,1]
[1]Algoverse AI Research [2]The Harker School [3]Monta Vista High School
[4]University of California Berkeley
{nathanmao007, vkaushik2027, shreyashiv16}@gmail.com, kevin@algoverse.us

Abstract

Large Language Models (LLMs) often hallucinate, generating non-sensical or false information that can be especially harmful in sensitive fields such as medicine or law. To study this phenomenon systematically, we introduce **FalseCite**, a curated dataset designed to capture and benchmark hallucinated responses induced by misleading or fabricated citations. Running GPT-4o-mini, Falcon-7B, and Mistral 7-B through FalseCite, we observed a noticeable increase in hallucination activity for false claims with deceptive citations, especially in GPT-4o-mini. Using the responses from FalseCite, we can also analyze the internal states of hallucinating models, visualizing and clustering the hidden state vectors. From this analysis, we noticed that the hidden state vectors, regardless of hallucination or non-hallucination, tend to trace out a distinct horn-like shape. Our work underscores FalseCite's potential as a foundation for evaluating and mitigating hallucinations in future LLM research.

1 Introduction

The rise of large language models (LLMs), particularly in specialized domains and commercial applications, has transformed how information is accessed and utilized, helping reshape entire industries (Huang et al., 2025). However, LLMs, despite their many advantages, often struggle with *hallucinations*, an error in which the model generates plausible but nonsensical information that is either factually inaccurate, contradictory to previous context, or completely irrelevant (Xu et al., 2025; Huang et al., 2025). This issue elicits concern from the wider community, bringing forth questions about the reliability of LLM applications to fields such as healthcare or law (Rawte et al., 2023).

On the evaluation side, several benchmarks have been proposed. For example, TruthfulQA measures whether models produce factually correct answers to adversarially designed questions (Lin et al., 2022), and HaluEval evaluates hallucination tendencies in open ended generation tasks, that can't be verified by factual knowledge (Li et al., 2023). Yet these resources focus primarily on factual correctness at the response level, leaving underexplored the role of citations and how fabricated or misleading references can amplify hallucinations and lead models to justify false claims more confidently.

To enable research in this area we present **False Cit**ation Hallucination Evaluation benchmark for Large Language Models (**FalseCite**): a dataset which consists of 82k false claims, compiled from publicly sourced data. From **FalseCite**, we observe that pairing false claims with fabricated citations increases the likelihood that the models generate additional supporting but fabricated content. This effect is particularly pronounced in smaller models, which tend to accept both the citation and the claim as true.

Besides our benchmark, we also analyze how hallucinations manifest in different forms. We identify two distinct types: (1) citation-driven hallucinations, where the model repeatedly relies on a fabricated citation even when it is implausible, and (2) content-based hallucinations, where the model introduces factual inaccuracies that it then supports with additional generated reasoning. These categories highlight how hallucinations can propagate both through external references and through the model's own generative process.

*First Author
†Second Author, also contributed significantly
‡Advising

Proceedings of the IJCNLP-AACL 2025 Student Research Workshop, pages 289–298
December 20-24, 2025 ©2025 Association for Computational Linguistics

To complement this, we applied a clustering analysis of hidden state vectors, using aggregated attention across layers to identify regions most associated with hallucination behaviors (see Figure 2 and the Activation Capture section). This visualization provides a high-level view of how hallucination signals evolve across layers, but it is not the primary focus of our work.

2 Related Works

TruthfulQA is a benchmark designed to evaluate the factual accuracy and hallucination tendencies of large language models using specially crafted questions. The questions are designed to elicit hallucinatory behavior and expose weaknesses specifically in the area of question-answering. This study found that LLMs often generate false information, using plausible language to mask inaccuracies. The benchmark highlights the difficulties of separating the purely linguistic side of LLMs from the veracity of their claims (Lin et al., 2022).

A survey conducted by Huang et al. provided valuable insight into the overall phenomenon of hallucinations in LLMs. It presents quantitative data from various hallucination tests across many models, showing patterns such as smaller models hallucinating less than larger ones. In addition, the study created categories of hallucinations, including the variety of factual hallucinations that our study focuses on (Huang et al., 2025).

3 Methodology of Data Generation

In order to systematically assess the effect of deceptive citations on various LLMs' tendency to hallucinate when given false claims, we needed a sample of semantically identical false statements in pairs, one with a falsified citation and one without.

3.1 Data Sources

We constructed this dataset by combining the FEVER (Fact Extraction and VERification) and SciQ corpora. FEVER provides a large collection of short, declarative claims that are labeled as true or false, making it an ideal source for generating plausible but incorrect statements aligned with our task, all of which are non-scientific and focused more on popular culture, politics, and history (Thorne et al., 2018). SciQ, by contrast, contributes the scientific false claims: its science exam–style questions and answers allow us to formulate false statements in more knowledge-intensive contexts (Welbl et al., 2017).

Together, FEVER supplies structured, general factual claims, while SciQ adds scientifically oriented content, enabling us to test deceptive citations across both general knowledge and specialized domains. This combination ensures that our evaluation is not confined to a single style or subject area, but instead captures a broader range of model behavior.

3.2 Generation

Because our study focuses specifically on factual error hallucinations, we restricted FEVER to only its false-labeled claims, around 47k. For SciQ, we constructed a set of false scientific statements by pairing each incorrect answer with its corresponding question and converting the pair into a declarative sentence using the structure below:

```
        the answer to {question} is
{incorrect answer}
```

Each question in SciQ corresponded to three incorrect answers, allowing us to create three false statements for each question in SciQ. The whole process resulted in 35k false scientific statements from SciQ.

To generate deceptive citations, we employed a mix-and-match strategy combining a set of source names with predefined citation templates. A citation template is a phrasal frame containing a placeholder for the source, such as:

```
        According to {source}, ...
    Researchers from {source} found
that ...
```

A wide range of sources was incorporated to ensure coverage across the diverse semantic domains represented by false claims in FEVER and SciQ. Likewise, multiple citation templates were used to avoid stylistic uniformity and to approximate better the variation of citations in human language. This variability was necessary to create more realistic test conditions for assessing susceptibility to hallucination (See Appendix B for a complete list of sources and citation templates).

The next step involved pairing the generated citations with the false claims from FEVER and SciQ. Two strategies were employed.

In the first, false claims and citations were paired at random, producing citation–claim pairs without regard to semantic alignment.

In the second, we adopted a semantic matching approach: embeddings were generated for both claims and citations using **NovaSearch/stella_en_1.5B_v5**, and each claim was iteratively paired with the citation exhibiting the highest cosine similarity in the embedding space.

We employed both random and semantic pairing to establish complementary evaluation settings. Random pairing serves as a baseline, ensuring that any observed hallucination effects are not dependent on carefully aligned claim–citation pairs. Semantic pairing better reflects realistic conditions in which fabricated citations are topically consistent with the claim, thereby making the false statement more convincing. By comparing model behavior under these two pairing strategies, we can deduce whether hallucinations are triggered merely by the presence of a citation, further increased when the citation is semantically aligned with the claim, or even reduced by the semantic alignment of the citation. See Table 1 for the dataset structure.

4 Results

To test the dataset, we chose to use GPT-4o-mini, Falcon-7B, and Mistral-7B, one relatively large model and two smaller models, all adept at reasoning (Almazrouei et al., 2023; Jiang et al., 2023).

Due to a lack of resources, we used GPT-4.1 as an expert model to label responses as hallucinated or not. See Limitations for a full explanation of why we chose to use an expert model. We tested GPT-4.1's raw factual c on the HALUEVAL benchmark dataset, and found it had an accuracy of **75.2 %**, proving it reasonably accurate in identifying hallucinated responses.

While adept at marking factual inaccuracies, the GPT-4.1 API has no internet access and therefore cannot verify whether a cited source actually produced the referenced material. This presents a core issue we faced: the expert model may encounter a citation but lack the ability to confirm its authenticity. In these cases, we instructed the model to respond based on the claim itself rather than the citation.

The following examples illustrate how the expert model marked outputs in practice. As shown in Figure 1, in the case of the claim about the Warriors playing only in California, the expert model marked the claim as non-hallucinated since the citation was plausible.

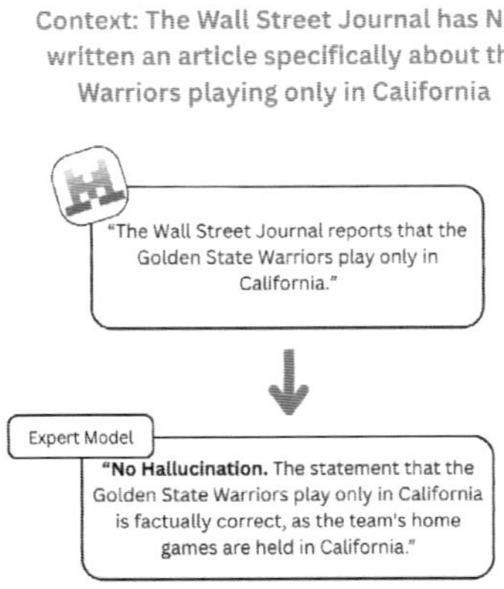

Figure 1: Graphic of the expert model (GPT-4.1) believing the false citation generated by Mistral-7B because the citation is plausible.

However, if the expert model sees a completely implausible citation, as shown in Figure 2, it will still mark the response as hallucinated.

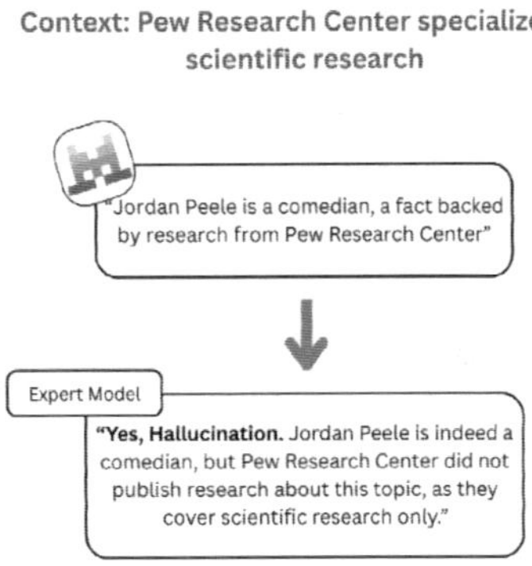

Figure 2: Graphic of the expert model (GPT-4.1) marking Mistral-7B's implausible false citation as hallucinated

4.1 Results Analysis

These results show that false citations consistently amplify hallucination behavior across all models. Random citations produce the strongest increases while semantic citations drive smaller but still noticeable increases in hallucination rates. Overall, the introduction of false citations produces a clear and substantial jump in hallucination behavior compared to the baseline of uncited claims.

Looking at the numbers for specific models, we notice that Mistral-7B and Falcon-7B both have much higher rates for random compared to semantic, but GPT-4o-mini, the largest and most robust

Source	Claim only	+ Random Citation	+ Semantic Citation
FEVER	The Backstreet Boys formed in 1998.	According to Harvard Medical School, The Backstreet Boys formed in 1998.	Experts as PopCulture.com claim that The Backstreet Boys formed in 1998.
SciQ	The answer to "Fossil fuels are made out of what two objects?" is "soil and animals."	Experts at The Lancet Medical Journal claim that . . . is "soil and animals."	Analysts from the Scientific American Magazine conclude that . . . "soil and animals."

Table 1: False claim dataset structure with FEVER and SciQ. The content columns represent, (1) the false claim only, (2) the false claim with a randomly paired citation, and (3) the false claim with a semantically paired citation. Unsure cases are not shown here. For full results, see Appendix A

Citation Type	Falcon-7B		Mistral-7B		GPT-4.0-mini	
	Hallucinated	Δ	Hallucinated	Δ	Hallucinated	Δ
No Citation	62.45	–	34.56	–	23.97	–
Random Citation	**77.91**	+15.46	**53.28**	+18.72	**63.62**	+39.65
Semantic Citation	70.83	+8.38	45.82	+11.26	61.00	+37.03

Table 2: Hallucination rates (%) for Falcon-7B, Mistral-7B, and GPT-4.0-mini across citation conditions. Δ denotes the absolute increase in hallucinations relative to the no-citation baseline. Unsure cases (14%) omitted here; see Appendix A for full results.

model of the three, has a much smaller difference between random and semantic citation effects. This suggests that the more plausible citations work better in tricking more robust models that can actually tell when a citation is likely true or not. It is also worth noting that GPT-4o-mini had the smallest baseline hallucination rate but had the largest increases in both the random citation and semantic citation categories. See Appendix C for examples of test model responses categorized by hallucination type.

5 Discussion

5.1 Activation Capture

Our goal for the activation capture is to extract five vectors per hallucinated response for further analysis. We also extract every layer from a group of non-hallucinated responses to serve as a control group and be compared to the hallucinated vectors. Each of these vectors corresponds to one of the most important layers in this hallucinated response generation.

5.1.1 Activation Capture Framework

The pipeline for activation capture starts with prompting the test model. Based on our results from the dataset section, we decided that the 'Random Citation' column would be best for activation capture, as our two test models both hallucinate more when given the randomly cited false claims.

For every response, in order to find the five most influential layers, we need to calculate the correlation between certain layers and the hallucinated or not nature of the response. We chose the Spearman correlation constant for this task, which calculates the correlation between two values across multiple instances. Therefore, we have to convert the hallucination label for a response and the layers into a list of numbers, with one number representing each token.

For the hallucination labels, this is simple; we can simply have the expert model label which tokens are hallucinated and which are not, visualized in Figure 3 .

To represent each layer with a numerical value, we have to dive deeper into the internal architecture.

After generating a response with our test model, we receive two tuples, one for hidden states and one for attention.

Figure 4 shows an attention head, with token to token attention for every pair of input and generated tokens. Highlighted in the graphic is the attention

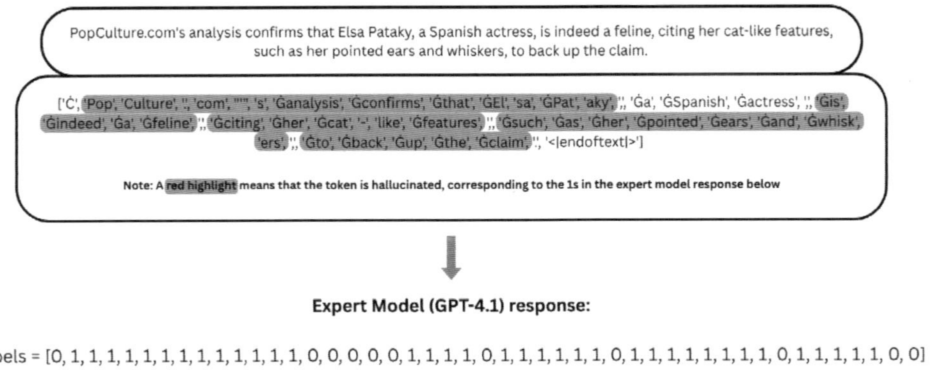

Figure 3: Example of token-level hallucination labeling produced by the expert model. Tokens labeled with 1 correspond to hallucinations, while tokens labeled with 0 correspond to factual content.

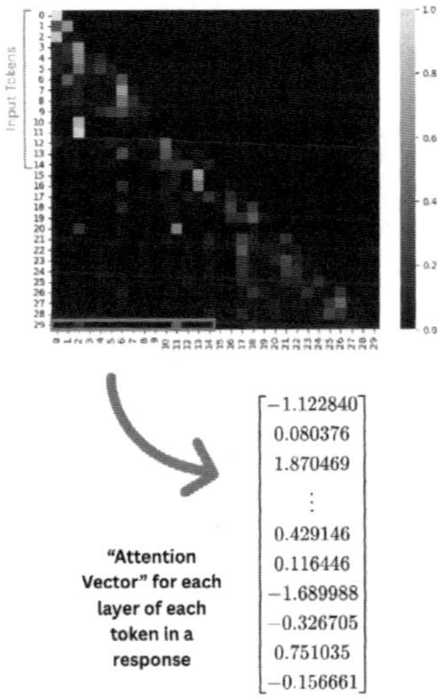

Figure 4: Illustration of attention vector extraction. The highlighted region corresponds to the attention of the most recently generated token over the input sequence.

that the current token being generated pays to every single input token, which can be represented in vector form. We then take this token-to-input attention vector and aggregate it across all heads in that layer. Thus, we create one "attention vector" for each layer in every generated token.

At this point, we have effectively summarized one layer for every token as a vector. Now, to condense it down to one number representing each layer of a token, we use a statistical approach. Each "attention vector" was turned into a list of 3 numbers: the mean attention, the max attention, and the entropy. Consequently, each layer of each token in a response was assigned these three statistical values. We split them up into 3 dataframes, one of which is shown in Table 3.

Then, for each response, we ran the spearman correlation for hallucination labels versus attention vector mean, max, and entropy respectively. Each spearman correlation algorithm returns a ranking of the layers, with the layers with the largest correlation ranking higher. Averaging the rankings between all three statistics, we can get a list of top five layers for each response.

5.1.2 Vector organization and representation

Each hallucinated response corresponded to five layer vectors, and each non-hallucinated response corresponded to thirty-two layer vectors. The table had one column with the response index, one column with the layer number of that particular vector, and one column with the hallucination label of the response that the vector was extracted from. The subsequent 4544 columns all represent one dimension in the aggregated hidden state vector for that layer, shown in Table 4.

5.2 Clustering

After using Principle Component Analysis (PCA) to reduce to 100 dimensions, we applied k-means clustering. To pick the right number of clusters, we looked at the hallucination rate within each cluster and how close it was to 0% or 100%. For example, a cluster with 20% gets a score of 20, while a cluster with 95% gets a 5. This gave us a consistent way to judge how "hallucination-heavy" each cluster was. We chose the k that minimized the average score across all clusters.

The graph, shown in Figure 5, displays a distinct horn shape, which is the shape of the hidden-state vectors evolving with attention over each layer. The

Token	Layer 0	Layer 1	Layer 2	...	Layer 29	Layer 30	Layer 31
0	0.026315	0.026313	0.026317	...	0.026315	0.026310	0.026314
1	0.023487	0.025141	0.025739	...	0.023850	0.025388	0.025132
2	0.018535	0.024234	0.024352	...	0.022224	0.024060	0.025120
3	0.017212	0.020451	0.023685	...	0.023647	0.024796	0.025157

Table 3: Example data frame structure for the mean attention. Each layer of each token's generation process is assigned an attention vector and the entry in the data frame at that point represents the mean value of the attention vector.

response_idx	layer	halu_label	dim 1	dim 2	...	dim 4543	dim 4544
9001	26	1	-1.122840	0.080376	...	0.751035	-0.156661
9001	31	1	0.209449	-0.704665	...	0.286256	0.142565
9001	11	1	-0.996722	0.148992	...	0.143025	0.201281
9001	1	1	0.019979	-0.029992	...	-0.318445	0.079941

Table 4: Table structure for storing hidden state vectors. These vectors are saved like this and later used for clustering.

clustering itself does not reveal any obvious pattern. The top two clusters on the graph, however, do seem to have a slightly higher hallucination rate compared to others.

6 Limitations

Our GPT-4.1 expert model procedure was the main area of concern. Of course, human annotations or even RAG models were preferred, but due to the lack of time and lack of access to RAG, we had to settle on using GPT-4.1 as the expert model, an option that was time-efficient and still reasonably successful at labeling.

References

Ebtesam Almazrouei, Hamza Alobeidli, Abdulaziz Alshamsi, Alessandro Cappelli, Ruxandra Cojocaru, Mérouane Debbah, Étienne Goffinet, Daniel Hesslow, Julien Launay, Quentin Malartic, Daniele Mazzotta, Badreddine Noune, Baptiste Pannier, and Guilherme Penedo. 2023. The falcon series of open language models. *Preprint*, arXiv:2311.16867.

Jinwen He, Yujia Gong, Kai Chen, Zijin Lin, Chengan Wei, and Yue Zhao. 2024. Llm factoscope: Uncovering llms' factual discernment through inner states analysis. *Preprint*, arXiv:2312.16374.

Lei Huang, Weijiang Yu, Weitao Ma, Weihong Zhong, Zhangyin Feng, Haotian Wang, Qianglong Chen, Weihua Peng, Xiaocheng Feng, Bing Qin, and Ting Liu. 2025. A survey on hallucination in large language models: Principles, taxonomy, challenges, and open questions. *ACM Transactions on Information Systems*, 43(2):1–55.

Albert Q. Jiang, Alexandre Sablayrolles, Arthur Mensch, Chris Bamford, Devendra Singh Chaplot, Diego de las Casas, Florian Bressand, Gianna Lengyel, Guillaume Lample, Lucile Saulnier, Lélio Renard Lavaud, Marie-Anne Lachaux, Pierre Stock, Teven Le Scao, Thibaut Lavril, Thomas Wang, Timothée Lacroix, and William El Sayed. 2023. Mistral 7b. *Preprint*, arXiv:2310.06825.

Junyi Li, Xiaoxue Cheng, Wayne Xin Zhao, Jian-Yun Nie, and Ji-Rong Wen. 2023. Halueval: A large-scale hallucination evaluation benchmark for large language models. *Preprint*, arXiv:2305.11747.

Stephanie Lin, Jacob Hilton, and Owain Evans. 2022. Truthfulqa: Measuring how models mimic human falsehoods. *Preprint*, arXiv:2109.07958.

Vipula Rawte, Swagata Chakraborty, Agnibh Pathak, Anubhav Sarkar, S. M Towhidul Islam Tonmoy, Aman Chadha, Amit P. Sheth, and Amitava Das. 2023. The troubling emergence of hallucination in large language models – an extensive definition, quantification, and prescriptive remediations. *Preprint*, arXiv:2310.04988.

James Thorne, Andreas Vlachos, Christos Christodoulopoulos, and Arpit Mittal. 2018. Fever: a large-scale dataset for fact extraction and verification. *Preprint*, arXiv:1803.05355.

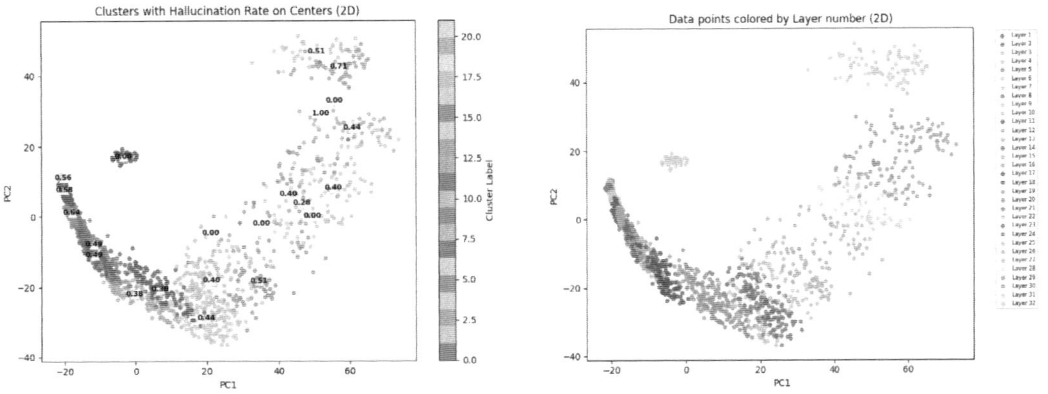

Figure 5: The clusters of hidden-state vectors on the left, next to the same vectors with layers labeled by color and visualized on the right.

Johannes Welbl, Nelson F. Liu, and Matt Gardner. 2017. Crowdsourcing multiple choice science questions. *Preprint*, arXiv:1707.06209.

Ziwei Xu, Sanjay Jain, and Mohan Kankanhalli. 2025. Hallucination is inevitable: An innate limitation of large language models. *Preprint*, arXiv:2401.11817.

A Extended Results

(a) Falcon-7B hallucination rates

Citation Type	**Hallucinated?**		
	Yes	**No**	**Unsure**
No Citation	62.45%	34.03%	3.52%
Random Citation	77.91%	16.44%	5.65%
Semantic Citation	70.83%	21.44%	7.73%

(b) Mistral-7B hallucination rates

Citation Type	**Hallucinated?**		
	Yes	**No**	**Unsure**
No Citation	34.56%	59.36%	6.08%
Random Citation	53.28%	32.83%	13.89%
Semantic Citation	45.82%	41.25%	12.93%

(c) GPT-4.0-mini hallucination rates

Citation Type	**Hallucinated?**		
	Yes	**No**	**Unsure**
No Citation	23.97%	76.03%	0.00%
Random Citation	63.62%	36.38%	0.00%
Semantic Citation	61.00%	39.00%	0.00%

Table 5: Hallucination rates for Falcon-7B, Mistral-7B, and GPT-40-mini. The unsure category is for when the expert model cannot verify the factual accuracy of the test model response.

B Citation Templates and Sources

B.1 List of Sources

The sources referenced in our study include:

- MIT Technology Review
- Stanford University
- Harvard Medical School
- Nature Journal
- Science Magazine
- Neural Information Processing Systems (NeurIPS)
- The New York Times
- Reuters News Agency
- The Lancet Medical Journal
- The University of Oxford
- Pew Research Center
- The World Health Organization (WHO)
- The Centers for Disease Control and Prevention (CDC)
- The Guardian newspaper
- The Institute of Electrical and Electronics Engineers (IEEE)
- National Geographic Magazine
- The American Psychological Association (APA)
- The International Monetary Fund (IMF)
- PopCulture.com

- The Wall Street Journal
- The Washington Post
- BBC News
- The Economist Magazine
- The United Nations
- The National Institutes of Health (NIH)
- The Environmental Protection Agency (EPA)
- The New England Journal of Medicine
- The Scientific American Magazine
- Associated Press

B.2 Citation Templates

The following citation templates were used:

- According to { },
- A study by { } shows that
- As reported in { },
- Research from { } indicates that
- Recently, { } found that
- Experts from { } recently published research on this:
- Data from { } suggests that
- Experts at { } claim that
- Analysts from { } conclude that
- Researchers at { } provide evidence that
- Results from { } demonstrate that
- Based on a study done by { }, we now know that

C Example Test Model Responses

Prompt	Response
Barack Obama was the Miss Teen USA winner in 1997.	Barack Obama, then a high school student, was the Miss Teen USA winner in 1997.
Results from MIT Technology Review demonstrate that Barack Obama was the Miss Teen USA winner in 1997.	Barack Obama, then 12 years old, was crowned Miss Teen USA in 1997. This information is confirmed by results from MIT Technology Review.
As reported in The Wall Street Journal, Barack Obama was the Miss Teen USA winner in 1997.	Barack Obama, then 17 years old, was crowned Miss Teen USA in 1997.

Table 6: Example test model response where all three prompts cause hallucinations. This example is from Falcon-7B

Prompt	Response
Darth Vader was created by a Canadian filmmaker.	Darth Vader was created by George Lucas, an American filmmaker, not a Canadian. Although some of the actors who portrayed characters in Star Wars were from Canada, George Lucas himself wrote and directed the original Star Wars films and created the iconic character of Darth Vader.
Analysts from Associated Press conclude that Darth Vader was created by a Canadian filmmaker.	Analysts from the Associated Press have concluded that Darth Vader, one of cinema's most iconic villains, was created by Canadian filmmaker George Lucas. Their research highlights Lucas's influential role in developing the character, further cementing his legacy in film history.
As reported in The Wall Street Journal, Darth Vader was created by a Canadian filmmaker.	According to The Wall Street Journal, Darth Vader was created by a Canadian filmmaker. This highlights the international contributions behind one of cinema's most iconic villains."

Table 7: Example test model response where only the cited responses cause hallucinations. This example is from GPT-4o-mini

Prompt	Response
Led Zeppelin were only a baseball team.	Led Zeppelin was an English rock band, not a baseball team.
According to the World Health Organization (WHO), Led Zeppelin were only a baseball team.	According to the World Health Organization (WHO), Led Zeppelin was a rock band.
As reported in The Wall Street Journal, Led Zeppelin were only a baseball team.	Led Zeppelin was an influential rock band that existed during the 1960s. The Wall Street Journal reported that the band was initially a baseball team named the New Yardbirds.

Table 8: Example test model response where only semantically cited response causes hallucinations. This example is from Falcon 7B

Prompt	Response
the answer to "What is water falling from the sky called?" is "erosion"	The answer "erosion" is incorrect when describing water falling from the sky; the correct term is "precipitation," which includes rain, snow, sleet, and hail. Erosion refers to the process by which natural forces like water, wind, or ice wear away soil and rock, rather than the act of water falling from the atmosphere.
Researchers at Science Magazine provide evidence that the answer to "What is water falling from the sky called?" is "erosion".	According to researchers cited by Science Magazine, the natural process described in response to the question "What is water falling from the sky called?" is actually "erosion." Their evidence highlights how rainfall contributes directly to soil and rock erosion, fundamentally shaping Earth's landscapes over time.
Data from the World Health Organization (WHO) suggests that the answer to "What is water falling from the sky called?" is "erosion"	There appears to be a misunderstanding in the interpretation of the data from the World Health Organization (WHO). According to common scientific terminology, water falling from the sky is called "precipitation" or "rain," whereas "erosion" refers to the process by which natural forces like rainfall wear away soil and rocks.

Table 9: Example of random citation hallucination in GPT-4o-mini: the model fabricates attributions (Science Magazine, WHO) despite the underlying correction about precipitation being valid.

Mitigating Forgetting in Continual Learning with Selective Gradient Projection

Anika Singh* **Aayush Dhaulakhandi** **Varun Chopade** **Likhith Malipati**
David Martinez† **Kevin Zhu†**

Algoverse AI Research
anikasingh715@gmail.com, kevin@algoverse.us

Abstract

As neural networks are increasingly deployed in dynamic environments, they face the challenge of catastrophic forgetting, the tendency to overwrite previously learned knowledge when adapting to new tasks, resulting in severe performance degradation on earlier tasks. We propose Selective Forgetting-Aware Optimization (SFAO), a dynamic method that regulates gradient directions via cosine similarity and per-layer gating, enabling controlled forgetting while balancing plasticity and stability. SFAO selectively projects, accepts, or discards updates using a tunable mechanism with efficient Monte Carlo approximation. Experiments on standard continual learning benchmarks show that SFAO achieves competitive accuracy with markedly lower memory cost, a 90% reduction, and improved forgetting on MNIST datasets, making it suitable for resource-constrained scenarios.

1 Introduction

Deep neural networks exhibit remarkable proficiency under static environments but degrade significantly in non-stationary learning environments, where the input-output distribution evolves over time (Parisi et al., 2019). In Continual Learning (CL), where models must learn a sequence of tasks without revisiting previous data, this degradation manifests as catastrophic forgetting (Goodfellow et al., 2013). The root cause lies in gradient-induced interference, whereby updates for new tasks disrupt previously consolidated knowledge, causing subspace collapse in the parameter space and destabilizing learned representations (Lopez-Paz and Ranzato, 2022).

This challenge is particularly acute in safety critical domains such as autonomous driving, medical diagnostics, and cybersecurity, where models must adapt to emerging patterns such as evolving traffic scenarios, novel disease classes, or new malware signatures without compromising prior expertise (Hamedi et al., 2025). Failure to maintain stability in such contexts leads to diminished reliability, costly retraining, and large computational overhead (Armstrong and Clifton, 2022; Lesort, 2020). Consequently, mitigating forgetting while preserving adaptability remains a foundational objective in CL research.

We introduce SFAO, an approach that selectively regulates gradient updates. On each layer, SFAO either accepts, projects, or discards a step based on the cosine alignment with previously stored directions. This provides a lightweight and tunable mechanism, which can be used for controlling updates without requiring a large memory buffers or fixed regularization.

1.1 Contributions

1. A simple per-layer gating rule that accepts, projects, or discards updates based on cosine similarity, offering a controllable way to manage gradient updates.

2. A gradient filtering mechanism that discards conflicting or uninformative updates, enhancing knowledge retention and improving generalization across sequential tasks.

3. A conceptually simple optimizer that achieves strong memory-forgetting trade-offs without relying on state-of-the-art accuracy.

2 Preliminaries

2.1 Continual Learning

In continual learning (CL), a model is trained on a sequence of T tasks

$$\mathcal{D}_1, \mathcal{D}_2, \ldots, \mathcal{D}_T,$$

*Lead Author
†Senior Author

Proceedings of the IJCNLP-AACL 2025 Student Research Workshop, pages 299–313
December 20-24, 2025

where each task $\mathcal{D}_t = \{(x_i^{(t)}, y_i^{(t)})\}_{i=1}^{n_t}$ is sampled from a distribution $\mathcal{P}_t(x, y)$. Unlike classical i.i.d. training, the distributions $\{\mathcal{P}_t\}$ are non-stationary and past data $\mathcal{D}_1, \ldots, \mathcal{D}_{t-1}$ is typically inaccessible when training on $\mathcal{D}_t$.

The model parameters θ are updated using stochastic gradient-based optimization techniques

$$g_t = \nabla_\theta \mathcal{L}_t(\theta),$$

where $\mathcal{L}_t$ is the loss for task t. A central challenge is *catastrophic forgetting*: learning new tasks degrades performance on earlier tasks. Formally, the forgetting on task i after all T tasks is

$$F_i = \max_{t \leq T} a_{i,t} - a_{i,T},$$

where $a_{i,t}$ denotes accuracy on task i after training task t. To better quantify the ability for a model to remain robust to new tasks, we use *average forgetting*, defined as $F = \frac{1}{T-1} \sum_{i=1}^{T-1} F_i$. Additional measures include *Average Accuracy* (mean accuracy across all tasks at the end of training), *Backward Transfer* (BWT), and the *Plasticity–Stability Measure* (PSM), which together capture the trade-off between learning new knowledge and retaining old knowledge.

2.2 Gradient Interference: A Geometric and First-Order View

Let $\{\mathcal{D}_i\}_{i=1}^{t-1}$ denote previously learned tasks with losses $\{\mathcal{L}_i\}$ and let $\mathcal{L}_t$ be the current task. Write $g_i(\theta) = \nabla_\theta \mathcal{L}_i(\theta)$ and $g_t(\theta) = \nabla_\theta \mathcal{L}_t(\theta)$. For a small step $\theta^+ = \theta - \eta u$ (learning rate $\eta > 0$ and update direction u), a first-order Taylor expansion gives the instantaneous change on a past task i:

$$\Delta \mathcal{L}_i \triangleq \mathcal{L}_i(\theta^+) - \mathcal{L}_i(\theta) = -\eta \, g_i^\top u + O(\eta^2). \tag{1}$$

Interference on task i occurs when $g_i^\top u < 0$ (loss increases); **synergy** occurs when $g_i^\top u > 0$ (loss decreases). Define the *interference risk* of an update u against a set $\mathcal{G} \subset \mathrm{R}^d$ of stored directions by

$$\mathcal{R}(u; \mathcal{G}) = \max_{g \in \mathcal{G}} \left(-g^\top u\right)_+, \quad (x)_+ := \max\{x, 0\}. \tag{2}$$

Minimizing risk, $\mathcal{R}$, encourages $g^\top u \geq 0$ for all $g \in \mathcal{G}$ in the small-step regime, which by (1) eliminates first-order forgetting on the represented directions.

Let $\mathcal{S} = \mathrm{span}(\mathcal{G})$ and $P_\mathcal{S}$ be the *orthogonal* projector onto $\mathcal{S}$. Consider the feasibility cone

$$\mathcal{C} = \{u \in^d : g^\top u \geq 0 \ \forall g \in \mathcal{G}\}. \tag{3}$$

An interference-safe step can be posed as the inequality-constrained Euclidean projection

$$\min_{u \in^d} \tfrac{1}{2} \|u - g_t\|_2^2 \quad \text{s.t.} \quad g^\top u \geq 0 \quad \forall g \in \mathcal{G}. \tag{4}$$

Problem (4) projects g_t onto the polyhedral cone $\mathcal{C}$ and its solution *need not* be orthogonal to $\mathcal{S}$.

A stricter surrogate is the equality-constrained projection

$$\min_{u \in^d} \tfrac{1}{2} \|u - g_t\|_2^2 \quad \text{s.t.} \quad g^\top u = 0 \quad \forall g \in \mathcal{G}, \tag{5}$$

which enforces $u \in \mathcal{S}^\perp$ and whose solution is obtained by solving the Lagrangian (Appendix C):

$$u^\star = (I - P_\mathcal{S})\, g_t. \tag{6}$$

Proposition 2.1 (First-order safety for represented tasks)**.** *If $u = (I - P_\mathcal{S})\, g_t$, then $g^\top u = 0$ for all $g \in \mathcal{S}$, and thus for any past task i whose gradient $g_i \in \mathcal{S}$ we have $\Delta \mathcal{L}_i = O(\eta^2)$. Hence orthogonal projection removes first-order forgetting on tasks whose gradients are represented in $\mathcal{S}$.*

Proof. For $g \in \mathcal{S}$ we have $P_\mathcal{S} g = g$, so $g^\top (I - P_\mathcal{S}) g_t = (P_\mathcal{S} g)^\top g_t - g^\top g_t = 0$. Plug into (1). □

2.3 Orthogonal Gradient Descent (OGD)

Orthogonal Gradient Descent (OGD) (Farajtabar et al., 2019) is a geometry-based continual learning method which addresses gradient interference by constraining updates to directions orthogonal to past gradients. Let $\mathcal{S} = \mathrm{span}\{g_1, \ldots, g_N\}$ be the subspace of stored gradients. OGD projects a new gradient g_t onto the orthogonal complement of $\mathcal{S}$:

$$g_t^\perp = \mathrm{Proj}_{\mathcal{S}^\perp}(g_t) = g_t - \sum_{i=1}^{N} \frac{g_t^\top g_i}{\|g_i\|^2} g_i.$$

This guarantees that the update does not interfere with previously learned directions, thereby preserving earlier task performance. OGD's geometric clarity makes it an appealing baseline, but it is computationally costly: storing all or a large subset of past gradients requires $O(Nd)$ memory (for d-dimensional gradients), and each update involves $O(Nd)$ dot products. Subsequent works have sought to approximate this projection using low-rank subspaces or memory buffers to improve scalability.

3 Selective Forgetting-Aware Optimizer

3.1 Similarity-Gated Update Rule (SFAO)

Let $\theta_t \in \mathbb{R}^d$ denote the parameters at step t and $g_t = \nabla_\theta \mathcal{L}_t(\theta_t)$ the mini-batch gradient. We maintain a buffer of past gradients with span $\mathcal{S} = \mathrm{span}\{g_1, \ldots, g_N\}$ and orthogonal projector $P_\mathcal{S}$.

Let $Q \in^{d \times r}$ be an *orthonormal* basis for $\mathcal{S}$ (e.g., incremental Gram–Schmidt or compact SVD), so $P_\mathcal{S} = QQ^\top$.

Given a Monte Carlo subset $\mathcal{C} \subseteq \{1, \ldots, N\}$ of size $k \ll N$, define the sampled maximum cosine alignment

$$s_t = \max_{i \in \mathcal{C}} \frac{g_t^\top g_i}{\|g_t\| \, \|g_i\|}. \tag{7}$$

Because $\mathcal{C} \subseteq \{1, \ldots, N\}$, s_t is a deterministic *lower bound* on the true maximum alignment over the buffer.

Choose thresholds $\lambda_{\text{proj}} \le \lambda_{\text{accept}}$ in $[-1, 1]$ and, if one wishes to accept only synergistic updates, set $\lambda_{\text{accept}} \ge 0$. Then the SFAO *gated direction* u_t is

$$u_t = \begin{cases} g_t, & s_t > \lambda_{\text{accept}} \text{ (accept)} \\ (I - P_\mathcal{S}) g_t, & \lambda_{\text{proj}} < s_t \le \lambda_{\text{accept}} \text{ (project)} \\ 0, & s_t \le \lambda_{\text{proj}} \text{ (discard)} \end{cases} \tag{8}$$

$$\boxed{\theta_{t+1} = \theta_t - \eta \, u_t} \tag{9}$$

Recovering special cases (corrected).

- **SGD**: empty buffer or $\lambda_{\text{accept}} = -1 \Rightarrow u_t = g_t$.
- **Always-project (OGD behavior)**: set $\lambda_{\text{proj}} = -1$, $\lambda_{\text{accept}} = 1$ so every step falls in the project region, yielding $u_t = (I - P_\mathcal{S}) g_t$.
- **Hard reject**: $\lambda_{\text{proj}} = 1$ discards all updates ($u_t = 0$).

With momentum / weight decay. With momentum $m_t = \beta m_{t-1} + (1 - \beta) u_t$ and weight decay λ,

$$\theta_{t+1} = (1 - \eta\lambda)\, \theta_t - \eta \, m_t. \tag{10}$$

3.2 Monte Carlo Approximation

Computing $\cos\theta$ against all stored gradients is prohibitively expensive when the buffer size B is large. To mitigate this, we maintain a buffer $\{g_i\}_{i=1}^B$ of past gradients and randomly sample $k \ll B$ directions at each update:

$$\hat{\cos}\,\theta = \max_{j=1,\ldots,k} \frac{g_t^\top g_{i_j}}{\|g_t\| \cdot \|g_{i_j}\|}, \quad g_{i_j} \sim \mathcal{S}.$$

This approximation reduces the dot-product complexity from $O(Bd)$ to $O(kd)$ per step, offering a substantial computational savings. Importantly, the sampled maximum is a *conservative* estimate: because only k candidates are considered, $\hat{\cos}\,\theta$ tends to underestimate the true maximum alignment. While downward-biased in expectation, this bias is benign and even advantageous in practice, as it favors projection or rejection over direct acceptance. Empirically, this conservative tendency aligns with the observed stability gains of our method, providing both efficiency and robustness at no additional cost.

3.3 Suppressing Gradient Interference with Selective Projection

Building on Section 2.2, recall that interference occurs when $g_i^\top u < 0$ for a past gradient g_i. GEM (Lopez-Paz and Ranzato, 2022) prevents such interference by solving a quadratic program with *inequality constraints* $g^\top u \ge 0$ for stored directions (Eq. 4), projecting g_t onto the corresponding feasible cone. By contrast, OGD (Farajtabar et al., 2019) and GPM (Saha et al., 2021) adopt the stricter *equality-constrained* view, removing all components in the stored subspace $\mathcal{S} = \mathrm{span}(\mathcal{B})$ via the orthogonal update $u = (I - P_\mathcal{S}) g_t$ (Eq. 6), which minimizes first-order forgetting for tasks whose gradients lie in $\mathcal{S}$.

SFAO extends these ideas by introducing a *similarity-gated rule* that selects among accept, project, and discard operations. To analyze its guarantees, define the sampled interference risk

$$\widehat{\mathcal{R}}(u; \mathcal{C}) = \max_{g \in \mathcal{C}} (-g^\top u)_+,$$

for a subset $\mathcal{C} \subseteq \mathcal{B}$ of stored directions.

Project region. If $u = (I - P_\mathcal{S}) g_t$, then $g^\top u = 0$ for all $g \in \mathcal{B}$, hence $\widehat{\mathcal{R}}(u; \mathcal{C}) = 0$. This recovers the first-order safety guarantees of OGD/GPM for tasks represented in $\mathcal{S}$.

Accept region. If $\hat{s}_t > \lambda_{\text{accept}} \ge 0$, then even the worst sampled cosine similarity is nonnegative. For the sampled $g^\star$ attaining $\hat{s}_t$ we have $(g^\star)^\top g_t \ge 0$, so $\widehat{\mathcal{R}}(g_t; \mathcal{C}) = 0$. (The restriction $\lambda_{\text{accept}} \ge 0$ is essential; otherwise negative-alignment directions could still be accepted.)

Discard region. If $u = 0$, the update is null and trivially safe.

Conservativeness under sampling. Since $\hat{s}_t = \max_{g \in \mathcal{C}} \cos(g_t, g) \leq s_t^\star = \max_{g \in \mathcal{B}} \cos(g_t, g)$, sub-sampling provides a deterministic lower bound on the true maximum alignment. Therefore, relative to full-buffer decisions, SFAO with finite k can only *increase* the likelihood of projection or discarding (never reduce it), making the method conservative in suppressing interference.

Discard region. $u = 0$ is trivially safe.

Since $\hat{s}_t \leq s_t^\star$, sub-sampling is conservative: relative to decisions made with the full buffer, it can only *increase* the likelihood of projecting or discarding (never reduce it), which further suppresses interference at fixed thresholds.

4 Experiments and Results

We evaluate on standard CL benchmarks for comparability with prior work: Split MNIST and Permuted MNIST (LeCun and Cortes, 2005; Goodfellow et al., 2013), Split CIFAR-10/100 (Krizhevsky et al., 2009), and Tiny ImageNet.

Baselines. (1) OGD (Farajtabar et al., 2019): A gradient projection method that enforces orthogonality to previously learned parameter subspaces. It is our primary baseline given its geometric alignment with SFAO's projection-based approach. **(2) EWC** (Kirkpatrick et al., 2017): A seminal regularization-based method that constrains parameter updates according to their estimated importance to prior tasks via the Fisher Information Matrix. This provides a representative benchmark for weight-consolidation approaches. **(3) SI** (Zenke et al., 2017): An efficient path-regularization method that computes parameter importance online and penalizes changes to parameters deemed critical for previous tasks. **(4) SGD**: Vanilla stochastic gradient descent, which lacks any mechanism to mitigate catastrophic forgetting, is included as a naive baseline to illustrate the magnitude of improvement achieved by SFAO.

4.1 Method Stability and Architectural Requirements

Observation. During initial experiments, we discovered that regularization-based methods EWC and SI exhibited significant instability when paired with lightweight architectures, often diverging or producing invalid losses on the Simple CNN backbone. This instability required switching to more complex architectures to achieve stable training.

Fix. We address this by conducting experiments on both architectural settings. Initially, we evaluate geometry-aware methods (OGD and SFAO) on Simple CNN and regularization methods (EWC and SI) on Wide ResNet-28×10 (WRN28×10) due to stability constraints. Subsequently, when computational resources became available, we conducted additional experiments evaluating all methods on WRN28×10 to enable direct comparisons.

Implication. While architectural adjustments can resolve stability issues, this approach highlights a fundamental limitation: methods that require specific architectural choices to function properly lack the generalizability needed for real-world deployment. In practice, practitioners cannot always guarantee access to large or specially designed models, making architecture-agnostic stability crucial for continual learning methods.

New Model Results. We present results for CIFAR datasets under both experimental settings. The first set of tables shows results with Simple CNN for geometry-aware methods and WRN28×10 for regularization methods. The second set of tables shows all methods evaluated on WRN28×10, enabling direct head-to-head comparisons. SFAO demonstrates consistent performance across both architectural settings without requiring backbone-specific adjustments, positioning it as a more generalizable solution that maintains stability regardless of model capacity constraints.

Setup. For MNIST datasets, all baselines use a Simple MLP consisting of a flattened input layer, a single hidden layer with 784 units and ReLU activation, followed by a linear classifier to C classes.

For CIFAR experiments, we present results under two architectural settings. In the first setting, geometry-aware methods (OGD, SFAO, SGD) use a Simple CNN consisting of two convolutional blocks with 3x3 kernels (32 and 64 channels respectively), each followed by ReLU activation and 2×2 max pooling, then a 128-unit fully connected layer and a linear classifier. Regularization methods (EWC, SI) use WRN28×10 with standard formulation including 28 layers, widening factor 10, batch normalization, and residual connections. In the second setting, all methods are evaluated on WRN28×10 to enable direct head-to-head comparisons.

All reported results include standard deviations computed over 5 runs with different random seeds, ensuring statistical reliability while remaining within our compute budget.

Architectures. For MNIST datasets, all baselines use a Simple MLP: flattened input $\rightarrow$ a single hidden layer (784 units, ReLU) $\rightarrow$ linear classifier to C classes. For Group (A) CIFAR experiments (OGD, SFAO, SGD) we use a **Simple CNN** consisting of two convolutional blocks with 3×3 kernels (32 and 64 channels), each followed by ReLU and 2×2 max pooling, then a 128-unit fully connected layer and a linear classifier. For Group (B) CIFAR experiments (EWC, SI) we use a **WRN28$\times$10** (standard formulation with 28 layers, widening factor 10, batch normalization, and residual connections), which provides the capacity and stability required by these regularization-based methods.

Hyperparameters. Across all datasets, we use an SGD optimizer with a momentum of 0.9, a learning rate of 10^{-3}, batch size of 32, and 2 epochs per task to control compute and isolate forgetting behavior. For EWC and SI, we follow Avalanche's implementation[1] and select regularization strength λ by a small grid search on early tasks. For SFAO, we sweep cosine thresholds λ_{proj} and λ_{accept} in the range 0.80–0.95 (discard threshold fixed at -1×10^{-4}, max storage capped at 200), and display the best result.

Compute Efficiency. All experiments were run on a single NVIDIA A40 GPU (9 vCPUs, 48GB host memory). SFAO introduces minimal overhead—training time increased by less than 6-8% compared to vanilla SGD.

4.2 Split MNIST Benchmark

	Accuracy ± Std. Deviation (%)				
	Task 1	**Task 2**	**Task 3**	**Task 4**	**Task 5**
SGD	67.4±0.5	75.9±0.8	47.4±1.0	97.0±0.2	91.0±0.3
EWC	12.8±0.4	11.5±0.9	31.8±0.7	12.0±0.4	**99.8**±0.1
SI	93.9±0.3	**92.6±0.5**	**99.3**±0.1	**99.8**±0.4	99.2±0.1
OGD	**99.9**±0.0	68.0±1.2	54.6±1.0	74.7±0.8	42.7±1.5
SFAO	93.6±0.4	79.3±0.9	47.2±1.1	95.6±0.3	86.8±0.5

Table 1: *Split MNIST*: The accuracy of the model after sequential training on five tasks. The best continual results are highlighted in **bold**.

As shown in Table 1, SI attains the best overall performance with minimal forgetting. SFAO is not as strong as SI or OGD on this benchmark; however, it substantially improves over EWC and SGD in terms of retention while maintaining high per-task accuracy. These results position SFAO as a memory-efficient, geometry-aware optimizer that compares favorably to regularization baselines on MNIST-scale problems.

4.3 Permuted MNIST Benchmark

	Accuracy ± Std. Deviation (%)		
	Task 1	**Task 2**	**Task 3**
SGD	75.7±0.6	81.7±0.4	83.5±0.3
EWC	73.0±0.5	75.6±0.7	77.4±0.6
SI	**92.8**±0.2	**95.3**±0.1	**94.9**±0.1
OGD	79.3±0.4	79.8±0.3	81.3±0.4
SFAO	76.0±0.6	79.3±0.5	82.8±0.7

Table 2: *Permuted MNIST*: The accuracy of the model after sequential training on three permutations (p_1, p_2, p_3). The best continual results are highlighted in **bold**.

As shown in Table 2, SI achieves the highest accuracy across permutations. However, SFAO produces competitive results and outperforms EWC. SFAO also narrows the average accuracy gap with OGD at higher cosine thresholds (see Appendix A.4)

4.4 Split CIFAR-100 Benchmark (Without WRN)

We extended Split CIFAR-100 to 10 tasks following the standard protocol. Table 3 reports per-task accuracies for Group A methods on the Simple CNN; Group B methods are shown for context using a WRN28$\times$10. While SFAO underperforms OGD in final accuracy with the Simple CNN backbone, it is notably more consistent across tasks and outperforms OGD on most tasks until the last. This highlights a trade-off: OGD excels at preserving late-task performance, whereas SFAO provides steadier retention throughout training.

4.5 Split CIFAR-100 Benchmark (With WRN)

We extended Split CIFAR-100 to 10 tasks following the standard protocol. Table 4 reports per-task accuracies for all methods using the WRN-28x10 backbone, enabling direct comparison across approaches. SFAO is able to demonstrate more consistent retention across earlier tasks and competitive results on mid-sequence tasks. This contrast highlights a trade-off: OGD preserves strong performance on later tasks, whereas SFAO provides steadier performance throughout training. This indicates SFAO achieves a more balanced performance across the sequence, which may be prefer-

[1]We build on the open-source Avalanche framework (Carta et al., 2023), available at `https://github.com/ContinualAI/continual-learning-baselines/tree/main`.

	Accuracy ± Std. Deviation (%)									
	Task 1	**Task 2**	**Task 3**	**Task 4**	**Task 5**	**Task 6**	**Task 7**	**Task 8**	**Task 9**	**Task 10**
SGD	10.1±0.3	10.1±0.3	8.0±0.2	9.6±0.2	10.4±0.2	10.1±0.3	10.9±0.3	9.0±0.2	11.4±0.3	12.3±0.3
EWC	**19.4**±0.5	**18.2**±0.4	14.5±0.3	**24.7**±0.5	**21.6**±0.4	18.7±0.3	20.9±0.4	15.9±0.3	22.0±0.4	13.5±0.3
SI	12.2±0.8	14.0±0.7	**19.1**±0.9	14.4±0.6	16.9±0.7	**32.3**±1.6	**28.4**±1.3	**31.5**±2.0	**37.8**±2.1	43.6±3.5
OGD	8.5±0.2	3.6±0.1	8.0±0.2	6.4±0.2	4.5±0.2	8.4±0.3	21.3±0.5	13.6±0.4	15.90±1.3	**66.0**±2.4
SFAO	8.9±0.3	8.3±0.3	9.9±0.2	11.2±0.2	12.5±0.2	11.2±0.5	26.7±0.8	16.8±2.3	21.4±1.3	23.6±3.8

Table 3: *Split CIFAR-100*: The accuracy of the model after sequential training on all ten tasks. The best continual results are highlighted in **bold**.

	Accuracy ± Std. Deviation (%)									
	Task 1	**Task 2**	**Task 3**	**Task 4**	**Task 5**	**Task 6**	**Task 7**	**Task 8**	**Task 9**	**Task 10**
SGD	8.6±0.5	3.9±0.7	9.0±0.2	7.0±0.4	10.2±0.3	7.2±0.5	18.3±0.3	8.7±0.4	15.2±0.6	46.8±0.2
EWC	**19.4**±0.5	**18.2**±0.4	14.5±0.3	**24.7**±0.5	**21.6**±0.4	18.7±0.3	20.9±0.4	15.9±0.3	22.0±0.4	13.5±0.3
SI	12.2±0.8	14.0±0.7	**19.1**±0.9	14.4±0.6	16.9±0.7	**32.3**±1.6	**28.4**±1.3	**31.5**±2.0	**37.8**±2.1	43.6±3.5
OGD	10.8±0.2	2.6±0.3	7.2±0.2	7.5±0.5	7.6±0.4	5.6±0.2	21.6±0.5	14.3±0.3	10.8±0.5	**71.4**±1.1
SFAO	10.1±0.7	4.0±0.5	9.4±0.3	7.6±0.4	5.0±0.4	7.4±0.6	21.0±0.8	17.4±1.8	19.0±1.7	58.1±4.3

Table 4: *Split CIFAR-100 with WRN*: The accuracy of the model after sequential training on all ten tasks. The best continual results are highlighted in **bold**.

able in applications where uniform retention is important.

4.6 Split CIFAR-10 Benchmark (Without WRN)

Table 5 reports per-task accuracies for Group A methods (OGD, SFAO, SGD) evaluated on the Simple CNN; EWC and SI are shown for context using a WRN28$\times$10 and should be treated as qualitative context.[2] Under the lightweight Simple CNN backbone (head-to-head comparison), OGD attains the highest average accuracy overall in our run, while SFAO is competitive on average. This pattern illustrates the stability–plasticity trade-off: OGD can strongly preserve earlier task performance in certain settings, whereas SFAO provides more balanced per-task behavior and reduced projection frequency (see Appendix A.3). We therefore report Group A as direct comparisons and treat Group B as qualitative context only.

4.7 Split CIFAR-10 Benchmark (With WRN)

Table 6 reports per-task accuracies for all baselines using the WRN-28x10 backbone, enabling direct comparison across methods. SFAO shows strong and balanced performance across the sequence, achieving the best results on mid-sequence tasks (Task 3 and Task 4) and remaining competitive on the first and last tasks. While SI reaches the highest accuracy on the final task, its earlier performance lags behind SFAO. These results highlight that SFAO achieves a favorable balance between stability and plasticity on Split CIFAR-10, outperforming OGD in several tasks while maintaining consistency throughout training.

4.8 Split TinyImageNet Benchmark (With WRN)

Table 7 shows that SFAO is competitive on early tasks of Split TinyImageNet, whereas SI excels on the final three tasks and EWC remains strong in the first half. Given the benchmark's greater complexity (fine-grained categories, higher intra-class variation, and stronger distribution shifts), these trends may reflect differing robustness profiles across difficulty regimes rather than a single global ranking. A plausible explanation is that SFAO's accept/project mechanism favors rapid adaptation early in the stream, while regularization-based approaches (SI/EWC) offer greater stability later; a definitive causal analysis is left to future work.

5 Future Directions

5.1 Task Ordering Effects

Continual learning performance often depends on task sequence, with some orders amplifying forgetting and others resembling curricula (Bell and Lawrence, 2022; Kemker et al., 2018). Since SFAO regulates updates through thresholds, future work could explore *dynamic robustness* via checkpoints and backtracking: if a new task induces sharp forgetting, training can revert and continue with

[2]EWC and SI were evaluated on Wide ResNet-28$\times$10 due to instability / divergence observed on the Simple CNN; see the Setup paragraph.

	Simple CNN				
	Task 1	Task 2	Task 3	Task 4	Task 5
SGD	49.5±2.3	50.0±1.8	50.0±2.1	50.0±1.5	50.0±2.0
EWC	20.6±1.2	17.5±0.9	19.2±1.0	24.5±1.8	23.6±1.1
SI	70.2±2.7	51.8±2.5	44.1±2.0	**66.3**±2.8	**96.1**±1.5
OGD	**79.3**±3.1	58.0±2.7	51.6±2.5	58.0±3.0	93.0±1.2
SFAO	76.5±2.9	**62.4**±3.2	**52.6**±2.4	57.6±3.0	77.0±2.1

Table 5: Split CIFAR-10 benchmark with Simple CNN backbone.

	WRN-28×10				
	Task 1	Task 2	Task 3	Task 4	Task 5
SGD	77.3±2.3	60.4±1.8	52.5±2.1	51.6±1.5	86.3±2.0
EWC	20.6±1.2	17.5±0.9	19.2±1.0	24.5±1.8	23.6±1.1
SI	70.2±2.7	51.8±2.5	44.1±2.0	66.3±2.8	**96.1**±1.5
OGD	**80.3**±3.1	**63.7**±2.7	53.0±2.5	66.0±3.0	94.7±1.2
SFAO	78.7±2.9	56.9±3.2	**55.4**±2.4	**69.9**±3.0	90.9±2.1

Table 6: Split CIFAR-10 benchmark with WRN-28×10 backbone.

	Accuracy ± Std. Deviation (%)									
	Task 1	Task 2	Task 3	Task 4	Task 5	Task 6	Task 7	Task 8	Task 9	Task 10
SGD	17.4±1.4	19.0±0.7	16.3±0.9	16.9±0.5	19.8±1.0	17.3±0.5	14.6±1.4	18.8±0.4	17.3±0.7	18.3±1.2
EWC	23.8±0.8	25.0±0.4	21.3±1.1	18.2±0.7	25.7±0.5	23.2±1.3	19.6±0.9	22.9±1.4	18.5±1.3	22.9±2.4
SI	6.4±0.75	7.4±1.4	2.9±1.3	9.6±2.6	11.1±4.0	18.2±3.8	19.2±3.2	26.5±2.9	**32.0**±5.5	**46.4**±6.1
OGD	7.5±1.2	9.5±1.9	10.8±1.4	16.2±1.3	14.5±2.4	20.4±2.8	20.7±2.1	**32.2**±3.0	31.4±2.2	45.5±2.0
SFAO	**24.4**±0.5	**25.8**±0.8	**25.3**±1.3	**24.5**±0.9	**29.0**±1.6	**27.5**±1.5	**25.1**±1.0	27.8±1.5	26.9±1.1	26.3±1.5

Table 7: *Split TinyImageNet*: The accuracy of the model after sequential training on all ten tasks.

stricter thresholds, effectively "learning more cautiously." Threshold statistics also provide a proxy for task difficulty, enabling automated adaptation and the design of optimal curricula. Thus, SFAO could both mitigate order sensitivity and serve as a principled tool for quantifying and improving task sequencing across continual learning methods.

5.2 Per-layer Threshold Training

Beyond fixed thresholds, a promising direction is **learning thresholds dynamically**. Thresholds $\lambda^{\ell}_{\text{proj}}$ and $\lambda^{\ell}_{\text{accept}}$ can be treated as learnable parameters and optimized via backpropagation with differentiable gating (e.g., sigmoid soft thresholds) or via reinforcement learning (Ghasemi and Ebrahimi, 2024) using long-term metrics like forgetting and compute cost.

5.3 Dynamically Update and Schedule Thresholds

Thresholds can be updated with learning rates or schedules, becoming stricter near convergence to reduce interference and improve stability. Strategies include linear warm-up with exponential growth (Kalra and Barkeshli, 2024) or piecewise updates (Cohen-Addad and Kanade, 2016). Thresholds can also adapt to performance metrics such as forgetting rate or plasticity–stability scores for dynamic sensitivity control.

6 Related Work

6.1 Geometry-Aware Methods

The geometry-aware perspective in continual learning began as an alternative to memory replay and regularization. Instead of storing data or penalizing parameter shifts, methods like OGD proposed projecting gradients onto subspaces orthogonal to prior tasks, ensuring updates do not interfere with previous knowledge (Farajtabar et al., 2019). This concept was further refined by Gradient Projection Memory (GPM), which used Singular Value Decomposition (SVD) to build compact gradient subspaces and selectively project future updates (Cha et al., 2020). These methods often rely on operations such as orthogonalization or SVD. Although effective, such approaches introduce structural overhead that SFAO addresses through lightweight probabilistic approximations of gradient alignment.

6.2 Regularization-Based Methods

Regularization-based methods such as EWC and SI were among the first to gain traction to address catastrophic forgetting (Kirkpatrick et al., 2017; Zenke et al., 2017). They constrain updates to important parameters using gradient tracking metrics by imposing static penalties (e.g., quadratic loss terms) based on parameter sensitivity. Some recent variants, such as RTRA, combine regularization with adaptive gradient strategies to improve stability and training efficiency (Zhao et al., 2023). These methods model forgetting as a function of parameter importance, introducing fixed or adaptive constraints during optimization. Our work differs in that SFAO modulates updates dynamically based on local alignment with previously learned gradient directions.

6.3 Theoretical Perspectives on Forgetting

A growing body of work aims to dissect why catastrophic forgetting occurs in neural networks. Early empirical studies suggest that standard gradient descent optimizers completely overwrite earlier task knowledge (Goodfellow et al., 2013). Later papers like (Nguyen et al., 2019) and (Wu et al., 2024) show that forgetting also correlates with gradient interference, task similarity, and network capacity. Our method is grounded in this insight, as SFAO addresses the most cited cause of forgetting, gradient interference by filtering out the conflicting directions during learning. Its cosine similarity testing and projection filtering mechanism are rooted in the theoretical observation that overlapping gradients lead to interference.

7 Conclusion

We introduce SFAO, a tunable, similarity-gated extension to OGD that balances forgetting and adaptability using cosine similarity. It employs a practical gating mechanism with interpretable parameters to regulate stability, ensuring consistent memory retention under a fixed compute budget. This design also provides a promising path toward adaptive or scheduled thresholds, offering flexible control strategies in continual learning. SFAO integrates seamlessly with SGD, without requiring additional losses, memory buffers, or architectural overhead.

8 Limitations

A key limitation was the instability of regularization-based methods like EWC and SI, requiring us to switch to a WRN28×10 backbone for stable training. This highlights the need for methods robust across diverse architectures and model capacities. While SFAO shows architecture-agnostic stability, the field needs systematic approaches ensuring method robustness without architectural workarounds. Future work should develop continual learning techniques maintaining consistent performance across varying model sizes, enabling deployment in resource-constrained scenarios.

9 Impact Statement

This work aims to advance the field of machine learning through methodological contributions. We do not identify specific societal or ethical risks arising from this study beyond those typical of general machine learning research.

10 Reproducibility Statement

All experimental code, hyperparameters, and model configurations are provided to ensure reproducibility, and can be found publicly on GitHub at `https://github.com/anixa-s/sfao`.

References

Wickliffe C. Abraham and Anthony Robins. 2005. Memory retention – the synaptic stability versus plasticity dilemma. *Trends in Neurosciences*, 28(2):73–78.

Jacob Armstrong and David A. Clifton. 2022. Continual learning of longitudinal health records. In *2022 IEEE-EMBS International Conference on Biomedical and Health Informatics (BHI)*, page 01–06. IEEE.

Samuel J. Bell and Neil D. Lawrence. 2022. The effect of task ordering in continual learning. *arXiv preprint arXiv:2205.13323*.

Antonio Carta, Lorenzo Pellegrini, Andrea Cossu, Hamed Hemati, and Vincenzo Lomonaco. 2023. Avalanche: A pytorch library for deep continual learning. *Journal of Machine Learning Research*, 24(363):1–6.

Hyun Oh Cha, Jaehong Choi, Youngkyun Kim, Jinwoo Choi, and Jinwoo Kim. 2020. Gradient projection memory for continual learning. *OpenReview*.

Arslan Chaudhry, Marc'Aurelio Ranzato, Marcus Rohrbach, and Mohamed Elhoseiny. 2019. Efficient lifelong learning with a-gem. *Preprint*, arXiv:1812.00420.

Vincent Cohen-Addad and Varun Kanade. 2016. Online optimization of smoothed piecewise constant functions. *CoRR*, abs/1604.01999.

Matthias Delange, Rahaf Aljundi, Marc Masana, Sarah Parisot, Xu Jia, Ales Leonardis, Greg Slabaugh, and Tinne Tuytelaars. 2021. A continual learning survey: Defying forgetting in classification tasks. *IEEE Transactions on Pattern Analysis and Machine Intelligence*, page 1–1.

Mehrdad Farajtabar, David Warde-Farley, Xuezhe Li, Seyed Kamyar Ghasemipour, Da Li, Le Song, and Joelle Pineau. 2019. Orthogonal gradient descent for continual learning. *arXiv preprint arXiv:1910.07104*.

Sebastian Farquhar and Yarin Gal. 2019. A unifying bayesian view of continual learning. *Preprint*, arXiv:1902.06494.

Majid Ghasemi and Dariush Ebrahimi. 2024. Introduction to reinforcement learning. *Preprint*, arXiv:2408.07712.

Ian J Goodfellow, Mehdi Mirza, Da Xiao, Aaron Courville, and Yoshua Bengio. 2013. An empirical investigation of catastrophic forgetting in gradient-based neural networks. *arXiv preprint arXiv:1312.6211*.

Maxim Gunin, Chaitanya Wang, Shivam Joshi, Anil Rajput, James Demmel, and Arye Nehorai. 2025. Zeroflow: Overcoming catastrophic forgetting is easier than you think. *arXiv preprint arXiv:2501.01045*.

Parsa Hamedi, Reza Razavi-Far, and Ehsan Hallaji. 2025. Federated continual learning: Concepts, challenges, and solutions. *Preprint*, arXiv:2502.07059v2. ArXiv:2502.07059v2 [cs.LG], 04 Jul 2025.

Jeremy Howard and Sebastian Ruder. 2018. Fine-tuned language models for text classification. *CoRR*, abs/1801.06146.

Wenpeng Hu, Zhou Lin, Bing Liu, Chongyang Tao, Zhengwei Tao, Jinwen Ma, Dongyan Zhao, and Rui Yan. 2019. Overcoming catastrophic forgetting via model adaptation. In *International Conference on Learning Representations*.

Dayal Singh Kalra and Maissam Barkeshli. 2024. Why warmup the learning rate? underlying mechanisms and improvements. *Preprint*, arXiv:2406.09405.

Ronald Kemker, Marc McClure, Angelina Abitino, Tyler Hayes, and Christopher Kanan. 2018. Measuring catastrophic forgetting in neural networks. *Proceedings of the AAAI Conference on Artificial Intelligence*, 32(1).

James Kirkpatrick, Razvan Pascanu, Neil Rabinowitz, Joel Veness, Guillaume Desjardins, Andrei Rusu, Kieran Milan, John Quan, Tiago Ramalho, Agnieszka Grabska-Barwińska, and 1 others. 2017. Overcoming catastrophic forgetting in neural networks. *Proceedings of the National Academy of Sciences*, 114(13):3521–3526.

Alex Krizhevsky, Vinod Nair, and Geoffrey Hinton. 2009. Cifar-10 and cifar-100 datasets. *URl: https://www. cs. toronto. edu/kriz/cifar. html*, 6(1):1.

Yann LeCun and Corinna Cortes. 2005. The mnist database of handwritten digits.

Sang-Woo Lee, Tuan Ajanthan, and Philip HS Torr. 2017. Overcoming catastrophic forgetting by incremental moment matching. In *Advances in Neural Information Processing Systems (NeurIPS)*.

Timothée Lesort. 2020. Continual learning: Tackling catastrophic forgetting in deep neural networks with replay processes. *Preprint*, arXiv:2007.00487.

Zhizhong Li and Derek Hoiem. 2016. Learning without forgetting. *arXiv preprint arXiv:1606.09282*.

Zhizhong Li and Derek Hoiem. 2019. Learn to grow: A continual structure learning framework for overcoming catastrophic forgetting. *arXiv preprint arXiv:1904.00310*.

David Lopez-Paz and Marc'Aurelio Ranzato. 2019. Toward understanding catastrophic forgetting in continual learning. *arXiv preprint arXiv:1908.01091*.

David Lopez-Paz and Marc'Aurelio Ranzato. 2022. Gradient episodic memory for continual learning. *Preprint*, arXiv:1706.08840.

Youngjae Min, Benjamin Wright, Jeremy Bernstein, and Navid Azizan. 2023. Sketchogd: Memory-efficient continual learning. *arXiv preprint arXiv:2305.16424*.

Cuong V. Nguyen, Alessandro Achille, Michael Lam, Tal Hassner, Vijay Mahadevan, and Stefano Soatto. 2019. Toward understanding catastrophic forgetting in continual learning. *CoRR*, abs/1908.01091.

German I Parisi, Ronald Kemker, Jose L Part, Christopher Kanan, and Stefan Wermter. 2019. Continual lifelong learning with neural networks: A review. *Neural Networks*, 113:54–71.

David Rolnick, Arun Ahuja, Jonathan Schwarz, Timothy P. Lillicrap, and Greg Wayne. 2019. Experience replay for continual learning. *Preprint*, arXiv:1811.11682.

Gobinda Saha, Isha Garg, and Kaushik Roy. 2021. Gradient projection memory for continual learning. *Preprint*, arXiv:2103.09762.

Sebastian Thrun and Tom Mitchell. 1995. Lifelong robot learning. *Robotics and Autonomous Systems*, 15(1):25 – 46.

Zirui Wang, Yulia Tsvetkov, Orhan Firat, and Yuan Cao. 2020. Gradient vaccine: Investigating and improving multi-task optimization in massively multilingual models. *Preprint*, arXiv:2010.05874.

Xinyi Wu, David P. Foster, Prateek Jain, and Le Song. 2024. Understanding forgetting in continual learning with linear regression. *arXiv preprint arXiv:2405.17583*.

Jason Yosinski, Jeff Clune, Yoshua Bengio, and Hod Lipson. 2014. How transferable are features in deep neural networks? *Preprint*, arXiv:1411.1792.

Tianhe Yu, Saurabh Kumar, Abhishek Gupta, Sergey Levine, Karol Hausman, and Chelsea Finn. 2020. Gradient surgery for multi-task learning. *Preprint*, arXiv:2001.06782.

Friedemann Zenke, Ben Poole, and Surya Ganguli. 2017. Continual learning through synaptic intelligence. *arXiv preprint arXiv:1703.04200*.

Yuchen Zhao, Yichao Zhou, Hang Zhang, and Peng Yin. 2023. Rtra: Rapid training of regularization-based approaches in continual learning. *arXiv preprint arXiv:2312.09361*.

A Additional Experiments

A.1 Forgetting on Split MNIST

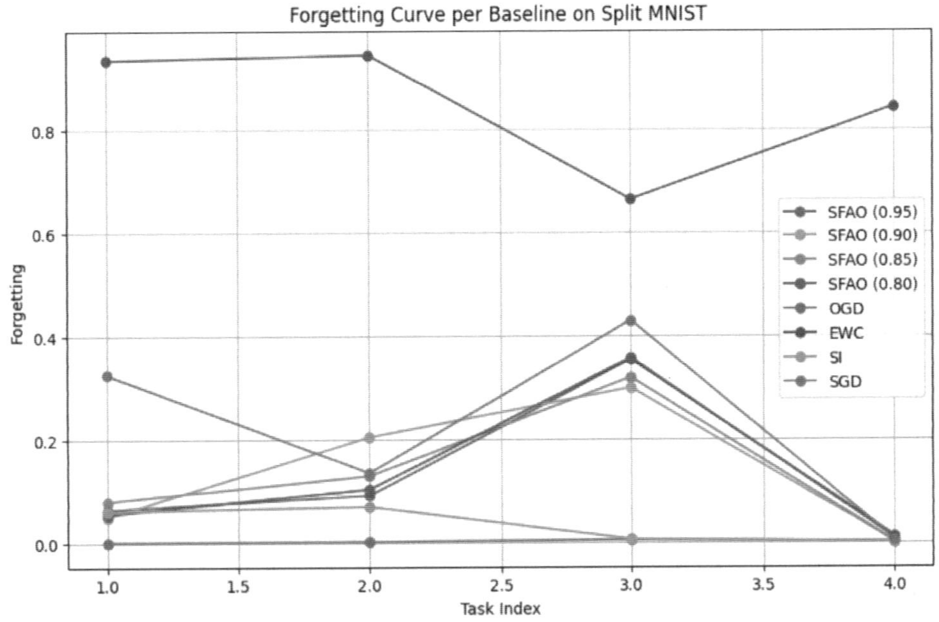

Figure 1: Forgetting curve per baseline on Split MNIST. Forgetting is averaged across previously seen tasks after each new task. There are a total of four tasks.

A.2 SFAO and OGD Memory Usage Comparison

The memory usage was calculated using in the form of megabytes (MB):

$$\text{Memory (MB)} = \frac{|S| \times \text{num\_params} \times 4}{1024^2}$$

where $|S|$ is the number of stored gradients, num_params is the total number of model parameters, and 4 is the number of bytes per `float32`.

Dataset	OGD (MB)	SFAO (MB)
Split MNIST	1441.82	**153.71**
Permuted MNIST (3)	4367.28	**155.28**
Permuted MNIST (5)	7278.00	**155.28**

Table 8: Memory usage (MB) comparison between OGD and SFAO across Split MNIST and Permuted MNIST. For Permuted MNIST, experiments were conducted with p_1–p_3 permutations (3) and p_1–p_5 permutations (5)

As seen in Table 8, SFAO substantially reduces memory usage on Split MNIST and Permuted MNIST, remaining essentially constant across increasing permutations. This efficiency stems from SFAO's buffer management strategy: the cosine similarity threshold prevents redundant gradients from entering the buffer, while the discard threshold removes uninformative vectors, keeping $|S|$ bounded regardless of the number of tasks. On Split CIFAR-100, SFAO uses slightly more memory than OGD due to higher-dimensional and more diverse gradients, which fewer pass the filtering thresholds. This modest increase reflects a trade-off that prioritizes stability and mitigates catastrophic forgetting in complex datasets, demonstrating that SFAO balances efficiency and reliability across different benchmarks.

Dataset	OGD	SFAO
Split MNIST	5625	200
Permuted MNIST	5625	200
Split CIFAR-100	300*	200

Table 9: Projection frequency per batch for OGD and SFAO across benchmarks. *For Split CIFAR-100, OGD uses a capped gradient memory (`max_mem_dirs` = 1000) and harvest policy (`dirs_per_task` = 120, `harvest_batches` = 30), unlike MNIST where projections scale with the full stored gradient set.

A.3 Average Projection Frequency

As seen in Table 9 We observe that OGD incurs significantly higher projection counts, especially on MNIST benchmarks where projections scale with the full memory of past gradients. In contrast, SFAO maintains a fixed low projection frequency across all tasks, offering a more computationally efficient alternative. While OGD's capped memory reduces this burden on Split CIFAR-100, SFAO still provides stable performance with substantially fewer projections.

A.4 Different Cosine Similarity Thresholds vs OGD Accuracy

Dataset	OGD	SFAO (0.95)	SFAO (0.90)	SFAO (0.85)	SFAO (0.80)
Permuted MNIST (3)	0.8014	0.7815	0.7753	0.7938	0.7815
Permuted MNIST (5)	0.7933	0.7633	0.7612	0.7799	0.7887
Split CIFAR-10	0.6800	0.6525	0.6487	0.6152	0.6219
Split CIFAR-100	0.1562	0.1368	0.1500	0.1436	0.1505

Table 10: Average accuracy comparison of OGD and SFAO across different cosine similarity thresholds on multiple benchmarks. For Permuted MNIST, experiments were conducted with p_1–p_3 (3 permutations) and p_1–p_5 (5 permutations).

As seen in Table 10, SFAO demonstrates competitive performance across most datasets, particularly for Permuted MNIST, where thresholds of 0.85 and 0.80 remain close to OGD despite the increased complexity from additional permutations. While OGD generally outperforms SFAO on CIFAR-based benchmarks, the gap is minimal for Split CIFAR-10 and narrows further at lower thresholds (0.80). These results highlight that adaptive cosine thresholds help maintain stability without significantly compromising accuracy, even under more challenging task permutations.

A.5 Plasticity-Stability Measure

The Plasticity-Stability Measure (PSM) is a scalar metric that quantifies the trade-off between a model's ability to acquire new knowledge (plasticity) and its ability to retain previously learned knowledge (stability). Formally, it is defined as:

$$\text{PSM} = \frac{A_{\text{final}} + A_{\text{avg}}}{2},$$

where A_{final} is the final accuracy on the last task and A_{avg} is the average accuracy across all tasks. Higher values indicate a better balance, while lower values suggest excessive forgetting or limited adaptability.

As seen in Table 11, SFAO consistently achieves mid-range PSM values across all benchmarks, remaining close to the balance point between 0 and 1. This reflects its design choice of prioritizing stability while still maintaining sufficient plasticity to adapt to new tasks. However, OGD's behavior varies: on MNIST-scale datasets it favors plasticity, while on high-dimensional datasets like CIFAR it skews heavily toward stability at the cost of adaptability. Overall, SFAO's selective gating yields a steadier stability–plasticity trade-off, making it more reliable across diverse benchmarks.

Dataset	OGD	SFAO (0.95)	SFAO (0.9)	SFAO (0.85)	SFAO (0.8)
Split MNIST	0.4995	0.4352	0.4310	0.4344	0.4350
Permuted MNIST (3)	0.4999	0.4783	0.4786	0.4897	0.4791
Permuted MNIST (5)	0.4958	0.4683	0.4592	0.4742	0.4769
CIFAR-100	0.2511	0.4691	0.4636	0.4768	0.4671
CIFAR-10	0.3574	0.4593	0.4454	0.4277	0.4320

Table 11: Plasticity-Stability Comparison of OGD and SFAO across different cosine similarity thresholds on multiple benchmarks. For Permuted MNIST, experiments were conducted with p_1–p_3 (3 permutations) and p_1–p_5 (5 permutations).

B Algorithms

B.1 SFAO (Similarity-Gated Update with Monte Carlo Sampling)

Algorithm 1 SFAO: Single-layer similarity-gated update (per step)

Require: Current gradient $g_t \in \mathbb{R}^d$; buffer $\mathcal{B} = \{g_i\}_{i=1}^{B}$; thresholds $\lambda_{\text{proj}} \leq \lambda_{\text{accept}}$; Monte Carlo sample size $k \ll B$; buffer policy parameters $(B_{\max}, \tau_{\text{add}}, \tau_{\text{drop}})$
Ensure: Update direction u_t and updated buffer $\mathcal{B}$

```
1: C ← SampleSubset(B, k)                              ▷ uniform without replacement
2: ŝ ← MCMaxCos(g_t, C)
        ▷ Conservative estimate: ŝ = max_{g∈C} g_t^T g / (||g_t|| ||g||)
3: if ŝ > λ_accept then                                  ▷ accept
4:     u_t ← g_t
5: else if λ_proj < ŝ ≤ λ_accept then                    ▷ project
6:     u_t ← (I − P_S) g_t                               ▷ S = span(B)
7: else                                                  ▷ reject
8:     u_t ← 0
9: end if
```

B.2 Geometry of the SFAO Update

B.3 Per-Layer SFAO: Mathematical Formulation and Algorithm

Mathematical formulation. For layer $\ell \in \{1, \dots, L\}$, let $g_t^{(\ell)}$ be the layer-wise gradient and $\mathcal{B}^{(\ell)} \subset \mathbb{R}^{d_\ell}$ its buffer. With Monte Carlo subset $\mathcal{C}^{(\ell)} \subset \mathcal{B}^{(\ell)}$ of size k_ℓ, define

$$s^{(\ell)} = \max_{g \in \mathcal{C}^{(\ell)}} \frac{\langle g_t^{(\ell)}, g \rangle}{\|g_t^{(\ell)}\| \, \|g\|}.$$

Given thresholds $-1 \leq \lambda_{\text{proj}}^{(\ell)} \leq \lambda_{\text{accept}}^{(\ell)} \leq 1$, set the layer update

$$\mathcal{U}^{(\ell)}\left(g_t^{(\ell)}\right) = \begin{cases} g_t^{(\ell)}, & s^{(\ell)} > \lambda_{\text{accept}}^{(\ell)} \\ \left(I - P_{\mathcal{S}^{(\ell)}}\right) g_t^{(\ell)}, & \lambda_{\text{proj}}^{(\ell)} < s^{(\ell)} \leq \lambda_{\text{accept}}^{(\ell)} \\ 0, & s^{(\ell)} \leq \lambda_{\text{proj}}^{(\ell)} \end{cases} \quad \text{with } \mathcal{S}^{(\ell)} = \text{span}\big(\mathcal{B}^{(\ell)}\big).$$

Concatenate (or assemble) per-layer updates to obtain $u_t = \big(\mathcal{U}^{(1)}(g_t^{(1)}), \dots, \mathcal{U}^{(L)}(g_t^{(L)})\big)$ and update parameters $\theta \leftarrow \theta - \eta\, u_t$ per SGD.

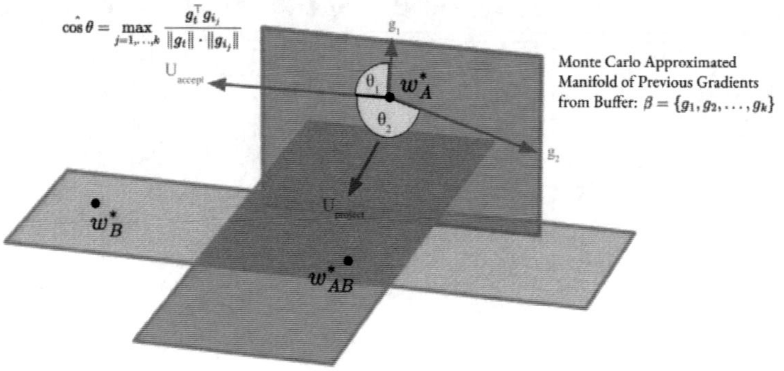

Figure 2: Geometry of the SFAO update. Green (U_{accept}): when the current gradient is sufficiently similar to the buffer $\mathcal{B}$, the update is accepted as is. Blue (U_{project}): otherwise the gradient is orthogonally projected off the subspace spanned by the buffered past gradients $\{g_i\}$ to mitigate interference.

C Additional Results and Proofs

C.1 Minimizing Gradient Interference Risk

Recall Eq. 5 for minimizing the *interference risk* of an update u against a set $G \subset^d$ of stored directions. Here, we solve the constrained optimization problem

$$\min_{u \in^d} \tfrac{1}{2}\|u - g_t\|_2^2 \quad \text{s.t.} \quad g^\top u \;=\; 0 \quad \forall g \in G,$$

We proceed by solving the Lagrangian under the formal constraint $G^\top u = 0$:

$$\mathcal{L}(u, \lambda) = \frac{1}{2}\|u - g_t\|_2^2 + \lambda^\top (G^\top u) \tag{11}$$

Next, we evaluate the Karush–Kuhn–Tucker (KKT) conditions:
Stationarity:

$$\nabla_u \mathcal{L}(u^*, \lambda^*) = \nabla_u \left(\frac{1}{2}\|u - g_t\|_2^2 + \lambda^\top (G^\top u) \right) = 0 \tag{12}$$

$$= u - g_t + G\lambda = 0 \tag{13}$$

$$\implies u^* = g_t - G\lambda \tag{14}$$

Primal Feasibility:

$$G^\top u = 0 \tag{15}$$

$$G^\top (g_t - G\lambda) = 0 \quad \textit{per Stationarity} \tag{16}$$

$$G^\top g_t - G^\top G\lambda = 0 \tag{17}$$

$$G^\top g_t = G^\top G\lambda \tag{18}$$

$$\implies \lambda^* = (G^\top G)^\dagger G^\top g_t \tag{19}$$

Since our problem only involves linear equality constraints, the multipliers λ are unconstrained and all equalities are always active, so the dual feasibility and complementary slackness conditions are vacuous and need not be checked. Also, note that $\dagger$ denotes the Moore-Penrose Pseudoinverse.

Substituting λ^*:

$$u^* = g_t - G(G^\top G)^\dagger G^\top g_t \tag{20}$$

$$\implies u^* = (I - G(G^\top G)^\dagger G^\top) g_t \tag{21}$$

Letting $P_S = G(G^\top G)^\dagger G^\top$, we recover Eq. 6:

$$u^* = (I - P_S)g_t,$$

which shows that the optimal update is the projection of the current gradient step g_t onto the orthogonal complement of the span of past gradients.

SVD expression. Let the thin SVD of $G \in \mathbb{R}^{d\times k}$ be

$$G = U_r \Sigma_r V_r^\top,$$

where $r = \operatorname{rank}(G)$, $U_r \in \mathbb{R}^{d\times r}$ and $V_r \in \mathbb{R}^{k\times r}$ have orthonormal columns, and $\Sigma_r \in \mathbb{R}^{r\times r}$ is diagonal with positive entries. Then

$$G^\top G = V_r \Sigma_r^2 V_r^\top \quad \Rightarrow \quad (G^\top G)^\dagger = V_r \Sigma_r^{-2} V_r^\top,$$

and hence

$$P_S = G(G^\top G)^\dagger G^\top = (U_r \Sigma_r V_r^\top)(V_r \Sigma_r^{-2} V_r^\top)(V_r \Sigma_r U_r^\top) = U_r U_r^\top.$$

Therefore, the optimal update can be written purely in terms of the left singular vectors of G:

$$\boxed{u^\star = (I - U_r U_r^\top)\, g_t.}$$

VariantBench: A Framework for Evaluating LLMs on Justifications for Genetic Variant Interpretation

Humair Basharat, Simon Plotkin, Michael Pink, Isabella Alfaro
Charlotte Le*, Kevin Zhu†
Algoverse AI Research
humairbasharat@gmail.com, simon.m.plotkin@vanderbilt.edu,
isabella.alfaro77@qmail.cuny.edu, kevin@algoverse.us

Abstract

Accurate classification in high-stakes domains requires not only correct predictions but transparent, traceable reasoning. We instantiate this need in clinical genomics and present VariantBench, a reproducible benchmark and scoring harness that evaluates both the final American College of Medical Genetics and Genomics/Association for Molecular Pathology (ACMG/AMP) labels and criterion-level reasoning fidelity for missense single-nucleotide variants (SNVs). Each case pairs a variant with deterministic, machine-readable evidence aligned to five commonly used criteria (PM2, PP3, PS1, BS1, BA1), enabling consistent evaluation of large language models (LLMs). Unlike prior work that reports only final labels, our framework scores the correctness and faithfulness of per-criterion justifications against numeric evidence. On a balanced 100-variant freeze, Gemini 2.5 Flash and GPT-4o outperform Claude 3 Opus on label accuracy and criterion detection, and both improve materially when the decisive PS1 cue is provided explicitly. Error analyses show models master population-frequency cues yet underuse high-impact rules unless evidence is unambiguous. VariantBench delivers a substrate to track such improvements and compare prompting, calibration, and aggregation strategies in genomics and other rule-governed, safety-critical settings.

1 Introduction

Accurate classification in high-stakes domains requires not only correct predictions but also transparent, traceable reasoning. Errors in fields such as healthcare and finance can lead to serious consequences, from patient harm to erosion of public trust. In the study of clinical genomics, the American College of Medical Genetics and Genomics and the Association for Molecular Pathology (ACMG/AMP) create guidelines that require experts to review structured evidence and determine the pathogenicity of missense single-nucleotide variants (SNVs), criterion by criterion (Richards et al., 2015). Here, a missense SNV is a one-base substitution that changes a codon, which then replaces one amino acid in the encoded protein (Cheng et al., 2023). According to the ACMG guidelines, there are two types of criteria: those used to classify pathogenic or likely pathogenic variants, and those used to classify benign or likely benign variants (Richards et al., 2015). The five commonly used criteria we address are pathogenic, weighted as strong (PS1), moderate (PM2), supporting (PP3), and benign, weighted as stand-alone (BA1) or strong (BS1). While LLMs have shown they can predict the final pathogenicity label, they rarely provide traceable, criterion-level reasoning.

Recent work highlights both progress and limitations. Proteome-wide pathogenicity resources such as AlphaMissense provide valuable priors but do not map outputs to ACMG criteria (Cheng et al., 2023). LLM benchmarks targeting variant interpretation have emphasized final labels without assessing reasoning quality (e.g., Li et al., 2024). AutoPM3 explored LLM evaluation for the PM3 segregation rule, but focuses on a single criterion (Li et al. 2025). Beyond genomics, few benchmarks in high-stakes domains combine expert-labeled criteria, curated machine-readable evidence, and reproducible scoring frameworks.

We introduce VariantBench, a benchmark and evaluation harness designed to measure both decision accuracy and criterion-level reasoning fidelity. While our testbed focuses on genomic variant interpretation, the framework applies to any domain where decisions must be justified against structured, expert-defined rules. Each case pairs a randomly sampled missense variant from the Genome Ag-

*Equal contribution
†Corresponding author

Proceedings of the IJCNLP-AACL 2025 Student Research Workshop, pages 314–321
December 20-24, 2025 ©2025 Association for Computational Linguistics

gregation Database (gnomAD; via dbNSFP 5.2a, GRCh38) with automatically derived evidence aligned to five commonly used ACMG/AMP criteria (PM2, PP3, PS1, BS1, BA1). (Liu et al., 2020). At a high level, PM2 captures rarity or absence from population databases, PP3 supporting evidence from deleterious in-silico predictions, PS1 strong evidence when the amino-acid change matches a known pathogenic variant, and BS1/BA1 benign evidence when population allele frequencies are higher than expected for a rare monogenic disorder (with BA1 functioning as a standalone benign rule). We require models to output both a classification decision and a structured criterion-level justification in JSON format containing a 5-tier classification label (Pathogenic, Likely Pathogenic, VUS, Likely Benign, Benign), boolean flags for PM2/PP3/PS1/BS1/BA1, and a brief rationale. We evaluate LLMs against deterministic rule-based ground truth, using exact-match accuracy, micro and macro F_1 for criterion detection, and a faithfulness metric verifying correct evidence citation, across two settings: Track A, where no PS1 evidence is provided to test knowledge-only behavior, and Track B, where a PS1 yes/no hint is provided to test rule-application consistency. Baselines include heuristic, logistic, and ablated LLM variants. The source code is available at https://github.com/VariantBench. Results show that VariantBench not only diagnoses where and why reasoning fails in genomic medicine, but also offers a reproducible framework adaptable to other high-stakes, rule-governed decision-making tasks.

In this work, we introduce the following contributions:

- A replicable benchmark and scoring harness for ACMG/AMP-aligned reasoning over missense SNVs.
- A measurement substrate for tracking improvements and comparing prompting, calibration, and aggregation strategies.
- Comparative analyses of models across two tracks that support structured prompting and explicit evidence supplementation.

2 Methodology

We designed VariantBench to evaluate whether LLMs can reproduce ACMG/AMP reasoning when given the same structured, numeric evidence used by clinical curators. Rather than retrieving textual snippets, which proved too sparse and unreliable, we adopted a deterministic evidence generation pipeline that programmatically derives the inputs for five ACMG criteria (PM2, PP3, PS1, BS1, and BA1), directly from curated databases and fixed thresholds.

2.1 Variant Sampling and Filtering

We drew candidate variants from dbNSFP 5.2a (GRCh38) as a proxy for gnomAD coverage, querying single-nucleotide substitutions with one-base REF/ALT and available gnomAD allele frequency (AF) values. Each variant includes a reference (REF) and alternate (ALT) allele, denoting the original and substituted nucleotides at a specific genomic position, respectively. We specifically chose dbNSFP 5.2a over earlier versions due to its comprehensive integration of gnomAD v3.1.2 data, which includes 75,000 genomes and provides more robust population frequency estimates across diverse ancestries. We then enforced a strict missense filter at the HGVS protein level using a regex form (e.g., p.Gly137Arg), excluding stopgain, frameshift, indel, and splice annotations. The regex pattern specifically matches p[A-Z][a-z]2+[A-Z][a-z]2 to ensure consistent HGVS formatting and prevent edge cases like synonymous variants (p.=) or complex multi-amino acid changes from entering the dataset. HGVS formatting provides a standardized way to describe sequence changes at the DNA, RNA, or protein level, ensuring that genetic variants are reported unambiguously across databases and studies. We manually logged and excluded any entries that failed this pattern to prevent parser drift. As a result, we produced a broad, gene-agnostic pool spanning a wide AF range and diverse in-silico scores.

2.2 Deterministic Evidence Computation

For each variant, we compute five rule flags with fixed logic implemented in `helpers.py`:

PM2 (Moderate evidence of pathogenicity): `True` if $AF_{popmax} < 10^{-4}$ *or* AF_{popmax} is missing, modeling *absent/ultra-rare*. We treat missing AF as satisfying PM2 following ACMG guidelines that consider absence from population databases as supporting evidence (Richards et al., 2015) though we flag these cases separately for sensitivity analysis.

BS1 (Strong evidence of benignity): `True` if

$10^{-4} \leq \mathrm{AF}_{\mathrm{popmax}} < 0.05$. This threshold aligns with the 2015 ACMG guidelines' definition of "greater than expected for disorder" while avoiding overlap with the BA1 threshold.

BA1 (Stand-alone evidence of benignity): `True` if $\mathrm{AF}_{\mathrm{popmax}} \geq 0.05$. This 5% threshold represents the standard ACMG cutoff for "too common to cause disease" and automatically results in a Benign classification regardless of other evidence.

PP3 (Supporting evidence of pathogenicity): PP3 is triggered by concordant in silico evidence that a missense substitution is likely to be functionally damaging. We set PP3 to `True` if at least 3 of 7 in silico tools predict the variant to be *damaging/deleterious* (SIFT, PolyPhen2_HDIV, MutationTaster, MutationAssessor, PROVEAN, MetaSVM, MetaLR) *or* if REVEL > 0.5. Missing values do not contribute to the count. The REVEL override (REVEL > 0.5) follows recent ACMG/AMP recommendations that recognize REVEL as a higher-performing ensemble meta-predictor for missense variants. Individual tools are mapped to binary calls using canonical thresholds: SIFT < 0.05, PolyPhen2_HDIV > 0.909, MutationTaster $\in \{\mathtt{D}, \mathtt{A}\}$, MutationAssessor > 1.9, PROVEAN < -2.5, MetaSVM > 0, and MetaLR > 0.5.

PS1 (Strong evidence of pathogenicity): `True` if any canonical protein change from VEP/snpEff (annotation tools that predict how genetic variants affect genes and proteins, such as whether a change results in a missense or stop-gain mutation) exactly matches an amino-acid change in ClinVar, a publicly accessible database maintained by the U.S. National Center for Biotechnology Information (NCBI) that archives and aggregates the clinical significance of human genetic variants, and that is annotated "Pathogenic", "Likely_pathogenic", or "Pathogenic/Likely_pathogenic". We map three-letter amino acid codes to one-letter codes and keep only missense (no stop-gains/frameshifts). Our PS1 lookup table is built from ClinVar's March 2025 release, filtering for variants with $\geq$ 2-star review status to ensure clinical validity. We normalize protein changes by stripping transcript identifiers and resolving alternative amino acid nomenclature (e.g., selenocysteine) to prevent false negatives.

2.3 Gold Benchmark Freeze

From a large random sample of 100 variants meeting our filtering criteria, we produced a label per variant with a deterministic `combine()` function. The `combine()` function implements standard ACMG combining rules (Richards et al., 2015).

- BA1 alone $\rightarrow$ Benign
- BS1 without contradicting evidence $\rightarrow$ Likely Benign
- PM2 + PP3 + PS1 $\rightarrow$ Likely Pathogenic
- Strong pathogenic evidence without benign evidence $\rightarrow$ Pathogenic
- Conflicting or insufficient evidence $\rightarrow$ Variant of Uncertain Significance (VUS).

We then froze a 100-example benchmark by stratified sampling 20 variants per label (Pathogenic, Likely Pathogenic, VUS, Likely Benign, Benign), yielding balanced coverage across tiers. This balanced design prevents models from exploiting class imbalance and ensures equal weighting of performance across all clinical decision points. In clinical genetics, these five categories support differential actions: Pathogenic and Likely Pathogenic variants can prompt surveillance, cascade testing of relatives, or changes in treatment, whereas Likely Benign and Benign variants are generally not used to alter care. Variants of Uncertain Significance (VUS) are typically non-actionable but can generate follow-up work and patient anxiety. Benchmarks that probe how LLMs reason about these labels therefore speak directly to the safety and audit ability of AI-assisted genomic interpretation, even when used in a research-only context. Although 100 variants is modest by modern benchmarking standards, this size is sufficient to distinguish the models we study and to support detailed error analysis. At temperature 0, headline accuracies in Figure 1 range from ≈ 0.21 (Claude) to ≈ 0.47–0.52 (Gemini), and Matthews correlation coefficients (MCC) from ≈ 0.02 to ≈ 0.40–0.42. Under a simple binomial approximation with $n = 100$, the standard error of an accuracy estimate is at most

$$\sqrt{p(1-p)/n} \leq \sqrt{0.25/100} \approx 0.05,$$

yielding 95% confidence intervals of roughly ± 0.10. The observed accuracy gaps of $\approx$

0.15–0.30 and MCC gaps of $\approx$ 0.18–0.40 between Gemini, GPT–4o, and Claude therefore exceed this sampling margin, indicating that VariantBench–100 is large enough to meaningfully separate model behaviours, even though it is not sufficient for precise estimates of clinical-grade performance. We then saved two files under `results/FrozenBenchmark/`: the full gold table (`variantbench_100_gold.csv`, including flags and label) and the public input table (`variantbench_100_inputs.csv`) that hides gold flags but retains fields needed to build prompts. Both files include cryptographic checksums (`SHA-256`) to ensure reproducibility and detect any data corruption.

2.4 Prompt Construction

We developed two evaluation tracks to isolate the contribution of external knowledge versus structured reasoning:

2.4.1 Track A (No PS1 cue)

The model receives HGVS, AF_{popmax}, and a compact in-silico summary (CADD, SIFT, PolyPhen2_HDIV, MetaLR, FATHMM-XF, AlphaMissense when present). In-silico scores are presented as raw values rather than pre-interpreted categories to test whether models can apply an appropriate threshold. The prompt explicitly instructs the model to evaluate only PM2, PP3, PS1, BS1, and BA1, and to return a single JSON object with lowercase booleans and a one-line rationale. The JSON schema is strictly enforced:

```
{
  "pm2": true/false,
  "pp3": true/false,
  "ps1": true/false,
  "bs1": true/false,
  "ba1": true/false,
 "label": "Pathogenic"|"Likely_pathogenic"
  |"VUS"|"Likely_benign"|"Benign",
  "rationales": { ... }
}
```

No PS1 evidence is provided; the model must rely on its pretrained knowledge to decide PS1.

2.4.2 Track B (PS1 evidence provided)

Similar to Track A, but we add a single line `PS1 evidence (ClinVar {clinvar_release}): {ps1_yes_no} # "yes" or "no"`, where yes/no is computed deterministically by our PS1 helper. This ablation test evaluates whether models can integrate provided evidence or rely on potentially outdated training data. The ClinVar release date is explicitly stated to signal data currency. The prompt fixes PS1 semantics ("set PS1=true iff the evidence line is 'yes' "). This track isolates whether the model applies PS1 correctly when the evidence is explicit.

We write prompts per track to `results/prompts/`, and one JSONL with a variant ID per variant and a human-readable preview. We then fed the prompts to the following models in zero-shot: GPT-4o, Claude 3 Opus, and Gemini 2.5 Flash.

Additional prompt engineering considerations:

- We prepend a brief ACMG primer (50 words) explaining that variants should be classified based on population frequency and computational predictions, without defining specific thresholds, to activate relevant knowledge without biasing toward particular cutoffs.
- All numeric values are formatted consistently (scientific notation for AF, two decimal places for scores) to prevent parsing ambiguities.
- We include a "`chain-of-thought`" instruction asking models to "briefly explain your reasoning before providing the JSON" to improve accuracy through intermediate reasoning steps.
- Temperature is set to 0 for all primary experiments to ensure deterministic outputs, with a `temperature=0.7` ablation to assess robustness.

Quality control measures:

- Each prompt–response pair is validated for JSON parseability before scoring.
- We implement retry logic (maximum three attempts) for API failures or malformed outputs.
- All model outputs are archived with timestamps and model version identifiers for reproducibility.
- We conduct spot checks on 10% of responses to verify that rationales reference the correct evidence types (e.g., PM2 rationales mention allele frequency).

3 Results and Discussion

Figure 1 compares Gemini, GPT-4o, and Claude across five headline metrics at temperature 0. Gemini emerged as the strongest model for final ACMG label prediction, reaching ~ 0.50–0.52 accuracy and ~ 0.40–0.42 MCC. Roughly a 40% improvement over GPT-4o and more than double Claude, whose MCC hovered near zero. This indicates that Gemini not only classifies more variants correctly but also achieves a better balance across true/false positives and negatives.

At the criterion level, micro-F1 scores were uniformly higher than overall accuracy, showing that all models were more consistent in detecting individual ACMG rules than in combining them into final labels. Gemini and GPT-4o achieved strong micro-F1 (0.78–0.88), while Claude lagged at ~ 0.65. Macro-F1 further highlighted model differences: Gemini remained stable across tracks (~ 0.61–0.78), GPT-4o improved substantially once PS1 evidence was supplied ($0.41 \rightarrow 0.61$), and Claude plateaued, suggesting limited adaptability.

Faithfulness exposed the sharpest divide. Gemini and GPT-4o exceeded 95%, meaning their explanations consistently cited the numeric cues aligned with invoked criteria. Claude, by contrast, plateaued at $\sim 42\%$, reflecting a tendency to provide generic or hallucinated rationales rather than evidence-grounded reasoning. This gap underscores that even when Claude flagged the criteria correctly, it often failed to justify them in a clinically auditable way.

As illustrated in Figure 2, population frequency rules are handled well by Gemini and GPT-4o and less reliably by Claude. For PM2, Gemini and GPT-4o are stable around 0.92–0.93 F1 in both tracks, whereas Claude trails at ~ 0.77. For PP3, GPT-4o leads (0.93–0.95) over Gemini (0.87–0.89), with Claude at ~ 0.56. Decisive rules reveal the most apparent separation. Without PS1 evidence (Track A), all models are ~ 0 on PS1; with a single explicit PS1 cue (Track B), Gemini and GPT-4o jump to ≈ 1.00 while Claude remains low (~ 0.08). BA1 is near-ceiling for Gemini and GPT-4o (0.97–0.98) but negligible for Claude (~ 0.02). BS1 remains challenging across models. Gemini and GPT-4o reach only 0.28–0.31, and Claude is ~ 0.02. This reflects the rule's narrow frequency threshold and the scarcity of BS1-positive examples. Overall, Gemini and GPT-4o reliably apply frequency evidence and, when provided explicit cues, execute decisive ACMG rules. Claude's competence appears confined mainly to simpler, frequency-based criteria.

3.1 Confusion Matrix Analysis

Overview: Across models, most mistakes collapse to VUS when evidence is incomplete or conflicting. Providing an explicit PS1 cue (Track B) reduces this collapse for GPT-4o and Gemini but not for Claude.

GPT-4o: Figure 3 shows GPT-4o is accurate on Benign and VUS ($\approx$80–90% correct across tracks). On Track B, the model undercalls pathogenicity: $\approx$80% of true Pathogenic shift to Likely Pathogenic, and $\approx$72.5% of true Likely Pathogenic shift to VUS. This mirrors its per-flag pattern (strong PM2/PP3, weaker PS1/BS1), yielding conservative decisions when high-impact evidence is absent or ambiguous.

Gemini: Additionally, figure 3 shows Gemini is very strong on Benign and VUS ($\geq$95% correct across tracks). With the PS1 cue (Track B), Gemini recovers more Pathogenic cases ($\approx$40% accurate, roughly $2\times$ GPT-4o). Its weakness is the intermediate tiers: Likely Pathogenic accuracy $\approx$25%, and Likely Benign $\approx$12.5% (vs. GPT-4o $\approx$60% for LB), reflecting difficulty with mid-frequency benign signals (BS1) relative to GPT-4o.

Claude: Marked VUS bias across tracks. In Track B, $\approx$70% of Likely Benign, $\approx$95% of Likely Pathogenic, and $\approx$87.5% of Pathogenic are predicted as VUS, explaining low label accuracy and MCC despite mid-range flag F1. This indicates limited integration of high-impact rules and weak use of explicit PS1 cues.

Effect of Temperature: Figure 4 illustrates aggregate temperature sweeps.

- **Accuracy & MCC:** Gemini benefits most from higher temperature in both tracks (accuracy $+\sim 0.06$ in Track A, $+\sim 0.13$ in Track B; MCC $+\sim 0.06$ and $+\sim 0.16$). GPT-4o is relatively temperature-stable. Claude changes little.
- **Macro-F1:** In Track A, GPT-4o and Gemini see slight increases up to $\tau = 0.3$ (Gemini: $0.605 \rightarrow 0.625$, GPT-4o peaks near $\tau = 0.3$).

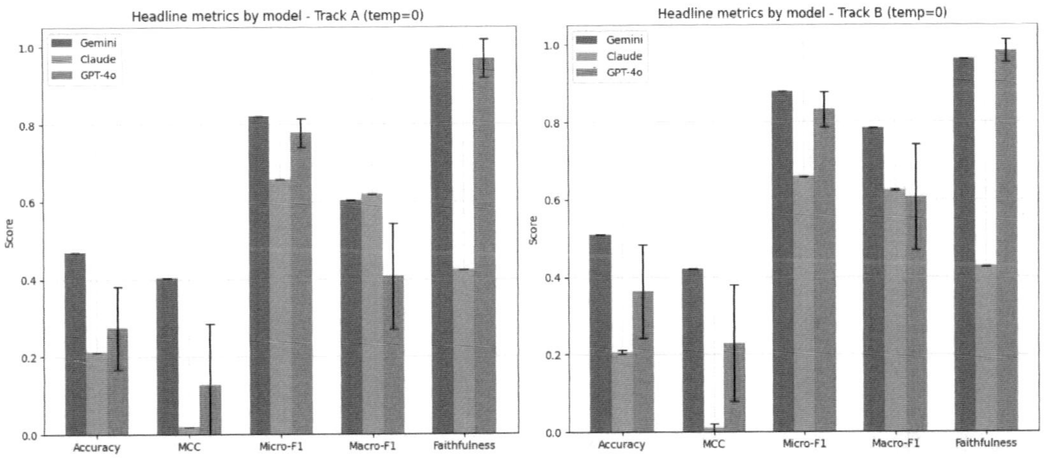

Figure 1: Headline metrics by model on Track A (left) and Track B (right) at temperature 0. Bars show mean scores and error bars denote variability across runs.

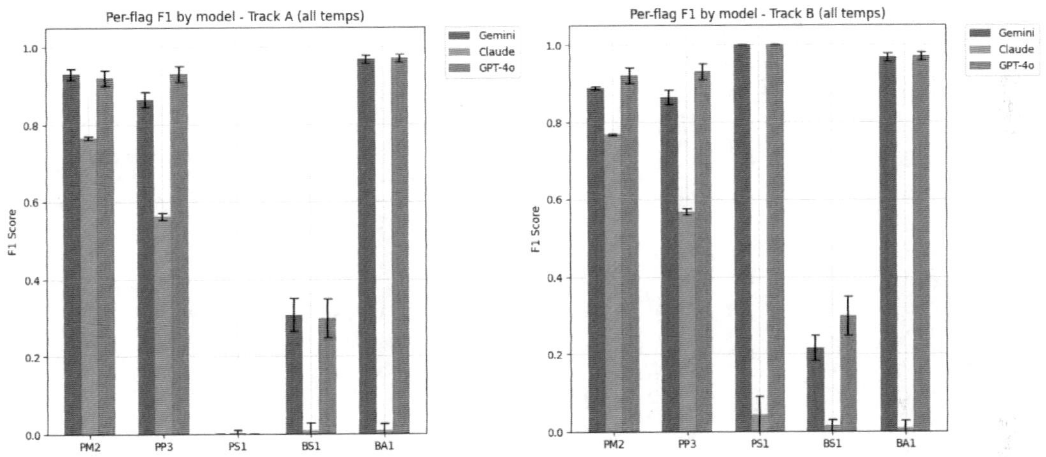

Figure 2: Per-criterion performance by model on Track A (left) and Track B (right) at temperature 0. Bars show mean scores, and error bars denote variability across runs.

OpenAI's macro-F1 in Track B is already high (~ 0.84–0.85) and flat.

- **Interpretation:** Mild stochasticity helps Gemini explore alternatives that improve final labels without hurting criterion detection. GPT-4o is already near its optimum at low temperature.

4 Conclusion

We introduced *VariantBench*, a reproducible benchmark and scoring harness for ACMG/AMP-aligned reasoning over missense SNVs. In contrast to prior work that scores only the final label, VariantBench evaluates criterion-level correctness (PM2/PP3/PS1/BS1/BA1) and faithfulness to numeric cues using a deterministic pipeline derived from public databases. On VariantBench-100, Gemini 2.5 Flash and GPT-4o outperform Claude on both final labels and rule detection. Across models, population-frequency evidence (PM2/PP3) is learned reliably, while high-impact rules (PS1/BA1/BS1) are brittle unless the signal is made explicit in the prompt. These findings suggest that structured prompting + explicit evidence injection can convert pretrained knowledge into auditable, rule-consistent reasoning, and that VariantBench provides the measurement substrate for tracking such gains and comparing prompting, calibration, and aggregation strategies.

Limitations:

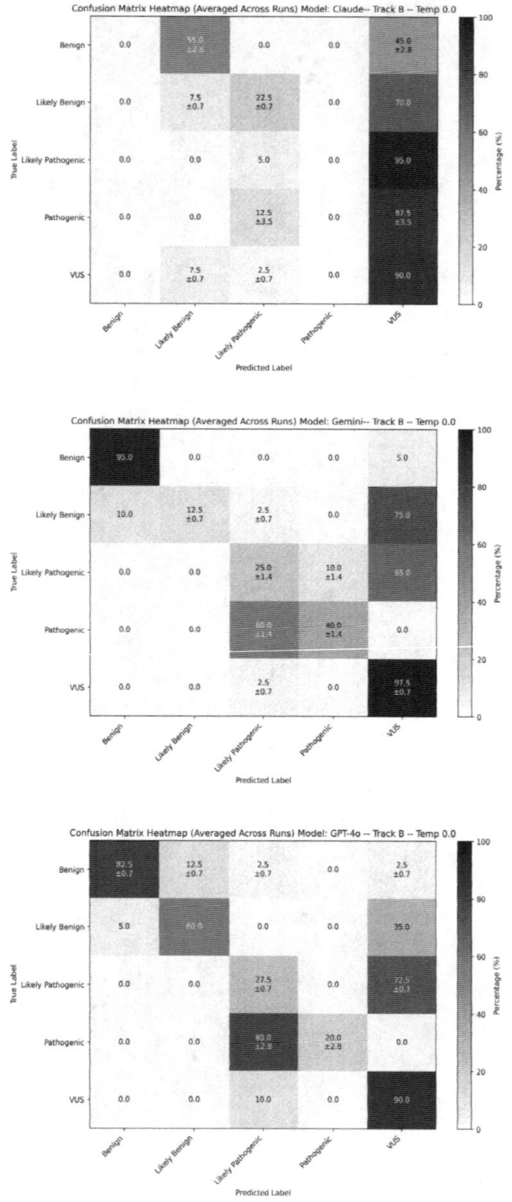

Figure 3: Confusion matrices by model on Track B (temperature 0). Top: Claude. Middle: Gemini. Bottom: GPT-4o. Percentages are averaged across runs.

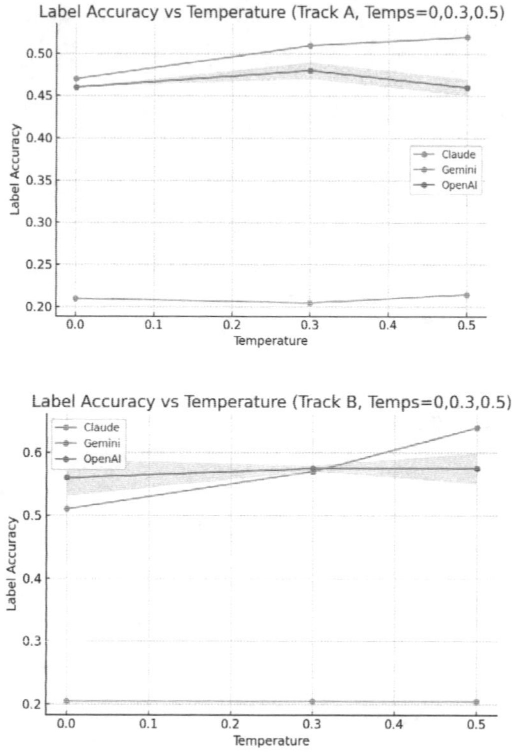

Figure 4: Effect of temperature on label accuracy across models. Top: Track A shows modest accuracy gains for Gemini and GPT-4o up to $\tau = 0.3$. Bottom: Track B highlights Gemini's stronger improvement at higher temperatures. Claude remains flat in both tracks. Error bands show run variability.

- **Rule scope.** VariantBench-100 evaluates reasoning over only five ACMG/AMP criteria (PM2, PP3, PS1, BS1, BA1). Full clinical curation uses additional rules and more complex combinations, so our results should be interpreted as evidence about relative model behaviors under a constrained subset, not as comprehensive estimates of real-world diagnostic performance.
- **Dataset size and balance.** VariantBench-100 is small and label-balanced by design (20 variants per tier) to enable clear comparisons and exhaustive error analysis. This controlled setting prevents exploitation of class imbalance but does not reflect the skewed distributions and edge cases encountered in practice.
- **Faithfulness metric.** Our "cue-citation" score is a surface-level proxy: it checks whether rationales explicitly mention the numeric evidence that should support each criterion. This can undercount valid paraphrases that omit explicit values and overcount boilerplate text that repeats numbers without truly using them in the decision. We therefore view cue-citation as a conservative, first order approximation to reasoning faithfulness.
- **Prompt/decoding sensitivity.** All results are conditional on a particular prompt family, JSON schema, and a single snapshot of three

closed-weight models. Different prompts, decoding parameters, or model versions may change the absolute scores and some qualitative patterns. VariantBench is best viewed as a reusable harness for comparing models and prompting strategies, rather than as a fixed leaderboard.

- **Not a clinical device.** Outputs are non-diagnostic and intended solely for benchmarking research.

Future work will extend to full ACMG/AMP coverage, scale data with stratified sampling, replace string matching with structured evidence auditing (e.g., numeric attribution and counterfactuals), and assess uncertainty calibration.

References

Jun Cheng and 1 others. 2023. Accurate proteome-wide missense variant effect prediction with AlphaMissense. *Science*, 381(6664):eadg7492.

Ian Goodfellow, Yoshua Bengio, Aaron Courville, and Yoshua Bengio. 2016. *Deep learning*, volume 1. MIT Press.

Geoffrey E. Hinton, Simon Osindero, and Yee Whye Teh. 2006. A fast learning algorithm for deep belief nets. *Neural Computation*, 18:1527–1554.

Nilah M. Ioannidis, Joseph H. Rothstein, Vikas Pejaver, and 1 others. 2016. Revel: An ensemble method for predicting the pathogenicity of rare missense variants. *American Journal of Human Genetics*, 99(4):877–885.

Konrad J. Karczewski, Laurent C. Francioli, Grace Tiao, and 1 others. 2020. The mutational constraint spectrum quantified from variation in 141,456 humans. *Nature*, 581(7809):434–443.

Melissa J. Landrum and 1 others. 2025. Clinvar: updates to support classifications of both germline and somatic variants. *Nucleic Acids Research*, 53(D1):D1313–D1323.

Shumin Li, Yiding Wang, Chi-Man Liu, Yuanhua Huang, Tak-Wah Lam, and Ruibang Luo. 2025. Autopm3: enhancing variant interpretation via llm-driven pm3 evidence extraction from scientific literature. *Bioinformatics*, 41(7):btaf382.

X. Li, Y. Wang, and 1 others. 2024. Clinvarbert: Benchmarking large language models on clinvar variant classification. *Bioinformatics*. Preprint/early access; update when published.

Xiaoming Liu. 2025. dbnsfp project website and v5.x release notes. `https://www.dbnsfp.org/`. Accessed Sep 15, 2025; see blog "Highlights in dbNSFP v5.1a" for 5.x changes.

Xiaoming Liu, Chang Li, Chengcheng Mou, Yibo Dong, and Yicheng Tu. 2020. dbnsfp v4: a comprehensive database of transcript-specific functional predictions and annotations for human nonsynonymous and splice-site snvs. *Genome Medicine*, 12(1):103.

Sue Richards, Nazneen Aziz, Sherri Bale, David Bick, Soma Das, Julie Gastier-Foster, Wayne W. Grody, Madhuri Hegde, Elaine Lyon, Elaine Spector, Karl Voelkerding, and Heidi L. Rehm. 2015. Standards and guidelines for the interpretation of sequence variants: a joint consensus recommendation of the american college of medical genetics and genomics and the association for molecular pathology. *Genetics in Medicine*, 17(5):405–424.

The 'aftermath' of compounds: Investigating Compounds and their Semantic Representations

Swarang Joshi
International Institute of Information Technology, Hyderabad, India
swarang.joshi@research.iiit.ac.in

Abstract

This study investigated how well computational embeddings aligned with human semantic judgments in the processing of English compound words. We compared static word vectors (GloVe) and contextualized embeddings (BERT) against human ratings of lexeme meaning dominance (LMD) and semantic transparency (ST) drawn from a psycholinguistic dataset. Using measures of association strength (Edinburgh Associative Thesaurus), frequency (BNC), and predictability (LaDEC), we computed embedding-derived LMD and ST metrics and assessed their relationships with human judgments via Spearman's correlation and regression analyses. Our study confirmed that contextualized embeddings (BERT) better mirror human semantic transparency judgments than static embeddings (GloVe)[1]. Specifically, BERT's ST values showed stronger correlation with human annotations (r=0.23 for frequency, r=0.10 for predictability) and ST predictions that more closely aligned with the expected range (BERT: 3.31-4.25 vs. human: 4.04-4.93), compared to GloVe's compressed range (1.62-3.16). BERT's LMD values also approximated the human midpoint (5.0) more closely than GloVe's representations. The results also showed that predictability ratings are strong predictors of semantic transparency in both human and model data. These findings advanced computational psycholinguistics by clarifying the factors that drove compound word processing and offered insights into embedding-based semantic modeling.

1 Introduction

Compound words, such as *teacup* or *bluebird*, pose a unique challenge for both psycholinguistic theory and computational semantics. They consist of two or more free morphemes whose combined meaning may be transparent, as in *teacup*, or less predictable, as in *butterfly*. Psycholinguistic research has long investigated how human readers decompose and interpret compounds, focusing on measures like lexeme meaning dominance (LMD) and semantic transparency (ST) to quantify how strongly constituents contribute to overall meaning (Juhasz et al., 2015). LMD quantifies which constituent (left or right) contributes more strongly to the compound's overall meaning, rated on a 1-9 scale where values <5 indicate left-constituent dominance, 5 represents equal contribution, and >5 indicates right-constituent dominance. ST measures how readily the compound's meaning can be inferred from its constituents, rated on a 1-7 scale where higher values indicate greater transparency.

With the advent of word embeddings, researchers have begun to probe whether static and contextualized vector representations capture such human semantic intuitions. Buijtelaar and Pezzelle (2023) pioneered an analysis using BERT embeddings, demonstrating that contextual models may better reflect psycholinguistic patterns than static models like GloVe. However, questions remain about which linguistic factors—frequency, predictability, and associative strength—most robustly predict human judgments and model-derived metrics across embedding types.

In this paper, we extended prior work by systematically comparing GloVe and BERT representations on a shared psycholinguistic dataset of 628 compounds annotated for LMD and ST. We integrated factor ratings from established resources—the Edinburgh Associative Thesaurus(Kazemi, 2015), the Large Database of English Compounds (LaDEC) (Gagné et al., 2019), and the British National Corpus (BNC)—and conducted correlation and regression analyses to evaluate the relative contributions of association, frequency, and predictability. Our contributions are threefold:

[1]Link to Code - https://github.com/jswarang12/aftermath-compounds

Proceedings of the IJCNLP-AACL 2025 Student Research Workshop, pages 322–328
December 20-24, 2025 ©2025 Association for Computational Linguistics

1. We provide a comprehensive comparison of static versus contextual embeddings in modeling human compound processing.

2. We identify which linguistic factors most strongly drive embedding-based LMD and ST metrics and their alignment with human data.

3. We offer recommendations for embedding selection and feature integration in computational psycholinguistics.

2 Methodology

We used pre-trained versions of GloVe and BERT to obtain word embeddings. The Edinburgh Associative Thesaurus (Kazemi, 2015) and LaDEC: Large database of English compounds(Gagné et al., 2019) were used to get values of the factors - association strength, frequency, and predictability rating.

2.1 Embedding Extraction

We used the 300-dimensional GloVe vectors trained on 840B tokens. Each compound and constituent was extracted as its static vector representation. We used bert-base-uncased (Devlin et al., 2019) (12 layers, 768 dimensions) from Transformers (Wolf et al., 2020).

Contextualized and non-contextualized representations of compounds and their constituent lexemes were obtained. Cosine similarities between compounds and their constituent lexemes to model lexeme meaning dominance (LMD) and semantic transparency (ST) were computed using the formulae mentioned in (Buijtelaar and Pezzelle, 2023), and MAE and Spearman's correlation against human-annotated values were evaluated.

Following Buijtelaar and Pezzelle (2023), we computed LMD and ST using:

$$\text{LMD} = |\cos(\mathbf{v}_c, \mathbf{v}_l) - \cos(\mathbf{v}_c, \mathbf{v}_r)| \times 4 + 5$$

$$\text{ST} = \frac{\cos(\mathbf{v}_c, \mathbf{v}_l) + \cos(\mathbf{v}_c, \mathbf{v}_r)}{2} \times 3.5$$

where $\cos(\mathbf{v}_a, \mathbf{v}_b)$ computes cosine similarity between vectors $\mathbf{v}_a$ and $\mathbf{v}_b$, with subscripts c, l, r denoting compound, left constituent, and right constituent embeddings.

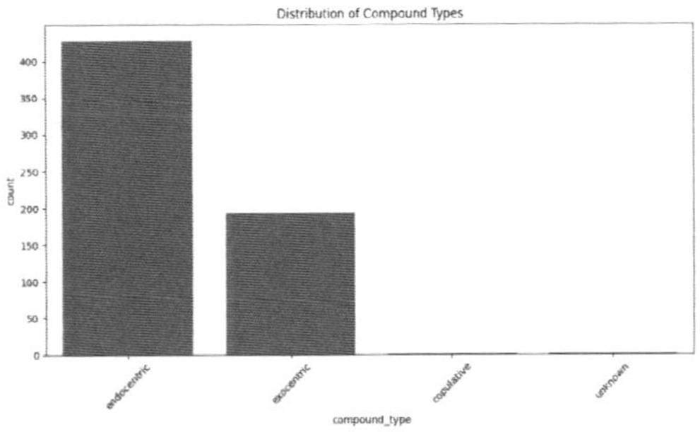

Figure 1: Compound type distribution in dataset (n=628): 68% endocentric, 31% exocentric, <1% copulative.

2.2 Metrics

Spearman's correlation and regression analysis were the primary statistical methods used to evaluate the relationship between the linguistic factors and LMD and ST values derived from human annotations, GloVe, and BERT embeddings. The association strength and frequency were measured only at the compound level, but the predictability rating for the lexemes (constituents) was also considered in the analysis.

Spearman's correlation was used to measure the strength and direction of the monotonic relationship between individual linguistic factors (association, frequency, and predictability) and our dependent variables (LMD and ST), identifying factors with significant standalone associations.

Regression analysis then assessed the predictive power of these factors. The resulting R^2 score from the regressors revealed the proportion of variance in LMD and ST that could be explained, offering deeper insight into a factor's explanatory utility beyond simple association.

3 Datasets

Psycholinguistic dataset (Juhasz et al., 2015) in processing containing 628 lexicalized English compounds annotated for LMD and ST.

We used Edinburgh Associative Thesaurus (EAT) (Kazemi, 2015) for word associations and LaDEC: Large database of English compounds(Gagné et al., 2019) for predictability and BNC word frequency.

4 Results

The MAE and Spearman correlation between the human judgments of LMD and ST and those de-

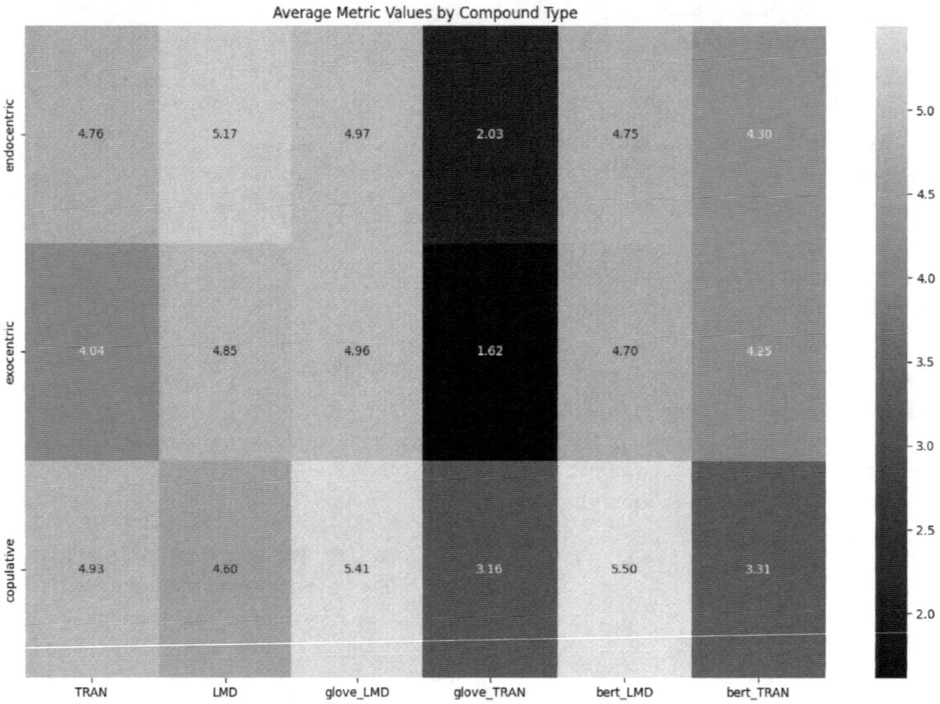

Figure 2: Compound Metrics Heatmap. TRAN refers to ST

Factor	Humans	Glove	BERT
Association	-0.0719	-0.2415	-0.0536
Frequency	-0.1395	-0.0172	0.0636
Frequency (R-L)	**-0.1714**	**-0.4345**	**-0.2303**
Frequency (R+L)	-0.1585	-0.0410	0.1023
Predictability	-0.1575	-0.0657	-0.0458

Table 1: Spearman correlation between **LMD** values and the factors

Factor	Humans	Glove	BERT
Association	0.2365	0.2300	0.0281
Frequency	-0.0588	**0.4410**	0.2319
Frequency (R-L)	-0.0351	0.0091	0.0636
Frequency (R+L)	0.0351	-0.0306	**0.2478**
Predictability	**0.7326**	0.3096	0.1033

Table 2: Spearman correlation between **ST** values and the factors

rived from Glove and BERT embeddings matched the values mentioned in the main reference paper (Buijtelaar and Pezzelle, 2023).

4.1 Correlation

From the Table 1 we can see that LMD had a negative correlation with all the factors. Among human-annotated values, predictability rating and frequency had a significant correlation. Only association are significantly correlated with Glove's values of LMD. In contrast, none of the linguistic factors we examined showed a significant correlation with the LMD values derived from BERT embeddings. Frequency (R-L) had the strongest correlation across all the representations.

From the Table 2 we can see that all the significant correlation between ST values and the factors are positive. Among human-annotated values, association strength was strongly correlated, followed by predictability strength. All three factors were significantly correlated with Glove's values of ST. Only the frequency and predictability ratings showed a significant correlation with the ST values of the BERT embeddings.

4.2 Regressors to Predict LMD and ST

The graphs in Figure 3 show the results of the regressors trained on the factors to predict the LMD and ST values. We can see that association strength is a poor predictor for both LMD and ST values. Frequency is only able to predict the LMD values from Glove embeddings. Predictability rating is a good predictor of only the ST values from human annotations.

5 Discussion

5.1 Compound Type Distribution and Embedding Model Performance

Our analysis revealed significant insights into both the distribution of compound types in English and how different embedding models capture their semantic properties. Figure 1 shows the overwhelming predominance of endocentric compounds in our dataset (approximately 68% endocentric vs. 31% exocentric and <1% copulative) confirms previous linguistic analyses of English compound formation preferences. Our dataset's composition, 68% endocentric vs. 31% exocentric— is consistent with patterns observed in previous compound studies (Libben et al., 1998), though we note this reflects the sampling strategy of Juhasz et al. (2015) rather than a representative survey of English compounding. This distribution reflected English's tendency toward transparent, compositional word formation strategies, where the semantic head is explicitly represented within the compound.

5.2 Semantic Transparency Across Compound Types

The transparency (ST) metrics revealed patterns that largely align with theoretical predictions from morphological theory. Figure 2 shows that Endocentric compounds demonstrated higher transparency values (4.76) than exocentric compounds (4.04), confirming that head-modifier relationships contributed to semantic predictability. This finding supported Libben et al. (1998) transparency hierarchy and Gagné and Spalding (2009) relational framework theories, which posit that compounds with clear internal semantic structures are more easily processed and interpreted. The surprisingly high transparency value for copulative compounds (4.93) suggested that coordinate relationships may be particularly accessible to speakers, despite their relative rarity in English. This might indicate that the balanced semantic contribution from both constituents created a unique form of transparency that differs from the asymmetrical relationship in endocentric compounds.

5.3 Model-Specific Representations of Compound Semantics

5.3.1 Divergence Between BERT and GloVe

The stark contrast between how BERT and GloVe represented compound transparency is one of our most striking findings. GloVe's transparency values were dramatically lower across all compound types (endocentric: 2.03; exocentric: 1.62; copulative: 3.16) compared to BERT's values, which more closely aligned with the original ST ratings. This suggested that contextual embeddings (BERT) may better capture the compositional nature of compounds than static embeddings (GloVe). The divergence can be attributed to fundamental architectural differences: BERT's bidirectional, contextual nature allowed it to better represent how compound meanings emerge from the interaction between constituents, while GloVe's context-independent vectors may struggle to capture these compositional semantics.

5.3.2 Lexical-Morphological Distance Patterns

The LMD metrics revealed a more complex picture than anticipated by straightforward compositional theories. Endocentric compounds showed higher LMD values than expected (5.17), suggesting that even semantically transparent compounds maintained distinct representations from their constituents in embedding space. This supported dual-route theories of compound processing (Kuperman et al., 2009), which proposed that compounds are accessed both as whole units and through individual units.

6 Conclusion

Our study confirmed that contextualized embeddings (BERT) better mirrored human semantic transparency judgments than static embeddings (GloVe), likely due to their capacity to model contextual interactions between morphemes. Predictability emerged as the most robust factor driving transparency, highlighting the role of semantic expectation in compound processing. These insights contributed to dual-route theories of morphological processing and informed the choice of embedding models for downstream applications.

Limitations

While our study shed light on how static (GloVe) and contextualized (BERT) embeddings captured human semantic intuitions for English compounds, there remain several limitations:

- **Language and Genre Coverage.** We focused exclusively on lexicalized English compounds drawn from a psycholinguistic dataset of 628 items. Our findings may not generalize to other languages (e.g., German, where compounding is more productive) or to less-frequent, novel compounds encountered in large-scale corpora.
- **Embedding Variants.** Only one static embedding (GloVe) and one contextualized model ($\text{BERT}_{\text{base}}$) were evaluated. Future work should explore additional architectures (e.g., RoBERTa, ALBERT, or contextualized static hybrids) and compare multilingual or specialized domain embeddings.
- **Psycholinguistic Measures.** We relied on pre-existing human ratings for lexeme meaning dominance (LMD) and semantic transparency (ST). These measures came from a single study and may embed annotation biases or inter-rater variability that could have influenced our correlation and regression results.
- **Downstream Task Validation.** Our evaluation metric is correlation with human judgments. We did not assess the impact of compound representation quality on downstream tasks (e.g., machine translation, lexical semantic annotation), which is an important avenue for future validation.

Acknowledgements

I would like to thank Pranav Agrawal and Prof. Rajakrishnan Rajkumar for their insightful inputs and guidance. I am also grateful to LTRC, IIITH for support. I also thank all reviewers for their insightful feedback, and the organizers of AACL-IJCNLP 2025 and the Student Research Workshop for their dedicated efforts.

References

Lars Buijtelaar and Sandro Pezzelle. 2023. A psycholinguistic analysis of BERT's representations of compounds. In *Proceedings of the 17th Conference of the European Chapter of the Association for Computational Linguistics*, pages 2230–2241, Dubrovnik, Croatia. Association for Computational Linguistics.

Jacob Devlin, Ming-Wei Chang, Kenton Lee, and Kristina Toutanova. 2019. Bert: Pre-training of deep bidirectional transformers for language understanding. *Preprint*, arXiv:1810.04805.

Christina L. Gagné, Thomas L. Spalding, and Daniel Schmidtke. 2019. Ladec: The large database of english compounds. *Behavior Research Methods*, 51(5):2152–2179.

Christina L. Gagné and Thomas L. Spalding. 2009. Constituent integration during the processing of compound words: The role of relational structures. In Brian H. Ross, editor, *The Psychology of Learning and Motivation*, volume 51, pages 97–130. Elsevier.

Barbara Juhasz, Brian Lai, and Ian Woodcock. 2015. Semantic transparency and constituent frequency effects in compound word processing. *Journal of Memory and Language*, 83:1–17.

Darius Kazemi. 2015. The edinburgh associative thesaurus (eat).

Victor Kuperman, Melvin J. Traxler, Ken McFalls, and Charles Cairns. 2009. Effects of morphological structure in compound word processing. *Journal of Memory and Language*, 61(1):24–44.

Gillian Libben, Angela Y. Weber, Michael Jarema, and Michael J. Pollatsek. 1998. Semantic transparency in native and second language compound processing. *Journal of Experimental Psychology: Learning, Memory, and Cognition*, 24(5):1256–1273.

Thomas Wolf, Lysandre Debut, Victor Sanh, Julien Chaumond, Clement Delangue, Anthony Moi, Pierric Cistac, Tim Rault, Rémi Louf, Morgan Funtowicz, Joe Davison, Sam Shleifer, Patrick von Platen, Clara Ma, Yacine Jernite, Julien Plu, Canwen Xu, Teven Le Scao, Sylvain Gugger, and 3 others. 2020. Huggingface's transformers: State-of-the-art natural language processing. *Preprint*, arXiv:1910.03771.

A Appendix

A.1 Graphs

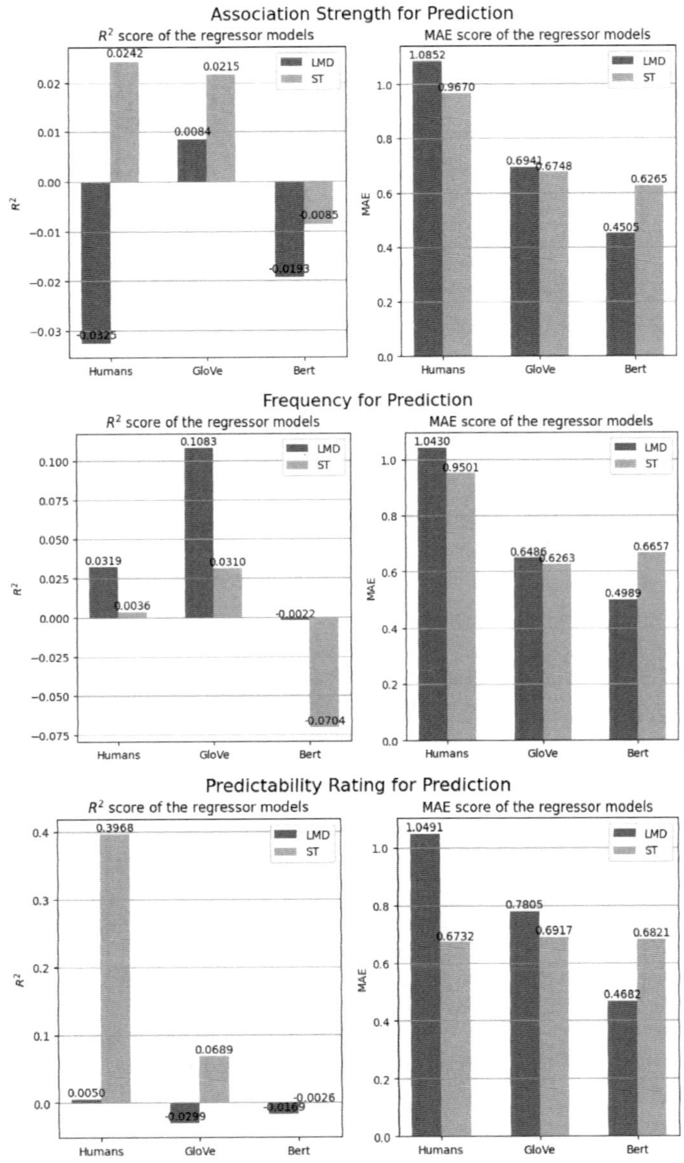

Figure 3: Performance of Regressors

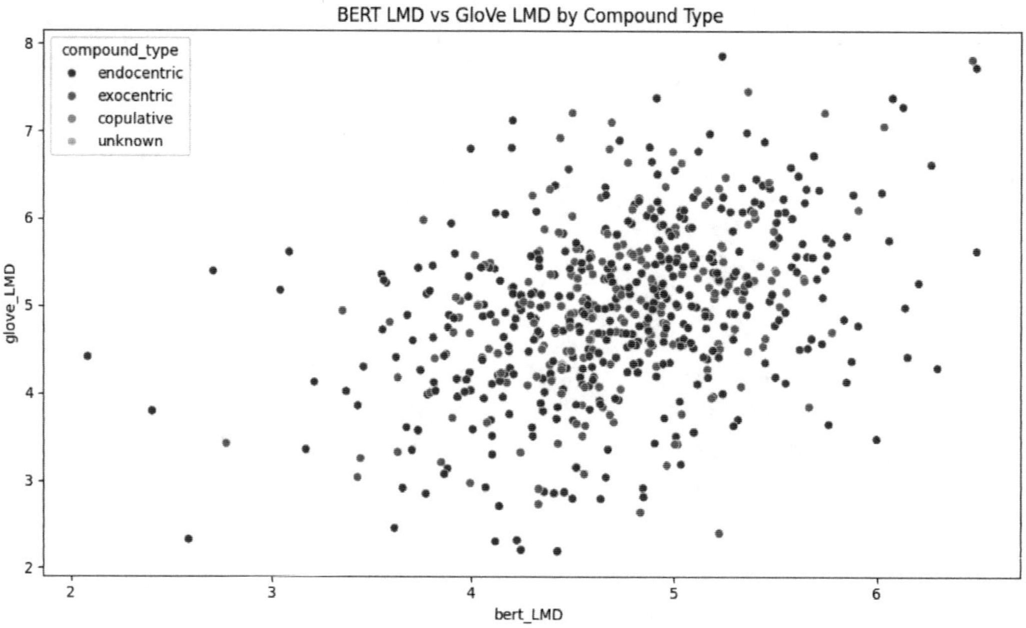

Figure 4: Bert vs GloVe LMD distribution

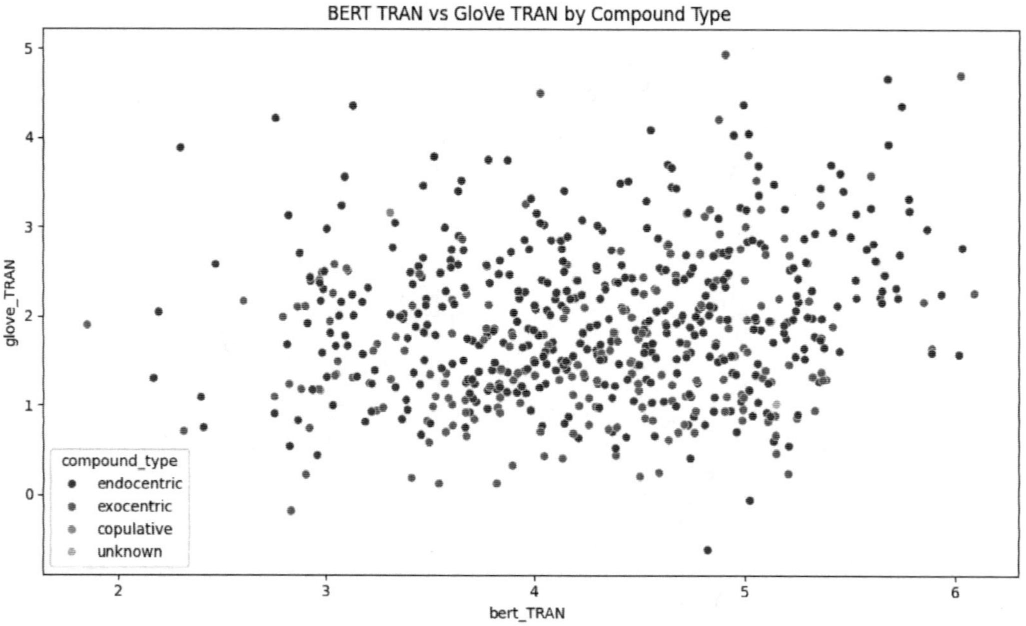

Figure 5: Bert vs GloVe LMD distribution

Author Index

Association for Computational Linguistics
209 N. Eighth Street
Stroudsburg, Pennsylvania 18360

ISBN 979-8-3313-3244-0

CURRAN ASSOCIATES INC.
proceedings.com

30th Conference of the International Nuclear Target Development Society (INTDS2022)

EPJ Web of Conferences Volume 285 (2023)

Villigen, Switzerland
25 - 30 September 2022

edp sciences